COWBOYS AND THE WILD WEST

COWBOYS AND THE WILD WEST

An A–Z Guide from the Chisholm Trail to the Silver Screen

Don Cusic

Facts On File®

AN INFOBASE HOLDINGS COMPANY

COWBOYS AND THE WILD WEST: An A–Z Guide from the Chisholm Trail to the Silver Screen

Facts On File, Inc.
460 Park Avenue South
New York, NY 10016

Library of Congress Cataloging-in-Publication Data
Cusic, Don.
    Cowboys and the Wild West : an A–Z guide from the Chisholm Trail to
  the silver screen / Don Cusic.
      p.   cm.
    ISBN 0-8160-2783-8 (acid-free paper). — ISBN 0-8160-3030-8 (pbk.
  : acid-free paper)
    1. Cowboys—West. (U.S.)—Encyclopedias. 2. Frontier and pioneer
  life—West (U.S.)—Encyclopedias. 3. West U.S.)—Encyclopedias.
    I. Title.
  F596.C975   1994
  978'.003—dc20   93-45584

All photographs, unless otherwise noted, are from the author's collection.

Facts On File books are available at special discounts when purchased in bulk quantities for businesses, associations, institutions or sales promotions. Please call our Special Sales Department in New York at 212/683/2244 or 800/322/8755.

Text and jacket design by Robert Yaffe
Printed in the United States of America

VB KA 10 9 8 7 6 5 4 3 2 1

This book is printed on acid-free paper.

This book is dedicated to
The Lone Ranger.

CONTENTS

PREFACE

In the midst of this project I ran into fellow author John Egerton at the Southern Festival of Books and told him my grandiose plans about this work. He replied, "People won't remember what you put in, they'll only remember what you left out." Those words have remained with me throughout the two years it took to write this book.

I have attempted to cover all aspects of "cowboys," from the historical background of the West, to the real cowboys who drove cattle up the cattle trails, to the people who became famous in the West like outlaws, lawmen and entrepreneurs. I have also covered films and TV cowboys, as well as important films and TV shows because these are as important as the historical cowboys in creating the "myth" of the West, or the West we have come to know in the latter part of the 20th century. Undoubtedly, I have left out somebody or something, but my attempt has been to include what I felt to be the most essential to understanding our contemporary ideas of cowboys.

The reason I wrote this book is simple: I wanted to own it. I had looked for a book like this and never found one, so I decided to write it. Had I known the blood, sweat, toil and tears at the beginning, I might never have tackled this project but, in the end, I'm glad I did. I'm a baby boomer and grew up with cowboys; my first ambition was to be a cowboy and this book is the dream of a lifetime. My childhood hero was the Lone Ranger and,

corny as it sounds, his "code" has stayed with me. It is most heartening to see my youngest son watching his favorite show, "Wild West C. O. W. Boys of Moo Mesa," and know he, too, is learning the "code of the West," where right and good always win.

A number of people should be thanked for their help and support. First, I would like to thank my wife, Jackie, for her encouragement and for providing a wonderful home life where I could go and forget about cowboys for a while. Next I thank my children, Delaney, Jesse, Eli and Alex, for diversions from this project that were not always welcome but were always good and therapeutic. I am particularly indebted to the baseball teams of Jesse and Eli for allowing me to be their first base coach.

At the Todd Library I especially thank Betty McCall and at the Center for Popular Music here I want to especially thank Ellen Garrison.

Members of the Country Music Foundation, particularly Ronnie Pugh, in Nashville gave invaluable help. The folks at the ProRodeo Hall of Fame in Colorado Springs, Colorado were extremely helpful, especially Sherry Compton and Steve Fleming. And Warner Western, the cowboy label for Warner Brothers, was a life saver, especially Reno Kling. Warner Western sent me the Michael Martin Murphey CD *Cowboy Songs,* which I played so much that it quit working—then sent me a fresh one to play some more. That album provided great inspiration while working on this project; I also listened to a good deal of Bob Wills, Gene Autry, Roy Rogers, Ernest Tubb, Sons of the Pioneers and Sons of the San Joaquin. For those albums I thank Roy Wunsch at CBS/Sony, Bruce Hinton at MCA, and Greg McCarn at BMG/RCA as well as Yumi Kimura at Warner Brothers. The Museum of Television and Radio was invaluable and researcher Jonathan Rosenthal always answered my queries quickly and efficiently or directed me to the best source.

Although during the course of this project I read countless books and articles, I will not list them all here. However, I do want to note several that were especially influential and informative. Doug Green's chapter on Gene Autry in *The Stars of Country Music* (University of Illinois, 1975) opened up a new perspective on singing cowboys for me. *Cowboy Culture* by David Dary (University of Kansas, 1989), *Cowboys of the Americas* by Richard Slatta (Yale, 1990), and *The Old Time Cowhand* by Ramon Adams (University of Nebraska, 1961) were the best at giving insight into cowboys in general. Jim Bob Tinsley's books *For a Cowboy Has to Sing* (University of Central Florida Press, 1991) and *He Was Singing This Song* (University Presses of Florida, 1981) were especially helpful in that area; Jon Tuska's book *The Filming of the West* (Doubleday, 1976) and David Rothel's book *The Singing Cowboys* (A.S. Barnes & Co., 1978) are both excellent. For reference books, I found myself constantly checking *Wild and Woolly: An Encyclopedia of the West* by Denis McLoughlin (Doubleday, 1975), *The Reader's Encyclopedia of the American West* edited by Howard R. Lamar (Harper and Row, 1977), *The*

Encyclopedia of Frontier Biography by Dan Thrapp (University of Nebraska, 1988) and *The Encyclopedia of Western Gunfighters* by Bill O'Neal (University of Oklahoma, 1979).

There has been a lot of revisionist history on the West recently and some of it is good. There are now books on blacks and women in the West—and it's hard to believe both groups were overlooked for so long. I was especially impressed by Jane Tompkins' book *West of Everything*. She provided the most clear-eyed look at Louis L'Amour I'd ever read, and captured the essence of the influence of literature in her chapter on Zane Grey.

Finally, the Time-Life series on the Old West gives an excellent overview of the West and I highly recommend the 26 book series to anyone who wants a general history.

A number of people have been kind and helpful with conversations, insight, favors and general enlightenment during this project; they include Don Reeves at the Cowboy Hall of Fame in Oklahoma City, The Country Music Association (especially Teresa George), Steve Eng, Doug Green, Charles Wolfe, Bob Pinson, John Rumble, Dave Debolt, Beth Mallen, Vernell Hackett and Jerry Bailey. A special thanks to Dave Debolt and Rick Freudenthal for help with pictures.

I'd like to thank Louis L'Amour for writing so many great cowboy books and John Wayne for making so many great cowboy movies—they have provided entertainment and relaxation through many an evening.

Finally, thanks to my agent, Madeleine Morel, and my editor, Susan Schwartz, for allowing me the privilege of doing this book.

A NOTE TO THE READER

In some instances, no information was available on where and when a person was born. In such cases a question mark appears in place of the location and date of birth. Similarly a question mark indicates that no information was available on the place and date of a person's death.

ABBOT-DOWNING COMPANY   This company made the famous Concord stagecoach. Established in Concord, New Hampshire in 1813 by Lewis Downing and J. Stephen Abbot, the company built its first Concord coach in 1826 and soon exported coaches all over the world. Lewis Downing was a perfectionist who only wanted the best materials used in painstaking efforts to produce the top stagecoaches. After the stagecoach declined, the Abbot-Downing Company made ambulances, gun carriages and circus and specialty wagons; however, in 1920 the company ceased production when the gasoline engine replaced horse-drawn vehicles. (See also CONCORD COACH).

ABILENE, KANSAS   Abilene, Kansas was the first railhead cattle town for the Texas cattle drives. From 1867 to 1872 it served as the shipping point for 1.5 million longhorns bound for Kansas City, Chicago and other cities in the East. Abilene was selected by livestock entrepreneur Joseph McCoy in 1867 because it was west of the quarantine line, was sparsely settled and had good water (the Smoky Hill River), plenty of grass and an area to hold large numbers of cattle. Nearby Fort Riley was a deterrent against Indian attacks, and the Kansas Pacific Railroad was building west from Kansas City toward Abilene. McCoy built the large Drover's Cottage, a hotel for cattlemen, and a number of cattle pens, barns, livery stables and other necessities for the cattle trade on a 250-acre area just outside Abilene. Abilene was the end of the Chisholm Trail and attracted an assortment of wild cowboys, gamblers, sporting houses, saloons and dance halls. It became well known for its wild and woolly vice and lawlessness. On the outskirts of town was the Devil's Addition, an area of vice. In 1870 Tom Smith became marshal and brought some law and order. As the town grew and prospered, the townsfolk increasingly saw the cattle trade as a threat to a peaceful settlement, as well as a threat to farmers, and so they insisted that the cattlemen move farther west. They extended the quarantine line, and Newton became the next famous cattle town. In addition, the Atchison, Topeka and Santa Fe Railroad had arrived in Newton, about 65 miles south of Abilene, which meant that cattle drives from Texas could take a week less. (See also CATTLE TOWNS; MCCOY, JOSEPH GEATING; QUARANTINE LINE; SMITH, TOM.)

ACE IN THE HOLE   Phrase that comes from stud poker, in which the first card, or "hole card," is dealt facedown. If it is an ace, the player is in good shape. In everyday language of the West, the phrase meant a particular advantage a person possessed, such as a gun in the boot or perhaps some secret knowledge nobody else had.

ACROBAT RANCH   Hosted by Jack Stillwell, this TV circus featured a western setting. Based in Chicago, the show premiered on August 19, 1950 on ABC and ran until May 12, 1951. Originally a 30-minute show, it became a 15-minute show in 1951 and was seen on Saturday mornings.

ACROSS THE WIDE MISSOURI   Film produced by Robert Sisk; directed by William Wellman; screenplay by Talbot Jennings from a story by Talbot Jennings and Frank Cavett; released in 1951 by MGM; 78 minutes in length. Cast: Clark Gable, Ricardo Montalban, John Hodiac, Adolphe Menjou, J. Carroll Naish and Alan Napier.

Flint Mitchell, a mountain man, hunts beaver pelts. He marries an Indian girl as a diplomatic gesture toward the Indians, but he actually falls in love with her and they have a son. His wife is killed, and Mitchell then takes their son and heads off into the mountains.

ADAMS, ANDY   (b. Whitley County, Indiana on May 3, 1859; d. Colorado Springs, Colorado on September 26, 1935)   Andy Adams is most famous for writing *The Log of a Cowboy* (1903), which is considered a classic in cowboy literature. The book came about after Adams, who had worked as a cowboy, saw the play *The Texas Steer*, which disgusted him with its portrayal of cowboys and cattle. Adams had left home at 18 and moved west, where he drove cattle and horses from Texas. Later he became a merchant in Rockport, Texas, then a miner in Cripple Creek, Colorado; he settled in Colorado Springs in 1894. Adams wrote five other novels after his first: *A Texas Matchmaker* (1904), *The Outlet* (1905), *Cattle Brands* (1906), *Reed Anthony, Cowman* (1907) and *Wells Brothers, the Young Cattle Kings* (1911).

ADAMS, GRIZZLY   (b. John Capen Adams, in Massachusetts 1812; d. October 25, 1860)   Grizzly Adams went west to California in the gold rush, but failing to strike it rich there, he became a trapper in the Sierra Nevada. He began catching and training grizzly bears, and zoos began to contact him for these animals. He trained two cubs, "Lady Washington" and "Benjamin Franklin," as companions and pack animals. Adams opened an exhibition at the Mountaineer Museum in San Francisco in 1855 and became a celebrity. He joined with P. T. Barnum as a partner in the early 1860s when he went to New York with his grizzlies.

ADOBE   A brick made from clay mixed with straw or grass and dried by the sun. The bricks were formed from the wet clay shaped by bare feet and then left in the sun to dry for a week or two. After a structure was built from

Andy Adams (*Western Archives*)

adobe bricks, it was then plastered over with more clay, making the interior cool. Adobe was a popular building material in the southwestern United States and Mexico. The material was first used by Native Americans and discovered by early Spanish explorers. Early Spanish missions, forts and trading posts were made of adobe. *Adobe* comes from the Spanish *adobar*, which means "to plaster." In addition to the material, "adobe" could mean the building itself. It could also mean anything inferior, a derogatory phrase directed against Mexicans and the Mexican culture.

ADOBE WALLS, BATTLES OF   (November, 1864; June 27, 1874)   There were actually two Battles of Adobe Walls, and both involved famous western figures. Both battles were fought at a trading post called Adobe Fort or Adobe Walls in the Texas panhandle on the north side of the Canadian River. The first took place in November 1864 and involved Kit Carson, who led a group of soldiers against several thousand warriors from the Kiowa and Comanche tribes. Carson's group had two mountain howitzers, which saved him and his men. The second Battle of Adobe Walls was on June 27,

1874 between a group of buffalo hunters, whose members included Billy Dixon and Bat Masterson, and Indians from the Comanche, Kiowa and Cheyenne tribes. The Comanche were led by Quanah Parker but were defeated by the Sharps buffalo rifles. The fighting began at dawn with a surprise attack from the Indians. Fortunately for those in this settlement—there were about 30 men and one woman (the wife of one of the businessmen there)—a wall on one of the sod houses collapsed during the night and awakened those inside. After this collapse, the men remained awake and about and thus were able to repulse the Indian attacks, which ended around 4 P.M. when Quanah Parker, wounded in the arm during the battle, withdrew his troops.

ADVENTURES OF BRISCO COUNTY, JR., THE   TV show starring Bruce Campbell as Brisco County, Jr., Julius Carry as Lord Bowler, Christian Clemenson as Socrates Poole, Bill Drago as John Bly, John Pyper-Ferguson as Pete Hutter, Kelly Rutherford as Dixie Cousins and John Astin as Professor Wickwire.

Brisco's father was a well-known marshal, and the son follows in his Dad's footsteps when five wealthy robber barons hire him to round up some outlaws. A humorous western set in the Old West, this show premiered on Friday, August 27, 1993 on the Fox network.

ADVENTURES OF CHAMPION, THE   TV show that starred Barry Curtis as Ricky North, Jim Bannon as Sandy North, Francis McDonald as Will Calhoun and Ewing Mitchell as Sheriff Powers.

A boy and his horse, a boy and his dog—both premises were part of this TV show, which starred Champion the Wonder Horse and a German shepherd named Rebel and was produced by Gene Autry's Flying A production company. The show's plots generally consisted of young Ricky North getting into trouble and the two animals saving the day. Set in the 1880s in the Southwest, the show premiered on September 30, 1955 and ended on February 3, 1956; it aired on Friday evenings on CBS. The half-hour show was later shown on Saturday mornings.

ADVENTURES OF JIM BOWIE, THE   TV show that starred Scott Forbes as Jim Bowie, Robert Cornthwaite as John James Audubon and Peter Hanson as Rezin Bowie.

Based on the novel *Tempered Blade* by Monte Barrett, this TV series was based on a real historical character, Jim Bowie, in the early 1830s in New Orleans. The premise is that Jim Bowie invented the famous Bowie knife after an encounter with a grizzly bear when his own knife broke. In truth, Bowie certainly popularized the knife—although he wasn't the only Bowie in the family to do so—but probably did not invent it. The knife made this show unique—a departure from the usual emphasis on guns in cowboy shows—but caused some consternation at the network, which was fearful of parental disapproval. Thus, the violence from the knife was played down. This show premiered on September 7, 1956 on ABC on Friday nights. The half-hour series ended on February 27, 1957 after 78 episodes, all in the same time slot. The show later appeared on Saturday mornings.

ADVENTURES OF KIT CARSON, THE   TV show that starred Bill Williams as Kit Carson and Don Diamond as El Toro.

This syndicated TV show, which bore little resemblance to the real Kit Carson's life and adventures, was aired for children. The 104 episodes were produced from 1951 to 1955 for syndication (it was never a network show). The heroes covered a lot of ground—from Wyoming to Texas—in the 30-minute episodes. Shot at the Republic studio as a budget series by MCA-TV, it reached more children in 1954 than any other show—3.5 million. Don Diamond played the Mexican sidekick El Toro; ironically Diamond was born in Brooklyn. Occasionally the character of Sierra Jack appeared, played by Hank Peterson.

ADVENTURES OF OKY DOKY   TV show that starred Wendy Barrie and Burt Hilber as hosts, Pat Barnard and the Mellodaires as regulars and Dayton Allen as the voice of Oky Doky.

A large puppet created by Raye Copeland, Oky Doky was first seen in New York at a kids' fashion show called "Tots, Tweens and Teens." Originally called "Adventures of Oky Doky," and later "Oky Doky Ranch," the TV series was set on a dude ranch where kids came to watch western adventures, participate in junior talent performances and play games. Oky always triumphed over his adversaries because of his magic strength pills, which contained milk. The show premiered as a half-hour feature in prime time on November 4, 1948 on Thursdays on the Dumont Network; in March 1949 it became a 15-minute show on Tuesday and Thursday evenings. Its last telecast was May 26, 1949.

ADVENTURES OF RIN TIN TIN, THE   TV show that starred Lee Aaker as Rusty, James Brown as Lieutenant Rip Masters, Joe Sawyer as Sergeant Biff O'Hara and Rand Brooks as Corporal Boone; Lee Duncan was the trainer.

There were two famous dogs in the movies and on TV in the 1950s: Lassie and Rin Tin Tin. Rin Tin Tin was a movie star back in the 1920s, and the original German shepherd that played the role died in 1932. The TV show Rin Tin Tin was played by the great-grandson of the original. The TV series premiered on network TV on October 15, 1954 on ABC on Friday nights and finished its run on August 28, 1959. It was also popular on Saturday morning TV, appearing on CBS from September 1962 to September 1964. The story line revolved around Rusty, who was orphaned after his parents were killed by Indians and was adopted by the cavalry troops at Fort Apache in Arizona. The nearby town was Mesa Verde, and conflicts occurred with Indians, townsfolk and various undesirables drifting through and within the cavalry itself. Rusty would yell "Yo, Rinty" when help was needed, and the dog would come. Actually, three different dogs were used on the series, all trained by Lee Duncan, who treated the dogs like stars. There were a total of 164 episodes shot, all in black and white. The

"The Adventures of Rin Tin Tin"   (Lee Aakers)

half-hour shows were filmed in Corriganville, Vasquez Rock and the Chatsworth Reservoir, all in California, with stock footage making it appear that scenes were shot on location. The show spawned a series of 38 comic books issued by Dell. In 1976 the series was repackaged and reissued, with actor James Brown doing introductions (in color) to each episode while the shows themselves were tinted brown.

ADVENTURES OF WILD BILL HICKOK, THE
TV show that starred Guy Madison as Marshal James Butler Hickok and Andy Devine as his sidekick, Jingles.

The real Wild Bill Hickok did not look like a movie star; Guy Madison, who played the legendary cowboy in the TV series, certainly did. The show began in syndication in 1951 (released in April that year) and continued until 1958. It was shown on the CBS network from 1955 to 1958 and on the ABC network from 1957 to 1958, usually in the daytime or late afternoon. There were 113 TV episodes and a concurrent radio program on Mutual from 1951 to 1956 (recorded at KHJ in Los Angeles), also starring the same duo. Wild Bill wore his gun "backward" (handles sticking out), which is the way the real Wild Bill carried his. However, the real Wild Bill stuck his in a wide belt; Guy Madison had his in beautiful, hand-tooled leather holsters specially constructed. The TV Wild Bill rode his trusty Appaloosa "Buckshot" through various adventures, with Jingles, on his black horse "Joker," yelling, "Hey! Wild Bill, wait for me!" as they rode off. The 30-minute show, sponsored by Kellogg, was incredibly popular during its first years but lost its luster in 1956 when Madison sought to expand the format from 30 to 60 minutes. All the shows were filmed in color, a rarity for early TV shows.

ALAMO, BATTLE OF THE (March 6, 1836) Relations between the Mexican government and Texas settlers had deteriorated after the Mexicans gained independence from Spain in 1821. This led to colonist dissent and an armed rebellion on October 28, 1835; in December Texans captured the Alamo, a former mission, in San Antonio. Originally begun about 1724 and named the Mission of San Antonio de Valero, the fort covered about three acres with a wall 10 feet high and two to three feet thick surrounding it. The mission was built across the San Antonio River from the village of San Antonio de Bexar and had been used as an industrial school where Indians were taught farming, weaving and building. The church was completed in 1757, but the roof and other parts soon collapsed. The mission was abandoned in 1793. It was called "the Alamo" beginning around 1805 because a grove of cottonwood trees (called *alamo* trees in Spanish) were located nearby. At the time of the Texas fight, the Alamo consisted of the church, the Long Barracks, a two-story stone building, and the Low Barracks, a one-story structure.

The Mexican army planned to march through Texas on the El Camino Real, the main road from the Rio Grande to the Sabine River. The army planned to march through San Antonio but expected no real resistance. The Texans were divided and divisive: One plan called for Texans to march south and capture Matamoros, but the government argued and split. General Sam Houston, in charge of an army he could not control, wanted a mobile army to attack and retreat against the huge Mexican army so it would be worn down as it marched. In January, Houston sent a message via Jim Bowie to abandon the Alamo and destroy the mission because he felt it was impossible to defend. But Bowie found the men at the Alamo ready to fight so he joined them. Meanwhile, farther south at Goliad, a group led by James Fannin was still considering a march to Matamoros.

On February 1, 1836 General Antonio Lopez de Santa Anna started his army north from Saltillo. On February 16 he crossed the Rio Grande with 5,400 men, 33 wagons, 200 carts, 1,800 pack mules and 21 cannon. The winter weather took its toll, and soon a number of animals were dead. Texans did not expect Santa Anna to continue marching forward—the conditions to support his huge army would have to wait for warmer weather—but the Mexican general kept coming and on February 20 was only 50 miles from San Antonio.

Meanwhile, at the Alamo 26-year-old William Barret Travis had arrived leading 25 men. Although Travis was put in command of the Alamo, an election among the men soon elevated Jim Bowie, who was suffering from tuberculosis, as their leader. Then, on February 14, Bowie and Travis agreed to command the Alamo jointly; Bowie would head the volunteers while Travis would head the regulars.

Green Jameson led the effort to make the Alamo a strong defensive position. There were 18 cannon positioned on newly built platforms, scaffolds and ramps. Horseshoes were cut up for ammunition, and a hospital was constructed in the Long Barracks. Davy Crockett, the legendary Tennessean, had arrived on February 8 with a dozen Tennessee volunteers and raised the troops' spirits. He turned down a command and served as a private at the Alamo.

The men in the Alamo knew that Fannin and his troops were 95 miles away in Goliad, so Travis sent a messenger on February 16 pleading for reinforcements. But Fannin and his group instead secured themselves in the Goliad mission (renamed Fort Defiance) to await a Mexican attack. That attack never came.

On February 21 Santa Anna camped about 25 miles from San Antonio and ordered his men to attack the city that evening, when the Texans had scheduled a fiesta. A quick rainstorm caused the river to rise, so the attack was called off. By dawn on February 23 a number of citizens were packing and fleeing San Antonio. Initially, the Texans could not believe the Mexican army was advancing; finally, scouts sighted the huge army, and the Texans moved into the Alamo with their families and Mexican friends. By the time the gates closed, there were 150 fighting men, about 25 women and children and some slaves. Travis dispatched messengers with pleas for help from Goliad and Gonzales, about 70 miles east. Then he assigned men to positions and acquired some steers and cows as well as dried corn from nearby farms.

When the people gathered inside the Alamo looked out toward the town of San Antonio, they saw a red flag flown from the church belfry: this was a message from Santa Anna that no prisoners would be taken—it would be a fight to the death. Travis answered with a shot from a cannon. Jim Bowie sent a message requesting surrender in exchange for safe passage for the Texans to their homes; Santa Anna's reply was unconditional surrender. Travis and Bowie disagreed over plans for fighting at this point, but Bowie had become so sick with fever that he collapsed and was placed on a cot.

On the morning of February 24 the Mexican army dug in about 400 yards from the Alamo and began firing cannon and howitzers. At this point, Travis wrote his historic message:

> To the People of Texas & all Americans in the world. Fellow citizens & compatriots—I am besieged, by a thousand or more of the Mexicans under Santa Ana—I have sustained a continual Bombardment & cannonade for 24 hours & have not lost a man—The enemy has demanded a surrender at discretion, otherwise, the garrison are to be put to the sword, if the fort is taken—I have answered the demand with a cannon shot, & our flag still waves proudly from the walls—*I shall never surrender or retreat.* Then, I call on you in the name of Liberty, of patriotism & everything dear to the American character, to come to our aid, with all dispatch—The enemy is receiving reinforcements daily & will no doubt increase to three or four thousand in four or five days. If this call is neglected, I am determined to sustain myself as long

as possible & die like a soldier who never forgot what is due to his own honor & that of his country—*Victory or Death.*

Travis underlined the last three words three times and sent the message out with Captain Albert Martin, who left the Alamo at dusk on the 24th.

When Fannin received this message in Goliad, he initially sent 320 men toward the Alamo, but a series of mishaps—a wagon broke, the oxen escaped—caused Fannin to decide to stay in Goliad. Twenty-five men from Gonzales, led by George Kimbell, came to the Alamo and arrived at 3 A.M. on March 1.

At this point no Texans had been killed, although the Mexicans sporadically bombarded the Alamo. Santa Anna's troops had charged but had been beaten back; however, as more soldiers arrived, the Mexican army surrounded the Alamo and every night came in closer and dug more earthworks.

Inside the Alamo the men stayed at their posts while Davy Crockett played his fiddle and performed duets with John McGrego, a Scot who played bagpipes. On March 3 Travis requested reinforcements again and sent the message via John W. Smith, who also carried a number of letters and messages written by those inside the Alamo to friends and families.

The Mexican army was firing from 200 yards away on Saturday, March 5, and those inside the Alamo began to feel a sense of doom. At five o'clock Travis called the men together and told them their choices were to surrender, attempt escape or fight to the end. He announced that his own choice was to fight but invited anyone who wanted to leave to do so. Only one, Louis Rose, a soldier of fortune who had come to the Alamo with Jim Bowie, chose to leave; the rest stayed.

Firing continued until 10 o'clock Saturday night. At this time, Santa Anna organized his troops for an attack in which he would use 4,000 men to storm the Alamo. The Mexican army slept a little and then rose and began moving into position around 1 A.M. on Sunday morning, March 6. At 5 A.M. someone yelled, "Viva Santa Anna," and a bugler signaled the attack. Travis's second in command, Captain John Baugh, yelled to alarm the Texans, who opened fire as the Mexican soldiers stormed the walls.

The Texans fought back the first wave, but Mexican soldiers kept coming. Travis was killed while on the walls encouraging his troops. On the third surge, the Mexican soldiers reached the walls and began climbing over. The army reserves then came into battle while the Texans continued to fire valiantly. Then in the northwest corner the Mexican soldiers broke through and the Texans fell back; hand-to-hand combat ensued for the next 45 minutes. In the open plaza the Texans retreated to the Long Barracks while the gun on top of the barracks raked the Mexican soldiers with grapeshot from the chopped-up horseshoes. The Texans made their final stand inside the Long Barracks, but the Mexicans got inside and finished the battle with bayonets.

The Mexican soldiers then ran throughout the Alamo, killing everyone until they found Susannah Dickerson, wife of an Alamo defender, and her young daughter Angelina. Because of pleading to Santa Anna from one of Mrs. Dickerson's friends, her life was spared and she was sent to the general. On the way to see the general someone shot her in the right calf. Joe, the slave of Travis, identified the bodies of Jim Bowie and Travis, while five surviving Texans who had hidden were found and executed. Alive were some women and children, the slave Joe, and a San Antonian who convinced the Mexicans he had been a prisoner in the Alamo. It was now about 6:30 A.M. and the sun was up; the fight had lasted about 90 minutes from the first charge.

General Santa Anna told Mrs. Dickerson to go to other Texans and tell them what had happened and warn them the same fate awaited all those who opposed him. With her daughter Angelina and Santa Anna's own servant, an American Negro, as her escort, she went to Gonzales and told the story of the Alamo.

In the end Santa Anna lost about 1,500 men in the fight and quickly buried them. The bodies of those killed defending the Alamo were then piled high and set afire by Mexican soldiers after the battle.

Mrs. Dickerson's story ignited the Texans, who quickly realized they had to fight the Mexican army and win or die. A deep thirst for revenge welled up in the Texans and on April 21, 1836—46 days later—the Texan army led by General Sam Houston defeated Santa Anna and his army at San Jacinto. When the Texans charged, their rallying cry was "Remember the Alamo." Houston's army lost only eight while killing 630 Mexicans and capturing Santa Anna. This created the Republic of Texas. (See also CROCKETT, DAVY; HOUSTON, SAMUEL; MEXICO; SANTA ANNA.)

ALAMO, THE   Film produced and directed by John Wayne; screenplay by James Edward Grant; released in 1960 by United Artists; 190 minutes in length. Cast: John Wayne, Richard Widmark, Laurence Harvey, Richard Boone, Carlos Arruza, Frankie Avalon, Patrick Wayne, Chill Wills, Ken Curtis, Denver Pyle, Aissa Wayne and Guinn "Big Boy" Williams.

This is the movie John Wayne mortgaged everything to make. Wayne wanted a patriotic film and got it; it covers the time period from the formation of the Republic of Texas to the Battle at San Jacinto. John Wayne plays Davy Crockett. The film cost over $12 million; Wayne wanted this to be one of his last movies, but instead he had to make a number of movies after this to recover his personal fortune.

ALASKANS, THE   TV show that starred Roger Moore as Silky Harris, Jeff York as Reno McKee, Ray Danton as Nifty Cronin and Dorothy Provine as Rocky Shaw.

Gold rushes attracted a horde of folks who wanted to get the gold without digging for it. The trio in "The Alaskans" was part of these folks: Rocky Shaw was a saloon singer, Silky Harris was a gambler and card shark and Reno was a con man. The show was set in Skagway, Alaska during the Alaskan gold rushes of the 1890s. The show premiered on October 4, 1959 on

Sunday nights. The hour-long show ended on September 25, 1960, with the last two months consisting of reruns.

ALIAS SMITH AND JONES

TV show that starred Peter Deuel as Hannibal Heyes (Joshua Smith) (1971–72), Roger Davis as Hannibal Heyes (Joshua Smith) (1971–73), Ben Murphy as Jed "Kid" Curry (Thaddeus Jones), Sally Field as Clementine Hale, Roger Davis as narrator (1971–72), and Ralph Story as narrator (1972–73).

The governor made a deal with two outlaws: stay straight for a year and all charges will be dropped. Easier said than done, and this show documents the escapades of the guys. The show began with actor Peter Deuel as Hannibal Heyes, traveling under the alias Joshua Smith, but the actor committed suicide after a couple of episodes. The show was quickly recast, with narrator Roger Davis getting the role and Ralph Story becoming the narrator. The show premiered on January 21, 1971 on ABC on Thursday evenings, then to Saturday nights in September 1972. It ended its run on January 13, 1973 after 48 episodes.

ALLEN, REX

(b. Wilcox, Arizona on December 31, 1922) Rex Allen was the last singing cowboy signed by Republic Pictures; beginning in 1949 with *The Arizona Cowboy*, Allen made 35 movies between 1950 and 1955 and then starred in the TV show "Frontier Doctor." Allen had come to Hollywood from the National Barn Dance on WLS in Chicago—the same place where Gene Autry had begun his career. Later, Allen did narration

Rex Allen

for a number of Walt Disney wildlife films. (See also SINGING COWBOYS.)

ALLISON, CLAY

(b. Robert A. Clay Allison in Waynesboro, Tennessee c. 1841; d. Pecos, Texas on July 3, 1887) A notorious gunman, especially when drunk, Clay Allison is the man who jerked some teeth out of a dentist's mouth in Rock Creek, Wyoming Territory after the dentist had extracted the wrong tooth from Allison's mouth. This is the same Allison who rode naked on his white horse up and down the streets of town and then invited everyone into the saloon for a drink. Allison left his family farm at 21 to fight for the Confederacy in the Civil War and after the war moved to Texas. He herded cattle for Charles Goodnight and Oliver Loving (possibly being one of the drovers who pioneered the Goodnight-Loving Trail) and others before establishing his own ranch in Cimarron, New Mexico. Allison killed a number of men, including Charles Kennedy, whose head he cut off and put on a pole in a saloon; Chunk Colbert; Pancho Griego; Cruz Vega; and Mason T. Bowman. Allison killed Bowman in a quick-draw fight, while Vega's body was dragged through rocks and brush by Allison after the killing. Wyatt Earp drew on him and forced him out of Dodge City—a major notch for the lawman. Allison died when he fell from a buckboard while drunk. (See also COLBERT, CHUNK; GRIEGO, PANCHO.)

ALVORD, BURT

(b. 1866; d. in Latin America c. 1910) Alvord witnessed the famous shootout at Tombstone's O.K. Corral (October 26, 1881) while working as a stable hand. He became deputy sheriff of Cochise County in 1886 and rustled some cattle in Mexico in the 1890s before serving as a constable in Fairbank, then Wilcox, Arizona. He was captured in 1904 after masterminding a series of train robberies and spent two years in the Yuma prison. Upon his release he went to Venezuela, then Honduras, and helped dig the Panama Canal.

AMERICANS, THE

TV show that starred Darryl Hickman as Ben Canfield and Dick Davalos as Jeff Canfield.

This was a Civil War drama in which two brothers fought against each other—one for the Confederacy and the other for the Union. The brothers starred in alternating weeks, so one week the Confederacy point of view was presented and the next the Union. The show premiered on January 23, 1961 on Monday nights on NBC. The hour-long show was last telecast on September 11, 1961.

ANDERSON, BRONCO BILLY

(aka Gilbert M. Anderson; b. Max Aronson in Little Rock, Arkansas on March 21, 1882; d. Woodland Hills, California on January 20, 1971) Bronco Billy Anderson was the first silent-screen cowboy star; he appeared in the first story western, *The Great Train Robbery*, and then joined Selig Polyscope Company as scriptwriter and director about 1904–5. In 1907 Anderson and George K. Spoor founded Essanay Film Manufacturing Company in Chicago (the name was derived from their initials, "S" and "A"). Around 1910, after some trial location filming in Colorado and New Mexico, Anderson moved Essanay productions to Niles, California (near Oakland) and thus became the first filmmaker to set up headquarters in the Golden State. From 1910 to 1915 Anderson starred as "Broncho Billy" in a series of westerns; some sources indicate the first film was in 1907, whereas others claim 1909. Anderson made over 400 of these two-reelers, often writing the script in the morning and filming in the afternoon, until he retired as an actor in 1920. The film industry lost track of Anderson until it decided to award him a special Academy Award in 1958 for his early contributions to the movies; it discovered he was living right in Hollywood. Anderson's last screen appearance came in 1965 when he had a cameo role in *The Bounty Killer.*

ANDERSON, HUGH (b. Texas; d. Medicine Lodge, Kansas in June 1873)   While on a cattle drive, Anderson became part of a group tracking murderer Juan Bideno to Bluff City, Kansas; Bideno was killed by John Wesley Hardin in a shootout there. Anderson was also in the group tracking Mike McCluskie, who had killed Texas gambler William Bailey, a friend of Anderson's. Anderson shot McCluskie at a dance hall, which ignited a bloody gun battle. McCluskie eventually died, as did several other cowboys when bullets flew. Anderson's friends whisked him out of town to Kansas City and then Texas, but he drifted back to Kansas, where he ran into McCluskie's brother. The two killed each other in a duel. (See also MCCLUSKIE, ARTHUR; NEWTON MASSACRE.)

ANGEL AND THE BADMAN   Film produced by John Wayne; directed by James Edward Grant; screenplay by James Edward Grant; released by Republic in 1947; 100 minutes in length. Cast: John Wayne, Gail Russell, Harry Carey, Bruce Cabot, Irene Rich, Lee Dixon and Stephen Grant.

This is the first film produced by John Wayne and concerns the gunfighter Quirt Evans (Wayne), who loves his gun so much that he sleeps with it. When he runs into some Quakers, a beautiful woman's love changes his ways. Evans learns to accept the ways of the Quakers but still must face a violent West and a shady past. In a showdown in town, Evans faces Laredo Stevens without his gun (he has given it to the young lady), but then Stevens is killed by Marshal McClintock when the outlaw draws to kill Evans. Evans then goes off with his new bride to become a farmer.

ANGORAS   Cowboy chaps made from the hide of a goat with the hair still on; these are worn with the hair on the outside.

ANNIE OAKLEY   TV show that starred Gail Davis as Annie Oakley, Brad Johnson as Deputy Sheriff Lofty Craig and Jimmy Hawkins as Tagg Oakley.

Gail Davis really could ride and shoot, which is how Gene Autry discovered her. The five-foot two-inch, 95-pound actress appeared in 20 of Autry's movies and 30 of his TV shows before his production company, Flying A Productions, created the "Annie Oakley" show for her. Riding her horse, Target, and accompanied by her

Gail Davis as "Annie Oakley"

brother Tagg on his steed, Pixie, and Deputy Sheriff Craig on his horse, Forest, Annie Oakley kept law and order around her town of Diablo. The group was sometimes helped by her uncle, Luke MacTavish, who was the seldom-seen town sheriff. The show was the second most popular kids' show on Saturday mornings in 1954. The show premiered in January 1954, sponsored by Canada Dry and T.V. Time Popcorn. The 81 episodes were produced from April 1953 to December 1956. The 30-minute shows were always syndicated and never a network production.

ANTELOPE   Antelope (*Antilocapra americana*) are actually *pronghorns*, a quick, fast (some clocked at 60 miles an hour) and high-jumping animal that travel in large-sized herds. At one time there were approximately 40 million, but as people expanded west, the numbers dwindled to 19,000 before being built back up to about 400,000. Like the buffalo, these were slaughtered by settlers and railroad crews.

ANTRIM, HENRY   See BILLY THE KID.

APACHE INDIANS   The term "Apache" comes from the Zuni word *Apachu*, meaning "enemy." The Indians of this tribe were nomads, very brave but very cruel. They were feared by other peaceful, settled Indians such as the Pueblo because of their raiding and killing throughout the southwestern area that is now Arizona and New Mexico. They lived in wickiups, small brush settlements. There were six main tribal divisions: Jicarilla Apache, Mescalero Apache, Chiricahua, Mimbreno, Sab Carkism and Cititeri. These groups were further divided into bands and these bands into groups of families related through the mother. The Apache fought the U.S. Army, Mexicans and American settlers. In 1875 most were rounded up and put on reservations, although some continued to raid until the surrender of Geronimo in 1886. Great Apache leaders included Geronimo, Mangas Coloradas and Cochise.

APACHE KID (b. c. 1867; d. c. 1894)   An outlaw Indian who served under Al Sieber as an Apache scout. He killed a man to avenge the murder of his father but was granted a pardon by President Grover Cleveland. Despite the pardon, he was sent to the Yuma penitentiary but managed to escape and lived as a hunted outlaw. In 1894 he was either killed or disappeared into Mexico—he may have been wounded in a gun battle and crawled off to die, but his body was never found.

APACHE PASS, BATTLE AT (July 1862)   At the old Apache Pass stage station in Arizona in July 1862, a detachment from the U.S. cavalry led by Captain Thomas L. Roberts left the group of 21 supply wagons to check on a spring for water. When they arrived at the spring, a group of Apache led by Cochise and Mangas Coloradas fired down on them from stone breastworks they had constructed on the slopes above the pass. The soldiers managed to engage a howitzer, which drove off the Indians, but the next day, when the wagons and escort were at the spring, the Indians fired again, and once again the howitzer drove them off and ended the fighting. Realizing the importance of this spring, the army established Fort Bowie at this site on July 28, 1862.

APPALOOSA HORSE   A horse that has been historically associated with the Nez Perce Indians of the Northwest. These spotted horses were brought to the Americas in the 16th century by the Spanish, and by 1730 the Nez Perce had them. The term derives from "a Palouse," or horse from the Palouse River country. After the Nez Perce War of 1877 the horse nearly disappeared, but the Appaloosa Horse Club was formed in 1938 to keep the horse from becoming extinct.

APPLE   The saddle horn or pommel of the saddle.

APPLEGATE, JESSE (b. Kentucky on July 5, 1811; d. Oregon on April 22, 1888)   A major figure in the history of the Oregon Trail, Applegate was captain of the "cow column" in the 1843 migration. This column was composed of about 2,000 cattle that were being driven to Oregon. Applegate's account of this trip, *A Day with the Cow Column*, was published in 1876. Applegate established a farm in the Willamette Valley and then became a leading figure in the history of Oregon, as a member of Oregon's provisional government in 1845. He established a large ranch in southern Oregon in 1849

and was instrumental in the construction of the Oregon and California Railroad.

ARAPAHO INDIANS   These Indians became a Plains tribe after migrating southwest from the Red River in Minnesota. The buffalo hunt was the center of their life and the sun dance an important ceremony. Their major enemies were the Shoshoni, Ute, Comanche, Kiowa, Pawnee, Crows and Sioux. The northern Arapaho were involved in the Battle of the Little Bighorn. They were placed in Oklahoma, then Indian Territory, in 1867 in the Treaty of Medicine Lodge. But the Arapaho wanted a reservation in Wyoming and, with an agreement from the Shoshoni chief Washakie, received one on the Wind River Reservation.

ARBUCKLE   A trade name of a coffee maker that came to be used as a general term for "coffee." It was also used as a term for a greenhorn, the logic being that the boss got him from trading some premium stamps that came with the coffee.

ARGONAUTS   Another name for the forty-niners who went to California during the gold rush that began in 1849. The term can mean any adventurer on a quest but was applied specifically to those who joined the gold rushes in the West. The term is rooted in Greek mythology: a group of heroes who sailed on the ship *Argo* with Jason to capture the Golden Fleece (the pure gold wool of a flying ram). According to the Greek myth, these men captured the golden fleece and received great honors.

ARIKARA INDIANS   The name "Arikara" comes from this group's method of wearing their hair with two pieces of bone standing up like horns on each crest. This was an agricultural tribe that lived in villages along the Missouri River in Nebraska until driven north. The Arikara grew crops of corn, beans and pumpkins and were expert swimmers and fishermen. Neighbors and allies of the Mandan and Hidatsa tribes, they were virtually wiped out in the smallpox epidemic of 1837. The survivors were placed on a reservation in North Dakota in 1870. The Arikara chief Bloody Knife was a favorite scout of General Custer and was killed in the Battle of the Little Bighorn.

ARKANSAS RIVER   Beginning in central Colorado in the Rocky Mountains, the Arkansas River flows across Kansas, Oklahoma and Arkansas for 1,450 miles to the Mississippi. Its principal tributaries are the Cimarron, Canadian and Neosho Rivers.

ARKANSAS TOM JONES (b. Roy Daugherty in Missouri c. 1878; d. Joplin, Missouri on August 16, 1924)   Raised in a religious household (his two brothers became preachers), Daugherty ran away from home to an Oklahoma ranch at 14 and claimed he was Tom Jones from Arkansas. He joined Bill Doolin's gang in the 1890s, and on September 1, 1893 the group of outlaws were in Ingalls, Oklahoma. Daugherty was ill in bed at the City Hotel when he heard gunshots; his cohorts had been drinking and playing poker in the saloon while lawmen gathered. Gang member Bitter Creek Newcomb and law officer Dick Speed traded shots. Newcomb was wounded by Speed, but Daugherty, standing at the hotel window, hit Speed in the shoulder and then killed him with a second shot. A hail of gunfire then erupted, killing one citizen and wounding four others.

Daugherty then went to the roof of the two-story building and commenced firing at lawman Tom Houston as the gang members were hightailing it out of town on their horses. Daugherty killed Houston, but a posse surrounded the hotel and demanded that Daugherty surrender; he held out for an hour, but at 2 P.M., after seeing two sticks of dynamite ready for him, he surrendered. He was sentenced to 50 years in prison for manslaughter but obtained a parole in 1910.

After his release, Daugherty ran a restaurant in Drumright, Oklahoma for a couple of years before going to Hollywood, where he appeared in western movies. In 1917 he came back to Missouri and helped rob a bank in Neosho. Thrown in prison again, he was released in 1921 and immediately went to Asbury, Missouri, where he held up another bank. Daugherty was pursued but avoided the law for three years until August 16, 1924 in Joplin, Missouri, when detectives found him at the home of Red Snow, babysitting. When Daugherty saw the lawmen approaching the house, he grabbed a pistol and shot twice before his gun jammed; lawmen then killed him. (See also DOOLIN, BILL; NEWCOMB, BITTER CREEK.)

ARKANSAS TOOTHPICK A type of knife with a long, tapering blade; sometimes called a "Bowie knife."

ARMSTRONG, JOHN BARCLAY (aka "Mc-Nelly's Bulldog"; b. McMinnville, Tennessee in January 1850; d. Armstrong, Texas on May 1, 1913) John Armstrong is the Texas Ranger who captured John Wesley Hardin on a train in Florida and brought him back to Texas to stand trial, resulting in Hardin doing time in prison. Armstrong had enlisted in the Texas Rangers in 1875 and served under the command of L. H. McNelly. He soon became known as "McNelly's Bull-dog" after accompanying the legendary lawman on some excursions into Mexico.

There was a $4,000 reward for Hardin, and Armstrong traveled throughout the Gulf states looking for the outlaw. On August 23, 1877 the Ranger entered a train coach with Hardin, drew his long-barreled .45 and ordered Hardin and his party to surrender. Hardin grabbed his guns, but the hammer of his pistol caught in his suspenders. Nineteen-year-old Jim Mann, sitting beside Hardin, drew his gun and shot a hole in Armstrong's hat; the Ranger then shot the youth through the chest. Mann leaped out the window but fell dead after staggering a few steps. Meanwhile, back in the coach Armstrong beat Hardin over the head with his pistol until the outlaw was unconscious; he then arrested him and his three companions and escorted them on a train back to Texas. After his days as a Texas Ranger, Armstrong established a ranch in Willacy County, Texas and then became a U.S. marshal for a while. He died peacefully on his ranch. (See also HARDIN, JOHN WESLEY.)

ARMY IN THE WEST Immediately after the Civil War the United States Army was reduced to about 57,000 troops; during the 1869–70 period it was reduced again to 37,000 troops, and then dropped to 24,000 troops by 1890. Since the United States was at "peace" and did not have to worry about outside threats to its security, the role of the army from the end of the Civil War to 1890 was to protect settlement in the West, and specifically to fight Indians.

Congress had first established a regular army in September 1789 with 840 men authorized; however, there were only 672 in the service. This army was supplemented by state militia and citizen volunteers who protected local areas; the army's job was to protect the frontier. The United States Military Academy at West Point, New York was founded in 1802 under Thomas Jefferson to provide a corps of officers, and this led to new roles for the army; it built roads, led explorations and conducted scientific surveys. The Corps of Topographical Engineers, created in 1838, played a major role in the exploration and mapping of the West before the Civil War. The army also established forts in the West that were usually the first settlements and served as markets as well as protection for settlers. The Bureau of Indian Affairs was created in 1832 to help "manage" Native Americans, and the army was charged with carrying out these policies; to this end it supervised the transfer of eastern Indians to Indian Territory (Oklahoma) after the Indian Removal Act of 1830 and engaged in several wars, including the Black Hawk War (1932) and the Seminole War (1834–42). By the 1840s the army was known as a place where immigrants could find work and learn English; at this point about 47% of recruits were immigrants. By the beginning of the Mexican War (1846) there were a little over 8,500 troops; at the end of the war in 1849 there were over 10,700 troops. During the Civil War the Army pulled most of its regular troops out of the West to fight in the East, and the number of troops swelled until the war was finished.

The army had been organized on a territorial basis since 1813, but after the Civil War a new system was established: there would be a Division of the Missouri, a Division of the Pacific and a Division of the East. The Division of the Missouri included the Departments of Arkansas (Arkansas and Indian Territory), Missouri (Missouri, Kansas and Colorado and New Mexico Territories), the Platte (Iowa and Nebraska, Utah and some of Dakota Territories along with some of Montana) and Dakota (Dakota and Montana Territories and Minnesota). There were some changes in the 1866–90 period, but this system remained basically intact in the West during the era of western settlement in the second half of the 19th century.

In 1868 there were about 2,600 army men in the West and around 200,000 Indians. Some posts had less than 50 men in isolated areas; still, the army was charged with defeating the Indians and managed to do so over the 25-year period because of organization, weapons and the simple fact that white settlement made it impossible for nomadic Indians to survive. During a significant part of this period (1866–76) the army was led by its commanding general, William Tecumseh Sherman.

Being a soldier was tough work; during the Civil War soldiers received $16 per month, but at the end of that war Congress was in a budget-cutting mode and reduced the soldiers' pay to $13 in 1871. The typical life of a soldier was divided between living on a post and being out looking for Indians. The army was very class conscious; officers and enlisted men did not socialize and had two different paths on the fort. (See also BUFFALO SOLDIERS; INDIAN WARS.)

ARNESS, JAMES (b. James Aurness near Minneapolis, Minnesota on October 22, 1921)   James Arness is most famous for playing Matt Dillon in the TV series "Gunsmoke." The show began in the fall of 1955 as a half-hour program and became a one-hour program in 1962; it remained on the air for 19 years, until 1975. Arness got the role because John Wayne turned it down; because Arness was signed to Wayne's production company, Wayne recommended him. Arness had appeared with Wayne in *Big Jim McLain* (1952) and had planned a career in the movies before he was sidetracked with a TV series. Arness and his younger brother, Peter Graves, both excelled in sports in high school (Arness in baseball and football); but after high school they took different paths: Graves went to college, and Arness joined the army and entered World War II, earning a Purple Heart after he was wounded at Anzio Beach. (See also GUNSMOKE; TELEVISION WESTERNS.)

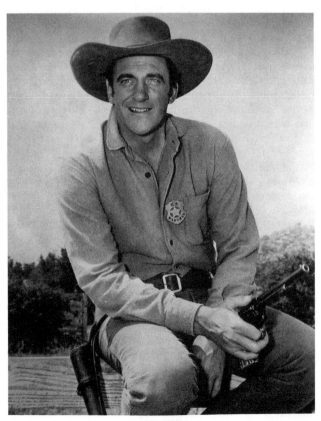

James Arness

ART Western art deals with themes of the western experience, specifically the area west of the Mississippi. The most popular and recurring picture themes involve Indians, cowboys, the frontier experience, mountain men, pioneer life and landscapes of the West.

Since its inception in the early 19th century, western art has undergone vast changes, reflecting the evolving story of the settling of the West.

After the Louisiana Purchase in 1803 the Lewis and Clark Expedition across the Rockies to the Pacific Ocean created tremendous interest among Americans, who were enthralled with stories brought back of natural wonders and Plains Indians. The Indians in the West were not like their eastern counterparts, and the diversity of cultures among the tribes intrigued the public as well as artists. During the first half of the 19th century, pictures of Indians and Indian life dominated western art.

These pictures served valuable purposes: they documented the Indians for anthropologists and ethnologists; they preserved a people and cultures that would soon disappear; and they gave this country an art that was distinctly American. Although the Hudson River school was established by this time, as a nation the United States was still an extension of Europe. The country's first artists were influenced by European portrait painters as well as landscapes. Western art would change that by giving artists distinctively American subjects: the West, cowboys, Indians, pioneers and the frontier life. Even though European influences would continue to be felt throughout the 19th and 20th centuries (some artists attempted to incorporate French impressionism in their works, while artists such as Georgia O'Keeffe were influenced by cubism and other European innovations), western art at its best would come to be defined as a distinct genre.

Critics of western art sometimes complain that it is more "illustration" than "art," and indeed the two dominant figures in western art, Frederic Remington and Charles Russell, were illustrators. A number of other western artists began as illustrators or made their living this way until their paintings could sell.

Western art is in harmony with the character of the West: it depicts life as it is—or was. The story of life in the West is strong, the truths overwhelming, and if carefully set down on canvas, it reflects great art.

Remington and Russell are good examples of this style—art that is powerful because it pictures a way of life that appeared only briefly. Even the landscapes of Albert Bierstadt and Thomas Moran helped create the myth of the West by conjuring the impact the landscape had on those who first saw it.

Western art may be subtle and sublime, but it must also have a literal appeal and value as well. One need not study art in formal academies or even introductory college courses to appreciate it: it is an art that one either likes or not at first glance.

However, to dismiss western art as only for those who cannot appreciate "true" art or as something second rate is to miss its true essence. The essential appeal of western art is that it captures the western experience.

This experience involves history, myth and a vanishing people, cultures and way of life. It includes the grandeur of the land, the heyday of the cowboy, the vanishing of the Indians and the buffalo, the time when the land was a second Garden, when the world was all before us, wild and untamed. It is an active art that captures viewers and transports them to a time past or a way of life they've never known—or perhaps know too well. At its best, western art mirrors the West itself. There is an inherent contradiction here: the West is many places, many stories and many images. The greatest challenge of western art is that it acknowledges this single identity while showing something separate from it, or perhaps unique to this identity. At its most basic, it deals with the conflict of people and nature. At its best, western art deals with people and nature through the stories of cultures clashing as the white settlers displaced the Native Americans as the dominant people in this land.

In chronological terms, the first "western" artists were those who accompanied early explorers on ships off the west coast. John Webber provided pictorial documentation on Captain Cook's third voyage in 1778, and John Sykes was an illustrator on Captain George Vancouver's Pacific expedition between 1790 and 1795. By this time, an artist was an important part of expeditions, serving to illustrate the reports written by explorers.

The first real examples of American western art are portraits of Indians painted early in the 19th century. The Indians had come to Washington, D.C. at the invitation of the government and while there posed for portraits. Charles B. J. F. de Saint-Memin (1770–1852), a young French nobleman, painted the earliest known portraits. The Osage Indian chiefs he painted had come to Washington at the behest of President Thomas Jefferson in an attempt to establish diplomatic relations in the newly purchased Louisiana Territory. Saint-Memin painted with the aid of a physiognotrace, a wooden device that enabled him to trace his subject's exact profile.

The first American artists to go into the West on an expedition were Titian Ramsay Peale (1799–1885) and Samuel Seymour (1796–1823), both from Philadelphia. Peale, only 19 at this time, was the son of the renowned Philadelphia artist Charles Wilson Peale. His job was to make sketches of geological formations as well as to collect, preserve and sketch specimens on the trip. Seymour painted landscapes and portraits of Indians engaged in ceremonial activities as well as in council. On this expedition, led by Major Stephen Long in 1820, Peale made the first sketches of a Plains Indian hunt and the first drawings of Plains Indian tipis. Seymour became the first artist to paint the snowcapped Rocky Mountains.

An early important figure in western art was not a painter but Thomas L. McKenney, superintendent of the Bureau of Indian Trade. Later, McKenney headed the Office of Indian Affairs when that organization was first formed. He established the Archives of the American Indian while at the Department of War; these archives included a number of Indian artifacts and were, in essence, the first museum of Indian people and Indian life. Beginning in 1822, McKenney commissioned portraits of Indian chiefs.

McKenney sent Otto Lewis (1799–1858) to treaty conferences on the frontier, and the artist sent McKenney some watercolors. Later, Lewis published *The Aboriginal Portfolio* (1835) with hand-colored lithographs done by printers Lehman and Duval of Philadelphia. These groups of prints were sold to subscribers, who were assured by Lewis Cass, a government agent, that the portraits were accurate and faithful to the original. This assurance came in the form of an endorsement, printed on the cover of these collections of lithographs. Lewis also supplied a text to accompany his pictures to help sell them to the public.

Thomas McKenney also produced some lithographs of Indian portraits that he published as *History of the Indian Tribes of the United States with Biographical Sketches and Anecdotes of the Principal Chiefs*. This was a three-volume set, published between 1836 and 1844, and featured pictures painted primarily by Charles Bird King (1785–1862) but also some by Lewis and others. McKenney compiled biographies of the Chiefs to accompany the portraits with the aid of James Hall, who authored most of the text. The book by McKenney and Hall achieved a fairly wide audience. Especially notable were the portraits done by Charles Bird King, an artist more polished than Lewis.

The first American artist to go west on his own was George Catlin (1796–1872), who spent the years 1830 to 1836 visiting over 50 Indian tribes. His collection of Indian paintings eventually numbered more than 600, and Catlin spent his life exhibiting his collection and trying to sell it, primarily to the government. Catlin also wrote several books, including *Letters and Notes on the Manners, Customs and Condition of the North American Indians* (1841), which featured engravings of some of his paintings.

In the East, Catlin had painted portraits of the Delaware, Shawnee and Iroquois. On his first visit to the West, he left St. Louis and went up the Missouri River to Fort Pierce, where he painted Sioux and Cheyenne, and then on to Fort Union at the mouth of the Yellowstone River—the American Fur Company's farthest post—painting a number of portraits of Blackfeet and Crow. Returning down the river, he painted wildlife and landscapes. In the Mandan villages, he painted portraits of leading figures as well as scenes from their daily and ceremonial life. It was fortunate Catlin painted the Mandan because he arrived as this once mighty tribe was being decimated by smallpox. First hit by the disease in 1787, the Mandan were struck again in 1837 in an epidemic that left only about 150 survivors from a population that once numbered over 12,000.

In the following years Catlin painted a number of Plains Indians, including the Osage, Kiowa, Comanche and Wichita. He paid excellent attention to ethnographic detail and left a valuable legacy for ethnologists and anthropologists. Critics of Catlin's work note that he was perhaps a better reporter than artist and paid less attention to composition than he did to recording the details of his subject's dress and culture.

From the earliest part of the 19th century many believed the Indians were a dying breed and that Indian life in the West would one day disappear. Catlin used this theme in his book, saying he felt his calling was "to rescue from oblivion . . . their primitive looks and customs," which he did with his paintbrush and pen.

Catlin became the preeminent artist and historian of Indians during the first half of the 19th century but could not convince the government to buy his works. For 30 years he toured American and European capitals with his "Gallery," but he lost ownership of his Indian gallery paintings because of bankruptcy. He then painted a second series to raise money and recover his losses. Eventually the Smithsonian purchased his Indian Gallery in 1879, seven years after his death. Catlin was the first artist to document the breadth and diversity of the native cultures in the West and became the first major American western artist.

Karl Bodmer (1809–93), a Swiss artist who accompanied the Austrian prince Maximilian of Wied-Neuwied to the United States in 1832, created a major publication on Indians. Maximilian loved natural history and on his trip out West wanted an artist to document the journey; Bodmer's watercolors illustrated the text written by Maximilian, and the work was published as *Travels in the Interior of North America*, first in German, then in French and English.

The high cost of reproducing the prints in book form made the audiences relatively small and exclusive. Still, these publications in the early 19th century presented to the American public for the first time authentic artistic images of the American Indian in the West.

Bodmer and Maximilian had begun their trip in the spring of 1833 on a steamboat up the Missouri River to Fort McKenzie at the mouth of Marias River. Here they saw a battle between the Blackfeet and combined Cree and Assiniboine tribes; during the fight Bodmer sketched. In the winter the group returned downstream and stayed at the Mandan and Hidatsa villages. Bodmer and Catlin are the outstanding painters of western Indian life in the pre–Civil War era. Technically Bodmer was a better painter, but Catlin was more prolific; like Catlin, Bodmer was valuable to anthropologists and ethnologists who studied Indians.

Sir William Stewart was a Scottish sportsman who made a grand tour of the Rockies in 1834, employing famed mountain man Jim Bridger to guide him from the Bighorn Mountains of Wyoming to an area south of Taos, New Mexico. In the fall of 1835, Stewart was in New Orleans, where he met painter Alfred Jacob Miller (1810–74) and invited him to join an expedition in the spring of 1837. During the expedition Stewart wanted Miller to paint pictures to serve as souvenirs, and the painter made a number of sketches that he developed into paintings in later years.

One of the most significant events witnessed by Miller was the trappers' rendezvous in 1837 on the Green River. Here, Miller did for the white trappers what Catlin did for the Indians: He recorded a vanishing way of life and preserved one of the major events for these men.

Miller returned with Stewart to Scotland, where he was artist in residence at Captain Stewart's castle. He finished a number of paintings from his initial watercolors there before returning to Baltimore, where he painted portraits and western scenes.

Miller only made one trip to the West, but this single trip provided him with an entire career. No longer would he be strictly a portrait painter; now he could sell patrons pictures of the West done from some of the same sketches he had done for Stewart. He painted in an early romantic style with mood lighting and an ethereal atmosphere that would come to dominate western landscape painting later in the century. But Miller was ahead of his time and not a great influence on his contemporaries; in fact, many of his paintings were unknown during his time and "discovered" 100 years after his death.

Although George Catlin, Karl Bodmer and Alfred Jacob Miller are considered three major painters in western art during the first part of the 19th century, they were certainly not alone. A number of other artists made significant contributions to western art during this period.

Peter Rindisbacher (1806–34) came to Canada from Switzerland in 1821 and continued his work in Fort Snelling, Minnesota, where a number of Swiss settlers migrated after the hardships of Manitoba winters. Rindisbacher is perhaps best known for painting *The Murder of David Tully and Family*, which documented the murder by the Sissetoon Sioux near Grand Forks. He died at the age of 28, and much of his best work was done before he was 20.

Seth Eastman (1808–75) graduated from West Point in 1829; one of his courses there was drawing. While stationed at Fort Snelling, Minnesota in 1841, he painted numerous pictures of Indian life, primarily the Santee Sioux. His paintings were so acclaimed that he was commissioned to illustrate *Indian Tribes of the United States*, by Henry Schoolcraft. After retiring from the army as a brevet major general, Eastman spent the rest of his life painting Indians, often with commissions from Congress.

Like George Catlin, John Mix Stanley (1814–72) attempted to secure government patronage but was rebuffed by Congress. Stanley also created an Indian gallery because he, too, believed the Indians were a disappearing people; unfortunately, all but a few of his works were destroyed by fire. Stanley began traveling in the West in 1842 when he went to Indian councils in present-day Oklahoma. He served in the army in the West as a draftsman, traveling to the Southwest and California. Stanley's final western journey came in 1853–54 when he was part of the expedition led by Isaac Stevens to survey a northern route for the Pacific Railroad. He made sketches of the Piegan division of the Blackfoot Indians. Stanley settled in Washington, D.C. in 1857 and began preparing his work to illustrate the book by Stevens, but a fire there in 1865 destroyed all but five of his Indian paintings. Stanley spent his final days in Detroit as a portrait painter.

Thomas Mickell Burnham (1818–66) moved to Detroit from his native Boston in the late 1830s and worked as a sign painter. In 1838 he opened a studio, painting portraits and other genre scenes. He probably painted his most famous picture at this time, a rendition of the Lewis and Clark Expedition.

Artists played an important role in expeditions by explorers and topographers in the West. The artists served the function later served by photographers—to document visually the land, people, flora and fauna—and to provide illustrations for the texts the explorers wrote. These artists were important because they allowed Americans to see the West for the first time.

William Jacob Hays (1830–75) went to the Missouri River basin in 1860—his only trip there—but painted a number of pictures, particularly of buffalo. Although Worthington Whittredge (1820–1910) is primarily associated with the Hudson River school artists, he made several trips west. His first, with Major General John Pope to New Mexico and Colorado, was in 1866, and there he produced a number of paintings of the plains.

George Caleb Bingham (1811–79) was born in Virginia but his family soon moved to Missouri, where he first studied the ministry and law, then art. He enrolled at the Pennsylvania Academy at 26 and then moved to Washington, where he painted portraits for four years before returning to Missouri and painting scenes of western life, including his well-known *Fur Traders Descending the Missouri.* Bingham liked painting everyday scenes; although he painted Indians, he was never really effective in their depictions. Bingham was one of the most popular painters of his time; additionally, he was the first major painter who actually lived in the West. Most other painters were easterners who visited the West.

John James Audubon (1785–1851) was the preeminent naturalist in America during the early 19th century. Audubon studied in France before returning to America in 1803 to manage his father's estate in Pennsylvania. After some failed businesses and a short period as a taxidermist at the Cincinnati museum, he began traveling the Ohio and Mississippi Rivers and the Great Lakes area studying and painting birds. Unable to find an American publisher for his paintings of over 1,000 birds, Audubon finally had the book published in England. Returning to the United States in 1831, Audubon explored the Texas coastline; in 1843 he went up the Missouri River to Fort Union, continuing to the Yellowstone River overland. Here, Audubon did for birds what Catlin did for Indians. He also painted deer, badgers and foxes and collected Indian artifacts before returning to his Hudson Valley estate.

John Woodhouse Audubon (1812–62) was the son of the artist-ornithologist John James Audubon. Born in Kentucky, the younger Audubon accompanied his father on a number of trips and helped his father with *Viviparous Quadrupeds of North America* along with his brother Victor. The three all worked on both text and color plates. John caught "gold fever" in 1849 and joined the gold rush; he did not strike it rich with gold but did return with some animal specimens.

William T. Ranney (1813–57) was born in Connecticut but moved south as a boy to North Carolina to work for an uncle as a tinsmith. After studying art in Brooklyn and serving with the army during the war with Mexico, he returned home to Brooklyn and painted portraits and western themes. His most famous painting is *Prairie Burial,* a sentimental picture of pioneers burying their young child.

Charles Deas (1818–67) grew up in Philadelphia and visited George Catlin's Indian Gallery, which inspired him about the West. He moved to St. Louis in 1841 and visited several Indian tribes. In 1844 he went to the Platte River headwaters with Major Wharton's expedition.

Rudolph Kurz (1818–71) was born in Switzerland but became enchanted with the West early in his life. He went to New Orleans in 1846 after three years studying in Paris and then moved to St. Joseph, Missouri, where he settled and made sketches of Indians—the Iowa, Oto, Pawnee, Osage and others. He obtained a position as clerk at Fort Berthold in 1851 and sketched Hidatsa and Mandan survivors until cholera broke out. He was advised to leave there because the Indians believed his drawings might be to blame. Kurz then moved west to Fort Union, near the mouth of the Yellowstone, where he sketched Crow, Assiniboin and Plains Cree Indians. Although Kurz sketched quite a bit, he did not convert his drawings into many finished works of art.

James Walker (1818–89) emigrated from England to New York City when he was young. During the Mexican War he was captured and imprisoned but escaped and became an interpreter for the U.S. Army. Walker sketched battle scenes in the Mexican War as well as the Civil War, during which he served in the Union. After the Civil War Walker went to California, where he painted the vaqueros.

Charles Nahl (1819–78) was born in Germany and went to New York in 1848 after studying in Germany and Paris. Nahl joined the California gold rush in 1850 and became a miner with his brother. However, Nahl spent more time sketching the activities of the miners and eventually became a full-time artist, exchanging his drawings for gold dust as well as selling them to newspapers, magazines and, later, books. *Sunday Morning in the Mines* is Nahl's most popular work. Few artists painted mining life in the West; Nahl is one of those few.

Arthur F. Tait (1819–1905) was born in England and moved to New York when he was 31. Tait never went to the West, but his western genre paintings were popular; the lithographers Currier and Ives published some of his prints. Newbold H. Trotter (1827–98) was born in Philadelphia and apparently traveled to the West (no details of his travels are known) because western themes began appearing in his works. Trotter was primarily an animal painter, and his most famous western paintings feature the buffalo.

Charles Wimar (1828–62) was a native German who moved to St. Louis with his parents in 1843. In 1852 Wimar returned to Dusseldorf, Germany to study painting. He traveled to St. Louis in 1856 and sketched around the area. His most well known works, such as *The Attack on an Emigrant Train,* are highly dramatic and show the German influence with light and shadow, while his landscapes rival Bierstadt's in grandiosity.

William Hays (1830–75) was a New Yorker who specialized in western wildlife after a trip up the Missouri River in 1860.

Albert Bierstadt (1830–1902) was the premier painter of landscapes in the American West during the 19th century. He had studied in Dusseldorf, Germany, and the European influences were obvious in his works, large landscapes that romanticized the West with depictions of the grandeur and awesomeness of mountains, canyons and other natural wonders. Bierstadt's people and animals were always dwarfed by the land, a perspective that made people seem insignificant in the West.

At the age of two Albert Bierstadt went to New Bedford, Massachusetts from Germany with his parents. He returned to Germany in 1853 to study art and returned to New Bedford when he was 27; two years later he joined General Frederick Lander's expedition to survey the Oregon Trail. In 1863 Bierstadt made his last trip west except for the 1871–73 period when he set up a studio in San Francisco.

Bierstadt's studio was in New York, and during his life he was immensely popular in America and Europe, receiving $25,000—more than most painters receive in their life—for his painting *The Rocky Mountains*, which measures over 6 feet by 10 feet.

Bierstadt visited Yellowstone in 1881 and painted some memorable pictures; some of his paintings of Yellowstone were lent to President Chester A. Arthur for the White House. The painter most identified with Yellowstone is Thomas Moran (1837–1926), who first visited Yellowstone in 1871 as part of the government-sponsored expedition led by Ferdinand Hayden.

Moran's paintings of Yellowstone, as well as the photographs taken by William Henry Jackson on the expedition, were shown to Congress by Hayden, who lobbied for a national park in the region; Congress proclaimed Yellowstone the first American national park on March 1, 1872 as a result of these efforts. Like Bierstadt, Moran painted the grandeur of the landscape, full of drama. Moran's final visit to Yellowstone came in 1892 when he painted the Golden Gate Canyon.

Thomas Moran was actually the first western landscape painter to capture the grandeur of the land. His work, which precedes Albert Bierstadt's, puts the human in rather insignificant perspective with the lofty mountains. Although his work came to be clouded with misty romanticism and dismissed during his lifetime, his awe-inspiring canvases created a sense of wonder among those who first saw the West through his paintings.

Born in England, Moran moved to Philadelphia as a child but returned to London when he was 21 to study art. His father was a weaver who apprenticed his son to an engraving firm. Moran was introduced to watercolors as a teenager by marine artist James Hamilton. He established a small engraving studio with his brother, Edward, and in 1861 the brothers went to England to study art under J. M. W. Turner.

Moran returned to America in 1862 and married Mary Nimmo. The couple began a two-year tour of Europe in 1866 where Moran studied the old masters. Returning to the United States, Moran taught painting and illustrated books and magazines. In 1870, at the age of 33, with a wife and three children and in need of money, he was assigned by *Harper's* magazine to illustrate an article by Montana native Nathaniel Langford about the Yellowstone country. Langford had been part of the Washburn expedition to Yellowstone and had collected some rough sketches done by some members of the party.

The assignment piqued Moran's curiosity; he had difficulty imagining the landscape from the sketches, and when he learned of a geological survey team going there in the summer of 1871 headed by Dr. F. V. Hayden, he requested to go along, stating he would pay his own way.

Moran was part of the first major expedition to Yellowstone in 1871. Going as a trained artist, he saw the opportunities for marketing his works and getting future commissions. He joined photographer William Henry Jackson and received money from Jay Cooke ($500) from the Northern Pacific Railroad (in return for a dozen future watercolors) and an advance from *Scribner's* magazine.

Moran was a thin man who did not look like he could take the rigors of the West. Indeed, he disliked eating wild meat so much that he spent a good deal of time fishing for his meals.

The expedition reached Devil's Slide on Cinnabar Mountain on July 19, 1871 and the following day saw the Mammoth Hot Springs, the first whites to do so. At each site, Moran made some quick sketches and color notations. He also helped Jackson with his photographic equipment, realizing the photographs would help his painting.

Moran returned to the East in early August with a sketchbook full of ideas and proceeded to paint all winter. The paintings, along with Jackson's photographs, were submitted to Congress and played a major role in its decision to make Yellowstone the first national park. The government also purchased several large oil paintings, including *Grand Canyon of the Yellowstone.*

Moran returned to the West in 1872, touring the Yosemite region with his wife, and in 1873 joined Major John Wesley Powell on an expedition through Utah and Arizona on the Colorado River. In 1874 Moran sketched the Mount of the Holy Cross in Colorado and in 1879 toured Idaho and Nevada. He returned to Yellowstone in 1892 to see a hotel erected at Mammoth Hot Springs. In 1916 Moran moved to Santa Barbara, where he died at the age of 89.

Thomas Hill (1829–1913), another artist known for his grandiose landscapes, emigrated from England to America when he was 15. In 1862 he moved to California after seeing the Yosemite Valley. He went to Paris in 1866 to study for two years; he then returned first to New England and then to California, where he spent his efforts and energies painting Yosemite landscapes. Hill not only painted large scenes, he used large canvases: his *Great Canyon of the Sierras* is 6 feet by 10 feet, and *The Driving of the Last Spike* is over 8 feet by 11 feet.

The two artists who dominate western art are Frederic Remington (1861–1909) and Charles Russell (1864–1926). All other western artists are compared with these two; indeed, western art itself is virtually defined by the works of Remington and Russell. Their work captures the end of the golden era of the cowboy, and these two artists reflected the myth of the cowboy at the same time they created it; the 20th-century cowboys on television and in the movies would look like their cowboys. Russell's and Remington's work achieved its initial fame in the late 19th and early 20th century, a time when the Old West was disappearing but had not quite gone. Russell and Remington were there during the final days of the Old West, and their paintings and sculptures have become a valuable bridge from the Old to the New West.

Frederic Remington grew up in upstate New York with an innate love for the outdoors. He first traveled to the West in 1881 and later lived briefly in Kansas. However, Remington's studio was in the East, and here he painted from sketches he compiled from his annual trips out West.

Remington first attracted attention as a popular magazine illustrator; this allowed him to earn money with his art and financed his travels to the West. His cowboy, cavalry and Indian pictures were usually dramatic narratives, telling a story while creating the image of the West for easterners. Later, Remington worked in oils to create works of art and then, in 1895, turned to sculpture.

Charles Marion Russell grew up in St. Louis with a love of the Wild West. After several futile attempts by his parents to change him, he was finally sent to Montana in 1880 to live with a family friend. Russell would remain in the West the rest of his life, working as a cowboy and then as an artist. Russell's artistic talents were all innate and self-taught, and he spent a number of years using his talents as a hobby to amuse his fellow cowboys, trading his drawings and paintings for some drinks or selling them for a few dollars. After his marriage in 1896, Russell's wife, Nancy, began to market his art back East, and the artist eventually was acclaimed as a major western artist.

Russell was at his best when drawing the working cowboy. Since he had worked as a cowboy himself, he knew intimately the day-to-day life of these men. He painted them in a way that captured their life as well as enhanced it, contributing to the myth of the cowboy as hero. Russell also had a sympathetic and deep understanding of the Indian, a result of having lived with the Bloods tribe during one winter.

Russell is also known for his sculpture works, of which he molded a large number.

A number of artists have been influenced by Russell's and Remington's painting style. For these artists, the cowboy joined Indians and western landscapes as an important, vital subject. Many of these artists were, like Russell and Remington, first illustrators, capitalizing on the market for western stories and articles. During the latter part of the 19th century and first part of the 20th, Americans wanted to know about

the West, and magazines and book publishers presented works to satisfy that demand. A number of artists benefited from their work, especially Olaf C. Seltzer (1877–1957), who went to Montana in 1892 and met Charles Russell in 1897. Russell befriended Seltzer and the two painted together, with Russell's style providing a great influence on Seltzer.

Charles Schreyvogel (1861–1912) was born in New York City to a poor family and taught himself to draw. Two patrons sent him to Europe when he was 19, and upon his return he was encouraged to go west for his health. He visited Colorado and Arizona and then returned to the East and painted portraits. His major break as an artist came in 1900 when he submitted *My Bunkie,* a western painting of a cavalryman rescuing his officer, to the National Academy of Design, where it won first prize. From this point Schreyvogel's career flourished, and he painted a number of cavalry pictures. Schreyvogel copied many of Remington's army themes—and incurred the wrath of Remington—but his fascination with the cavalry produced a number of fine paintings as well as the excellent sculpture *The Last Drop.*

J. Edward Borein (1872–1954), known as the "cowpuncher artist," traveled to Mexico in 1897–99 and sketched. He returned to California to become a staff artist on the *San Francisco Call* in 1899, and in 1901, with Maynard Dixon, he went to the Sierras, Carson City, Oregon and Idaho and sketched. Borein returned to Oakland in 1904 and set up a studio. He stayed there until 1907, when he moved to New York City. There he became a successful illustrator for popular magazines as well as for advertisers. Finally, Borein moved back to California in 1919, where he remained until his death.

Artist N. C. Wyeth (1882–1945) was one of the premier illustrators during his time, and his experiences on a Colorado ranch in 1904 (where he worked as a ranch hand) led to a series of paintings on the life of a cowboy. Wyeth then wrote a text for his painting entitled *A Day at the Round-up* which was published by *Scribner's.* Wyeth was born in Needham, Massachusetts and moved to Delaware at 20. In 1906 he settled in Chadd's Ford, Pennsylvania. He became one of America's greatest illustrators, with his work appearing in numerous magazines and children's and adult classic books. Gradually, however, Wyeth began to move away from painting about the West, feeling stereotyped as a western artist and wanting to be known as well for other things.

W. H. D. Koerner (1879–1938) was born in Germany but grew up in Iowa. He obtained a job with the *Chicago Tribune* as an illustrator when he was 17 and later studied in New York. Koerner did not go west until 1924 when he visited Montana; later he traveled to California and the Southwest. Koerner's illustrations appeared often in the *Saturday Evening Post.* He had a studio in New Jersey and used western artifacts in his studio for book covers and magazine illustrations until he finally went to Montana on a family vacation.

Frank Tenney Johnson (1874–1939) was born in Iowa and grew up in a frontier environment near the Oregon Trail. He moved to Milwaukee with his family in 1884 and then studied in New York. He went to Colorado and the Southwest as an illustrator for *Field and Stream.* Eventually, he moved to California where he painted full-time, earning enough to give up illustrating. One of Johnson's specialties is nocturnal scenes. Johnson was attracted to Yellowstone, spending his summers from 1931 to 1938 at the Rimrock Ranch, about 30 miles from Yellowstone Park. Johnson's paintings of Yellowstone are more impressionistic than descriptive, while the work of John Henry Twachtman (1853–1902) is almost completely impressionistic. Twachtman's Yellowstone paintings were based on his single visit to the West in 1895.

Rosa Bonheur (1822–99) was a painter Buffalo Bill Cody met in Paris in 1889 when he was touring for his Wild West show. Bonheur painted a famous portrait of Cody on a white horse that hung in his North Platte, Nebraska home. This painting was supposedly one of Cody's favorites. Harvey T. Dunn (1884–1952) was born in a sod house in South Dakota and painted western subjects for book covers and magazine illustrations. Irving R. Bacon (1875–1962), who was trained in Munich, was known for his painting *The Conquest of the Prairie,* which glorified Buffalo Bill Cody. In this symbolic painting, the Indians sit on their horses watching Cody lead a wagon train across the plains.

Carl Rungius (1869–1959) first went to Wyoming in 1895 as a hunter. He is known for his work on wildlife. Hermann Herzog (1831–1932) was another artist born in Germany who studied at Dusseldorf. In 1869 he left Europe for Philadelphia and traveled throughout the United States; he was most widely known for his landscapes. William Cary (1840–1922) was born in New York and grew up in New York City. On a trip to the West, he spent six weeks at Fort Union and then joined a wagon train headed for Fort Benton that was captured by Crow Indians. The group was released when a Crow chief recognized one of the captives, a fur company man. After Fort Benton, Cary went to Oregon Territory and then San Francisco.

Henry Farny (1847–1916) came to this country from France and settled in Cincinnati with his family in 1852. He traveled to Europe to study art and then returned as an illustrator for magazines. He made his first trip to the West in 1881 and began bringing back Indian artifacts for his studio.

Ralph Albert Blakelock (1847–1919) was born in New York and traveled west in 1869 making notes and sketches. Specializing in landscapes, he painted in an impressionist style ahead of his time. Blakelock's works are interesting today for their moody and mystical use of light and shadow, but during his time his paintings did not sell and he became financially destitute.

Elbridge Ayer Burbank (1858–1949) went west around 1895 and began painting Indians. His portraits are of interest to ethnologists and anthropologists because of his attention to detail.

Winold Reiss (1888–1953) was born in Germany and read James Fenimore Cooper's *Leather-Stocking Tales,* which enthralled and intrigued him about Indians. He headed for the American West at 25 but ran out of money in New York City. Six years later he visited the Blackfoot Indian reservation in Montana and made portraits. He returned to Montana a number of times to paint the Blackfeet and was commissioned by the Great Northern Railroad to do portraits for its calendar—which he did for 31 years.

Olaf Wieghorst (1899–) was born in Denmark and moved to New York at 19. He enlisted in the Fifth Cavalry, which was patrolling the Mexican border. After three years as a soldier he worked as a cowboy in New Mexico on the Quarter Circle 2 C Ranch before returning to New York City, where he joined the New York City Mounted Police.

Perhaps no other event in American history has captured artists' attention like Custer's fight at the Little Bighorn when he and his troops were soundly defeated by a gathering of Sioux. The event occurred on June 25, 1876, and within a month W. M. Cary's picture of Custer appeared in the *New York Graphic and Illustrated Evening Newspaper.* But F. Otto Becker's copy of Cassily Adams's version of the event became more famous.

Cassily Adams (1843–1921) was born in Zanesville, Ohio and studied in Boston and Cincinnati. His painting *Custer's Last Fight,* which measured 12 by 32 feet, was acquired by Anheuser-Busch, Inc. in 1890 when it took over the assets of a bankrupt saloon. The firm hired Otto Becker (1854–1945) to paint a smaller version, and 150,000 lithographs were made and presented to saloons all over America; it became one of the country's most famous paintings. The picture shows Custer, long hair flying in the wind, wearing buckskin and brandishing a sword as Indians charge him. However, there are a number of factual errors: for example, Custer had short hair—he had just had it cut—at the time of the fight; no officers were known to carry sabers; the Indians did not carry Zulu shields; and Custer was wearing a blue flannel shirt—not buckskin—at the encounter. Still, this painting defined the image of Custer at his last stand for millions of viewers.

In all there have been over 800 paintings of the battle—and more are still being painted. More books and pamphlets and articles have been written about it than any other battle in U.S. history. Remington and Russell both painted versions of the events; so did Sharp, William Dunton, N. C. Wyeth and Walt Kuhn.

In addition to paintings, a number of artists made some fine sculptures. These include Remington and Russell as well as Solon Borglum (1868–1922), the son of Danish immigrants who moved to Nebraska in search of religious tolerance; Sally James Farnham (1876–1943), a friend and colleague of Remington's; Hermon Atkins MacNeil (1866–1947); Alexander Phimister Proctor (1862-1950), who made 37 life-size sculptures of animals and other figures for the 1893 Columbia Exposition at Chicago; Henry Merwin Shrady (1871–1922), who specialized in animals—particularly the buffalo—studying the animals at the Bronx Zoo after finishing his law studies at Columbia; and James Earl Fraser, who created the memorable *End of the Trail* sculpture in 1898, constructing a heroic-sized version for the Panama-Pacific Exhibition in 1915.

An artists colony developed in Taos, New Mexico at

the end of the 19th century, and this community has had a significant impact on western art throughout the 20th century.

Joseph Sharp (1859–1953), one of the founders of the Taos Society of Artists, was born in Connecticut and studied in Cincinnati and then Europe. Two years after he returned from Europe, he traveled to Albuquerque and Santa Fe, New Mexico. Enthralled by the landscape and the Indians, he encouraged two other artists, Bert Phillips and Ernest Blumenschein, to go to Taos and Santa Fe to paint. Sharp moved to Taos in 1902 after a period of time when he taught at the Cincinnati Art Academy and spent his summers in Taos and Montana. He viewed Indians as thoughtful, gentle, contemplative people.

Ernest Blumenschein (1874–1960), born in Pittsburgh, was an accomplished violinist before he became an artist. While studying in Paris he met Joseph Sharp and Bert Phillips and, with their encouragement, went to the Southwest to paint, spending his summers in Taos and winters in New York teaching. Blumenschein moved to Taos in 1919 and became an important figure in the Taos Society of Artists.

Oscar Berninghaus (1874–1952) studied art in St. Louis while working as a lithographer. He first went to the Southwest when he was 25 and visited Taos, meeting Bert Phillips. From this time Berninghaus spent his summers in Taos and winters in St. Louis before moving to Taos in 1925, where he was one of the founders of the Taos Society of Artists.

Walter Ufer (1876–1937) was born in Louisville but went to Germany to study art. He returned to the United States and settled in Chicago, where the mayor encouraged him to visit Taos—and even paid his way. Ufer arrived in New Mexico when he was 38 and was immediately asked to join the Taos Society of Artists.

W. Herbert Dunton (1878–1936) grew up in Maine and made his first trip to the West at 18. Eventually, he made a number of trips, working as a ranch hand and cowboy, and moved to Taos when he was 34. There he joined the Taos Society of Artists and painted a number of action-filled cowboy pictures.

Ernest Martin Hennings (1886-1956) was born in New Jersey and studied in Germany. He returned to America at the outbreak of World War I, painting murals in Chicago. He visited Taos in 1919 and moved there in 1921, becoming a member of the Taos Society of Artists in 1924.

E. Irving Couse (1866–1936) was born in Saginaw, Michigan and studied in France, where he met Joseph Sharp and Ernest Blumenschein, who encouraged him to go to the Southwest. In 1902 Couse visited New Mexico and set up a studio in Taos in 1906 where he painted Indians in idealized and romantic portraits.

A number of other artists are affiliated with the Southwest, and their paintings reflect the light and images of that region of the country.

Maynard Dixon (1875–1946) was born in Fresno, California and worked as an illustrator for the most popular magazines of the day. When he was 37, Dixon gave up illustrating and turned to painting. His most famous painting is *Medicine Robe*, completed in 1915.

Robert Henri (1865–1929) was born in Cincinnati but studied in Paris. In 1891 he returned to America and taught in Philadelphia and New York; he then broke with his colleagues and became a member of "the Eight" (also known as the Ashcan school), a group that also included John Sloan, William Glackens and George Luks. His first trip west was in 1916, which marks the beginning of western themes in his paintings.

William R. Leigh (1866–1955) was born in West Virginia and spent 12 years in Munich, Germany. In 1897 he went west for the first time on assignment for *Scribner's* magazine. Leigh's best paintings are of the Southwest and Pueblo Indians, although he also painted cowboys and Plains Indians.

Gerald Cassidy (1879–1934) was born in Cincinnati and moved first to New York and then to Albuquerque, where he became acquainted with the Indians. He moved to Denver and then back to New York to study painting. In 1912 he moved to Santa Fe, where he specialized in murals.

Nicolai Fechin (1881–1955) was born in Russia and moved to New York City in 1923. He moved to New Mexico because of his health (he had tuberculosis) and built a house in Taos. He returned to New York in 1934.

Henry C. Balink (1882–1963) was born in Amsterdam and moved to New York City at 22. In 1917 he made his first visit to Taos and moved to Santa Fe 13 years later. His fascination with Indians led to his making a number of paintings with them as his subjects.

Georgia O'Keeffe (1887–1986) was one of the most individualistic painters to be considered "western." Born in Wisconsin, she studied in Chicago and New York. For a while she gave up art but then took a job teaching art in the Amarillo, Texas school system in 1912. Later she taught at the University of Virginia and achieved success in New York when photographer Alfred Stieglitz began showing her pictures in his studio. She married Stieglitz in 1924, and between then and his death in 1946 she spent her winters in New York and summers in New Mexico. After Stieglitz's death, she moved to Abiquiu, New Mexico. O'Keeffe used symbolism, abstraction, hard-edged realism, neocubism and surreal juxtapositions in her work. She is known for her paintings of enormous flowers and for white animal skulls.

Thomas Hart Benton (1889–1975) was born in Missouri and studied in Chicago and Paris, where he finally rejected all "isms" and concentrated on a wholly American style of art, devoted to folksy subjects. Benton's forte was small-town, rural America, and the West was part of this. He has been described as a "fabulist," and his figures tend to "writhe" in his pictures.

Other artists who have had an impact on western art include:

Will James (1892–1942)
Harold von Schmidt (1893–1982)
Peter Hurd (1904–84)
Frank Mechau (1904–46)
John Clymer (1907–)

Tom Lovell (1909–)
Oscar Howe (1915–)
R. Brownell McGrew (1916–)
Newman Myrah (1921–)
Harry Jackson (1921–)
Tom Ryan (1922–)
James Bama (1926–)
Don Spaulding (1926–)
Fritz Scholder (1937–)
Ned Jacob (1938–)
Michael Coleman (1946–)

See also REMINGTON, FREDERIC; RUSSELL, C. M.

ASHLEY, WILLIAM HENRY   (b. Chesterfield County, Virginia c. 1778; d. in Missouri on March 26, 1838)   Ashley formed the Rocky Mountain Fur Company, which was the first association of American fur trappers in the Rockies, in order to make money to pursue a political career. He formed his company with partner Andrew Henry by placing an ad in Missouri newspapers in March 1822. A number of initial recruits would become famous mountain men, including Jim Bridger, Jedediah Smith, Bill Sublette and Hugh Glass. Because he did not have money for wages, the normal way to pay trappers, Ashley outfitted the trappers and then took a share of their furs. This marked the first time that mountain men provided beaver furs; previously, the fur companies purchased the furs from Indian trappers. Ashley also began the rendezvous system, whereby a meeting place in the wilderness was established for trappers to bring their furs, instead of taking them to established forts. Ashley sold his interest to Jedediah Smith and two partners in 1826 and retired from the fur business. He served in Congress from 1831 to 1837.

ASSINIBOIN INDIANS   Part of the Yanktoniai Sioux, these Plains Indians lived in the Lake Winnipeg region.

ASTOR, JOHN JACOB   (b. Waldorf, Germany on July 17, 1763; d. New York City on March 29, 1848) Because Astor was heavily involved in the beaver fur business during the prime early years of that business, he became the wealthiest man in the United States during his lifetime. Born in Germany, Astor went to the United States in 1784 as a salesman for flutes and through a chance encounter became aware of the fur business. Astor moved into the Old Northwest (what is now Ohio and Indiana) in 1796 when the British abandoned that area; in 1808 he organized the American Fur Company and set up operations at the mouth of the Columbia River in Astoria. This venture folded during the War of 1812, and Astor shifted his fur business to the Northwest; by 1812 the South West Company, which he had helped form, dominated the fur trade in this region. In 1821 Astor persuaded Congress to abolish fur posts and leave the field to private firms; obviously, this benefited Astor a great deal. In 1823 he began trading operations on the plains and in the Rockies and in 1826 established the western department of the American Fur Company. Astor saw the decline of the

beaver trade and left the fur business in 1834; from this point on he concerned himself with realty investments in New York City, where he lived.

ATEN, IRA   (b. Cairo, Illinois on September 3, 1863; d. Burlingame, California on August 5, 1953)   Aten joined the Texas Rangers when he was 20 and was assigned to border duty. He was involved in a shootout with cattle rustlers in May 1884 but ended up spending 27 days in the Webb County jail on trumped-up charges brought by a crooked sheriff. He also pursued murderer Judd Roberts and wounded him twice during gunfight encounters. Aten and John Hughes ambushed Roberts in July 1887 in the Texas panhandle ranch house of a girl he had been courting. Roberts tried to shoot his way out but was killed, dying in the arms of his sweetheart. In 1889 Aten was involved in the gunfight that killed cattle rustlers Alvin and Will Odle. Later (1895–1906) Aten became superintendent of 600,000 acres of the XIT ranch and then moved to California with his wife and five children. Aten lived until he was nearly 90.

AUSTIN, STEPHEN FULLER   (b. Wythe County, Virginia on November 3, 1793; d. Austin, Texas on December 27, 1836)   Stephen Austin is the true founder of the colony in Texas that later became a republic and then a state. His father, Moses Austin, had been granted permission by Spanish authorities to establish a colony of 300 families in the area now known as Texas in 1820. But before he could carry out his plans, he died, and

Stephen Austin (*Daughters of the Republic of Texas Library*)

Stephen took over. Educated at Yale and Transylvania Universities, Stephen had managed his lead-mining business and been a member of the Missouri territorial legislature for six years (1814–20) before taking up the settlement of Texas. Austin selected a site, and colonists began arriving in December 1821; in January 1822 the first legal Anglo-American colony had been established. During this same period Mexico became independent from Spain, and the Mexican government refused to recognize the Spanish grant; it was Stephen Austin's persistence and diplomatic skills that kept the colony going during these early years. The colony elected a government in 1828, and Stephen Austin became law-maker, chief judge and military commander and man-aged to keep a steady flow of immigrants into Texas. But in 1830 the Mexican government sought to stop the Anglo-American immigrants (by 1832 there were ap-proximately 8,000 people in Austin's colonies), which brought about the Texas War of Independence. Austin traveled to Mexico to mediate this dispute but was imprisoned and finally released in 1835; this ended his hope of an Anglo-American state within Mexico. Austin returned to Texas in June 1836—after the Battle of the Alamo and Battle of San Jacinto—but was defeated for the presidency of the Republic of Texas by Sam Houston. Austin accepted the post of secretary of state but died in December 1836 at the age of 43.

AUTRY, GENE   (b. Orvon Gene Autry near Tioga, Texas on September 29, 1907)   Gene Autry popular-ized the singing cowboy during the 1930s. Prior to Autry,

Gene Autry singing

Gene Autry

westerns sought to be realistic with cowboy actors found in rodeos, in Wild West shows and from western ranches. Autry was not rugged; in his appearance he was the antithesis of the frontier cowboy. But he was the cowboy America loved most during the 1930s and, in-deed, until the 1950s when he hung up his guns as a movie and TV star.

Autry was born on a small farm in Texas. His father, Delbert, who was a livestock dealer and horse trader, often took him to cities like Fort Worth and Kansas City where he purchased records and was exposed to a wide variety of music. His mother, Elnora Ozmont Autry, taught him to play guitar, and Autry did his first public singing in the Indian Creek Baptist Church where his grandfather, the Reverend William Autry, served as pastor.

Autry toured briefly with the Fields Brothers medi-cine show while in high school and played saxophone in the school band. When he graduated in 1925, he took a job as a telegrapher for the Saint Louis and Frisco Railroad where he spent the next three years. Stationed near Chelsea, Oklahoma, just outside Tulsa, Autry was on duty in 1928 when Will Rogers came in to wire his newspaper column to his editor in New York. Autry was singing and playing his guitar at the time, and the two sang some songs together before Rogers filed his col-umn. Rogers encouraged the young man to try singing professionally, so taking advantage of a free railway pass and vacation time, Autry went to New York to audition for recording companies.

On this first trip to New York, Autry did not find instant success, but in late 1929 he did make recordings for a variety of labels—Victor, Grey Gull, Columbia, Cova, OKeh and Gennett—under a number of pseudonyms. Autry was invited to record because he sounded so much like Jimmie Rodgers, the reigning king of country music at the time and one of Victor's top sellers. In fact, his most successful early recording was "Left My Gal in the Mountains" b/w "Blue Yodel No. 5," a Rodgers song, for the Columbia Records group.

Autry signed with the American Record Corporation (ARC), under the direction of Arthur E. Satherley. In October 1931 Autry recorded "That Silver Haired Daddy of Mine" for ARC, a song he wrote with Jimmy Long that sold half a million copies. This record would establish Autry as a hillbilly singer. Autry also obtained a spot in Chicago on radio station WLS. "Oklahoma's Singing Cowboy," as Autry called himself, appeared on the WLS Barn Dance, then the most popular country music program in the nation and one that reached a huge audience in the Midwest. He also appeared on the "Conqueror Record Time" on the same station.

Autry made good use of his western background and increasingly sang songs with western themes, moving away from his initial influence of Jimmie Rodgers and the "Blue Yodel" numbers. Sears, the giant mail-order company that owned WLS, sold Gene Autry records, songbooks and "Round-Up" guitars in its catalog, merchandise that spread his name throughout the rural heartland.

Autry spent the years 1931 to 1934 in Chicago performing on radio and recording for ARC Records under "Uncle Art" Satherley.

Autry got his first break onto the silver screen when cowboy star Ken Maynard became too difficult to work with and was replaced by Autry.

There was no thought that Autry would become a major cowboy star—in fact, it was thought that it was impossible for a clean-cut cowboy to become a western star. The producer decided to name the lead character "Gene Autry" instead of the original script name because Autry had a following in the Midwest and South, the prime market for cowboy movies, from his exposure on WLS, through the Sears catalog and through his recordings. It was a move based on simple finance: The name Gene Autry might sell a few tickets. Later that year Autry starred in his first feature film, *Tumbling Tumbleweeds* from Republic Studio. Also in the film with Autry was a western singing group, the Sons of the Pioneers, with a young singer named Leonard Slye, who would later become Roy Rogers.

Once he got his break in the movies, Autry's fame soared. In 1936 he was voted the number three western star, behind longtime favorites Buck Jones and George O'Brien, and by 1937 was firmly ensconced as the number one western movie star in the nation. In addition to his roles in movies, Autry also continued to record and sold millions with western songs like "Tumbling Tumbleweeds," "South of the Border," "Mexicali Rose," hillbilly songs like "Have I Told You Lately That I Love You," "Be Honest with Me," and "At Mail Call Today." After World War II Autry had his greatest success as a recording artist with children's classics like "Here Comes Santa Claus," "Peter Cottontail" and "Rudolph the Red Nosed Reindeer." In fact, of the more than 25 million records that Gene Autry sold, "Rudolph" accounted for about nine million of that total.

In 1937 Gene Autry walked off the Republic set over a contract dispute and took off on a concert and personal appearance tour.

In 1939 Autry began a CBS radio show entitled "Melody Ranch" that was sponsored by Wrigley's gum and ran for 17 years. This show featured a combination of music, comedy and a 10-minute dramatic feature, complete with sound effects, in which Autry played the role of the cowboy hero. Autry's stage shows were also popular during this period, and he made a number of appearances with rodeos.

During World War II Autry served in the Army Air Corps, flying a supply plane in Asia, and at this time Roy Rogers replaced him as "King of the Cowboys." When he returned to the movie sets after the war, Autry viewed his show business career as a business while diversifying his investments. As a result Autry became a fabulously wealthy man.

In 1947 Autry moved to Columbia Studios from Republic. Also in the late 1940s he began Flying A Productions, which produced a number of shows for television, including "Annie Oakley" and his own TV series between 1950 and 1955. But the 1950s marked the end of the show business career of Gene Autry. In 1953 Autry filmed his last feature, *Last of the Pony Riders*, and in 1956 he stopped production on his "Melody Ranch" radio series and his weekly TV show. He stopped personal appearances in 1961 and the following year did his last major recording, "Gene Autry's Golden Hits" for RCA.

Gene Autry made more movies than any other singing cowboy. Although Autry's movies were romanticism and escapism, he insisted on high quality in the production and new songs for each picture. It was this insistence on quality that allowed Autry to become a top recording artist with songs from his movies.

Gene Autry became a household name between 1935 and 1956 because of his exposure in the movies, on recordings, on radio and on television, as well as through his personal appearances. He made the cowboy a romantic hero and made country music respectable and national. His success created the demand for singing cowboys, and Tex Ritter, Roy Rogers, Rex Allen, Eddie Dean, Jimmy Wakely, the Sons of the Pioneers and others reaped the benefits of the trail blazed by Autry. He also blazed the trail with merchandising, selling his name for holsters, cap pistols, sweatshirts, games, comic books, hair oils, spurs, chaps, wristwatches and the Autry Stampede Suit, which was promoted as "Western Made for Western Man."

In 1969 Gene Autry was elected to the Country Music Hall of Fame.

(See also BURNETTE, SMILEY; B WESTERN MOVIES; COWBOY COMMANDMENTS; GENE AUTRY SHOW, THE; MOVIES; REPUBLIC STUDIO; SINGING COWBOYS.)

Following are listed Gene Autry's movies:

In Old Santa Fe (1934)
Mystery Mountain (1934)
Phantom Empire (1935), serial
Tumbling Tumbleweeds (1935)
Melody Trail (1935)
Sagebrush Troubadour (1935)
Singing Vagabond (1935)
Red River Valley (1936)
Comin' Round the Mountain (1936)
The Singing Cowboy (1936)
Guns and Guitars (1936)
Oh, Susanna (1936)
Ride, Ranger, Ride (1936)
The Big Show (1936)
The Old Corral (1936)
Roundup Time in Texas (1937)
Git Along, Little Dogies (1937)
Rootin' Tootin' Rhythm (1937)
Yodelin' Kid From Pine Ridge (1937)
Public Cowboy No. 1 (1937)
Boots and Saddles (1937)
Manhattan Merry-Go-Round (1937)
Springtime in the Rockies (1937)
The Old Barn Dance (1938)
Gold Mine in the Sky (1938)
Man from Music Mountain (1938)
Prairie Moon (1938)
Rhythm of the Saddle (1938)
Western Jamboree (1938)
Home on the Prairie (1939)
Mexicali Rose (1939)
Blue Montana Skies (1939)
Mountain Rhythm (1939)
Colorado Sunset (1939)
In Old Monterey (1939)
Rovin' Tumbleweeds (1939)
South of the Border (1939)
Rancho Grande (1940)
Shooting High (1940)
Gaucho Serenade (1940)
Carolina Moon (1940)
Ride, Tenderfoot, Ride (1940)
Melody Ranch (1940)
Ridin' on a Rainbow (1941)
Back in the Saddle (1941)
The Singing Hills (1941)
Sunset in Wyoming (1941)

Under Fiesta Stars (1941)
Down Mexico Way (1941)
Sierra Sue (1941)
Cowboy Serenade (1942)
Heart of the Rio Grande (1942)
Home in Wyomin (1942)
Stardust on the Trail (1942)
Call of the Canyon (1942)
Bells of Capistrano (1942)
Sioux City Sue (1946)
Trail to San Antone (1947)
Twilight on the Rio Grande (1947)
Saddle Pals (1947)
Robin Hood of Texas (1947)
The Last Round-Up (1947)
The Strawberry Roan (1948)
Loaded Pistols (1949)
The Big Sombrero (1949)
Riders of the Whistling Pines (1949)
Rim of the Canyon (1949)
The Cowboy and the Indians (1949)
Riders in the Sky (1949)
Sons of New Mexico (1950)
Mule Train (1950)
Cow Town (1950)
Beyond the Purple Hills (1950)
Indian Territory (1950)
The Blazing Sun (1950)
Gene Autry and the Mounties (1951)
Texans Never Cry (1951)
Whirlwind (1951)
Silver Canyon (1951)
Hills of Utah (1951)
Valley of Fire (1951)
The Old West (1952)
Night Stage to Galveston (1952)
Apache Country (1952)
Barbed Wire (1952)
Wagon Team (1952)
Blue Canadian Rockies (1952)
Winning of the West (1953)
On Top of Old Smokey (1953)
Goldtown Ghost Riders (1953)
Pack Train (1953)
Saginaw Trail (1953)
Last of the Pony Riders (1953)

AZTEC LAND AND CATTLE CO. See HASH-KNIFE OUTFIT.

BACA, ELFEGO   (b. Socorro, New Mexico in 1865; d. Albuquerque, New Mexico on August 27, 1945)   At the age of two, Elfego Baca was kidnapped by Apache Indians, who returned him to his family two days later—unharmed. His family moved to Kansas when he was a boy and then returned to New Mexico, where, at the age of 19, he ordered a badge from a catalog firm and named himself a deputy sheriff. In October 1884 in Frisco, New Mexico, when a cowboy named McCarty from John B. Slaughter's ranch was drunk and shooting up the town, making people "dance" by firing at their feet, Baca pinned on his badge, pulled out his pair of six guns and "arrested" McCarty. Several of the cowboy's friends confronted Baca and demanded that McCarty be released; Baca gave them to the count of three to leave—then counted and began shooting, injuring some cowboys. One cowboy, named Young Perham (the foreman for Slaughter's ranch), was killed during the gunfire when his horse reared and then fell on him. The next morning local citizens demanded that Baca turn over the prisoner to the local justice of peace, who fined McCarty $5. Meanwhile, outside the courthouse were 80 cowboys led by ranch owner Tom Slaughter. Shots were fired when Baca came out; the self-appointed lawman ducked into an alley and then ran to a small building. Inside the building was a woman and two children; Baca pushed them outside. Rancher Jim Herne tried to get in, but Baca killed him. Thus began a siege. The gang of cowboys began firing at the flimsy building while inside Baca crouched low on the floor, which was about 18 inches below ground level. Now and then Baca raised up and shot back at the cowboys; he had deadly aim, killing four men and wounding several others. The cowboys continued to pour bullets into the house, shooting up the walls and causing the roof to cave in. But Baca, crouched low in a corner, dug himself out of the rubble. At midnight a stick of dynamite destroyed half the building, but Baca was in a far corner and was unhurt. The next morning, Baca cooked himself breakfast. Finally, at 6 P.M. Baca surrendered to a deputy sheriff, who allowed him to keep his guns. Baca then rode to Socorro, where he was acquitted of murder. Baca continued to lead a charmed life: He was run over by a fire truck, stabbed several times and survived three automobile crashes. He became a lawman, then a lawyer, and his reputation caused a number of bad men to not test their luck against him. He died at the age of 80.

BACK IN THE SADDLE AGAIN   Song written by Gene Autry (September 29, 1907–) and Ray Whitley (December 5, 1901–February 21, 1979). Published by Western Music in 1940.

In 1938 Ray Whitley got an early morning call from a movie executive telling him that another song was needed for a movie Whitley was to sing in that starred George O'Brien. Whitley had come to Hollywood as a singing cowboy, which was the rage of this period after Gene Autry created this type of western hero in 1935. Whitley had to come up with a song in two hours, and he told his wife, "I'm back in the saddle again." When she commented that that was a good title, he sat down and composed the song quickly. The song was first performed in the movie *Border G-Man* and later recorded by Whitley with his group, the Six Bar Cowboys, for Decca in 1938. For Gene Autry's movie *Rovin' Tumbleweeds*, Autry and Whitley rewrote the song; in 1940 Autry began using it as the theme song for his radio show "Melody Ranch." (See also AUTRY, GENE; WHITLEY, RAY.)

BACK-TRACK   Going opposite to the signs on a trail or going back over a trail.

BADLANDS OF DAKOTA   Located in North and South Dakota, these areas have rocks, ridges and crumbly soil in an arid region that is difficult to travel across. Bitterly cold in winter, extremely hot in summer, the Badlands possess their own beauty with unusual rock formations and shades of colors. These are now part of the Theodore Roosevelt National Memorial Park.

BAKER, CULLEN MONTGOMERY   (b. Weakly County, Tennessee on June 22, 1835; d. southwestern Arkansas on January 6, 1869)   Cullen Baker, who served in and deserted both the Confederate and Union armies during the Civil War, had killed a number of men as a member of a gang of bandits. But in 1869 he was hunted by a group led by Thomas Orr, a schoolteacher with a crippled right hand that Baker had bullied. The group found Baker and a companion having lunch beside the road; they opened fire and killed both men. After the shooting, they found a shotgun, four revolvers, three derringers and six pocket knives on Baker's body.

BAKER, JIM   (b. Belleville, Illinois on December 19, 1818; d. on May 15, 1898)   Jim Baker learned Indian culture so well he dressed like one, adopted Indian customs and mannerisms and married six Indian squaws. At 19 he joined a group of trappers recruited by Jim Bridger for the American Fur Company and trapped beaver in the Rocky Mountains. Later, after the fur trade had declined, Baker worked for General Harney at Fort Laramie as chief scout and guided an army against the Mormons in 1857. In 1873 Baker

BASS, SAM

23

settled down in Wyoming in the valley of the Little Snake River, where he built a home and raised livestock.

BALLAD OF CABLE HOGUE, THE

Film produced and directed by Sam Peckinpah; screenplay by John Crawford and Edmund Penny; released in 1970 by Warner Brothers; 120 minutes in length. Cast: Jason Robards, Stella Stevens, David Warner, Strother Martin, Slim Pickens, L. Q. Jones, Peter Whitney, and R. G. Armstrong.

Cable Hogue, abandoned in the desert, miraculously discovers water, realizes a stage route goes by this water hole and decides to make money from this discovery. He sets up a stage stop and then engages in business, killing a customer who won't pay, overcharging, cheating customers and running a restaurant where the plates are nailed to the table (it makes washing easier; he just throws a bucket of water on them). In this comedy Cable, an irascible but likable rogue, dies when a car runs over him, symbolic of the end of the Old West.

BANDANA

A cowboy's neckerchief, or cloth worn around his neck. This bandana protects the back of the neck from sunburn, keeps the dust out of a cowboy's mouth, filters water and serves to hold on hats and cover the ears during cold storms. It can also hide a man's face if he wants to rob a bank.

BANNOCK INDIANS

A branch (also called the Basnnack) of the Shoghonean family that once lived in Idaho and Wyoming, also going into Oregon. Their primary source of food was the camas root. The Bannock War began in 1878 when about 1,500 Indians (Bannock and Paiute) led by Chiefs Buffalo Horn and Egan fought the U.S. Army. The war came about because the livestock of settlers were eating the camas roots, depriving the Indians of their food.

BAR

When referring to a brand on a horse or cow, a straight horizontal line.

BARBARY COAST, THE

TV show that starred Doug McClure as Cash Conover, William Shatner as Jeff Cable, Richard Kiel as Moose Moran and Dave Turner as Thumbs, the piano player.

Set in San Francisco's wildest section during the 1870s, this show featured a casino owner (Jeff Cable) and a government secret agent (Cash Conover) who try to bring some criminals to justice in the midst of this mayhem. The show premiered on September 8, 1975 on ABC on Monday nights. The hour-long show moved to Friday nights in October 1975 and ended its run there on January 9, 1976.

BARBED WIRE

During the 1870s barbed wire was introduced to the western plains, ending the era of the open ranges. Barbed wire made it possible to divide the range; previously fences were made of stone or wood, but in the West these materials were scarce and the region too large to make this practical. The most popular barbed wire was developed by an Illinois farmer, Joseph F. Glidden, in 1874; his type was a special barbed spur twisted through the double-strand wire. Also called "bob" wire, it doomed the large cattlemen who used open range—often public lands—for their own cattle. This led to "fence wars" in which fences were cut. By 1890 most of the private range land was fenced. The barbed wire helped cattle breeding because it controlled the breeding process. It also gave a new job to the cowboy: riding fence to check for breaks or repairs. It also reduced rustling, established boundaries and allowed farmers to plant crops without fear of cattle overrunning them.

BARLOW KNIFE

A pocketknife; also called a Russell barlow knife, barlow pocketknife and barlow pen knife.

BARNES, SEABORN

(b. Cass County, Texas; d. Round Rock, Texas on July 19, 1878) Barnes (aka "Seab" and "Nubbins Colt") was the chief lieutenant and trusted accomplice of infamous Texas outlaw Sam Bass. Raised near Fort Worth, Barnes spent a year in the Fort Worth jail when he was 17 and then joined a gang of thieves organized by Bass in the Dallas area. In four train robberies, Barnes was shot in his legs four times. His end came in Round Rock, Texas, where the Bass gang had planned to rob the bank. The group, consisting of Bass, Barnes, Frank Jackson and Jim Murphy, rode into town on Friday, July 19, to look the place over for the robbery planned the next day. But Murphy had become a secret informant for the Texas Rangers and tipped off authorities. Barnes, Bass and Jackson were in the store next to the bank when Deputy Sheriffs Morris Moore and Ellis Grimes came in. The lawmen grabbed Barnes and asked if he was armed. Barnes immediately pulled his gun and opened fire, killing Grimes and wounding Moore. The outlaws then ran out of the store for their horses, but local citizens opened fire. Texas Ranger Dick Ware was in the barbershop getting a shave but ran out with his face still covered with lather and shot Barnes in the head. He died on the street and was buried in the Round Rock cemetery, next to the campsite they were using. Sam Bass died a few days later from his wounds and was buried next to Barnes. (See also BASS, SAM.)

BASS, SAM

(b. Mitchell, Indiana on July 21, 1851; d. Round Rock, Texas on July 21, 1878) In 1870 Sam Bass moved to Denton, Texas and was hired by Sheriff W. F. Eagan, but Bass preferred horse racing. In 1876, with Joel Collins and Jack Davis, he drove some cattle from Texas to Kansas but failed to hand over the money to the Texas rancher who owned the cattle. Bass and Collins then went to Deadwood, where they indulged in high living with booze and floozies until the money ran low. The three cowboys then set up their own brothel but drank the profits and gambled away the rest of the money. Desperate, they recruited three others and began robbing stagecoaches and trains. Their first big haul was on September 19, 1877 when they got $60,000 from a Union Pacific train in Big Spring, Nebraska. Pursued by posses, three of the outlaws were gunned down; one revealed the names of the others involved. This put the Pinkertons and others on their trails, but Bass continued to recruit gang members and rob in the Dallas area. They planned to rob the bank in Round Rock, Texas, but one of the members, Jim Murphy, was an informer and had alerted the Texas Rangers, who were waiting for the gang. On their way to rob the bank, Murphy dropped behind to buy corn for their horses; the others went into a store where a gunfight ensued. One gang member, Seaborn Barnes, was killed in the store, but Bass and Frank Jackson got on their horses. Texas Ranger George Harrell pumped a bullet into Bass that ripped into the right side of his spine and left by his naval; Bass rode a short way before falling out of his saddle. Gang member Frank Johnson picked him up, but Bass couldn't go on. When the posse found Bass the next morning, the outlaw was sitting under a tree. He was taken back to Round Rock, where he lingered for a day and then died on his 27th birthday, his lips sealed about any useful information for the law officers. (See also BARNES, SEABORNE; SAM BASS (song)).

BAT MASTERSON   TV show that starred Gene Barry as Bat Masterson.

The real Bat Masterson was a bit of a dandy, and he actually had a derby, cane and special gun given to him by the citizens of Dodge City after his tenure as sheriff. But the real Bat Masterson was never quite as glamorous as Gene Barry's version, who used his wits, charm and cane to charm ladies and extricate them from undeserved accusations. The half-hour show began on October 8, 1959 on NBC on Wednesday evenings. In October, 1959 it moved to Thursdays, where it ended its run on September 21, 1961.

BAXTER, WARNER   (b. Columbus, Ohio on March 29, 1891; d. Beverly Hills, California on May 7, 1951)   Baxter won an Academy Award as "the Cisco Kid" in the first major western with sound, *In Old Arizona* (1929). This was Baxter's second film and made him a star. Baxter began his stage career in Louisville, Kentucky and went to Los Angeles with a stock company after working in vaudeville. In 1936 Baxter was Hollywood's top moneymaking actor, but he suffered a nervous breakdown and was inactive from 1941 to 1943, which ended his career. Other westerns Baxter appeared in include *Romance of the Rio Grande* (1929), *The Cisco Kid* (1931), *The Squaw Man* (1931) and *The Return of the Cisco Kid* (1939).

BAY   A horse with a chestnut red-brown color. Usually these animals have a black mane and tail.

BEADLE AND ADAMS   See DIME NOVELS.

BEAN, JUDGE ROY   (b. Mason County, Kentucky c. 1825; d. Langtry, Texas on March 16, 1903)   The son of Francis and Anna Bean, Roy left home in 1847 with his brother Sam. He killed a man in a bar in Chihuahua, Mexico but escaped to San Diego, where he lived with his brother Joshua. After Joshua was killed by gunman Joaquin Murietta, Roy took over his brother's saloon in San Gabriel. He killed a Mexican officer after quarreling over a woman and was hung, but

he managed to get cut down by the girl (fortunately, the rope stretched during the hanging) in the nick of time. However, because of an injury to his neck from this incident, Roy Bean was never able to turn his head again.

Bean worked briefly in a New Mexico bar and then moved to San Antonio, where he became a blockade runner during the Civil War and prospered for 16 years. On October 28, 1866 he married Virginia Chavez, and they had four children.

After selling his property for $900 in 1882, Bean established a tent saloon in Eagle's Nest and then moved to Vinegaroon between the Rio Grande and the Pecos River. Bean was appointed justice of the peace there on August 2, 1882 by Texas Ranger Captain T. L. Oglesby. Because he was recognized by the Texas Rangers, Bean took the liberty to ply his trade as both saloon keeper and judge—although he was nearly illiterate.

Bean established a town named Langtry, after the English actress Lily Langtry (Bean had a lifelong infatuation with her), and set up a saloon called the Jersey Lilly. Judge Roy Bean ruled this town in west Texas for 20 years and died there of heart and lung complications.

During these later years, Judge Roy Bean became known as the "Law West of the Pecos." Actually, it was his own version of the law, a rather colorful mixture of common sense and unbridled egotism. He made a number of legendary verdicts, like convicting a dead railroad worker for carrying a concealed weapon when a gun and $40 was found on the corpse; the fine imposed: $40. At another time, a lawyer used the term *habeas corpus* in his courtroom and Bean almost hanged him for using profanity.

The judge conducted weddings and divorces, although he was not legally entitled to do the latter. However, Bean reasoned he should be able to "correct his mistakes." At one time, he charged two Mexican couples $2 apiece for their divorces. When he noticed them changing partners on their way out, Bean informed them he was going to arrest them for fornication if they didn't get married on the spot; he then charged each couple $5 for the marriage.

During elections, which were held every two years, Bean would stand outside the schoolhouse with a sawed-off shotgun, asking each voter how he planned to vote.

Since he was such a legendary figure, a number of people came all the way to Langtry to see him. One time a New Yorker came by, bought a pint of whiskey for 35 cents and paid for it with a $20 gold piece. Bean refused to make change, and the New Yorker responded by calling Bean a bastard, whereupon the judge promptly levied a fine of $19.65 for disturbing the peace.

Bean finally ran afoul of the law in 1892 when it was discovered that the number of votes cast in an election for Bean exceeded the number of people in his jurisdiction, so he lost his office. Thereafter, he served the area as a private citizen.

In 1896, Bean decided to host the Bob Fitzsimmons–Peter Maher championship fight, which had been banned in Texas, New Mexico, Arizona and Chihuahua.

Bean had the match fought on a sandbar in the Rio Grande, outside Ranger jurisdiction.

Judge Roy Bean spent most of his life infatuated with the English actress Lily Langtry. In addition to naming a town and his saloon after her, Bean also wrote her numerous fan letters and each Christmas sent her a turkey. A large portrait of her hung on his wall. The highlight of his life occurred when he saw her perform in San Antonio in 1888, although, sadly, no one would introduce him to her so he left without meeting her. His greatest ambition was for her to visit the town he named for her; she did so 10 months after he died and was presented with his pistol at this time.

BEAR, GRIZZLY   There are several different kinds of grizzly bears *(Ursus horribilis)*, from the 350-pound types in the inland areas of the West to the 1,500-pound types in coastal areas. Usually a shy animal, the female grizzly can be ferocious when protecting her young, and a male grizzly is ferocious when wounded or threatened or when it has a toothache (called "soreheads"). A huge carnivore that averages eight feet in height and 800 pounds, the grizzly is so strong that it can kill a person with a single blow from its heavy paw or carry a 200-pound deer under its arm. The grizzly will kill a person—and many have been killed by grizzlies—but the bear will not eat him or her. In California, the Spanish would often pit grizzlies against fierce bulls at fiestas; often a grizzly could break a bull's neck with one swipe. The hair on the grizzly bear was gray or grayish.

BEARCAT, THE   See STARR, HENRY.

BEARCATS   TV show that starred Rod Taylor as Hank Brackett and Dennis Cole as Johnny Reach.

It was a classic Stutz Bearcat and not a horse that these two adventurers traveled around in about 1914 in the Southwest, foiling dastardly deeds and stopping crooks. In each episode they requested a blank check; at the end of the episode they filled in the blanks for what they felt they were worth. The show premiered on September 16, 1971 on CBS on Thursday evenings. The hour-long show ended on December 30, 1971 after 13 episodes.

BEARD, RED   (b. Edward T. Beard in Beardstown, Illinois c. 1828; d. Wichita, Kansas on November 11, 1873)   Beard was well educated and came from a prominent family; he had married a cultured woman and was the father of three children. In 1861 he suddenly pulled up stakes and headed west, traveling to California, Oregon, Arizona and then Kansas, where he opened a dance hall in Wichita during the cattle boom. Usually drunk, he was involved in a series of shootouts in 1873, the final one occurring on October 27.

Beard and Rowdy Joe Lowe were at odds; Lowe owned a dance hall and whorehouse next to Beard's place. On this night Beard got drunk, quarreled with a prostitute named Jo DeMerritt then fired through the window at Joe Lowe. Beard then shot Annie Franklin in the stomach, mistaking her for DeMerritt, just before Lowe, also drunk, came after Beard with a shotgun. Lowe fired at

Beard and Beard fired back, hitting Lowe in the neck. Lowe then chased Beard to the river bridge, shattering his right arm and hip with buckshot. Beard lay in agony but held on for two weeks before dying on November 11. (See also LOWE, ROWDY JOE.)

BEAVER   A river rodent with a highly prized silky-smooth fur undercoat that was used for fashionable hats and trimming in the early 1800s in Europe and major American cities, the beaver *(Castor canadensis)* was hunted by mountain men who were responsible for the early exploration of the West by white men. The beavers were generally caught by steel traps set underwater, which caused them to drown. An adult beaver weighed an average of 30 to 50 pounds, and its cured pelt would bring $5 to $6 for a trapper. By 1840 the beaver was nearly extinct.

BECKNELL, WILLIAM   (b. Amherst County, Virginia c. 1788; d. Red River County, Texas on April 30, 1865)   Becknell was the American trader who first used the Santa Fe Trail, which led to it becoming a major freight trail in the West. Becknell and four others took some pack animals to trade with the Comanches, but were persuaded to go to Santa Fe where they made huge profits from their goods. The following summer, on April 4, 1822, Becknell took 30 men and $5,000 in merchandise over the Santa Fe Trail and arrived in Santa Fe on November 16. On this trip he took a wagon from Missouri to the Arkansas River near what later became Dodge City and crossed the Cimarron, which established this route as the Santa Fe Trail. After trading for a number of years Becknell settled near Clarksville, Texas.

BECKWITH, HENRY   (b. Hugh M. Beckwith in Alabama c. 1824; d. Presidio, Texas around 1892)
Henry Beckwith, whose real name may have been José Enriquez, had a store and ranch near Santa Fe around 1849 and ran a saloon in New Mexico near Fort Stanton during the Civil War; he was arrested by the Union Army during the war and charged with treason. He moved to a ranch in Lincoln County, New Mexico near Seven Rivers, where he killed his son-in-law, William Harrison Johnson, a former Union soldier with a double-barrelled shotgun. During the altercation (over land management and a long-time seething resentment) John Wallace Olinger shot Beckwith in the face but the rancher recovered. Beckwith was the father of John and Bob Beckwith, who were both involved in the Lincoln County War with the Murphy-Dolan faction. Ironically, Henry Beckwith almost killed his son John during the altercation when he killed Johnson. Later the elder Beckwith opened a hotel in Fort Stockton, Texas and then a store at Presidio, Texas, where he was reportedly beaten to death by outlaws who robbed his store. (See also OLINGER, JOHN WALLACE.)

BECKWITH, JOHN H.   (b. New Mexico c. 1855; d. Seven Rivers, New Mexico on August 26, 1879)   John and his brother Bob Beckwith were heavily involved in the Lincoln County War. The brothers had started a cattle ranch and were deputized to fight Billy the Kid and the rest of Alexander McSween's "Regulators." John Beckwith was killed in a gun battle with rustler John Jones over ownership of a herd of cattle, a year after Bob Beckwith had been killed in a shootout in Lincoln. (See also LINCOLN COUNTY WAR.)

BECKWITH, ROBERT W. (b. New Mexico on October 10, 1850; d. Lincoln, New Mexico on July 19, 1878) The major battle in the Lincoln County War occurred July 15–19, 1878 at Alexander McSween's house. During this four-day siege, McSween and his "Regulators," who included Billy the Kid, were pinned in the house. On July 19 the house was set ablaze while Beckwith and others moved in. Beckwith, then 20 years old, yelled out that he would protect those inside the house, but as he approached the door, they began shooting. Beckwith attempted to shoot back but his gun jammed; meanwhile McSween and his men came out shooting. Beckwith was hit in the wrist and left eye and killed; McSween was killed and fell dead on top of Beckwith. (See also LINCOLN COUNTY WAR.)

BECKWOURTH, JIM (b. James Pierson Beckwourth (or Beckwith) in Fredericksburg, Virginia on April 26, 1798; d. with the Crow Indians in 1866 or 1867) Beckwourth was the son of a black slave and white planter in Virginia but spent his adult life in the West. A member of the Ashley fur expedition in the 1820s, he lived with the Crow Indians in 1829 and

Jim Beckwourth

became a member of the Dog Soldiers; according to his autobiography, he then became a chief with the tribe. He lived with the Crows a number of years. In 1846 he served as a guide to Colonel Stephen W. Kearny in the Mexican War. He lived in Denver for a while and was involved in the Sand Creek Massacre after being drafted by Colonel John M. Chivington. Beckwourth, by this time old with failing eyesight, was threatened with hanging by Chivington if he refused to guide the bloodthirsty group to the Indian camp. Along the way, Beckwourth was replaced by another guide, a half-breed Cheyenne, Jack Smith. In 1866 Beckwourth returned to the Crows and died with them a year later.

BED ROLL A cowboy's bed, generally composed of one or more blankets and tarp. The cowboy kept most of his possessions in his bedroll.

BEECHER ISLAND, BATTLE OF (September 17, 1868) On a small island in the Republican River in Colorado, Major George A. Forsyth and 50 troops dug in against about 1,000 Indians on September 17, 1868. Major General Philip Sheridan had directed Forsyth to hunt for Indians and fight when he found them. The Sioux and Cheyenne war party attacked the army's camp, and the soldiers quickly retreated about 400 yards to a small sandbar in the middle of a shallow river. With all their horses dead, the soldiers could not escape, so they had to dig in. The fight lasted nine days, and the soldiers and scouts had the best weapons: a seven-shot Spencer repeating carbine and Colt Army percussion revolvers. The Indians charged at dawn; Forsyth was wounded and his second in command, Lieutenant F. H. Beecher, was killed. Indian war chief Roman Nose was also killed in this fight, during a charge he led that evening. A pair of volunteers, Jack Stillwell and Hank Trueau, left to summon help from Fort Wallace, about 125 miles away. The next night two more volunteers, Allison Pliley and Jack Donovan, unsure if the first two volunteers had gotten through the Indian lines, also went for help. But the first two had slipped past the Indian lines and summoned a rescue force of 70 black troopers from the 25th Infantry—the buffalo soldiers—led by Captain L. H. Carpenter. On September 27 the relief force arrived, but the Indians had left a few days earlier. The fight left five soldiers dead, but more than 70 Indians died. There were about 30 other wounded soldiers; it is unknown how many Indians were wounded.

BEECHER'S BIBLES These were the Sharps rifles that famous antislavery preacher Henry Ward Beecher cited when he said they had more moral power "so far as the slave-holders were concerned than in a hundred Bibles." (See SHARPS RIFLES.)

BEEF A steer over four years old, although originally this meant any steer at all.

BEEF BOOK The ranch book that keeps track of the beef.

BEEF TEA Water—usually shallow—stirred up by cattle.

BELL, TOM (b. Thomas Hodges in Rome, Tennessee c. 1824; d. near Merced River, California on October 4, 1856) Thomas Hodges was a doctor practicing medicine in Nashville when he caught "gold fever" and joined the rush to California. Not having much luck prospecting, Hodges took the alias "Tom Bell" and began holding up stagecoaches in the area. On August 11, 1856 near Marysville, California the Tom Bell Gang attempted to rob a stage carrying a shipment of gold, but gunfire erupted and a woman passenger was killed. Posses pursued Bell's gang, which was finally captured near the Merced River on October 4, 1856. After being allowed to write letters to his mother and to his mistress (and partner in crime) Elizabeth Hood, Bell was strung up by the mob at 5 P.M.

BENT'S FORT About 100 miles from the foot of the Rocky Mountains, on the Santa Fe Trail in southwestern Colorado, Bent's Fort was established by brothers Charles and William Bent in 1833. It became one of the major trading posts for the fur trade for 15 years.

BEST OF THE WEST TV show that starred Joel Higgins as Marshal Sam Best, Carlene Watkins as Elvira Best, Meeno Peluce as Daniel Best, Leonard Frey as Parker Tillman, Tom Ewell as Doc Jerome Kullens, Valri Bromfield as Laney Gibbs, Tracey Walter as Frog and Macon McCalman as Mayor Fletcher.

This was a satire on westerns, a comedy of errors that spoofed the genre. "Best" was Marshal Sam Best, a Civil War veteran, who lived with his wife, Elvira, a fluttery southern belle he'd met while burning down her plantation, and his son, Daniel, a smart-aleck punk kid. Best had gotten the job after accidentally running off the Calico Kid and had to patrol a town owned and controlled by the shady, avaricious, effeminate Parker Tillman who owned the Square Deal Saloon. The half-hour show debuted on September 10, 1981 on Thursdays on ABC; it then moved to Friday nights in February, 1982 before landing on Monday nights in June, 1982, where it ended its run on August 23, 1982.

BETWEEN GRASS AND HAY Adolescence, or the time of a male's life when he's between manhood and boyhood.

BIBLE-PUNCHER Religious man or preacher.

BIERSTADT, ALBERT See ART.

BIG ANTELOPE Phrase used for a cow killed by a cowboy that didn't belong to him or his outfit.

BIG COUNTRY, THE Film produced by Gregory Peck and William Wyler; directed by William Wyler; screenplay by James R. Webb, Sy Bartlett and Robert Wilder; released in 1958 by World Wide/United Artists; 156 minutes in length. Cast: Gregory Peck, Jean Simmons, Carroll Baker, Charlton Heston, Burl Ives, Charles Bickford and Chuck Connors.

Gregory Peck leaves the sea (he was a former sea captain) for the West and marries a woman; they become embroiled in a conflict over water rights.

BIGHORN SHEEP Wild mountain sheep of the West that have huge horns up to about 40 inches long, which sweep back in a spiral. Bighorn sheep *(Ovis canadensis)* are about five feet long, three feet high and agile in high elevations. The males butt horns when they fight during the mating season.

BIG-NOSE KATE (b. Mary Catherine Elder in Budapest, Hungary on November 7, 1850; d. Prescott, Arizona on November 2, 1940) Big-Nose Kate was reportedly the wife of Doc Holiday; although no records exist of their marriage, Kate claims to have married Doc in 1870 at the Planter's Hotel in St. Louis. Married or not, she did travel with Doc to Fort Griffin, Texas in 1877 and then to Dodge City, Las Vegas, New Mexico and Tombstone, Arizona. Born in Hungary, she moved to the United States with her family and settled in Davenport, Iowa in 1853; two years later her parents were dead. Kate ran away in 1867 and took the name "Fisher"; she worked in sporting houses, including one in Wichita run by the Earp women in 1874, and in 1875, she worked in Tom Sherman's dance hall in Dodge City. In 1880 Kate moved to Globe, Arizona when Doc went to Tombstone to join up with the Earps; during the gunfight at the O.K. Corral she was visiting Doc in Tombstone. She married George M. Cummings but left him and lived with John J. Howard until 1930; she entered the Pioneers' Home in Prescott in 1931, where she died.

BIG SKY, THE Film produced and directed by Howard Hawks; screenplay by Dudley Nichols from the novel *The Big Sky* by A. B. Guthrie; released in 1952 by Winchester/RKO; 122 minutes in length. Cast: Kirk Douglas, Dewey Martin, Elizabeth Threatt, Arthur Hunnicutt, Buddy Baer, Steven Geray and Hank Worden.

A group of white men save an Indian woman and then take her along on their journey up the Missouri River.

BIG TRAIL, THE Film directed by Raoul Walsh; screenplay by Maria Boyle, Jack Peabody and Florence Postal from a story by Hal G. Evarts; released by Fox in 1930; 125 minutes. Cast: John Wayne, Marguerite Churchill, Ian Keith, Tyrone Power, Sr., Ward Bond, El Brendel, Tully Marshall, Charles Stevens and Chief Big Tree.

This is the movie that transformed Marion Michael Morrison into John Wayne. Named after General Anthony "Mad Dog" Wayne, Wayne played a trapper who worked as a scout for a wagon train on the Oregon Trail. This character, Brick Coleman, also sought revenge for his brother's murder as the story of the Oregon Trail is retold.

BIG VALLEY, THE TV show that starred Barbara Stanwyck as Victoria Barkley, Richard Long as Jarrod Barkley, Peter Breck as Nick Barkley, Lee Majors as

The cast of "Big Valley": Lee Majors, Peter Breck, Richard Long, Barbara Stanwyck and Linda Evans

Heath Barkley, Linda Evans as Audra Barkley and Napoleon Whiting as Silas.

Victoria Barkley owned and ran the huge Barkley ranch during the 1870s. The ranch was located in California's San Joaquin Valley near the town of Stockton. The matriarch was helped by her four sons and daughter, who battled an assortment of con artists, thugs and wheeler-dealers. The show lasted four years, filming 112 episodes, all in color. The show premiered on September 15, 1965 on Wednesday nights on ABC. In July 1966 the hour-long show moved to Monday nights, where it completed its run on May 19, 1969.

BILLY THE KID (aka Henry McCarty, William Bonney, Henry Antrim, Kid Antrim and William Antrim; b. Patrick Henry McCarty in New York City on September 17, 1859; d. Fort Sumner, New Mexico on July 14, 1881) Legend has it that Billy the Kid killed 21 men in his 21 years; in truth, he was a gunfighter for about four years and probably only killed about six. But he was a famous gunman and killer in his time, a result of being actively involved in the Lincoln County War, one of the bloodiest conflicts in the Old West. Here, the Kid's exploits were reported in the *National Police Gazette*, bringing him fame nationwide. Then, about three weeks after his death, the book *Authentic Life of Billy the Kid* was published, a quick biography listing Pat Garrett, the Kid's killer and former friend, as the author. (Actually, the book was ghostwritten by Ash Simpson, Gar-

rett's friend.) This story was published at a time when dime novels as well as inflated stories about real Wild West figures were blanketing the eastern media, and it found a ready audience. Thus the seeds for the legend of Billy the Kid were planted and watered; they have grown to gigantic proportions since that time.

The Kid was born in New York City, the second son of Patrick and Catherine McCarty. In the early 1870s, Catherine appeared in New Mexico without Patrick, who apparently died before or during the trek west. Catherine married William H. Antrim in Santa Fe, New Mexico in 1873; the couple and Catherine's two sons moved to Silver City in New Mexico Territory, where Antrim worked in the silver mines while Catherine ran a boardinghouse. Catherine died on September 16, 1874, and young Henry moved into the Star Hotel, where he worked for his room and board. About a year later came McCarty's first brush with the law when he was arrested for stealing clothes from two Chinese; but McCarty escaped from jail and went to Arizona, where he worked as a cowboy.

Billy the Kid was known as Kid Antrim when he killed his first man on August 17, 1877. The 17-year-old Kid quarreled with Irishman F. P. Cahill in Fort Grant at George Adkins's saloon. Cahill, a blacksmith, had taunted and bullied young Billy; in the saloon, there was a fistfight in which Cahill threw the Kid on the floor and slapped his face. Billy responded with his gun blazing; the next day Cahill died and the Kid was charged with murder. The Kid again escaped from jail.

Billy the Kid's major fame comes from his part in the Lincoln County War after he left Arizona and went back to New Mexico. There, he hooked up with a boyhood friend, Jesse Evans, and they rustled cattle. At this point it is difficult to determine whether he went to work for rancher John Chisum; however, in November 1877 he met George and Frank Coe (they were cousins) and stayed at their ranch during the winter. This, in turn, led to his working for John H. Tunstall, a wealthy Englishman who had a ranch on the Rio Feliz, about 30 miles south of Lincoln, New Mexico. The Kid began working for Tunstall in January 1878, and a friendship developed between the English gentleman and the Kid.

But there was trouble brewing in Lincoln County. There were two major factions: One was headed by Lawrence Murphy and James J. Dolan, who controlled the town, and the other was headed by Tunstall, John Chisum and attorney Alexander McSween. On February 18, 1878 Tunstall was stopped by a group from the Murphy-Dolan faction, and they gunned down the rancher. The Kid watched helplessly from a nearby ridge. This started the shooting part of the Lincoln County War, initially headed by Tunstall's ranch foreman, Dick Brewer.

The Kid was in a posse led by Dick Brewer and composed of Charlie Bowdre, William McCloskey, John Middleton, Frank McNab, Henry Brown, J. G. Scurlock, Wayt Smith and Jim French. The group captured two of Tunstall's killers, Frank Baker and William Morton, after a five-mile chase. Undecided whether to kill the two men or not—Brewer wanted them taken to the Lincoln jail—the group rode on; about 25 miles later, the next day, Morton grabbed William McCloskey's pistol and killed him, and then he and Baker made a run for it. But a hail of gunshots killed the two prisoners. Although Billy was firing—and later claimed he killed both—there was no proof of which bullet—or whose bullets—actually inflicted the fatal wound.

The next major event in the Lincoln County War occurred on April 1, 1878 in Lincoln, New Mexico when the Kid, with Henry Brown, John Middleton, Fred Wait and Jim French, set up an ambush behind a low adobe wall that overlooked the main street in Lincoln. Sheriff William Brady and his deputy, George Hindman, walked by about midmorning, trailed by Billy Matthews, Jack Long and George Peppin. When the firing started, the sheriff and his deputy were killed. The Kid and Wait were wounded when they went into the street and attempted to steal the dead men's Winchesters, but all got away.

A few days later, on April 4, 1878 at Blazer's Mill, New Mexico, the Regulators stopped for a meal and met Buckshot Roberts, a member of the opposing faction, in the tavern. Roberts was heavily armed but was surprised by the Regulators; Charlie Bowdre pulled a gun on him and ordered him to surrender. Roberts opened fire and wounded George Coe and John Middleton; he then was hit by Bowdre's gunfire. Roberts scrambled out and holed up inside a building next door. Sitting against a wall, he blew off the top of Dick Brewer's head when the Regulator tried to get into position to snipe him. Finally the Regulators rode off, and Roberts died from his wounds.

More gunplay followed. On May 1, 1878, shots were exchanged in the streets of Lincoln, and on May 14 the Kid stole 27 horses. On July 4, 1878 in Roswell, New Mexico in Ash Upson's store, the Kid and Frank and George Coe ran into some enemies and had a running gun battle on their way back to John Chisum's ranch. Deputy Sheriff Jack Long was carrying warrants for the arrest of this gang on July 13, 1878 near San Patricio, New Mexico when he ran into the Kid and 10 other Regulators. The lawman managed to escape the gunfire that erupted, although his horse was killed.

During the big battle in the Lincoln County War, on July 15–19, 1878 at Alexander McSween's adobe house, the Kid was in the house with 10 others when they were surrounded and laid under siege by the opposing forces. They spent the first day ducking bullets and occasionally returning some fire. But on the final day McSween's house was set afire, and the Kid and others had to make a run for it after dark. McSween was cut down with a burst of gunfire when he walked outside holding a Bible to his chest. Tom O'Folliard was wounded, and Harvey Morris was killed. Three others were killed, but the Kid somehow managed to escape unscathed. He may have killed 19-year-old Bob Beckwith during the escape—athough in the dark and chaos it is hard to know.

Civil War hero Lew Wallace replaced Samuel B. Axtell as governor of New Mexico Territory after the big shoot-out and, in an attempt to restore peace to the area, offered a general pardon to those involved if the shooting would stop. At this time the Kid lived at the Chisum ranch, but the pardon would not apply to him because he'd killed Sheriff Brady. In February 1879 a truce was called, but then someone with the Murphy faction killed a lawyer named Chapman. Wallace arranged a meeting with the Kid in which he promised a full pardon in exchange for testimony against Chapman's murderers. The Kid agreed, and he allowed himself (with Tom O'Folliard) to be arrested and placed in jail. Then Chapman's killers escaped, and the Kid was left waiting with his concerns unanswered by Wallace, primarily because Wallace was busy working on his epic novel *Ben Hur* at the time. Since the pardon was stalled, and the Kid was tired of waiting—and worried he might be set up to be killed—he walked away from his guards one day, got on his horse and rode away, which made him a fugitive again.

With the Kid's notoriety came the usual group of gunslingers who wanted to make a name for themselves with a notch on their gun. On January 10, 1880 at Fort Sumner, New Mexico in Bob Hargrove's Saloon, Joe Grant was drinking heavily and had let some people know he intended to kill the Kid. Tipped off, the Kid asked Grant if he could see his ivory-handled pistol; Grant let him look at it, and the Kid set the cylinder so it would next fire on an empty chamber. A little later Grant challenged the Kid to a gunfight, pulled his gun and stuck it in Billy's face; he then pulled the trigger on the empty chamber. The Kid pulled out his revolver and shot Grant in the head, killing him.

On November 29–31, 1880 near White Oaks, New Mexico, an eight-man posse caught up with the Kid and Billy Wilson, and there was a running gun battle in which the posse killed the outlaws' horses. But the Kid and Wilson escaped on foot and caught up with Dave Rudabaugh; the next day the three rode down the main street of White Oaks, fired at Deputy Sheriff James Redman and then hightailed it out of town. A posse was formed and chased the outlaws to the ranch of Jim Greathouse. The outlaws held Greathouse hostage, but Deputy Sheriff James Carlyle, who led the posse, convinced the outlaws to let him trade places with the rancher. They did so, and Carlyle tried to talk the outlaws into surrendering. Around midnight, Carlyle tried to escape by jumping through a window but was killed. Nobody knows if Carlyle was killed by the outlaws or the posse, but when the posse discovered Carlyle was dead, they burned the house down. Meanwhile, the outlaws escaped.

Pat Garrett, an old friend of the Kid's, was elected sheriff of Lincoln County and given as his top priority the capture of the Kid. On December 19, 1880 at Fort Sumner, New Mexico, the Kid, along with Rudabaugh, Wilson, Charlie Bowdre, Tom O'Folliard and Tom Pickett, rode into town, but they were ambushed at the Old Post Hospital by a posse led by Garrett. The Kid originally was at the front of the group riding in but had moved to the rear to get a chaw of tobacco from Wilson. O'Folliard was killed but the rest escaped.

On December 23, 1880 in Stinking Springs, New Mexico, the Kid and four others were hiding out in a rock house. Garrett and his posse trailed them there, and Garrett ordered his men to kill the Kid on sight. When

Charlie Bowdre walked out of the house, he was shot by Garrett and the posse; he staggered back inside but the Kid pushed him back out, where he died in Garrett's arms. Garrett then killed one of the outlaws' horses; the dead beast blocked the doorway, forcing the outlaws to surrender. And so the Kid was brought in to stand trial for the murder of Sheriff Brady. He was found guilty and scheduled to hang on May 13.

On April 28, 1881 the Kid was in jail in the two-story courthouse in Lincoln. On this day, deputy J. W. Bell stayed with the Kid while the other prisoners went across the street to eat. Bell let the Kid use the outhouse, and on the way back the Kid got his hands out of his handcuffs and forced open the weapons closet from which he grabbed a six-gun, which may have been planted there by a friend, Jose M. Aguayo. Bell tried to get away but the Kid killed him. Then Billy grabbed the shotgun of Deputy Bob Olinger and sat at the window as Olinger walked up. Olinger had tormented and taunted the Kid while in jail; the Kid said "Hello, Bob," and then killed the deputy with his own gun before he threw the gun into the dust beside Olinger's body. The Kid then took a Winchester and gun belt, tried to get off his leg chains (he was unsuccessful), got on a horse and rode out of town.

On July 14, 1881 in Fort Sumner, New Mexico, the Kid went into town to see his sweetheart, Celsa Gutierrez. He had been hiding out at a nearby sheep ranch. At the fort, Pat Garrett, John Poe and Tip McKinney were looking for the Kid. Billy went to Celsa's quarters and at midnight decided he was hungry, so he went to Pete Maxwell's house to ask for the key to the meat house. On Maxwell's porch, the Kid pulled out the double action .41 he had put into his waistband (he also had a butcher knife) and asked, "Quein es? Quein es?" when he saw McKinney and Poe. Meanwhile, Garrett had gone inside and awakened Maxwell to ask the whereabouts of the Kid. When the Kid came into the darkened bedroom, Maxwell told Garrett, "That's him." Garrett opened fire—and his first bullet entered Billy's heart. The Kid died from a bullet from his former friend's gun and never knew who killed him. That night Maxwell and Garrett put together a coffin for Billy and buried him the next day at noon in the post cemetery between Tom O'Folliard and Charlie Bowdre. (See also BOWDRE, CHARLIE; GARRETT, PAT; LINCOLN COUNTY WAR; O'FOLLIARD, TOM; OLINGER, BOB; TUNSTALL, JOHN HENRY.)

BILLY THE KID   There have been a number of songs about Billy the Kid; the most popular version was recorded in 1927 for Brunswick/Vocalion by Vernon Dalhart. The song recorded by Dalhart was written by Andrew Jenkins and Irene Spain of Atlanta, Georgia in 1927; it supposedly was based on the book *The Saga of Billy the Kid* by Walter Noble Burns. However, folklorists later noted that this song was actually based on an old traditional song—a fairly common occurrence with early songwriters who used and adapted folk songs for early recordings. Songs about Billy the Kid have been collected and published by John Lomax (1916) and Jack Thorp (1921). The song "The Finger of Billy the Kid" was written by Phil LeNoir, and a long poem, "Billy Thuh Kid" was written by Harold Hersey. In 1928 two song-poems about Billy the Kid were published by S. Omar Barker, "The Cycle of Sudden Death" and "When Billy the Kid Rides Again." "The Ballad of Billy the Kid" was published by Henry Herbert Knibbs in 1930, and another song, "Billy the Kid," with words by Milton Bethwyn and music by Sterling Sherwin, was published in 1933. In 1935 a poem "Billy the Kid," written by William Felter, was published, and an other song titled "Billy the Kid" was written by Waldo O'Neal in 1938.

BISON   See BUFFALO.

BIT   (1) The metal part of a bridle that is inserted into a horse's mouth. This term is also used to describe a triangle cut made into a cow's ear as a mark. (2) In money this was 12 1/2 cents, which meant "two bits" was a quarter.

BITE THE DUST   Could mean being killed, although it usually meant coming off a horse involuntarily.

BLACK, BAXTER   (b. Las Cruces, New Mexico on January 10, 1945)   With the publication of his first book, *The Cowboy and His Dog,* in 1980, Black became a best-selling cowboy poet. Black became a veterinarian and entertained cowboys with his poetry and songs while making his rounds. He became known as a popular speaker and shifted to entertainment as demand increased for his appearances. After his first book, Black published *A Rider, a Roper and a Heckuva Windmill Man* (1982), *On the Edge of Common Sense, the Best So Far* (1983), *Doc, While Yer Here* (1984), *Buckaroo History* (1985), *Coyote Cowboy Poetry* (1986), *Croutons on a Cow Pie* (1988), *Buckskin Mare* (1989), *Cowboy Standard Time* (1990) and *Croutons on a Cow Pie Vol 2* (1992). He has also done a number of cassette albums.

BLACK BART   (b. Charles E. Bolton (or Boles) probably in Jefferson County, New York c. 1830; d. 1917)   Black Bart plagued Wells Fargo for eight

Baxter Black   *(Coyote Cowboy Company)*

Black Bart

years beginning in 1877, robbing 28 stagecoaches over a period of six years and leaving doggerel after the robberies in which he identified himself as "Black Bart the Po8" (poet). He was captured in 1883 by Wells Fargo's chief of detectives James B. Hume, who found a handkerchief left by Bart at a holdup. Tracking down the laundry mark to a San Francisco hotel, where Bolton lived quietly when he wasn't robbing stagecoaches, Hume arrested Black Bart, who served some time in San Quentin and then was released and vanished. Legend has it that Wells Fargo put him on a $200 a month pension after his release from prison so he would leave them alone, but the company has always denied this claim. It is believed that he died in New York City.

BLACKFOOT INDIANS One of the first tribes to move from the northeastern United States to the West, the Blackfeet became the strongest military power on the buffalo plains. A seminomadic buffalo culture, they were famous horsemen and hunters, brave and savage warriors. Their enemies included the Sioux, the Crows and the Flatheads. The Blackfeet were a confederacy composed of the Piegan, the Bloods and the Siksika. Their territory ranged from the North Saskatchewan River in Canada to the Missouri River in Montana and from the eastern border of Montana to the edge of the Rocky Mountains. In 1855 the United States made a treaty with the tribe; when this treaty was broken by traders, gold prospectors and settlers, the Blackfeet attacked ranches, forts and stagecoaches. Whites then destroyed Indian villages and camps. At Piegan, Chief Red Horn's camp, 170 Blackfeet were massacred in January 1870. The tribe was reduced because of the

decline of the buffalo, and by 1888 all Blackfeet were on a reservation in northwest Montana.

BLACK HILLS OF DAKOTA The Black Hills have thick, ponderosa pines and are located primarily in South Dakota, although some spread into southeastern Wyoming. They were part of the Great Sioux Reservation from the Fort Laramie Treaty in 1868 and are considered sacred by the Sioux. However, General George Custer led an expedition there in 1874 and reported that gold had been found, which precipitated a gold rush. The federal government then retracted its treaty of 1868 for the gold miners. The town of Deadwood was established in this region in 1876. Here in these hills is Mount Rushmore, where sculptor Gutzon Borglum carved out the heads of Washington, Jefferson, Lincoln and Theodore Roosevelt. In addition, sculptor Korczak Ziolkowski began carving out the mounted figure of Sioux chief Crazy Horse in 1948.

BLACK RODEO Film produced and directed by Jeff Kanew; screenplay by Jeff Kanew; released in 1972 by Cinerama Releasing Corporation; 87 minutes in length. Cast: Muhammad Ali, Woody Strode, Bud Bramwell, Cleo Hearn, Skeets Richardson, Moses Fields, Nat Purefoy and Lisa Bramwell.

This is a documentary of a rodeo on Randall's Island, New York in September 1971 in which all the participants were blacks. Narrated by Woody Strode (who was in John Ford's *Sergeant Rutledge*), the film had the first starring role given to a black actor in a Hollywood western.

BLACK SADDLE TV show that starred Peter Breck as Clay Culhane, Russell Johnson as Marshal Gib Scott and Anna Lisa as Nora Travers.

The "black saddle" was actually the saddlebags where Clay Culhane kept his law books as he traveled around. Culhane came to study the law after his brothers were gunned down; he decided there must be a better way to settle differences, so he began to study law and help others. Some of the conflict was provided by Marshal Gib Scott, who kept a close eye on Culhane, not totally convinced that the former outlaw had given up his gunfighting ways. Culhane operated out of Latigo, New Mexico and stayed at the Marathon Hotel, run by Nora Travers. The half-hour show debuted on January 10, 1959 on Saturdays on NBC. In October it switched over to ABC, where it was shown on Friday nights. The final telecast was September 30, 1960 after 44 episodes.

BLACKS IN THE WEST For some blacks, the West was a chance for a new beginning, a land of opportunity where many fled to escape southern hostility and violence; however, blacks soon discovered that the racism prevalent in the eastern United States was just as prevalent in the West. There were laws against blacks (like the Black Codes of the South), and a number of former southerners carried their racial hatreds into the West; but in a land so vast with law enforcement so lax and sporadic, blacks often escaped persecution. Still, blacks were lynched at the slightest provocation, they were tarred and feathered and they could not find protection with the law; indeed, a number of lawmen actively singled out blacks for persecution. Overall, whites in the West simply did not want blacks around; therefore, they did all they could to discourage blacks from settling in the West.

There were Africans in what became the United States before there were white English settlers; a black man came over with Columbus, and in 1501 a group of African slaves were brought to America by the Spanish. Spanish explorer Vasco Nunez de Balboa had 30 Africans in 1513 when he sighted the Pacific Ocean; there were also Africans with Hernando Cortes during his expedition in 1519. But these Africans were slaves; the only difference between the Africans in the early 1500s and the Africans in the early 1600s is that the Spanish brought the former over to the Southwest and West whereas the latter were brought over by the English on the East Coast.

The most famous early African in what became the United States was Estevan (sometimes called Esteban, Estevanico or Stephen Dorantes), who was a slave and on the 1527 expedition that began in Florida; but Estevan survived and gave the Spanish the first reports of what the Southwest was like (he claimed to have found the Seven Cities of Gold). On the first white American exploration into the West, York, the slave of William Clark, accompanied the group on the Lewis and Clark Expedition. When fur traders entered the Rockies to trap beaver, two famous trappers—Jim Beckwourth and Edward Rose—were black. Beckwourth discovered Beckwourth Pass just north of what is now Reno, Nevada and guided settlers through the pass. But his story is indicative of the history of blacks in the West; the historians and chroniclers simply denied the existence of blacks in the West. Proof of this came when Hollywood made a movie in 1950 on the 100th anniversary of the discovery of Beckwourth Pass; in this movie Beckwourth ("Tomahawk") is played by white actor Jack Oakie, and there is absolutely no acknowledgment that Beckwourth was black. For Hollywood and historians alike, it was as if the blacks never existed.

Before the Civil War the story of blacks centered on slavery; from this issue we have the stories of the Underground Railroad, of freed blacks and of slave uprisings. By the time of the Civil War, blacks accounted for about 20% of the population in the United States, but it was unevenly distributed; in New England blacks were about 2% of the population, but in the Deep South they could be 70% of the population in certain areas. But during this period some blacks ventured west. George Washington, born to a white mother and black father, was given to a white family who moved from his native Virginia to Ohio, then Missouri and then out to Oregon Territory, where he married the black widow Mary Jane Cooness and founded the town of Centerville. Another black, George Washington Bush, came to Oregon Territory in 1844 and introduced the first sawmill, gristmill, mower and reaper to the area; one of his sons served in the Washington legislature twice. Aunt Clara Brown became a leading citizen in Central City, Colo-

rado and, through her work as a laundress and nurse, earned enough money to sponsor a black wagon train from Fort Leavenworth to Denver and helped establish a church.

Although these are good, noble stories, they are the exception and not the rule. Western territories quickly enacted laws against black migration; people at the time believed that blacks were inferior and whites simply did not want them as neighbors. Even the pro- and antislavery forces had one thing in common: Both wanted to control blacks. The slavery question was of great political concern to the South because southerners depended on slaves for their economic power. And southerners wanted to keep their strong political base so they could continue slavery; many other politicians opposed slavery not for the benefit of blacks but as a way to diminish or abolish the power of white politicians.

Slavery did not fit into the West; the culture of slavery was important to the southern states because they needed slaves for the large plantations that grew cotton and tobacco and other labor-intensive crops. These crops were unsuited to the West.

Blacks first came to the West as Spanish slaves; later they mixed through marriages and, as Spain lost Mexico to independence, became free. In 1790 about 18% of Californians were black or mulatto; in fact, Los Angeles was founded by 44 persons (11 families) of which 26 were black. Pio Pico, governor of California from 1845 to 1846, was the son of a mulatto mother.

But that did not help the freed blacks who came to California in the gold rush (about 2,000 blacks joined the forty-niners). In the gold fields, blacks found themselves discriminated against, unable to file claims or obtain any legal protection. Whites who brought black slaves to the gold fields caused laws to be enacted that barred blacks from the diggings; at issue here was the "unfair advantage" of having slaves help dig while other miners had to swing a pick and shovel on their own. The only advantage that blacks had in the gold fields was that 17,000 Chinese were also there in the diggings, and whites feared the Chinese more than they feared the blacks.

Still, some blacks did well in California; Alvin Coffey and Daniel Rogers were gold diggers, George Monroe became a respected stagecoach driver, William Robinson became a Pony Express rider and Mifflin W. Gibbs established the first black newspaper in California and later became the first black judge in United States history.

Because Texas was a slave state, there were a number of blacks there at the end of the Civil War. And since the state was so decimated (about a fourth of the white male Texans who served in the Civil War were killed or wounded), blacks were involved in early cattle roundups and trail drives. On these trail drives blacks enjoyed less discrimination than anywhere else; on ranches or on drives it was impossible to have segregation, and the trials of the trail forced a man to prove himself regardless of color. On the trail, white cowboys got to know black cowboys as individuals, so there was much less violence. But there was discrimination in the towns, although the early cattle towns enforced a rather easy-going discrimination. Black cowboys were expected to gather at one end of the bar and were not allowed in white prostitution houses. Still, the early cattle drives treated blacks fairly well; about 5,000 blacks went up the Chisholm Trail, and on most early crews of eight men, about two would be black.

In the wild and woolly West there were some famous black characters. The first cowboy killed in Dodge City was Tex, a black cowboy who got caught in the crossfire of a gunfight between two whites. Dick Shafer was the black marshal of Boley, Oklahoma (which was a town composed of only blacks) who stood down some whites. Britton Johnson was a well-known black cowboy, and Jessie Stahl was a good bronc rider. Nat Love was probably a fake, but he provided a colorful autobiography in which he claimed to have met all the big "names" of the West and been christened "Deadwood Dick." Cherokee Bill (Cranford Goldsby) was a brutal killer, and Ben Hodges was a master con man in Dodge City.

Isom Dart was a cattle rustler in the Gault Gang who was probably killed by Tom Horn; Bill Pickett achieved fame for inventing bulldogging and being one of the first great Wild West and rodeo performers. Ironically, Pickett had to dress like a Mexican in order to compete in rodeos, which barred blacks, until his fame and reputation were so great that no one noticed his color.

Like white settlers, blacks dreamed of owning their own homestead and establishing their own communities. Since violence and hatred were so prevalent in the South during Reconstruction, a number of blacks fled to the West, especially Oklahoma (Indian Territory), where they established communities. These "Exodusters," led by Benjamin "Pop" Singleton, migrated into Kansas in such great numbers (20,000–40,000 blacks were in this migration) that they overwhelmed the communities. The black migrants managed to purchase 20,000 acres of land and build 300 homes; their most famous town was Nicodemus.

Although Kansas initially received the most Exodusters in the westward movement of 1870–1910, in general the black population in western territories doubled during this period; in Montana, Idaho, Wyoming, Colorado, New Mexico, Arizona, Utah and Nevada the black population increased 13-fold, while in Washington, Oregon and California it increased five times. By 1910 there were almost a million blacks living in the West, although Texas, with 690,000 blacks, and Oklahoma, with 137,600, had the majority. In the Mountain and Pacific states blacks accounted for only 0.7% of the population.

Perhaps the most famous blacks in the West were the buffalo soldiers. These soldiers (the 9th and 10th Cavalry and the 24th and 25th Infantry) served well in the West. The buffalo soldiers accounted for about 20% of the cavalry in the West, had the lowest desertion rate of any army units and saw 11 of their black soldiers earn the Medal of Honor while serving with the most decrepit horses and poorest equipment.

The story of blacks in the West is a reflection of the story of blacks in the United States. Intense racism from whites produced discrimination, manifested in laws that barred blacks and attempted to create a segregated society. There was random violence in which blacks were victimized with no recourse and denied basic citizenship rights. Historians ignored blacks for years when they wrote the history of the West; in general whites in the West did all they could to not allow blacks in the region; when this proved impossible, whites ignored blacks as much as possible in everyday life and then ignored them and their contributions when the histories were written.

Blacks struggled in the West, and a few succeeded. But for most it was a period of unending tribulation; still, blacks in general believed in the idea of the United States and hoped their children would see a day when life would be much better. Despite all the racism, hatred and discrimination, blacks in the West saw the potential for a new land and a new day. Because they persevered against these odds, and in many cases rose above them, the "black West" has been discovered by contemporary historians, the United States Army no longer tries to ignore or discredit the buffalo soldiers and the stories of black cowboys, rodeo performers and Exodusters are told as an example of a people's strength and courage and used as an example of black achievement in the United States. (See also BUFFALO SOLDIERS.)

BLAKE, AMANDA   (b. Beverly Louise Neill in Buffalo, New York on February 20, 1929; d. Sacramento, California on August 16, 1989)   Amanda Blake played "Miss Kitty" on "Gunsmoke." Blake's movie debut was in *Duchess of Idaho* (1950), and she also appeared in *Stars in My Crown* (1950), *Lili* (1953), *Sabre Jet* (1953), *A Star Is Born* (1954), *About Mrs. Leslie* (1954) and *High Society* (1956). (See also ARNESS, JAMES; GUNSMOKE; TELEVISION WESTERNS.)

BLAKE, TULSA JACK   (b. William Blake c. 1862; d. near Dover, Oklahoma on April 4 or 5, 1895)   Tulsa Jack was a member of the Doolin Gang. Lawman Chris Madsen led a posse that found the gang camping on the Cimarron River near Dover, Oklahoma; the crew was asleep while Tulsa Jack stood guard. Blake spotted Deputy William Banks and fired at the lawman, awakening the gang and starting a gunfight. Blake was killed when Banks fired a shot that hit Tulsa Jack's cartridge belt, causing a shell to explode. The rest of the gang escaped.

See also DOOLIN, BILL.

BLAZING SADDLES   Film produced by Michael Hertzberg; directed by Mel Brooks; screenplay by Mel Brooks, Norman Steinberg, Andrew Bergman, Richard Pryor and Alan Unger, from the story by Andrew Bergman; released in 1974 by Warner Brothers; 94 minutes in length. Cast: Cleavon Little, Gene Wilder, Slim Pickens, David Huddleston, Liam Dunn, Alex Karras, John Hillerman, George Furth, Claude Ennis Starrett, Jr., Mel Brooks, Harvey Korman, Madeline Kahn, Carol Arthur, Charles McGregor, Robyn Hilton, Dom DeLuise, and Count Basie.

This is the spoof of all spoofs on westerns, a classic caricature of classic movies. Black Bart (Cleavon Little)

Dan Blocker

is black and rides into Rock Ridge, an all-white town, as sheriff. Later, he must disguise himself as a Ku Klux Klan member to break out an outlaw ring.

BLEVINS, ANDY   See COOPER, ANDY

BLOCKER, DAN   (b. Texas on December 10, 1932; d. Hollywood, California on May 14, 1972)   Dan Blocker played Hoss Cartright on "Bonanza." He graduated from Hardin-Simmons University and received an M.A. from Sul Ross State College; he then did postgraduate work at the University of California–Los Angeles. Blocker served in the Korean War (1950–52) and was a schoolteacher in Sonora, Texas and Carlsbad, New Mexico before he went to Hollywood, where he was a substitute teacher at Glendale High School. Blocker appeared in the "Cimarron City" television show, which led to his being cast in "Bonanza." His success on "Bonanza" led to several movie roles, including appearances in *Come Blow Your Horn* (1963), *Lady in Cement* (1968) and *The Cockeyed Cowboys of Calico County* (1969). (See also BONANZA; TELEVISION WESTERNS.)

BLOOD ON THE SADDLE   This song, a story of a cowboy killed by a bronc that landed on him, may be traced back to an old song from the Middle Ages that inspired the Scottish ballad "Halbert the Grim," first published in 1827 by William Motherwell. "Blood on the Saddle" was heard in 1905 on a Canadian ranch, and the standard form of this song was popularized by Tex

Ritter, George B. German and Everett Cheetham. German published a booklet of cowboy songs in 1929 that contained some verses of this song. Cheetham and Ritter appeared in *Green Grow the Lilacs,* the folk play that became the basis of *Oklahoma* while both were in New York in 1931. The duo sang this song during an interlude between scenes; Cheetham made up some lyrics based on a rodeo accident that injured cowboy Orville Fisher and copyrighted it in 1936. In the 1937 movie *Hittin' the Trail,* star Tex Ritter featured this song.

BOB-TAIL GUARD   The first two-hour shift of the evening during a trail drive.

BODMER, KARL   See ART.

BOILED SHIRT   A white shirt or "city shirt," with a hint toward snobbishness and the easy life.

BOLES, CHARLES   See BLACK BART.

BOLTON, CHARLES   See BLACK BART.

BONANZA   TV show that starred Lorne Greene as Ben Cartwright, Michael Landon as Little Joe Cartwright, Dan Blocker as Eric "Hoss" Cartwright (1959–72), Pernell Roberts as Adam Cartwright (1959–65), Victor Sen Yung as Hop Sing, Ray Teal as Sheriff Roy Coffee (1961–71), David Canary as Candy (1967–70, 1972–73), Lou Frizzel as Dusty Rhoades (1970–72), Mitch Vogel as Jamie Hunter (1970–73) and Tim Matheson as Griff King (1972–73).

Next to "Gunsmoke," "Bonanza" is the top western TV series of all time. Premiering on September 12, 1959 on the NBC network on Saturday evenings, it ran for 14-1/2 years. Its most enduring slot was on NBC on Sunday nights (September 1961–September 1972), when it replaced "The Dinah Shore Show." Later, it also ran on Tuesday evenings (May 1972–January 1973). During the summer of 1972, reruns were shown under the title "Ponderosa." "Bonanza" was the first western to be shown in color (although "The Cisco Kid" and "The Lone Ranger" were the first to be filmed in color, they were shown in black and white), and for three consecutive seasons, 1964–67, it was the top-rated program on TV. This success came after an inauspicious start: In its first season "Bonanza" had dismal ratings and was in danger of being canceled.

The show was set on the Ponderosa Ranch, a 1,000-acre spread in Nevada near Virginia City and the newly discovered Comstock Lode to which silver miners were rushing for riches. The plots concerned encroaching civilization and the problems from all those newcomers in the region. The core group was a widowed father and his three sons, each from a different wife: father Ben Cartwright, played by Lorne Greene; eldest son Adam Cartwright, played by Pernell Roberts, a serious, thoughtful son who would probably follow in his father's footsteps; Hoss Cartwright, played by Dan Blocker, a big, gentle, albeit rather slow-witted, son with a heart of gold; and Little Joe, played by Michael Landon, hot-headed and impetuous. During the show's run, Roberts quit the show (at the end of the 1964–65 season) and

The cast of "Bonanza": Dan Blocker, Lorne Greene, Pernell Roberts and Michael Landon *(Western Archives)*

was written out, and Blocker died (just prior to production on the 1972–73 season's episodes).

BOND, JOHNNY (b. Cyrus Whitfield Bond in Enville, Oklahoma on June 1, 1915; d. in Burbank, California on June 12, 1978) Johnny Bond and Jimmy Wakely began singing on radio station WKY in Oklahoma City. In 1937 they were joined by Scotty Harrell to form the Cowboy Trio, which was sponsored by the Bell Clothing Company. Broadcast on WKY as well as KVOO in Tulsa, the group soon became known as the Bell Boys; also in 1937 Bond changed his first name to Johnny. The Bell Boys were part of the singing-cowboy craze led by Gene Autry in his singing-cowboy movies and the Sons of the Pioneers with their western songs and tight harmonies. Bond wrote the song "Cimarron" in 1938, which became a theme song for the group, and in 1939 the group went to California and appeared in the Roy Rogers movie *Saga of Death Valley.* In early 1940 the group returned to California as the Jimmy Wakely Trio

on Gene Autry's "Melody Ranch" show. By this time the group was usually billed as Jimmy Wakely and His Roughriders, with Dick Reinhart replacing Scotty Harrell. Bond signed a recording contract with Okeh/Columbia in 1941 and recorded with his group called the Red River Valley Boys. In 1943 on the CBS radio network he was a star on the "Hollywood Barn Dance" and remained with this show until 1947. Bond and Tex Ritter both performed on "Town Hall Party" over the NBC radio network beginning in 1953 and stayed with that show until it closed in 1961. Bond composed about 300 songs, appeared in some B westerns and recorded some hits, including "Ten Little Bottles," "Divorce Me C.O.D," "So Round, So Firm, So Fully Packed" and "Sick, Sober and Sorry." (See also CIMARRON (song).)

BOND, WARD (b. Denver, Colorado on April 9, 1903; d. Dallas, Texas on November 5, 1960) After he finished his education at the University of Southern California, where he went to school with John Wayne,

Ward Bond

Ward Bond became a key member of John Ford's stock company. Wayne and Bond debuted as movie actors in the film *Salute* when director John Ford needed some USC football players. Between 1929 and 1959 Bond appeared in about 200 films, mostly in supporting roles. Westerns Bond appeared in include:

The Big Trail (1930)
The Sundown Rider (1933)
The Fighting Ranger (1934)
Frontier Marshal (1934)
Western Courage (1935)
The Cattle Thief (1936)
Gun Law (1938)
The Law West of Tombstone (1938)
The Cisco Kid and the Lady (1939)
Dodge City (1939)
Drums Along the Mohawk (1939)
Frontier Marshal (1939)
The Oklahoma Kid (1939)
The Santa Fe Trail (1940)
Wild Bill Hickok Rides Again (1941)
Tall in the Saddle (1944)
Dakota (1945)
Canyon Passage (1946)
My Darling Clementine (1946)
Fort Apache (1948)
Three Godfathers (1949)
Riding High (1950)

Singing Guns (1950)
The Great Missouri Raid (1951)
Hondo (1953)
The Searchers (1956)
Rio Bravo (1959)
Alias Jesse James (1959)

Bond had also starred in *Wagonmaster* (1950), the movie that served as the inspiration for the popular TV series "Wagon Train." Ward Bond died during the time he was starring in "Wagon Train."

BONNEY, WILLIAM   See BILLY THE KID.

BOOMER   Someone who got an early start on a land rush; also known as a sooner.

BOONE, DANIEL   (b. near Reading, Pennsylvania on November 2, 1734; d. St. Charles County, Missouri on September 26, 1820)   Daniel Boone was the first American hero pioneer. A "long hunter" (so called because their hunts in the wilderness might last for over a year), Boone loved Kentucky, an Indian hunting ground, and wanted to make this his home. Born to Quaker parents, young Boone had no schooling but learned to read and write phonetically. In 1750 the family moved south to North Carolina; here he was told about Kentucky by John Finley. Boone first explored in

Daniel Boone   *(Cumberland Gap National Historical Park)*

Kentucky in the fall of 1767; then in spring 1769 he and five others went through the Cumberland Gap and spent two years exploring this wilderness. In September 1773 Boone, his family and five other households left North Carolina for Kentucky; they reached the Clinch River, and Boone became an agent for a land development project for Judge Richard Henderson. But the trip also had its tragedy; Indians killed six of the travelers on this journey, including Boone's eldest son, James. Boone and 30 others laid out the Wilderness Road and helped establish Boonesborough on the Kentucky River. This Wilderness Road was the road that settlers used in the first great migration to the West. Captured by the Shawnee Indians in January 1778, Boone escaped in June to warn the settlers of an impending attack and thus saved the village. In 1799, Boone moved to Missouri, where he was granted about 8,000 acres, but he lost this claim in the Louisiana Purchase. In fact, Boone's life was a series of efforts at land development and a series of disasters with land titles. His biggest disaster was having $50,000 stolen from his saddlebags while he slept in an inn. In debt most of his life, Boone was granted 850 acres in Missouri in 1814 by Congress; he sold this land and paid off his Kentucky debt. Boone's wife, Rebecca, died in 1813, but Daniel lived seven more years; he died at the ripe old age of 86 in his son's farmhouse in Missouri. Later, Kentucky arranged to have his body reinterred in Frankfort, Kentucky.

BOONE, RICHARD (b. Los Angeles, California on June 18, 1917; d. St. Augustine, Florida on January 10, 1981) Richard Boone starred as Paladin in the TV series "Have Gun, Will Travel" and later in "Hec Ramsey." In between he spent time in Hawaii or in St. Augustine, Florida, where he taught students acting. Kicked out of Stanford University, Boone worked in the oil fields near Long Beach and then became an artist. During World War II he joined the navy and afterward studied drama at the Neighborhood Playhouse in New York on the GI Bill. He appeared in western films such as *Way of a Gaucho* (1952), *Return of the Texan* (1952), *City of Badmen* (1953), *The Siege at Red River* (1954), *The Raid* (1954), *Ten Wanted Men* (1955), *Robbers' Roost* (1955), *Star in the Dust* (1956), *The Tall T* (1957), *The Alamo* (1960), *A Thunder of Drums* (1961), *Rio Conchos* (1964), *Hombre* (1967), *Madron* (1970), *Big Jake* (1971), *Against a Crooked Sky* (1975) and John Wayne's final film, *The Shootist* (1976). (See also HAVE GUN, WILL TRAVEL.)

BOOT HILL A generic name for a cemetery in a wild cattle town where cowboys and others were buried with little ceremony in a pauper's grave. The original Boot Hill may have been in Dodge City, Kansas, although almost all of the wide-open towns eventually had their own "Boot Hills."

BOOTS See CLOTHING, COWBOY.

BOOTS AND SADDLES TV show that starred John Pickard as Captain Shank Adams, Michael Hinn as Luke Cummings (scout), John Alderson as Sergeant Bullock, Gardner McKay as Lieutenant Kelly, Michael

Richard Boone *(Western Archives)*

Emmett as Corporal Davis and Patrick McVey as Commander Colonel Wesley Hays.

This show told of the trials and tribulations of the U.S. cavalry during the 1870s at Fort Lowell in Arizona Territory. The show had a good dose of realism as a result of being filmed on location in Kanab, Utah. The show was never a prime-time series but appeared on NBC's daytime schedule in 1957. There were 39 episodes filmed, all in black and white, of the 30-minute shows.

BORDER DRAW A type of gun draw in which a right-handed cowboy kept his gun on his left side, butt out, so he could draw it across his body. It was not quite as fast as the fast draw, but it was probably more practical if the gunslinger wore a coat or was on horseback.

BORDER SHIFT Passing a gun from one hand to another during a gunfight. Could happen from being wounded in the gun hand.

BORN TO THE WIND TV show that starred Will Sampson as Painted Bear, A. Martinez as Low Wolf, Dehl Berti as One Feather, Rose Portillo as Star Fire, Linda Redfearn as Prairie Woman, Emilio Delgado as White Bull and Guillermo San Juan as Two Hawks.

A short-lived summer series, the program was about an Indian tribe around 1800, before the white settlers arrived, and dealt with Indian life from the Indian perspective—no whites in sight. The show premiered on August 19, 1982 and was last telecast on September 5, 1982. The one-hour show jumped around on the NBC network, appearing on Thursday, Saturday and then Sunday before it left the air.

BOUNTY HUNTER Someone who got money from tracking down animals or humans. Often bounties were offered for wolves in cattle country as well as for Indian scalps.

BOWDRE, CHARLIE (b. Mississippi or Tennessee c. 1848; d. Stinking Springs, New Mexico on December 21, 1880) Bowdre was a close friend of Billy the Kid's and a member of the Kid's band of rustlers. During the Lincoln County War he was aligned with Alexander McSween's "Regulators." Bowdre married and tried to settle down, becoming foreman of a ranch near Fort Sumner, New Mexico, but eventually rejoined the Kid. On December 19, 1880 the Kid's gang was surprised by a posse led by Pat Garrett, and two members of the gang were killed. The rest of the gang retreated to a rock house near Stinking Springs, where they nearly froze. On the morning of December 23 Bowdre walked out of the house and was shot in the chest; he staggered back inside but soon died. He is buried with Billy the Kid in Fort Sumner. (See also BILLY THE KID; LINCOLN COUNTY WAR.)

BOWIE, JAMES (b. Elliott Springs, Tennessee in 1795 (although some say in Burke County, Georgia in 1796); d. at the Alamo in San Antonio, Texas on March 6, 1836) Jim Bowie is famous for two reasons: He is thought to have developed the "Bowie knife," and he fought valiantly at the Alamo although confined to a cot because of illness. Bowie was versed in English, French and Spanish; he moved to Louisiana when he was 18 and, with his brother Rezin, formed a partnership to run sugar plantations as well as speculate in Louisiana lands. The Bowie brothers also engaged in the slave trade, which was very profitable for them. Bowie then moved to Texas and settled in San Antonio (then Bexar) and in 1830 became a Mexican citizen. He married the daughter of the vice governor of San Antonio in April 1831 and became a wealthy landowner. However, during the cholera epidemic in 1833 he lost his wife, two infant children and mother- and father-in-law. (Bowie was away in New Orleans at the time of their deaths.) Bowie became a captain in the Texas rebels and, with the rank of colonel, held joint command at the Alamo with Colonel Travis (Bowie was in charge of the volunteer forces; Travis commanded the regular) until he was bedridden with fever from typhoid-pneumonia. Jim Bowie reportedly died in his bed, fighting. Bowie did have a hand in the development of the Bowie knife but was not its sole developer. (See ALAMO, THE; BOWIE KNIFE.)

BOWIE KNIFE Although this term was used for a variety of knives, the real Bowie knife was heavy with a long blade that tapered to a double-edged point. Since the shape of the knife—with its broad spine and long blade—made it possible to throw, it was often used as a lethal weapon. The Bowie knife had a broad blade made

Jim Bowie *(Daughters of the Republic of Texas Library)*

of the finest steel, and the blade and point were ground razor sharp. This blade could be from seven to 14 inches long; the handle of the blade was wrapped around the "tank" or "shank," which made it very solid and sturdy. Carried in a leather scabbard reinforced with brass or silver, this knife was a lethal instrument and incredibly versatile; it was used for fighting, skinning animals, cutting up meat, shaving, and shaping wood. The Bowie knife *may* have been developed by Jim Bowie and made by blacksmith James Black. However, some say Black himself originated the blade, while others contend that Rezin P. Bowie, Jim's brother, designed the knife. A number of Bowie knives were made in Sheffield, England for the American market in the mid-1800s.

BOX CANYON An enclosed canyon with only one opening to either enter or exit.

BOYD, BILL (b. William Boyd in Fannin County, Texas on September 29, 1910; d. Dallas, Texas on December 7, 1977) A guitarist who recorded instrumental versions of cowboy songs, Boyd had his most successful song in 1935—"Under the Double Eagle." Bill and his brother Jim formed the Cowboy Ramblers in the late 1920s and began recording in 1935. Raised on a ranch, they appeared in a number of movies.

BOYD, WILLIAM (b. Cambridge, Ohio on June 5, 1898; d. South Laguna Beach, California on September 13, 1972) William Boyd played Hopalong Cassidy, the first cowboy TV star when that medium was in its infancy. Boyd had first starred as Hop-A-Long (later spelled Hopalong) Cassidy in a western series in 1935; the original character created by novelist Clarence Mulford had a strong limp from a bullet wound and was full of vices such as smoking and drinking. Boyd turned this character into a matinee hero for kids, dressed in black on his white horse, Topper. A total of 66 Hopalong movies were done; 54 were made from 1935 to 1943; the last 12 were produced by Boyd after the original producer, Harry Sherman, dropped the series. After the movies stopped production, Boyd spent his life savings to acquire the TV rights for these movies, and the first Hoppys on TV were actually edited versions of the old movies. The deal made Boyd a rich man; after he acquired all the television, radio and commercial rights in 1948, he consolidated them under one enterprise and began to market the character, and when it was over, there were Hopalong Cassidy lunch boxes, comic strips and various other merchandise. His last film appearance was a cameo role as circus attraction "Hopalong Cassidy" in Cecil B. DeMille's *The Greatest Show on Earth.*

Pat Brady

BOZEMAN TRAIL Named after John M. Bozeman, who mapped the trail in 1863–65, this was intended to be a direct route to the Montana gold fields. The trail started in Julesburg, Colorado, headed north past Fort Laramie, crossed the Powder River (at Fort Connor), then moved to the Yellowstone River (past the Bighorn Mountains) and headed west to Virginia City and then the gold fields. The Sioux objected to the trail, which cut through the heart of their territory, and when the army built Forts Reno, Phil Kearny and C. F. Smith, the Sioux, led by Red Cloud, went to war (Red Cloud's War). The Indians won this one (Fetterman's Massacre and the Wagon Box Fight were part of this war), and the trail was abandoned by 1868. Later, the trail was used for Texas cattle headed toward the northern ranges in the late 1870s and 1880s.

BRADY, PAT (b. Robert Ellsworth O'Brady in Toledo, Ohio on December 31, 1914; d. Green Mountain Falls, Colorado on February 27, 1972) TV fans remember Pat Brady on "The Roy Rogers Show" with his jeep "Nellybelle." Brady and Rogers had a long professional relationship before the half-hour TV series; Brady had replaced Rogers in the Sons of the Pioneers on October 16, 1937 when Rogers (then Leonard Slye) was signed to Republic as a singing cowboy. The only child of vaudeville performers, Brady was known as "Bob," but since the Sons of the Pioneers already had a "Bob" (Nolan), Brady then became "Pat." Brady had moved to

Hopalong Cassidy (William Boyd)

California when he was 12 and played bass with pop and jazz groups before he joined the Pioneers; with this group he appeared in Charles Starrett's movies (1937–41); his debut film was *Outlaws of the Prairies* (1937). In 1941 the Pioneers signed with Republic to costar with Rogers in a series of movies that began with *Red River Valley* (1941) and ended with *Night Time in Nevada* (1948). During World War II Brady served with General George Patton's Third Army in France and won two Purple Hearts. In 1948 the naturally comic Brady joined Roy Rogers as a sidekick after Andy Devine left. Brady returned to the Sons of the Pioneers from 1959 to 1967 after the Roy Rogers TV series ended in 1957. (See also NELLYBELLE; ROGERS, ROY; ROY ROGERS SHOW, THE; SONS OF THE PIONEERS.)

BRAHMA CATTLE   Cattle descended from Asian-Indian stock and known for the hump above their shoulders. The King Ranch in Texas experimented with Brahmas, originally introduced into South Carolina in 1849, and bred them with longhorns in order to produce an animal with more beef. Brahma bulls are ridden in rodeo contests.

BRAND, MAX   (b. Frederick Schiller Faust in Seattle, Washington on May 29, 1892; d. Europe near Santa Maria Infante on Italian front during Allied offensive on May 12, 1944)   Max Brand was one of the most successful commercial writers in 20-century America; he wrote under at least 19 different pen names and turned out an estimated 30 million words. Brand's most popular westerns were *The Untamed* (1919), *Trailin'* (1920) and *Destry Rides Again* (1930), although he is most famous for creating Dr. Kildare for the movies. Brand always wanted to write classic poetry and serious literature. He attended the University of California at Berkeley and then joined the Canadian army during World War I before he entered the American army. Brand's works are certainly plentiful, though not particularly noteworthy. Unlike Zane Grey and Louis L'Amour, he offered no sense of realism and did not advance the western beyond an interesting story for mass consumption. Brand was killed while working as a war correspondent for *Harper's* magazine in World War II.

BRANDED   TV show that starred Chuck Connors as Jason McCord.

Jason McCord was a captain in the cavalry and a West Point graduate. At the Battle of Bitter Creek he was knocked unconscious; later, at a court-martial he was drummed out of the military for "cowardice." McCord pieced together the truth: Another officer had set him up to cover that officer's desertion. But that didn't help McCord, who had to search the West for the mean, lowdown true coward while wearing the "brand" of cowardice himself. This is the basic story line, which ran throughout the 48 episodes of this half-hour show. The series premiered on January 24, 1965 and ended on September 4, 1966, always on Sunday nights on NBC.

BRANDING   Branding is done by placing a hot iron onto the hide of cattle so that a distinguishing mark is made. When branding began in the West, the first brands covered nearly the entire side of a cow; however, because the hide needed to be preserved for leather, the brands began to be placed on the hip. Branding is necessary to keep track of the ownership of cattle, especially on an open range when a number of cattle are grazing. In Texas, each county had an official brand book in which brands were registered. In addition to the brands on the side, the ears of cattle were usually cut in a particular way. The calf branding was done primarily during the spring roundup; however, if a calf was born after this time, or overlooked, it was branded in the fall roundup. Brands are composed of letters, numbers and symbols and are always read from left to right, from top to bottom or from outside to inside. In addition to regular brands, cattle were usually given a "road brand" for cattle drives because several herds might be mixed on a drive and because drives from several different outfits could occur at the same time, resulting in a mingling of cattle.

BRAVE EAGLE   TV show that starred Keith Larsen as Brave Eagle, Keena Nomkeena as Keena, Kim Winona as Morning Star and Bert Wheeler as Smokey Joe.

"Brave Eagle" was unique because it attempted to tell the story of the westward expansion from the Indian's point of view, a progressive attitude in the mid-1950s, when it was produced by Roy Rogers Productions. The stars had Indian ancestors: Keith Larsen was part Cheyenne, Kim Winona was full-blooded Sioux and Keena Nomkeena was full-blooded Hopi and Klamath. The stories dealt with some peaceful Cheyenne Indians in the Southwest during the mid-1800s who attempted to resolve the conflicts with white settlers on their lands. The show premiered September 28, 1955 and ended June 6, 1956 on Wednesday evenings on CBS. Twenty-six episodes of the half-hour show were filmed.

BRAVE STALLION   This was the syndicated title of the TV show "Fury." (See FURY.)

BREAKENRIDGE, WILLIAM MILTON   (b. Watertown, Wisconsin on December 25, 1846; d. Tucson, Arizona on January 31, 1931)   William Breakenridge is the man responsible for Curly Bill Brocius's hanging up his guns. Breakenridge had walked into a saloon in Tombstone, where he was insulted by Jim Wallace, a gunman in the Lincoln County War, who drew on Breakenridge. Breakenridge made light of the situation and bought drinks for everybody. But when Breakenridge tried to leave, Curly Bill started to quarrel and followed him out to his horse. Breakenridge drew his gun as he mounted while Curly Bill continued to shout abuse. As Breakenridge swung into his saddle, he fired a slug through the left side of Curley Bill's neck that came out his right cheek, knocking out a tooth. When he recovered, Curly Bill never wore a gun again and left Arizona.

Breakenridge had served with the Union during the Civil War and then moved west to Denver. He participated in the Sand Creek Massacre with Chivington's Third Colorado Cavalry in 1864. Late in life he published his memoirs, titled *Helldorado*. (See also BROCIUS, CURLY BILL.)

Walter Brennan

BRENNAN, WALTER (b. Swampscott, Massachusetts on July 25, 1894; d. Oxnard, California on September 21, 1974) Walter Brennan played the wizened old codger in a number of films, winning an Academy Award for his portrayal of Judge Roy Bean in *The Westerner* (1940). Later in life he starred in the TV series "The Real McCoys" (1957–63) and "The Guns of Will Sonnett" (1967–69). His first film appearance was in *Tearin' into Trouble* (1927), and his last was in *Smoke in the Wind* (1971). He appeared in a number of western films, including *The Lariat Kid* (1929), *The Long, Long Trail* (1929), *Smilin' Guns* (1929), *Law and Order* (1932), *Texas Cyclone* (1932), *Law Beyond the Range* (1935), *The Three Godfathers* (1936), *The Cowboy and the Lady* (1938), *The Texans* (1938), *My Darling Clementine* (1946), *Red River* (1948), *Curtain Call at Cactus Creek* (1950), *Singing Guns* (1950), *Return of the Texan* (1952), *Rio Bravo* (1959), *How the West Was Won* (1962), and *Support Your Local Sheriff* (1969). Walter Brennan was the first actor to win three Academy Awards, all of which he won in 1936 to 1940. Brennan studied engineering in school and then appeared in vaudeville before he tried the movies. His early parts were small, but his roles increased until his major break came in *Come and Get It* (1936), which gave him his first Academy Award for Best Supporting Actor. Brennan's movie career peaked in the 1940s; his greatest fame occurred in the 1950s and 1960s as a TV star. (See also MOVIES.)

BRET MAVERICK TV show that starred James Garner as Bret Maverick, Ed Bruce as Tom Guthrie, Stuart Margolin as Philo Sandine, Darleen Carr as Mary Lou Springer, Richard Hamilton as Cy Whittaker, Davis Knell as Rodney Catlow, John Shearin as Sheriff Mitchell Dowd, Ramon Bieri as Elijah Crow, Jack Garner as Jack, the bartender, Luis Delgado as Shifty Delgrado, Tommy Bush as Deputy Stufgess, Priscilla Morrill as Mrs. Springer, Marj Dusay as Kate Hanrahan and Simone Griffeth as Jasmine DuBois.

Maverick grows up was the general theme of this show, done 20 years after the original Maverick. Bret Maverick had become an upstanding citizen of Sweetwater, Arizona, owning a ranch and part of the Red Ox Saloon. No longer traveling from town to town in search of a good poker game, Maverick tried to capture the wit and charm of the original but didn't attract the same large audience. The show premiered on December 1, 1981 on Tuesday evenings on NBC and finished its run on August 24, 1982 after just one season and 22 episodes.

BREWER, DICK (b. Richard M. Brewer near St. Albans, Vermont on January 10, 1852; d. in Blazer's Mill, New Mexico on April 4, 1878) On April 4, 1878 Brewer led a group of Lincoln County "Regulators" that included Billy the Kid, Frank and George Coe, Bill Scroggins, Tom O'Folliard, Stephen Stevens, Henry Brown, Jim French, Fred Wait, John Middleton and Doc Scurlock into Blazer's Mill to get a meal. Buckshot Roberts came into the mill with a Winchester and two pistols, which Charlie Bowdre demanded he give up. Roberts refused and Bowdre fired, hitting Roberts in the abdomen; Roberts then shot back and wounded John Middleton and George Coe before he staggered into another building. Here, he propped himself up on a mattress by the room's only window with his Sharps .50 buffalo gun. Dick Brewer crawled in close and got off several shots while he hid behind logs. But when Brewer raised his head, Roberts shot off the top of it. Roberts then died from his wounds. Dick Brewer and Buckshot Roberts were buried side by side after the fight was over by mill owner Dr. J. H. Blazer. (See also BILLY THE KID; LINCOLN COUNTY WAR.)

BRIDGER, JIM (b. Richmond, Virginia on March 17, 1804; d. near Little Santa Fe, Missouri on July 17, 1881.) One of the greatest mountain men was Jim Bridger, who lived in the Rocky Mountains for about 20 years, beginning in 1822, and worked for various fur trading companies. Bridger was the first white person to see the Great Salt Lake in Utah, the geysers and other wonders in Yellowstone National Park. He blazed several important routes, including Bridger's Pass over the Continental Divide, which the Union Pacific Railroad later used, and several other routes used by wagon trains. He established Fort Bridger in southwestern Wyoming in 1843, which became a major trading post for those on the Oregon Trail, as well as a military center and Pony Express station. Bridger was ousted from his post in 1853 by the Mormons; later, during the Mormon War (1857–58), he was the major guide for Colonel Albert Sidney Johnston. Bridger also served as a scout and guide for other military expeditions during the 1860s. Although Bridger was illiterate, he could speak about a

Jim Bridger *(Library of Congress)*

dozen different Indian languages as well as French, Spanish and English. He married three Indian squaws but outlived them all. Bridger also had a hand in the ownership of some major fur trading companies. He originally trapped for William Ashley and in 1830 became one of the organizers of the Rocky Mountain Fur Company; in 1834, when this company dissolved, he joined the Sublettes in a new partnership. In 1838 he was with the American Fur Company. Bridger was in the Battle of Pierre's Hole (July 18, 1832) and was shot in the back with an arrow; he carried this arrowhead in his back for three years before Dr. Marcus Whitman cut it out in 1835 during the mountain men's rendezvous. Bridger bought a farm south of Westport, Missouri and settled there in 1868. His health failed, and by 1873 he was blind; four years later he died.

BRIDLES Headgear for a horse in order to control it. There are three types: (1) the split-ear consists of a leather strap over the animal's head and down the side to a metal bit in the horse's mouth. The top of the bridle is split so that part of the bridle is in front of the ears and the other part in back; (2) the California bridle consists of a leather strip down the horse's forehead in addition to the basic design of the split-ear bridle; (3) the hackamore does not have a bit; instead it has a noseband (generally of braided rawhide) with two leather strips running down each side of the horse's

face. This type of bridle can easily be made from rope, and a bridle can be assembled quickly on the range.

BRISCO COUNTY, JR. See ADVENTURES OF BRISCO COUNTY, JR., THE.

BROCIUS, CURLY BILL (b. probably in Texas but possibly in Missouri c. 1857–82; d. c. 1890s) Curly Bill Brocius got his nickname from a cantina singer in New Mexico. One of the leaders in the Clanton cattle-rustling gang, Curly Bill had a rather inflated reputation as a gunslinger. However, he did clash with the Earp faction in Tombstone on several occasions.

On October 28, 1880, Curly Bill and a number of other cowboys decided to "buffalo" the town of Tombstone, Arizona, taking over the saloon and riding up and down the streets shooting their revolvers. Marshal Fred White—the first marshal of Tombstone—deputized Virgil Earp, and the two attempted to restore peace. They found Curly Bill in an alley, and Bill's gun went off during the ensuing struggle, hitting White in the stomach. But Marshal White gasped out that it was an accident, and Curly Bill was acquitted during his trial. It is possible Curly Bill did not hear the Marshal say it was an accident—he had been clubbed over the head by Wyatt Earp brandishing his Buntline Special.

On May 25, 1881 in Galeyville, Arizona, Curly Bill was again drinking heavily with a group of cowboys when Tombstone deputy sheriff Billy Breakenridge came into the saloon. One of the rowdies, Jim Wallace, drew his gun on Breakenridge, but Breakenridge laughed and bought drinks for the house. When the lawman went outside, Curly Bill followed him, exchanging words. Breakenridge knew of White's death and cautiously drew his gun while he mounted his horse; he then shot at Curly Bill. The bullet went in the neck on Curly Bill's left side and came out his right cheek, removing a tooth. That was all for Curly Bill; after healing, he left Arizona forever.

Since Brocius was a member of the Clanton Gang of cattle rustling, there was bad blood between him and the Earps. Wyatt Earp reportedly scoured the countryside looking for Brocius, claiming later he killed him in a gunfight. Curly Bill supposedly heard the story of his death about 10 years later while going through Arizona on his way to Texas. (See also BREAKENRIDGE, WILLIAM MILTON.)

BROKEN ARROW Film produced by Julian Blaustein; directed by Delmer Daves; screenplay by Michael Blankfort (from the Elliott Arnold novel *Blood Brother*); music by Alfred Newman; released in 1950 by Twentieth Century–Fox; 93 minutes in length. Cast: James Stewart, Jeff Chandler, Debra Paget, Basil Ruysdael, Will Geer and Jay Silverheels.

Based on the novel by Elliott Arnold *(Blood Brother)*, this movie tells the story of the Apache chief Cochise and Indian agent Tom Jeffords. It marks a changing point in the image of Indians in westerns, seeing them for the first time as wholly human and equal to whites instead of as feared savages. Jeffords and Cochise try to keep peace between the two peoples; Jeffords marries an Indian woman but she is murdered by white men.

Michael Ansara *(left)* and John Lupton *(right)* of "Broken Arrow"

Director Julian Blaustein attempted to make the movie as accurate as possible, with real Apache doing dances and music. This film led to a number of movies that portrayed Indians in a more sympathetic light, as well as to the creation of the television series "Broken Arrow."

BROKEN ARROW TV show that starred John Lupton as Tom Jeffords, Michael Ansara as Cochise, Tom Fadden as Duffield and Steven Ritch as Nukaya.

Based on the novel *Blood Brother* by Elliott Arnold and later a movie in 1950, this story centers on an Indian agent, Tom Jeffords, who becomes blood brothers with Cochise. The two then unite against bad Indians and bad white folks. On the first five shows, Sue England played Sonseeray, Tom Jeffords's wife, who was killed in an ambush by White Eyes. In the pilot, an hour-long show that appeared on the "Twentieth Century Fox Hour," Rita Moreno played Sonseeahray. The show premiered on September 25, 1958 on ABC on Tuesday evenings. In April 1960 it was moved to Sunday evenings, where it finished its network run on September 18, 1960. There were 78 episodes of the 30-minute series, shot in black and white, mostly on location at Vasquez Rocks and the Fox Ranch in Malibu Canyon near Los Angeles.

BROKEN LANCE Film produced by Sol Siegel; directed by Edward Dmytryk; screenplay by Richard Murphy (based on a story by Philip Yordan); released in 1954 by Twentieth Century–Fox); 96 minutes in length. Cast:

Spencer Tracy, Richard Widmark, Hugh O'Brian, Earl Holliman, Robert Wagner and Katy Jurado.

The story of a domineering cattle baron and his Indian wife. The first three sons of the rancher came from a white mother, so they hate their stepmother and half brother. In addition, miners are moving in, and the baron sets out to stop civilization from advancing. This movie is a remake of the 1949 movie *House of Strangers,* which starred Edward G. Robinson.

BRONC, OR BRONCO An unbroken horse.

BRONCO TV show that starred Ty Hardin as Bronco Layne. Bronco Layne first appeared on the TV show "Cheyenne." He was a former Confederate captain wandering the West who became the star of "Cheyenne" when Clint Walker left that show over a salary dispute with Warner Brothers. Later, a separate show emerged, "Bronco," which alternated weeks with "Sugarfoot" in 1958–59 and 1959–60, then with "Sugarfoot" and "Cheyenne" in 1960–61 and, in the final season, with "Cheyenne." "Bronco" premiered on September 23, 1958 and ended its run on August 20, 1962. The hour-long show was seen on Tuesday evenings on ABC until October 1960, when it began its run on Monday nights on the same network. The final show aired on August 20, 1962.

BRONCO BUSTER Film produced by Ted Richmond; directed by Budd Boetticher; screenplay by Horace McCoy and Lillie Hayward; released by Universal-International in 1952; 80 minutes in length. Cast: John Lund, Scott Brady, Joyce Holden, Chill Wills, Don Haggerty, Bill Williams and Casey Tibbs.

This rodeo movie featured legendary rodeo rider Casey Tibbs in real performances. The story is about a

Ty Hardin as Bronco Layne

rodeo champ who teaches a newcomer the trade; the newcomer then turns into a monster and goes after the champ's girl. The newcomer rides a bull that kills the girl's father (who is a rodeo clown), and the old champ and newcomer set out to settle their differences. This same theme was also used in a 1972 movie, *When Legends Die.*

BRONCO BUSTING   The way to tame a wild horse so it can be ridden is to rope the horse, tie it to a "snubbing post" to hold it and then put the saddle on the horse's back, tie it down, get in the saddle and hang on until the horse does not try to get rid of you. The purpose of this exercise is to break the wild spirit of a horse so it becomes domesticated and can become part of ranch work. Bronco busting is usually done when the horse is about four years old. In the old days there were a number of professional bronco busters who went from ranch to ranch breaking horses. Other times a particular cowboy on a ranch might be known for being especially good at breaking horses, and his job would be to bust the broncos. This is now part of a rodeo, with the horse being made to buck from a strap tied tightly around its flanks. The term *bronco* means "rough" in Spanish.

BROOKS, BUFFALO BILL   (aka "Bully"; b. William L. Brooks c. 1849; d. Wellington, Kansas on July 29 or 30, 1874)   Brooks was hung by a mob after being caught for stealing mules. The stealing and hanging were part of a feud between two rival stage companies, the South Western Stage Company and Vail and Company. Brooks had apparently been hired by the South Western Stage Company to help run the other line out of business. But he was caught and captured by a posse of about 150 men and, along with Charley Smith and L. B. Hasbrouck, was thrown into the Wellington, Kansas county jail. At midnight a mob rushed the jail and hauled the three off to a hanging tree. The two others died quickly, but Brooks died slowly and painfully, strangled to death by the noose as his wife watched.

BROOKS, GARTH   (b. Tulsa, Oklahoma on February 7, 1962).   Singer and songwriter Garth Brooks grew up in Yukon, Oklahoma, outside of Oklahoma City, and attended Oklahoma State University, where he was inspired by George Strait's recordings to become a country singer. In 1987 Brooks and his band moved to Nashville and in 1988 signed with Capitol (now Liberty) Records. The following year his first single "Much Too Young (To Feel This Damn Old)" and his first album were released. Brooks' first album and all following albums sold Platinum and in 1990 he won the Country Music Association's "Horizon Award." His tours are increasingly successful and he released a string of hit singles, including "Friends in Low Places," "The Dance" and "Rodeo." In 1991 Brooks was named "Entertainer of the Year" by the CMA and the following year won his first Grammy and the "Entertainer of the Year" from the Academy of Country Music. Brooks sings contemporary country music but often uses cowboy imagery in his songs and wears cowboy clothes. In the 1990s he became the biggest superstar in country music.

BROWN, HENRY NEWTON   (b. Cold Spring Township, Missouri in 1857; d. Medicine Lodge, Kansas on April 30, 1884)   Henry Newton Brown and Billy the Kid had a cattle-rustling gang in New Mexico, and Brown was part of the Lincoln County War with the McSween's "Regulators." He had headed west in 1875 after his early years on his uncle's farm in Missouri to hunt buffalo in Colorado. He then headed down to New Mexico, where he worked for Major L. G. Murphy and was caught up in the bitter feud that involved Murphy, John Chisum, lawyer Alexander McSween and rancher John Tunstall. Brown was indicted in the murder of Sheriff William Brady and Deputy George Hindman in Lincoln. Brown was also involved with Buckshot Roberts' murder. Brown then left the area and moved to Tascosa, Texas, where he became town constable before he moved to Caldwell, Kansas and pinned on a badge as deputy marshal in July 1882. With Ben Wheeler (real name, Ben Robertson), Brown helped clean up Caldwell, and the town presented him with a specially engraved rifle. Brown, in fact, was an upstanding citizen of Caldwell, so when he told the local citizens that he and Wheeler were going out looking for a murderer, nobody asked questions. That was not the case when it was discovered that Brown and Wheeler, along with two others, actually went over to Medicine Bow, about 40 miles away, and robbed the bank. The two had left on April 30, 1884, a Sunday afternoon, and hooked up the next day with two cowboys, William Smith and John Wesley. On Wednesday morning the four rode into Caldwell about nine in the morning during a driving rainstorm. They went into the Medicine Valley Bank, where Brown killed the bank president, E. W. Payne, during this holdup while another gang member killed a teller, George Geppert. This led to a posse chasing them into a box canyon where, trapped, they shot it out for two hours before being captured. They were taken into town and thrown into the local jail, where they ate two meals and had their pictures taken. Brown wrote a moving note to his young bride saying he did this all for her. Around nine that night a lynch mob came by, overpowered the guards and then hauled the prisoners out. Brown managed to break away, but a farmer loosed both barrels of a shotgun and blew him in half. The other three were taken to a tree where they were strung up. (See also LINCOLN COUNTY WAR; WHEELER, BEN.)

BROWN, JOHNNY MACK   (b. Dothan, Alabama on September 1, 1904; d. Woodland Hills, California November 14, 1974)   Brown was a football star at the University of Alabama; in the 1926 Rose Bowl game he caught the game-winning touchdown. The following year he was an All-American and during the Rose Bowl scored on an intercepted pass to win the game. After the Rose Bowl, Brown took a screen test and was signed to a studio contract. Between 1930 and 1952 Brown appeared in over 130 cowboy movies as a no-nonsense hero with his horse, Rebel. His first film was *Bugle Call*

Johnny Mack Brown

(1927), and he made his western debut in *Montana Moon* (1930). He then appeared in *Billy the Kid,* which made him a star. He starred in two western serials, *Fighting with Kit Carson* (Mascot, 1933) and *Rustlers of Red Dog* (Universal, 1935). In the 1960s he appeared in *The Bounty Hunter* (1965) and *Requiem for a Gunfighter* (1965), and his last movie was *Apache Uprising* (1966). (See also B WESTERN MOVIES; MOVIES.)

BROWNING, JOHN MOSES (b. Ogden, Utah on January 29, 1855; d. Liege, Belgium on November 26, 1926) John Browning invented most of the major breakthroughs and improvements in firearms, and his patents were licensed and sold under the names Winchester, Colt, Remington, Savage and others. The son of a gunsmith, Browning held 128 patents for firearms and invented 80 firearm models. In 1879 he received his first patent for a single-shot rife, which became Winchester's single-shot model of 1885. Browning also invented the lever-action repeating rife, marketed by Winchester in 1886, a single-action shotgun, a punch-action shotgun, and lever and pump action for single-shot rifles. Browning's big breakthrough came when he figured out how to use expanding gases and the recoil from ammunition exploding to automatically eject, reload and fire a weapon. Browning developed this idea when he noticed that the grass reeds between a man firing and the target were blown vigorously by escaping gun gases during local competition. In 1892 Browning received his first

patents for an automatic weapon and in 1895 invented the automatic machine gun. Browning also invented the semiautomatic pistol, and in 1911 his .45 automatic pistol was the government's standard military sidearm. During World War I Browning's automatic machine gun and automatic rife were used in battles. In World War II Browning's .50 caliber machine gun was used. Since Browning's death in 1926 there have been no fundamental changes in the firearms industry.

BRUSHPOPPING Term used by cowboys to mean combing brush thickets for cattle during round-up time.

BRYANT, BLACK FACED CHARLIE (b. Charles Bryant; d. near Waukomis, Oklahoma on August 23, 1891) As a youth, Bryant was hit in the face by grains of black powder from a point-blank pistol shot; this permanent disfigurement gave him his nickname. He joined the Dalton Gang in 1891 and was arrested in Hennessey, Oklahoma while in a hotel room sickbed. Deputy U.S. Marshal Ed Short was transporting him by train to Wichita, Kansas when Short went to the smoker and, after checking Bryant's handcuffs and handing the outlaw's pistol to the express messenger, left Bryant in the custody of the railroad worker. The messenger put the six-gun into a pigeonhole in his desk, but Bryant sneaked to the desk and seized the gun just as Short returned to the car. Bryant shot Short in the chest, but Short fired his rifle at the outlaw, the bullet severing Bryant's spinal column. Bryant managed to empty his pistol at Short before he died. Then Short laid down on a cot and died.

BUCK AND THE PREACHER Film produced by Joel Glickman; directed by Sidney Poitier; screenplay by Ernest Kinoy from a story by Ernest Kinoy and Drake Walker; released in 1972 by Columbia; 102 minutes in length. Cast: Sidney Poitier, Harry Belafonte, Ruby Dee, Cameron Mitchell, Denny Miller, Nita Talbot, Tony Brubaker and Pamela Jones.

The first movie directed by Sidney Poitier, this film is about the Exodusters, groups of formers slaves who went west after the Civil War to settle. Poitier plays a former Union cavalryman who becomes a frontier scout, guiding slaves west. Harry Belafonte is the preacher, a con man. The wagon train of black pioneers faces white southern labor recruiters in addition to the usual troubles.

BUCKAROO A rider on the back of a bucking bronc. A derivation of the Spanish term for cowboy, *vaquero.*

BUCKBOARD (aka buck wagon) A four-wheeled horse-drawn vehicle made to carry two to four people and pulled by one or two horses. A light wagon, it tended to "buck" on rough ground, hence its name.

BUCKING STRAP The strap around the flank of a rodeo horse that makes it buck; also used on rodeo bulls.

BUCKSKIN Leather dressed from deer or elk (also the bighorn sheep) and worn as clothing. The Indians used buckskin for shirts, moccasins, bags and dresses; the mountain men had pants and shirts made from buckskin. In describing a horse, the term means one with a buckskin—or tannish—color with a black mane and tail.

BUCKSKIN TV show that starred Tommy Nolan as Jody O'Connell, Sallie Brophy as Mrs. Annie O'Connell, Michael Road as Marshall Tom Sellers, and Michael Lipton as Ben Newcomb.

The hub for social and business activities in Buckskin, Montana in 1880 was the boardinghouse run by Mrs. Annie O'Connell, a widow with a 10-year-old son, Jody. The show was seen through the eyes of Jody, who watched the comings and goings of the prominent and not-so-respectable of the town. This show premiered on July 3, 1958 as a summer replacement for "The Tennessee Ernie Ford Show." It was shown on NBC on Thursday nights until October 1958, when it switched to Friday evenings. The half-hour show moved to Monday nights in January 1959 and ran there until September 1959. The show ended as it began—as a summer re-run—in 1965, with its last telecast on August 29, 1965.

BUCK THE TIGER Another name for the game faro. The term is derived from the pictures of tigers painted on the cards; an alternate name is *fight the tiger.* (See FARO.)

BUFFALO The American buffalo (*Bos bison americanus*) ranged on the prairies from the Gulf of Mexico to the Canadian border, from the Rocky Mountains to the belt of forests along the Mississippi; some even lived in the Southeast in Kentucky, Tennessee and the tidewater areas of the Carolinas and Virginia and in the Ohio Valley. There were actually several types of buffalo: The plains buffalo adult bull weighed about 2,000 pounds and stood about seven feet tall at the shoulder; the female cows weighed 700–900 pounds and stood about five feet tall at the shoulder. The wood or mountain buffalo, bigger and darker than the plains variety, wintered in the Rockies; it reached a weight of about 2,500 pounds for bulls and 1,600 pounds for cows. The buffalo bred from mid-July to the end of August, and their calves were born about nine and a half months later. Fast animals, buffalo could run 35–40 miles an hour over about a quarter of a mile and often outran their enemies over long distances. At one time in the 17th century there were probably 40 million buffalo in the present-day United States.

The buffalo were the main food supply for the Plains Indians, who hunted them on foot with limited success (usually trying to stampede them off a cliff or box them into a canyon) until horses came to the plains. On horseback, a new culture was created because buffalo could be hunted all year long and the men had more leisure time; women had to care for the hides and meat, and one good hunter could keep four or five women busy. The advent of horses also caused the Plains Indians to become nomads, following the buffalo. In fact, the whole Plains Indian culture was centered on the buffalo; everything on a buffalo was used, and the animal was considered sacred.

The end of the buffalo came when white settlers moved into the plains. First, the homesteaders fenced the farms and ranchers and added livestock, keeping out Indians and limiting the buffalo's territory. Buffalo hunters killed buffalo for their hides to ship back East; later, when the railroad crews moved into the West, the buffalo were killed for their meat, although hunters often killed large numbers of buffalo, stripped their hides off and cut out the tongue, a tasty delicacy, and left the rest of the carcasses to rot.

The beginning of the end for the buffalo came during the 1840s when settlers went west on the Oregon and California Trails. These trails divided the plains into northern and southern areas for the buffalo. The final disaster for the buffalo occurred from 1870 to 1883. First, buffalo hunters killed large numbers for railroad workers and for the hide market back East, but the army and white settlers also encouraged the elimination of the buffalo in order to eliminate Indians from the plains. Since the Indians depended on buffalo for food, clothing, blankets, tipis and, in fact, an entire way of life, the elimination of the buffalo meant a solution to the "Indian problem." Between 1872 and 1874, buffalo hunters killed almost four and a half million, and the last large kill of buffalo occurred in 1883; after this, the bones of the buffalo became valuable for fertilizer and bone china. The buffalo were easy to slaughter because if their leader was killed, the rest of the herd just remained quietly in the area. The eyes of a buffalo are on the sides of its head, so it cannot see in front; a dumb animal, it would just stand in a field while hunters slaughtered hundreds if the hunter stayed downwind. The sounds of gunfire did not bother them; neither did the dead bodies of other buffalo.

From 1883 to 1900 the only buffalo that survived were those protected independently by western ranchers; at this point the United States government began to preserve buffalo.

BUFFALO BILL, JR. TV show that starred Dick Jones as Buffalo Bill, Jr., Harry Cheshire as Judge Ben Wiley and Nancy Gilbert as Calamity.

Buffalo Bill, Jr. was the fictional son of the legendary Buffalo Bill Cody, who, with his sister Calamity, lived in Wileyville, run by Judge Ben Wiley. The show was a Saturday morning favorite, aimed at children and produced by Gene Autry's Flying A Productions. Jones had starred in the "Range Rider" series and seven Autry films before being cast in this series, which ran on CBS during 1955. Fifty-two episodes of the half-hour show were shot, all in black and white.

BUFFALO BILL AND THE INDIANS; OR, SITTING BULL'S HISTORY LESSON Film produced and directed by Robert Altman; screenplay by Alan Rudolph and Robert Altman; released in 1976 by United Artists; 123 minutes in length. Cast: Paul Newman, Burt Lancaster, Joel Grey, Kevin McCarthy, Harvey Keitel, Allan Nicholls, Geraldine Chaplin, John Considine, Robert Doqui, Mike Kaplan, Denver Pyle and Shelley Duvall.

Show biz meets the Wild West in this movie, directed by Robert Altman, and the western myths are debunked. Based on Arthur Kopit's 1969 Broadway play *Indians*, the movie portrays Cody as a showman and not much more. Sitting Bull is in marked contrast to Cody; the theme involves the superficiality of the myth created by Cody with his Wild West shows versus the dignity and "reality" of the Indians, symbolized by Sitting Bull, who must endure the shallow showmanship to make a living. The message is clear: The Wild West is more a press release than real history.

BUFFALO BILL'S WILD WEST SHOW   Buffalo Bill Cody was adamant that his "Wild West" was not a "show" but was rather an "authentic" representation of the Wild West. Known officially as "Buffalo Bill's Wild West and Congress of Rough Riders of the World" during its most popular period, the show toured for over 30 years, although the final years saw the original show dismantled, with Cody touring in the Sells-Floto Circus.

The "Wild West" was a three-hour extravaganza that featured shooting exhibitions, military exhibitions, dramatic spectacles, races, riding and horse acts and specialty acts. Its most important contribution was the creation of the West as "myth" and the cowboy as a genuine American hero.

Cody's "Wild West" was not the only touring show of its kind in the late 19th century and early 20th; there were about 80 companies similar to Cody's that toured, including "Pawnee Bill's Wild West," "Doc W. F. Carver's Wild America" and the "Miller Brothers' 101 Ranch and Wild West Show."

The genesis for Cody's Wild West show was "The Old Glory Blowout" on July 4, 1882 in North Platte, Nebraska. This event featured the first rodeo with cash prizes given to cowboys, although it was not really defined as a "rodeo" at this time. Cody offered the cash prizes to attract cowboys to participate. Hoping to get about 100 cowboys interested, he was surprised when about 1,000 appeared for the riding and roping contests.

Cody and Dr. W. F. Carver went into partnership to organize the first Wild West show, which premiered on May 19, 1883 in Omaha, Nebraska as "Hon. W. F. Cody and Dr. W. F. Carver's Rocky Mountain and Prairie Exhibition." That first Wild West show featured the core of all the Wild West shows to follow: some shooting exhibitions (including those by Cody), the attack on the Deadwood mail coach in which passengers were rescued by Cody, the reenactment of the Pony Express, a race between an Indian on horseback and an Indian on foot as well as a horse race between cowboys, a "Great Hunt" that featured some buffalo as well as a simulated fight with Indians, and some rodeo events, such as riding Texas steers, roping and riding buffalo, and "Cowboy Fun" that featured cowboys riding bucking horses and performing rope tricks.

In addition to Cody and Carver, others in the show included interpreter Gordon Lillie, who would later form his own Wild West show as "Pawnee Bill," Buck Taylor,

the "King of the Cowboys," and the "Cowboy Kid," Johnny Baker.

Carver dropped out of the Wild West partnership in 1884, but Cody joined with Nate Salsbury and Captain Bogardus as new partners. At this time the name of the show was changed to "Buffalo Bill's Wild West, America's National Entertainment." Also in this year Annie Oakley joined the show after auditioning in New Orleans. Annie and her husband, Frank Butler, formed a core act for Buffalo Bill's show that featured her shooting glass balls thrown in the air by her husband, shooting the ashes off a cigarette in his mouth and shooting an apple off the head of her poodle.

In 1885 Chief Sitting Bull was added to the show, and from this point on Cody would always feature a famous Indian chief in his show.

Initially, the "Wild West" played one-night stands, but beginning in 1886, it began playing long engagements on permanent grounds. The first long engagement was from June to September 1886 at Staten Island in New York. Cody's show also played Madison Square Garden during the winter in another long engagement and began touring Europe the following year.

Cody's first international tour began in 1887 when he played London and performed before Queen Victoria on May 11, 1887 in a royal command performance. He received instant international acclaim.

The apex of fame for Buffalo Bill's Wild West show came in 1893 during the Chicago World's Fair. Here, Cody set up in a lot opposite the fair's entrance and enjoyed huge crowds attracted by the fair. He had not been in the United States with his Wild West show since 1889, when he first played Paris for a six-month stand (and introduced popcorn to the Parisians), then Germany, Belgium and England again. It was at this time the name of the show was changed to "Buffalo Bill's Wild West and Congress of Rough Riders of the World."

After the Chicago show, James Bailey of the Barnum and Bailey Circus became a partner and improved the travel arrangements. Bailey organized the show like a circus, able to set up and tear down quickly as it moved from town to town. The "Wild West" returned to Europe in 1902 and then went back to the United States, where it began a series of tours. The show became a financial drain, and in 1907 Cody sold two-thirds of the show to Bailey. He also began making it a more "western" show, replacing a number of circus acts and performers added by Bailey with western acts and dramas.

In 1908 Gordon Lillie purchased Bailey's two-thirds portion and formed "Buffalo Bill's Wild West and Pawnee Bill's Far East" show, which turned the event into more of a circus. The show was on shaky ground financially, and the duo began a series of farewell tours in 1910. In 1912 Cody joined the Sells-Floto Circus owned by Harry Tammen (who was also part owner of the Denver Post) and became financially obligated to Tammen. When the circus played Denver in 1913, Cody was sued by Tammen for moneys owed, and Cody's organization went bankrupt; this led to the Wild West show being auctioned off on September 15, 1913.

In order to pay off debts and be released from his

financial obligation to Tammen, Cody began touring with the Sells-Floto Circus in 1915, which was the low point of his professional career. Tired, worn out, run down and financially strapped, Cody spent his final days playing out his mythic role on one-night stands. By the end of 1916 Cody had performed for more than five million people in over 1,000 cities and 12 countries. Cody had missed only nine performances during the first 26 years of the show and had probably been seen by more people than any other living person.

At the height of the show, in 1897, there were about 300 people and 500 horses traveling with the show. The one-night stands were generally played on empty lots, baseball fields, race tracks and driving parks, and seats were set up to accommodate about 15,000 fans. The show performed in rain or shine during these events in an area about 150 feet wide by 320 feet long. By this time the show's cast and support crew had grown from about 300 people to about 700 people.

BUFFALO CHIPS Buffalo dung that, when dried, was used as fuel for fires.

BUFFALO GRASS See GRASSES.

BUFFALO GUN Any kind of rifle that could drop a buffalo, which meant the gun had to have range, velocity and penetrating power so a buffalo could be killed with one shot—a difficult task. The first famous buffalo gun was the Sharps rifle with .40 to .50 caliber cartridges.

BUFFALO SOLDIERS The "buffalo soldiers" were the African American soldiers in the United States Army who served in the West after the Civil War. They were given the name "buffalo soldiers" by the Indians, who thought their hair was like the buffalo's. One group of buffalo soldiers, the 10th Cavalry, used the buffalo as part of its emblem on its regimental banner. The idea that blacks could serve in the army in the West came about because during the Civil War almost 180,000 blacks had served in the Union army; 33,380 had been killed. This involvement proved to the government and the army that African Americans could be good soldiers, so when the post–Civil War army was organized, it was agreed there would be some regiments of Negro troops. The authorized strength of the post–Civil War army was 54,641 officers and men (the actual number was much smaller), and on July 28, 1866 Congress passed an act to authorize six regiments of Negro troops; two regiments would be cavalry (the 9th and 10th), and four would be infantry (there would only be two, the 24th and 25th). Congress required white officers to lead the black troops (the reasoning was that there were no experienced Negro officers); further, all officers must have had active field service in the Civil War. The leaders of the cavalry units were Edward Hatch of Iowa, who was to head the 9th Cavalry, and Benjamin Grierson of Illinois, who headed the 10th Cavalry. (George Armstrong Custer refused an assignment with the 9th and managed to obtain a spot with the 7th.) The 24th Infantry was organized in 1869 from two regiments stationed in Louisiana, Texas and New Mexico. Their commanding officer was Lieutenant Colonel William R. Shafter. The 25th Infantry was organized in New Orleans in 1869 from remnants of the 39th from North Carolina and the 40th stationed in Louisiana. The troops signed up for an enlistment of five years; most were illiterate, and the army set about teaching them to read and write by assigning a chaplain to the task.

From the beginning, the buffalo soldiers were not treated equally with white soldiers by the government. First, they received the poorest horses and most broken down equipment; on troop inspections, the black troops were required to stay at least 10 to 15 yards from white troops, and the Negro troops were not allowed to march in review. Meals were generally coffee, bread, beans and beef; occasionally there might be molasses, corn bread and sweet potatoes. Often the bread was sour and the beef was of poor quality. At other posts for white soldiers, molasses, canned tomatoes, dried apples, dried peaches, sauerkraut, potatoes, onions and canned peas were eaten regularly. Flour was only provided for officers of the buffalo soldiers. Extended furloughs were denied and discipline was unusually severe, much greater than for white soldiers. Further, the buffalo soldiers were usually given the most lonely and isolated posts. By August, 1867 eight companies of the 10th were in the field; three were assigned to Indian Territory, and the others were sent to post and camps in central Kansas where the Kansas Pacific Railroad was being constructed. The spring and summer of 1867 meant the 9th and 10th Cavalry moved west; they would be on the Great Plains or in the southwest of west Texas, Arizona and New Mexico for the next 20 years. They were there to patrol the Mexican border, to fight Indians and to protect citizens on the frontier, but most citizens (especially in west Texas) hated the Negro soldiers. The buffalo soldiers had a thankless task.

By 1891 the Buffalo soldiers had fought Indians on the Kansas plains and in the Red River War in Indian Territory. They helped keep boomers out of Indian Territory. They had served in west Texas, where they protected the frontier and helped defeat Victorio, and patrolled along the Rio Grande into New Mexico and Arizona, where they helped defeat the Apache and capture Geronimo and were even involved in the Lincoln County War against Billy the Kid. Finally, they were in Colorado and the Dakotas, where they came to the rescue of the 7th Calvary during the Wounded Knee uprising, which ended the Indian Wars. The buffalo soldiers had the lowest desertion rate in the army, and chronic drunkenness, a major problem with most regiments, was almost unheard of in these regiments. Later, buffalo soldiers served in the Spanish-American War in Cuba at San Juan Hill and fought against Pancho Villa in Mexico. Eleven buffalo soldiers were awarded the Medal of Honor. Twenty blacks were admitted to West Point in the 19th century, but only three graduated. The first graduate, Henry Flipper, was court-martialed and drummed out of the army for "conduct unbecoming to an officer" because he had gone riding with a white woman in Texas; later he had a distinguished career and served as a translator for the United States Senate

Committee on Foreign Relations and in the Department of the Interior.

BUFFALO WALLOW Buffalo crave being rubbed, but on the plains there was a shortage of trees, so the buffalo wallowed on the ground, creating large saucer-shaped indentations in the land. These wallows would often collect water and, on some occasions, serve as defense works for men under attack.

BULLDOGGER A rodeo cowboy who bulldogs steers; also called a "dogger." (See STEER WRESTLING.)

BULLDOGGING See STEER WRESTLING.

BULL DURHAM Popular brand of tobacco that cowboys either rolled into papers or put in a pipe.

BULLION, LAURA (Might be the alias of Della Rose; b. Knickerbocker, Texas c. 1876; d. unknown, after 1912) Laura Bullion rode with Butch Cassidy's Wild Bunch because she was the girlfriend (later, possibly the wife) of gang member Ben Kilpatrick. Bullion grew up on a sheep ranch in Concho County, Texas, met Kilpatrick and accompanied him to Browns Hole, Colorado, a hideout for the Wild Bunch, in 1895. She apparently took part in some robberies dressed as a man (the Great Northern train robbery in Wagner, Montana on July 3, 1901 was one). Laura and Ben were sentenced to the Jefferson City, Montana penitentiary at the end of 1901, after which they returned to outlawry. Kilpatrick was killed during a 1912 train robbery; Bullion disappeared after this event.

BULLWHACKER The bullwhacker was in charge of the wagon trains of linked wagons pulled by ox teams. He usually walked beside his team and carried a bull-whip, which could be over 20 feet long, and cracked it over the heads of the oxen to keep them moving. A mule skinner had the same task with mules hooked to the wagons instead of oxen. Oxen were cheaper and stronger than horses and mules but were slower.

BUNTLINE, NED (b. Edward Zane Carroll Judson in Stamford, New York on March 20, 1923; d. New York on July 16, 1886.) The dime novel brought the Wild West to easterners, and Ned Buntline was a most prolific—and perhaps the most influential—of the western dime novelists. It was Buntline who found Buffalo Bill Cody and began writing the books about his exploits that gave Cody his initial national fame; Buntline also wrote a play for Cody, *The Scouts of the Plains*, that launched Cody's show business career.

Ed Judson ran away to sea when he was 10 and collected experiences as well as a pen name. A "buntline" is a rope at the bottom of a square sale. He used the name because his first published work, *The Captain's Pig* (1842), had an unflattering portrait of his captain and young Carroll did not want him to know who wrote it. The captain offered a reward for the identity of the author; Judson resigned his commission and fled.

Buntline then began a magazine in Pittsburgh, *Ned Buntline's Magazine,* that folded after two issues; he then moved to Cincinnati, where he started the *Western Literary Journal* to publish his own works. He moved the publication to Nashville, Tennessee in 1844 and began printing names and scams of gamblers working the area. Buntline became involved with a married woman and then shot her husband when the cuckolded mate pursued the writer with a pistol. To escape a lynch mob, Buntline jumped from a high window (giving himself a lifelong limp) but was caught and strung up; luckily his friends cut him down just in time. He then moved to Philadelphia and began a magazine, *Ned Buntline's Own,* and served a year in prison for inciting a riot in New York (which claimed 34 lives). Still he cranked out stories.

Ned Buntline was the highest-paid writer in America by the summer of 1849, making about $20,000 a year, or more than Twain, Melville or Whitman. He traveled west to find Major Frank North, who had just become a hero at an Indian battle. Arriving in North Platte, Nebraska, Buntline met North, who did not like writers or talking about his exploits. According to one story, North pointed out a young man under a wagon who was sleeping off a hangover, and suggested the writer talk to him. The young man was 23-year-old Bill Cody.

Cody and Buntline spent the next 10 days drinking and trading yarns. Buntline then went back to New York and wrote "Buffalo Bill: The King of the Border Men. The Wildest and Truest Story I Ever Wrote" for Street & Smith's *New York Weekly.* The story, which was mostly fiction, thrilled Cody, and a star was born.

Ned Buntline

The theatrical debut for Buffalo Bill occurred in Chicago at a theater managed by Jim Nixon. Cody arrived with "Texas Jack" Omohundro, a fellow ex-scout, five days before showtime. Nixon had been promised 26 Indians but instead found himself with two hopeful actors who did not know their lines. Further, no play had yet been written and the house was sold out. So Buntline sat down and wrote a script for the December 12, 1872 opening. In the show, "The Scouts of the Plains," Buntline appeared as scout Cale Durg and spent the evening feeding lines to his two costars, who were suffering severe stage fright. In the second act, Durg was killed and so Buntline watched his death avenged. Bill and Jack did not deliver a single line as written, and the whole spectacle would have gone down as one of the great disasters in the history of show business except that the audience loved it. The group traveled on to St. Louis and then New York, where Cody kicked Buntline out of the show and replaced him with Wild Bill Hickok, who did not last long.

Buntline was quite a character, married at least five times and perhaps eight (twice simultaneously) and reportedly kept six mistresses. He supposedly once wrote 610 pages in 62 hours.

BUNTLINE SPECIAL A line of guns made by Colt for Ned Buntline in 1876. They were "Peacemakers" with 16-inch barrels; approximately 30 were made, and they sold for $26 each. Buntline presented guns to Wyatt Earp, Charlie Bassett, Bat Masterson, Bill Tilghman and Neal Brown. The guns had shoulder stocks but were mostly for show; Earp, Masterson and Tilghman had the barrels cut down on their guns, and only Bassett and Brown kept their originals intact. In 1957 Colt produced a pistol with a 12-inch barrel called the "Buntline Special," which was popularized by the TV show "The Life and Legend of Wyatt Earp."

BURNETTE, SMILEY (b. Lester Alvin Burnette in Summum, Illinois on March 18, 1911; d. in Los Angeles, California on February 16, 1967)   Smiley Burnette was most famous as Gene Autry's sidekick, although he also starred with Charles Starrett and was a talented actor and musician in his own right. The son of ministers, Burnette began public musical performances when he was nine in Astoria, Illinois. He landed a job for WDZ, a 100-watt radio station, as announcer and entertainer and, as a result, came to the attention of Gene Autry, who was looking for an accordion player to join him on the "National Barn Dance" on WLS in Chicago. When Autry went west to Hollywood in 1934, Burnette went with him and wrote "Ridin' Down the Canyon" with Autry while the two were traveling in the car to California. Beginning with *The Phantom Empire*, Burnette was in 50 features with Autry from 1934 to 1942; in fact, he appeared in every Autry picture except two during this time, *Melody Ranch* and *Shooting High*. Burnette, playing the character "Frog Millhouse," created the mold for all cowboy comic sidekicks. At 289 pounds, he served as a comic foil for Autry, and the two created the basic plot of the sidekick getting the cowboy

Smiley Burnette

in more trouble than the outlaws. Burnette was also an excellent musical addition to Autry, writing over 300 songs, including "Song of the Range," "It's My Lazy Day" and "Call of the Canyon," in addition to being an excellent musician. After Autry joined the armed services in World War II, Burnette worked with Roy Rogers, Eddie Dew, Bob Livingston and Sunset Carson. In 1946 Burnette moved from Republic to Columbia Studios to costar with Charles Starrett in 56 films in the *Durango Kid* series but rejoined Autry in 1952 and worked with the singing cowboy on his final features. In 1963 Burnette starred as Charlie Pratt on "Petticoat Junction." Burnette's horse was as famous as he was: "Black Eyed Nellie" (also called "Ringeye") was a white horse with a black circle painted around its eye; it was done with shoe polish. Burnette got so popular that this sidekick even had a sidekick, a young kid named "Tadpole." (See also AUTRY, GENE.)

BURRO Spanish word for "donkey." These animals were especially valuable for prospectors because they could carry up to 300 pounds on their back; but their value as a pack animal is often offset by the stubbornness, stupidity (they can swim but will often drown because they won't try to swim while crossing a river or stream) and wanderlust.

BURROWS, REUBEN HOUSTON (b. Lamar County, Alabama on December 11, 1854; d. Linden, Alabama on October 8, 1889)   Burrows and his brother Jim were farmers in Texas scratching by until, inspired by the exploits of Sam Bass, they began robbing trains in the 1880s. In 1888 Burrows killed a newspaperman in Alabama and was involved in a shootout on a train in Nashville. Burrows had moved south after robbing a number of trains in Texas, which put the Pinkertons on his tail. On September 1, 1890 Rube held up the Louisville and Nashville train at Flomaton, Alabama and then took shelter in the home of Jesse Hildreth, a large black man, who overpowered him and handed him over to lawmen. In jail in Linden, Alabama, Burrows got hold of a pistol and tried to shoot his way out; instead he was gunned down.

BURY ME NOT ON THE LONE PRAIRIE
See O BURY ME NOT ON THE LONE PRAIRIE.

BUSHWHACK A surprise ambush with the target often shot in the back while the attacker hid behind cover.

BUTCH CASSIDY AND THE SUNDANCE KID
Film produced by John Foreman; directed by George Roy Hill; screenplay by William Goldman; music by Burt Bacharach; released in 1969 by Twentieth Century–Fox; 110 minutes in length. Cast: Paul Newman, Robert Redford, Katharine Ross, Strother Martin and Cloris Leachman.

This movie, a megahit at the box office, is about the

Butch Cassidy and the Sundance Kid *(Western Archives)*

real-life legendary outlaws but also about friendship; Newman's and Redford's appeal as "friends" explains a great deal about the popularity of this movie. Witty repartee and plenty of comedy make this film enjoyable and the fact that these two likable fellows are in a dangerous, illegal business—robbing trains. During one robbery, Butch and Sundance are surprised by a posse that relentlessly pursues them. They decide to go to South America, along with Sundance's girlfriend, Etta Place (Katharine Ross). After a few robberies in Bolivia, Etta returns to the States, Butch and Sundance go straight for a while and then return to the outlaw trade. Their activities lead to a shootout in a public square; the films ends in freeze frame when Butch and Sundance run out firing, surrounded by thousands of South American soldiers whose guns are aimed at them. The ending avoids the sticky question of whether Butch and Sundance (either or both) survived South America and returned to the United States, a matter of some dispute among historians.

BUTTE A hill, generally created by erosion of the land around it.

BUTTERFIELD, JOHN See BUTTERFIELD OVERLAND MAIL.

BUTTERFIELD OVERLAND MAIL This was the longest stagecoach line, traveling 2,800 miles from St. Louis, Missouri to San Francisco, California and covering Arkansas, Indian Territory, Texas, New Mexico, Arizona and southern California in the process. It was begun in 1857 by John Butterfield (1801–69), who received a government contract to provide mail service between the Mississippi River and San Francisco. Each trip took 25 days one way. There were 1,000 horses, 500 mules, 750 men (150 drivers) and 100 Concord stages in this line with way stations established at regular intervals. The first trips were made on September 1858. The fare was $100 across the continent. In 1861 the route was reestablished as the Central Route in federal controlled territory after the outbreak of the Civil War.

John Butterfield was born in Berne, New York and became a stagecoach driver in Albany at the age of 19. Butterfield was an energetic, ambitious man who established a number of transportation businesses before the Overland Mail. The firm succeeded in establishing daily (rather than semiweekly) mail service but incurred large financial losses, even though the federal government gave it a $600,000-per-year subsidy. Finally, the board of directors removed Butterfield from the presidency in 1860 and replaced him with William B. Dinsmore. Butterfield then went to New York City and engaged in some business enterprises until he was felled by a stroke in 1867; he was moved to his home in Utica and never recovered, dying two years later.

BUTTRAM, PAT (b. Addison, Alabama in 1917 d. Los Angeles, California on January 8, 1994) Pat Buttram was Gene Autry's sidekick after Smiley Burnette (Frog Millhouse) left. Actually, Buttram joined Autry after World War II when the singing cowboy returned

Pat Buttram

BUZZARD A vulture that disposes of dead animals, the buzzard (*Cathartes aura*) has a wingspan of nearly six feet and soars high in the air with open wings on air currents. Also called a turkey vulture, the buzzard has a negative connotation because of the image of it circling a dying man in the desert.

B WESTERN MOVIES There were different types of movies produced in Hollywood from the 1930s through the 1950s: The "A" movies were big-budget, big-production features produced by the major studios. These played top theaters in top cities; since the movie companies owned theaters through most of this period, they controlled the access and distribution, so they were guaranteed that these movies would be shown. The second kind of movie was the "B," which could stand for "budget" and was second to A. These movies were relatively inexpensively made and satisfied the demand from movie audiences for two movies in an evening and for movies on Saturday matinees. Major studios often had a division where "Bs" were made, but it was usually up to independent studios to make these "Bs." These Bs were made and sold in groups for a flat fee and played in second-run theaters or in small towns. The heart of the western movie business from the 1930s through the 1950s was "B" movies; it was in these movies that most western stars got their start and the formula for the western was developed and perfected. The "B" western was not shown in large, first-run theaters; instead, it was usually shown in neighborhood theaters in small towns for Saturday matinees; it was known for having lots of action. The "Bs" were straightforward: There were good guys and bad guys, and it was easy to tell the difference; the plot was a basic morality play in which the good guys win and the bad guys lose. These movies were generally set in the American West in late 19th century and were aimed at kids and rural audiences. The top studio for "B" westerns was Republic, and their major audiences were in the South, Midwest and Southwest. (See also REPUBLIC STUDIOS).

from the service; Buttram had met Autry when the two were both on the "National Barn Dance" on WLS in Chicago. Buttram and Autry appeared on radio together for 15 years and then in Columbia movies and the "Gene Autry" TV show; Buttram's first film with Autry was *The Strawberry Roan* (1948), and he was Autry's sidekick for 16 films through 1952. Later, Buttram played Mr. Haney on the TV show "Green Acres." Buttram's grandfather was Admiral James Harmon Ward, one of the founders of Annapolis.

CACTUS JIM TV show that starred Clarence Hartzell as Cactus Jim (1949–51) and Bill Bailey as Cactus Jim (1951).

A children's program in the very early days of television, this show was actually a series of western movies introduced by old-time range rider Cactus Jim. The prime-time version debuted on October 31, 1949 on NBC every day, Monday through Friday. The half-hour show ended on October 26, 1951. The show originated in Chicago at WNBQ and later was on Saturday mornings on NBC, where it enjoyed a brief run from January to March 1952.

CADE'S COUNTY TV show that starred Glenn Ford as Sam Cade, Edgar Buchanan as J. J. Jackson, Taylor Lacher as Arlo Pritchard, Victor Campos as Rudy

Davillo, Peter Ford as Pete, Sandra Ego as Joannie Little Bird (1971) and Betty Ann Carr as Betty Ann Sundown.

Movie cowboy Glenn Ford came to the small screen in this contemporary western, set in Madrid County, California. Ford played Sheriff Sam Cade, a contemporary figure with Old West ways and a Wild West sense of justice. The show premiered on September 19, 1971 on Sunday nights on CBS. In August 1972 it was shifted to Monday nights. The hour-long show ended on September 4, 1972 after 24 episodes.

CAHILL, UNITED STATES MARSHAL Film produced by Michael Wayne; directed by Andrew V. McLaglen; screenplay by Harry Julian Fink and Rita M. Find from the story by Barney Slater; released in 1973 by Warner Brothers; 103 minutes in length. Cast: John Wayne, George Kennedy, Gary Grimes, Neville Brand, Clay O'Brien, Marie Windsor, Morgan Paull, Don Vadis, Denver Pyle, Jackie Coogan and Harry Carey, Jr.

Cahill (John Wayne) joins up with an Indian half-breed to chase some outlaws. He must also face the fact that his sons, growing up in his absence, are heading toward the wrong side of the law; in the final showdown, Cahill must clear up the outlaw problem and involve his sons in the danger as well.

CAHOOTS Phrase used for partnership or people teamed together.

CALABOOSE Anglicized version of a Spanish term for jail.

CALAMITY JANE (b. Martha Jane Canary (or Cannary) in Princeton, Missouri on May 1, 1852; d. a few miles from Deadwood on August 1, 1903). Calamity Jane drank hard, lived hard and died broke. She was tough, wore buckskins, cussed, and worked like a man. Supposedly, the great love of her life was Wild Bill Hickok, whom she met in 1876 and by whom she reportedly had a daughter.

Nobody knows for sure why she was called "Calamity Jane," although several ideas have been offered: (1) She saved an army officer from Indians; (2) her own misfortunes gave her this name; or (3) she created such a stir wherever she went. Another version says she received her nickname "Calamity" from Wild Bill Hickok when the two met in Laramie, Wyoming and, according to legend, Wild Bill said to her, "You're the Jane that's always on hand when somebody's sick or wounded. I figure you're always there for a calamity. I'm going to call you Calamity Jane." There is another story that says she received her nickname after rescuing her commander during an Indian raid. At any rate, the nickname was certainly colorful, and it fit her well.

Born Martha Jane Canary, she moved with her family from Missouri to Utah after the Civil War; during the trek her mother died. Shortly after arriving in Salt Lake City, her father died as well, leaving the younger children with foster parents and Jane on her own. Jane worked as a nurse, a dishwasher, an ox-team driver, waitress and cook—all by the time she was 18. She also gained the reputation of being able to stand up to a man

Calamity Jane *(Library of Congress)*

and back him down. Like a cowboy, she learned to shoot a Springfield rifle and ride with the best of them.

Calamity and Wild Bill were supposedly secretly married on September 1, 1870, and she gave birth to their daughter on September 25, 1873. However, just after the birth Wild Bill rode off, and she did not see him again for several years. Apparently, she and Wild Bill were reunited briefly in 1876 after he had remarried and just before he was killed.

According to her own story, she married Clinton Burk in Texas in 1885 but Burk left her and she began to drift and drink. In 1893 she joined Buffalo Bill's Wild West show, in which she rode her horse while demonstrating her sharpshooting skills. During the 1870s she was the subject of several dime novels, bringing her national fame. Calamity Jane lived her final years in poverty with failing eyesight. She is buried in Deadwood, near Wild Bill Hickok.

CALF-WAGON Also called a blattin' wagon or blattin' cart, this is a wagon for calves born during a cattle drive. Since these calves cannot keep up with the herd, they have to be carried on a wagon, although they were often given to farmers along the way or killed. The calf-wagon was used on later trail drives; early trail drives didn't have them, probably because cowboys herded only steers about the same age up the trail. Later, some cowboys and ranchers felt that having some cows and young calves along helped steady the herd.

CALICO   Term that refers to a woman because of her calico dress; if it referred to an activity, the cowboy meant paying a visit to court a lady. If a cowboy used this term when referring to a horse, it meant a pinto.

CALIFORNIA JOE   (b. Moses Milner in Kentucky in 1829; d. Fort Robinson, Nebraska in October 1876) California Joe came to California in 1849 and became an army scout during the Indian Wars. He was appointed chief of scouts to the Seventh Cavalry by General Custer but was fired because of drunkenness. Known for always smoking his pipe, California Joe took part in the Battle of Washita (1868) and carried the news of victory from Custer to General Phil Sheridan through 100 miles of snowbound, hostile country on his mule in 18 hours. He was killed by a man named Newcomb who carried a grudge against him.

CALIFORNIANS, THE   TV show that starred Adam Kennedy as Dion Patrick (1957–58), Sean McClory as Jack McGivern (1957–58), Nan Leslie as Martha McGivern (1957–58), Herbert Rudley as Sam Brennan (1957–58), Richard Coogan as Matthew Wayne, Howard Caine as Schaab (1957–58), Carole Mathews as Wilma Fansler (1958–59) and Arthur Fleming as Jeremy Pitt (1958–59).

Set in San Francisco during the 1850s when "gold fever" was at its peak, this show dealt with the clash between honest men—represented by a crusading newspaper reporter and newly elected marshal—trying to run a good, clean town that was inhabited by cheats, scoundrels and other lowlifes. The show premiered on September 24, 1957 on NBC on Tuesday evenings and ran there until June 1959, when it switched to Thursday evenings. The last show was telecast August 27, 1959, by which time the half-hour series had filmed 69 episodes in black and white.

CALIFORNIA TRAIL   The California Trail followed the Oregon Trail from Missouri to Soda Springs, Idaho and then veered southwest to the Humboldt River. From there, the trail continued southwest along the Carson and Walker Rivers and across the Sierra Nevada into California. It was first used in 1841 when John Bartleson led a group down this offshoot. The original group on the Oregon Trail included Jesuit missionary Pierre De Smet and was led by famed guide Thomas Fitzpatrick. The group was ill prepared for the trip, and Bartleson and a group left the party along the way; the group was then led by John Bidwell, who led the group of 33 people into California. Nobody used this trail the next year, but in 1843 Joseph B. Chiles, a member of the Bartleson-Bidwell party, went back East and led a group of 30 men with a number of women and children in wagons on this overland route to California. But they met with disaster after they were unable to purchase provisions along the way. The group divided at Fort Hall, Idaho, and Chiles led 13 men on horses to Fort Boise and then west along Malheur River trying to get around the Sierra Nevada and into northern California, but the journey was too long and took

too much time. Meanwhile, Joseph Walker led the wagon train down the Humboldt River, south through the Walker Pass (named after him) and into the southern part of the San Joaquin Valley. The group arrived safely but had to abandon their wagons in favor of packhorses along the way.

The most popular route on the California Trail was pioneered in 1844 by the Stephens-Murphy party. When this group reached the sink of the Humboldt River, it headed west to cross the Sierra Nevada and became the first group to get wagons into California when it opened up the Truckee River and went through Emigrant Gap into Bear Valley. Later, this route would be used by highway and railroad builders. In 1845 there were five or six parties, or about 250 people, who traveled the California Trail; the largest group was led by William B. Ide and had about 100 people, but this group was plagued with violence and brutality. The California Trail opened up when the Mexican War ended in 1846 and California officially became American territory. In this year there were 1,000–1,500 men, women and children with about 200 wagons on the trail. Included in this group was the Donner party. (See also DONNER PARTY.)

CALL OF THE WEST   This TV show is a rerun of the popular "Death Valley Days" TV show with John Payne serving as host. (See DEATH VALLEY DAYS.)

CALUMET   Long-stemmed pipe used by Indians for tobacco smoking.

CANARY, MARTHA JANE   See CALAMITY JANE.

CANTINA   Mexican term for a barroom or saloon.

CANTON, FRANK   (b. Joe Horner near Richmond, Virginia in 1849; d. Edmond, Oklahoma on September 27, 1927)   Frank Canton was a "Regulator" during the Johnson County War. He had accepted the job of field inspector for the Wyoming Stock Growers' Association; in 1882 he was elected sheriff of Johnson County, Wyoming. But what the citizens did not know was that Frank Canton was actually Joe Horner, a Texas cowboy who was a fugitive from justice and former bank robber. Horner had killed one soldier and wounded another in Jacksboro, Texas on October 10, 1874.

In Wyoming, Canton was active in curtailing "rustling," at least "rustling" as defined by the big ranchers. After he retired as sheriff of Johnson County in 1886, he took another job with the Wyoming Stock Growers' Association as well as a commission as deputy U.S. marshal. In these positions, he played a major role in the Johnson County War of 1892.

Canton was with Tom Smith, Joe Elliott and Fred Coates on November 1, 1891 on the Powder River in Wyoming when the group tried to kill Nate Champion, whom the Wyoming Stock Growers' Association considered to be the leader of the Johnson County "Rustlers." The four men surrounded the cabin where Champion and Ross Gilbertson lived; then, just before dawn, they rushed inside firing at Champion, who leaped out of his bed with his pistol blazing and hit two lawmen.

Canton and Tom Smith were chief lieutenants, under Major Frank Wolcott, of the Regulators, gunmen hired by

Yakima Canutt

the Wyoming Stock Growers' Association to rid the area of "rustlers" and small homesteaders. On April 9, 1892 at the KC Ranch over 50 gunfighters surrounded the home leased by Nate Champion. Just before dawn Canton arrested Ben Jones and Bill Walker when they went outside; the two had spent the night with Champion. But when Nick Ray went outside, the Regulators opened fire. Champion came out and helped Ray get back inside the cabin; a siege began, but Ray died about 9 A.M. Outside help came after Jack Flagg, also wanted by the Regulators, came by the ranch and surprised the group; he escaped into Buffalo and gathered up a group to help rescue Champion. But the Regulators lit a wagon filled with hay and sent it into the cabin, flushing out Champion, who was riddled with bullets when he tried to escape. The Regulators then went to another ranch where they were trapped for several days by a group led by Sheriff Red Angus. Finally, the Regulators were rescued by the cavalry after several of the influential ranchers pulled some strings in Washington. They were all eventually let off.

In 1893, after the Johnson County War, Canton became superintendent of the Nebraska City Packing Company; he then moved to Oklahoma Territory, where he was deputy U.S. marshal under the hanging judge, Isaac Parker. In 1897 he became deputy U.S. marshal in Alaska but in 1899 became snow-blind, which caused him to move back to Oklahoma to recover his sight. He became a lawman again and was employed by the Cattle Raisers' Association of Texas to track down rustlers who came to Oklahoma. He was appointed adjutant general of the

Oklahoma National Guard in 1907 and built up that organization. (See also CHAMPION, NATE; JOHNSON COUNTY WAR.)

CANUTT, YAKIMA (b. Enos Edward Canutt in Colfax, Washington on November 29, 1895; d. North Hollywood, California on May 24, 1986) Yakima Canutt pioneered such stunts as dropping down between the horses of a racing stagecoach and then hand-walking under the wagon until he dropped off the end of it. For his stunt work he was given a special Oscar in 1966. Canutt's walk was copied by John Wayne, who worked with Canutt in a number of movies. Canutt was a star rodeo performer before he went to Hollywood; between 1917 and 1923 he was a champion rodeo rider five times and was later elected to the Rodeo Hall of Fame. Canutt worked as an actor in a number of westerns and was also an important second-unit director; he held that job for the classic *Stagecoach*. He doubled many actors, including John Wayne, Clark Gable and Gene Autry, in addition to appearing in a number of movies, usually as a villain until 1985, when he made his last appearance in *High on the Range*.

CANYON A valley or area cut away (often by a river) between two mountains. Originally a Spanish term, *canon*.

CAREY, HARRY (b. Henry DeWitt Carey II in the Bronx, New York on January 16, 1878; d. Brentwood, California on September 21, 1947) Harry Carey became a star of western films in the 1920s during the silent era. A native easterner, Carey fell in love with the West. He began acting in films for Biograph in 1909 and was in a number of D. W. Griffith's films; he acted in

Harry Carey

about 25 films directed by John Ford. Some of the major westerns he appeared in include *Law and Order*, (1932), *Last of the Mohicans* (1932), *The Thundering Herd* (1933), *Powdersmoke Range* (1935), *Wagon Trail* (1935), *The Law West of Tombstone* (1938), *El Diablo Rides* (1939), *Angel and the Badman* (1947), *Duel in the Sun* (1947) and *The Last Outlaw* (1936).

CAREY, HARRY, JR. (b. Henry DeWitt Carey, Jr. in Saugus, California on May 16, 1921) Like his father, Harry Carey, Jr. appeared in a number of Hollywood westerns as a character actor; also like his father, Carey appeared in a number of movies directed by John Ford. Movies Carey has appeared in include:

 Red River (1948)
 She Wore a Yellow Ribbon (1949)
 Three Godfathers (1949)
 Copper Canyon (1950)
 Rio Grande (1950)
 Wagonmaster (1950)
 San Antone (1953)
 The Searchers (1956)
 Seventh Cavalry (1956)
 From Hell to Texas (1958)
 Rio Bravo (1959)
 Two Rode Together (1961)
 The Way West (1967)
 Death of a Gunfighter (1969)
 Cahill, United States Marshall (1973)
 The Long Riders (1980)
 Back to the Future III (1990)

Leo Carillo

Harry Carey, Jr.

CARILLO, LEO (b. Leo Antonio Carillo in Los Angeles, California on August 6, 1881; d. Santa Monica, California on September 6, 1961) Leo Carillo was 75 years old when he began the part of "Pancho" on TV's "The Cisco Kid." Carillo actually didn't want the part—he thought it would make him appear to be a buffoon—but was convinced to take it (and played the character like a buffoon!). The exaggerated Spanish accent he used came from a gardener he knew. Carillo's great grandfather was Carlos Antonio Carillo, the governor of California in 1837; Leo received his degree from St. Vincent of Loyola and was a newspaper cartoonist before he began acting in vaudeville and on Broadway. Carillo starred in 176 half-hour TV programs and five features for United Artists in his role as "Pancho" on his horse, "Loco." (See also CISCO KID, THE) (TV show).

CARSON, KIT (b. Christopher Houston Carson in Kentucky on December 24, 1809; d. Fort Lyon, Colorado on May 23, 1868) One of the greatest frontiersmen, scouts and mountain men in the history of the West, Kit Carson became famous through his work with John Fremont and then as a legend through dime novels, in which his name was used for a fictional hero whose exploits were so outlandish that they were said to embarrass Carson.

 The son of Lindsey and Rebecca Carson, whose ancestors came from North Carolina and Virginia, Carson

Kit Carson (Library of Congress)

was born near Richmond, Kentucky, but the family moved to a Missouri farm in mid-1812. Apprenticed at 14 to David Workman, a saddle maker, he fled and joined a caravan headed for New Mexico in 1826. After a brief stay in Santa Fe, Carson moved to Taos, headquarters and resort for mountain men. He accompanied Ewing Young, a famous trapper, from 1828 to 1831 through southern Arizona and California and learned about trapping beaver. He then spent time in the Rocky Mountains and Far West as a mountain man and trapper.

In 1835 Carson attended the Green River rendezvous with Jim Bridger, where he killed French trapper John Shuman in a duel on horseback over an Indian girl. He married the Arapaho girl and they had a daughter. Carson probably had another Indian wife later, a Cheyenne, who probably cast his belongings outside their tipi, thereby divorcing him.

Carson served as a hunter at Bent's Fort from 1841 to 1842 and then went to St. Louis in 1842. Carson's Arapaho wife had died, and he took his daughter back East to be educated. There he had a chance encounter with John C. Fremont. At this time, Fremont, son-in-law of Senator Thomas Hart Benton, a western expansionist, was organizing a western expedition. Fremont needed a guide so he engaged Carson, who proved to be a valuable addition for the "Pathfinder." Carson eventually served as guide for three different expeditions led by Fremont: through the Rockies, the Great Basin in Oregon and in California.

Carson became famous through Fremont's reports from his travels, edited by Fremont's wife, Jessie. Carson was acclaimed for his skill as a scout as well as his courage and loyalty; in a short time he became a national hero.

Carson became involved in the Mexican War during Fremont's third expedition to California (1845–46) and was involved in the establishment of the Bear Flag Republic. Carson also guided the army of General Stephen Watts Kearny to California from New Mexico during this war.

Carson became a rancher in spring 1849 when he returned to Taos, and set up a ranch in nearby Rayado with Lucien Maxwell. He made a $30,000 profit in 1853 when he drove a herd of 6,500 sheep to California; later that same year he became Indian agent for the tribes of northern New Mexico; he held that position until 1861.

During the Civil War Carson was a colonel in the First New Mexico Volunteer Infantry and was involved in the Battle of Valverde on February 21, 1862. In the winter of 1862–63 he was sent to southeastern New Mexico, to Fort Stanton, to wage war on the Mescalero Apache. After successfully subduing that tribe, he began a campaign against hostile Navajo in western New Mexico and Arizona. In the summer of 1864 Carson forced about 8,000 Navajo to surrender after destroying their crops and livestock. Carson was a particularly vicious Indian fighter, although some insist he understood Indians better than most whites and was sympathetic to their plight.

Carson served briefly as commander of Fort Garland, Colorado and then moved to Boggsville, Colorado with his third wife, a Mexican named Josefa Jaramillo of Taos, whom he had married on January 6, 1843 when she was 15. Carson's wife died in April, 1868 in Boggsville. About a month later, Carson died at nearby Fort Lyon, a result of internal injuries suffered after he fell from a horse.

CARSON, SUNSET (b. Michael James Harrison in Plainview, Texas on November 12, 1927; d. Reno, Nevada on May 1, 1990) Carson was a rodeo star and worked as a trick rider, roper, bulldogger and bronco rider before he enrolled in the Pasadena Playhouse to become an actor. His first film was *Stagedoor Canteen* (1942), and he was then signed to Republic where he appeared in a number of "B" westerns. Carson appeared on "The Black Bandit" radio series in 1950 and on the TV series "Six Gun Heroes," which showcased "B" westerns.

CASEY JONES TV show that starred Alan Hale as Casey Jones, Eddy Waller as Red Rock, Dub Taylor as Wally Sims, Mary Lawrence as Alice Jones, Bobby Clark as Casey Jones, Jr. and Paul Keast as President Carter.

Casey Jones was an engineer for the Illinois Central Railroad Company and the driver of 382—the Cannon-

Sunset Carson

ball Express in this syndicated series set in Jackson, Tennessee around 1880. Accompanied by his dog, Cinders, Casey had to get the train to its destination while carrying an assortment of famous passengers or treasures and overcoming obstacles along the way. There were 26 episodes of this half-hour series, which was syndicated and never part of regular network programming, although it enjoyed some success on Saturday mornings in 1957.

CASSIDY, BUTCH (aka Robert LeRoy Parker, George Leroy Parker, George Cassidy and possibly William T. Phillips; b. Beaver, Utah on April 13, 1866; d. either in San Vincente, Bolivia in 1907 or in Spangle, Washington on July 20, 1937) Young Robert LeRoy Parker idolized a rustler named Mike Cassidy, who hung out near the family's ranch near Circleville, Utah. Cassidy gave young Parker a saddle and a gun, and at 16 Parker joined Cassidy's gang. Parker adopted the alias "George Cassidy" and joined the McCarty Gang, which robbed banks and trains. Cassidy worked as a cowboy in Wyoming and then as a butcher in Rock Springs in 1892, which led to his nickname "Butch." In 1894 he stole horses with Al Rainier, was caught and spent 18 months in the state penitentiary in Laramie, Wyoming. When he was released, in January 1896, he headed out to the Hole in the Wall area—where Utah, Wyoming and Colorado meet and where bandits hung out—and began the associations that would become the Wild Bunch, a gang that included Harry Longabaugh (better known as

the "Sundance Kid" and Cassidy's closest cohort), Elza Lay, William Carver, Camilla Hanks, Harvey Logan, Deaf Charley Hanks, Blackjack Ketchum, Ben Kilpatrick and Harry Tracy.

This group robbed a number of trains and banks in the ensuing years in Utah, Wyoming, Colorado, Montana, Nevada and New Mexico and then often headed to a city such as Denver, San Antonio or Fort Worth afterward for a vacation. Butch's sweetheart during this time was Mary Boyd. After they robbed the Great Northern train at Matla, Montana on July 3, 1901, the Wild Bunch (Sundance, Bill Carver, Kid Curry and Ben Kilpatrick) went to Fannie Porter's brothel in Fort Worth; then Butch and Sundance, along with Sundance's girlfriend, Etta Place, went to New York, where in early 1902 they left for South America. The group first went to Uruguay and then to Argentina, where they operated a cattle and sheep ranch, selling their stock to miners in Chile. Sundance took Etta back to Denver in 1907 for an operation on her appendix. When he returned, the two bandits moved to Bolivia, where they robbed payroll shipments and banks and worked in the Concordia tin mines.

In 1908, on a Bolivian jungle trail, Butch and Sundance stole a mule train with the payroll from the Alpoca Mine and then went to San Vincente, about 15 miles away, for dinner. They tied their animals to a hitching post in the plaza, but a young Bolivian boy recognized a mule—it was a well-known silver and gray mule owned by the superintendent of the mine—and reported it to authorities. A troop of soldiers were camped nearby and were notified; a large number soon surrounded the plaza. Then an army captain came up and demanded their surrender and was shot by Sundance. The outlaws barricaded themselves in the restaurant, but the pack animals held their rifles and ammunition. At dark Sundance made a run for the guns and ammo but was shot down on the way back. Butch pulled him inside. Around nine or 10 that night, Butch put on the uniform of one of the dead soldiers, shot Sundance in the head to put him out of his misery and slipped through the soldiers and escaped.

There is another story, based on "The Bandit Invincible" manuscript William T. Phillips wrote. Here, Butch Cassidy, the Sundance Kid and two other accomplices robbed a pack train and were jumped by some Bolivian soldiers. A fight broke out, and the outlaws hid behind some boulders. Butch and Sundance killed several soldiers; the soldiers killed the other two accomplices and hit Sundance. Sundance told Butch he'd married Etta, gave him a letter to Etta and asked Butch to give Etta his money. Sundance then died as Butch watched. Butch apparently shot another soldier, then crawled away and, after about an hour, got to their horses, which had not been found by the soldiers. Butch then rode out in the darkness. Since there were three dead Americans and three horses tied—and some identification left behind—Butch was convinced that authorities would believe Butch Cassidy was dead. So, when Butch got to the coast, he sailed to Europe, had facial surgery in Paris and returned to the United States.

The story continues that he returned to the United States and took the alias of William Thadeus Phillips, who had been a mechanical engineer from Des Moines, Iowa. Phillips married Gertrude Livesay in Adrian, Michigan on May 14, 1908 and moved to Globe, Arizona and then Seattle, Washington, where he established a company that made adding machines and other business equipment. Phillips became a respectable member of the community, an Elk and a Mason, and bought some fine cars. Apparently he returned to some of his old haunts in 1910, 1925 and 1934, where he was seen by friends, including his former sweetheart, now the widowed Mary Boyd Rhodes. During the Great Depression, Phillips's company went broke, and in 1934 he tried to sell his autobiography, "The Bandit Invincible." He also developed a scheme to kidnap a wealthy Spokane citizen for ransom, but the plan never materialized. Phillips developed cancer and died in Spangle, near Spokane, Washington, at Broadacres, the county poor farm. (See also SUNDANCE KID, THE.)

CAT BALLOU   Film produced by Harold Hecht; directed by Elliot Silverstein; screenplay by Walter Newman and Frank R. Pierson from a story by Roy Chanslor; released in 1965 by Columbia; 96 minutes in length. Cast: Jane Fonda, Lee Marvin, Michael Callan, Dwayne Hickman, Nat "King" Cole and Arthur Hunnicutt.

This is a spoof on the West and was one of the westerns from the 1960s that humorously punched holes in the cherished images nurtured through the years. Catherine Ballou (Fonda) has a run-in with Tim Strawn (Lee Marvin), a crook who wears a badge. When some land-grabbing businessmen and Strawn (who is their hired gun) murder Ballou's father, she sends for famed gunfighter Kid Shelleen (also played by Marvin), a hero in dime novels. Trouble is, Shelleen has a severe drinking problem and is not in shape for gunplay. So Ballou becomes "Cat," forms a gang, robs a train and heads to the Hole in the Wall where the over-the-hill Wild Bunch is convinced by Ballou to join her in exacting revenge. The scene of the drunken Shelleen on his drunken horse leaning against a wall is a classic; Marvin won an Oscar for his dual role.

CATLIN, GEORGE   See ART.

CATTALO   An animal that is the result of longhorns crossed with buffalo or domestic cattle. The development of this animal was pioneered by Charles Goodnight. Unfortunately, these cattalo were difficult to control, the meat wasn't as good as beef and a number of males were sterile.

CATTLE CALL   Song written by Tex Owens (June 15, 1892–September 9, 1962) and published by Forster Music in 1934.

Tex Owens was born and raised in Bell County, Texas and worked on ranches as a youth. But he was more interested in show business and worked in a number of shows in the area. In 1928 he worked as an entertainer on KMBC in Kansas City; one day while watching snow fall outside his window he composed "Cattle Call" to the tune of "The Morning Star Waltz." Tex Owens later appeared in the John Wayne movie *Red River* and was injured during the filming of the cattle stampede. "Cattle Call" was made famous by Eddy Arnold, who used it as his theme song.

CATTLE DRIVES   The first markets for Texas cattle were in Louisiana—Shreveport got some Texas cattle perhaps as early as 1839; others may have been shipped to Mobile, Alabama. There were very few markets for Texas cattle before the Civil War; the southern states to the east of Texas already had plenty of cattle, and the area to the west of Texas was so sparsely settled that there was no demand; the Mexicans to the south also had plenty of cattle, and Indian country was to the north. But several events created a market for beef before the Civil War: (1) the early settlers in Oregon; (2) the gold rush prospectors who flooded California beginning in 1849 and later other sites such as Colorado and Montana; (3) army posts established in the West that needed to feed their soldiers; and (4) Indian reservations and government contracts to feed Indians for treaty obligations. Thus a market for Texas cattle opened up before the Civil War.

The first real market for beef before the Civil War was during the gold rush 1,500 miles from Texas. Still, Walter Cross drove about 500 cattle from Missouri to California in 1850; it took him about five months to get them there. There were also herds driven from Missouri to California in the years 1850 to 1853, and Texas cattle also were driven west, although it took five to six months to get them to California. The California gold seekers and settlers received their first cattle from Spanish rancheros already in California who drove their herds north to the San Francisco area; but the high prices paid for cattle caused the ranchers to sell off all their available stock and not save any for breeding. By 1855 there were about 7,000 cattle in southern California; in addition, American immigrants were running off Mexicans with Spanish and Mexican land grants, disregarding the rancher's property claims because of gold fever; thus the cowboy culture declined seriously in California until, by the end of 1856, it was over.

A number of settlers were also moving to Texas in 1850, primarily east and central Texas. Cattle ranchers established a trail to St. Louis in the 1840s, later called the Shawnee Trail (it was also known as the Osage Trace and Kansas Trail); this was the first cattle trail north out of Texas. By the early 1850s a cattle trail from Texas to Missouri was well established, with the first drive to Missouri by Thomas Candy Ponting and Washington Malone, who drove cattle from Illinois to Wisconsin. They eventually ended up in New York City with about 150 head. In the fall of 1854, herds were being driven northward from Texas across Indian Territory (now Oklahoma), and Indians were charging tolls. Kansas Territory was created in 1854 by Congress, and the eastern Kansas border was a route for Texas cattle from Baxter Springs, Kansas northward to Westport and Kansas City. These areas had become central for freighters heading out over the Santa Fe Trail.

In June 1853 Missouri turned back Texas cattle because of "Texas fever," which caused cattle other than Longhorns to die. This meant Texas cattle had to travel on trails farther west and avoid Missouri farms. The trails first shifted over to Kansas, but as the Kansas legislature enacted "quarantine laws" forbidding Texas cattle into its state, they shifted farther and farther west until they were moving up Colorado to get to the northern ranges.

In 1854 about 50,000 Texas cattle were herded to Chicago; in 1857 over 50,000 were sold in Kansas City and another 48,000 in 1858 (two-thirds from Texas). At this point, Kansas City was established as the largest cattle market. The first cattle town in Kansas was Baxter Springs, established by John J. Baxter in 1855. There Baxter built corrals, a tavern and a tannery, and cattle were driven there to be slaughtered primarily for their hides.

The first cattle drive from Texas to the Colorado gold fields occurred in 1860 when Oliver Loving and Charles Goodnight drove cattle up what became known as the Goodnight-Loving Trail. During the spring of 1860 cattle were driven to Kansas and Missouri; these were crude cattle drives, but they taught cattlemen a number of things about cattle drives that would benefit them later. But in April 1861 the Civil War began, and the nation would focus on this war for the next four years.

There were a few cattle drives during the Civil War in an attempt to get cattle to Confederate troops (Texas was part of the Confederacy), but these generally proved to be inefficient; it was much easier to drive cattle from Florida and the South during the early part of the war because this area had plenty of cattle. Too, the blockades established by Union troops helped cut Texas off from the Confederacy.

The major cattle-driving period was 1866–85, when Texas drovers first took cattle to the railheads in Kansas for shipment to eastern states and then took cattle west and north to the northern ranges of Wyoming and Montana. In 1860 it was estimated there were 3.5 million cattle in Texas. But in the summer of 1861—the first summer of the Civil War—there was a terrible drought in Texas that extended to 1864 and killed a number of cattle; there were also a series of northers in 1863 that drove Texas cattle south into southern Texas. These factors are what led so many loose cattle (an estimated five or six million) to be in southern Texas after the Civil War.

The Civil War devastated Texas in several ways: First, about a fourth of the white male population in the state was either dead or crippled. After the war, men got together in south Texas and began "cow hunts" to locate their cattle. Word soon came that the North, whose cattle population had been devastated by the war, needed beef, so these rather useless cattle in Texas suddenly became quite valuable. The problem of how to get them back to the large eastern markets was solved by the railroads, which were building tracks west; these railroads had gotten to Kansas by 1867, so Texas cattle could be driven there, loaded up and shipped back to the eastern markets. And along with the story of the trail drives came the story of cowboys who let off steam from the long drives once they hit these cattle towns, which created a new dimension in cowboy lore: the brave lawman, the hell-raising cowboy, the gamblers and showdowns.

The first year for cattle drives to Abilene, a town established as a "cattle town" by Joseph McCoy, was 1867; during that year about 35,000 were brought there to be shipped. The next year about 75,000 Texas cattle went to Abilene, and in 1869 about 350,000 were driven up the trail. In 1871, the last year Abilene was a cattle town (the quarantine line was moved west of the town after this year), there were 700,000 cattle driven up the trails.

The first cattle drive into the northern ranges was headed by Nelson Story, who purchased a herd of Texas cattle in June 1866, hired 22 cowboys and headed north in early August; by September he was in Fort Laramie, and in December he reached his destination of the Gallatin Valley in Montana. Story was a prospector in the Alder Gulch gold fields and knew firsthand the need for beef there, but he did not sell all his cattle to the miners; instead he kept some select cattle for breeding and established a ranch in Montana. Story had driven his cattle over the Bozeman Trail and had to fight Indians on the way; after his drive this trail was closed, so no more Texas cattle came up to Montana for a number of years. Most of the cattle driven into Montana during 1869–75 came from Oregon along the Oregon Trail; over 250,000 head reached Montana this way.

The major cattle drives to the Wyoming ranges occurred in 1870; at the beginning of that year there were only 8,143 cattle in Wyoming, but in 1871 over 32,000 cattle, mostly longhorns, were in southeastern Wyoming. Some Texas cowboys stayed on the northern ranges and started their own ranches, and by 1875 most of the southern Wyoming grasslands were stocked; by 1883 the buffalo were virtually gone from the northern ranges, leaving the area open for cattle.

The cattle drives ended around 1885 for several reasons: (1) The railroads had reached into the West so that long cattle drives were no longer necessary; (2) most of the ranges had been stocked by then; (3) Kansas had closed its borders to Texas cattle because of "Texas fever"; (4) barbed wire began to appear in the West in the late 1870s, sealing off much of the land and making it impossible to drive cattle through; (5) the West was becoming populated by settlers who resisted cattle being driven through their farms and lands; (6) the gold and silver rushes were just about finished, and those still going on could get cattle from nearby ranchers; (7) the refrigerated railroad car, developed in the 1870s, meant cattle could be slaughtered and carried long distances, so live cattle did not have to be driven; and (8) the homesteaders had taken over much of the public lands and ended the era of the large ranches whose land and water was supplemented by public lands.

CATTLE KATE   (b. Ella Watson in Lebanon, Kansas c. 1862; d. near Independence Rock in Wyoming on July 20, 1889)   A prostitute, Cattle Kate was hung by vigilantes in Johnson County, Wyoming after she was accused of stealing cattle; this hanging was one of the opening shots fired in the Johnson County War. Kate was not a cattle thief, although she probably took some cattle as payment for her services as a prostitute. She married James Averell in 1886; he was a surveyor, store owner, saloon keeper and justice of the peace in Johnson County. Kate apparently continued her previous occupation after the marriage and claimed a homestead next to her husband's in the middle of the lands of Albert J. Bothwell, a big-time rancher and cattleman. Averell was active in drumming up public opinion against Bothwell and other big cattlemen; he wrote letters to newspapers accusing Bothwell of a variety of faults. Obviously, these accounts incurred the wrath of Bothwell, who then accused Kate and Averell of rustling cattle and, with five other vigilantes, pulled Watson and Averell from their homes and lynched them.

CATTLE QUEEN OF MONTANA   Film produced by Benedict Bogeaus; directed by Allan Swan; screenplay by Howard Estabrook and Robert Blees (from a story by Thomas Blackburn); released in 1954 by RKO; 88 minutes in length. Cast: Barbara Stanwyck, Ronald Reagan, Gene Evans, Lance Fuller, Anthony Caruso, Jack Ingram, Yvette Dugay, Morris Ankrum, Chubby Johnson, Myron Healey and Rodd Redwing.

A herd of 2,500 steers are driven to Montana from Texas by Barbara Stanwyck and her father. Along the way an Indian tribe stampedes the herd and kills her father; some white men rustle most of the remaining herd. Finally, the rustlers and Indians are brought to justice, and Barbara Stanwyck wins a husband to help her build her empire.

CATTLE TOWNS   The most famous cattle towns were those in Kansas, established after the Civil War, because that is where the railroads had their western terminus. Texas cattle drivers, who needed to get their cattle to eastern markets, drove the cattle north to Kansas, let them fatten up on some grass there and then shipped them east. But as the cattle trade prospered, so did the lawless element; prostitutes and gamblers regularly plied their trade, and a number of saloons and sporting houses sprang up to accommodate thirsty Texas cowboys who were anxious to let off steam at the end of a long trail drive. As time progressed, the town usually grew to include a number of citizens who wanted to rid their town of this lawless element, so they would organize an effort to keep cattle and cowboys out of their town; thus one town would eliminate the cattle trade, whereas another town would seek to attract it to build up its economy. The cattle themselves also caused problems, trampling crops planted by farmers who had moved into the area. But the biggest problem was the dreaded "Texas fever." This fever, carried by a tick on longhorns that were immune to its poison, infected other cattle brought from theEast and killed them. Thus a "quarantine line" was established by the Kansas legislature whereby no cattle were allowed into a certain area; the cattle towns in Kansas were always west of the

quarantine line, and when the time came to shut down the Texas cattle trade in a town, the legislature simply shifted the quarantine line farther west.

Abilene, the first post–Civil War Kansas cattle town, began when Charley Thompson arrived in 1860 and surveyed the area for a town and gave it its name. In 1867 Joseph G. McCoy looked for a town from which Texas cattle could be shipped east and found it in Abilene. McCoy bought 250 acres and established a stockyard; when the Kansas Pacific Railroad arrived there in 1867, so did the first cattle. By the end of the year, 35,000 head had been shipped east, with the money attracting a number of businesses, bankers and boomers.

As the town grew, farmers moved into the surrounding areas and planted crops. When the Texas cattle arrived, crops and farms were often destroyed, so farmers began organizing an end to the cattle trade; by 1870 the farmers around Abilene had succeeded—aided by the upright citizens who wanted to rid the town of gambling, vice and the rowdy and lawless elements. Real estate speculators also had a hand in getting rid of the cattle trade because land could not be sold or developed as long as cattle came through it.

When the cattle trade ended for Abilene in 1871, it had become a prosperous town with a good year-round agricultural base. The next cattle town would be Ellsworth, about 60 miles southwest of Abilene—and at the end of railroad tracks that took cattle back East. Ellsworth had been founded in May 1867 and prospered the first year because the Kansas Pacific Railroad line ended there. But when the line pushed on, the town looked as though it would be abandoned. This abandonment caused a number of citizens in the town to try to lure the cattle trade back in order to save the town. Using their influence with Kansas legislators, entrepreneurs laid out a cattle trail from Fort Cobb (in Indian Territory) to their town and began promoting their town to Texas cattle drovers. They also made sure the quarantine line was east of them.

The Kansas Pacific Railroad had been promoting Ellsworth as a cattle town, and in 1872 a number of cattle were shipped from there. But the 1871–72 winter in the area had been harsh, so the cattle destroyed crops foraging for food, which created anticattle feelings among the farmers. The farmers then organized into protective associations, and as a result the cattle trade moved on to Wichita.

Wichita, located about 85 miles south of Abilene, was organized by William Greiffenstein. By 1869, a couple of hundred people had moved into the area; the next year citizens organized a company, so the Santa Fe Railroad decided to extend its line to the town; this line was completed in 1872, which began Wichita's fame as a cattle town.

Over 70,000 Texas cattle were shipped east that first year. Although opponents of the cattle trade (which included farmers) sought to have the quarantine line extend to include Wichita, the legislature kept the line east of the town. The town then enacted stringent laws against cattle in 1876, the last year when Wichita was a cattle town; only about 12,380 cattle were shipped east from there that year. But the railroad industry had looked ahead and developed a line to Dodge City, which would be the next major cattle town.

Dodge City was formed in 1872. At first, the town served as a center for buffalo hunters, who shipped their hides east the first year. Cattle pens were constructed by the Santa Fe Company, and 9,540 cattle were shipped in 1876. There was no settlement to the south of Dodge City, so the cattle industry was welcomed and the heyday of Dodge City as a cattle town began. About 22,940 cattle were shipped east in 1877. In 1879–80 a drought slowed the cattle-driving business, but business picked up in 1882. Again, the anticattle forces sought to keep Texas cattle out of a town cattle had created and gradually they were successful. But this time, it meant the end of Kansas as a place for Texas cattle; in 1884 the Kansas government quarantined the entire state. This made Caldwell, on the Kansas-Oklahoma (then Indian Territory) border the final cattle town.

Located about 50 miles south of Wichita, Caldwell was established in 1871 by Charles H. Stone and James H. Dagner, who surveyed and sold the land. Farmers attracted to the area quickly sought to stop the cattle business, but a recession overruled their objections. The Santa Fe Railroad built a line to the town, which was completed in 1880, so cattle could be shipped east. But the Kansas City, Lawrence and Southern Railway, which also wanted the cattle trade, built a line to Hunnewell, on the Indian Territory border, which took away some of Caldwell's cattle trade.

After 1886, Caldwell declined as a cattle town because the railroads had then built lines into Texas so Texas cattlemen did not have to drive the cattle all the way to Kansas to ship them east. The trail drives after this period were to get cattle either to northern and western ranges or to Indian reservations.

Kansas was not the only state with cattle towns; Ogallala, Nebraska; Cheyenne, Wyoming; and Fort Worth, Texas also became cattle towns. But the Kansas cattle towns are the ones that created the myth of cowboys raising hell after a long cattle drive up from Texas. (See also ABILENE, KANSAS; CATTLE TRAILS; DODGE CITY, KANSAS; ELLSWORTH, KANSAS; NEWTON, KANSAS; QUARANTINE LINE; TEXAS FEVER; WICHITA, KANSAS.)

CATTLE TRAILS The first cattle trail was the Shawnee Trail (sometimes called the Osage Trace or Kansas Trail), which took cattle into Missouri. What became known as the Shawnee Trail began in south Texas and headed north-northeast into Kansas City, Sedalia and St. Louis until Texas cattle were forbidden to enter Missouri because of Texas fever, a disease spread by ticks carried by Longhorns. The most famous trail, the Chisholm Trail, was actually a series of trails from south Texas into Kansas. The original Chisholm Trail was only the last leg of the trail in Kansas, but the entire route soon became known by that name. A number of shorter trails from various points in south Texas fed into a main trail at the Red River on the Texas border,

and from there the trail went through Indian Territory (now Oklahoma) and then branched off either east to Abilene (later Newton, Wichita and Caldwell), north to Ellsworth, or west to Dodge City. The Western Trail also started in south Texas but headed north-northwest up to Dodge City, then on into Ogallala, Nebraska and from there either west to Cheyenne and then north to Miles City, Montana or from Ogallala almost straight north into Dakota Territory and Fort Buford. The Goodnight-Loving Trail began in central Texas, went west to the Pecos River, then north through New Mexico Territory and up into Colorado (Pueblo and Denver) and then to Cheyenne. The cattle trails moved west because first Missouri, and then Kansas, outlawed Texas cattle in their states, so cattle drives took an increasingly western route until the final Western Trail went up through Indian Territory, then over to Colorado, just west of the Kansas border, and into the northern ranges. (See also BOZEMAN TRAIL; CHISHOLM TRAIL; COLORADO TRAIL; GOODNIGHT-LOVING TRAIL; JIM STINSON TRAIL; NATIONAL CATTLE TRAIL; SHAWNEE TRAIL; TEXAS-MONTANA TRAIL; WESTERN TRAIL, THE.)

CAYUSE A horse descended from mustangs, although the term originally was derived from the Cayuse Indians and meant a wild horse.

CAYUSE INDIANS These Native Americans lived in Washington and Oregon and were closely associated with the Nez Perce Indians. A small tribe, they had fine horses, and "cayuse" came to mean "horse" for cowboys in the Northwest. Marcus Whitman established a mission among the Cayuse in 1838 but a smallpox epidemic hit in 1847 and resulted in the warriors' killing Whitman and others, whom they blamed for the illness. The Cayuse War of 1847–50 ended when five Cayuse surrendered, were tried and hanged for the murders.

CENTENNIAL TV miniseries that starred Robert Conrad as Pasquinel, Richard Chamberlain as Alexander McKeag, Raymond Burr as Bockweiss, Sally Kellerman as Lisa Bockweiss, Barbara Carrera as Clay Basket, Michael Ansara as Lame Beaver, Gregory Harrison as Levi Zandt, Stephanie Zimbalist as Elly Zahm, Cristina Raines as Lucinda, Stephen McHattie as Jake Pasquinel, Kario Salem as Mike Pasquinel, Chad Everett as Maxwell Mercy, Alex Karras as Hans Brumbaugh, Mark Harmon as John McIntosh, Dennis Weaver as R. J. Poteet, Timothy Dalton as Oliver Seccombe, Richard Crenna as Colonel Frank Skimmerhorn, Cliff DeYoung as John Skimmerhorn, Glynn Turman as Nate Person, Les Lannom as Bufe Coker, Brian Keith as Axel Dumire, Adrienne LaRuss as Clemma, Rafael Campos as Nacho, Anthony Zerbe as Mervin Wendell, Doug McKeon as Philip Wendell, Lynn Redgrave as Charlotte Cukland Seccombe Lloyd, William Atherton as Jim Lloyd, Lois Nettleton as Maude Wendell, Andy Griffith as Lew Vernor and Sharon Gless as Sidney Enderman.

Based on James Michener's epic novel *Centennial,* this lavish miniseries reportedly cost over $20 million and featured 24 hours of programming. Michener appeared at the beginning of each episode to introduce it and talk about the significance of America's past actions. The story centers on a piece of land in the Rocky Mountain area from 1795 to the present. First, some white men stake a claim—two French trappers and a Scottish trader. Eventually the place becomes Centennial, Colorado, a town that attracts a variety of inhabitants who displace the original Cheyenne and Pawnee inhabitants. The resulting history is the story of American settlement: good-hearted settlers, greedy merchants, honest lovers of the land, self-righteous reformers and the rest of humanity who settled the West. The miniseries originally aired from October 1, 1978 to February 1979 on NBC on Sundays and Saturdays at various times. It was shown again from September to October 1980 during the actors' strike—again on NBC at various times during the week.

CENTRAL PACIFIC RAILROAD　　The Pacific Railroad Act was signed by President Abraham Lincoln in July 1862. It authorized the construction of a railroad between the Missouri River and the Pacific coast that would open up the Far West and give the United States its first transcontinental railroad. Building the railroad were two separate companies; the Union Pacific was to begin at the Missouri River and build westward toward California, and the Central Pacific would begin in California and build eastward until the two met. A number of land grants and subsidies were given to the railroads based on the amount of track laid, inspiring a race. The "Big Four" of the Central Pacific were Collis P. Huntington, Leland Stanford, Mark Hopkins and Charles Crocker; they incorporated on June 28, 1861, and work began in January 1863 in Sacramento. In December 1863 ground was broken in Omaha, Nebraska by the Union Pacific, but railroad construction did not go full steam ahead until the Civil War ended. From 1865 to 1869 the forging of the railroad to link the entire United States was the dominant endeavor. To cross the Sierra Nevada, Charles Crocker, who was the driving force, imported 12,000 Chinese workers. The Union Pacific had Irish immigrants doing most of its work. Using hand tools, wheel barrows, horse-drawn wagons and black powder, "Crocker's Pets," as the Chinese were called, worked feverishly. The two railroads were joined on May 10, 1869 at Promontory Point, Utah, after covering 1,775 miles in the largest engineering project ever undertaken in America. Here the Golden Spike was driven by Leland Stanford and a Union Pacific official. The Central Pacific was absorbed by the Southern Pacific Railroad in 1885.

CHAMPION, NATE　　(b. Nathan D. Champion in Williamson County, Texas on September 29, 1857; d. at the KC Ranch in Johnson County, Wyoming on April 9, 1892)　Nate Champion was the cowboy killed on the first day of the Johnson County War. But Champion did two things to ultimately defeat the cattle barons who organized this war: (1) He held off the group of ranchers and gunmen for a whole day, which led to others becoming alerted to the war, and (2) he kept a journal while under siege that was later given to a newspaperman and

published, ultimately leading to a greater awareness of what actually happened during the shootout.

Champion and his twin brother, Dudley, had been born into a respected family in Texas. The two drove cattle up the Goodnight-Loving Trail in 1881 and decided to settle in Wyoming. Champion may have put his brand on some stray cattle while he was trying to establish a small ranch—most ranchers (large and small) did this. But his major crime was that he was a small rancher in an area in which the large ranchers wanted to dominate, so they put him on their "hit list" of people to be eliminated.

Champion's first encounter with the "Regulators," the gunslingers hired by the large ranchers, occurred while he was living on the Powder River in a line shack with Ross Gilbertson. One morning before dawn, four men— Joe Elliot, Tom Smith, Frank Canton and Fred Coates— planned to surprise Champion and kill him. The group kicked the door in, but Champion had a pistol in a holster hanging on his bedpost; shots were fired, and Champion wounded two.

On April 8, 1892 Champion and Nick Ray were at the KC Ranch near Hole in the Wall country. That evening two men, an unemployed cowboy named Bill Walker and Ben Jones, an unemployed chuck wagon cook, came by and spent the night. At dawn the next morning Jones went outside for some water and was immediately captured by about 50 Regulators, who had surrounded the house. When Walker went out, he too was captured; neither of these two men was on the Regulators' hit list so they were not harmed. But when Nick Ray went outside, the Regulators opened fire and Ray crumpled to the dirt. Champion immediately came out firing and dragged Ray back inside. Champion traded shots with the Regulators while he nursed Ray, and began writing a journal. At 9 A.M. Ray died from his wounds, but Champion hung on. Around three that afternoon, Jack Flagg, another man on the hit list, came by and the Regulators fired on him. But Flagg escaped and hightailed it to Buffalo, where he spread the alarm, and a group of men, headed by Sheriff Red Angus, headed out to the KC.

In order to flush out Champion, the Regulators finally set fire to a wagon loaded with hay and sent it into Champion's house. Champion came out blazing with his guns and headed for a ravine about 50 yards away but was shot down in a hail of bullets. In the house, his journal was found and given to Sam Clover, a correspondent from the *Chicago Herald* who accompanied the Regulators and ranchers; Clover later printed the journal. Before the Regulators left Champion, they pinned a note to his body, "Cattle thieves, beware." When found by the group from Buffalo, Champion's body had 28 wounds. (See also JOHNSON COUNTY WAR.)

CHAPARRAL　　Place where scrub oaks grew, although it later came to mean any country or area covered by thick scrub brush, usually intertwined and full of thorns, where longhorns could hide out.

CHAPS　　Chaps are worn by cowboys to protect their legs from thick brush, cactus, rope burns and steer horns and to protect their pants. The Mexican vaqueros introduced chaps (*chaparejos* in Spanish). There are several types of chaps: Shotgun chaps are narrow, closed legs that resemble a double-barrel shotgun; batwing chaps are those that have wraparound backs fastened to the legs with snap locks and wide, flapping fronts (a cowboy can put these on without removing his boots or spurs); goat or bearskin chaps sometimes have the hair worn on the outside and are popular on the northern ranges because of their warmth.

CHEROKEE BILL   (b. Crawford Goldsby in Fort Concho, Texas on February 8, 1876; d. Fort Smith, Arkansas on March 17, 1896)   Part Cherokee, part Mexican, part black and part white, Cherokee Bill first got into trouble at a dance in Fort Gibson, Oklahoma when he was 18. He quarreled with Jake Lewis, a black, and a fistfight followed; Bill drew a gun and wounded Lewis. He joined up with Jim and Bill Cook, two young hoodlums, and in June 1894 Cherokee Bill killed lawman Sequoyah Houston at Four Mile Creek near Tahlequah, Oklahoma when the lawman, with a posse, attempted to arrest Jim Cook. Later that same year Cherokee Bill killed his brother-in-law, George Brown, after Brown had beaten Cherokee Bill's sister, Maude.

Also in 1894 Cherokee Bill, with some accomplices, was robbing a store in Lenapah, Oklahoma when he killed Ernest Melton, a killing that led to Bill's original sentence of execution by the "hanging judge" Issac Parker. The sentence was delayed, and while in jail at Fort Smith, Cherokee Bill killed a guard while trying to escape. Fellow convict Henry Starr convinced Cherokee to give up his gun; he did, and Judge Parker immediately had the 24-year-old killer hung. (See also STARR, HENRY.)

CHEROKEE STRIP   Area also known as the Cherokee Outlet that was set aside as communal property of the Five Civilized Tribes in an 1866 treaty. Located in the northwestern part of what is now Oklahoma, this area was ceded to Native Americans by the federal government and was known as Indian Territory. This arrangement lasted until 1889, when the tribes sold this tract and the Oklahoma land rush began. The area known as the Cherokee Strip was opened to a land run on September 16, 1893. Prior to the land rush, outlaws escaped to this area because it was outside the jurisdiction of state law enforcement officers. (See also OKLAHOMA LAND RUSH.)

CHEYENNE   TV show that starred Clint Walker as Cheyenne Bodie and L. Q. Jones as Smitty (1955–56).

This one-hour show premiered on September 20, 1955 on ABC (a Tuesday evening) and was last telecast on September 13, 1963, a Friday evening, on ABC. From September 1959 to December 1962 the show aired on ABC on Monday evenings. "Cheyenne" starred six-foot six-inch Clint Walker as the "loner" Cheyenne Bodie who held various jobs from week to week—a ranch foreman, army scout, deputy sheriff—in the period right after the Civil War. He faced conflicts in these roles, and inevitably the big guy would get thumped; TV fans would

regularly see him take a beating before emerging victorious. The show premiered as "Warner Brothers Presents," a series of three rotating shows that was the studio's first TV venture. "Cheyenne" was the most popular of the three shows and so it emerged, although it was rarely ever seen weekly because hour-long shows were difficult to produce. Later it alternated weeks with "Sugarfoot" (1957–59) and "Conflict" (1956–57). The show had other problems as well: Star Clint Walker left the series in 1958 because of disagreements with the studio and did not return until 1959. In the meantime, the show ran under the title "Cheyenne" but starred Ty Hardin as Bronco Layne. In 1960–61 the show became known as "The Cheyenne Show," an anthology that was interspersed with the shows "Bronco" and "Sugarfoot." The show was based on the 1947 movie *Cheyenne* starring Dennis Morgan. The 107 black-and-white episodes also featured a series of comic books—25 issues— published by Dell.

CHEYENNE AUTUMN   Film produced by Bernard Smith; directed by John Ford; screenplay by Joseph R. Webb from a story by Mari Sandoz; released in 1964 by Warner Brothers; 160 minutes in length. Cast: James Stewart, Richard Widmark, Carroll Baker, Ricardo Montalban, Karl Malden, Sal Mineo, Dolores Del Rio, Gilbert Roland, Arthur Kennedy, Patrick Wayne, Elizabeth Allen, John Carradine, George O'Brien, Ken Curtis, Edward G. Robinson, Harry Carey, Jr., Ben Johnson and Denver Pyle.

This was director John Ford's last western and shows him reexamining his thinking about the West; specifically, Ford is revising his view of Indians in this movie. The story, based on an actual incident, is about 300 Cheyenne Indians on a reservation in Indian Territory in 1878 who decide to walk to their home in Wyoming because they are suffering from disease and malnutrition. In addition to being faced with the daunting physical feat of walking 1,500 miles, the Native Americans are chased by the cavalry and harassed by settlers; very few survive the trek.

CHEYENNE INDIANS   The Cheyenne are a tribe of Plains Indians, originally from Minnesota where they built permanent villages. However, when they moved west to North Dakota, they became nomadic. They eventually moved farther west to South Dakota's Black Hills; Lewis and Clark first encountered them there in 1804. As the Cheyenne moved farther west, the Kiowa and Sioux had to move south. The tribe was divided into the southern Cheyenne and northern Cheyenne in 1832 after a treaty with the United States allowed for an army fort in southern Colorado. The "Dog Soldiers" were a group of young braves trained for war, a highly skilled and elite organization. Under Chief Black Kettle, the southern Cheyenne were slaughtered in the Sand Creek Massacre in 1864 by Colonel Chivington; and in the Battle of the Washita, General Custer attacked Black Kettle's camp in 1868 and killed the chief. From this point on, the Cheyenne were openly hostile to white people. The northern Cheyenne took part in the Battle of the Little Bighorn, allied with the northern Arapaho and Sioux. After Custer's defeat, a number of northern Cheyenne were put on a reservation in Indian Territory where they sickened and died in the alien climate. Pleas to return to their homeland were refused; thus, led by Chiefs Dull Knife and Little Wolf, about 300 Cheyennes left the reservation in September 1878 for their homeland. They were pursued by army troops. At Fort Robinson, Nebraska, Dull Knife and his followers were captured and imprisoned; they attempted to escape, but most (including Dull Knife) were killed. Little Wolf and his group surrendered in Wyoming.

CHIEF JOSEPH   See JOSEPH, CHIEF.

CHIEF THUNDERCLOUD   (b. Victor Daniels in Muskogee, Oklahoma on April 12, 1889; d. Ventura, California on November 30, 1955)   Chief Thundercloud was the first Tonto in the Republic series *The Lone Ranger* (1938) and *The Lone Ranger Rides Again* (1939). He began his career in rodeos and Wild West shows and then worked in Hollywood as a film stuntman. He starred in the film *King of the Stallions* (1942) and appeared in movies with Harry Carey, Buck Jones, Johnny Mack Brown and Dick Foran and worked with Gary Cooper in *The Plainsman*.

CHINESE IN THE WEST   Large numbers of Chinese first went to the United States during the 1849 gold rush. During the 1850s and 1860s large numbers of Chinese emigrated, primarily from the Pearl River Delta in the province of Kwangtung in South China. The Chinese played an important role in the history of the West, particularly in the building of the railroads and in mining because so many Chinese worked in these two endeavors. However, the Chinese were available as workers because of a trade in indentured servants that left most Chinese virtual slaves while businessmen had the advantage of cheap labor.

Unlike most immigrants who came to the United States to live, most Chinese came to the United States intending to work for a while, earn some money and then return to their native land. Thus, the Chinese remained apart from most immigrants and established tight communities in cities, social clubs and secret societies called "tongs" that could be organized crime groups. "Tong wars" developed from Chinese group rivalry.

There was strong anti-Chinese feeling from Americans, which led to the Chinese Exclusion Act in 1882; prior to this time the United States and China agreed on free emigration for each of their citizens. By 1882 there were about 100,000 Chinese men and 5,000 Chinese women in the United States (a result of immigration restrictions on women), and three-fourths of these Chinese lived in California, with San Francisco the most populous city. Violence against Chinese erupted in the 1880s; the worst outbreak occurred on September 2, 1885 in Rock Springs, Wyoming at Union Pacific Coal mines when 150 whites killed 28 Chinese and wounded 15 others. That same year in Pierce, Idaho five Chinese were lynched after a white merchant was murdered. After the 1880s the Chinese population in the United

States began to decline, and work opportunities were severely restricted. Restaurants and laundries replaced railroads and mines as the primary places of employment for Chinese by the beginning of the 20th century.

CHINOOK   Warm wind coming from the Southwest that will melt winter snows, important to cowboys because a Chinook allows cattle to get to the grass under the snow. In the winter of 1886–87, there were no Chinooks and thousands of cattle died. This situation was popularized by artist Charlie Russell in his famous drawing *"Waiting for a Chinook."* In addition, Indians who lived along the Columbia River were called "Chinooks."

CHISHOLM, JESSE   (b. Tennessee either 1805 or 1806; d. near Geary, Oklahoma on March 4, 1868) The Chisholm Trail is named after this man, a trader, whose other claim to fame is that his aunt married Sam Houston. Born to a Cherokee mother and Scottish father, Chisholm moved to Oklahoma, near Fort Gibson, and in 1832 laid out a wagon road with Robert Bean Chisholm from Fort Smith, Arkansas to Fort Towson, Oklahoma. Chisholm lived in Arkansas as a trader before he moved to present-day Oklahoma City and opened a trading post. There he learned a number of Indian languages and traded with the Osage, Wichita, Kiowa and Comanche, interpreting for them in treaty sessions. During the Civil War Chisholm traded around present-day Wichita, Kansas and often traveled on the route between Wichita and the North Canadian River. When the first herd of longhorns in 1867 used it to travel

Jesse Chisholm   *(Library of Congress)*

from south Texas to the Kansas cattle towns, it was referred to as the "Chisholm trail." Unfortunately, Jesse Chisholm died of cholera in 1868 before his name was widely associated with the Texas cattle drives.

CHISHOLMS, THE

TV miniseries that starred Robert Preston as Hadley Chisholm, Rosemary Harris as Minerva Chisholm, Ben Murphy as Will Chisholm, Brian Kerwin as Gideon Chisholm (1979), Brett Cullen as Gideon Chisholm (1980), James Van Patten as Bo Chisholm, Stacey Nelkin as Bonnie Sue Chisholm (1979), Delta Burke as Bonnie Sue Chisholm (1980), Susan Swift as Annabel Chisholm (1979), Susan Swift as Mercy Hopwell (1980), Mitchell Ryan as Cooper Hawkins (1980), Victoria Racimo as Kewedinok, Charles Frank as Lester Hackett (1979), Reid Smith as Lester Hackett (1980), Devon Ericson as Betsy O'Neal (1980), Guich Koock as Frank O'Neal (1980), Les Lannom as Jeremy O'Neal (1980), Frank Noel as McVeety (1980) and Nick Ramus as Tehohane.

This was originally a four-part miniseries that was telecast several times. The show told the story of the Chisholm family, poor Virginians who lost their land in the 1840s and thus went to California for a new start. During the trip from Virginia to Fort Laramie, Wyoming, an Indian attack killed youngest daughter, Annabel; son Will married an Indian woman, and con man and gambler Lester Hackett got daughter Bonnie Sue pregnant, and she had an illegitimate child. CBS added some more twists and turns to the series the second time it was broadcast, and in this series the family had joined a wagon train from Fort Laramie to California led by Cooper Hawkins. During this trip, family patriarch Hadley Chisholm died. The show originally aired on March 29 and ran to April 1979 on Thursday nights on CBS. The hour-long show ran again from January 1980 until March 15, 1980 on Saturday nights.

CHISHOLM TRAIL

The Chisholm Trail was actually a series of cattle trails from southern Texas to the Kansas cow towns of Dodge City, Ellsworth, Abilene, Caldwell, Wichita, Newton and Junction City. The trails or cow paths led from various ranches and areas in south Texas until they came together around 1867 when the first cattle went up the trail from Texas to the Kansas railheads. The original Chisholm Trail was used by trader Jesse Chisholm and only covered about 220 miles between Wichita and the North Canadian River. The first longhorns used this at the end of their journey, but cowboys began to refer to the whole journey as the Chisholm Trail. Ironically, Jesse Chisholm never knew his name was linked to the most famous trail in cowboy history; he died in 1868 from cholera before the trail had received widespread recognition. The first terminus for the trail was Abilene, Kansas, created by Joseph McCoy in 1867 when he purchased land, erected cattle pens and forged an agreement with the railroad to build its lines there. (See CATTLE TOWNS; CHISHOLM, JESSE; MCCOY, JOSEPH GEATING.)

CHISHOLM TRAIL, THE

See OLD CHISHOLM TRAIL, THE.

CHISUM

Film produced by Andrew J. Fenady; directed by Andrew V. McLaglen; screenplay by Andrew V. McLaglen; released in 1970 by Warner Brothers; 111 minutes in length. Cast: John Wayne, Forrest Tucker, Christopher George, Ben Johnson, Glenn Corbett, Andrew Prine, Bruce Cabot, Patric Knowles, Richard Jaeckel and Lynda Day George.

Based on the story of legendary New Mexico rancher John Chisum (who employed Billy the Kid briefly), the movie is more about John Wayne than about John Chisum, as it espouses the conservative philosophy of Wayne. The real Chisum built his empire from ruthless behavior; he was big business in the cowboy's West. But Wayne's Chisum believes in law and order, a fair deal done by honest men. The Lincoln County War is virtually overlooked, and Chisum is the model of the ethical businessman until things get out of hand; he then puts on his guns and solves the problems. You have to fight fire with fire, and Chisum knows this; but at bottom he is the kind of man who built the West and made it a decent place to live.

CHISUM, JOHN

(b. John Simpson Chisholm in Hardeman or Madison County, Tennessee on August 15, 1824; d. Eureka Springs, Arkansas on December 20, 1884) John Chisum may have been the largest cattle rancher in the United States at one time, with between 60,000 and 100,000 head of cattle. He had moved to Lamar County, Texas in 1837 and was first a contractor (he built the courthouse in Paris, Texas); he entered the cattle business in 1854, selling beef to Indian reservations. He moved to South Spring in Old Lincoln County, New Mexico in 1867 and was a friend of attorney Alexander McSween and cattleman J. H. Tunstall in the Lincoln County War (1878–79). One of Chisum's gunfighter cowboys was Billy the Kid, but Chisum himself kept out of the gunplay. The brand for Chisum was the Long Rail (a long, straight mark from shoulder to flank), and a "jingle-bob" ear cut, in which the ear was cut so that the bottom half flopped like the jingle bob on a spur; for this reason Chisum's ranch was called the "jingle-bob" outfit. Chisum never married, and his holdings were passed along to relatives who could not perpetuate the empire Chisum founded. Chisum's original name was Chisholm, and he is often confused with Jesse Chisholm of the Chisholm Trail fame. It is not known whether the two Chisholms were related. (See also BILLY THE KID; LINCOLN COUNTY WAR.) .

CHRISTIAN, BLACK JACK

(aka "202"; b. Will Christian near Fort Griffin, Texas in 1871; d. Black Jack Canyon, Arizona on April 28, 1897) Christian picked up the nickname "202" in Sulphur Springs Valley, Arizona because of his weight. He was known mostly as "Black Jack," although he also worked under the alias Ed Williams. He and his brother, Bob, had broken out of jail in Oklahoma in 1895 and headed west. He joined a gang, the "High Fives," and robbed stagecoaches, trains and bands in 1896 and 1897. Christian was hiding in a cave with two others when a five-man posse found them on April 28, 1897. The posse set up an

John Chisum *(Western Archives)*

ambush and hit Christian when the outlaw was on his horse. Black Jack laid on the ground dying for most of the day. After he was dead, the men threw his body on a load of timber, where he was hauled into town.

CHRISTIANSON, WILLARD ERASTUS   See MORMON KID, THE.

CHRISTIE, NED   (b. near Tahlequah, Oklahoma on December 14, 1852; d. Ned's Fort Mountain, Oklahoma on November 3, 1892)   Christie was a Cherokee pursued for a number of years by lawmen intent on stopping his whiskey running. In 1886 Christie killed a lawman who tried to arrest him for this illegal act and spent the next seven years driving lawmen away from his stronghold, about 15 miles southeast of Tahlequah. In 1889 Christie's home and shop were destroyed by a posse, but he rebuilt his operation about a mile away on a cliff that

became known as Ned's Fort Mountain. That same year Christie's nose was shattered when a bullet struck his face and put out his right eye. His son was also wounded in the lung and hips by deputy marshals in an early morning surprise. Deputy marshals raised posses of Indians and attacked Christie's fort in 1891 and 1892. At dawn on November 2, 1892 Deputy Marshal Paden Tolbert led a 16-man posse to Christie's fort. The lawmen had a three-pounder cannon and six sticks of dynamite for their assault. They fired all the first day but that night dynamited the building. Christie and another man ran into the woods trying to escape, but a rifle slug caught Christie behind the ear and killed him.

CHUCK WAGON   A restaurant on wheels used during cattle drives to feed the cowboys. It came into use during later cattle drives (on the early drives the cowboys were expected to carry their own food) and became the social center during the drive as men gathered to eat, talk and bed down for the evening. The development of the chuck wagon is credited to Charles Goodnight, who took an old army wagon and put a "chuck" box for food at the rear with a drop-down gate to be used for a table where the cook worked. The wagon carried a water barrel, flour box, coffee grinder, tool box and other assorted essentials. Inside the wagon the cowboys kept their bedrolls and other equipment. Under the wagon a leather sling carried the wood and dried buffalo dung for the fire. This fire was made in a pit to avoid prairie fires. Major meals included steak (well done) and coffee (black and strong and hot). A favorite dish was "son-of-a-bitch" stew, and a real delicacy was "prairie oysters," which were the broiled testicles of a steer. The cook was in charge of the chuck wagon and the second highest paid member of a crew; the highest paid was the trail boss.

CHUTE   Narrow fenced area used for driving cattle to be dipped or loaded. In rodeo it is also, the small fenced area in which a bull or bronc is penned until the cowboy is mounted and the gate thrown open to let the animal into the ring.

CIMARRON   Film produced and directed by Wesley Ruggles; screenplay by Howard Estrabrook from Edna Ferber's novel; released by RKO-Radio in 1931; 124 minutes in length. Cast: Richard Dix, Irene Dunne, Estelle Taylor, William Collier, Jr., Nance O'Neil, Edna May Oliver and Rosco Ates.

Based on Edna Ferber's novel by the same name, this film won an Academy Award for best picture. Set against the land rush in the Cherokee Strip, the story follows one family through the history of Oklahoma. Yancey Cravat (Richard Dix) is idealistic and restless and serves as a lawyer and editor; he has the courage of a pioneer with the soul of a poet. Another version was released by MGM in 1960 (147 minutes) that was produced by Edmund Grainger, directed by Anthony Mann, with a screenplay by Arnold Schulman. The cast in this version included Glenn Ford, Maria Schell, Anne Baxter, Arthur O'Connell, Russ Tamblyn, Mercedes McCambridge, Vic Morrow, Harry Morgan, L. Q. Jones, Edgard Buchanan, Dawn Little Sky and Eddie Little Sky.

CIMARRON Song written by Johnny Bond and published by Peer in 1942.

The movie *Cimarron*, based on the book with the same title by Edna Ferber, was a major hit in 1931; however, there was no song by that title. Back in Oklahoma a singing group known first as the Cowboy Trio and then the Bell Boys had crossed that river a number of times during its travels. This group, composed of Johnny Bond, Jimmy Wakely and Scotty Harrell, had often commented on the fact that "Cimarron" would be a good title for a song. In 1938 group member Johnny Bond sat down to write a song in his room at the YMCA in Oklahoma City; the result was "Cimarron," and the group began performing it during appearances in and around Oklahoma. The group moved to Hollywood in 1940 and changed its name to the Jimmy Wakely Trio and joined Gene Autry's radio program, "Melody Ranch." In 1941 the group performed "Cimarron" in the movie *Twilight on the Trail*, which starred Bill Boyd. In the 1942 Gene Autry movie *Heart of the Rio Grande* it performed the song again, and Jimmy Wakely recorded the song for Decca. Later, Les Paul and Mary Ford and the Billy Vaughn Orchestra both had hit recordings of this song. (See also BOND, JOHNNY; WAKELY, JIMMY.)

CIMARRON CITY TV show that starred George Montgomery as Matthew Rockford, Audrey Totter as Beth Purcell, John Smith as Lane Temple, Stuart Randall as Art Sampson, Addison Richards as Martin Kingsley, Fred Sherman as Burt Purdy, Clarie Carleton as Alice Purdy, Dan Blocker as Tiny Budinger, George Dunn as Jesse Williams, Pete Dunn as Dody Hamer, Tom Fadden as Silas Perry and Wally Brown as Jed Fame.

Oklahoma Territory boom town Cimarron City was vying to become the capital of Oklahoma—not yet a state—in the 1890s after oil and gold had been discovered in the area. The series was narrated by star George Montgomery, who told the stories as an older man reflecting back on his younger days. Only 26 episodes were filmed of the hour-long series, which lasted only two full seasons, premiering on October 11, 1958 and ending on September 16, 1960. The show originally appeared on NBC on Saturday nights before being moved, in June 1960 (as a rerun), to Friday nights.

CIMARRON STRIP, THE TV show that starred Stuart Whitman as U.S. marshal Jim Crown, Percy Herbert as Mac Gregor, Randy Boone as Francis Wilde and Jill Townsend as Dulcey Coopersmith.

The second 90-minute western series ("The Virginian" was the first) was "The Cimarron Strip," which took its title from the 1,000-mile area between Indian Territory (later Oklahoma) and Kansas. The strip was patrolled by U.S. marshal Jim Crown; the romantic interest was Dulcey Coopersmith, who ran an inn built by her deceased father. There were 23 episodes of this big production, which premiered on September 7, 1967 on Thursday nights on CBS and ran until September 7, 1971.

CISCO KID, THE The character "the Cisco Kid" came from a short story, "The Caballero's Way," by O.

The Cisco Kid (Duncan Renaldo)

Henry (William Sydney Porter) in 1906. In movies, the character was first played by Warner Baxter in *In Old Arizona* (1929), the first major western talking picture (Baxter won an Academy Award for this role). Baxter eventually made three "Cisco Kid" pictures; Cesar Romero then starred in six, and Gilbert Roland starred in six before Duncan Renaldo took over the role for the last eight pictures in the Columbia series. Renaldo then became the TV "Cisco Kid." Sidekicks for Cisco included Chris-Pin Martin, Martin Garralaga, Frank Yaconelli and Leo Carillo, the most famous "Pancho" when the Cisco Kid became a TV show. (See also CARILLO, LEO; CISCO KID, THE (TV show); IN OLD ARIZONA; RENALDO, DUNCAN.)

CISCO KID, THE TV show that starred Duncan Renaldo as the Cisco Kid and Leo Carillo as his sidekick, Pancho.

"The Cisco Kid" was produced by ZIV Television for syndication; it was never a network show. However, it was incredibly popular, and the 156 episodes filmed between 1950 and 1956 appeared on a number of network stations in local markets. (Interestingly, all these shows were filmed in color but generally shown in

Pancho in "The Cisco Kid"

black and white.) Duncan Renaldo was 50 and Leo Carillo 71 when this series was shot, and though they rode their trusty horses (Diablo and Loco, respectively) and fought bandits, it was not with wild abandonment. Impeccably dressed in black with fancy embroidered shirts and a large Mexican hat, the Cisco Kid charmed ladies but only kissed them lightly before waving his hat and riding off into the sunset. Pancho consistently fractured the English language as these Mexican adventurers established a warm, funny relationship that was the key to the show's success. "The Cisco Kid" has a long history before TV; it was originally an O. Henry story, "The Caballero's Way," and then was featured in movies beginning in 1929 with *In Old Arizona* starring Warner Baxter as Cisco—who won an Academy Award for this portrayal. Other films featured Cesar Romero, Gilbert Roland and Duncan Renaldo in the lead; during the 1940s "The Cisco Kid" was a radio series, and there was a newspaper comic strip that began with the TV series and ended in 1968.

CLAIBORNE, BILLY (b. William F. Claiborne in Yazoo County, Mississippi on October 21, 1860; d. Tombstone, Arizona on November 14, 1882)
Claiborne was in the gunfight at the O.K. Corral (October 26, 1881) on the Clanton-McLaury side. He was wounded but escaped by following Ike Clanton, who ran into C. S. Fly's photography studio next door. Claiborne was drinking at the Oriental Saloon in Tombstone on November 14, 1882 when he had words with Buckskin

Frank Leslie. Claiborne went outside and hid behind a fruit stand to ambush Leslie, but Frank crept out the side door and surprised him. Claiborne fired wildly, but Leslie plugged him in the left side. He was taken to a private home, where he died cursing Buckskin Frank. (See also GUNFIGHT AT THE O.K. CORRAL; LESLIE, BUCKSKIN FRANK).

CLANTON, BILLY (b. William Clanton in Hamilton County, Texas in 1862; d. Tombstone, Arizona on October 26, 1881) Billy Clanton was one of those killed at the O.K. Corral by the Earps and Doc Holliday. The youngest of Old Man Clanton's sons, Billy was only 19 years old when he was cut down. The Clantons were known for cattle rustling; they generally raided ranches in Mexico and sold the cattle to Arizona ranchers. Among those in this gang of rustlers were the McLaury brothers, Curly Bill Brocius, Johnny Ringo, Buckskin Frank Leslie, Bill Leonard, Jim Crane, Harry the Kid, Billy Claiborne and Frank Stilwell. This was one of the reasons for bad blood between the Earps and the Clantons.

On the afternoon of October 26, 1881, Billy and Ike Clanton, Billy Claiborne and the McLaury brothers were at the O.K. Corral getting ready to leave town. They were approached by Doc Holliday and the Earp brothers—Morgan, Virgil and Wyatt. The Earps drew their guns and ordered everyone to drop their weapons; Billy Clanton threw up his hands and shouted, "Don't shoot me; I don't want to fight." But Morgan Earp shoved his gun toward Clanton and fired point-blank; the bullet struck Billy just below his left nipple. Billy Clanton and Frank McLaury then drew their guns and wounded Virgil and Morgan Earp and Doc Holliday. Billy, whose right wrist was broken in the gunfight, drew and fired with his left hand with the gun propped on his knee while he lay on his back. But a final, fatal bullet struck him in the stomach. Photographer C. S. Fly ran over to him and took his gun away and then helped take him into an adjacent building. In agony and writhing from pain, Billy said, "Pull off my boots. I always told my mother I'd never die with my boots on," as he was being carried. He began to cry out when he was laid down, "They've murdered me! Clear the crowd away from the door and give me air; I've been murdered." A doctor came and injected two syringes of morphine into Billy Clanton; 10 to 15 minutes after this he uttered, "Drive the crowd away," and died. (See also GUNFIGHT AT THE O.K. CORRAL.)

CLANTON, IKE (b. Joseph Isaac Clanton in Callaway County, Missouri in 1847; d. Bonita, Arizona on June 1, 1887) Ike Clanton survived the Gunfight at the O.K. Corral, although his brother, Billy, was killed. Ike was the son of N. H. "Old Man" Clanton, who moved his family to Fort Thomas, Arizona from California; in 1877, they moved on to Tombstone. Ike and his brother Phineas ran a freight line but were also involved in cattle rustling, stage robbing, some ranching and various illegal or suspicious activities. Old Man Clanton was a well-known cattle rustler and headed a ring of outlaws; when the old man died, Ike took over the ring. Since the

Earp brothers were lawmen, this led to a growing feud between the two families; however, it is also strongly suspected the Earps may have also been involved in some shady dealings and had run afoul of the Clantons.

On October 25, 1881 Ike and Tom McLaury went into Tombstone to buy some supplies; that night they were eating in a saloon when Doc Holliday, backed up by Virgil, Warren and Wyatt Earp, approached the table and challenged Clanton to fight. Ike got up and left, saying he was unarmed. Later that night, after a poker game that included city marshal Virgil Earp, Ike was cursed and pistol-whipped by Earp. The next day, October 26, Ike and Billy Clanton, Billy Claiborne and the McLaury Brothers, Frank and Thomas, were outside the O.K. Corral when they were approached by three Earps and Doc Holliday. Ike was not armed and, when the gunfire began, grabbed Wyatt Earp's left hand and implored him to stop. Earp replied, "The fighting has now commenced. Go to fighting or get away." Ike made a dash for C. S. Fly's photography studio and got inside, thus escaping being killed, although Wyatt supposedly shot at him five times and Clanton did receive a wound in the neck.

Ike Clanton was killed in Bonita, Arizona in 1887 by Deputy Sheriff J. V. Brighton when Brighton and Deputy George Powell tried to arrest Ike and his brother Phineas for cattle rustling at Peg Leg Wilson's cabin; Ike resisted arrest and was shot down. (See also GUNFIGHT AT THE O. K. CORRAL.)

CLARK, JIM CUMMINGS (b. Clay County, Missouri in 1841; d. Telluride, Colorado on August 7, 1895) Clark was christened Jim Cummings but changed his name when his widowed mother married a man named Clark. He was a member of William Quantrill's raiders in the Civil War, becoming one of Quantrill's most trusted lieutenants. About midnight on August 6, 1895 in Telluride, Colorado, Clark was walking toward his cabin with a character named Mexican Sam. As the two passed the Columbo Saloon, a gunshot was heard. Clark fell from a slug that tore through a lung and severed an artery. He died the next day.

CLARK, WILLIAM (b. Carolina County, Virginia on August 1, 1770; d. St. Louis on September 1, 1838) William Clark was the "Clark" of Lewis and Clark, the first white Americans to explore the West to the Pacific and bring back a report about their findings. William Clark was a distinguished soldier before the expedition, and after the expedition his reputation and fame continued to grow. Brother of Revolutionary hero George Rogers Clark, he grew up on an upper-class Virginia plantation and was nicknamed "Red Head." Too young to serve in the Revolution, Clark moved with his family to present-day Louisville when he was 14 and in 1789 began his army career; in 1790 he was commissioned a captain of the militia. Clark was part of Mad Anthony Wayne's campaign against Indians and participated in the Battle of Fallen Timbers (August 20, 1794) along with a young ensign, Meriwether Lewis. In 1796 Clark resigned his commission and moved back to manage his

family's plantation, which he owned in 1799 after his parents died. In 1803 Clark received a letter from Meriwether Lewis telling him about the expedition to the Pacific and asking him to join. Lewis promised Clark he would be commissioned a captain; however, Clark was actually commissioned a second lieutenant but was always considered an equal—and treated likewise—by Lewis during the expedition. For his part, Clark never let the official title stand in the way on this trip. Lewis and Clark complemented each other well: Lewis was more educated and scientifically trained, but Clark was a practical man, with plenty of frontier savvy and management expertise; he also had a good knowledge of Indians. The Lewis and Clark journey began on May 14, 1804; they went up the Missouri River to a Mandan village where they settled for the winter on October 26. On April 7, 1805 the group continued westward and reached the Pacific Ocean on November 7. They wintered on the coast and began their return journey on March 23, 1806. On this return trip the two explorers split up. Clark took a group and explored the Yellowstone River and rejoined Lewis on August 12. They arrived back in St. Louis on September 23, 1806 to the surprise of most of the people in the country, who never expected to see them again. The trip had taken two years, four months and nine days. On February 27, 1807 Clark resigned from the army and was named brigadier general of the militia for Louisiana Territory

William Clark *(Western Archives)*

and principal Indian agent at St. Louis, where he would marry, have a family and live until his death. After Meriwether Lewis died, Clark was offered Lewis's position as governor of Louisiana Territory but declined. Clark spent most of the rest of his life concerned with Indian affairs. During the War of 1812 he took part in the northern frontier defense and was named governor of Missouri Territory (Louisiana Territory after the State of Louisiana had been created) in 1813 by President Madison. The next two presidents, James Monroe and John Quincy Adams, recommissioned Clark to this position. However, when Missouri became a state in 1821, Clark lost the election for governor. Clark laid out the town of Paducah, Kentucky and negotiated several Indian treaties. He held the job of superintendent of Indian Affairs until his death.

CLARKE, RICHARD   See DEADWOOD DICK.

CLEMENS, SAMUEL LANGHORNE   See TWAIN, MARK.

CLEMENTS, MANNEN   (b. Emmanuel Clements on February 26, 1845; d. Ballinger, Texas on March 29, 1887)   Clements was a cousin of outlaw John Wesley Hardin and helped the outlaw escape from jail in 1872. Hardin stayed on the Clements's ranch in 1871 and helped them drive a herd up the Chisholm Trail, also helping out in the Sutton-Taylor feud. Clements developed large horse and cattle herds but was accused of rustling. He ran for sheriff of newly formed Runnels County, Texas in the 1887 election that had a heated campaign. In the Senate Saloon in Ballinger, Texas on March 29, 1887, Clements was approached by city marshal Joe Townsend; the two had words and gunfire erupted, killing Clements. (See also HARDIN, JOHN WESLEY; SUTTON-TAYLOR FEUD.)

CLEMENTS, MANNIE   (b. Emmanuel Clements, Jr. in Brown or Gonzales County, Texas in 1869; d. El Paso, Texas on December 29, 1908)   Both the younger Clements and his father were killed in saloons. In 1894 the son had gone to El Paso where he spent the following 14 years as deputy constable, constable and deputy sheriff. He was reunited with his cousin John Wesley Hardin when the outlaw was released from prison. Clements was killed on December 29, 1908 in the Coney Island Saloon in El Paso. The killing was thought to have been connected with a racket to smuggle Chinese immigrants into the country.

CLIFTON, DAN   See DYNAMITE DICK.

CLOTHING, COWBOY   The contemporary cowboy is defined more by his clothing than anything else. The essential elements of the cowboy "look" are boots and hats, although jeans, vests, spurs, belt buckles, bandanas, coats and shirts may also be part of the contemporary look. These clothes set the contemporary cowboy apart from others and make him distinctive, but the clothing for the original cowboys consisted of work clothes, practical and pragmatic.

Contemporary cowboy hats come in a variety of styles and shapes from a number of manufacturers, but the hats worn by cowboys in the 1865–85 period were usually less flashy, more likely to have a flat brim, and served more as a head covering than as fashion. In the northern ranges the brim was likely to be shorter than that of the hats worn in the Southwest because the winds in the north would blow off a wide-brimmed hat; in addition, the southwestern cowboys needed a wide brim for shade from the sun. The hat crown for southwestern cowboys was also generally larger to allow more air circulation, whereas the smaller crowns of northern cowboys helped keep the hat on and the heat in. Cowboy hats became distinctive when John B. Stetson developed his "Stetson" in 1865 at his hat-making shop in Philadelphia. Prior to this time—and even during the 1865–80 period—most working cowboys wore a ragtag assortment of hats whose primary role was to protect the head from heat and rain rather than make them "look" like a cowboy. The cowboy hat was further developed and popularized by Buffalo Bill Cody (who was responsible for the large "ten-gallon" hat) and movie cowboys, who used the hat as a fashion statement. But for the working cowboy, a hat served as protection from the sun and rain, as a drinking gourd for him and his horse, to fan himself or the campfire and to signal to other cowboys. For the working cowboy in the 19th century, hats generally cost $10 to $20.

Boots were developed for men on horses, not for the man on foot, so they were often uncomfortable if someone had to do a great deal of walking. Made of leather, the boots had thin soles and high heels (usually one and one half or two inches) to enable the wearer to stay in the stirrup yet feel the horse. The large heel also served as a brake for the cowboy when he was roping; on the ground he could dig in, while in the saddle he could stay on. Easy to pull on— and devoid of cumbersome shoestrings—the boots had high tops (about 17 inches) to protect the legs; early cowboys usually stuffed their pants inside the boots to protect the pants as well. Later, fancy embroidery began to appear on the boot tops. The most popular early boot maker was Joe Justin, whose boots became so popular that the term "Justins" meant boots. Handmade boots (and working cowboys always preferred handmade boots over factory boots) generally cost the 19th-century working cowboy $20 to $30. For the working cowboy, spurs were added; for the contemporary cowboy they are optional but generally rare.

The preferred pants of historical as well as contemporary cowboys are jeans or dungarees; the first brand popularized was Levi's, developed by Levi Strauss in San Francisco. The working cowboy also wore chaps over his pants to protect both his pants and legs.

Because shirts in the Old West did not have collars, working cowboys used the bandana to protect their necks. Shirts were usually made of cotton and had no pockets, thus the necessity for vests, which had pockets to hold the cowboy's cigarettes (or tobacco and papers) and other assorted odds and ends. The bandana served a number of other purposes, from a washcloth or rag to a covering for the mouth and nose to protect against dust. Coats were rare in the Southwest; most cowboys avoided them. When they were worn, they were usually short and made of denim. On the northern ranges coats were a necessity and often worn long for maximum warmth. Long rain coats, or yellow slickers, were kept tied to the saddle or in the chuck wagon until rain came; they kept a cowboy dry and generally covered the cowboy as well as the saddle. Gloves with long flared cuffs were a necessity for the working cowboy to protect against rope burns.

Big bright belt buckles, string ties with fancy slides, hand-carved belts and ornate hatbands were extremely rare in the West; a working cowboy might use some ornaments when he dressed up, but generally his clothing was plain. The contemporary cowboy is full of ornamentation, a direct descendant of movie cowboys and rodeo cowboys (the winners in rodeos are given large belt buckles). But even the working cowboy of the 19th century liked to make a fashion statement with his clothes when he came off the range; at the end of a trail drive, cowboys usually took their money straight to the boot maker and general store for some brand new duds and then went to the photographer and had their picture made. (See also LEVI'S; SPURS; STETSON, JOHN B.)

COCHISE (b. c. 1815; d. Chiricahua, Arizona on June 9, 1874)   Cochise, a chief of the Chiricahua Apache, fought against Mexicans but was basically

Three cowboys dressed up

friendly toward white settlers until Mickey Free, a half-breed boy, was abducted in 1861 and the Chiricahua were wrongfully accused of the crime. This led the army to seize Cochise and several of his relatives; Cochise escaped, captured three white men and offered to exchange them for his relatives. The offer was refused and so he killed his captives; the army responded by hanging the Apaches. From this point forward, Cochise sought revenge against whites and particularly the United States Army. Cochise and Mangas Coloradas (chief of the Mimbreno Apache) fought General Carleton and 3,000 California volunteers at Apache Pass in 1862 but had to retreat because of the howitzers. Cochise became principal chief of the Apache when Mangas died; after the Civil War the army mounted a major campaign against Cochise, who moved into the Dragoon Mountains with 200 warriors. For more than 10 years, Cochise and his band continued to raid settlements and keep the army away; he was finally hunted down by Lieutenant Colonel George Crook, who used Apache scouts to track down the fugitives. In September 1871 Cochise surrendered and lived on the Chiricahua Reservation in Arizona until 1874, when he died.

CODY, BUFFALO BILL   (b. William Frederick Cody in Le Claire, Iowa on February 26, 1846; d. Denver, Colorado on January 10, 1846)   The facts and myth of the Old West are combined in Buffalo Bill Cody more than in any other single individual. Buffalo Bill Cody brought the Wild West to easterners, popularizing the cowboy all over the world, creating an image of the westerner and uniting the reality of the West with show business in a way that made the cowboy a genuine American hero and the Old West a place and time of mythic proportions.

The fourth born of eight children, young Bill moved with his family to Kansas in 1850, and the Codys established a sawmill business. In 1857 his father, Isaac, died; to help the family William got a job as messenger boy with Russell, Majors and Waddell, a freighting firm based in Leavenworth, Kansas. Initially, Cody's job involved carrying messages between wagon trains; later, when the firm established the Pony Express, Cody became a rider on the Julesburg section of the route. During this period he met Wild Bill Hickock, who became a lifelong friend.

In 1861 Cody returned home and stayed until his mother died in 1863. In early 1864 he joined the Union army and served with the Seventh and Ninth Kansas regiments before taking on hospital duties in St. Louis. Out of the army in 1865, Cody became a stagecoach driver. On March 6, 1866 he married Louisa Frederici. The couple established a boardinghouse, but this failed, so Cody became an army scout working for General George Armstrong Custer at Fort Larned and then worked as a buffalo hunter for the Kansas Pacific Railroad. Cody got his first taste of fame when he bettered Buffalo Bill Comstock by killing more buffalo in one day: 69 versus 46. This feat gave him his moniker "Buffalo Bill."

Cody continued to gain more fame on the plains from

A young Buffalo Bill Cody with rifle

Buntline in 1872 that had been adapted from a Buffalo Bill story. Later, Cody appeared in one of Buntline's plays, *Scouts of the Plains*, which opened at the St. Louis Opera House, and from this point on was involved in show business when he wasn't working on the plains as a scout.

For the Great Royal Buffalo Hunt in 1872, Cody served as guide for Grand Duke Alexis of Russia. While serving as chief scout with Colonel Merritt and the Fifth Cavalry, Cody killed and scalped Yellow Hand, the Cheyenne chief, in a battle in July 1876—just after Custer's defeat at the Little Bighorn. Cody went back to the stage to promote this exploit. Also in 1876 Cody and his family moved into a large home in Rochester, New York; a few years later he built "Welcome Wigwam" in North Platte, Nebraska and moved there.

On July 4, 1882 Cody organized the "Old Glory Blowout" in North Platte. This spectacle, part rodeo and part buffalo hunt, inspired the first Wild West show in 1883, which toured North America and Europe during the next 25 years, attracting fame, fortune and then bankruptcy.

Cody had domestic problems in the 1890s. Fond of women and drink, he fell in love with an English actress, Katherine Clemmons, and invested $80,000 in her ca-

Buffalo Bill Cody *(Annie Oakley Museum)*

the Indian Wars (in all, he would take part in 16 different Indian fights, including the Battle at Summit Springs on July 11, 1869), but his real fame occurred in 1869 while working as chief of scouts for the army when he met Ed Judson (Ned Buntline), and the dime novelist soon made Cody the hero of some Wild West novels. Buntline fictionalized Cody and his exploits when he wrote "Buffalo Bill: King of the Bordermen" for the *New York Weekly*, but the series was an immediate success and Cody quickly became a national hero. A number of other sensationalist novels followed, some written by Buntline but most by Prentiss Ingraham. In addition to capturing the public's fancy, these dime novels also captured Cody's fancy, and he set out to live the image created about him.

Invited to Chicago and New York because of his newfound fame, Cody went to a play in New York with reer. Cody planned to marry her when his divorce from Louisa became final, but it never did. The court antics and Lulu's tantrums created much publicity in the media as well as personal misery for Cody, but in the end he turned back to her. Katherine finally married someone else.

Although Cody made a great deal of money during his lifetime, he also spent freely on pleasures as well as suspect business ventures. Inclined to get-rich-quick schemes and grandiose ambitions, he invested heavily in his 4,000-acre Scout's Rest Ranch in Nebraska and bought 400,000 acres in Wyoming's Bighorn Basin that included the TE Ranch and the city of Cody, which he founded, a hotel, newspaper, hunting lodge, waterworks and gold and silver mines.

At the end of his life Buffalo Bill Cody was a tired, sick man, exhausted from so much performing, unable to escape debt or creditors and forced to become a parody of himself with the Sells-Floto Circus, paraded out each night to doff his hat and be seen by the crowds.

Cody's last performance was in Portsmouth, Virginia in November 1916. After this he entered a Colorado sanatorium before going to Denver and the home of his sister, Mrs. May Decker, where he lay in bed until his death just after noon on January 10, 1917. The day before, he had requested and received last rites from the Catholic Church.

Cody's death pushed the news of World War I off the front pages, and his body lay in state in the Colorado state capitol before being taken to a mortuary. Cody requested that he be buried on Cedar Mountain above Cody, Wyoming, but $10,000 was needed for this. Because Cody died broke, there was no money, and Henry Tammen, owner of the Sells-Floto Circus and *Denver Post*—and a creditor of Cody's who had forced the Wild West show to be auctioned off—convinced the city of Denver and Cody's widow to have him buried on Lookout Mountain, west of Denver. Cody was buried five months after his death—after a steel vault had been constructed so the body would not be stolen—while a huge parade of automobiles, Sells-Floto wagons, speakers and old girlfriends gathered in a raucous farewell to the man and the legend. (See also BUFFALO BILL'S WILD WEST SHOW.)

COE, FRANK   (b. probably in Iowa on October 1, 1857; d. Lincoln County, New Mexico on September 16, 1931)   Frank Coe was with the McSween faction during the Lincoln County War. He was at the shootout in 1878 at Blazer's Mill where Buckshot Roberts and Dick Brewer were killed, and was ambushed by the "Seven Rivers Crowd" later that month. Coe was also with Billy the Kid on July 4, 1878 when a running gunfight erupted. Coe moved to San Juan County in 1884 and lived a long life, leaving six children and his wife of 50 years when he died in 1931. (See also LINCOLN COUNTY WAR.)

COE, GEORGE WASHINGTON   (b. Brighton, Iowa on July 13, 1856; d. Lincoln, New Mexico on November 12, 1941)   Coe joined the "Regulators," the

group that included Billy the Kid, during the Lincoln County War after he was arrested by Sheriff William Brady. Coe was at Blazer's Mill during the confrontation between Buckshot Roberts and Dick Brewer. Coe was hit by a shot from Roberts that ricocheted off Charlie Bowdre's cartridge belt, shattering Coe's hand and taking off his trigger finger. Roberts shot at Coe three times when Coe charged him, but the bullets only hit Coe's shirt and vest. On July 4, 1878 Coe was with Billy the Kid and others at Ash Upson's store near Roswell, New Mexico when they were chased by 15 to 20 men in a running gun battle back to John Chisum's ranch. During the siege on the McSweens' house from July 15 to 17, 1878, Coe fought with Billy the Kid, Henry Brown and Joseph Smith and escaped the burning house under a hail of violent gunfire. After the Lincoln County War, Coe left the area but returned in 1884 and developed the Golden Glow Ranch. (See also LINCOLN COUNTY WAR.)

COE, PHIL   (b. Phillip Haddox Coe in Coe Valley, Gonzales County, Texas on July 17, 1839; d. Abilene, Kansas on October 9, 1871)   Coe was killed in the famous gunfight with Wild Bill Hickok in Abilene, Kansas in which Hickok also killed one of his own best friends. After the Civil War, Coe and Tom Bowles had opened a saloon in Austin, Texas and installed Ben Thompson as house gambler. In 1871 Coe and Thompson opened the Bull's Head Saloon in Abilene, Kansas. A picture over the Bull's Head upset the townsfolk, who considered the graphic image of the bull's anatomy obscene, even though Abilene was a major cattle town at this time. Nevertheless, city marshal Wild Bill Hickok was sent to get the sign changed. When Coe and Thompson resisted, Hickok sent some painters to paint over the offensive section of the painting, but when the paint dried, the offending part could still be seen. Worse, Coe was greatly offended that Hickok would do such a thing. Problems were exacerbated when Coe and Hickok had eyes on the same girl and got into a fistfight in which Coe floored Hickok and the marshal swore revenge.

On October 5, 1871 Hickok treated Coe and about 50 of his rowdy friends from Texas to a drink at the saloon but warned them not to get too carried away. Around 9 P.M. Coe fired a shot in the street, and Hickok came out to check on the disturbance. Coe admitted he had fired his gun, saying he had shot at a dog, but the marshal drew. Coe shot first, putting a hole in Hickok's coat and sending another shot between his legs. Meanwhile Hickok had shot Coe with a bullet that went into his stomach and came out his back. It was at this point that Hickok's friend, Mike Williams, came around the corner to aid Hickok, but the marshal—surrounded by a hostile crowd and understandably jumpy—turned and drilled two bullets in Williams's head, killing his friend immediately. Wild Bill then closed down the town.

Coe was shot on a Thursday and died the following Sunday. (See also HICKOK, WILD BILL; THOMPSON, BEN.)

COFFEYVILLE RAID, THE   On October 5, 1892 at 9:30 in the morning Bob, Emmett and Grat Dalton, along with Dick Broadwell and Bill Powers, rode into the Kansas town of Coffeyville in the southeastern corner of the state, right on the Oklahoma line. Bill Doolin had started out with the gang, but apparently his horse had become limp so he stayed behind. Workers in the town square had taken down the hitching rails, so the group tied up their mounts in an alley. A local citizen, Aleck McKenna, recognized the Daltons and quietly spread the word throughout town when he saw them enter town. Bob and Emmett Dalton went into the First National Bank and gathered $21,000 from the cashier and some customers; Grat Dalton, Dick Broadwell and Bill Powers entered the Condon Bank but only got $1,500. Meanwhile, word was spreading throughout the town about the Daltons in the banks, and citizens were arming themselves.

Bob and Emmett Dalton had three hostages in front of them when they left the bank they had just held up but were forced back inside from the citizens' gunfire. Slipping out the back door, they were spotted by Lucius Baldwin, a young man who tried to block their getaway; Bob Dalton killed him with a rifle shot into his heart. At Rammel's drugstore were boot makers George Cubine and Charles Brown, who had known the Daltons as boys. Bob killed both when Cubine held a rifle on him. One of the hostages, bank cashier Thomas G. Ayres, had gone from the bank to Isham's hardware store; when he came out, Bob killed him with a bullet in the left cheek.

The five bandits met up in the alley, where they tried to mount their horses for a getaway, but the mounts of Bob Dalton and Powers were killed, leaving the men without horses. Just then a former schoolteacher, Charles Connelly, came firing his gun into the alley; he was killed by Grat Dalton. Next, a livery stable owner, John J. Kloehr, came into "Death Alley" and Bob Dalton whirled around, only five feet away. Kloehr shot before Dalton could, hitting the outlaw in the chest; Dalton staggered back and then died after sitting down and rolling over. Meanwhile Powers was shot in the heart as he jumped onto Grat Dalton's horse and landed dead on the ground. Broadwell was on his horse taking off with only a wound in his arm when a rain of bullets killed him.

Emmett Dalton tried to pick up his brother Bob after he mounted his horse with the money, but barber Carey Seaman and John Kloehr each shot at him, and the outlaw fell out of the saddle. Finally the firing stopped, with citizens Charley Gump and T. A. Reynolds both wounded and Emmett Dalton full of bullets but still alive. Locks from Bob's head were quickly snipped by some souvenir hunters and the outlaws were laid out and photographed. (See also DALTON GANG, THE.)

COLBERT, CHUNK (b. ?; d. Colfax County, New Mexico on January 7, 1874)   Colbert was a legendary gunfighter, supposedly killing seven men in the early 1870s, but in 1874 he ran into Clay Allison, who killed him. Colbert had challenged Allison to a horse race, and the race was declared a tie. Colbert and Allison, both unhappy, went for a meal and then began drinking coffee. Colbert decided to shoot Allison and, while reach-ing with one hand for the coffee pot, quietly began getting his pistol into firing position under the table. Allison spotted the ruse and grabbed his own revolver. Colbert rushed his shot and the bullet went into the table top; Allison was more careful and put his bullet just above Colbert's right eye, killing him instantly. (See also ALLISON, CLAY.)

COLGATE WESTERN THEATRE   This was a summer TV series of western films. Most of these films had originally been on "G. E. Theater" and "Schlitz Playhouse."

COLLINS, BEN   (b. ?; d. near Emet, Oklahoma on August 1, 1906)   Collins, an Indian policeman in Indian Territory, was appointed deputy U.S. marshal in 1898 and in 1905 had to arrest an influential resident, Port Pruitt. Fighting broke out during the arrest, and Pruitt was shot and partially paralyzed by Collins. Pruitt and his brother Clint swore revenge and hired a gunman to kill Collins, paying the gunman $200 with the promise of an additional $300 when the job was done. But the hired gun hightailed it with the money. The next year another hired gun, Killin' Jim Miller, lay in ambush for Collins at the marshal's home near Emet, Oklahoma. Miller fired a shotgun blast at Collins, knocking the lawman out of the saddle. Collins fired some shots at Miller, but the killer sent another load of buckshot in Collins's face. Collins's wife rushed outside to her husband, but he was dead by the time she reached his side. (See also MILLER, KILLIN' JIM.)

COLORADO TRAIL   This cattle trail left the Western Trail in southern Oklahoma and headed northwest through the Texas panhandle and into Colorado. This was not a particularly well marked trail, and because it was used to bring cattle in to stock the Colorado ranges, it had various points of destination. The trail crossed the Neutral Strip and went across the southwest corner of Kansas and into the Cimarron River area before going into Colorado, where the main trail generally ended at La Junta.

COLT, SAMUEL   (b. Hartford, Connecticut on July 19, 1814; d. Hartford, Connecticut on January 10, 1862)   Sam Colt invented the first practical revolving pistol, which ultimately became the western six-shooter. Colt had gone to sea in 1830 and during a voyage to Singapore whittled a revolving handgun model; in 1831 he built two pistols with this pattern and obtained a patent. Colt established his first company at Paterson, New Jersey, where he made five-shot revolvers, rifles, carbines and shotguns, but problems with army and navy purchases caused the company to go out of business. However, Colt's guns were popular with the public, and the Texas Rangers began to use them. Samuel H. Walker came to purchase guns for the new Republic of Texas, and he and Colt worked out a pattern for a new gun, called the Walker Colt, which was a six-shot pistol. In 1847 the U.S. government ordered 1,000 of these revolvers, which put Colt back in business. Colt then set up his firm in Hartford, Connecticut,

Wade Preston as Christopher Colt in "Colt. 45"

and during the Civil War the company manufactured more than 300,000 revolvers and over 100,000 rifles and muskets.

COLT .45   TV show that starred Wayde Preston as Christopher Colt and Donald May as Sam Colt, Jr. (1959–60).

Secret government agent Christopher Colt told people he was a representative of his famous family, carrying his Frontier Model Colt .45 to "demonstrate" as part of the gun- selling business. Later, he was joined by Sam Colt, Jr., also in the same business. The show premiered on October 18, 1957 on ABC on Friday nights. During its three-year run it also appeared on Sundays and Tuesdays. Star Wayde Preston walked out over a disagreement with Warner Brothers and was replaced as the lead character by Donald May. There were 67 black-and-white episodes of the half-hour series, which ended its run on September 27, 1960.

COLTER, JOHN   (b. near Staunton, Virginia c. 1774; died Missouri in November 1813)   A member of the original Lewis and Clark Expedition in 1804–6, John Colter is most famous for his "run for life" from the Blackfoot Indians in 1808. Colter became the first white man to see Yellowstone when he explored Wyoming, Montana and Idaho in a solo exploration in 1807–8. Colter and a companion, John Potts, were trapping beaver in Montana in the fall of 1808 when a large party of Blackfeet attacked them and killed Potts. Colter was

set to be tortured, and the first stage was for him to run for his life while the Blackfeet chased him before killing him. The Indians stripped Colter naked and gave him a 400-yard head start. The 500 warriors then began pursuing him. Colter outran every Indian except one—blood streaming from his nose and mouth—and he finally turned and killed this Indian with the Blackfoot's own lance. Then Colter walked for seven days to reach a trading post. In 1810 Colter quit fur trapping in the Rockies and went to St. Louis, where he married and settled near Daniel Boone. A few years later, Colter died of jaundice.

COMANCHE INDIANS   An offshoot of the Shoshoni Indians in Wyoming, the Comanche were known as the finest horsemen on the plains. The Comanche fought the Mexicans and then the early Texans, wreaking fear and havoc. Living in tipis, the Comanches were nomadic buffalo hunters who lived in the Southwest until the Treaty of Medicine Lodge sent them to a reservation in Indian Territory. The most famous chief was Quanah Parker, son of a Comanche chief and a captured white girl, Cynthia Ann Parker.

COMANCHE MOON   Comanche were said to raid during a September moon. Beginning around 1830 and lasting until about 1870 or so, those who lived in west Texas and Mexico dreaded and feared the Comanche moon.

COMANCHEROS   The Comancheros were traders who moved between the Mexicans and the Comanche. The trade agreements came about after a peace agreement between Comanche chiefs and Spanish officer Don Juan Bautists de Anza in New Mexico. Often of mixed descent (Mexican and Indian hybrids), these men were neutral, carrying goods and messages between the Indians, Mexicans and whites.

COMANCHE TRAIL   The trail into Mexico from the Staked Plains in Texas, on which the Comanche rode for their raids.

CONCORD COACH   The stagecoach built by the Abbot-Downing Company that replaced the heavy, awkward British coach. Abbot-Downing used leather thoroughbraces instead of steel springs in its coaches, which made the ride more "flexible" on backwoods roads. The Concord coach body stood 8 feet, 6 inches above ground; the rear wheels were 5 feet 1 inch high, the front wheels 3 feet 10 inches. The coach weighed almost 2,500 pounds, and the framework was made from white ash, kiln dried; the side panels were made of poplar forged into shape by steam. There was Norway iron on the axle bars, tires, brake rods, fittings and collars for wheel hubs. On the wheels there were no bolts or screws, and the outside of the coaches were known for having multiple coats of red, blue, yellow or green paint, covered with two coats of varnish. On the outside of the coach a landscape was usually painted on each door; the colorful coaches had red paint on the wheel

"Concrete Cowboys" TV show   (Jerry Reed)

spokes and yellow running gear, with the steps and top rail shiny black. (See also ABBOT- DOWNING COMPANY.)

CONCRETE COWBOYS   TV show that starred Jerry Reed as Jimmy Lee (J.D.) Reed and Geoffrey Scott as Will Ewbanks.

This is the old "Route 66" show of the 1960s updated in the 1980s. J.D. and Will dressed like cowboys and were carefree in their beat-up old camper. Country music singer Jerry Reed served as narrator and star. He picked and grinned along the way, including the theme song "Breakin' Away," which he wrote and recorded. This show premiered on February 7, 1981 on Saturday night on CBS; its last telecast was on March 21, 1981.

CONESTOGA WAGON   All covered wagons have come to be called "Conestogas," a term not entirely correct. The authentic Conestoga wagon was developed in Lancaster County, Pennsylvania in the Conestoga River valley and was used as far back as 1717. The product of Pennsylvania Dutch craftsmen, the original Conestogas were used to haul furs from Lancaster to Philadelphia. The authentic Conestoga had a wagon bed 42 inches wide that bowed downward in the middle, with the front and rear panels built outward so that it resembled a boat. There were bows of bent wood for a canvas or Osnaburg cloth covering; a tool box was located on the left side, and a feedbox was on the rear. The Conestoga was not made for the driver to ride; he either walked beside the wagon or rode on the left-wheel horse.

Moravian craftsmen in Salem, North Carolina manufactured a variation of this wagon. The heyday for the Conestoga was from 1820 to 1850, or before the railroads replaced them for passenger travel. Although some called all covered wagons "Conestogas," in truth most of those wagons on the Santa Fe, Oregon and California Trails were not authentic Conestogas. (See also PRAIRIE SCHOONER.)

CONNORS, CHUCK   (b. Kevin Joseph Connors in Brooklyn, New York on April 10, 1921; d. Los Angeles, California on November 10, 1992)   Chuck Connors was a popular TV actor, appearing in a number of western series, beginning with "The Rifleman." The six-foot five-inch actor attended Seton Hall College on an athletic scholarship—one of 25 offers he received—and played baseball and basketball; he then signed with the Brooklyn Dodgers in June 1942. Connors was sold to the Chicago Cubs in 1951, and they farmed him to their minor league team in Los Angeles in the Pacific Coast League. This led to screen tests and a career in films and TV, beginning with his first role in the Spencer Tracy film *Pat and Mike*. (See also RIFLEMAN, THE; TELEVISION WESTERNS.)

CONQUISTADORES   The conquistadores were the early Spanish conquerors. The most famous conquistadores were Hernando Cortes, who conquered Mexico (1519–21); Hernando de Soto, who explored Georgia, Florida, the Carolinas, Tennessee, Alabama, Mississippi, Arkansas, Texas and Oklahoma (1539–42) and led the first Spanish group who saw the Mississippi River; Francisco Vasquez Coronado, who searched for the Seven Cities of Gold (1540–42) and explored New Mexico, Texas, Oklahoma, Arizona and Kansas; Don Juan de Onate, who began the first settlement in New Mexico beginning in 1598; Sebastian Vizcaino, who explored California; and Alonso de Leon, who explored Texas in 1690. It was the Spanish conquistadores who claimed most of the West for Spain and later became Mexicans by mixing and intermarrying with native Indians. They introduced cattle and horses to the Americas.

COOK   Also called "cookie," "beanmaster," "doughbelly" or "sourdough," the man who presided over the chuck wagon or, back at the ranch, was in charge of the kitchen. Out on the trail the chuck wagon had a back that dropped down to a table. There were shelves and drawers for coffee, flour, salt, soda, baking powder, sugar, beans, lard, rice, dried fruit and a jar or crock of sourdough to make flapjacks and bread. There were boxes for tin plates, cups, spoons, knives and forks and space for cast-iron cooking utensils. There was also a drawer for medicines such as quinine, horse liniment, calomel and the inevitable whiskey or brandy. Inside the wagon were the cowboys' bedrolls as well as grain for the horses; on the side of the wagon was usually a water barrel with a wooden spigot; beneath the wagon were heavier cooking utensils (such as Dutch ovens), shovels or spades, an axe and large pans or tubs for the dishes. The cook ruled over all of this equipment. The cook's job was to get up ahead of the cowboys and fix their morning meal; then he packed up his wagon and moved ahead of the crew to find a suitable spot for lunch; after lunch he would again pack up, move ahead of the cowboys and find a suitable place for dinner, which he would have ready for the cowboys. The chuck wagon was the social center on the cattle drive, and the cook was often the doctor and father confessor as well as entertainer, if he could play the fiddle. A good cook attracted cowboys; the best outfits generally had excellent cooks, whose pay was equal to the top hand's monthly draw of around $40 to $50.

COOLEY, SCOTT (b. in 1852; d. Blanco County, Texas in 1876) Cooley was a central figure in the Mason County War (Texas) in 1875. Formerly with the Texas Rangers, he quit to go ranching. Cooley was living in a neighboring county but returned to Mason County for revenge when friend Tim Williamson—whose wife had nursed Cooley back to health when the cowboy contracted typhoid fever—was killed. The war was essentially between Germans and Anglos; Cooley killed two Germans soon after his arrival and then joined up with some other gunman. The first man killed by Cooley was Deputy Sheriff John Worley, who was working on a well when Cooley arrived at his home. Worley was pulling a helper out of the well when Cooley asked the lawman his name; when the lawman replied, "Worley," Cooley had confirmed his target; he shot the lawman, scalped him and fled. The helper plunged back down into the well during all this. The Rangers stopped the feud, but Cooley avoided arrest. However, back in Blanco County, Cooley became ill and died.

COOL WATER Song written by Bob Nolan (April 1, 1908–June 16, 1980) and published by Unichappel in 1936.

Bob Nolan formed the Sons of the Pioneers with Leonard Slye (Roy Rogers) and Tim Spencer, and the group was soon a hit on radio and in the movies, appearing with top singing-cowboy stars and recording for Decca. Their popularity created a constant demand for songs, generally written by Bob Nolan and Tim Spencer, for their movies, recordings and performances. Nolan had written a number of poems in his youth, and "Cool Water" was originally a poem he wrote in the mid-1920s while a student at Tucson High School. It was inspired by Nolan's fascination with the desert after he moved there from his native Canada to join his father. This song has been recognized as the best-known western song of all time. (See also NOLAN, BOB; SONS OF THE PIONEERS.)

COOPER, ANDY (b. Andy Blevins in Texas c. 1861; d. Holbrook, Arizona on September 4, 1887) A son of Mart Blevins, Andy took the name "Cooper" while in Texas. He had trouble with the law most of his life—in Indian Territory he was wanted for selling liquor to Indians, in Texas for rustling and maybe for murder. He joined his family in Pleasant Valley, Arizona and became involved in the Graham-Tewksbury feud. A violent man, Cooper hired himself out to cattlemen against sheepherders. On September 2, 1887 Cooper opened fire on John Tewksbury and Bill Jacobs at a sheep camp and killed both men. Cooper, who was with several others in this killing, then allowed hogs to eat the two bodies. Two days later Andy was visiting his mother, who had moved to Holbrook with his brother Jim after his father and another brother had been killed in the Pleasant Valley War. It was a Sunday afternoon, and Cooper looked out the window and saw Sheriff Perry Owens coming to the house. Andy fired at the sheriff from the front door, but Owens hit Cooper and killed him. Andy's mother dragged him back while older brother John opened fire. Mose Roberts, a brother-in-law, came out and was killed. Sixteen-year-old Sam Houston Blevins then came out with a revolver and was killed by Owens. Only John Blevins and two women at the house survived. (See also OWENS, COMMODORE PERRY; PLEASANT VALLEY WAR.)

COOPER, GARY (b. Frank James Cooper in Helena, Montana on May 7, 1901; d. Los Angeles on May 13, 1961) Gary Cooper was the classic cowboy star in the earliest sound westerns, but perhaps his greatest fame in westerns rests with his portrayal of Will Kane in *High Noon*, which garnered him an Academy Award in 1952; he was also given a special Academy Award in 1961. A native westerner, Cooper attended Wesleyan College in Bozeman, Montana and Grinnell College in Iowa and then became a newspaper cartoonist. His first movie appearance was as an extra in *The Eagle* (1925). Cooper starred in the first sound version of the classic *The Virginian* (1929), and this role made him a western

Gary Cooper

star. Cooper was not limited to westerns; he starred in a number of them in the 1920s, only one in the 1930s, and eight between 1948 and 1956.

COOPER, JAMES FENIMORE   (b. Burling, New Jersey on September 15, 1789; d. September 14, 1851.) Cooper is considered the first of the western novelists. His *Leather-Stocking Tales,* with heroes Natty Bumpo and his Indian companion Chingachgook, inspired the dime novel heroes and the first generation of western fiction writers. The son of Quakers, Cooper moved with his family to Cooperstown, New York, where he grew up. He was expelled from Yale and then went by sea to Europe, but he returned when his father died and left him an inheritance. Cooper then became a gentleman farmer and began writing for money. His first novel was a failure, but *The Spy* (1821), his next, began his success. The *Leather-Stocking* series began with *The Pioneers* (1823) and was followed by *The Last of the Mohicans* (1826), *The Prairie* (1827), *The Pathfinder* (1840) and *The Deerslayer* (1841).

CORRAL   A fenced-in area used to pen horses or cattle. Sometimes made of wood, it can also be made of rope or adobe walls.

CORRIGAN, RAY "CRASH"   (b. Raymond Bernard in Milwaukee, Wisconsin on February 14, 1907; d. Brookings Harbor, Oregon on August 10, 1976)   Corrigan was one of the "Three Mesquiteers" in a series of

Ray "Crash" Corrigan

films with Bob Livingston and Max Terhune and then starred in *The Range Busters* series. He retired from movies in 1944 to concentrate on his business, Corriganville, an authentic western town that was used as a movie set. In the 1950s he appeared on a children's TV series. (See also CRASH CORRIGAN'S RANCH.)

COTTONWOOD   A type of tree belonging to the poplar family, named because of the cottonlike fluff around its seeds. These trees grow all over the West and, for settlers and travelers, were often the sign of water nearby.

COUGAR   See MOUNTAIN LION.

COULEE   Also spelled *cooley* or *coolly,* this is a cut in the earth—a valley, ravine or gully—with steep sides. Water often collects here.

COURTRIGHT, LONGHAIRED JIM   (b. Timothy Isaiah Courtright in Sangamon County, Illinois in 1848; d. Fort Worth, Texas on February 8, 1887)
Courtright, a detective, was killed by Luke Short in a Texas gun battle over "protection" payments. Courtright had served in the Civil War for the Union and went to Texas afterward. He was appointed city marshal of Fort Worth in 1876 and then went to Lake Valley, New Mexico before moving back to Fort Worth and opening up a detective agency. Because of some gun trouble in New Mexico, Courtright was served extradition papers; however, friends fastened two six-guns underneath a cafe table and stationed a saddled mount outside, allowing Courtright to escape. After wandering to New York, Canada and Washington, Courtright returned to New Mexico and cleared his name; he reopened his detective agency, the T. I. C. Commercial Agency, in Fort Worth. The agency was actually a protection racket that charged the town's gambling joints. Luke Short owned a one-third interest in the White Elephant Saloon; on February 8, 1887 Luke Short refused a payment demanded by Courtright. Later that evening, Short and Bat Masterson met Courtright, and Short reached inside his coat after words had been exchanged. Courtright told Short not to go for his gun, but Short replied he never carried a pistol there. Meanwhile, Courtright pulled his revolver and shot, but the hammer caught in Short's watch chain, stopping the firing. This gave Short time to draw and shoot at Courtright. The first shot shattered the cylinder of Courtright's gun; three of the next five hit Courtright—in the right thumb, right shoulder and heart. Within minutes Courtright was dead. Short was cleared for "self-defense." (See also SHORT, LUKE L.)

COVERED WAGON   See CONESTOGA WAGON.

COVERED WAGON, THE   Silent film produced by Famous Players Lasky; directed by James Cruze; released by Paramount in 1923.
   This silent movie is the first western epic. The story involves a girl and two suitors, a good guy and a bad guy, and a 2,000-mile journey over the Oregon Trail in 1849. The wagon train is beset with numerous perils—

Indian attacks, fires, buffalo and a rising river—and the settlers are shown against the backdrop of the awesome western landscape (it was filmed in Nevada).

COWBOY CHRISTMAS The Fourth of July, so named because this was the most prominent holiday celebrated in the West. Fourth of July celebrations gave rise to the rodeo and Wild West show. (See also BUFFALO BILL'S WILD WEST SHOW; RODEO.)

COWBOY CLOTHING See CLOTHING, COWBOY.

COWBOY COMMANDMENTS These were the commandments, written by Gene Autry for his fans, that all cowboys were expected to follow:

1. He must not take unfair advantage of an enemy.
2. He must never go back on his word.
3. He must always tell the truth.
4. He must be gentle with children, elderly people and animals.
5. He must not possess racially or religiously intolerant ideas.
6. He must help people in distress.
7. He must be a good worker.
8. He must respect women, parents and his nation's law.
9. He must neither drink nor smoke.
10. He must be a patriot.

COWBOY G-MEN TV show that starred Jackie Coogan as Stoney Crockett and Russell Hayden as Pat Gallagher.

This show was never a network series but was produced independently. The 39 half-hour shows began filming in color in 1951 and debuted in 1952, sponsored by Taystee Bread. The show was later popular on Saturday morning TV. The general theme of the show was that the two stars were secret government undercover agents in the 1870s.

COWBOY IN AFRICA TV show that starred Chuck Connors as Jim Sinclair, Tom Nardini as John Henry, Ronald Howard as Wing Commander Howard Hayes and Gerald Edwards as Samson.

Rich English landowner Howard Hayes had a game ranch in Kenya. He hired rodeo cowboy Jim Sinclair to come over to the African country and introduce ranching methods. Sinclair brought along his Navajo blood brother, John Henry. Based on the movie *Africa—Texas Style*, the show premiered on September 11, 1967 on Monday evenings on ABC. The one-hour show ended on September 16, 1968.

COWBOYS The cowboy as Americans have come to know him in the 20th century is derived from several sources: (1) the real-life cowboys who drove cattle north from Texas to the Kansas rail towns after the Civil War; (2) the heroes of dime novels in the 19th century (and their descendants, the pulp magazines of the early 20th century); (3) Wild West shows, most notably the one by Buffalo Bill Cody; (4) movies, especially the singing-cowboy and "B" movies of the 1930s and 1940s; and (5)

television shows, particularly those in the late 1950s and early 1960s, when westerns dominated the networks. There are, of course, other sources for our images of cowboys: cowboy songs, the number of country music singers who dress like cowboys and sing western themes, rodeos, western novels, western clothing stores, western dance clubs, advertisements (particularly the Marlboro Man), museums, historical centers, books about the West and a variety of other sources, including the simple fact that cowboys still exist and work in the West and that, for many westerners, the clothing style of the cowboy is an essential part of their everyday wear.

The Spanish gave the United States its first cowboys, called "vaqueros," its first cattle and its first horses. These cattle and horses, like the Spaniards, moved first into Mexico and then northward at the end of the 15th century. The Spanish gave the cowboy the idea of raising cattle on ranches, working on horses, the saddle, the rope (or lariat), the idea of the roundup, and much of what evolved as cowboy clothing and the "look" of the cowboy.

The Mexican sombrero, for example, with its straight, stiff brim and low, flat crown, was developed by these vaqueros to protect themselves from the hot sun. These early cowboys also wore bandanas; shirts were either cotton or wool, depending upon the weather and climate. However, by the late 16th century, they wore leather jackets, knee breeches over long underwear, and leather leggings that covered the lower leg to the ankle. Shoes were buckskin (although most early vaqueros did not have any), but they also wore an early version of chaps and high-topped cowboy boots. The first spurs were iron and often strapped to bare feet for the vaqueros.

In the 1550s the cattle roundups began, in which vaqueros would "hunt" for cattle and bring them to a ranch; their major working tools were lances or long, iron-tipped poles that were used to push and prod the cattle. The cattle were valuable because of their hides, so when cattle were rounded up, the vaqueros would kill them while on horseback; using a hocking knife on a lance, the vaquero would cut the animal's right hind leg and sever the tendon, which caused the animal to fall to the ground helpless; then the vaquero drove the knife into the spinal cord, just behind the horns on the head. The dead cattle were then skinned and the hides pegged out on the ground to dry. Gradually, the rope replaced the hocking knife, and during the 16th century the vaquero learned to put a loop on his lance and capture cattle by the horns. These early ropes were usually leather, made from braided untanned cowhide. Northern Mexico, in the area of Chihuahua, Coahuila, Nuevo Leon and Durango, is the home of the original Mexican vaqueros. This area had large ranches that covered thousands of acres; by the early 17th century the hacienda system developed, in which a ranch house was established as headquarters for the operation.

Horses were essential for cowboys working cattle on ranches—indeed, the horse is what separated the Spanish working cattlemen from the eastern British colonists who settled on farms and worked with cattle on foot. Saddles were developed by leather workers on haciendas, and saddle making became an art; further, new practical saddles were manufactured for the purpose of working cattle. Saddlebags also came along; a large saddle horn was added to anchor the rope tossed around the horn (known as *da la vuelta*, which became anglicized as "dally"). Thus, the major working tool of the vaquero shifted by the end of the 17th century from the lance to the rope. New terms would eventually come into the English vocabulary: *reata* means "rope," a *lariat* was a short rope (usually for picketing horses) and a *lazo* was a long rope with a slip knot; lasso and lariat would come to be used by the English.

The California vaquero—and ranch owner—provided the "look" of later-day movie cowboys with their bright colors, ornate dress and saddles and flashy personalities. It is no wonder the movie cowboys of Hollywood so closely resemble the ranchero owners and vaqueros of southern California 100 years earlier. But the cattle culture as we know it developed in Texas, where the Mexican-Indian vaquero on horseback gathered cattle on the open range.

Since the word "cowboy" implies someone who works with cattle, it is not surprising that the term was used long before Anglo-Americans were in the West. In fact, the term first appeared around A.D. 1000 in Ireland; during the period of the American Revolution the term "cow boy" was fairly widely used, although it usually referred to British loyalists who stole cattle from American farmers and sold them to the British army. During the late 1830s the term was first used in Texas, although the term "vaquero" was the most widely used term from this period until the Civil War. After the Civil War, the term "cow-boy" came into general use for those actively involved in working cattle on ranches and driving cattle north to the Kansas railheads. Around 1900 "cow-boy" became "cowboy."

There were some cattle drives before the Civil War. In the 1840s Texas cattle were driven to St. Louis on the Shawnee Trail (also called the Osage Trace and Kansas Trail). By the early 1850s a cattle trail from Texas to Missouri was well established, and there was even a cattle drive to New York City by two enterprising souls. These cattle drives altered some of the equipment used by the cowboy; the saddle got smaller, slimmer and lighter (12 or 13 pounds in the early 1850s.) In addition, the cantle fit better and the stirrups became wider, but the heavier Mexican-style saddle would still be popular until after the Civil War.

During the spring of 1860, cattle were driven to Kansas and Missouri; these were crude cattle drives. Wagons and carts hauled some supplies; but the drovers generally had to buy food from Indians and settlers or live off the land; there were no chuck wagons.

After the Civil War men returned to Texas, which had been a Confederate state. The land had been decimated by neglect and drought; however, there were a number of cattle roaming around that had multiplied during the Civil War. Further, the North needed cattle because its herds had been decimated; there were big markets for

Five Cowboys

beef in the eastern cities. The railroads had been building westward and would soon reach Kansas; thus a cow whose hide was worth more than its meat—and which was only worth $4 to $5 walking around in south Texas—was worth $40 to $50 if it could get to an eastern market. The answer was for the cattle to be rounded up, branded for ownership and driven about 1,000 miles north to the railheads in Kansas, where the cattle would be loaded on trains and shipped east. This was the real beginning of the American cowboy.

The heyday for the American cowboy was from 1865 to 1890; during this period the cattle drives began in earnest, the cattle industry in the West developed to become a major industry, the West opened up to settlement and, finally, the open range era ended as railroads brought more settlers into the West, which ultimately caused the decline of large cattle ranching and the end of the cowboy in this first phase.

The large cattle drives to Kansas began in 1867 when Joseph McCoy established stockyards and a business structure to make Abilene the first "cattle town." Abilene would remain the major cattle town until 1871, when other towns replaced it, chiefly because the Kansas legislature established a "quarantine line" to keep Texas cattle out of Kansas farmland so the "Texas fever" spread by the longhorns would not affect Kansas domestic stock. The cattle drives would continue to a series of Kansas towns—Ellsworth and Dodge City— until they ended in 1885.

There were a number of significant changes in the life of the real working cowboy during this period. The term "roundup" replaced "cow hunt" around 1870; and the open range style of ranching, in which large ranchers claimed public lands as their own, gave way to homesteaders claiming smaller parcels of land. The introduction of barbed wire to the range in the 1870s forever ended the old roaming cowboys. After barbed wire, the work of the cowboy included riding line and mending fences; the fences created major changes for ranchers, too, who could now develop their breeding practices with cattle and horses.

By the early 1870s the cowboy was firmly established as a hired man on horseback. Also in the 1870s the cowboy became an established part of literature through the dime novels. Writers came to the West looking for subjects to write about; the cowboy, with his different look and lifestyle, was a romantic figure, so these writers wrote books for eastern audiences—dime novels, about 30,000 words long—that glamorized the cowboy and the West. Some of the "cowboys" glamorized were real people like Buffalo Bill Cody and Wild Bill Hickok as well as other scouts, adventurers and lawmen.

The discovery of gold and silver created a number of "boom towns," and some of these towns—Virginia City, Tombstone, San Francisco, Denver and others—enhanced the image of the wild and woolly West. Lawmen and gamblers played a large part of the history of these towns and became part of the "history" of the cowboy and the history of the West.

In 1883 Buffalo Bill Cody and W. F. Carver created the first Wild West show and took it on the road; this show took the cowboy away from the boring and mundane—though dangerous—job of looking after cattle and put him into an arena as a romantic hero. Buck Taylor became "King of the Cowboys" in Cody's show and the subject of some dime novels as well.

During the 1870s the West expanded with settlers moving onto homesteads. Cattle had first come to the northern ranges with settlers on the Oregon Trail who brought them from Iowa, Missouri and Illinois. But these eastern cattle generally were not capable of withstanding the long, frigid hard winter, and many died; it would take the sturdy Texas longhorn to flourish there. For the cowboy this meant the northern ranges in Wyoming and Montana were opened to cattle raising, and cattle drives moved some Texas cattle from Texas to these ranges. About 40% of the Texas cowboys stayed in Wyoming and Montana, but these cowboys developed a slightly different look and culture. In Texas about 15–20% of cowboys were black, a result of Texas being a slave state before the Civil War and the fact that ranchers needed any able-bodied men they could find for these cattle drives. But not as many blacks stayed in the North.

The cowboy's clothing underwent major changes: The pocket in his pants was made straight down (instead of with a narrow side opening) so that items would

Cowboys on horses running and waving hats   (*Library of Congress*)

not slip out when he rode a horse or branded cattle. The slicker made of oilskin became part of the northern cowboy's range clothing as well as angora chaps, which kept his legs warm. The narrow-brimmed hat with a high crown was popular in the North because the wide-brimmed Texas hats caught too much wind. A vest was added for warmth as well as for pockets, since shirts did not have pockets. Boots for both northern and southwestern cowboys were about the same—about 17 inches tall. And the average wage for all cowboys in the 1880s was $35 to $45 per month.

The cattleman and the cowboy began to emerge as two different creatures—with social and cultural distinctions—after the Civil War. Cattlemen began to hire cowboys; the term "cowboy" referred to the hired hands. There wasn't much "glamour" or appeal in being a cattleman—who was actually a businessman—whereas there was plenty of appeal in being a footloose and fancy-free cowboy. Gradually, the character of the cowboy began to emerge—remarkably like the heroes in the dime novels. The cowboy became a rugged individualist who was always cheerful and courageous, did not quit or complain, helped a friend or stranger in distress, had a "live and let live" attitude, didn't pry into other people's business and worshiped decent women and put them on a pedestal ("other" women were tenderloin—but even those deserved to be treated with respect).

The cowboy's appearance was helped along by having a wad of money in his pockets when he hit a cattle town after a long drive. Cowboys would pay $25 for a pair of boots hand made, buy a pearl-handled six-shooter, silver bridle, fine saddle, leather chaps, hatband, felt hats and other assorted accoutrements that made them look like what easterners thought cowboys should look like. Then a cowboy might go have his picture made at a local photography studio to immortalize the occasion. In short, the cowboy changed from a dusty hired hand to a dandy when he hit town.

The decline of the traditional, working American cowboy occurred for several reasons: (1) The ranges became overstocked with cattle, and prices declined sharply in the late 1880s; (2) the terrible winter of 1886–87 virtually wiped out the cattle industry on the northern ranges; (3) homesteaders moved in, increasing the population and taking away large tracts of land for cattle; (4) barbed wire fenced off property, creating fixed boundaries for ranches and farms; and (5) the railroads linked the country, making cattle drives unnecessary and bringing in settlers, who populated the ranges. But the cowboy as a romantic hero continued to develop, aided by the cowboy's involvement in popular entertainment and his portrayal in the mass media.

The rodeo developed about the same time as the Wild West show—and from some of the same sources—and in the 20th century the rodeo replaced the Wild West show as the major example of cowboy entertainment. In 1898 the first western "movie" was filmed; *Cripple Creek Barroom* showed a vignette of an old Wild West saloon. The first story movie, *The Great Train Robbery* in 1903, was a "western," and the first major successful feature filmed in Hollywood, *The Squaw Man*, was also a western; thus western themes were important to the history of the movie industry at the same time the movie industry was shaping an image and vision of the West. This shaping continued through the "talkies" and then the singing cowboys and "B" westerns of the 1930s and 1940s. When television was introduced to the American public in 1947, some of the first popular shows were westerns, and the 1950s—the era in which television became a dominant part of American culture—were also noted as the era of TV westerns.

The contemporary cowboy is identified by attitude and clothing; the "rugged individualism," yearning for freedom and devil-may-care exhibited are carried by individuals wearing jeans, western shirts, cowboy boots and cowboy hats. The contemporary cowboy is more likely to drive a pickup truck, the contemporary version of a horse, and to listen to country music. Like the traditional cowboy, the contemporary cowboy views himself as a superior being, a loyal hardworking individual who is a free spirit. The contemporary cowboy may not ride a horse or work with cattle but still views himself as a cowboy; indeed, it is the clothes and attitude that make a man a "cowboy" today—not the work he does or where he lives. (See also BLACKS IN THE WEST; B WESTERN MOVIES; CATTLE DRIVES; CATTLE TOWNS; CATTLE TRAILS; COWBOY'S PAY; LONGHORN CATTLE; MOVIES; RODEO; SINGING COWBOYS; TELEVISION WESTERNS; TRAIL DRIVES; WOMEN IN THE WEST.)

COWBOYS, THE Film produced and directed by Mark Rydell; screenplay by Irving Ravetch, Harriet Frank, Jr. and William Dale, based on the book by William Dale Jennings; released in 1972 by Warner Brothers; 128 minutes in length. Cast: John Wayne, Roscoe Lee Browne, Bruce Dern, A. Martinez, Alfred Barker, Jr., Nicolas Beuvy, Steve Benedict, Robert Carradine, Norman Howell, Jr., Stephen Hudis, Sean Kelly, Clay O'Brien, Sam O'Brien, Colleen Dewhurst and Slim Pickens.

John Wayne was 65 when he starred in this movie about a Montana cattleman who has to drive 1,500 head of cattle without his cowboys, who've all quit to go dig gold. The old man hires 11 schoolboys and they set off. There are some adventures along the way, and Wayne gets killed (the first time that happened to him in a movie since *The Alamo* 12 years earlier) and is buried along the trail. The boys deliver the goods, and on their way back, they look for Wayne's grave but can't find it.

COWBOYS, THE TV show that starred Moses Gunn as Jebediah Nightlinger, Diana Douglas as Mrs. Annie Andersen, Jim Davis as U.S. marshal Bill Winter, A. Martinez as Cimarron, Robert Carradine as Slim, Sean Kelly as Jimmy, Kerry MacLane as Homer, Clint Howard as Steve, Mitch Brown as Hardy and Clay O'Brien as Weedy.

Based on the novel by William Dale Jennings and the movie starring John Wayne, this series showed young boys (ages nine to 17) working on a cattle ranch in New Mexico in the 1870s. The series was short—only 12 episodes filmed—and premiered on February 8, 1974 on Wednesday evenings on ABC. The half-hour series ended on August 14, 1974.

COWBOYS & INJUNS A children's program during TV's early years hosted by Rex Bell.

Originally a local program in Los Angeles, the show was filmed at an outdoor corral and an Indian village as well as on an indoor stage and consisted of live demonstrations of cowboy and Indian folklore. The show was first telecast on October 15, 1950 on Sunday nights at 6 on ABC. The half-hour program was last telecast on December 31, 1950.

COWBOY'S LAMENT, THE The lyrics to this song, also known as "The Streets of Laredo," were written by a cowboy, Francis Henry Maynard, in 1876 during a trail drive. It was inspired by "The Dying Girl's Lament," a song about a girl betrayed by her lover, and the melody is basically the same for both. This melody may also be traced back to the Irish ballad "The Unfortunate Rake." Another American version of this song (based on "The Dying Girl's Lament") is the sailor's song "Wrap Me Up in My Tarpaulin Jacket." The original "scene" for this song was Tom Sherman's barroom in Dodge City, Kansas; the other setting is Laredo, Texas. This song was popular with cowboys in the West from the time it was written.

COWBOYS OF MOO MESA See WILD WEST C. O. W. BOYS OF MOO MESA.

COWBOY'S PAY The working cowboy never got rich; he was always a hired hand. In 1885 the monthly wage for working cowboys averaged $38.72, but it dropped in 1890 to $32.24. During the 1890s the average was $32 to $33, with top hands getting $40 to $45 and the range foreman or wagon boss $125. A wagon cook got the same amount as a top hand. (See also COWBOYS.)

COWBOY THEATRE TV show hosted by Monty Hall.

This was an anthology of edited western films from the 1930s and 1940s hosted and narrated by Monty Hall. The show premiered on Saturday afternoons in September 1956 and moved to prime time on June 9, 1957, when NBC broadcast the show on Sunday evenings. Originally a half-hour show, the series ran as a one-hour show from June to September 1957; it ended its run on September 15. Later, the show appeared on Saturday morning TV.

COW FEVER The insatiable yearning to follow cows and be a cowboy.

COWGIRL This term was first applied to Lucille Mulhall, daughter of Zack Mulhall and expert roper and trick rider in the Miller Brothers' 101 Wild West Show, by President Teddy Roosevelt about 1901. However, the term "cowgirl" was previously not complimentary; women saw themselves as "women," and being called a "girl" was an insult. (See also WOMEN IN THE WEST.)

COWHAND A cowboy or someone who takes care of cows.

COWHIDE The cow's skin, which is used for everything from saddles to holsters to coats to beds.

COW HUNT Early term used to describe gathering up cows; it was replaced by the term "roundup" about 1870.

COWJUICE Milk.

COWMAN Someone who owns cattle. A cowman is different from a cowboy, who takes care of cows.

COWMAN'S PRAYER, THE A song first published as an unsigned poem in the *Socorro Bullion* in 1886 in Socorro, New Mexico. A melody was later adopted, and the song was collected by John Lomax for his book *Cowboy Songs* in 1910. It expresses the sincere request of the western cattleman.

Lord, please help me, lend me Thine ear,
The prayer of a troubled cowman to hear.
No doubt my prayer to you may seem strange,
But I want you to bless my cattle range.
Bless the roundups year by year;
Please then don't forget the growing steer.
Water the land with brooks and rills,
For my cattle that roam on a thousand hills.
Now O Lord, if you'll be so good,
See that my stock has plenty of food.
Our mountains are peaceful, the prairies serene,
O Lord, for the cattle, please keep them green.
Prairie fires, won't you please stop?
Make thunder roll and water to drop.
It frightens me to see the dread smoke,
Unless it is stopped, I'm bound to go dead broke.
As you O Lord my fine herds behold,
They represent a sack of pure gold.
I think that at least five cents on the pound
Would be a good price for beef the year round.
One thing more, and then I'll be through:
Instead of one calf, let my cows have two.
I may pray different from all other men,
But I've had my say, and now, amen.

COWPOKE Workers at the railroad station who had to keep the penned cattle on their feet while awaiting shipment by train. Since the workers used long poles to keep the cattle up, they were called "cowpokes," although the term later became synonymous with cowhand and cowboy.

COW SENSE Anyone or anything good at understanding or working cattle. The term could be applied to a man, woman, dog or horse.

COWTOWN RODEO TV show that featured Marty Glickman and Howard "Stony" Harris as commentators.

This was a summer show in which rodeo performers were shown competing for prizes in rodeo events. One of the commentators, Stony Harris, owned the Cowtown Ranch in New Jersey, which produced the program. The show was first telecast on August 1, 1957 on Thursdays on ABC. The hour-long program was shown during the 1957 summer and on Mondays in the summer of 1958. The last telecast was on September 8, 1958.

COYOTE A small wolf *(Canis latrans)* that feeds on small animals such as rabbits, ground squirrels, poultry and mice or on berries if no meat is available. A fast animal that can run about 40 miles an hour, it is about four feet long (the male) and resembles a small collie dog. Coyotes have been a nuisance to ranchers and farmers because they kill domestic livestock, but Indians admired them for their cunning and intelligence. For Indians and mountain men, the coyote has always had a spiritual aura, and a coyote's howl on a moonlit night is an integral part of the sounds of the West.

CRABBE, BUSTER (b. Clarence Linden Crabbe in Oakland, California on February 7, 1908; d. Scottsdale, Arizona on April 23, 1983) Buster Crabbe's first fame came as an Olympic swimming champion in 1928 when he won a Bronze medal; in 1932 he won an Olympic Gold Medal and would eventually hold 16 swimming records. Crabbe passed a screen test with Paramount and was cast in a Western series on Billy the Kid in which he made 36 "B movies" with Fuzzy St. John (1941-46). But Crabbe's greatest movie fame came in the Flash Gordon series and, later on television, as Captain Gallant of the Foreign Legion.

CRASH CORRIGAN'S RANCH TV show hosted by Ray "Crash" Corrigan.

A children's program created when TV programmers were trying to figure out how to fill the airwaves, this was a variety show in a western setting with songs and skits,

Buster Crabbe

presided over by Crash Corrigan. The half-hour show premiered on July 15, 1950 on Saturday nights on ABC. It ended its run on September 29, 1950.

CRAVENS, BEN (b. Lineville, Iowa in 1868; d. September 19, 1950) Cravens has been called the last of the notorious Oklahoma outlaws. In Indian Territory he tore up a local school and was jailed; this led to a series of arrests for whiskey running, train robbing and horse stealing, but he always managed to escape, finally living in Missouri under an alias. Cravens had already killed several men during a prison break in 1897 in Kansas when, in 1901, he and a former convict, Bert Welty, robbed a store in Red Rock, Oklahoma. Cravens killed the postmaster, and the two thieves escaped in a buggy during a thunderstorm. When the buggy overturned, Cravens shot Welty with a shotgun, but Welty later recovered and identified Cravens. At this time Cravens was in jail under an alias; he was given a life sentence but was paroled as an old man.

CRAWFORD, ED (b. ?; d. Ellsworth, Kansas on November 7, 1873) Crawford was on the police force of Ellsworth, Kansas during the heyday of this cattle town. When Sheriff C. B. Whitney was killed by some Texans, Crawford vowed revenge and killed Texan Cad Pierce after an encounter on the street. Crawford was fired from the police force for killing Pierce, and some Texans warned him to get out of town. He did but returned later and was drunk in Lizzie Palmer's whorehouse when he shot through a door and then kicked it open to face a lady of the evening with a man named Putnam, who was Cad Pierce's brother-in-law. Crawford shot Putnam in the hand, but Putnam emptied his six-gun into Crawford. Putnam hit Crawford four times, but the disturbance attracted a number of other Texans, who also shot at Crawford. The dead Crawford had 13 bullets in his body when the shooting stopped.

CRAZY HORSE (b. Tashunka-uitco c. 1840; d. at Red Cloud Agency at Fort Robinson, Nebraska on September 5, 1877) Crazy Horse, a chief of the Oglala Sioux, was present at a number of key battles during the Indian Wars. He took part in the Fetterman Massacre, the Battle of the Rosebud, the Battle of the Little Bighorn and Red Cloud's War against the army over the Bozeman Trail. He received his name from a dream when he pictured his horse performing a wild, crazy dance. A mystic, he was victorious against the U.S. Army until January 1877 when General Nelson A. Miles launched a surprise attack against his winter camp, leaving the Indians without food, clothing or shelter on the cold plains. This led Crazy Horse and his people to surrender at the Red Cloud Agency in Nebraska. Crazy Horse was killed by a soldier at Fort Robinson, Nebraska on September 5, 1877 after he was arrested amid rumors he was planning to escape.

CRAZY WEED See LOCO WEED

CROCKETT, DAVY (b. near Rogersville, Tennessee on August 17, 1786; d. at the Alamo in San Antonio on March 6, 1836)   Davy Crockett became the first "western hero" in America, largely through the writings about him (often attributed to him but, in fact, drummed up as tall tales by others). Crockett had little formal schooling and ran away from home when he was 12. He married Polly Findlay and became a farmer in Lincoln County, Tennessee. But Crockett was an indifferent farmer; he preferred hunting and adventure. During the Creek War of 1813–14 he served as a scout under General Andrew Jackson. In 1821 he was elected to the Tennessee legislature; Crockett had moved to Giles County, Tennessee and become justice of the peace there after his wife died in 1815. He was also elected a colonel of the militia. Crockett served in the Tennessee legislature until 1827, when he was elected to Congress, where he served in 1827–31 and 1833–35. In April 1834 he toured the Northeast and came to national attention as a backwoods "character." After he was defeated for Congress, Crockett headed west to Texas to join the fight for independence there; he arrived at the Alamo in February 1836 and helped organize the group of fighting men, playing his fiddle as entertainment. In March he

Davy Crockett *(Western Archives)*

was in the fort when General Santa Anna's troops overran it. (See also ALAMO, BATTLE OF THE.)

CROOK, GEORGE (b. near Taylorsville, Ohio on September 23, 1829; d. Chicago on March 21, 1890) General George Crook was one of the premier Indian fighters in the Indian Wars on the plains. But he was also one of the most fair, honest and scrupulous, and the Indians respected him and called him "Chief Grey Wolf." Crook did not look like an ordinary soldier: He wore a cork sun helmet and a canvas suit, preferred to ride a mule instead of a horse and did not swear, smoke or drink liquor or coffee. A West Point graduate (1852), he served in the Civil War; afterward he was sent to Boise, Idaho and in 1871 was put in command of the Department of Arizona. There he had to quell the Apache and introduced the use of Apache scouts. After serving in the Sioux War of 1876 and commanding the Department of the Platte, he was sent back to Arizona in 1882 to capture Geronimo. Crook did manage to capture Geronimo, but the Apache chief escaped, and the ensuing criticism forced Crook to resign this command. Crook was a kind, sympathetic man whose word with the Indians was good.

CROSS HOBBLE   To tie one of the horse's front feet to one of its back feet on the opposite side so it cannot roam.

CROW INDIANS   The Crow Indians were an agricultural tribe when they lived in the area that is now North Dakota along the Missouri River but became a nomadic tribe when they moved to the Rocky Mountain area near Yellowstone. A warrior tribe, they placed great honor and glory in battle and often fought the Blackfeet, Sioux and Cheyenne. The Crows were generally friendly to whites, especially when the whites fought one of their traditional enemies. The Crows served as scouts in the U.S. Army, including several who served with General Custer in the 1870s during the Indian Wars.

CRUZ, FLORENTINO   (aka "Indian Charley"; b. Mexico; d. Tombstone, Arizona on March 22, 1882) Cruz, an Indian-Mexican involved with cattle rustlers and stage robbers, was aligned with the Clantons and other anti-Earp factions. With four other men Cruz approached Campbell and Hatch's Billiard Parlor at 10:50 P.M. on the night of March 18, 1882 while Morgan Earp was playing pool. Earp was standing with his back to a glass door while his brother Wyatt sat nearby. Cruz, Pete Spence, Frank Stilwell, a gambler named Freis and Indian Charlie opened fire. Morgan Earp was hit in the back, and another slug landed in the wall near Wyatt's head; within half an hour Morgan Earp was dead. Four days later, on March 22, Wyatt and Warren Earp, Doc Holliday, Sherman McMasters and Turkey Creek Jack Johnson gunned down Frank Stilwell in Tucson; they then returned to Tombstone, where they went to Pete Spence's wood camp about 11 A.M., where Cruz was chopping wood. The Earp group went out to pay Cruz a visit; wood camp worker Theodore Judah heard about a dozen shots and went out to find Cruz's body full of bullets. (See also EARP, WYATT; HOLLIDAY, DOC.)

CUMMINGS, DOC (b. Samuel M. Cummings near Westville, New York on September 20, 1861; d. El Paso, Texas on February 14, 1882)

Cummings was the brother-in-law of Texas gunman Dallas Stoudenmire. In April 1881 Cummings and Stoudenmire (who was El Paso's marshal) gunned down Bill Johnson, who had previously shot at the two with a shotgun. In February 1882 Cummings went into the Coliseum Variety Theater in El Paso and ran into Jim Manning, whom Cummings suspected of being one of those behind the assassination attempt. Cummings goaded the reluctant Manning into a fight; when Cummings went for his guns, Manning and bartender David Kling both beat him to the draw. Doc fired wildly and then staggered into the street, where he collapsed and died.

See also MANNING, JAMES; STOUDENMIRE, DALLAS.

CURRY, FLAT NOSE (aka Big Nose Curry; b. George Curry in Prince Edward Island, Canada on March 20, 1871; d. Castle Gate, Utah on April 17, 1900) Curry's nose was smashed when a horse kicked him in the face, earning him his nickname. He joined the Wild Bunch, a group of outlaws headed by Butch Cassidy, and was involved in some train and bank robberies and was wounded in 1897 by a posse. Taken prisoner, he escaped and worked with the Sundance Kid and Harvey Logan in Nevada for a while. Curry took part in a train robbery at Wilcox Siding, Wyoming in 1899; he was finally cornered on April 17, 1900 in Castle Gate, Utah by a posse led by Sheriffs Jesse Tyler and William Preece. After a six-mile running gunfight, Curry was hit in the head with a shot from a long-range rifle. He got behind some rocks and the posse surrounded him; when there was no action, the posse crept in and discovered Curry dead, slumped against a rock with his rifle in his lap.

CURRY, KID (b. Harvey Logan in Rowan County, Kentucky c. 1875; d. Glenwood Springs, Colorado on June 8, 1904) When Kid Curry was 19, he went west with two of his brothers and a cousin and landed in Wyoming, where they became rustlers. They then started a ranch near Landusky, Montana in 1888 with some stolen cattle. During the Johnson County War they hired out as gunmen with Nate Champion's Red Sash Gang. Kid Curry's first killing took place on Christmas Eve in 1894 when he and two others were drunk and shooting up the town of Landusky, Montana, founded by Pike Landusky. Curry was the father of an illegitimate child by one of Landusky's stepdaughters, so there was no love lost between them. Curry struck Landusky, which led to a fistfight in which Curry easily beat the 55-year-old Landusky. Landusky drew his pistol, but Curry drew his and shot first, killing the old miner, who was on his knees. Curry and his friends escaped on a stolen buckboard.

Kid Curry joined the Wild Bunch and hid out in the Hole in the Wall area with Butch Cassidy. During this period he robbed trains and banks and killed sheriffs in Wyoming, Utah and Arizona, as well as Jim Winters, a Montana rancher who had killed Curry's brother five years before. Curry was always on the run from the law from his years with Cassidy's gang and sought to escape by moving to Knoxville, Tennessee. But in a saloon on December 13, 1901 he got into a fight and then a shootout. Curry was hit in the shoulder during his escape, and lawmen trailed the blood, capturing him about 30 miles away. Put on trial, he was sentenced to prison in Columbus, Ohio. But before he was transported, Curry made a small lasso from the wire on a broom; when a guard walked too close to his cell, the wire ended up around the guard's neck. Curry then tied up the guard with strips of cloth, got his keys and two pistols, used a second guard as a shield and got outside, where he stole the sheriff's horse and got out of town.

Curry reportedly attempted to join up with Butch Cassidy and the Sundance Kid in South America at this time, but was unable to make the connections, so he headed out to Colorado, where he formed another gang. On June 8, 1904, near Glenwood Springs, Colorado, Curry's gang was trapped by a posse after a train holdup near Parachute, Colorado. Wounded, Curry apparently committed suicide with his .45 behind a rock during the gun battle. He was dropped into a grave in Glenwood Springs—the lawmen did not know who he was—but he was later exhumed and identified.

CURTIS, KEN (b. Curtis Wain Gates in Lamar, Colorado on July 2, 1916; d. Fresno, California on April 28, 1991) For 11 years, Curtis was known as Deputy Festus Hagen on "Gunsmoke." A talented singer who joined the Sons of the Pioneers in 1949 (he replaced founding member Tim Spencer), Curtis stayed with the musical group until 1953. From 1945 to 1947 he appeared in musical westerns for Columbia and in 1964 replaced Dennis "Chester" Weaver on "Gunsmoke." He costarred on the NBC series "The Yellow Rose." (See also GUNSMOKE; SONS OF THE PIONEERS.)

CUSTER TV show that starred Wayne Maunder as Lieutenant Colonel George A. Custer, Slim Pickens as California Joe Milner, Peter Palmer as Sergeant James Bustard, Michael Dante as Crazy Horse, Robert F. Simon as Brigadier General Alfred Terry and Grant Woods as Captain Miles Keogh.

This show was based on the legendary George Armstrong Custer between 1868 and 1875, the year before his fatal mishap at the Little Bighorn. During this time Custer commanded the Seventh Cavalry regiment, which hunted down Indians through the use of Indian scouts from other tribes as well as by other, more conventional methods. The show premiered on September 6, 1967 on Wednesday nights on ABC. The hour-long show ended on December 27, 1967.

CUSTER, GEORGE ARMSTRONG (b. New Rumley, Ohio on December 5, 1839; died at the Little Bighorn River in Montana on June 25, 1876) General George Armstrong Custer has become the major symbol of the Indian Wars in the 1870s, a figure wrapped in legend, awe and notoriety who achieved the fame and glory he sought in a way he never dreamed it would be achieved. As the leader of the Seventh Cavalry,

Custer commanded this group of 225 men into a huge Indian encampment at the Little Bighorn River in Montana. Everyone in this group, including Custer, was killed, thrusting both Custer and this battle into national prominence.

Custer graduated at the bottom of his class at West Point and then served in the Civil War, in which he distinguished himself as a cavalry officer. He was made brevet brigadier general at the age of 23, the youngest to hold that rank since Lafayette. Later he was promoted to brevet major general, then major general of volunteers. Custer led a cavalry charge at the Battle of Gettysburg that stopped Jeb Stuart and proved decisive in the northern victory. He also led the way when Sheridan ravaged the Shenandoah Valley and played a decisive role in cutting off Lee's final retreat. General Sheridan gave him the table on which the historic surrender of the Civil War was signed in appreciation of his efforts.

When the regular army was reorganized after the Civil War, Custer was appointed captain, then lieutenant colonel, but he continued to be called "General" because of military custom and courtesy. He was placed second in command of the Seventh Cavalry, but since the colonel in charge was kept on detached service, Custer was the active commander of the Seventh from his appointment in 1866 until his death 10 years later. A strict disciplinarian who drove his men hard, Custer turned the Seventh Cavalry into the best horse soldiers on the plains.

Custer was successful as an Indian fighter, although he was also vain, relentless and sometimes cruel. He led his troops to victory when he attacked Chief Black Kettle's village in the Battle of the Washita in 1868, but during this battle Major Joel Elliot and 19 men did not return from pursuing some Indians. Custer did not bother to look for them; later their bodies were discovered about two miles away. They had fought valiantly and held off their attackers for a day—during which time Custer could have come and rescued them if he had chosen to do so. After this, Custer never commanded the loyalty of his officers.

Custer had a thirst for fame or, as he put it, wanted to "link [his] name not only to the present but to future generations." A moody man, Custer could be incredibly childish in his behavior—smashing furniture in his home—or withdrawn and prone to temper tantrums. He possessed an abundant, frenetic energy and was generally conceded to be egomaniacal and to put his personal glory above the concern for his troops or commanding officers. Custer was known for attacking without reconnoitering, so he never really knew what he was getting into. But these surprise attacks often proved effective. This recklessness led Custer to be questioned continually by his superiors, and he once was court-martialed, but General Phil Sheridan managed to override the court's verdict.

Custer led the exploration of the Black Hills on the Sioux Reservation in 1874, which led to the discovery of gold and, ultimately, the Sioux War of 1876, during which Custer was killed. In the fall of 1875 General Phil

General George Armstrong Custer

Sheridan planned a massive campaign on the northern plains against the Cheyenne and Sioux to finally defeat the Indians. The Battle of the Little Bighorn was part of this campaign. (See also LITTLE BIGHORN, BATTLE OF.)

CUTTING HORSE   A horse trained to isolate a cow or steer in a herd and separate it from the herd, an essential skill for working cattle because a good cutting horse can manipulate cattle. (See also QUARTER HORSE.)

D

DAKOTAS, THE   TV show that starred Larry Ward as Marshal Frank Rogan, Jack Elam as Deputy J. D. Smith, Chad Everett as Deputy Del Stark and Mike Greene as Deputy Vance Porter.

This short-lived show premiered on January 7, 1963 and was last telecast on September 9 of the same year, airing on ABC on Monday nights. There were only 19 hour-long episodes of "The Dakotas," whose plot consisted of four lawmen in Dakota Territory after the Civil War. One of the factors that purportedly led to ABC's dropping the show was that one of the episodes featured Deputy J. D. Smith (played by actor Jack Elam) chasing an outlaw into a church and killing him there. The hue and cry from audiences was intense, overwhelming and apparently as fatal as the shot itself.

DALLY   A roping technique in which the rope is wrapped around the saddle horn after a catch is made, as opposed to having the rope tied to the saddle horn at all times. This "dally" gives more leverage and control of the rope to ease the pressure brought from a steer pulling hard.

DALTON, BILL   (b. William Marion Dalton in Cass County, Missouri in 1866; d. near Ardmore, Oklahoma on September 25, 1895.)   Bill Dalton was never a member of the Dalton Gang, but after his brothers Bob and Grat were killed in the Coffeyville raid—and Emmett was injured—Bill returned from California and joined up with Bill Doolin and his gang, known as the "Oklahombres." Bill had some brushes with the law in the past. Bob and Grat Dalton had gone to visit Bill in California while they were fleeing the law, and Bill was arrested when Grat showed up at his house wounded after a holdup with a posse chasing him. But Bill was soon freed and remained in California until the Coffeyville raid. By this time three of his nine brothers had died violently; older brother Frank Dalton had been killed by some whiskey runners while serving as a deputy U.S. marshal.

Bill Dalton was second in command to Doolin in the Oklahombres and they committed a series of robberies in 1893 and 1894. Doolin's gang broke up in 1895, but lawmen still pursued the members. On September 25, 1895 Bill Dalton was hiding on a ranch about 25 miles from Ardmore, Oklahoma at his wife's house. A posse had surrounded him while he was on the porch playing with his crippled daughter; they yelled out to him to surrender, but Dalton reached for his Winchester. When he turned for the rifle, Deputy Marshal Loss Hart fired, and the bullet went into Dalton's back and out his heart; within moments he was dead. (See also DOOLIN, BILL.)

DALTON, EMMETT   (b. Cass County, Missouri in 1871; d. Los Angeles, California on July 13, 1937)   Emmett Dalton was part of the Dalton Gang, which raided Coffeyville, Kansas in 1892, and was the only gang member to survive. Doctors wanted to amputate Emmett's arm because of the wounds suffered in the bank robbery, but Emmett refused and gradually the arm healed. After recovering, Emmett pleaded guilty to a second-degree murder charge from the Coffeyville holdup and was sentenced to the Kansas state penitentiary to a life term but received a pardon in 1907. Emmett then married and went straight. In 1920 he moved to Los Angeles and sold real estate, appeared in some bit parts in movies and wrote a popular book, *When the Daltons Rode,* which was made into a movie. Ironically, he vigorously crusaded for law and order and prison reform until his peaceful death in 1937. (See also COFFEYVILLE RAID, THE; DALTON GANG, THE.)

DALTON, GRAT   (b. Grattan Dalton in Cass County, Missouri in 1865; d. Coffeyville, Kansas on October 5, 1892)   After spending his early years in Missouri, Kansas and Oklahoma, Grat Dalton went to California to join brothers Littleton and Bill after having to resign as a deputy U.S. marshal because of rumors of cattle rustling. In California Grat was joined by his brother Bob, and the two attempted a train robbery in February 1891. In the getaway, Grat's horse fell and the outlaw was injured; lawmen trailed the blood to Bill Dalton's home in Tulare, where Grat was hiding. Convicted and sentenced to 20 years, Grat was on a train for the penitentiary on April 1, 1891 when he managed to escape. Grat got back to Oklahoma and joined brother Bob's gang of thieves. After several holdups, the Dalton Gang attempted to rob two banks in Coffeyville, Kansas. The bloody shootout that ensued left Grat Dalton dead (See also COFFEYVILLE RAID, THE; DALTON GANG, THE .)

DALTON GANG, THE   Bob Dalton was the leader of the Dalton Gang, which terrorized the Oklahoma-Kansas area for a year and a half (1890–92) and whose members included Bob's brothers Grat and Emmett, Bill Doolin, Dick Broadwell, Black Faced Charley Bryant, William McElhanie, Bitter Creek Newcomb, Charley Pierce and Bill Powers. Eugenia Moore, who was Bob's girlfriend, worked as the gang's advance agent until she died of cancer before their infamous raid in Coffeyville.

The Dalton family had 15 children, who grew up on a farm in Missouri; the family moved to Indian Territory in 1882. Ironically, they lived within a few miles of Coffeyville for a while. Frank Dalton, an older brother of Bob's, was a deputy U.S. marshal and served under Isaac Parker, the "hanging judge." Frank was killed by some whiskey runners when Bob was a teenager. This prompted Bob, Emmett and Grat to become deputy marshals themselves, although they soon resigned amid rumors of cattle rustling by Emmett and Grat and the taking of bribes by Bob.

Bill, Littleton and Grat Dalton went to California for a while; Bob and Emmett went to New Mexico. The latter two held up a faro game there and became fugitives, so Bob hightailed it to California while Emmett headed to Oklahoma. Bob then decided to move back to Oklahoma and Kansas because he knew the area; he formed his outlaw band and committed four train holdups (in Wharton, Lelietta, Red Rock and Adair) before he made plans to rob two banks in Coffeyville in 1892. There the gang met its end when Bob and Grat Dalton, Dick Broadwell and Bill Powers were all killed and Emmett Dalton was wounded. (See BRYANT, BLACK FACED CHARLIE; COFFEYVILLE RAID, THE; DALTON, BILL; DALTON, EMMETT; DALTON, GRAT; DOOLIN, BILL; NEWCOMB, BITTER CREEK; PIERCE, CHARLEY.)

DANCES WITH WOLVES   Film produced by Jim Wilson and Kevin Costner; directed by Kevin Costner; screenplay by Michael Blake; music by John Barry; released in 1990 by Orion Pictures; 181 minutes in length (video form). Cast: Kevin Costner, Mary McDonnell, Graham Greene and Rodney A. Grant.

After the Civil War, a soldier is assigned to an outpost in the Far West where he meets and befriends a tribe of Indians. The story of the clash of cultures—the army versus Native Americans—is tied together by a romance between the soldier and a white woman who had been captured by the Indians and was part of their tribe. This movie won seven Academy Awards and signaled a reemergence for the western as a major Hollywood subject.

DANIEL BOONE   TV show that starred Fess Parker as Daniel Boone, Albert Salmi as Yadkin (1964–65), Ed Ames as Mingo (1964–68), Patricia Blair as Rebecca Boone, Veronica Cartwright as Jemima Boone (1964–66), Darby Hinton as Israel Boone, Dal McKennon as Cincinnatus, Robert Logan as Jericho Jones (1965–66), Don Pedro Colley as Gideon (1968–69),

Roosevelt Grier as Gabe Cooper (1969–70) and Jimmy Dean as Josh Clements (1968–70).

When Davy Crockett became a national phenomenon—but did not become a regular series—actor Fess Parker looked around for something to capitalize on his fame. He found it in Daniel Boone, who looked and acted amazingly like Davy Crockett, even though the two historical figures were quite different. The Boone series was successful, running for six seasons, and premiered on September 24, 1964 on Thursday nights on NBC. The show ended on August 27, 1970 after 165 episodes on the same network in the same time slot.

DARK COMMAND, THE   Film produced by Sol Siegel; directed by Raoul Walsh; screenplay by F. Hugh Herbert, Grover Jones and Lionel Houser from a story by W. R. Burnett; Released by Republic in 1940; 94 minutes in length. Cast: Claire Trevor, John Wayne, Walter Pidgeon, Roy Rogers, George Hayes, Porter Hall, Margorie Main, Raymond Walburn, Trevor Bardette, Yakima Canutt, Hal Taliaferro and Glenn Strange.

This was Republic Pictures' (the home of the "B" westerns) attempt at a major "A" motion picture. Starring John Wayne, along with Republic's B western stars Roy Rogers and Gabby Hayes, the film tells the story of Civil War guerrilla leader William C. Quantrill's raid on Lawrence, Kansas in 1863 in which innocent townspeople were slaughtered. Based on the novel by W. R. Burnett, the movie is especially notable for Walter Pidgeon's portrayal of Quantrill.

DAUGHERTY, ROY   See ARKANSAS TOM JONES.

DAVY CROCKETT: KING OF THE WILD FRONTIER   TV show that starred Fess Parker as Davy Crockett, Buddy Ebsen as Georgie Russell and Jeff York as Mike Fink.

The Davy Crockett series was part of "Walt Disney Presents," which consisted of a rotating series of shows from Tomorrowland, Fantasyland, Adventureland and Frontierland, introduced by Walt Disney. The original Crockett shows were "Davy Crockett, Indian Fighter," on December 15, 1954, "Davy Crockett Goes to Congress," on January 26, 1955, and "Davy Crockett at the Alamo," on February 23, 1955. This series spawned a Crockett-mania that swept the nation and resulted in Crockett merchandise and a number one hit song, "Ballad of Davy Crockett." (There were several versions of that song, including one sung by the series star, Fess Parker.) The Crockett series never spawned a regular series, in large part because Crockett was killed at the Alamo, and the Disney group had produced that show as part of the original trilogy. However, they did go back and film some more Crockett shows about his earlier adventures, including his encounter with legendary riverboat helmsman Mike Fink. In the 1980s the Disney group filmed some new Davy Crockett shows with Tim Dunigan starring as Crockett and Gary Grubbs as Georgie Russell.

DEAD MAN'S HAND   A poker hand with aces and eights, which is what Wild Bill Hickok was holding when he was killed in Deadwood by Jack McCall, who shot him in the back.

DEADWOOD, SOUTH DAKOTA   Deadwood is the town where Wild Bill Hickok was killed and also where Calamity Jane lived, tending to those during a smallpox epidemic. It was laid out in April 1876 in Deadwood Gulch after gold was discovered in the Black Hills. A mining town whose soaring slopes hemmed in growth, it nevertheless had a population of 25,000 a year after it was founded. Wyatt Earp, Poker Alice, Sam Bass, Doc Holliday, Calamity Jane and Wild Bill Hickok all went to Deadwood. The town nearly perished in fire in 1879, and in 1883, floods carried away over half its buildings. The town is now a popular tourist attraction, with the Adams Museum the site of Wild Bill's last card game and the graves of Hickok and Calamity Jane duly marked in the Mount Moriah Cemetery.

DEADWOOD DICK   (alias of Richard Clarke; b. Waterford, Ireland c. 1848 or Hansborough, England c. 1845; d. near Deadwood, South Dakota c. May 10, 1930)   Deadwood Dick was actually a fictional character created by dime novelists in the late 19th century, but because a number of other dime novel characters (Buffalo Bill, Wild Bill Hickok, Buck Taylor and Calamity Jane, for example) were based on real people, it was often assumed Deadwood Dick was a real person; thus a number of people claimed to be "Deadwood Dick" through the years. During the 1920s the Deadwood Chamber of Commerce began to sponsor "Days of '76" parades and celebrations to commemorate the 1876 gold rush and attract new attention and business to the area. Richard Clarke, who had come to the Black Hills during the 1876 gold rush, rode in the parade as "Deadwood Dick." In 1927 Clarke was sent to Washington, D.C. as a publicity gimmick to invite President Calvin Coolidge to Deadwood; this led Clarke to take himself seriously as "Deadwood Dick," and he began to make up stories about himself. The Chamber of Commerce indulged Clarke and built a cabin for him where he greeted visitors.

DEADWOOD STAGE   The Deadwood Stage was a Concord stagecoach that became famous during the Wild West shows of Buffalo Bill. During these shows, the Deadwood Stage would be attacked by Indians, and Cody would then ride to the rescue on a white horse. Cody bought authentic Deadwood Stagecoaches for his shows; these stagecoaches originally ran between Deadwood, South Dakota and Cheyenne, Wyoming.

DEAN, EDDIE   (b. Eddie Dean Glossup in Posey, Texas in 1910)   Dean received fame as a singing cowboy; he was a talented singer and composer (he wrote "One Has My Name, the Other Has My Heart") and began his career in 1930 on radio in Tulsa, later joining the "National Barn Dance" on WLS in Chicago. His first major movie was *The Harmony Trail* (1944), and between 1945 and 1948 he made 18 films; in the 1960s he appeared on "The Beverly Hillbillies." (See also SINGING COWBOYS.)

Buffalo Bill and the Deadwood Stage   *(Western Archives)*

DEATH VALLEY   The hottest, lowest and driest place in North America, Death Valley is a desert surrounded by mountains in California on the Nevada border. It was named by a group of emigrants in 1849 who crossed it as a shortcut to California; they suffered terribly, and 13 of their members died. A number of mines and ghost towns are in Death Valley, a result of some minerals being found. But the biggest "treasure" there was borax. The Death Valley National Monument was established in 1933 and covers about 3,000 miles.

DEATH VALLEY DAYS   TV show hosted by Stanley (the "Old Ranger") Andrews (1952–65), Ronald Reagan (1965–66), Robert Taylor (1966–68), Dale Robertson (1968–72) and Merle Haggard (1975).

There were 558 episodes of this 30-minute show produced from 1952 to 1975. The show began as a radio series in the 1930s and ran until 1945. It was created by Ruth Woodman, a New York advertising agency scriptwriter, to promote one of the agency's clients, the Borax Company. The show featured the famous opening of a bugle call and then the mule team hauling the borax wagons out of the desert. The homey commercials were done by Rosemary DeCamp. Interestingly, Woodman had never seen Death Valley when she began writing the radio scripts, but she later made a number of trips to

Eddie Dean

the area, uncovering Wash Cahill, a grizzled desert rat who served as her guide and spun numerous yarns about the place and its people. Woodman insisted that every script was based on some fact about the area and the show was indeed a series of vignettes. There was no regular cast or story line; instead, the unifying character was the host, Stanley Andrews, known as the "Old Ranger," who introduced each week's story. Andrews was replaced after 13 years by Ronald Reagan, who quit as host after being elected governor of California. Hosts that followed were Robert Taylor, Dale Robertson and country singer Merle Haggard, who hosted the final year of filming, 1975. The show, which was never a network production, has been repackaged and syndicated under a number of titles with a variety of hosts. Some examples are "Call of the West" with host John Payne; "Frontier Adventure" with host Dale Robertson; "The Pioneers" with host Will Rogers, Jr.; "Trails West" with host Ray Milland; and "Western Star Theatre" with host Rory Calhoun. Interestingly, the show featured performances from a wide variety of actors and actresses, such as Fess Parker, Clint Eastwood, Rory Calhoun, Jane Russell, Guy Madison, Don Barry, Hank Worden, Roy Barcroft, Harry Lauter, Jim Davis, Gloria Talbott, Richard Anderson, William Smith, Rudy Vallee, Richard Simmons, Mary Murphy and Ronald Reagan.

DEATH VALLEY SCOTTY   (b. Walter Edward Scott near Cynthiana, Kentucky on September 20, 1872; d. January 5, 1954)   Death Valley Scotty was one of the all-time great con men of the West. At 14 he ran away to Wells, Nevada and joined his two brothers, who were cowboys. Scotty learned to ride broncs and toured with Buffalo Bill's Wild West show during the 1890s, where he learned to be a huckster. Scotty came to fame in 1905 when he chartered a three-car train from the Santa Fe Railroad for a 2,265-mile run between Los Angeles and Chicago; he made it in 44 hours and 54 minutes. He conned financiers Albert M. Johnson, Julian Gerard and E. Burdon Gaylord repeatedly; the result was a $2.5 million "castle" in Death Valley, which is now a major tourist attraction. Scott regularly went to Death Valley during the winter months, when the Buffalo Bill show wasn't playing, and prospected, although he usually came home empty handed. Still, he used his "experience" as a prospector to con eastern financiers into staking him money in exchange for a portion of his findings.

DEER   There are two basic kinds of deer in the West: the white-tailed deer *(Odocoileus virginianus)*, which grows to about 230 pounds, and the black-tailed *(O. hermionus)* or mule deer (so named because of its large ears), which can grow up to 400 pounds. Indians used every part of a deer; hunters liked the meat and the buckskin made from the deer's hide, and settlers used deer fat for candles and soap.

DELANEY, ARTHUR   See MCCLUSKIE, MIKE.

DELLA ROSE   See BULLION, LAURA.

DENVER, COLORADO   Located where the Great Plains meet the Rocky Mountains, the town began when William Green Russell found gold near the mouth of Cherry Creek and the South Platte River in 1858. It became a major center for outfitting miners and by 1870 had 5,000 inhabitants. It also created its own mint for 10- and 20-dollar gold pieces. Denver became a major cultural center of the Old West, partly a result of the Tabor Grand Opera House and Windsor Hotel, built by mining king Horace Tabor.

Fueled by exaggerated reports of the find, the "fifty-niners" created a gold rush to the area in 1859 and set up crude log huts and tents to await the spring thaw. Entrepreneurs and town promoters then moved into the area to establish towns; many sites were promoted but a few survived, including Denver, Colorado City, Central City, Golden and Boulder. Named after the territorial governor of Kansas, General James Denver, this town first became the county seat of Arapahoe County and then merged with Auraria, its rival located on the other side of Cherry Creek, in 1860. The chief architects of this merger were promoter William Larimer and printer William Byers, who founded the *Rocky Mountain News* in 1859. Colorado was accorded territorial status in 1861, and Byers promoted the town in his newspaper, telling one and all that the land was excellent for farming. More settlers came to Colorado after the Homestead Act. The key to Denver's survival was the railroad: If it came to their town, it would survive; if it bypassed it, the town would die. The Union Pacific elected to go to Cheyenne, Wyoming, and some speculators moved out; however, some power brokers built a railroad line, the Denver Pacific, to Wyoming to connect to the Union Pacific. This line was completed in 1870, about the same time the Kansas Pacific completed its line to Denver. Once the town was connected to the east and north, promoters then constructed a line to the southwest to Pueblo, which was completed in 1872 and gave the city access to coalfields there.

Because businessmen were so successful in getting railroads to connect the town, the area began to dominate the finance and commerce of the region. In the 1870s and 1880s, when the mining industry discovered valuable ore in the Rockies, the city took advantage of its propitious location.

Denver was voted the state capital of Colorado in 1881, and in 1890 the population was about 100,000, or about a fourth of the population in Colorado.

DEPUTY, THE
TV show that starred Henry Fonda as Marshal Simon Fry, Allen Case as Clay McCord, Wallace Ford as Marshal Herk Lamson (1959–60), Betty Lou Keim as Fran McCord (1959–60) and Read Morgan as Sergeant Hapgood Tasker (1960–61).

Simon Fry, played by movie actor Henry Fonda, was the Arizona territorial marshal based in Silver City. The basic conflicts in the series occurred between Fry, who was quick to use a gun for justice, and storekeeper Clay McCord, who did not like gunplay (although he was sometimes forced to use a gun to enforce justice), and between the young people in the town, who wanted a settled law-and-order town, and the old timers, who liked the wild and woolly days. It was considered a real coup to get Henry Fonda on television, although there were some drawbacks. Fonda narrated all the shows, but after the first season he only appeared sporadically because of other commitments—much to the disappointment of the audience. After two seasons the show was discontinued because of Fonda's movie commitments. "The Deputy" premiered on September 12, 1959 on Saturday nights on NBC. The half-hour series remained in that time slot during its entire two-year run, which ended September 16, 1961 after 76 black-and-white episodes.

DERRINGER
Also spelled "deringer," a small pocket pistol first developed by Henry J. Deringer, Jr. (1786–1868) in 1825. After this small pistol appeared, a number of other gun manufacturers, including Colt and Remington, produced small pocket pistols, called "derringers." These pistols were anywhere from three and three-fourth inches to six inches long and deadly only at very short range. They were easy to conceal, which made them the weapon of choice for gamblers and women. The major problem with the derringer was its inaccuracy at anything but the closest range and sometimes its unreliability.

DESERTS
There are four major deserts in the United States: the Great Basin, the Mojave, the Sonoran and the Chihauhuan. The first is a cold desert, whereas the rest are warm. The Great Basin Desert covers most of Nevada and Utah; it extends northward to southern Idaho and southeastern Oregon and southward to southern California and western Arizona and even into Mexico. Rainfall there is four to eight inches a year, and sagebrush dominates the plant life. The Mojave Desert is almost totally in California; the Sonoran Desert includes the upper Gulf of California from Baja into southwestern Arizona, and the Chihuahuan Desert extends from Mexico northward into parts of New Mexico and west Texas.

DESTRY
TV show that starred John Gavin as Harrison Destry.

Destry's humor came out of his challenge to the macho stereotype of western heroes; instead of standing up to trouble like a real man, Harrison Destry looked for ways out. Harrison was the son of legendary lawman Tom Destry, who originally appeared in the Max Brand novel *"Destry Rides Again."* He was then a character in the movies played by Tom Mix, James Stewart and Audie Murphy, and on Broadway, played by Andy Griffith. The series was brief—only 13 episodes—and began on February 14, 1964 on Friday evenings on ABC. The hour-long show ended its run on September 11, 1964.

DESTRY RIDES AGAIN
Film directed by George Marshall; screenplay by Felix Jackson, Gertrude Purcell and Harry Myers from the book by Max Brand; released in 1939 by Universal; 94 minutes in length. Cast: Marlene Dietrich, James Stewart, Charles Winninger, Mischa Auer and Brian Donleavy.

There are several versions of this movie. The 1932 movie starred Tom Mix, but the 1939 version is considered the classic. It was made again in 1955 as simply *Destry.* With this story, Hollywood added sex and humor to the western. Frenchy is a saloon girl whose headquarters is the Last Chance Saloon in Bottleneck. She spends her time destroying men and hires a drunk sheriff to run the town. Thomas J. Destry, Jr. is the antithesis of the hardened cowboy; he orders a glass of milk at the Last Chance. The 1932 version was released by Universal (61 minutes)and directed by Ben Stoloff, with screenplay by Richard Schayer and Isadore Bernstein. In addition to Tom Mix, the cast included Claudia Dell, Zasu Pitts, Stanley Fields, Earle Fox, Francis Ford, John Ince and Tony (Mix's horse), Jr. The 1955 version was released by Universal-International (95 minutes) and directed by George Marshall, with screenplay by Felix Jackson, Edmund H. North and D. D. Beauchamp. The cast included Audie Murphy, Mari Blanchard, Lyle Bettger, Lori Nelson, Thomas Mitchell, Edgar Buchanan, Wallace Ford, Alan Hale, Jr., Lee Aaker and Trevor Bardette.

DEVINE, ANDY
(aka "Jingles"; b. Flagstaff, Arizona on October 7, 1905; d. Ventura, California on February 18, 1976)   The TV audiences remember Andy Devine as Wild Bill Hickok's sidekick with the famous line "Hey, Wild Bill, wait for me" in his high-pitched voice, a result of a childhood accident when he

Andy Devine

put a curtain rod down his throat. Devine was a big man (over 300 pounds) who played professional football briefly after he attended Santa Clara University. Devine first appeared as an extra in *The Collegians* (1927), and his first role in a sound movie was *Law and Order* (1932). Beginning in 1930 he was with Universal for 17 years; in *Stagecoach* (1939) he was the stagecoach driver. In 1947 Devine went to Republic, where he starred as "Cookie Bullfincher," the sidekick for Roy Rogers in nine films. The "Wild Bill Hickok" series made Devine a wealthy man because he received 10% of the profits as well as $250 per episode. Devine starred in "Andy's Gang" on NBC beginning in 1955 after the death of Smilin' Ed McConnell (the show was originally titled "Smilin' Ed's Gang"). Devine was in *The Man Who Shot Liberty Valance* (1962) and appeared in the "Flipper" TV series (1964–65); he was also mayor of Van Nuys, California for 17 years. (See also ADVENTURES OF WILD BILL HICKOK, THE.)

DE MORES, MARQUIS   See MARQUIS DE MORES.

DIAMOND DICK   (b. Ernest St. Leon; d. Texas in 1891) Named "Diamond Dick" because of the diamonds he wore, this Texas Ranger was dismissed from that force because of his drinking but was later reinstated after a successful undercover operation in which St. Leon posed as an ore thief. Assisted by Rangers John

Hughes and Lon Oden, Diamond Dick cut down the three real thieves in a gunfight at a mine shaft. In 1891 St. Leon had arrested three cowboys but then turned them loose and repaired to a saloon with the trio for a drink. But a gunfight erupted, and Diamond Dick died the next day from his wounds. (See also HUGHES, JOHN REYNOLDS.)

DICK POWELL'S ZANE GREY THEATER   TV show hosted by and starring Dick Powell.

Western author Zane Grey's stories were adapted for the early shows in this series; later, other authors' works were used. Dick Powell served as host and occasionally acted in some of the shows. The shows featured a who's who of Hollywood as top-name actors and actresses appeared in episodes. The show premiered on October 5, 1956 on CBS on Friday evenings. It moved to Thursdays in October 1958, where it remained until its final telecast on September 20, 1962. There were 145 episodes of the half-hour show, and for the last season all the shows were reruns.

DIME NOVELS   These were the short (about 30,000 words) adventure books that appeared weekly during the 19th century. Intended to be mass entertainment, these series included westerns, mysteries, science fiction and other adventure narratives; there were actually more than 30 different series. The "dime novel" was the brainchild of Erastus Beadle, who launched this series in June 1860; he had moved from Buffalo to New York City in 1858 and patterned his series (published in an orange cover) after another series of adventure tales published since 1844 in Boston. About five million copies of Beadle's dime novels were sold from 1860 to 1865. The firm (Beadle and Adams) employed writers who wrote a novel in about three days, and the books were edited by Orville J. Victor. It was the dime novel that introduced Buffalo Bill, Calamity Jane, Deadwood Dick and Hurricane Nell to the American book public. Among the more successful dime novelists were Ned Buntline (who "created" Buffalo Bill), Prentiss Ingraham (who wrote over 600 novels) and Edward L. Wheeler (who "created" Deadwood Dick, Hurricane Nell and Calamity Jane). The inspiration for these stories and characters was James Fenimore Cooper's novels as well as southwestern humor. These books, published in the East, were important to the history of the West because they made the western experience a grand adventure, inspired many easterners to move west and were the first step in creating the "myth" of the West by providing glamour and excitement to the western experience and making heroes out of western characters.

DIRTY SALLY   TV show that starred Jeanette Nolan as Sally Fergus and Dack Rambo as Cyrus Pike.

In a wagon pulled by her trusty mule, Worthless, crusty old hard-drinking Sally made her way west toward the California gold fields with young ex-gunfighter Cyrus Pike. The half-hour show's run was brief: from January 11 to July 19, 1974 on CBS on Fridays.

DIXON, BILLY   (b. Ohio County, West Virginia on

September 25, 1850; d. Texline, Texas on March 9, 1913)   Billy Dixon is most famous for firing his Sharps buffalo rifle at an Indian about a mile away and knocking the man off his horse during the June 1874 Battle of Adobe Walls. Dixon was also involved in the Buffalo Wallow Fight on September 12, 1874 with five others in Hemphill County, Texas. The group was saved when a flash flood filled up the wallow with much-needed water and temporarily drove off the Indians. Dixon managed to rescue the group from 125 Kiowa and Comanche Indians when he found an army supply group, but they only allowed a surgeon to help bandage the wounded. Finally, around midnight, a trumpet signaled a relief force of soldiers as the men's ammunition was running out. Dixon served as an army scout until 1883 and then homesteaded a claim in Hutchison County, Texas, where he became the first sheriff of that county. Dixon later wrote a book—dictated to his wife—about his life that was published after his death.

DOAN'S STORE   This was the general store located on the Texas side of the Red River owned by Judge C. F. Doan and his nephew Corvin on the Western Cattle Trail. This store served as an important stopping point for cattle drives going north. Here, cowboys could purchase equipment, clothing, bedding, food, guns and whiskey.

DOBIE, J. FRANK   (b. James Frank Dobie in Live Oak County, Texas on September 26, 1888; d. Austin, Texas on September 18, 1964)   J. Frank Dobie was a University of Texas professor who published some of the most important works in western history, including *A Vaquero of the Brush Country* (1929), *Apache Gold and Yaqui Silver* (1939), *The Longhorns* (1941), *The Mustangs* (1952), *Up the Trail from Texas* (1955) and *Cow People* (1964). Dobie was a teacher and principal of public schools in Alpine, Texas and managed a ranch in southwest Texas before he became head of the English department at Oklahoma A&M from 1923 to 1925. He then rejoined the University of Texas, where he stayed until his retirement, serving as visiting professor of American history at Cambridge (England) in 1943–44. Dobie was known for going out among the cowboys to collect material, and his histories are imbued with a strong sense of fact rooted in both academic research and fieldwork.

DOC   In the Old West this could mean any man with an education and book learning. It was also applied to any medical doctor as well as most saloon pianists.

DODGE, GRENVILLE MELLEN   (b. Danvers, Massachusetts on April 12, 1831; d. Council Bluffs, Iowa on January 3, 1916)   From 1866 Dodge was the chief engineer for the Union Pacific Railroad and was responsible for laying the track for the eastern segment of the first transcontinental railroad. Dodge did his job well; his crew laid 568 miles of track in one year. Dodge established Council Bluffs, Iowa as the division point along the Union Pacific route; his home there was lavish and is now a historic landmark. Dodge loved railroads

and later became chief engineer for the Texas and Pacific, building 9,000 miles of track from 1873 to 1883. Dodge served in the Civil War for the Union and was wounded in 1854 in Atlanta; while in the Civil War he supervised bridge construction and the rebuilding of railroad track that had been destroyed in the South. Dodge served one term in Congress as a Republican (1867–69) and later in life lectured on the Civil War and wrote *How We Built the Union Pacific Railroad* (1910).

DODGE CITY   Film directed by Michael Curtiz; screenplay by Robert Buckner; released by Warner Brothers in 1939; 104 minutes in length. Cast: Errol Flynn, Olivia De Havilland, Ann Sheridan, Bruce Cabot, Frank McHugh, Alan Hale, Guinn "Big Boy" Williams, Charles Halton, Ward Bond and Monte Blue.

This is Errol Flynn's first western. It is 1866 in Kansas, and a group of businessmen led by Colonel Dodge are on their way to a new town; they engage in a race between a train and a stagecoach, and the train wins. The town grows but in 1872 is a bastion of lawlessness; then Flynn arrives and the taming of the town begins. A huge saloon brawl made this movie famous, and much stock footage is inserted. A little boy is killed during a school picnic when a street gunfight erupts, and Hatton (Flynn) decides it's time to clean up the town, marry a good woman and settle down. But then Colonel Dodge shows up and tells him that Virginia City needs his help, so the couple heads out to a new adventure. This new adventure would become *Virginia City* (Warner Brothers, 1940) and then *The Santa Fe Trail* (Warner Brothers, 1940), a trio of westerns all directed by Michael Curtiz, which starred Errol Flynn, with screenplays by Robert Buckner and music by Max Steiner.

DODGE CITY, KANSAS   Before Dodge City, located in the southwest quadrant of Kansas, became famous on the TV series "Gunsmoke," it was a well-known cattle town from which 250,000 cattle were shipped east each year from 1876 to 1886. Originally founded in the summer of 1872 about five miles from the army post of Fort Dodge, the town was built for buffalo hunters and named Buffalo City. The Atchison, Topeka and Santa Fe Railroad stopped there so buffalo hides—about 1.5 million in all—could be loaded and shipped east. A boom town quickly emerged and was rechristened Dodge City. In 1876 the town had about 1,200 citizens and about 20 saloons, as well as dance halls, theaters and sporting houses. Because the quarantine line in Kansas was moved farther west, Dodge City became the major railhead for cattle driven up the trails from Texas. As a cattle town it developed a well-earned wild reputation, and such colorful figures as Wyatt Earp, Bat Masterson and Bill Tilghman lived there and served as lawmen. The heyday for Dodge City was 1877–87, when people like Doc Holliday, Belle Starr, Luke Short, Wyatt Earp and Bat Masterson stayed for a while. (See also EARP, WYATT; MASTERSON, BAT; QUARANTINE LINE.)

DOGIE   Also spelled dogy or doggie, a dogie is a calf without its mother. It is sometimes called a doby.

DOG SOLDIERS   A special warrior society in the Cheyenne tribe, although for those unfamiliar with the Cheyenne, it came to refer to any Cheyenne warrior.

DOG TROT   A covered area between two small cabins that provided shade and a breezeway. It was also called a dog run.

DONNER PARTY   One of the most famous tragedies of emigrants going west involved the Donner party, a group of 89 people who headed toward California in the summer of 1846, became caught in the Sierra Nevada with an early snow and resorted to cannibalism after a number had died and before rescue parties carried out the survivors. Jacob and George Donner, two wealthy brothers, organized the group in Springfield, Illinois and used the *Emigrant's Guide to Oregon and California* by Lansford W. Hastings as their map. This map led them to abandon the Oregon Trail at Fort Bridger and head toward the San Francisco Bay. The group expected to find Hastings at Fort Bridger, but he was leading another party west when the Donner party arrived; still, the group pushed on. Perhaps the first tragedy for the Donner party was the fact that they waited for Hastings at the head of Weber Canyon for eight days, a fateful delay. Then the group decided to follow a different trail that proved unpassable and wasted another 18 days as they wandered south of the Great Salt Lake. Hastings had written an ill-conceived narrative; he estimated it would take two days to cross the desert, but it took the group six days. This time delay caused the group to lose most of their livestock and four wagons and abandon their valuables; two men then left the party for California to bring back food. The group was beset with constant bickering and quarreling from exhaustion. One man, John Reed, was banished from the wagon train after he stabbed a man to death; his wife and five children remained with the wagon train. On October 19 one of the men who had gone ahead came back with five mules, supplies and two Indian guides from Sutter's Fort, and on October 23 the group began to climb the Sierra Nevada. But on October 28, while the group was at a lake high in the mountains, an early winter storm struck and blocked the pass, leaving the group snowbound. The group did what they could to survive; they made tents out of wagon canvas and held on until December 16 when they sent some volunteers ahead with six days' rations to get help; it would be the beginning of a 32-day ordeal for those who remained. On Christmas night a violent snowstorm hit and four died; the survivors, desperate and out of food, ate them; then two more died and were eaten. The Indians refused to eat human flesh, so the emigrants killed and then ate them. Seven survivors came into an Indian village on January 10, 1847, setting out the alarm for help. Several rescue parties went to help the emigrants, and the first arrived on February 19 with food; they discovered 45 survivors out of the original 89 in the party.

DONNER TRAIL   The Donner Trail is the one taken by the Donner party in 1846–47 when they left the Oregon and California Trails. The trail was the ill-conceived idea of Lansford Hastings, who had written a book, *Emigrant's Guide to Oregon and California,* describing this trail, which he claimed would shorten the trip to California to 120 days and 2,100 miles. The trail followed the Oregon and California Trails, but instead of crossing north of the Great Salt Lake toward Fort Hall, the Donner Trail left Fort Bridger and went southwest through the Wasatch Range and toward the Humboldt River by traveling south of the Great Salt Lake. From the Humboldt Sink in western Nevada, the trail followed the Truckee River into the Sierra Nevada up to Donner Lake, which is where the Donner party became snowbound. From here the trail went down to the Sacramento Valley and Sutter's Fort.

DO NOT FORSAKE ME, O MY DARLING   See HIGH NOON THEME SONG.

DON'T FENCE ME IN   Song written by Cole Porter (June 9, 1891–October 15, 1964) and published by Warner Brothers in 1944.

This original lyrics to "Don't Fence Me" were written by Robert Henry Fletcher (March 13, 1885–November 20, 1972) in the fall of 1935 after he was asked by Hollywood producer Lou Brock to write some dialogue for a planned musical western, *Adios Argentina.* Fletcher was a native of Montana and had written a number of stories, poems and songs about that area. Cole Porter was assigned to do the music for the movie, and Fletcher gave him the lyrics; however, the movie was never done, and Porter offered Fletcher $250 for the rights to the song. Fletcher agreed but wanted recognition if the song was ever published. Cole Porter then rewrote the lyrics and music, and the song was sung by Roy Rogers in a movie musical, *Hollywood Canteen,* in 1944 and again the following year in his own movie named *Don't Fence Me In.* Hit recordings by Roy Rogers, Kate Smith, Bing Crosby and the Andrews Sisters followed, and the song reached number one on "Your Hit Parade." The story of Bob Fletcher was revealed by columnist Walter Winchell 20 years after the song became a hit, and Fletcher managed to receive a financial settlement from Cole Porter's representatives.

DOOLIN, BILL   (b. William M. Doolin in Johnson County, Arkansas in 1858; d. Lawson, Oklahoma on August 25, 1896)   Bill Doolin grew up on an Arkansas farm and went to Indian Territory in 1881 to work for the H-X Bar Ranch as a cowboy. He joined the Dalton Gang after a run-in with the law in 1891 in Coffeyville, Kansas. Doolin was drinking beer with a group of cowboys when two constables came up and asked who owned the beer. Doolin replied, "It's free," and invited the lawmen to partake; they informed the cowboys it was illegal to drink beer in Kansas and began to roll the barrels over to pour the beer out. Shooting ensued and the two lawmen were killed. Afraid of being blamed for the incident, Doolin joined up with the Dalton boys.

In the Coffeyville Raid, Doolin started out with the gang but did not take part; rumors say either his horse went lame on the way to the holdup or he had a quarrel with Bob Dalton over how the money was to be split, which caused him to drop out. After the Dalton Gang was wiped out in 1892, Doolin married a preacher's daughter in 1893 but soon formed his own gang, the "Oklahombres," with Bill Dalton, Charley Pierce, Red Buck (George Weightman), Little Bill Raidler, Bob Grounds, Tulsa Jack Blake, Little Dick West, Dynamite Dick (Dan Clifton), Arkansas Tom Jones (Roy Daughterty), Bitter Creek George Newcomb, Alf Sohn and Ol Yantis.

The Oklahombres spread terror from 1893 to 1895 robbing trains in Adair, Oklahoma and near Ashland, Kansas. The gang escaped a shootout in Ingalls, Oklahoma when lawmen tried to arrest them, and they fled from another posse in Dover, Oklahoma. But on August 25, 1896 in Lawson, Oklahoma, Doolin ran out of luck escaping lawmen.

Doolin had previously been caught by lawmen Chris Madsen, Heck Thomas and Bill Tilghman in Eureka Springs, Arkansas at a health resort where the outlaw had gone to get some relief from his chronic rheumatism. But Doolin managed to escape before going to jail and then went to New Mexico, where he hid out on writer Eugene Manlove Rhodes's ranch. He returned to Lawson to get his wife and son, who were staying at the farm of his father-in-law.

Doolin was walking down the road at night under a bright moon, leading his horse and carrying his Winchester, when lawman Heck Thomas, who had been tipped off, ordered him to stop. Lawmen were lying in wait on both sides of the road, and somebody's bullet knocked the rifle from Doolin's hand when he began firing. Doolin fired a few shots from his pistol before posse member Bill Dunn unloaded a shotgun at him. When the shooting stopped, there were twenty-one holes in the body of the dead Bill Doolin. (See also ARKANSAS TOM JONES; BLAKE, TULSA JACK; COFFEYVILLE RAID, THE; DALTON GANG, THE; DUNN, WILLIAM B.; DYNAMITE DICK; NEWCOMB, BITTER CREEK; PIERCE, CHARLEY; RAIDLER, LITTLE BILL; RED BUCK; THOMAS, HECK .)

DRAG The end of a herd of cattle. The cowboy who rode drag had the worst job on a trail drive because all the dust of the herd settled on him. In addition, the cowboy in this position had to look out for the calves, sick cows and others who could not keep up with the herd. Sometimes riding drag was punishment for some offense, although it was generally part of the job of driving cattle and given to the least experienced cowboy.

DRAW To "draw" (or to "clear leather" or "draw iron") is to pull a pistol out of a holster. It can also mean a gully that ran off from a canyon.

DROVER The lead drivers who moved cattle up the trails. In time the term "cowboy" replaced "drover," although this term remained popular until the 1870s; it was significant that a "drover" was a professional working cowboy and not the ranch owner.

DR. QUINN, MEDICINE WOMAN TV show starring Jane Seymour as Dr. Michaela "Mike" Quinn, Joe Lando as Byron Sully, Chad Allen as Matthew Cooper, Erika Flores as Colleen Cooper and Shawn Toovey as Brian Cooper.

This is the story of a young female medical school graduate from Boston who moves west to set up a practice in a small town. When she arrives, she adopts three young children whose mother had died and moves into a home built by Sully, whose young wife had died in childbirth. The difficulties of being a woman in the West and the primitive state of medicine in the 19th century are the central themes, with a subtle romantic thread provided by handsome Sully dressed like an Indian helping Dr. Quinn. The hour-long show premiered on January 1, 1992 and appeared on Saturday night on CBS.

DRURY, JAMES (b. New York City on April 18, 1934)   Actor James Drury starred in "The Virginian" TV series. The original pilot for this series had Drury play the Virginian as a dandy, but the idea didn't sell; four years later Drury played the role as a man's man dressed in black, and this is the character that appeared 1962–71. Drury's father was a professor at New York University; the family had a ranch in Oregon and the young man spent summers there. Drury was signed to MGM in 1954 and appeared in *Love Me Tender* with Elvis Presley, *Bernadine* with Pat Boone and *Pollyanna* with Hayley Mills; on TV he appeared in "Gunsmoke," "The

James Drury

Rebel" and "The Rifleman" before "The Virginian." After "The Virginian" series ended, Drury appeared briefly in "Firehouse" as Captain Spike Ryerson. (See also TELEVISION WESTERNS; VIRGINIAN, THE.)

DRY GULCH An ambush or surprise attack.

DUDE RANCHES Dude ranches are western ranches that accept paying guests. The Rocky Mountain states (Wyoming, Montana, Colorado, Arizona and New Mexico) form the backbone of this important western enterprise, while other western states (Idaho, Oregon, Washington, Texas, California and Nevada) have a lesser number of dude ranches.

Dude ranching grew out of western hospitality and the vacation industry. The term "dude" became popular in the 1880s and meant someone who came from somewhere other than the West. Other popular definitions of "dude" included someone who wore outlandish clothing or who was a greenhorn or a tenderfoot. But for dude ranches, sometimes known as *guest ranches,* the term simply meant a paying guest.

Ranch owners originally welcomed anyone who showed up at their door and, because most ranches were in remote areas, enjoyed the outside company. But as the ranches became popular places for Easterners to visit or vacation, the idea of hosting paying guests evolved as a way to ensure the ranchers' economic survival. Major factors in the development and growth of dude ranches were the opportunities available for hunting parties who came West, the scenic appeal of the West and the hospitality of ranchers. The ranches attracted the sons of the rich (particularly Europeans) who had no place in the family business or whom the family wanted to send into the world, as well as remittance men who had drinking problems, those who needed to "toughen up," those who were family embarrassments or those who just had the misfortune to be born late in the family. All had money coming from home and all needed a place to stay when they came West. Dude ranches filled this need.

Dude ranching originated in the states of Montana, Wyoming and Colorado. There, the appeal of hunting and fishing lured Easterners and legendary western figures such as mountain man Jim Bridger, Bill Sublette, Buffalo Bill Cody and General Philip Sheridan. Two famous guests from Europe were Lord Dunraven of Ireland, who came in 1869 and 1871, and the Grand Duke Alexis of Russia, who came in 1873. Also in 1873 Isabella Bird traveled in the West and wrote a book about her adventures, *A Lady's Life in the Rocky Mountains,* which proved popular and influential. Ten years later President Chester Arthur made a trip to Yellowstone that brought national attention to the West. But the two most influential Easterners to visit the West were Owen Wister and Theodore Roosevelt. Roosevelt came West after the death of his first wife and Wister came West for his health and stayed at a ranch owned by Major and Mrs. Frank Wolcott. Wister later used this area as the backdrop for his novel *The Virginian* (1902), which was a huge success during the same time Theodore Roosevelt was president.

The first dude ranch was run by the Eaton brothers, who were born in Pittsburgh, then moved to Medora, in Dakota Territory, where they established the Custer Trail Ranch in 1879. In 1904 the brothers moved to a ranch near Sheridan, Wyoming. The Eatons had led hunting parties and pack trips and opened their doors to all comers until they discovered one year they had provided 2,200 free meals to their guests. In 1882 the Eatons hosted their first paying guest and by 1891 paying guests were a regular business.

The access to Yellowstone National Park was a key feature in the development of dude ranches in Montana and Wyoming and a major reason this area developed first and fastest. The United States had made Yellowstone a national park in 1872 and people wanted to visit the site; the Eatons included a pack trip to Yellowstone each year for their guests.

Later, dude ranches developed in the Southwest, particularly New Mexico and Arizona, but a different kind of dude ranch developed there. First, the ranches were more likely to be called "guest ranches," the clientele tended to be older, and recreation and relaxation were stressed. The northern dude ranches were mostly working ranches and dudes became part of the family, helping with ranch work, while in the southwest the ranches tended to be resorts and guests relaxed. Swimming pools and tennis courts (and, later, golf courses) were often a part of southwestern guest ranches but seldom found on northern ranches.

The heyday for dude ranching was 1895–1929, particularly during the 1919–29 period. The problems in Europe following World War I made it unattractive to vacationing Americans. During this time, the national parks in the United States instituted an advertising campaign to "see America." Further, the roaring twenties provided the atmosphere and economic stimulus to travel to the West.

For Westerners there were reasons to attract Easterners: beef prices fell and hay prices rose, so paying guests became an economic necessity for individual ranchers. In addition, people who visited dude ranches were often enticed to buy other ranches in the area, which led to economic expansion. Finally, the cowboy as a romantic hero was at a crossroads; although the movies projected a glamorous image, ranch work by this point had become the work of farm hands—driving tractors, mending fences, baling hay. Jobs were getting scarce for cowboys, but the dude ranches provided an opportunity for employment as well as a chance to fulfill the romantic myth for cowboys who were outgoing, could rope and ride and entertain guests.

In 1926 the Dude Ranchers Association was formed, led by the efforts of A. B. Smith, passenger traffic manager of the Northern Pacific railroad. The first president of the organization was Larry Larom and the executive secretary was Joe Cahill. Railroads, in an effort to attract passengers in the West, also led in the development of other dude ranch organizations in Colorado and the Southwest. The Dude Ranchers Association engaged in active recruitment of guests with the executive secretary traveling East to meet with prospective clients. At this point, most guests came from New York, Boston, Chicago and Philadelphia, and dude ranchers kept a list of guests, visited them during the winter months back East and depended on word of mouth to attract more guests. Since ranchers preferred to think of their guests as part of the ranch and family and not just customers this personal contact was important. In 1924 it was estimated that dude ranching accounted for $12 million of the Wyoming economy. In 1936 there were 356 Dude ranches listed by the dude Ranchers Association: 114 in Montana, 95 in Wyoming, 65 in Arizona, 26 in New Mexico and 25 in Colorado. Over 90 percent of the dude ranches were in these five states, while the rest were in California, Nevada, Texas, Oregon and Canada. Ironically, one appeal of Nevada dude ranches was the state's liberal divorce laws: a person only had to be in Nevada for six weeks to qualify for a divorce and a dude ranch was a good place to spend those six weeks.

After World War II dude ranching changed a great deal. First, the automobile became the major means of transportation for dude ranching guests, replacing the railroad. The people who came to dude ranches before World War II tended to be rich and they stayed one to three months; after World War II the middle class increasingly came to dude ranches, but they came by car and stayed only one or two weeks. The post-World War II guest brought different demands: they wanted shorter vacations and more entertainment, and they wanted to rough it with a degree of comfort. These people tended to like nature but not the wilderness and, when they traveled, wanted to remain in their cars. Therefore horseback riding, the central activity for dude ranching, changed from all day or week-long trips to one- to three-hour excursions.

For dude ranchers there were also major changes after World War II as quality brochures replaced word of mouth as the major way to attract guests. Many dude ranchers found that soaring land values after World War II made ranching economically difficult; they could sell their ranches, invest their money elsewhere and make a larger profit. Cowboys found employment if they could sing, play a guitar and socialize well with guests; in short, become more like movie cowboys than ranch hands. Still, dude ranches have remained a vital and important part of the western economy and a way for those outside the West (or those living in cities in the West) to experience a taste of the Old West and life on a ranch.

DUEL IN THE SUN   Film produced by David O. Selznick; directed by King Vidor; screenplay by Oliver H. P. Garrett and David O. Selznick (from the Niven Busch novel and script); music by Dmitri Tiomkin; released in 1946 by Selznick Releasing Organization; 138 minutes in length. Cast: Jennifer Jones, Joseph Cotten, Gregory Peck, Lionel Barrymore, Lillian Gish, Walter Huston, Harry Carey, Butterfly McQueen and Orson Wells.

Called "Lust in the Dust" by its detractors and "trash" by those who found the steamy love story morally offensive, this movie concerns Senator McCanles, a dictatorial cattle baron, and his alcoholic wife and a dysfunctional family with a good son (Jesse) and a bad one (Lewt). The beautiful half-breed, Pearl Chavez, is the object of both sons' love and lust. The railroad is coming, and Senator McCanles tries to stop it. Meanwhile, there's no stopping the love story; Lewt shoots his brother and Sam Pierce, and then Lewt and Pearl shoot each other. The movie was produced by David O. Selznick as a vehicle for his wife, Jennifer Jones (Pearl), and cost over $6 million to produce and $2 million to promote. But it was worth it; by 1952 the movie had grossed $17 million.

DUNDEE AND THE CULHANE   TV show that starred John Mills as Dundee and Sean Garrison as Culhane.

British actor John Mills (later Sir John) starred as British attorney Dundee, who with his partner, the Culhane, had law offices in Sausalito, California, just across the bay from San Francisco. Their activities and adventures took them throughout the Wild West, however. The show was brief—only 13 episodes of the hour-long show were filmed—and it premiered on September 6, 1967. The show ended on December 13, 1967 in the same time slot: Wednesday nights on CBS.

DUNLAP, THREE-FINGERED JACK   (b. Jack Dunlap; d. 1900?)   Three-Fingered Jack Dunlap joined the bandit gang of Black Jack Christian and later was part of the Burt Alvord–Billy Stiles gang of train robbers. A notorious outlaw, he had been captured in 1895 but escaped. On February 15, 1900 in Fairbank, Arizona, Dunlap, George and Louis Owens, Bravo Juan Yoas and Bob Brown met to rob an incoming train at dusk. The outlaws opened fire, but express messenger Jeff Milton, who had been hit in his left arm, grabbed a shotgun and opened fire. Three-Fingered Jack was hit by 11 buckshot in his side; he collapsed while the other outlaws continued firing. Finally, the outlaws gathered up Dunlap, put him into a saddle and rode out of town, where he probably died.

DUNN, WILLIAM B.   (b. ?; d. Pawnee, Oklahoma on November 6, 1896)   Bill Dunn was in the posse that trapped outlaw Bill Doolin. Dunn himself reportedly pulled the trigger on the shotgun blast that killed Doolin. Dunn and his brothers had owned a road ranch near Ingalls, Oklahoma, and rumors abounded of solitary travelers being robbed and murdered there. Dunn also owned a meat market in Pawnee, Oklahoma, where stolen cattle were taken for disposal. Dunn had run-ins with lawman Frank Canton over these thefts, and there was bad blood between them, with Dunn vowing to kill Canton. On November 6, 1896 in Pawnee, Dunn ran into Canton on the street and immediately cursed him and then put his hand on his pistol. Canton grabbed his .45

revolver, which was tucked into his waistband, and put a slug into Dunn's forehead. (See also CANTON, FRANK; DOOLIN, BILL.)

DURHAM   A type of cattle. Cowboys out West referred to these cattle as "shorthorns." They were imported from County Durham, England to upgrade the longhorn stock. Around the 1880s the Durhams were replaced by Herefords.

DUSTY'S TRAIL   TV show that starred Bob Denver as Dusty, Forrest Tucker as Mr. Callahan, Ivor Francis as Mr. Brookhaven, Lynn Wood as Mrs. Brookhaven, Jeannine Riley as Lulu McQueen, Lori Saunders as Betsy and Bill Cort as Andy.

"Gilligan's Island" set in the West, also starring Bob Denver and the basic "Gilligan's Island" cast. The wagon train led by Dusty was lost on the prairie with a cast of characters who struggled for direction and laughs. This was a syndicated show produced and released in the fall of 1973. The half-hour series ran for 26 episodes.

DYNAMITE DICK   (b. Dan Clifton in Texas; d. near Checotah, Oklahoma on December 4, 1896)   Dynamite Dick was in Bill Doolin's gang, the "Oklahombres." He was captured with Doolin and put in jail in Guthrie, Oklahoma, where they bribed a guard in July 1896 and escaped. In a shootout with lawman Lafe Shadley, Dynamite Dick was hit in the neck and the bullet had to be cut out, which left a nasty scar. He was involved in several other shootouts—one in September 1893 in Ingalls, Oklahoma, in which he escaped from a posse, and another in May 1895 in Southwest City, Missouri while he was part of a bank robbery. Dynamite Dick was killed in Checotah, Oklahoma on Sid Williams' farm about 16 miles outside Newkirk. He was found by lawmen George Lawson and W. H. Bussey; they opened fire and knocked him out of his saddle. Dynamite Dick escaped through the brush to a cabin in the woods but was trailed by the lawmen; they got to the cabin and burst through the door, guns blazing, and finished off the outlaw. (See also DOOLIN, BILL.)

E

EAGLE   The eagle has always had spiritual or religious significance to Indians. The tail feathers of eagles were used in war bonnets of the Sioux and others. Two types of eagles are found in the United States: the bald eagle, which is primarily dark brown with white head feathers and eats fish; and the golden eagle, which is brown with a goldish tint on the feathers on its head and shoulder and eats snakes and small mammals. Both eagles have wingspans of up to seven feet. The eagle is a vulture and bird of prey.

EARMARK   A cut in the ear of cattle that is part of the brand of an outfit.

EARP, MORGAN   (b. Pella, Iowa on April 24, 1851; d. Tombstone, Arizona on March 18, 1882)   Morgan Earp joined his older brothers Jim, Virgil and Wyatt in Tombstone in early 1880. He had grown up in Iowa, gone to California with his parents in 1864 and returned east to Missouri with his brothers. He went to Wichita, Kansas, then to Deadwood and then Butte, Montana (where he killed Billy Brooks) before going to Ford County, Kansas where he served as a deputy sheriff before moving on to Tombstone in January 1880.

Morgan got a job as a shotgun guard for Wells Fargo, replacing his brother Wyatt, who had just been named a deputy sheriff. Morgan quit this job and began dealing faro in the Occidental Saloon, but when the Wells Fargo stage was held up and two men murdered, Morgan joined the posse that captured Luther King, who named Jim Crane, Harry Head and Bill Leonard as the guilty parties. This became part of the feud between the Earps and Clantons-McLaurys. Morgan was involved in the gunfight at the O.K. Corral on October 26, 1881, firing the first shot into Billy Clanton, the 19-year-old who was standing a few feet away and who had just shouted, "Don't shoot me; I don't want to fight." Clanton died from a bullet through the heart. Morgan also killed Frank McLaury with a bullet under the right ear, ending the fight. Morgan himself took a bullet in the left shoulder.

On March 18, 1882 at Campbell and Hatch's Billiard Parlor in Tombstone, Morgan and Bob Hatch were playing a game of billiards. The place was crowded on this Saturday night around 10:50 P.M., and the onlookers watched while Morgan chalked his cue. Suddenly two shots rang out; the first hit Morgan on the right side of his stomach and shattered his spinal column. That same bullet wounded one of the onlookers when it exited Morgan. Earp had been standing with his back to a glass door and did not see the gunmen, who had crept up to the rear of the pool hall and shot.

Brother Wyatt, who had narrowly missed being hit by another shot, rushed to his brother's side and, with the help of Dan Tipton and Sherman McMasters, stretched Morgan out. Three doctors looked him over but could do nothing. Morgan was then carried into a card room and

Morgan Earp

had been in a poker game. After the game, Virgil pistol-whipped Ike Clanton. The next day Virgil, Wyatt, Morgan and Doc Holliday were in the gunfight at the O.K. Corral, where Virgil was hit in his leg. Because of this gunfight, Virgil was discharged from being marshal.

On December 29, 1881 Virgil walked out of the Oriental Saloon in Tombstone around 11:30 at night and was ambushed by some assailants with shotguns. The buckshot was in his left side, back and arm; the doctor removed the buckshot and four inches of bone after Virgil forbid the amputation of his arm. After his brother Morgan was killed in March by some ambushers, Virgil and his wife went to Colton, California to bury his brother, and then they stayed with his parents. Later, he returned to Arizona to prospect for gold. In 1900 he went to Wilcox, Arizona after his brother Warren was killed, and he killed the killer. Virgil and his wife, Allie, lived in a number of mining camps until 1905, when he joined brother Wyatt in Goldfield, Nevada, where Virgil died of pneumonia. (See also GUNFIGHT AT THE O. K. CORRAL.)

EARP, WARREN   (b. Pella, Iowa on March 9, 1855; died Wilcox, Arizona on July 7, 1900)   Young Warren was living in Tombstone, gambling at the Oriental Sa-

put on a sofa. Surrounded by his brothers Wyatt, Virgil, James and Warren and the Earp women, Morgan died less than an hour after being shot, a month short of his 31st birthday. (See also EARP, WYATT; GUNFIGHT AT THE O.K. CORRAL; STILWELL, FRANK C.)

EARP, VIRGIL   (b. Hartford, Kentucky on July 18, 1843; d. Goldfield, Nevada on October 19, 1905) Virgil Earp served in the Union army with his brothers Newton and James during the Civil War. Ironically, it was reported that he was killed during the war, so his wife moved to Walla Walla, Washington with their daughter and remarried. In 1899 his daughter, Jane, finally located him in Kirkland, Arizona, and they had a happy reunion; she later buried him. After the war, he lived in Council Bluffs, Iowa, where he drove a stagecoach. He was on the police force in Dodge City in the 1870s and then moved to Prescott, Arizona before moving with his brothers to Tombstone, where he became deputy marshal. In June 1881 he was appointed marshal of Tombstone and fought at the O.K. Corral in October of that year. The gunfight occurred the day after Virgil, Ike Clanton, Tom McLaury and two other men

Virgil Earp

loon, during the time of the gunfight at the O.K. Corral but wasn't in the fight. He was at the revenge killings of Frank Stilwell and Florentino Cruz, though. In fact, Stilwell was killed in Tucson after he was spotted by the Earp party—Wyatt, Warren, Doc Holliday, Sherman Masters and Turkey Creek Jack Johnson—and cornered just moments after the train pulled out carrying Virgil and his wife to California. There are several stories of Warren's demise. One states that in 1900 Warren was drunk in a saloon in Wilcox, Arizona when he ran into Johnny Boyet. Boyet and Earp had words before; Earp challenged him to a gunfight, so Boyet drew and fired. Unfortunately, Earp had forgotten he didn't have his gun with him—it was in his hotel room—and he died from Boyet's bullet. Another story states he worked for a cattlemen's association and was killed by two rustlers. Brother Virgil reportedly went to Wilcox and killed the man who killed his brother.

EARP, WYATT (b. Wyatt Berry Stapp Earp in Monmouth, Illinois on March 19, 1848; d. Los Angeles, California on January 13, 1929) The most famous of the Earp brothers, and the only one who wasn't wounded at the famous gunfight at the O.K. Corral in Tombstone, Arizona, Wyatt Earp owes his fame and legend to several factors: (1) He outlived all his brothers, dying at the age of 80; (2) before he died, he told his life story to novelist Stuart Lake, who published *Wyatt Earp: Frontier Marshal* after Earp's death in 1929; and (3) the book was so fanciful and popular that Earp became the popular subject of movies and TV shows, and in fact, "The Life and Legend of Wyatt Earp" was one of the most popular TV shows of the 1950s. Further, Earp's version of the gunfight at the O.K. Corral was the basis of John Ford's movie *She Wore a Yellow Ribbon* (1949). However, Allie Earp, Virgil's wife and Wyatt's sister-in-law, read the book and said it was hogwash.

Wyatt Earp's life is shrouded in legend and fancy; still, he managed to spend his life roaming throughout the West and was present at some historic spots and events. He reportedly met and knew a wide variety of western legends, from Jim Bridger and Wild Bill Hickok to Bat Masterson and Doc Holliday.

He was born in Illinois and named after his father's Mexican War commander Wyatt Berry Stapp. The Earps were a close family who stuck together; they moved to Missouri, Iowa and then California before Wyatt and his brothers moved back to Missouri. Wyatt defeated his half brother Newton for town constable of Lamar, Missouri and married his first wife, who died three and a half months after their wedding.

Wyatt went to Indian Territory and became a buffalo hunter, got arrested for horse stealing and gambled quite a bit in Hays City. He was a city policeman in Wichita in 1875 but ran into some trouble. He collected fines from prostitutes but forgot to turn them in, was arrested for fighting and almost shot himself with his own gun. He finally had to leave town, so he headed for Dodge City, where he became a policeman in May 1876. That same year Wyatt and a large cowboy named Red Sweeney got in a fight over a dance hall girl; Wyatt was

Wyatt Earp *(Western Archives)*

beaten senseless. He left Dodge for a while and wandered around Texas.

Wyatt became a church deacon of the Union Church and assistant marshal of Dodge in 1878. He went to Mobeetie, Texas and then to Las Vegas, New Mexico in 1879. Late in 1879 Earp married his second wife, Mattie, and in late 1879 or very early 1880 Wyatt with brothers James and Virgil moved to Tombstone, Arizona. In 1882 Wyatt abandoned his wife; she became a prostitute for several years before committing suicide in Pinal, Arizona on July 3, 1888.

Wyatt's first job in Tombstone was as a shotgun guard for Wells Fargo before he was appointed deputy sheriff in July 1880. Meanwhile, brothers Morgan and Warren, along with Doc Holliday, moved to Tombstone.

Wyatt obtained an interest in the Oriental Saloon but continued as a deputy sheriff of Tombstone while Virgil was marshal. The other Earp brothers were deputized from time to time; one of those times was on October 26, 1881 for the gunfight at the O.K. Corral. At the gunfight, Wyatt shot Frank McLaury in the stomach and ignored Billy Claiborne's plea to not shoot.

After the O.K. Corral shootout, some ambushers wounded Virgil Earp in December and then killed brother Morgan in March. Wyatt was in on the revenge killings. The Earp faction continued to "control" Tombstone, although Wyatt and Doc Holliday were arrested several times but released on bail.

Hugh O'Brien as Wyatt Earp in "Wyatt Earp"

Angeles, where he settled down permanently, although he often visited Parker, Arizona.

In his later years in Los Angeles Wyatt Earp visited some movie sets where the silent cowboy movies were filmed, trying to interest William S. Hart in his life story. Finally, just before his death, he met his biographer, Stuart N. Lake, and the result was the posthumously published *Wyatt Earp: Frontier Marshal* (1931). Interestingly, Wyatt also visited Tombstone again during his final years—anonymously—and walked around as a tourist. In 1957 when the "Wyatt Earp" TV show was a hit, some thieves stole his tombstone. (See also EARP, MORGAN; EARP, VIRGIL; GUNFIGHT AT THE O.K. CORRAL; HOLLIDAY, DOC; MASTERSON, BAT; STILLWELL, FRANK C.)

EASTWOOD, CLINT (b. Clinton Eastwood, Jr. in San Francisco, California on May 31, 1930)   Clint Eastwood replaced John Wayne as the top western actor after Wayne's death in 1979. Eastwood also brought fame and respectability to "spaghetti westerns" with his portrayal of the "Man with No Name" in Serge Leone's trio of westerns filmed in Spain, *A Fistful of Dollars* (1964), *For a Few Dollars More* (1965) and *The Good, the Bad and the Ugly* (1966). Prior to these films, Eastwood had starred as Rowdy Yates in the television series "Rawhide" (1959–66). Educated at Los Angeles City College, Eastwood had his first film role in a Francis the Talking Mule movie, *Francis in the Navy* (1955). Other western films for Eastwood include *Ambush at Cimarron Pass* (1958), *Hang Em High* (1968), *High Plains Drifter*

After he left Tombstone, Wyatt went to California, where he married Josie, his third wife, in 1882 in San Francisco. The next year he was in Colorado, and he then joined Luke Short in Dodge City, where he was a member of the Dodge City Peace Commission. He was at the Coeur d'Alene gold rush in Idaho in 1884; there he owned some saloons and staked some mining claims and became involved in some claim-jumping activities. He spent some time in Wyoming and Texas before he returned to San Francisco, where he ran a saloon from 1886 to 1890. Then he raised thoroughbred horses in San Diego.

In 1896 Wyatt was involved in another scandal when he refereed the Bob Fitzsimmons–Tom Sharkey prizefight and was accused of throwing the fight to Sharkey. Wyatt had agreed to referee only after he was allowed to wear his gun in the ring.

Wyatt Earp went to Nome during the Alaskan gold rush and ran a saloon there from 1897 to 1901. He continued to get into scraps now and then; in Alaska he was slapped and disarmed by U.S. marshal Albert Lowe when he pulled a revolver, and in San Francisco he was beaten badly in a fistfight with prizefighter Mike Mulqueen, who was 20 years younger.

The Earps had gold fever and Wyatt was no exception; he went to the Southwest in 1901 and prospected with his wife in Nevada, opening a saloon in Tonopath. He went to Goldfield, Nevada and visited brother Virgil shortly before his brother's death; he then moved to Los

Clint Eastwood

(1973), *The Outlaw Josey Wales* (1975), *Pale Rider* (1985), and *Unforgiven* (1992), which won the Academy Award for Best Picture for 1992 and also garnered Eastwood the Best Director Oscar.

EBSEN, BUDDY   (b. Christian Rudolph Ebsen in Belleville, Illinois on April 2, 1908)   Buddy Ebsen was a cowboy sidekick for Rex Allen in 1950–51 before he became famous as Georgie Russell, Davy Crockett's sidekick in the Walt Disney movies. Ebsen later starred as Jed Clampett in "The Beverly Hillbillies" and as Barnaby Jones in the TV series of the same name.

EDWARDS, DON   (b. Boonton, New Jersey on March 20, 1939)   Edwards has preserved the traditional cowboy songs with his recordings and books. Son of a vaudeville musician, Edwards was influenced by "B" westerns and Tom Mix. In 1961 he worked as an actor, singer and stuntman at a theme park, Six Flags over Texas, settled on a ranch near Fort Worth (the Sevenshoux) and became part owner of the White Elephant Saloon. He became nationally known through his involvement in the Cowboy Poetry Gatherings in Nevada and in the West Fests organized by Michael Martin Murphey.

ELDER, KATE   See BIG-NOSE KATE.

EL DORADO   Film produced and directed by Howard Hawks; screenplay by Leigh Brackett (from the novel *The Stars in Their Courses* by Harry Brown); music by Nelson Riddle; released in 1967 by Paramount; 126 minutes in length. Cast: John Wayne, Robert Mitchum, James Caan, Charlene Holt, Paul Fix, Arthur Hunnicutt, Edward Asner and Johnny Crawford.

This movie is another version of *Rio Bravo*, with Robert Mitchum playing the role of the alcoholic that Dean Martin played in the previous film. John Wayne plays Cole Thornton, an old gunfighter with a bullet lodged near his spine. The prisoner is Ed Asner, and they have to protect the prisoner until a federal marshal can arrive.

ELFEGO BACA   See WALT DISNEY PRESENTS.

ELK   The second largest member of the deer family (the moose is largest), adult male elk *(Cervus canadensis)* can weigh from 500 to 1,000 pounds. A relative of the European red deer, this animal had been nearly exterminated by the end of the 19th century, a result of being killed for its meat, hide and for sport. The remaining members of this group migrated to the north-central Rockies. Indians used the elk's hide for tipis and clothing, its large antlers for tools and its teeth for ornaments.

ELLIOTT, WILD BILL   (b. Gordon Nance in Pattonsburgh, Missouri on October 16, 1903; d. Las Vegas on November 6, 1965)   A "B" western cowboy star, Elliott had his first starring role as Wild Bill Hickok, which gave him his nickname; later he starred as Red Ryder. Elliott got his start in rodeos and then went to Rockhurst College and Pasadena Playhouse, where he

Wild Bill Elliot

changed his name from Gordon Nance to Gordon Elliott. His first movie was *The Plastic Age* (1925), and he appeared in over 60 movies before he acted in his first western, *Trailin' West* (1936). After this movie he appeared with Gene Autry in *Boots and Saddles* (1937). In 1946 Elliott changed his billing to William Elliott; his last starring western was *The 49ers* (1954). (See also B WESTERN MOVIES; MOVIES.)

ELLSWORTH, KANSAS   Ellsworth was a major cattle town from 1871 to 1873. During this time it gained a reputation for being wild and woolly, especially the community of Nauchville, about half a mile east of town, which housed the red light district. Ellsworth was first laid out in spring 1867. At one time it had the biggest stockyard in Kansas as well as a legendary solid sidewalk made of limestone rock that was 12 feet wide and ran the length of the Texas cattlemen's favorite stopping place, the Grand Central Hotel. Ellsworth was the scene of the spectacle of Prairie Rose walking naked down the main street with a revolver in each hand for a $50 bet.

EMPIRE   TV show that starred Richard Egan as Jim Redigo, Terry Moore as Constance Garret, Anne Seymour as Lucia Garret, Ryan O'Neal as Tal Garret, Warren Vanders as Chuck Davis and Charles Bronson as Paul Moreno.

This was a contemporary western set on the half-million-acre Garret Ranch in New Mexico, a multimillion-dollar empire that included cattle, sheep, horses, crops, oil, mining and lumber. Like "Dallas" and "Dynasty" 15 years later, this show had elements of a soap opera, of the Wild West and of big business all rolled in one. The show premiered on September 25, 1962 on Tuesday evenings on NBC. In March 1964 the show moved to ABC, where it was shown on Sunday nights. The hour-long show ended on September 6, 1964, at which point it was renamed "Redigo" after the tough foreman and became a short-lived half-hour series. (See also REDIGO.)

EQUALIZER A gun, usually a pistol, that creates all men equal.

EVANS, DALE (b. Frances Octavia Smith in Uvalde, Texas on October 31, 1921) Dale Evans is the only actress to emerge as a star from "B" westerns. She was raised in Arkansas and married her childhood sweetheart at 14, but the marriage did not last long. She then began singing on radio stations, first in Memphis and then at WHAS in Louisville, Kentucky, where the program director changed her name to Dale Evans. She next went to Dallas on WFAA and then became a big-band singer with the Jay Mills and Anson Weeks Orchestra. In 1942 she was signed by Twentieth Century–Fox; she also worked on the Edgar Bergen/Charlie McCarthy Radio Show. In 1943 she signed with Republic Pictures and made her first western, *In Old Oklahoma* (1943), which starred John Wayne. Her first starring role with Roy Rogers was in *The Cowboy and the Senorita,* and the duo soon became a hot screen ticket; between 1944–1947 they made 20 films together. In 1946 Rogers's wife died after childbirth, and Roy and Dale began courting; they were married on December 31, 1947, at which time Republic removed Evans from the Rogers series and replaced her with Jane Frazee. But pressure from fans caused the studio to relent, and in 1949 she returned to star with Rogers in eight movies. From December 1951 until 1957 she starred with Roy on the Rogers TV show (along with her horse Buttermilk) and in the early 1960s costarred with Roy on a one-hour

Dale Evans

variety show. (See also ROGERS, ROY; ROY ROGERS AND DALE EVANS SHOW, THE; ROY ROGERS SHOW, THE; WOMEN IN B WESTERN MOVIES.)

EXODUSTERS These were the black settlers on an "exodus" generally from the South after the Civil War into Oklahoma and Kansas to establish settlements. The most famous leader was Benjamin "Pap" Singleton, and the most famous black settlement was Nicodemus, Kansas, established in 1877.

F

FAN A GUN A method of shooting in which the trigger of a pistol is pulled back and kept there while the other hand knocks the hammer back repeatedly. Several shots can be fired quickly like this, but they are not accurate. The technique is most effective in TV shows, cowboy movies and at short range.

FANDANGO Any kind of party or good time gather-

ing, for whatever reason, although it originally meant a fast dance.

FARGO, WILLIAM G. See WELLS, FARGO & COMPANY.

FARO This was the most popular casino game in the West. Faro was played on a table with cards affixed to it; a bettor would place a chip on top of the card he was betting (e.g., ace, six; suits did not matter). The dealer then dealt two cards from a box, and if the first card dealt was the one bet, the bettor lost; if the second card dealt was the one bet, the bettor won. If a bet was placed on a card that was not dealt, the bettor either let the bet stay or withdrew it. When a pair was drawn, the bank took half the money won. (See also GAMBLING.)

FATHER MURPHY TV show that starred Merlin Olsen as John Michael Murphy, Moses Gunn as Moses Gage, Catherine Cannon as Mae Woodward Murphy, Timothy Gibbs as Will Adams, Lisa Trusel as Lizette Winkler, Scott Mellini as Ephram Winkler, Chez Lister as Eli (1982), Charles Tyner as Howard Rodman, Ivy Bethune as Miss Tuttle, Richard Bergman as Father Joe Parker, Warren Munson as Dr. Thompson and Charles Cooper as the sheriff.

A family show created and produced by Michael Landon, this TV series featured John Michael Murphy, who ran an orphanage in Dakota Territory for children whose parents were miners blown up by the town boss. Murphy had to pretend to be a priest, hence Father Murphy, in order to keep the 25 children. During the second season at the Gold Hill School the cover was blown, and Murphy married Mae Woodward and adopted all the children. The show premiered on November 3, 1981 and was shown on Tuesday nights on NBC. The hour-long show moved to Sundays in March 1982, then back to Tuesdays in July 1982, before returning to Sundays in April 1984, where it ended its run on June 17.

FAUST, FREDERICK See BRAND, MAX.

FENCES Fences out West are all aimed at keeping others out and individual property protected as well as boundaries established. The most popular fence in the West was the barbed wire fence because it was relatively cheap, could be maintained by line riders (or fence riders) and put up quickly. There was also the rail fence (sometimes called the "snake fence" because it snaked along in a crooked line) and board fence (often painted white around large ranch houses).

FETTERMAN MASSACRE (December 21, 1866) Captain W. J. Fetterman once bragged that with 80 men he could defeat any group of Indians, an indication of the low regard he held for Indians and their fighting methods. Ironically, 80 men left Fort Phil Kearny on December 21, 1866 after a group from the fort, who had been gathering wood, was attacked by a group of Indians that included Sioux, Cheyenne and Arapaho. Fort Phil Kearny guarded the Bozeman Trail, which branched off the Oregon Trail northward through Wyoming and ended in Virginia City, Montana at gold diggings. Chief Red Cloud had vowed to defend his land, rich in buffalo, antelope and other game, which had been ceded to the Indians by the government.

The fort's commander, Colonel Henry Carrington, was better skilled at administration than fighting; indeed, he was not known for leading his men into any battles. Fort Phil Kearny was in northeastern Wyoming in the Rockies, and Carrington had overseen the build-

ing of this fort, which contained 30 buildings. The major problem with the fort was that it was several miles away from the timber needed for the buildings, stockade and fuel. So every day a small "wood train" drove out to the nearest forest, cut wood and returned. It took about an hour for the wood train to get to the timber, and it was constantly attacked by Indians, so the fort's soldiers were used to riding out to rescue the wood-gathering group and return to the fort. Captain William Fetterman, 33 years old, had joined the fort in November and quickly developed a disdain for Carrington and the defensive tactics used with the wood train. Fetterman also had special contempt for Indians, who refused to face the soldiers in battle but instead would hit and run. Fetterman wanted to attack the Indians in the area aggressively, arguing that the fort was under siege as long as Indians could hit the wood trains and then escape. Many of the Fort Phil Kearny soldiers liked this idea, which led Fetterman to brag openly that he could defeat the entire Sioux nation while ridiculing Carrington and accusing him of cowardice and timidity. Carrington did not rein Fetterman in and thus lost some control over his men.

On December 6, the Cheyenne, under Roman Nose, and the Sioux, under Red Cloud, attacked a wood train; Carrington went out to counterattack and found himself surrounded by a large number of Indians. He managed to get back to the fort and ordered his men not to chase fleeing Indians or engage in any future battles. The Indians struck again on December 19, when Red Cloud led about 2,000 warriors on another decoy attack on the wood train; Carrington made a better escape this time when Captain James Powell rescued the wood train but refused to be lured into a trap. The next day, the wood train had an especially heavy guard and came home safely. On December 21 Carrington planned for the wood train to make its final trip, gather wood and then close down operations for the winter. Ironically, Red Cloud set up his most elaborate attack and decoy trap on this date.

The Indians set their attack on some flats along a creek about five miles from the fort. The trail ran through some tall grass where Indians hid, while others waited on horses behind rocks. A group of Indian decoys were positioned to lure soldiers over Lodge Trail Ridge and into a trap where they would be surrounded.

The Indian attack occurred about 11 A.M. on a bitingly cold day; Carrington again sent Captain Powell, but Fetterman confronted him and demanded the right to lead the soldiers. Carrington should have rebuked Fetterman, but he let the insubordinate soldier leave with 48 infantry, 27 cavalry, the quartermaster and regimental armorer, and two civilian employees—a total of 80 men. Carrington ordered Fetterman in clear terms not to pursue the Indians or fight them but to help the wood train get back to the fort. But Fetterman had no intention of following Carrington's orders and quickly rode after the Sioux warriors. The Indians stopped their attack on the wood train and fled—not very fast—behind a young warrior named Crazy Horse, who led the braves in taunting the soldiers. Fetterman's troops chased them right into the trap and were quickly surrounded by 2,000 Indian warriors. A furious attack by the soldiers followed, and frantic fighting by the soldiers left some Indians dead, but the soldiers were doomed. The entire fight lasted only 15–20 minutes; Fetterman and Captain Brown apparently killed each other to avoid being captured and tortured by the Indians.

Meanwhile, back at the fort, Carrington heard the gunfire and immediately sent a 75-man force under Captain Tenedor ten Eyck, who were soon joined by another 40 men—almost the entire fighting force at the fort—who were also attacked by Indians. This force arrived after the Indians had finished killing and mutilating the soldiers under Fetterman's command and were starting their victory dance. The Indians taunted and beckoned the soldiers, who were about three miles away on a ridge overlooking the carnage, but Ten Eyck waited until the Indians left the valley and then went down to collect the dead and take them back to the fort.

Although Fetterman was considered a national hero for his foolhardy actions, army brass questioned the use of this fort in defending the Bozeman Trail, especially since a railroad was then being constructed that would make this trail obsolete. A deal was struck with Red Cloud: If the Indians would allow the railroad to go through south of this area, the army would abandon the fort. Red Cloud agreed, and on July 31, 1868 the troops pulled out of Fort Phil Kearny. The Indians immediately burned the fort to the ground, convinced that as long as it stood, the soldiers could come back, and adamant that no soldiers be allowed to have a fort in this rich hunting ground.

FIFTY-NINERS   The group who headed to Denver looking for gold in 1859. (See also GOLD RUSH, THE.)

FILLY   A young female horse, although the term was often applied to a girl or young lady.

FISHER, JOHN KING   (b. Sugar Grove Creek, Upshur County, Texas in 1854; d. San Antonio, Texas on March 11, 1884)   Fisher was known as a dandy, a gaudy dresser and a cattle rustler. He was arrested several times in San Antonio and Uvalde and supposedly killed several men. (In 1878 Fisher admitted killing seven, "not counting Mexicans.") In Eagle Pass, Texas he nailed up a sign at a crossroads: "This is King Fisher's Road—Take the other one."

Fisher got into several gunfights, the most famous occurring in 1877 on his Pendencia Ranch when some Mexicans were caught stealing a horse. One Mexican shot at Fisher, who promptly jumped off his horse onto the man, took the gun away and began to shoot; he killed three Mexicans.

Fisher got married in 1876 and fathered four daughters. Although he was arrested a number of times for murder and theft, he managed to be released because the charges were dismissed or he was found not guilty. He gradually became more law abiding and became deputy sheriff, then acting sheriff of Uvalde County.

On March 11, 1884 in San Antonio, Texas, King and Ben Thompson got off the train from Austin, rather drunk. After seeing a play at the Turner Hall Opera House, they went to the Vaudeville Variety Theater, where Thompson had killed owner Jack Harris two years earlier. In the upstairs box King and Thompson were joined by Billy Simms and Joe Foster, former partners of Harris's, and bouncer Jacob Coy. The rowdy Thompson alluded to Harris's death before putting a six-gun into Foster's mouth and cocking the hammer. Coy immediately grabbed the cylinder while Fisher backed off, saying he wanted to leave before trouble started. But a hail of gunfire erupted and Thompson was killed. King was hit 13 times in his head, chest and leg—dying on the spot—though he never drew his gun. (See also THOMPSON, BEN.)

FISHER, KATE   See Big-Nose Kate.

FISTFUL OF DOLLARS, A   Film produced by Cinecitta Studios; directed by Serge Leone; music by Ennio Morricone; filmed in Spain and Italy; released in 1967 by United Artists; 100 minutes in length. Cast: Clint Eastwood as the "Man with No Name."

A Fistful of Dollars came along when the western was in serious decline. It was made in Europe by Italian director Sergio Leone; interestingly, Leone used the moniker "Bob Robertson" so that Americans would not be put off by a foreign director. Known as a "spaghetti western" (because it was made by an Italian) and memorable because of the bleak landscapes (indicative of a moral wasteland) and the haunting scores by Ennio Morricone, this was the first of a trilogy starring Clint Eastwood (the others were *For a Few Dollars More* and *The Good, the Bad and the Ugly*). These films made Eastwood a star; prior to this movie his major fame came from playing Rowdy Yates on the TV series "Rawhide." Eastwood was not the first choice for the film; that honor belonged to Henry Fonda, but Eastwood fit the role perfectly. Starring as the Man with No Name, Eastwood works for money and for himself—nothing more or less. The plot came from Yojimbo, a Japanese film by Akira Kurosawa. The Man with No Name comes to a small town where two families are in conflict; violence and brutality follow.

FITZPATRICK, BROKEN HAND   (b. Thomas Fitzpatrick in County Caven, Ireland in 1799; d. Washington, D.C. on February 7, 1854)   Broken Hand Fitzpatrick is one of the truly great heroes of the Old West; unfortunately, he came along before dime novels were in the business of making popular mass-market heroes out of real-life westerners, so most of the public is unaware of him and his accomplishments. Born in Ireland, Fitzpatrick went to the United States around 1816; he signed up with William Ashley as a fur trapper in 1823 and soon became a legendary mountain man who trapped with Jedediah Smith, William Sublette and David Jackson. In 1830, with four others, he purchased the Rocky Mountain Fur Company and became head of that new organization; in 1836 this firm sold out to the American Fur Company. Fitzpatrick was in the fur trade until 1841 and was in the Battle of Pierre's Hole (July 18, 1832). He was sometimes referred to as

Thomas "Broken Hand" Fitzpatrick *(Library of Congress)*

"White Hair" because his hair turned gray in 1832 when he narrowly escaped from the Gros Ventres Indians. In 1841 Fitzpatrick guided a wagon train over the Oregon Trail from Fort Laramie to Fort Hall, and in 1843 he served as guide for John Charles Fremont's second expedition. He served as guide to Stephen Watts Kearny in 1845 during events that led to the Mexican War and, after his position was taken over by Kit Carson, was dispatched to Washington, D.C. Fitzpatrick impressed Washington politicians and became Indian agent for the Upper Platte and Arkansas Rivers; he recommended the construction of Fort Laramie, Fort Hall and others and was instrumental in the organization of the great Fort Laramie Treaty conference of 1851, at which Arapaho, Cheyenne, Shoshoni, and Sioux all met and established the format for Indian-white relations on the Great Plains. Later, he took a delegation of Indians to Washington. Fitzpatrick got his nickname because his left hand was crippled as a result of an accident with a gun. Fitzpatrick died in Washington, D.C. of pneumonia while there on business related to Indian matters.

FIVE CIVILIZED TRIBES   This is an Indian confederacy, created in 1843, of the Cherokee, Creek, Choctaw, Chickasaw and Seminole, who originally lived in the southeastern United States and who actively traded with white settlers. These tribes became agricultural, and many owned slaves before the Civil War, but the tribes were removed to Indian Territory with the Indian Removal Act (1830). The headquarters for the tribes is Tahlequah, Oklahoma.

FLANK   Also called flank riders, the cowboys on a cattle drive who are stationed about two-thirds from the front of the herd. These cowboys ride between the "swing" riders and the "drag," who ride at the end of the herd.

FLATT, GEORGE W.   (b. Tennessee in 1852 or 1853; d. Caldwell, Kansas on June 19, 1880)   George Flatt established quite a reputation in Caldwell as a gunman, first on July 7, 1879 when, as a member of a posse, he encountered cowboys George Wood and Jake Adams in the Occidental Saloon. Wood and Adams were drunk and shooting up the town when they were confronted by some lawmen and a posse. Wood and Adams pointed their guns at the lawmen, but Flatt stepped forward; the cowboys shot at him but missed. Flatt then drew his pistols and shot Wood, killing him with a bullet that clipped the end off Flatt's forefinger, took out the trigger of his gun and then went through both of Wood's lungs before coming out under his right shoulder blade. He then hit Adams with a bullet in the right side and watched as Deputy John Wilson finished off the outlaw with two more shots.

Around 1 A.M. on June 19, 1880 after a Saturday night filled with drunken carousing, Flatt was headed toward Louis Segerman's restaurant to eat. On his way to the restaurant, Flatt was hit by a blast in the base of his skull that severed his spinal cord. As he lay dead in the street, three more slugs were pumped into his body. Nobody was ever convicted of the killing, although Flatt's former business partners, Frank Hunt and William Horseman, were always suspected. Four days after Flatt's death, his wife gave birth to a baby son. (See also HUNT, J. FRANK.)

FLICKERBOB   Part of the brand of an animal in which the same mark is made on both sides of the ears.

FONDA, HENRY   (b. Henry Jaynes Fonda in Grand Island, Nebraska on May 16, 1905; d. Los Angeles, California on August 12, 1982)   Henry Fonda was a versatile actor whose image extends beyond westerns; still, he made a number of memorable westerns, including *The Trail of the Lonesome Pine* (1936), *Drums along the Mohawk* (1939), *Jesse James* (1939), *The Return of Frank James* (1940), *The Ox-Bow Incident* (1943), *My Darling Clementine* (1946), *Fort Apache* (1948), *The Tin Star* (1957), *How the West Was Won* (1962), *Firecreek* (1968), *Once upon a Time in the West* (1969), *The Cheyenne Social Club* (1970) and *Wanda Nevada* (1979). In westerns Fonda generally played good characters who had integrity, even when they were on the wrong side of the law. But in Sergio Leone's *Once upon a Time in the West* he gunned down nine-year-olds with relish. Fonda began acting in his native Nebraska and then moved to New York in 1928. He made his Broadway debut the following year but did not star in a hit until *The Farmer Takes a Wife*, which also became his first film role. He began an association with director John Ford in 1939 that led to some memorable performances in westerns. Fonda also starred in a TV series, "The Deputy."

FOR A FEW DOLLARS MORE   Film produced by Alberto Grimaldi and Arturo Gonzales; directed by Sergio Leone; screenplay by Sergio Leone and Luciano Vincenzoni; music by Ennio Morricone; based on the movie *Sanjuro* by Akira Kurosawa; released in 1967 (in the United States; 1965 in Europe) by United Artists; 130 minutes in length. Cast: Clint Eastwood, Lee Van Cleef, Gian Maria Volonte and Jose Egger.

This is a story of two bounty hunters who kill for money. The sequel to *A Fistful of Dollars* stars Eastwood again as well as Lee Van Cleef. The two are merciless as they track the same bounty; they don't trust each other but eventually work together to kill their prey.

FORD, BOB   (b. Robert Ford in Virginia in 1861; d. Creede, Colorado on June 8, 1892)   The "dirty little coward who shot Mr. Howard" is Bob Ford, who shot the notorious outlaw Jesse James (aka Thomas Howard) on April 3, 1882 in St. Joseph, Missouri.

Ford became involved with the James Gang through his brother, Charlie, who was a member of the gang. In January 1882 Ford killed Wood Hite, a member of the James Gang, during an argument at breakfast. That

Glenn Ford

same month, Ford met with Missouri governor T. T. Crittendon, who promised a $10,000 reward and full pardon if Jesse James was killed. With that, Bob persuaded his brother to get him into the gang.

The gang was at Jesse's home on a Monday morning. James complained of the heat, took off his coat and guns and climbed into a chair to straighten a picture on the wall. With that, both brothers drew their pistols, and from about four feet away, Bob put a bullet into the back of the outlaw's head, killing him.

The public viewed the Ford brothers with contempt and distaste, causing Charlie to commit suicide in 1884. But Bob went on a stage tour, telling audiences how he killed Jesse James; he was generally met with boos. He spent two years in P. T. Barnum's freak show before moving to Las Vegas, New Mexico and buying a saloon. When that deal went bad, he moved to Creede, Colorado, where he opened another saloon.

On June 8, 1892 in Creede, Ford accused Ed O. Kelly of stealing his diamond ring; Kelly came into Ford's saloon with a shotgun and killed Ford with a blast. (See also HITE, WOOD; JAMES, JESSE; KELLY, ED O.)

FORD, GLENN   (b. Gwyllyn Samuel Newton in Quebec, Canada on May 1, 1916)   Glenn Ford took his stage name from Glenford, a town in Canada. His wealthy family moved to southern California when Ford was a child, and he grew up in Santa Monica. Ford was signed to Columbia before World War II and then joined the Marine Corps during the war. He made his film

Bob Ford   *(Western Archives)*

debut in a western, *Heaven With a Barbed Wire Fence* (1939). Later he appeared in westerns such as *Go West, Young Lady* (1941), *Texas*, (1941), *The Desperadoes* (1943), *The Man From Colorado* (1948), *Lust For Gold* (1949), *The Redhead and the Cowboy* (1950), *The Man From the Alamo* (1953), *The Fastest Gun Alive* (1956), *3:10 to Yuma* (1957), *Cowboy* (1958, and *Cimarron* (1960). He starred in the TV mini series *The Sacketts* in 1979 and had his own television series, *Cade's Cove*.

FORD, JOHN (b. Sean Aloysius O'Feeney in Cape Elizabeth, Maine on February 1, 1895; d. Los Angeles, California on August 31, 1973) John Ford is the most famous and influential director of westerns in the history of Hollywood. He directed 112 movies and was the major influence on the career of John Wayne. Ford began working in films in 1914 with his brother, Francis Ford, who had moved to Hollywood to work for Universal. Since his older brother changed the Irish family name to "Ford," John did the same. Ford began directing in 1917 after working as a movie laborer, stuntman and actor; his first westerns were silents, starring Harry Carey, Sr. In 1921 Ford joined Fox, where he directed *The Iron Horse* (1924), a silent epic about the building of the railroads. The success of this movie assured Ford of a Hollywood career, and he made the shift into talking movies in the 1930s. Ford won an Oscar for Best Director in 1935 (for *The Informer*) and directed *The Grapes of Wrath* (1940), which became a classic. He also directed *Stagecoach* (1939), his first western since his silent-movie days. During World War II he worked as a filmmaker for the government; after the war he directed such hits as *My Darling Clementine* (1946) and his cavalry trilogy: *Fort Apache* (1948), *She Wore a Yellow Ribbon* (1949) and *Rio Grande* (1950). Other films he directed include *Wagonmaster* (1950), *The Searchers* (1956), *The Man Who Shot Liberty Valance* (1962), and *Cheyenne Autumn* (1964). Ford made Monument Valley famous because he filmed so many of his movies there, the first director to do so. Throughout his career he worked on a number of movies with a group of actors that included John Wayne, Ward Bond, Ben Johnson, Harry Carey, Jr. and Henry Fonda.

FORT APACHE Film produced and directed by John Ford; screenplay by Frank Nugent (from the James Warren Bellah story "Massacre"); music by Richard Hageman; released in 1948 by Argosy Pictures/RKO; 127 minutes in length. Cast: John Wayne, Henry Fonda, Shirley Temple, John Agar, Victor McLarglen, George O'Brien, Anna Lee, Dick Foran and Ward Bond.

This is the first of the cavalry trilogy made by director John Ford (the following two were *She Wore a Yellow Ribbon* [1949] and *Rio Grande* [1950]). Here Colonel Owen Thursday (Henry Fonda) is sent west to take charge of Fort Apache, where he is confronted by an undisciplined troop of soldiers who don't even wear the right dress; Thursday is a straight, by-the-book soldier and sets out to straighten up this messy outfit. Thursday goes after Indian chief Cochise as a way to gain fame and fortune, convincing Yorke (Wayne), who is friendly with the chief, to set up a talk. Thursday comes to the meeting with a cavalry troop and charges into a disaster. The movie then shifts to years later when Yorke is head of the fort and is being interviewed by newspaper reporters about Thursday's battle. A highly fictionalized version is presented to Yorke, who replies that it's all true. The Yorke at the end of the movie bears an eerie resemblance to Thursday—spit and polish and intimidating one and all with his "Any questions?" barked at the end of his statements.

FORT BRIDGER, WYOMING Built by mountain man Jim Bridger on the Green River in southwestern Wyoming, this fort was situated on the Oregon and California Trails and enabled emigrants to get rest and supplies. Bridger and his family had to flee the fort in 1853 when it was attacked by Mormons angry over Bridger's selling arms to the Indians. In 1857 Bridger led army troops against the Mormons, and the religious group burned his fort. The U.S. Army rebuilt the fort, and it was later used as a stopping point for the Pony Express and stagecoach lines.

FORT GRIFFIN-FORT DODGE TRAIL See WESTERN TRAIL, THE.

FORT LARAMIE, WYOMING This was a major fur trading post, acquired by the American Fur Company in 1826. It was built by fur traders William Sublette and Robert Campbell in 1834 and originally named Fort William, after Sublette. However, the area was generally known as "Laramie" after French trapper Jacques La Ramee, who was killed there in 1821 by Indians. In 1841 adobe buildings replaced the rotting logs, and that same year the first settlers on the Oregon Trail stopped by. This fort would remain a key stopping spot for emigrants on the Oregon Trail. In 1849 it became a large army fort, and important Indian treaties were signed there in 1851 and 1868. General George Crook used this fort in 1876 as his base of operations against the Sioux. The fort was abandoned in 1890.

FORT PHIL KEARNY, DAKOTA TERRITORY Built by the army in 1866 at the foot of the Bighorn Mountains in northern Wyoming to protect the Bozeman Trail, the fort was under the command of Colonel Henry Carrington during the Fetterman Massacre in December 1866. Carrington sent John "Portugee" Phillips out with a message to telegraph to his superiors after this massacre, and Phillips managed to ride the nearly 200 miles on a mule in a snowstorm in 18 hours. In August 1867 the Wagon Box Fight took place outside the fort when Indians attacked a wood-cutting group. Finally, in 1868 Red Cloud burned it down after signing a treaty at Fort Laramie declaring the area as a reservation for his people.

FORTS Forts were established by the United States Army as a base of operations, for trading purposes and to house troops. There was a wide variety of forts; some were enclosed by walls, but most were simply camps or barracks built at strategic sites. Indians seldom attacked forts; they preferred more isolated hit-and-run tactics. But the forts served to establish the American presence in an area and, in a sense, to "claim" the land.

FORT WORTH, TEXAS
Fort Worth was originally established in 1849 as an army fort by Major Ripley and his company of Dragoons in 1849 about 30 miles west of Dallas to protect emigrants in the new state of Texas. Named after General W. J. Worth, commander of the Department of Texas, the fort was abandoned by the army in 1853, but by this time a number of settlements had been established in the area. It was incorporated as a city in 1873, and in 1874 the Texas and Pacific Railroad reached there, making it an important shipping point for cattle.

FORTY-NINERS, THE
These are the people who headed to California from 1849 to 1852 for the first gold rush. About a quarter of a million people came to this area over a five-year period, and $200 million in gold was discovered. The forty-niners were inexperienced farmers from the eastern United States, Latinos, Chinese (about 25,000 Chinese were in San Francisco in 1852) and people with mining skills and experience from Germany, Wales, England, South America and Mexico. Before the gold rush, there were not even 14,000 Anglo-Americans and Latinos in California; by the end of 1849 there were more than 100,000 in California, and by 1852 there were 250,000.

FOUNTAIN, ALBERT JENNINGS
(b. Albert Jennings in Staten Island, New York on October 23, 1838; d. White Sands, New Mexico on February 1, 1896) A prominent but controversial politician and lawyer, Fountain had settled in California in the 1850s and became a journalist for the *Sacramento Union* in 1859. He joined the California Infantry Volunteers during the Civil War and went to New Mexico with this group; there he married Marian Perez in Mesilla and had 12 children.

Fountain organized a militia company to fight Indians after the war and was wounded in a skirmish in 1865. He became an attorney in El Paso after this and in 1868 was elected to the Texas Senate. He had a turbulent career in Texas, including a gunfight on December 7, 1870 in which he killed lawyer B. F. Williams after being seriously injured by the attorney. Judge Gaylord Judd Clarke also died in that gunfight. Fountain then moved back to Mesilla in 1875.

Fountain was a member of the New Mexico House of Representatives and was a prominent, respectable citizen at the same time he was controversial and turbulent. He was involved in a bitter power struggle with Albert B. Fall, who eventually became involved in the notorious Teapot Dome Scandal while he was secretary of the interior. In 1896 in White Sands, Fountain and his nine-year-old son were killed; their bodies disappeared, and no killers were ever found. This incident became one of the great mysteries of the Southwest and was a dangerous subject to discuss in the area for a number of years. (See also GARRETT, PAT.)

FOY, EDDIE
(b. Edwin Fitzgerald in New York City on March 9, 1856; d. Kansas City on February 16, 1928) One of the most popular entertainers on the western circuit, Foy played saloons, theaters and gambling houses as a comic song-and-dance man. Foy played a number of the rough and rowdy cattle towns, such as Dodge City, and such boom towns as Leadville, Tombstone, Butte and San Francisco. During his time Foy was probably the best-known entertainer on this circuit.

FRAZER, BUD
(b. G. A. Frazer in Fort Stockton, Texas on April 18, 1864; d. Toyah, Texas on September 14, 1896) Bud Frazer and Killin' Jim Miller had run-ins for a number of years, beginning in 1890 when Frazer was sheriff of Reeves County, Texas and Killin' Jim was one of his deputies. Miller killed a Mexican prisoner and claimed the Mexican was trying to resist arrest, but in truth the Mexican knew Miller had stolen a pair of mules. Frazer fired Miller, and the two ran against each other for sheriff in 1892. Miller lost the election but was appointed city marshal of Pecos, the county seat. On April 12, 1894 in Pecos, Miller was talking in front of a hotel when Frazer opened fire and struck him in the right arm; he then emptied his pistol into Miller's chest. Frazer walked away and was amazed to discover later that Miller had miraculously recovered.

On December 26, 1894 in Pecos, Frazer came back and ran into Miller in front of a blacksmith shop. Frazer again shot Miller twice in the chest, but Miller did not fall. Frazer was arrested and then discovered that Miller had a hidden steel breastplate that had protected him.

On September 14, 1896 in Toyah, Texas, Frazer was in a saloon at 9 A.M. playing cards. Miller looked in the doorway, saw Frazer and blasted him with a shotgun. (See also MILLER, KILLIN' JIM.)

FREE, MICKEY
(b. Santa Cruz, Sonora c. 1847; d. summer, 1915) Mickey Free was a young boy captured by the Apache, an incident that led to the arrest of Cochise—who had nothing to do with the abduction—and then to Cochise's waging war on whites. Free, son of an Irish father, John Ward, and Mexican mother, Jesus Martinez, lived with his parents as Felix Ward on their ranch in Arizona. After his capture in 1861, Free lived with the Apache until 1872, when he became an Indian scout at Fort Verde, Arizona. He lived for the next 20 years as Mickey Free, a scout, interpreter and Indian policeman. He returned to the Apache and lived with them on the Fort Apache Reservation after his discharge in 1893.

FRÉMONT, JOHN CHARLES
(b. Savannah, Georgia on January 21, 1813; d. New York City on July 13, 1890) Frémont first came to fame as the "Pathfinder" when he explored the West as part of the U.S. Topographical Corps. Beginning in 1838, when he explored between the upper Mississippi and Missouri Rivers, Frémont led five expeditions in the West. On his second expedition he teamed with legendary scout Kit Carson and charted the best course to Oregon (this became the Oregon Trail). In 1842, again with Carson, Frémont crossed the plains between the Rockies and the

Sierra Nevada; his return to St. Louis in 1844 created national news. Frémont's third trip led to his involvement in the Bear Flag Revolt in California against Mexico, and Frémont and his group played a key role in helping California defeat the Mexicans. During this revolt, Frémont served under Commodore Robert F. Stockton; but there was infighting between Stockton and Brigadier General Stephen Watts Kearny, who challenged Frémont's authority. After Stockton named Frémont governor of California, Kearny stepped in and sent him back to Washington, where he was court-martialed and dismissed from the Army. President James Polk canceled the court-martial, but Frémont resigned from the army. An ambitious politician, Frémont ran for president against James Buchanan on the newly formed Republican ticket in 1856 but lost. He became a major general in the Union army during the Civil War and was put in charge of the Department of the West but often clashed with Lincoln, so he was relieved of his command. Born to unmarried parents, Frémont was successful in large part because of his wife, Jessie Benton, whom he married on October 19, 1841. Jessie was the daughter of the powerful senator Thomas Hart Benton, who was an ardent expansionist and promoted Frémont and his exploring expeditions. Jessie helped Frémont write several books about his travels, which received wide national attention; it was these books that brought

Kit Carson to fame. After the Civil War Frémont lost his fortune in railroad schemes; because of this Congress appointed him governor of the Territory of Arizona from 1878 to 1883.

FRONTIER   TV show, a western anthology, narrated by Walter Coy.

This show attempted to depict the westward expansion of the country, with pioneer settlers facing a variety of difficulties each week. Created by producer Worthington Miner, the show is memorable from narrator Walter Coy's opening lines: "This is the West. This is the land of beginning again. This is the story of men and women facing the frontier. This is the way it happened." At the end of each show, narrator Coy closed with, "It happened that way—moving west." In addition to serving as narrator, Coy also acted in some shows. The half-hour show premiered on September 25, 1955 and ended on September 9, 1956 on Sunday nights on NBC. There were 39 episodes filmed in black and white.

FRONTIER ADVENTURE   This TV show is a rerun of the popular "Death Valley Days" with Dale Robertson serving as host. (See DEATH VALLEY DAYS.)

FRONTIER CIRCUS   TV show that starred Chill Wills as Colonel Casey Thompson, John Derek as Ben Travis and Richard Jaeckel as Tony Gentry.

The T & T Circus was a traveling troupe in the 1880s, going from town to town in the Old West. This program was yet another attempt to provide a western with a new twist for TV viewers who were saturated with westerns. The show premiered on October 5, 1961 on Thursday evenings on CBS; the half-hour show finished its run, after 26 episodes, on September 20, 1962.

FRONTIER DOCTOR   TV show that starred Rex Allen as Dr. Bill Baxter.

This was a syndicated show, filmed in 1957 and sold to individual TV stations. Legendary cowboy movie star and singer Rex Allen starred as a doctor who never carried a gun but dispensed frontier justice as well as medicine. These 39 half-hour shows were shot in black and white.

FRONTIER JUSTICE   TV show hosted by Lew Ayres (1958), Melvyn Douglas (1959) and Ralph Bellamy (1961).

This western anthology was a summer replacement for "December Bride" in 1958, "The Danny Thomas Show" in 1959 and "Dick Powell's Zane Grey Theater" in 1961. The show actually consisted of reruns of "Dick Powell's Zane Grey Theater" with different hosts during each of the summers. The show premiered on July 7, 1958 and was last telecast on September 28, 1961. In 1958 the show ran from July to September on CBS on Monday nights. During the summer of 1959 the half-hour series ran on Monday nights, and in 1961 the show was broadcast on Thursday evenings.

FRONTIER THEORY   Theory about the western frontier and the American character presented by historian Frederick Jackson Turner in 1893 at the Ameri-

John Charles Frémont   *(Library of Congress)*

can Historical Association meeting in Chicago. The paper Turner read to the group in July was titled "The Significance of the Frontier in American History" and was published in the *Proceedings* of the State Historical Society of Wisconsin in December 1893. Turner stated in his thesis that America had been defined by the frontier, which had produced a uniquely American character, helped foster democracy and developed American society by providing an "escape valve" for people who sought a brighter future. Turner's thesis presented the idea that after 1890 the United States no longer had a "frontier" within its own boundaries. (See also TURNER, FREDERICK JACKSON.)

FROST, LANE (b. Kim, Colorado on October 12, 1963; d. Cheyenne, Wyoming on July 30, 1989) Lane Frost lived a short but colorful life as a bull rider until he was killed, at the age of 25, during the Cheyenne Frontier Days rodeo. Frost only won one bull-riding championship—in 1987 with $105,697 in earnings—but he finished in the top 10 from 1984 until his death. In the annual Bull Riding Championship, Frost finished ninth in 1984, third in 1985, third in 1986 and sixth in 1988. The movie *Eight Seconds* is based on Frost's life. Frost in buried in Hugo, Oklahoma beside Freckles Brown, a great bull rider and one of Frost's heroes.

F TROOP TV show that starred Ken Berry as Captain Wilton Parmenter, Forrest Tucker as Sergeant Morgan O'Rourke, Larry Storch as Corporal Randolph Agarn, Melody Patterson as Wrangler Jane, Frank deKova as Chief Wild Eagle, Don Diamond as Crazy Cat, James Hampton as Bugler Hannibal Dobbs, Bob Steele as Trooper Duffy and Joe Brooks as Trooper Vanderbilt.

This comedy western was a slapstick look at the army at Fort Courage after the Civil War. The Hekawi Indians were in cahoots to sell tourists souvenirs while the Shugs made trouble now and then. The army was shown as either bumbling incompetents or conniving profiteers, and there were plenty of laughs. The show premiered on September 14, 1965 on ABC on Tuesday nights. In September 1966 it was moved to Thursday nights. The final telecast for the half-hour show was August 31, 1967.

FURY TV show that starred Bobby Diamond as Joey, Peter Graves as Jim Newton, William Fawcett as Pete, Roger Mobley as Packy, Tom Keene as the sheriff and Ann Robinson as Helen.

Only young Joey, son of ranch owner Jim Newton, could ride the wild mustang Fury—a key theme in the show, set at the Broken Wheel Ranch. This was a contemporary western and was never a prime-time series but rather a Saturday morning show for children. The 30-minute show began on September 15, 1955 on NBC and ran for five years, ending in 1960 after 114 episodes. Fury, 15 hands high, was a coal black stallion whose real name was Beauty. He was trained by Ralph McCutcheon and had appeared in the movies *Giant* (ridden by Elizabeth Taylor), *Lone Star* (ridden by Clark Gable) and *Johnny Guitar* (ridden by Joan Crawford). The show was filmed in black and white in Chatsworth, California at the Iverson Ranch. The show was retitled "Brave Stallion" when it was syndicated in 1959.

G

GABBY HAYES SHOW, THE TV show hosted by Gabby Hayes.

One of the very early shows in TV's history, this progam consisted of old, heavily edited western films. It was broadcast daily over NBC from June 1950 until the summer of 1952 and ran for 45 minutes just before the evening news. The show only ran in major cities and was sponsored by Quaker Oats.

GADSDEN PURCHASE The Gadsden Purchase (1853), negotiated by James Gadsden, the U.S. ambassador to Mexico, completed the continental United States and would be the next to last purchase of territory by the United States (the last was Alaska in 1867). This territory gave the United States more than 29 million acres of land between California and Texas in what became the southern part of Arizona and New Mexico.

The negotiations had been instigated in order to obtain a railroad route to the Pacific coast from the Mississippi River, necessitated by the large number of Americans in California and much of the western half of the United States after the war with Mexico and the discovery of gold in California. The deal was consummated under the administration of President Franklin Pierce and instigated by Secretary of War Jefferson Davis, who wanted a southern, rather than central, route for stagecoach mail service to the West Coast. The deal cost the United States $10 million and was signed in Mexico City on December 30, 1853 and ratified by the Senate on June 29, 1854.

GALL (b. Moreau River, South Dakota c. 1840; d. Oak Creek, South Dakota on December 5, 1894) As the chief lieutenant (and adopted brother) of Sitting

Bull, Gall, a war chief of the Hunkpapa Sioux, played a major role in the Battle of the Little Bighorn. Gall was an orphan named Pizi who tried to eat the gall of an animal carcass while scavenging for food, thus earning him his new name. After the Little Bighorn, Gall and Sitting Bull escaped to Canada but returned in 1880. After a battle with U.S. soldiers in January 1881 in Montana, Gall surrendered and lived in South Dakota on the Standing Rock Reservation. His memories of the Battle of the Little Bighorn were secured by an interview when he attended the 10th anniversary of that battle.

GALOOT   A phrase used to show derogatory affection for another person. "Hombre" is a synonym.

GAMBLING   Gambling was the most popular and favorite form of recreation for 19th century cowboys. These cowboys would bet on just about anything (this was part of the reason roping and riding contests, which developed into rodeos, began), and their favorite games on the ranch involved horse races and cards, especially poker. Games with dice were also popular. In towns, saloons generally had gambling, and popular games included keno, faro, roulette wheels and billiards as well as the old standbys of cards and dice. The horse race was always popular throughout the West, as well as any kind of sport that produced a winner and loser (boxing, shooting contests and cockfights were all popular). Professional gamblers plied their trade on riverboats and in boom towns in the West, although every major town had gambling saloons and professional gamblers. A professional rarely played it "straight" because his living depended on his wins, so there was a variety of cheating, from loaded dice, to marked cards, to gamblers working together against "marks" or unsuspecting victims. (See also FARO; KENO; MONTE.)

GARNER, JAMES   (b. Norman, Oklahoma on April 7, 1928)   For western fans, James Garner is best known as the star of the TV series "Maverick." James Garner and Bret Maverick are apparently a lot alike: suave, smooth, humorous and knowledgeable about slick deals. Garner left "Maverick" because his contract paid him only a maximum of $1,250 for each episode in the series, although the show brought in over $8 million for Warner; in addition, the studio "owned" him and controlled his other appearances, but a series of lawsuits got him out. Later, Garner starred in the ill-fated western series "Nichols" and then the hugely successful "Rockford Files." Western movies he appeared in include *Shoot-Out at Medicine Bend* (1957), *Cash McCall* (1960), *The Great Escape* (1963), *Duel at Diablo* (1966), *Hour of the Gun* (1967), *Support Your Local Sheriff* (1969), *A Man Called Sledge* (1971), *Skin Game* (1971), *Support Your Local Gunfighter* (1971), *One Little Indian* (1973) and *The Castaway Cowboy* (1974). Garner grew up in Norman, Oklahoma but left at 18 and traveled around before he was drafted into the army and served in the Korean War, for which was decorated by General Douglas MacArthur. (See also MAVERICK (TV show); NICHOLS; TELEVISION WESTERNS.)

James Garner

GARRETT, PAT   (b. Patrick Floyd Garrett in Chambers County, Alabama on June 5, 1850; d. near Las Cruces, New Mexico on February 29, 1908)   Pat Garrett is most famous for killing Billy the Kid, but that event was only part of this remarkable man's life. Pat Garrett went west in 1869 at the age of 18 and became a cowboy and then a buffalo hunter in the Texas panhandle. In 1878 he went to Fort Sumner, New Mexico, where he worked as a hog rancher and then opened a small restaurant. In January 1880 he married Apolinaria Gutierrez, and they had eight children. One child, Elizabeth, was blind; he lavished much attention on her, and she would become a close associate of Helen Keller, a popular speaker and the writer of the official New Mexico state song.

Pat Garrett knew Billy the Kid during these early days in New Mexico, as the two often gambled together; in fact, they were nicknamed Big Casino and Little Casino for their relative sizes. Billy was a major figure in the Lincoln County War, and Garrett was elected county sheriff in 1880 to restore order by capturing his former friend. By this time, Billy the Kid had formed a gang of outlaws, rustlers and fugitives.

On December 19, 1880 Garrett and a posse set a trap for the Kid and his gang; gang member Tom O'Folliard was killed but the rest escaped. Two days later, Garrett killed another gang member, Charles Bowdre, at Stinking Springs; the Kid and the rest of his gang surrendered, and Garrett put him in jail in Lincoln to await trial. But on April 28, 1881 the Kid killed two guards and blasted his way out of jail, forcing Garrett to chase him again.

On July 14, 1881 Garrett went to Fort Sumner, accompanied by Frank Poe and Tip McKinney. Garrett went into Pete Maxwell's bedroom and awakened Maxwell, asking if the Kid was around. While they were talking, Billy walked into the dark room, wanting to ask Maxwell for a key to the meat house. Billy was hatless, in his stocking feet, carrying a butcher knife with his revolver in his waistband. Billy entered Maxwell's bedroom asking, "Quien es? Quien es?" Maxwell whispered, "That's him," and Garrett pulled his pistol and sent a bullet into Billy's heart. Garrett and Maxwell then fled the room, but the Kid died where he lay. He was buried in the Fort Sumner cemetery the next morning.

Garrett told his side of the story in a biography of Billy the Kid ghostwritten by Ash Upson, a journalist. For his success in killing Billy, Garrett was not even renominated by the Republican party for sheriff and had to hire a lawyer to get the reward money.

Garrett then went into ranching, finally operating his own spread near Roswell, New Mexico. He was defeated for sheriff of Chaves County in 1890, moved to a horse ranch in Uvalde, Texas and was elected county commissioner in 1894. In 1896 he left Texas for Mexico to join in the search for Judge Albert J. Fountain's killers in the White Sands area. Garrett worked hard but the case was never resolved, and Garrett was not renominated for sheriff of Dona Ana County. Garrett opened a livery stable in Las Cruces, New Mexico before receiving an appointment to be a customs collector in El Paso; but he was refused appointment in 1905 and returned to ranching near Las Cruces.

On February 29, 1908 Garrett stopped his buggy about four miles outside Las Cruces to urinate. He had been involved in a feud with Wayne Brazel over a herd of goats grazing on a tract leased by Garrett to Brazel. Carl Adamson had offered to lease the land, and Garrett, Brazel and Adamson were all together on the buggy. As Garrett was urinating, a bullet was shot into the back of his head, coming out above the right eye. Garrett spun around and caught a second bullet in the belly and fell to the ground, dying within moments. It was widely believed that Killin' Jim Miller had ambushed Garrett, although Wayne Brazel claimed he killed Garrett in self-defense. (See also BILLY THE KID; BOWDRE, CHARLIE; FOUNTAIN, ALBERT JENNINGS; LINCOLN COUNTY WAR; MILLER, KILLIN' JIM; O'FOLLIARD, TOM .)

GENE AUTRY SHOW, THE   TV show that starred Gene Autry and Pat Buttram.

Gene Autry had been a movie hero long before television came along. His TV show premiered on July 23, 1950 on CBS on Sunday nights. It ran in this slot until July 1953, when it was switched to Tuesday; CBS switched it one more time, in September 1954 to Saturday evenings, before it ended its network run on August 7, 1956. Eighty-five episodes were filmed, all produced by Autry's own Flying A production company with sidekick Pat Buttram and trick horse Champion. The backdrops were often Pioneer Town, Lone Pine and Melody Ranch, and the theme song was Autry's own "Back in the Saddle." Since the TV show was filmed during the same time some of Autry's feature films for Columbia were made, actors Sheila Ryan, Alan Hale, Jr., Harry Lauter and Gail Davis often appeared in his TV shows.

GENERAL ELECTRIC THEATRE   TV show hosted by Ronald Reagan (1954–62) .

This anthology featured a wide variety of shows each week, including westerns such as "Saddle Tramp in the Old West" starring James Stewart and "Too Good with a Gun" starring Robert Cummings and Michael Landon. The show began on February 1, 1953 and originally ran on alternate weeks with "The Fred Waring Show." In 1954 Ronald Reagan became the host, introducing the show each week and occasionally starring in a drama. Some of the early shows were broadcast live, but later all were filmed. The show was seen on CBS on Sunday evenings. The half-hour show was last telecast on September 16, 1962.

GERONIMO   (b. Goyahkla c. 1823; d. near Fort Sill, Oklahoma on February 17, 1909)   Geronimo became famous in the 1880s when he was the last Apache to surrender to the government, leading a band of renegade Apache in the mountains of southeastern Arizona. Mexicans gave Goyahkla (One Who Yawns) the name Geronimo, or Jerome. The Mexicans also killed Geronimo's

Pat Garrett   *(Western Archives)*

Geronimo *(National Archives)*

mother, wife and three children during a raid, and the Indian hated Mexicans with a vengeance his whole life. Geronimo joined the Chiricahua band through marriage and served under Cochise as a warrior. When Cochise died in 1874, Geronimo took over leadership among the Chiricahua. The U.S. government rounded up the Chiricahua in 1876 and sent them to the San Carlos Reservation, but Geronimo refused to go. The U.S. Army sent General George Crook to capture Geronimo and he did so twice, but each time the Apache fled, which prompted Crook's resignation and the U.S. Army to assign General Nelson A. Miles to the task. In September 1886 Miles captured Geronimo, who spent the rest of his years on reservations. During the 1904 St. Louis World's Fair, Geronimo sold autographed pictures of himself for 50 cents each and often posed for pictures with tourists. He dictated his autobiography in 1906 and died on a reservation in Fort Sill, Oklahoma at the age of 80.

GHOST DANCE   A religious movement led by Wovoka, an Indian prophet, that promised that dead Indians would rise, the buffalo would return and whites would leave. It was a mystical religion whose adherents wore shirts with mystic symbols that were supposed to repel the bullets of white men. These adherents danced in a circle for days at a time. Whites were alarmed and upset by the ghost dance because they feared Indians were preparing for war with this movement. By the end of 1890 about 3,000 soldiers were in Sioux country ready to quell this alleged rebellion. This military build-up led to the slaughter at Wounded Knee in December

1890 when 300 Sioux in the ghost dance movement were massacred by soldiers.

GHOST RIDERS IN THE SKY   Song written by Stan Jones and published by Edwin H. Morris and Company in 1949.

A veteran cowboy named Cap Watts and a young cowpoke named Stan Jones were working for the D Hill Ranch near Douglas, Arizona when storm clouds came up. The quickly moving clouds seemed to form figures riding through the sky, and Watts yelled, "Ghost riders." Later he told young Jones the story of "ghost riders" who tried to "catch the devil's herd" when cold air and hot air currents collided, often resulting in tornadoes. Jones remembered the story and later wrote the song "Ghost Riders in the Sky" about the experience. In 1949 while working as a park ranger in Death Valley, Jones helped a movie company scout locations for its movie *Three Godfathers.* One night he sang this song to the Hollywood crew by campfire, and it made an immediate impression; later that year the song became the title for the Gene Autry movie, in which Stan Jones and "Ghost Riders in the Sky" were first seen and heard by the American public. (See also JONES, STAN.)

GHOST TOWN   A town that was inhabited and then abandoned, with the buildings still standing. In the boom days of the Old West, a strike of gold or silver could create a town literally overnight; when the inhabitants heard about another strike somewhere else, they would abandon the former town wholesale and create another. The town left behind was a "ghost town."

GIANT   Film produced and directed by George Stevens; screenplay by Peter Packer; released in 1956 by Warner Brothers; 201 minutes in length. Cast: Elizabeth Taylor, Rock Hudson, James Dean, Carrol Baker, Chill Wills, Jane Withers, Mercedes McCambridge, Sal Mineo, Dennis Hopper, Paul Fix, Rod Taylor, Earl Holliman, Monte Hale, Sheb Wooley, Ray Whitley and Max Terhune.

Based on the book by Edna Ferber, this movie tells the story of 30 years in the life of one Texas family (1923–53) as it moves from cattle to oil. The owner of the 595,000-acre Reata Ranch (Rock Hudson) marries a Maryland girl (Elizabeth Taylor) and takes her to Texas to live in a Victorian mansion in the midst of a barren Texas plain. Here a series of intrigues, jealousies and power struggles occur in a soap opera that presaged the TV series "Dallas." This was James Dean's last film, for he died in a car crash two weeks after he finished filming. Dean stars as the young man who goes from kicking up dust to being the king of Texas from an oil strike.

GIBBON, JOHN   (b. near Holmesburg, Pennsylvania on April 20, 1827; d. Baltimore, Maryland on February 6, 1896)   The troops of Gibbon and General Alfred Howe Terry arrived to save the remnants of the Seventh Cavalry after Custer's slaughter at the Little Bighorn. Gibbon had served in the Civil War and led a force of mixed infantry and cavalry against the Sioux and Cheyenne forces. After the Battle of the Little Big-horn, Gibbon led a force against Chief Joseph and the Nez Perce, highlighted by the Battle of the Big Hole on August 9, 1877. Gibbon and his troops attacked the Indian camp at dawn but were then forced in a defensive position when the Indians regrouped and counterattacked. The wounded Gibbon and his men held on for three days until the Indians saw a relief column of cavalry approaching and fled.

GIBSON, HOOT   (b. Edmund Richard Gibson in Tekamah, Nebraska on August 6, 1892; d. Woodland Hills, California on August 23, 1962)   Hoot Gibson was one of the major movie cowboy stars during the silent era; between 1912 and 1929 he made more than 120 movies and during the mid-1920s was making $14,500 a week in cowboy pictures. He got his nickname from his love of owl hunting. A rodeo performer (he was Best All-Round Cowboy at Pendleton Rodeo in 1912), Gibson was part of the Miller Brothers' 101 Ranch in 1906 and in 1907 joined the Stanley-Atkinson Wild West Show. He served in the U.S. Army Tank Corps during World War I; afterward he worked with John Ford. In 1931–33 he did 11 films for Allied; he appeared in seven Trail Blazers films with Ken Maynard but retired in 1939. Later, he made a comeback of sorts when he appeared in *The Horse Soldiers* (1959), directed by John Ford and starring John Wayne. Gibson's hobby was racing planes. (See also MOVIES.)

Hoot Gibson

GILA MONSTER   The largest and only poisonous lizard in the United States, the Gila *(Heloderma suspectum)* averages about 19 inches in length. It bites its victims (snakes, ground squirrels and rats), and its poisonous saliva comes up from glands at the roots of its teeth into its victim. The Gila's poison is generally not fatal to humans, although it can cause intense sickness. This animal inhabits the Gila River valley in Arizona as well as desert regions in Utah, Nevada and New Mexico.

GIRLS OF THE GOLDEN WEST   (b. Dorothy Laverne (Dolly) Goad on December 11, 1915, d. November 12, 1967; b. Mildred Fern (Millie) Goad on April 11, 1913, d. May 2, 1993)   This female duo consisted of sisters who were popular singers of cowboy songs during the 1930s. Dolly and Millie Goad (later they changed it to "Good") debuted on WIL and then moved to KMOX in St. Louis in 1930. Their greatest fame came on WLS's "National Barn Dance" in 1933–37, in which their harmony singing and cowgirl outfits made them hits. In the programs, their hometown was listed as "Muleshoe, Texas," even though they'd never been there; the change was made to make them more "authentic" to listeners. After the "National Barn Dance," the Girls of the Golden West (given that name by radio executive Walter Richards at KMOX in St. Louis after an old cowboy story by Bret Harte) moved to the Boone County Jamboree and then the Midwestern Hayride on WLW in Cincinnati. Dolly always sang lead and Millie sang harmony in their shows and on recordings on Victor's Bluebird label and the American Record Company. The sisters worked until 1949 and were briefly united in 1963 for some albums. They worked with Gene Autry and Smiley Burnette in Chicago and helped popularize cowboy songs and the cowboy image.

GIRLS OF THE LINE   Prostitutes, also called ladies of the line, hookers, call girls and girls of the evening. The "girls of the line" set up shop in tents or rough shacks on the edge of a mining camp, cow town or railroad camp.

GIT ALONG LITTLE DOGGIES   Veteran folk song collector John Lomax first published the song "Whoopee Ti-Yi-Yo, Git Along Little Dogies" in his landmark book of western folksongs, *Cowboy Songs and Other Frontier Ballads,* in 1910. A couple of lines of this song had also appeared in *The Log of a Cowboy* by Andy Adams in 1902, which was about an 1882 cattle drive from Texas to the Canadian border. Lomax had heard the song sung by a Gypsy woman in Fort Worth. The journals of Owen Wister, author of the novel *The Virginian,* also recorded some verses to this song in 1893. The song has been traced by Alan Lomax to an Irish song, "The Old Man's Lament," which he heard from folksinger Seamus Ennis in Dublin in 1950. This lullaby has been traced back to an English song, "I Father a Child That's None of My Own," dated 1672.

GLASS, HUGH   (b. c. 1785; d. Yellowstone River c. 1833)   Hugh Glass was a mountain man who survived an incredible mauling by a grizzly bear and was left for dead. Glass's wounds were so severe that John Fitzgerald and Jim Bridger, who were left by the party of mountain men led by Andrew Henry to take care of Glass, believed there was no way for him to recover, so they took his rifle and the supplies and left him. But Glass did recover and managed to crawl about 100 miles to Fort Kiowa. Glass had sworn vengeance on Fitzgerald and Bridger, but when he found them, he got his rifle back and forgave them. Nobody knows when Glass was born or when he died, although it is believed he was killed in spring 1833 by Indians on the Yellowstone River.

GOLDEN SPIKE The Golden Spike was the ceremonial railroad spike driven by Leland Stanford of the Central Pacific Railroad and Thomas C. Durant of the Union Pacific Railroad on May 10, 1869 at Promontory Point, Utah to commemorate the joining of the two railroads that connected the continent after seven years of intense work. The ceremony involved four special spikes, two of silver and two of gold, and a last spike connected to the telegraph so the sledge hammer would send the signal proclaiming the job was complete. But Stanford and Durant both missed when they swung at the spike. The telegraph operator sent the message anyway, and two locomotives, the Jupiter of the Central Pacific and No. 119 of the Union Pacific, moved forward until they touched. Then champagne bottles were broken and pictures were taken.

GOLD RUSH, THE There were a number of "gold rushes" in the West, but the first is the most famous: the one in 1849 to California after gold was discovered at Sutter's Mill near present-day Sacramento. But the gold rushes that began in 1849 did not end until the end of the century, 1896–97, when the final gold rush to Alaska occurred. By this point, gold could only be obtained by mining companies with elaborate equipment, and the days of the prospector striking a vein or groups of miners panning for gold and getting rich were gone. Indeed, the days of a single miner striking it rich were rare; most miners worked long days just to find enough to get by. The big money was made by the merchants and others whose work collected the miner's money (gamblers, restaurants, lawyers, con men), speculators and, later, the mining companies.

Thousands upon thousands of Americans caught "gold fever" during this 50-year period; most were totally inexperienced in mining gold (or silver); still, they dropped everything they were doing and headed for the gold fields where, with dreams of striking it gloriously rich bouncing in their heads, they proceeded to pan and dig for gold in the hope of landing the big strike. The whole event was rather dramatic, though unplanned and highly uncoordinated. A number of "boom towns" were created in the gold and silver rushes, but often these same towns were quickly abandoned when word got around about another strike somewhere else.

Miners looked for "placers," which were flakes or nuggets originally encased in veins in rocks. The gold in these veins was loosened through weather and then carried by rains and streams in nuggets, chunks, dust or thin flakes. Miners generally put some dirt or gravel in water in a pan and "sloshed" it out; the gold was heavier and stayed on the bottom. "Rockers" or "cradles" were also used, which were faster; some miners used mercury to amalgamate with the gold, and others built a "long tom," or a series of long wooden boxes through which the gravel was washed while the gold was caught behind in "riffle bars" that were built across the bottoms. These became standard tools. The prospectors were the pioneers, usually solitary figures (sometimes they worked in twos and threes) who often found gold first; then the miners who dug came, and then the mining companies.

After the gold rush to California, there was one to the Fraser River in British Columbia in 1858 that attracted 25,000 people. There were two rushes in 1859: one to the Comstock Lode in Nevada and then one to Colorado for the "Pikes Peak" rush. This Pikes Peak rush by the fifty-niners was the second most popular gold rush, and more than 50,000 came (1859–79); there was also a rush to Leadville, Colorado in the mid-1870s and to Cripple Creek, Colorado in 1890–91.

By the mid-1860s it was pretty much over for the single miner; the Comstock Lode was silver, which required a different type of mining, not suitable to picks and shovels. There were gold rushes in the 1860s to Idaho and Montana, but because of the inaccessibility of the area and the severe winters, this area attracted fewer miners. Gold in the Black Hills led to the creation of the towns of Deadwood and Lead; a silver strike in 1877 led to the creation of Leadville, Colorado, and another silver strike that same year led to the creation of Tombstone, Arizona. The final gold rush was to Bonanza Creek in Alaska in 1896; over 100,000 started for the Yukon Valley but fewer than half arrived, and the severe conditions led this to be the last and shortest gold rush.

Miners in these gold rushes would come and stake "claims," usually a 10-foot-square area, where they would "mine" until they gave it up. Often they could make a great deal of money, but prices were so inflated that they soon spent it all; in California the average daily income of a miner was $20 in 1848 and $16 in 1849; it then decreased to $5 a day in 1853 and about $3 after that.

GOLDSBY, CRAWFORD See CHEROKEE BILL.

GOOD, THE BAD AND THE UGLY, THE Film produced by Cinecitta Studios; directed by Serge Leone; music by Ennio Morricone; released in 1967 by United Artists; 180 minutes in length. Cast: Clint Eastwood, Lee Van Cleef and Eli Wallach.

The third film in the Sergio Leone trilogy (after *A Fistful of Dollars* and *For a Few Dollars More*), this film also stars Clint Eastwood as the Man with No Name (the "good"), his costar from the second film, Lee Van Cleef (the "bad") and Eli Wallach (the "ugly"). Set in the Civil War, the film uses the carnage of war to explain the ruthlessness of the search for gold by the three men, who are amoral, changing sides whenever it suits their advantage. The movie ends with a three-way shootout.

GOODBYE OLD PAINT This song and "I Ride an Old Paint" are remarkably similar and often interchangeable. "Goodbye Old Paint" was first collected by folk song collector John Lomax in Cheyenne, Wyoming. Although the original author is unknown, a version has been traced back to black cowboy Charley Willis, who learned it on a cattle drive from Texas to Cheyenne in 1871. Willis taught this song to Jesse Morris of Bell County, Texas, and Morris later recorded it in 1947 for John Lomax when he was collecting songs for the Library of Congress. (See also I RIDE AN OLD PAINT.)

GOODNIGHT, CHARLES (b. Macoupin County, Illinois on March 5, 1836; d. Tucson, Arizona on December 12, 1929)   A legendary rancher and cattleman, Charles Goodnight pioneered the Goodnight-Loving Trail, developed the chuck wagon, developed the JA Ranch in the Texas panhandle and crossed Herefords with longhorns to develop better beef animals. Goodnight also crossed cattle with buffalo and created the "cattalo," an infertile failed breed, but by saving and nurturing some buffalo on his ranch, he helped those animals avoid extinction. Goodnight moved to Texas in 1846 and served in the Texas Rangers during the Civil War. His first cattle herd was in Palo Pinto County, Texas

Charles Goodnight *(Archives Division: Texas State University)*

with Oliver Loving. When they decided to drive their herds to market in 1866, they pioneered a new trail that avoided Indian Territory and Kansas and moved their cattle to Colorado and the northern ranges. He established a ranch in Colorado in 1869 and then, in 1877, formed a partnership with John Adair for the JA Ranch in the Palo Duro Canyon in the Texas panhandle. The ranch had over a million acres of land and 100,000 cattle. Goodnight also blazed a trail from his ranch to Dodge City and formed the Panhandle Stockmen's Association to stop cattle thieves and improve breeding. Along the way Goodnight developed the chuck wagon for trail drives, modifying an old army wagon to feed his crew. Previously each cowboy brought along his own food wrapped in his sleeping bag.

GOODNIGHT-LOVING TRAIL   This cattle trail was pioneered by Oliver Loving and Charles Goodnight in 1866 when they drove about 2,000 cattle west from Texas first to Navajo and Apache Indians on a reservation in Fort Sumner, New Mexico and then north to the Colorado gold fields to deliver beef to miners. The trail started in Texas, around Fort Belknap, and moved southwest to Horsehead Crossing, then northwest to Pope's Crossing and then paralleled the Pecos River north up through New Mexico to Fort Sumner, Las Vegas, Raton Pass and then on into Colorado to Trinidad, Pueblo and Denver. This trail was treacherous over the Staked Plains, where there was a waterless stretch for 96 miles that took from 30 to 40 hours to cross. The trail Loving pioneered stopped at Bosque Redondo or Fort Sumner in Mexico; after Loving's death in 1867 Goodnight continued the trail up into Colorado and in 1868 took a drive all the way to Cheyenne, Wyoming. In 1866 rancher John S. Chisum used this trail to Bosque Grand; in 1867 Chisum went up the trail on the west side of the Pecos River, and this was called the Chisum Trail (not to be confused with the Chisholm Trail).

GO WEST, YOUNG MAN   This phrase, attributed to Horace Greeley, founder of the *New York Tribune* and western promoter, was actually originated by J. L. B. Soule in 1851 in an article in the *Terre Haute* (Indiana) *Express*. Greeley, however, popularized the phrase when he wrote in a *Tribune* editorial, "Go West, young man, and grow up with your country," in July 1865.

GRAHAM-TEWKSBURY FEUD   See PLEASANT VALLEY WAR.

GRAND CANYON   Cut by the Colorado River over a period of 2.6 to 10 million years, the Grand Canyon is a mile deep, 217 miles long and between four and 18 miles wide. It was first seen by whites when Francisco Vasquez de Coronado and his conquistadores explored it in 1540. Major John Wesley Powell led the first expedition by whites down the river in 1869. The Navajo, the Paiute and the Hopi are the Indian tribes most closely associated with the canyon, living and hunting in the area for a number of years. It was established as a national park in 1919.

Kirby Grant

GRANT, KIRBY (b. Kirby Grant Hoon in Butte, Montana on November 24, 1911; d. near Cape Canaveral, Florida on October 3, 1985)

Kirby Grant's greatest fame came as Sky King on the TV series by the same name. Born on a Montana ranch, Grant was a violin child prodigy; at 12 he debuted with the Seattle Symphony Orchestra. Grant played semi-professional baseball, attended the University of Washington and Whitman College and moved to Chicago, where he worked in radio and sang with a Chicago dance band. In 1937 he entered a "Gateway to Hollywood" talent contest and won first prize, a six-month RKO film contract. During World War II he was an air force flight instructor; afterward he resumed his movie career and appeared in a number of westerns, although he did not particularly care for the genre. During the time he was appearing in "Sky King," Grant lived in Highland Park, Illinois, a suburb of Chicago, and would fly west to shoot the series. In his later years Grant did publicity for Florida's Sea World and lived in southern Florida. In the 1970s he operated the Sky King Young Ranch of America for homeless teenagers. (See also SKY KING; TELEVISION WESTERNS.)

GRASSES There are three major types of grasses that dominate the prairies, divided roughly into tall, short and mixed grasses. The tall grasses grow over six feet in height and need the most rain; major grasses in this group include porcupine grass (*Stipa spartea*), big bluestem (*Andropogon gerardi*) and yellow Indian grass (*Sorghastrum nutans*). Medium grasses include little blue stem (*Andropogon scoparius*) and side oats grama (*Bouteloua curtipendula*), and short grasses include blue grama (*B. gracilus*) and hairy grama (*B. hitsuta*). Short grasses, located primarily in the area east of the Rockies in "buffalo country," are dominated by blue grama or little grama grass and "buffalo grass" (*Buchloe dactyloides*). Other grasses in the north are needle-and-thread grass (*Stipa comota*), western wheat grass (*Agropyron smithii*) and red three-awn (*Aristida longiseta*). In the southern prairies from Texas through western Oklahoma, Kansas, Nebraska and the central Dakotas up to Canada, there are mixed grasses that include June grass (*Koeleria cristata*), blue grama, hairy grama, little blue stem, porcupine grass and needle-and-thread. Climate and rainfall are the primary determinants of the size of grasses.

GRATTAN MASSACRE See LARAMIE, TREATY OF.

GRAY GHOST, THE TV show that starred Tod Andrews as Major John Singleton Mosby and Phil Chambers as Lieutenant St. Clair.

A Civil War show, this series featured the exploits of southern hero John Singleton Mosby, whose raids led to him being nicknamed the "Gray Ghost." Based on the book *Gray Ghosts and Rebel Raiders* by Virgil Carrington Jones, the show had to be syndicated because sponsors backed out several times before network telecasts. The 39 episodes of the half-hour show were produced in 1957 and released in October of that year.

GREASY SACK OUTFIT A cattle outfit that was poor. This term developed because cowboys who worked for poor outfits didn't have a chuck wagon, so they had to carry all their food in a greasy sack.

GREAT ADVENTURE, THE TV show narrated by Van Heflin.

Assisted by the National Education Association, this series attempted to be historically accurate as it presented a significant historical event each week in an episode. Taken from the annals of American history, shows included "The Massacre at Wounded Knee" starring Joseph Cotten and Ricardo Montalban; "Wild Bill Hickok—The Legend and the Man" starring Lloyd Bridges; and "The Testing of Sam Houston" starring Robert Culp. The show premiered on September 27, 1963 on CBS on Friday evenings and finished its run on April 23, 1965.

GREAT AMERICAN DESERT The Great American Desert is the area bordered by the Rocky Mountains on the west and roughly the middle of what is now North Dakota, South Dakota, Kansas, Nebraska, Oklahoma and Texas on the east (the 100th meridian). In 1806 Zebulon Pike explored the West and labeled it the "Great Sandy Desert"; he likened it to the Sahara, stating it would be a barrier to civilization. In 1820 Major Stephen Long explored the area and named it the Great American Desert, a name that remained in use until after the Civil War; the area is now called the Great Plains. Both explorers were wrong—it was not a "desert" at all, although the annual rainfall was less than 20 inches a year (the eastern area of the country was used to having about 40 inches of rain per year). There was a lack of trees in the area, as well as other vegetation, and long hot summers. The area did not look promising for agriculture, although the explorers seemed to believe it would be a good place for the "uncivilized" Indians to roam. Explorer John Fremont challenged and changed the notion that the Great American Desert was uninhabitable during his trips in 1838 and 1843–44. Fremont, who traveled there during a period of unusually high rainfall, noted that the area could support livestock. Fremont also noted that the area between the Rockies and the Sierra Nevada actually was a desert and named it the Great Basin. Settlers began dotting the Great Plains after the Civil War, encouraged by the railroads and the Homestead Act (1862). There was also a theory promoted that "rain follows the plow," which led many to believe that rain would increase on the plains when settlement increased; this notion was proven false.

GREAT NORTHERN RAILWAY   Originally called the Minnesota and Pacific Railroad Company when it received its charter in 1857, this line was developed by noted railroad entrepreneur James J. Hill, who gained control of the line in 1878 and built it from Minnesota into the Dakota Territory. He then went on to Great Falls, Montana in 1887 before crossing the Rockies and Cascade Mountains and finishing the line in Washington in January 1893. Along the way Hill, who did not have the benefits of government land grants and subsidies like his competitors, opened up Dakota Territory by providing cheap rates of transportation, importing purebred livestock and establishing credit for farmers and experimental farms with new strains of seeds.

GREAT NORTHFIELD, MINNESOTA RAID, THE Film produced by Jennings Lang; directed by Philip Kaufman; screenplay by Philip Kaufman; released in 1972 by Universal; 91 minutes in length. Cast: Cliff Robertson, Robert Duvall, Luke Askew, R. G. Armstrong, Dana Elcar, Donald Moffat, John Pearce, Matt Clark, Wayne Sutherlin, Robert H. Harris and Jack Manning.

This is a movie about the James and Younger brothers trying to rob Northfield, Minnesota. This film reflects the 1970s as much as the 1870s; the "myths" of Jesse James and other famous people are debunked. Instead, we see murderous, self-absorbed, neurotic characters.

GREAT SALT LAKE This lake in northwestern Utah is where the Mormons settled to establish their domain. The saltiest body of water in the Americas—it is four or five times as salty as the oceans—the Great Salt Lake is fed by four rivers: the Jordan, Weber, Ogden and Bear. The lake is 75 miles long, 30 miles at its widest point and between 10 and 30 feet deep, and it covers an area of 1,500 square miles. First discovered by whites when mountain man Jim Bridger found it in 1824, the lake is salty because it is fed by mountain streams that bring down minerals and salts. Because there is no outlet, the water evaporates, leaving the salt and minerals in a highly concentrated form (27% saline content). The Great Salt Lake lies just east of the Great Salt Lake Desert, a 4,200-square-mile wasteland that claimed the lives of a number of forty-niners who tried to use this area as a shortcut to the California gold fields.

GREAT TRAIN ROBBERY, THE   Silent film produced and directed by Edwin S. Porter; released in 1903 by Edison; screenplay by Edwin S. Porter; about 12 minutes in length.

Because Edwin S. Porter made a film for the Delaware, Lackawanna and Western Railroad in 1903, the railroad firm let him use its railroad and trains for his own film. Porter decided to film a four-act play, *The Great Train Robbery*. The play, written by Scott Marble, had opened in New York City in 1896. Porter gathered up a crew and headed to rural New Jersey, near Dover. The movie he made was 12 minutes long and told a story; earlier films had just shown action and short subjects. This would be the beginning of the movie industry because it was the first time a "complete" movie was made. The movie took two days to film and had 14 scenes. The plot is simple but timeless: A telegraph operator is tied up by outlaws, who stop the train and shoot the guard. Then, in a saloon, some bully makes a tenderfoot dance by shooting at his feet. Then comes the chase where riders pursue the train outlaws, guns blazing. Finally, there is a final shootout where the bad guys are killed and the good guys win. The film was first shown in Manhattan at the Eden Musee on 14th Street to an enthusiastic audience; it then moved to the Hammerstein Theater on 42nd and Broadway—a vaudeville theater. *The Great Train Robbery* would become the top-grossing film until *The Birth of a Nation* by D. W. Griffith in 1915. Thus, the birth of western movies was also the birth of the movie industry itself.

GREELEY, HORACE   (b. Amherst, New Hampshire on February 3, 1811; d. New York City on November 29, 1972)   Horace Greeley was the New York editor who popularized the saying, "Go West, young man." Greeley also popularized the West, taking celebrated trips to the area in 1859 and writing articles about his travels that led to a book, *An Overland Journey from New York to San Francisco in the Summer of 1859* (1860). Greeley made another trip west in 1866. Greeley was the major newspaperman of his day and engaged in active journalism, letting his newspaper, the *New York Tribune*, serve as a moral leader as well as political broker. Before the Civil War, Greeley and his paper had national impact (Greeley was a major force in the nomination of Abraham Lincoln in 1860), but after the war the paper's influence (and Greeley's) declined.

After working for a newspaper in Vermont and as a printer in Erie, Pennsylvania and upstate New York, Greeley arrived in New York City at the age of 20 in August 1831 and obtained some jobs as a typesetter. He began to write for newspapers and edited several and on April 10, 1841 launched the *New York Tribune;* he soon formed a partnership with Thomas McElrath that allowed Greeley to involve himself in politics while the business decisions of the paper were handled by McElrath. Greeley always had political aspirations but failed to be elected to a number of offices; his final quest was to unseat Ulysses S. Grant as the Republican nominee for his second term as president in 1872. Greeley suffered a crushing defeat in the October primary, then watched his wife die and, when he returned to the *Tribune*, found he was no longer editor or had the power he once had; this led to a nervous breakdown, insanity and his death. His elaborate funeral was attended by the president, vice president and numerous other dignitaries.

GREENE, LORNE (b. Ottawa, Ontario, Canada on February 12, 1915; d. Santa Monica, California on September 11, 1987)   Lorne Greene was best known as Ben Cartright on "Bonanza." Green spent 14 years on this show; after it ended, he starred in another TV series, "Griff," as a private detective. Greene was born into a theatrical family; at Queen's University he studied chemical engineering but appeared in a number of stage productions. He then attended Neighborhood Playhouse in New York before he returned to Canada and a job with an advertising agency. This job led him to the job of chief news broadcaster for the Canadian Broadcasting Corporation; he also did a number of "Voice of America" broadcasts. He served as an officer in the Royal Canadian Air Force in World War II and then returned to Canadian radio and helped found the Jupiter Theatre in Toronto. Greene went to New York, where he was offered a role in *1984* by producer Fletcher Markle; he then starred in three Broadway plays, *The Prescott Proposals, Speaking of Murder* and *Edwin Booth.* From there he went to Hollywood, where his first major movie was *The Silver Chalice* (1954). During his run on "Bonanza" Green recorded a hit song, "Ringo," and an album, "Welcome to the Ponderosa." In addition to his success on "Bonanza," Green also appeared in the western films *The Hard Man* (1957), *The Last of the Fast Guns* (1958), *Waco* (1966), *Nevada Smith* (1975) and *Lewis and Clark Expedition* (1976). (See also BONANZA; TELEVISION WESTERNS.)

GREENHORN   Also called a greener, a man totally lacking in firsthand knowledge or experience in the West, usually an Easterner but always someone lacking in the ways and skills of real cowboys.

GREY, ZANE   (b. Pearl Zane Gray in Zanesville, Ohio on January 31, 1875; d. Altadena, California on October 23, 1939)   Zane Grey became one of the most popular writers of his time and the first great western novelist; his novels influenced countless other writers, and his success proved that there was a huge public demand for realistic westerns. When Grey died at the age of 65, he had published 66 novels; another 26 were published posthumously. More than 130 movies have been made from his books, and by 1975, the 100th anniversary of his birth, his book sales had tallied over 50 million copies.

Grey's father was a somber and serious preacher-dentist who burned his 14-year-old son's first manuscript and then beat the boy for writing it. Young Pearl Gray earned a baseball scholarship to the University of Pennsylvania, where he studied dentistry; after graduation in 1896 he set up a dental practice in New York City. When he met 17-year-old Lina Roth in 1900, she told him she wanted to marry a writer, so he began writing. She would be his major supporter and provide the encouragement he needed.

Grey first wanted to become a fishing writer because he loved fishing. His first story, "A Day on the Delaware," was published in 1902 in *Recreation* magazine. His first novel, *Betty Zane,* was rejected by publishers but published with his future wife's inheritance; his second novel, *The Spirit of the Border,* was published after he'd first received a crushing rejection. With this he quit dentistry for good, married "Dolly" (his wife's nickname) and moved to Lackawaxen, Pennsylvania to write full-time.

Known as Pearl Gray since boyhood, he changed his name to Zane Grey. In 1907, when he was 35, he attended a lecture by Arizona cattleman Buffalo Jones and decided to take a trip to the Grand Canyon. He

Zane Grey

arrived in the West on March 27, 1907. This trip would be his inspiration to write westerns.

Grey's first western manuscript, "The Last of the Plainsmen," was turned down; his next, *The Heritage of the Desert,* was purchased by Harper and Brothers. His third, in 1912, was *Riders of the Purple Sage;* this story would become a western classic and launch Grey's career as a major writer. His income increased dramatically: In 1909 he made $423, in 1913 he made $100,000 and by the end of his life Grey had made about $37 million from his writing. After *Riders,* Grey had continued success: In 1913 *Desert Gold* was published, and in 1917 *Wildfire* was published, reaching number three on the best-seller list; in 1920 his novel *The U.P. Trail* reached number one.

Grey bought a 25-room Spanish mansion in Altadena, California and a fishing yacht worth half a million dollars and continued his love of fishing. He could turn out 100,000 words (all written in longhand) per month, or two or three books a year. Grey suffered a stroke in 1937 that left him paralyzed; in 1939 he suffered a heart attack while finishing *Western Union* and died.

GRIEGO, PANCHO (b. Francisco Griego; d. Cimarron, New Mexico on November 1, 1875) On May 30, 1875 in Lambert's Saloon in the St. James Hotel in Cimarron, New Mexico, Griego got into an argument with some men of the Sixth U.S. Cavalry. When the soldiers tried to flee, Griego killed two with his pistol and finished off a third with his Bowie knife. On November 1, the same year, Griego ran into Clay Allison at the St. James Hotel. Griego was angry over the death of Cruz Vega from a lynch mob headed by Allison. Inside, the two men had drinks together and then went over and sat at a table talking. Suddenly, Allison pulled his pistol, shot Griego three times and bolted. (See also ALLISON, CLAY.)

GRINGO Derogatory term used by Mexicans for an Anglo, or white person. Some have thought the term came from the song "Green Grow The Lilacs," which was often sung by Anglos, but this is not ture.

GRIZZLY BEAR See BEAR, GRIZZLY.

G.T.T. This term is an abbreviation for "Gone To Texas." Those who left for Texas (especially those from the southeastern United States, particularly Tennessee) often left a sign on their door that said "G.T.T."

GUADALUPE HIDALGO, TREATY OF This is the treaty that officially ended the Mexican War in 1848, gave the United States most of its western territory, established the United States' southern border with Mexico as the Rio Grande and obligated the United States to pay Mexico $15 million. This was an important treaty because the United States acquired 1.2 million square miles and increased its size by 66%. Future states included in this treaty were all of California, Nevada and Utah, most of New Mexico and Arizona and parts of Colorado and Wyoming. The treaty was negoti-

ated by State Department chief clerk Nicholas P. Trist with the assistance of General Winfield Scott. The treaty was signed in Mexico on February 2, 1848 and ratified by the Senate on March 10, 1848. Ironically, the terms of this treaty were the maximum terms authorized by envoy James Slidell in 1846 before the Mexican War.

GUESTWARD HO! TV show that starred Joanne Dru as Babs Hooten, J. Carrol Naish as Hawkeye, Mark Miller as Bill Hooten, Flip Mark as Brook Hooten, Earle Hodgins as Lonesome, Jolene Brand as Pink Cloud and Tony Montenaro, Jr. as Rocky.

Set on a dude ranch in New Mexico, which the Hootens bought sight unseen after deciding to flee the hustle and bustle of New York, the show consisted of the humorous encounters between the family and Hawkeye, an old Indian and the only source of supplies for the run-down ranch. The show premiered on September 29, 1960 on Thursday nights on ABC. The last telecast for the half-hour show was September 21, 1961.

GULCH A deep gully with steep sides and a small river or stream usually flowing through.

GUNFIGHT, A Film produced by A. Ronald Lubin and Harold Jack Bloom; directed by Lamont Johnson; screenplay by Harold Jack; released in 1971 by Paramount; 90 minutes in length. Cast: Kirk Douglas, Johnny Cash, Jane Alexander, Raf Vallone, Karen Black, Eric Douglas, Philip Mead and Keith Carradine.

This is a movie where the Old West meets show biz. Two aging gunfighters (Kirk Douglas and Johnny Cash) decide to hold a gunfight in an arena and sell tickets. It's winner take all, and though the men are friends, they're broke so they fight it out. They want to satisfy the public curiosity about who is the fastest draw as well as give the winner some much needed money and put the loser out of his misery.

GUNFIGHT AT THE O.K. CORRAL (October 26, 1881) The gunfight at the O.K. Corral in Tombstone, Arizona happened on October 26, 1881 and lasted about 30 seconds. But there were a number of events leading up to it, and the repercussions have lasted years.

The gunfight occurred between two factions. On one side were the clannish Earp brothers, Virgil, Morgan and Wyatt, along with friend Doc Holliday. On the other side were the McLaury brothers, the Clanton brothers and Billy Claiborne.

The Clantons, Ike and brother Billy, were known cattle rustlers, a calling they inherited from their father N. H. ("Old Man") Clanton, who had been killed just two months previously (August 13), reportedly for rustling cattle from Mexico and selling them to Arizona ranchers. (One report had Old Man Clanton and four others shot while asleep in their blankets, but there were also rumors that the Earps had been involved in the killings.) The Clantons also were known to be friends with some stagecoach robbers. Apparently Wyatt was running for sheriff and made a deal with Ike Clanton. For several thousand dollars, Ike was supposed to bring the robbers into an ambush for Wyatt, but the robbers were killed before this happened. Ike betrayed either Earp or his friends; either way, it was damaging for both Wyatt Earp and Clanton. There were also rumors that Doc Holliday, a friend of the Earps', was involved in a stagecoach robbery but was drunk and bungled the job. In addition, the Clantons were southerners, whereas some of the Earps had served in the Union army, a continual cause of western conflicts after the Civil War. At any rate, there was a running feud between the Clantons and Earps, and each had threatened the other; it is possible the Clantons were planning to kill the Earps.

At the time of the O.K. Corral gunfight, Virgil Earp was marshal of Tombstone, a position he had held since June of that year. Virgil would deputize his brothers, and other men, as the need arose; thus Wyatt and Morgan Earp and Doc Holliday were deputized just before the gunfight.

Ike Clanton and Tom McLaury came into Tombstone on October 25 to buy some supplies and stayed that evening, eating in a saloon. While having dinner, Doc Holliday—with Wyatt, Warren and Virgil Earp behind him—came up, cursed Clanton and challenged him to a fight. Ike pointed out that he was unarmed and left the saloon. But Ike was in a poker game later that evening with Virgil Earp, Tom McLaury and others. After the game, Virgil Earp cursed Ike and then beat him with his pistol before taking him to night court.

The next morning Wyatt Earp ran into Tom McLaury on the streets; Earp drew his gun and challenged Tom to fight. When Tom refused, Wyatt slapped him with his left hand and then hit him over the head with his foot-long Buntline Special, knocking McLaury down in the street.

Just before noon on October 26 Billy Clanton and Frank McLaury rode into town. When Frank came out of a store, he saw Wyatt Earp pulling his horse by the bit and said, "Take your hands off my horse." Wyatt replied, "Keep him off the sidewalk. It's against the city ordinance." McLaury then rode down to the O.K. Corral, where he tied his horse.

McLaury went into several stores and was stopped by Sheriff John Behan, who was trying to head off trouble and disarm everyone. Frank refused to give up his gun; Behan then requested the whole Clanton-McLaury party to give up their guns. Frank again refused, while Ike Clanton and Tom McLaury replied that they were unarmed. Tom had turned in his revolver and gun belt to local saloon keeper Andy Mehan earlier that afternoon because he didn't want any trouble. At this point the Earp party appeared, and Behan tried to calm both factions.

Later that afternoon Ike and Billy Clanton, Frank and Tom McLaury and Billy Claiborne were ready to leave town. They were near the O.K. Corral when Morgan, Virgil and Wyatt Earp, along with Doc Holliday, approached. The lawmen had gone there on the pretense of disarming the rustlers, and Virgil shouted, "Throw up your hands," as they approached. Nineteen-year-old Billy Clanton immediately threw up his hands and yelled, "Don't shoot me; I don't want to fight!" Tom McLaury showed the lawmen he had no guns by opening his coat. But Morgan Earp fired his gun point-blank into Billy Clanton, hitting him in the heart. This started the gunfire.

Billy Clanton was knocked backward but was still alive; another shot broke his right wrist, but he drew his Smith and Wesson revolver and began firing with his left hand, the gun propped on his knee, but he was stunned again when a bullet hit him in the stomach.

Ike Clanton, who was unarmed, grabbed Wyatt Earp's left hand and begged him to stop fighting. Wyatt replied, "The fighting has now commenced; go to fighting or get away." Ike then ran into photographer C.S. Fly's studio, next door to the O.K. Corral, followed by Billy Claiborne.

Wyatt wounded Frank McLaury in the stomach and McLaury began staggering forward, holding his middle while firing his gun. Morgan Earp managed to shoot Frank under his right ear and yelled, "I got him," as Frank dropped lifeless on the street. Doc Holliday pulled a shotgun from under his coat and aimed at Tom McLaury, who was standing behind his horse. McLaury was unarmed, although a rifle was in the saddle scabbard. Doc had just been grazed by a shot from Frank McLaury's gun, which had been meant for Wyatt Earp, whose bullet had just hit Frank. McLaury was hit under his right arm by 12 buckshot and died there; Holliday then fired his pistol at Ike Clanton, who was running into the photography studio. Virgil Earp was hit in the leg, Morgan Earp was hit in the shoulder and Doc Holliday was grazed in the side. Only Wyatt of the Earp clan was not hit. Photographer C. S. Fly ran out and grabbed Clanton's gun away from him as Billy lay there. Billy was then carried into an adjacent building in agony and died about 15 minutes later after being injected with morphine by a doctor and crying out, "They've murdered me!"

Wyatt refused to be taken in when Sheriff John Behan tried to arrest them. On December 1, 1881 a justice of the peace ruled that the Earps were innocent because they had been acting as law officers.

The gunfight led to the decline of the Earps' popularity and some revenge killings. Virgil Earp was severely wounded in December, and the following March Morgan Earp was killed. Wyatt led a group that killed Deputy Sheriff Frank Stilwell in Tucson and killed Indian Charley and others in and around Tombstone. (See also CLAIBORNE, BILLY; CLANTON, BILLY; CLANTON, IKE; CRUZ, FLORENTINO; EARP, MORGAN; EARP, VIRGIL; EARP, WARREN; EARP, WYATT; HOLLIDAY, DOC; MCLAURY, FRANK; MCLAURY, THOMAS; STILWELL, FRANK; TOMBSTONE, ARIZONA.)

GUNFIGHT AT THE O.K. CORRAL Film produced by Hal B. Wallis; directed by John Sturges; screenplay by Leon Uris, from a story by George Scullin; released in 1957 by Paramount; 122 minutes in length. Cast: Burt Lancaster, Kirk Douglas, Rhonda Fleming, Jo Van Fleet, John Ireland, Lyle Bettger, Frank Faylen, Earl Holliman, Dennis Hopper, DeForest Kelley, Lee Van Cleef and Jack Elam.

The movie and the actual gunfight at the O.K. Corral

are a world apart. Here, Wyatt Earp (Burt Lancaster) and Doc Holliday (Kirk Douglas) star as he-men for right; in real life these men were much shadier.

GUNFIGHTER, THE Film produced by Nunnally Johnson; directed by Henry King; screenplay by William Bowers and William Sellers (from a story by Andre De Toth and Bowers); music by Alfred Newman; released in 1950 by Twentieth Century–Fox; 84 minutes in length. Cast: Gregory Peck, Helen Westcott, Millard Mitchell, Jean Parker and Karl Malden.

A famous gunfighter is always confronted by some young whippersnapper who wants to make a name for himself by killing a legend. Jimmy Ringo (Gregory Peck) wants to get a ranch and settle down with his wife and son but can't. When he rides into town, he has to kill a young gunslinger in a saloon, and then he is faced with the gunman's three brothers tracking him down. Ringo surprises them and sets them on foot, but they keep coming. Still, Ringo goes to his wife and son in Cayenne and, when he arrives, parks himself in a saloon. The marshal is an old friend of Ringo's, but he wants the gunfighter to leave town so there'll be no danger; Ringo agrees to do so after he sees his wife. Ringo's wife won't go with him to California but agrees to meet up with him a year later; meanwhile, the three brothers are after him, as well as another young gunslinger wanting to kill a legend.

GUNFIGHTERS The modern myth of the western gunfighter was created by movies and TV; the idea of a man standing in the middle of the street beating someone to the draw isn't the way the West really was. In fact, there were few, if any, of these "showdowns" on Main Street at high noon, and the "quick-draw" artist was virtually unheard of; what mattered was the ability to be cool, deliberate and cold-blooded when a confrontation occurred.

A "gunfighter" was known as a "shootist" if he was a good marksman; he would carry a pocket pistol that might be "pulled" and perhaps a holstered weapon, but the most deadly weapon was a sawed-off shotgun. The most popular revolver was the Colt 1873 Army model, known as the "Peacemaker," which was a six-shot single-action, which meant the hammer had to be cocked for each shot. Fully loaded, this gun weighed a little over three pounds. It was the revolver that made the gunfighter possible.

The "gunfighters" were divided between lawmen and outlaws, and often there was a very thin line between them. Some men walked on both sides of that line at different times during their lives, but an essential difference remained: The lawman fought and killed in defense of the law, whereas the outlaw fought and killed outside the law.

The lone lawman who cleaned up a town was a myth. Lawmen were never alone; they were always part of a group, although a particular incident might involve a single lawman. Most of the legendary lawmen came out of the cattle towns of Abilene, Ellsworth, Wichita, Caldwell and Dodge City from 1870 to 1885: During this period 45 men were killed by violence, a much lower number than the movies would have us believe. Still, this was a period when lawmen had to stop violence with violence, and shootouts occurred, although most gunfights erupted over booze, gambling, women, revenge or a threat to personal honor. The outlaws and killers were divided into several categories: those who killed in self-defense, those who killed in private quarrels and those who had a mean streak and were bloodthirsty. These last men were often sadistic and enjoyed killing. There is also the idea of the "good bad man," or Robin Hood type (Jesse James falls into this category), whereby the public perceived some people to be outside the law because of forces greater than them; these men were fighting "evil" even though "evil" might technically have the law on its side.

When men knew they were facing violence, they generally had their guns already drawn and ready. The element of surprise counted and so did coolness, deliberation and excellent reflexes; most people hesitate to kill someone, but the killers did not. Self-preservation was a major motive in pulling the trigger in the final second; up to that point the gunfighter's major concern was to get the killing over with as efficiently and effectively as possible. There wasn't much thought to consequences and certainly not to philosophy; the killer did the deed and allowed the future to take care of itself. The idea of a gunfighter as a "lone wolf" is inaccurate as well; most gunfighters were good mixers and highly sociable. Though they rarely engaged in gunfights with other professionals (most gunfights occurred between professionals and inexperienced braggarts), they enjoyed marksmanship contests with other shootists of reputation.

The idea of the "fast draw" came from Hollywood: In 1954 Dee Woolem "robbed" trains at a tourist exhibition in Orange County, California; he also built an electric timer to time his speed, and by the mid-1960s there were "fast-draw" contests. These contestants were helped by the steel reinforced holsters, which no real cowboy in the 19th century every saw. "Fanning" the gun wasn't done in the West either; it hurt the firing mechanism and was too inaccurate. What counted in a gunfight was the ability to keep one's cool, take deliberate aim and have no hesitation in pulling the trigger. Most gunfighters carried several guns but only used one at a time; the second gun was used as a backup. The shotgun was the most deadly weapon because it scattered buckshot; the derringer was handy because it was hidden, whereas the rifle was more accurate and deadly at a distance. But the revolver was a gunfighter's main tool. The gunfighters who killed the most men all had an indifference to human life and an arrogance about them; they were also likely to have large doses of fear, anger, resentment and jealousy in their personalities.

GUNNYSACKER Someone with a cloth bag or gunnysack over his head to hide his identity.

GUNS There were three major types of guns in the West: revolvers, rifles and shotguns. Each had its special use and purpose; revolvers were good for close range and could be carried on an individual; rifles were deadly at long distances; shotguns covered a wide area with their buckshot. The rifle was developed in Europe but refined in the United States; the Kentucky rifle was the first American firearm. The stock on the Kentucky rifle went up to the muzzle, but the Plains rifle's stock only went halfway up the barrel, making the rifle lighter and easier to handle and lessening the effect of the extremes in temperature out West that caused the wood to crack. Revolvers were first developed by Samuel Colt in 1836 with improvements made by Texas Ranger Captain Samuel Walker; eventually Colt became the dominant maker of revolvers. The revolver that could shoot six bullets replaced the cap and ball pistols, which were awkward and cumbersome; and the development of metallic cartridges that encased the gunpowder were a vast improvement over the loose powder and ball, which had to be carried and packed individually. The breech-loading single-shot rifle was developed by Christian Sharps in 1848, but until the metallic cartridge was developed, the rifle was also a clumsy weapon with its percussion caps and paper. B. Tyler Henry patented a breech-loading repeating rifle in 1860; Oliver Winchester was president of this company and oversaw further development of the rifle initiated by the inventions of John Browning. The Winchester became the first repeating rifle, and the 1873 Winchester rifle with its .44 caliber became known as "the gun that won the West." Shotguns could be either single or double barrel and were used primarily by stagecoach and bank guards, although law enforcement officers often used them, too. The primary suppliers of guns to the West were the Edward K. Tryon Company of Philadelphia and the Great Western Gun Works of Pittsburgh, Pennsylvania. Major gun manufacturers included Colt, Remington, Savage, Smith and Wesson, Merwin and Hulbert, Sharps, Henry, and Winchester; Adirondack, Whitney, Marlin, Stevens, Wesson and Ballard also provided guns.

GUN SHY TV show that starred Barry Van Dyke as Russell Donovan, Tim Thomerson as Theodore Ogilvie, Geoffrey Lewis as Amos Tucker, Keith Mitchell as Clovis, Adam Rich as Clovis, Bridgette Anderson as Celia, Henry Jones as Homer McCoy, Janis Paige as Nettie McCoy and Pat McCormick as Colonel Mound.

A comedy western set in Quake City, California in 1869, this show was based on the Walt Disney films *The Apple Dumpling Gang* and *The Apple Dumpling Gang Rides Again*. The central theme is that a gambler must take care of two young children he won in a card game. The short-lived half-hour show debuted on March 15, 1983 on Tuesdays and was last telecast on April 19 of that year on CBS.

GUNSLINGER TV show that starred Tony Young as Cord, Preston Foster as Captain Zachary Wingate, Charles Gray as Pico McGuire, Dee Pollock as Billy Urchin, Midge Ware as Amby Hollister and John Picard as Sergeant Major Murdock.

Working for Captain Zachary Wingate, commandant

at Fort Scott, New Mexico, gunslinger Cord (no other name was used) settled the problems assigned to him in the post–Civil War setting. The theme song was sung by Frankie Laine, who also sang the theme to "Rawhide," and the show was produced by Charles Marquis Warren, the same person who did "Gunsmoke" and "Gunslinger." The hour-long show was a midseason replacement, premiering on February 9, 1961 on Thursday nights on CBS. The show ended on September 14, 1961 after just 12 episodes.

GUNSMOKE TV show that starred James Arness as Marshal Matt Dillon, Milburn Stone as Dr. Galen (Doc) Adams, Amanda Blake as Kitty Russell (1955–74), Dennis Weaver as Chester Goode (1955–64), Ken Curtis as Festus Haggen (1964–75), Burt Reynolds as Quint Asper (1962–65), Glenn Strange as Sam, the bartender (1962–74), Roger Ewing as Clayton Thaddeus (Thad) Greenwood (1965–67), Buck Taylor as Newly O'Brien (1967–75), Dabbs Greer as Mr. Jones (1955–60), James Nusser as Louie Pheeters, Charles Seel as Barney, Howard Culver as Howie, Tom Brown as Ed O'Connor, John Harper as Percy Crump, Hank Patterson as Hank (1957–75), Sarah Selby as Ma Smalley (1962–75), Ted Jordan as Nathan Burke (1964–75), Roy Roberts as Mr. Bodkin (1965–75), Woody Chamblis as Mr. Lathrop (1966–75), Charles Wagenheim as Halligan (1967–75) and Fran Ryan as Miss Hannah (1974–75).

"Gunsmoke" is the most popular western TV series of all time, running 20 years on the CBS network. For four years, 1957–61, it was the top-rated TV program, and it consistently finished in the top 10 programs during its run. In fact, "Gunsmoke" is the *only* TV series to run 20 years with the same basic set of characters, making it not only the top western but the top TV program of any format in the history of the medium. By the time it ended its run in 1975, it was the only western on network TV.

"Gunsmoke" debuted on September 10, 1955, and the first episode was introduced by John Wayne. Wayne had originally been offered the role of Marshal Matt Dillon but turned it down; he suggested James Arness, who took the role. In its first season it was scheduled on Saturday evenings at 10 P.M. against the "George Gobel Show" and did not fare well. It did break some new ground and, along with "The Life and Legend of Wyatt Earp," which premiered the same week as "Gunsmoke," transformed that genre from escapism aimed at children to serious, adult drama. Soon the program was so successful that a deluge of westerns was on the air; at one time 30 westerns were on network television trying to capture the success of "Gunsmoke."

Originally a 30-minute show, it was extended to 60 minutes for the 1961 season, while keeping its Saturday night slot; meanwhile, the reruns of the half-hour version were broadcast over CBS on Tuesday evenings under the title "Marshal Dillon." The show was in serious decline when CBS decided to give it one last shot before the 1967 season and switched it to Monday evenings; it rebounded miraculously again into the top ratings and ran until September 1975.

The cast of "Gunsmoke" (from left to right): James Arness, Milburn Stone, Amanda Blake, Ken Curtis and Burt Reynolds (seated)

"Gunsmoke" began as a radio program on CBS radio in spring 1952 with William Conrad starring as Marshal Dillon. It lasted nine years on radio before CBS decided to move it to TV; the major casualty of the move was Conrad, who apparently did not have the look the producers wanted for the show. The plots involved Marshal Dillon taking care of Dodge City, Kansas, a wild cow town of the 1880s to which cowboys regularly came to let off steam after they drove their herds to the railroad line, which had stopped in Dodge City for some years before extending farther into the West. Most of the characters ended up at the Long Branch Saloon, run by Miss Kitty. Although history would tell us her character would be a prostitute, and the radio show hinted at this, on TV Miss Kitty was a good businesswoman with a heart of gold; and though she might have been interested in romancing Marshal Dillon, they only exchanged smiles. Appropriately, she was a redhead, a nice compromise from the stereotypes of sexy, sultry dark-haired women and the pure, innocence of blonds.

During the last years, "Gunsmoke" often had stories that did not involve Marshal Dillon, who managed to be out of town (and thus off the screen) for a number of episodes. In its run it attracted the top writers and actors in Hollywood, with people such as Chill Wills, Nick Nolte, Mercedes McCambridge, Rory Calhoun, Victor French, Jon Voight, Darren McGavin, John Russell, Cameron Mitchell, Charles Bronson, Ruth Roman, Gene Evans, Bette Davis, Anthony Caruso and Richard Jaeckel appearing in episodes. In 1987 a special two-hour "Gunsmoke" TV movie, starring James Arness, Amanda Blake, Ken Curtis and Buck Taylor, was shown. "Gunsmoke" was produced by Leonard Katzman, who also produced "Dallas," and two actors remained during the entire 20-year run: James Arness as Matt Dillon and Milburn Stone as Doc Adams.

GUNS OF PARADISE See PARADISE.

GUNS OF WILL SONNETT, THE TV show that starred Walter Brennan as Will Sonnett and Dack Rambo as Jeff Sonnett.

"No brag, just fact" were the words uttered by Will Sonnett on more than one occasion, and he always backed them up. Will Sonnett was played by Walter

Walter Brennan as Will Sonnett and Dack Rambo as Jeff Sonnett in "The Guns of Will Sonnett"

Brennan, who was 73 when this series began. The plot involved Will and his grandson, Jeff Sonnett, roaming the West in search of Will's son and Jeff's father, James Sonnett. James had left tiny Jeff with Will, and now the grown Jeff wanted to find his father, who had become a notorious gunfighter. They never did find him, but they ran into a number of folks who had known him—some with fond memories and others who had been done in by him. The show premiered on September 8, 1967 on ABC on Friday nights. It moved to Monday nights in June 1969, where it finished its run on September 15, 1969. Fifty episodes of the half-hour show were shot.

HACKAMORE Horse's bridle without a bit for the mouth. When trained for a hackamore, the horse responds to the reins against his neck.

HALE, MONTE (b. Ada, Oklahoma on June 8, 1921) Monte Hale was a "B" western cowboy star who appeared in some singing-cowboy movies. He grew up

Monte Hale

on a ranch in San Angelo, Texas and was in several country bands; during World War II he served in a USO troop. His first film was *Steppin' in Society* (1944), and he then signed with Republic in 1946, where his first film was *Home on the Range* (1946); he did 19 films for the studio. (See also SINGING COWBOYS.)

HALIDAY, WINDY   See HAYES, GABBY.

HALL, RED   (b. Jesse Lee Hall in Lexington, North Carolina on October 9, 1849; d. San Antonio, Texas on March 17, 1911)   Considered one of the greatest Texas Rangers, Hall helped end the Sutton-Taylor feud and managed to arrest King Fisher. Before the Rangers, he was city marshal of Sherman, Texas and then a deputy sheriff of Denison, Texas. Later in life he managed a ranch, served as an Indian agent and served in the Philippines as head of the Macabebe Scouts. (See also SUTTON-TAYLOR FEUD.)

HAND   A measurement used for horses, a "hand" equals four inches. In card games, the term refers to the cards dealt to an individual ("three aces in his hand") as well as all the cards dealt for a single game ("we'll play a final hand of poker"). On a ranch, a worker is known as a "hand," while a worker giving help is said to be "lending a hand." It can also mean "to give," as in "hand me that gun," or be used as a compliment, such as "I've got to hand it to you."

HANG 'EM HIGH   Film produced by Leonard Freeman; directed by Sergio Leone (listed as Ted Post); screenplay by Leonard Freeman and Mel Goldberg; released in 1968 by United Artists; 114 minutes in length. Cast: Clint Eastwood, Inger Stevens, Ed Begley, Pat Hingle and Arlene Golonka.

After Clint Eastwood finished the three spaghetti westerns for Sergio Leone, he came back to the United States and began making westerns; this was his first. Based on Judge Isaac Parker (the "hanging judge"), the story tells about Oklahoma Territory in 1873. Cooper (Eastwood) is accused by a posse of stealing the cattle he is driving; they hold court quickly and hang him, but he is saved by a passing cowboy. Then he is taken to Fort Grant (read: Fort Smith) where he is tried before Judge Fenton (read: Judge Parker), who believes Cooper and hires him as marshal. Cooper then sets out to track down the nine men in the posse who arrested and hung him in the first place; the theme emerges here of public justice versus private revenge.

HAPPY HUNTING GROUND   A phrase used by white people to mean the Indians' heaven.

HAPPY TRAILS   Song written by Dale Evans and published by Paramount–Roy Rogers Music in 1951.

Roy Rogers had often used the phrase "Happy Trails" when signing autographs or as a parting phrase. In 1950 his wife, Dale Evans, began humming the phrase "Happy Trails" and then composed the song, which was soon adopted as the theme song for "The Roy Rogers Show" on television. (See also EVANS, DALE; ROGERS, ROY; ROY ROGERS SHOW, THE.)

HARDIN, JOHN WESLEY   (aka "Wes" and "Little Arkansas"; b. Bonham, Texas on May 26, 1853; d. El Paso, Texas on August 19, 1895)   One of the most notorious gunmen in the West, John Wesley Hardin reportedly killed 30 to 40 men; later in life he wrote his autobiography, which told of a number of these killings. John Wesley Hardin came from a prominent Texas family: One ancestor fought at San Jacinto; another signed the Texas, Declaration of Independence; his grandfather, Judge William B. Hardin, served in the Congress of the Republic of Texas and Hardin County is named after him. But Wes, son of a Methodist circuit preacher, got into trouble early in life, stabbing a boy when he was 11. In November 1868, at the age of 15, he killed a former slave and then ambushed and killed three soldiers who were attempting to arrest him. After this, the 16-year-old boy was taken to Navarro County School at Pisgah Ridge.

On December 25, 1869 in Towash, Texas, Hardin was winning big in a card game when a man named Bradly threatened him with a knife. Wes got his gun, and later that evening when he ran into Bradly, the two exchanged shots with Bradly being killed and Hardin escaping. A short while later Hardin got into an argument with a circus man in Horn Hill, Texas and shot the man. That same month in Kosse, Texas, Hardin killed a man who had tried to rob him, first throwing his money on the floor and then shooting the robber between the eyes when he bent to pick it up.

In February 1871 in Gonzales County, Texas, Wes and some other cowboys were in a Mexican camp playing monte when an argument erupted; Wes wounded two Mexicans in the shootout. Later that same year, while on a cattle drive on the Chisholm Trail, Hardin killed an Indian "just for practice." On July 6 in Abilene, Kansas, at the end of a trail drive, Hardin killed Charles Cougar after a quarrel. The next day, in Bluff City, Kansas, Hardin killed Mexican Juan Bideno in a cafe. Bideno had killed cowboy Bill Cohron, who was friends with Hardin, Jim Rodgers and Hugh Anderson. The trio had obtained a warrant and, with John Cohron (Bill's brother), were searching for Cohron. Two months later, in September 1871, Hardin walked up to two black state policemen, Green Parramore and John Lackey, who were eating crackers and cheese in the general store. The outlaw asked if they knew John Wesley Hardin; they replied they'd never seen him but wanted to find him and arrest him. Hardin replied, "Well, you see him now!" as he drew his gun and shot both, killing Parramore. Lackey, wounded in the mouth, ran out of the store.

In July 1872 in Trinity City, Texas, a man named Sublette engaged Hardin in a game of bowling for five dollars a set. Sublette berated Hardin after losing six straight, so Hardin pulled a gun and made him finish the last game. A few moments after leaving the building, Sublette came back with a shotgun and shot Hardin in the side; Hardin shot Sublette in the back trying to escape. Hardin was then carried into hiding. The next month, in Angelina County, Texas, Wes was laying in a room in a farmhouse, two state policemen crept up to the window and fired into the room, hitting Hardin in the thigh. The outlaw grabbed a shotgun and crawled to the door, running the men off.

In April 1873 in Cuero, Texas, Wes and J. B. Morgan began quarreling in a saloon; outside Morgan went for his gun and was shot dead by Hardin. In July of the same year in Albuquerque, Texas, Wes and Jim Taylor saw Jack Helm, a leader in the Sutton-Helm feud. When Helm and six cohorts approached the two, he was gunned down.

On Hardin's 21st birthday, May 26, 1874, he was in Comanche, Texas at a horse race. In a saloon, Comanche County deputy sheriff Charles Webb and Hardin had words; guns were drawn and Webb was killed, although Hardin got a bullet in his side. A crowd soon gathered to run the outlaws out of town. Hardin's brother Joe, along with Bud and Tom Dixon, were lynched, although John Wesley escaped. After the death of Webb, Texas put a $4,000 "dead or alive" reward on Hardin's head. This led the Texas Rangers to begin tracking him. Meanwhile, Hardin took the alias "J. H. Swain, Jr." and, with his wife and daughter, went to Florida. Hardin spent three years in Florida and Alabama as a businessman, living quietly, buying and selling cattle and horses and operating a saloon and a logging business. But on August 23, 1877 Hardin was returning to Pensacola from Alabama by train with four cohorts when Texas Ranger John Armstrong, with several others, entered the train just outside Pensacola. Armstrong entered Hardin's coach and pulled his .45 as Hardin shouted, "Texas, by God," and went for his gun in the waist of his pants. But the gun caught in Hardin's suspenders, and the outlaw couldn't shoot. Meanwhile Jim Mann, sitting next to Hardin, drew his pistol and shot a hole in Armstrong's hat before the Ranger shot the 19-year-old Mann in the chest. Mann jumped out the train window, ran a few steps and fell dead. Hardin had his gun taken away by Armstrong, who then clubbed the outlaw until he was unconscious. With that, Hardin was taken back to Texas by train.

Sentenced to the penitentiary in Huntsville, Texas, Hardin studied law, and when he was released, in February 1894, he went to Gonzales, Texas and opened a law office. He moved his practice to Junction and married a young girl who left him the day of the wedding (Hardin's wife had died while he was in prison). Hardin then moved on to El Paso, where he opened a law office and defended Killin' Jim Miller (Miller's wife was Hardin's cousin). Hardin practiced law in El Paso but could not avoid trouble. On August 19, 1895 Hardin was drinking and gambling in the Acme Saloon. Hardin had run-ins with peace officer John Selman and John Selman, Jr. over Mrs. Martin McRose, a married woman and former prostitute Hardin had been seeing. The younger Selman had arrested Mrs. McRose, and Hardin threatened to kill both father and son. A little after 11 P.M. while Hardin was shooting dice with H. S. Brown, the senior Selman walked into the saloon; Hardin's back was to the door and he did not see the officer. Selman came over and put a slug into the back of Hardin's head. When Hardin was on the floor, Selman fired shots in Hardin's arm and chest. Hardin never got off a shot. (See also ARMSTRONG, JOHN BARCLAY; HELM, JACK; SELMAN, JOHN.)

HARKEY, DEE (b. Richland Springs, Texas on March 26, 1866; d. New Mexico c. 1948) Three of Harkey's brothers were killed in gunfights before they were 21. Young Dee was a deputy at 16 for his brother Joe, the sheriff of San Saba County. This was the beginning of an action-packed career as a law officer.

In Richland Springs, Texas in 1884, a mule thief named Quinn was arrested by Harkey and another deputy named Davis. The two accompanied Quinn to his hotel room for a change of clothes. Harkey had been courting Quinn's daughter Mary, and, in the hotel room, Mary and her mother burst in, with Mary holding a pistol saying, "Dee, that's my father and I'm going to protect him." She then shot her suitor in the stomach. Deputy Davis ran from the room while Harkey knocked Mary to the floor and grabbed the pistol; meanwhile Quinn grabbed a machete and a standoff ensued; it was broken by Davis leading a mob of citizens into the room. Harkey was restrained from shooting Quinn; a doctor determined that the bullet Mary fired had only caused a blister burned on Harkey's abdomen when it hit his watch.

Harkey killed a neighbor named George Young with a knife in a corn patch, and in 1890 as a butcher in Carlsbad, New Mexico, he had a shootout with a customer named George High. For this, the townsfolk got him appointed deputy U.S. marshal to clean up the area.

In 1895 in Phoenix, New Mexico, Harkey and three other lawmen rode into Phoenix on bicycles, encountering Tranquellano Estabo on the way. Estabo had been shooting up the town, and the lawmen ordered him to stop. The Mexican shot and Harkey shot back; then Estabo tried to run over the lawmen with his horse. Harkey got a horse and chased Estabo for about three miles before catching him. When caught, Estabo threw up his hands and said, "Don't kill me, don't kill me! I will go with you."

In 1908 near Sacramento Sinks, New Mexico, Harkey and four other lawmen trailed an outlaw band led by former Dalton Gang member Jim Nite, a recent escapee from the Texas penitentiary. The lawmen found the outlaws' camp, but the outlaws grabbed their guns and began firing. Harkey and the posse charged downhill on their horses toward the camp, but the outlaws answered with heavy fire and drove everyone but Harkey away. On foot, Harkey held his ground and continued to fire. Finally the outlaws surrendered, and the rest of the posse joined Harkey as the fugitives were led away.

Dee Harkey was a New Mexico lawman until 1911, when he began holding a variety of official positions. Later in his life he was a rancher in Eddy County, dying when he was in his 80s.

HARRY THE KID   (b. Harry Head; d. Eureka, New Mexico in June 1881)   Harry the Kid was part of Ike Clanton's gang of cattle rustlers around Tombstone, Arizona. On March 15, 1881 in Contention, Arizona—about 12 miles from Tombstone—Harry, Bill Leonard and Jim Crane held up a stagecoach carrying $26,000 in Wells Fargo money. During the holdup, driver Budd Philpot was killed. Holding the horses for the outlaws was Luther King; he was captured the next day by Morgan Earp and spilled the names of his cohorts. A reward of $2,000 each for Head, Leonard and Crane was offered by Wells Fargo. Wyatt Earp secretly offered Ike Clanton $3,600 if he'd set up the outlaws in a trap. The outlaws avoided capture until June 1881, when two attempted to rob a store in Eureka, New Mexico. Harry the Kid and Bill Leonard were killed by store owners Bill and Ike Haslett. (See also CLANTON, IKE; EARP, WYATT.)

HART, WILLIAM S.   (b. William Surrey Hart in Newburgh, New York on December 6, 1870; d. Newhall, California on June 23, 1946)   William S. Hart was the first true star of western movies; he achieved his fame in the silent era and retired from movie making before sound films. Hart was a stage actor who starred in western plays before he came to Hollywood; he starred in *The Squaw Man* on Broadway in 1905 and had the lead in *The Virginian* in 1907–8. Hart's first starring film was *In the Sage Brush Country* (1914). Hart had roomed with Thomas Ince in New York; when Ince became a movie

William S. Hart

mogul in Hollywood, Hart went west and persuaded Ince to let him write and star in westerns. Hart's westerns were realistic in some ways; they had primitive sets, he wore authentic clothes and the movies have a dusty, shabby look about them. But Hart was also a romantic; his men were always rugged individualists, and his women were always pure, sweet and innocent. Hart's last film was a talkie and was his best, the classic *Tumbleweeds* (1928). After this film, Hart retired to his ranch and wrote his autobiography and some other books.

HARTE, BRET   (b. Francis Brett Harte in Albany, New York on August 25, 1836; d. Camberley, Surrey, England on May 5, 1902)   Harte is best known as a western writer for his California gold rush short stories; the best are "The Luck of Roaring Camp," "The Outcasts of Poker Flat" and "The Heathen Chinee," all published in 1870 in his first book of short stories. Harte moved to California in 1854 and lived there for 17 years. He worked as a newspaper reporter, obtained some government positions and founded *Overland Monthly* and served as its editor. When Harte left the West, he moved back East and then lived abroad.

HARTS OF THE WEST   TV show starring Beau Bridges as Dave Hart, Harley Jane Kozak as Alison Hart,

Lloyd Bridges as Jake Tyrell, Saginaw Grant as Auggie Velasquez, Meghann Haldeman as L'Amour Hart, O-Lan Jones as Rose McLaughlin, Sterling Macer, Jr. as Marcus St. Cloud, Sean Murray as Zane Grey Hart, Stephen Root as R. O. Moon, Talisa Soto as Cassie Valesquez, Nathan Watt as John Wayne "Duke" Hart, Dennis Fimple as Garral, Alan Haufrect as Fred and Peter Kozak as the marshal.

Dave Hart lived in Chicago and sold lingerie but always had a dream to be a cowboy. So he packed up his family (a wife, two sons and a daughter) and moved to the Flying Tumbleweed Ranch in Sholo, Nevada, which he had purchased. The ranch doesn't look like the brochure; it is a run-down place, but Hart is determined to make it work. The children, meanwhile, face a tough adjustment and wish they were back in the city. The theme song, "In a Laid Back Way" was written and sung by Clint Black. A contemporary western, the show premiered on Saturday evening, September 25, 1993 on CBS.

HASHKNIFE OUTFIT The Aztec Land and Cattle Company was called the "Hashknife outfit" because of its brand. Established in Arizona Territory in 1883 and 1884, the ranch had over 80,000 head of cattle and was headquartered on the Little Colorado River near St. Joseph in the Pleasant Valley, also known as the Tonto Basin. Hashknife cowboys were involved in the Pleasant Valley War on the side of the Coopers and Grahams. Andy Blevins (Cooper) and the Grahams, along with some Hashknife cowboys, were involved in rustling livestock to build up their own herds. The Tewksburys were victims of this rustling. (See also PLEASANT VALLEY WAR.)

HATS See CLOTHING, COWBOY.

HAVE GUN, WILL TRAVEL TV show that starred Richard Boone as Paladin, Kam Tong as Hey Boy (1957–60; 1961–63) and Lisa Lu as Hey Girl (1960–61).

Set in the West after the Civil War, this show featured Paladin, a West Point graduate who had grown tired and disillusioned with the army. Residing in the plush Hotel Carlton in San Francisco, he was a man of high culture who often quoted poets such as Keats and Shelly and squired ladies to the San Francisco Opera when he wasn't chasing crooks and criminals. His assignments were delivered with the morning paper by Hey Boy while he ate in the hotel dining room. Paladin dressed all in black when he was on assignment—quite different from his cultured, dapper dress in San Francisco—and was noted for his strong ethics. At times, Paladin hunted down the one who had hired him, a result of uncovering some shady dealings. A paladin is a white chess knight, and "Paladin" was the only name this character was known by. His business card read "Have Gun–Will Travel wire Paladin, San Francisco."

The show premiered on September 14, 1957 on CBS on Saturday nights. The show kept that time slot for its entire run, concluding on September 21, 1963 after six seasons because star Richard Boone decided to leave. The show was a ratings success, finishing only behind "Gunsmoke" and "Wagon Train" during the 1958-61

period. The theme song, "The Ballad of Paladin" was a hit single for Johnny Western.

HAWKEYE AND THE LAST OF THE MOHICANS TV show that starred John Hart as Hawkeye and Lon Chaney, Jr. as Chingachgook.

Based on the *Leather-Stocking Tales* by James Fenimore Cooper, this series was shot in Canada and produced by the Canadian Broadcasting System and the Independent Television Corporation. Cooper wrote the first "western" novels in American literature, although the "West" at that time was the Allegheny Mountains and upstate New York. This half-hour show was never a network series; its 39 episodes were syndicated in 1956–57.

HAWKS, HOWARD (b. Howard Winchester Hawks in Winchester Hawks, Goshen, Indiana on May 30, 1896; d. Palm Springs, California on December 26, 1977) Movie director Howard Hawks was educated at Cornell University and began his career in the movies during summer vacations as a prop boy for Famous Players Lasky. He went on to direct John Wayne in *Red River*, the film that Wayne credited with making him an actor. Hawks worked with Wayne on a number of other films, including *Rio Bravo* (1959), *El Dorado* (1967), and *Rio Lobo* (1970). Other westerns he directed include *The Outlaw* (1943) and *The Big Sky* (1952). Hawks was also a proficient screenwriter whose work often went uncredited, particularly on movies he directed.

HAYES, GABBY (b. George Francis Hayes in Wellsville, New York on May 7, 1885; d. Burbank, California on February 9, 1969) Legendary cowboy sidekick Gabby Hayes worked with Hopalong Cassidy, Roy Rogers, Bob Steele, Rex Bell, Tom Tyler, Hoot Gibson, Harry Carey, John Wayne and Randolph Scott. Hayes played a variety of characters; he was Windy Haliday with Hopalong (as well as Ben, Spike and Shanghai) but had to change his name to "Gabby" when he joined Republic Pictures because he could not use "Windy" legally. Gradually, Hayes developed the character of "Gabby," first when he worked with John Wayne in *West of the Divide* (1933) and *Blue Steel* (1934). After Smiley Burnette developed the role of the requisite comic sidekick in his performances with Gene Autry, the comic sidekick became a bankable feature of westerns and Gabby's career took off. Gabby's character wore a plaid shirt, old leather vest and tattered black hat, a slovenly image that did not match the impeccable dresser that he was offscreen.

Hayes was originally a vaudeville performer and moved to Hollywood in the 1920s. His first sound picture was *The Rainbow Man* (1929), and he did not get cast into cowboy movies until he was in his 40s. Hayes's major fame came as Roy Rogers's sidekick, and in *Southward Ho!* (1939) he developed the "Yur durned tootin'!" line that became his motto; he was also famous for his "Durn persnickety females!" line as well. Hayes and Rogers starred in 28 pictures between 1939 and 1942; Gabby was then teamed with Wild Bill Elliott, and Smiley Burnette joined Rogers. After some pictures with

Gabby Hayes

Elliott, Hayes was teamed with Sunset Carson before rejoining Rogers in *Lights of Old Santa Fe* (1944) and 13 more. During the mid-1940s Gabby Hayes was at the peak of his popularity; he made his last movie when he was 65, *The Caribou Trail* (1950), starring Randolph Scott. After his movie career, Hayes hosted a television show for children, "The Gabby Hayes Show," sponsored by Quaker Oats on Sunday afternoon. He also hosted the "Howdy Doody" show in 1954–55 after Buffalo Bob had a heart attack. (See also ROGERS, ROY.)

HAYS, BOB (aka Sam Hassell and John West; b. Iowa c. 1874; d. San Simon Valley, Arizona on November 18, 1896) On August 6, 1896 in Nogales, Arizona, Black Jack Christian's gang came to rob the International Bank of Nogales. Bob Hays and Jess Williams went inside, held up the bank clerk and began stuffing money into sacks. Newspaperman Frank King walked in and started shooting. The two outlaws dropped the money and ran, escaping even though two of their horses were wounded and King was chasing them. Later, an eight-man posse found the gang's hideout in San Simon Valley in Arizona and ambushed them. Hays leaped off his horse when it was killed and shot at posse member Fred Higgins. But Higgins was the more deadly shot, and Hays was killed; Black Jack and two other outlaws escaped.

HAYS, JOHN COFFEE (b. Little Cedar Lick, Wilson County, Tennessee on January 28, 1817; d. near Piedmont, Alameda County, California on April 25, 1883) Hays was a famous leader of the Texas Rangers whose pioneering use of the Colt five-shot pistols ensured the success of Sam Colt's company as well as the defeat of the Comanche Indians. Hays was a captain in the Rangers stationed in San Antonio in 1840 when, with 13 other Rangers, he was attacked by about 70 Comanche warriors. Accustomed to single-shot weapons, the Comanche charged after the Rangers shot once, intending to cover them with arrows while the Rangers were reloading. But Hays led a charge at the Comanche and killed about 30 startled warriors before the tribe fled. In 1841 at the Battle of Bandera Pass, about 500 Comanche attacked Hays and 40 Texas Rangers, and the Rangers killed about 60. During the Mexican War, Hays commanded a regiment of Rangers; he later moved to California and became sheriff of San Francisco County.

HAYWIRE OUTFIT An inefficient and predominantly hopeless ranch outfit or crew.

HAZER In rodeo, the cowboy who rides alongside a steer to keep it going straight so the bulldogger, or steer wrestler, riding on the other side of the steer can drop down on the steer.

HEAD, **HARRY** See HARRY THE KID.

HEAVEN'S GATE Film produced by Joann Carelli; executive producers: Denis O'Dell and Charles Okum; directed by Michael Cimino; screenplay by Michael Cimino; released in 1980 by United Artists; 150 minutes in length. Cast: Kris Kristofferson, Christopher Walken, John Hurt, Sam Waterston, Brad Dourif, Isabelle Huppert, Joseph Cotten, Jeff Bridges, Ronnie Hawkins, Paul Koslo, Geoffrey Lewis, Rich Masur, Tom Noonan, John Conley, Robin Bartlett, Mary C. Wright, Terry O'Quinn, Margaret Benczak, James Knobloch and Erika Peterson.

A colossal failure for Hollywood, this movie cost $40 million and symbolized all the waste and egotism of Hollywood; it also seemed to represent the end of westerns. The story concerns the Johnson County War in Wyoming and features breathtaking scenery, but its cost over runs and lack of box-office success made it a financial disaster.

HEC RAMSEY TV show that starred Richard Boone as Hec Ramsey, Richard Lenz as Sheriff Oliver B. Stamp, Harry Morgan as Doc Amos Coogan and Dennis Rucker as Arne Tornquist.

Hec Ramsey was a detective in the Old West, learning the science of criminology after his gunfighting days were mostly over. Hec served a deputy in New Prospect, Oklahoma and solved mysteries with Sheriff Oliver B. Stamp. The show was produced by Jack Webb's Mark VII Productions and was part of the "Sunday Mystery Movie" series, alternating with "McCloud," "McMillan and Wife" and "Columbo." The 90-minute shows were first seen on October 8, 1972 and last seen on August 25, 1975 on Sunday nights on NBC.

HELENA, MONTANA Helena was originally named "Last Chance Gulch" in 1864 because prospector John Cowan decided to give the spot one last dig for gold before giving up. The site became a gold rush hot spot when he discovered a vein that would yield $16 million by 1868. Its name was later changed to Helena, and it became the capital of Montana Territory in 1875, then the capital of the state when Montana entered the Union in 1889. "Last Chance Gulch" where the gold was found is now the town's main street.

HELM, JACK (d. Albuquerque, Texas in July 1873) Jack Helm worked as a cowboy for rancher Shanghai Pierce before the Civil War. After the war he was involved in the Sutton-Taylor feud in South Texas and became one of the leaders of the Sutton "Regulators." Texas Governor E. J. Davis appointed Helm to the Texas State Police on July 1, 1869, but shortly after this appointment Helm and C. S. Bell, another Regulator, encountered two Taylor men, John Choate and his nephew Crockett Choate. The two Regulators gunned down the Choates. For this, and because he levied a tax of 25 cents a person to defray his hotel expenses, Helm was permanently dismissed from the State Police.

On August 23, 1869 Helm, Bell and several other gunmen ambushed Hays and Doboy Taylor, sons of Creed Taylor, outside their father's ranch. Hays was killed; Doboy was wounded. Three days later Helm decided to arrest brothers Henry and William Kelly, who were responsible for causing a disturbance in Sweet Home. The Kelly brothers were killed while the posse Helm headed was bringing them in.

Helm was elected sheriff of DeWitt County but moved to Albuquerque, Texas in April 1873. There he worked as an inventor, trying to perfect a device to combat cotton worms. In 1873 he and six friends were on the street when Helm spotted John Wesley Hardin and Jim Taylor at a blacksmith shop. Helm went over to the two; as he approached, Hardin blasted him with a shotgun while Taylor emptied his revolver into Helm's head. (See also SUTTON-TAYLOR FEUD.)

HEREFORD Cattle with white heads, red bodies and white markings that originated in Herefordshire, England and were brought into the West in the 1880s to breed with longhorns.

HICKOK, WILD BILL (b. James Butler Hickok in Troy Grove, Illinois on May 27, 1837; d. Deadwood, Dakota Territory on August 2, 1876) Wild Bill Hickok came to fame when newspaperman Henry Morton Stanley (of "Dr. Livingston, I presume" fame) came to the West in 1867, met him and wrote articles for the *Weekly Missouri Democrat,* the *New York Tribune* and *Harper's* that contained some far-fetched and rather embellished facts about Hickok. The article in *Harper's,* published in February 1867, reached a large national audience and did the most to create the legend of Wild Bill Hickok.

"Wild Bill" was the fourth son of an abolitionist actively involved in the Underground Railroad, and his early memories were of whisking slaves away. He may have received his nickname in his hometown as a way for people to differentiate between him and his brother Lorenzo; Lorenzo became "Tame Bill" and James became "Wild Bill." In another version of how he came to be known as "Wild Bill," legend has it that the moniker was applied after he had single-handedly forced a lynching mob to back down. Still another story has him acquiring the name "Bill" while driving freight on the Santa Fe Trail and then the "Wild" after he killed Dave McCanles. At any rate, James Butler Hickok became the legendary "Wild Bill" during his lifetime, and his reputation has grown since his death.

During the Civil War, Hickok served with the Union army as a civilian volunteer, working as a wagon master in Sedalia, Missouri and then as a spy and guide under General Samuel P. Curtis. He probably fought at the Battle of Pea Ridge, Arkansas in 1862. Hickok began scouting for Custer's Seventh Cavalry on January 1, 1867. Later that year he ran for sheriff of Ellsworth County, Kansas—and lost—but he obtained employment as a deputy U.S. marshal, chasing army deserters and thieves who stole government livestock.

During his travels as a scout, gambler and lawman, Hickok met a number of Old West legends, including Buffalo Bill Cody. In 1872 he was a member of the royal Russian buffalo hunt in Kansas and in 1873 tried his hand at show business back East when he appeared for seven months in *Scouts of the Plains* with Cody, a pallid play written by Ned Buntline that played to enthusiastic audiences. Hickok shot out the stage lights twice during the run and finally, bored and disgruntled, left the stage for the real thing out West.

Hickok's legend as a gunman began in his early 20s. Hickok was working for Russell, Majors and Waddell, driving freight on the Santa Fe Trail, when he was mauled by a bear; still, he managed to kill the bear with his Bowie knife and then was sent to a way station in Nebraska, the Rock Creek stage depot, run by Horace Wellman and his common-law wife and stable hand Doc Brink. He worked as a stock tender while he nursed his wounds and recovered. Trouble soon arose between Dave McCanles, who lived with his family on a nearby ranch, and Hickok over a woman, Sarah Shull. Shull was McCanles's mistress; Hickok had been secretly seeing her. The problems were exacerbated by McCanles's financial difficulties with Russell, Majors and Waddell. McCanles began calling Hickok "Duck Bill" and other slurs. On July 12, 1861 McCanles came to the stage station but Hickok refused to come out. "Come out and fight fair," said McCanles, before threatening to drag Hickok outside. "There will be one less son-of-a-bitch when you try that," answered Hickok. McCanles then came inside the depot; Hickok, who was behind a curtain, put a bullet through McCanles's heart. When McCanles was shot, his 12-year-old son Monroe, cousin James Woods and ranch employee James Gordon ran toward the station. Hickok shot Woods twice and then hit Gordon. While Monroe cradled his father's head, the other two attempted to flee, followed by Wellman and Brink; Wellman killed Woods with a hoe—hacking him to death—while Brink killed Gordon with a shotgun.

Other gunplay followed Hickok in his life. In Springfield, Missouri on July 21, 1865, another fight over a woman occurred, this time between Dave Tutt and Hickok. Tutt knew Hickok because the two were both courting Susanna Moore. On the previous evening, Hickok and Tutt exchanged threats over a card game; the next day at 6 P.M. they faced each other in the town square in front of a large crowd. Hickok said, "Don't come any closer, Dave," when they were 75 yards apart; Tutt replied with a shot from his pistol. Hickok used two hands—his left had to steady the revolver—and put a bullet into Tutt's chest. He died instantly; Hickok was acquitted in his trial.

In Hays City, Kansas a drunken cavalryman, John Mulrey, refused to be arrested, so Hickok shot him. He died the next morning. On September 27, 1869—a month later—about 1 A.M. Hickok and Deputy Peter Lanihan went to a beer palace where Samuel Strawhim was leading a drunken group in tearing up the place. Hickok order the revelers to stop; Strawhim refused and a riot ensued; Hickok then shot Strawhim in the head—he died instantly—and the trouble stopped.

On July 17, 1870 in Hays City, Kansas, Wild Bill was drunk and became involved in a brawl with five drunk soldiers from the Seventh Cavalry, led by Tom Custer, the famous general's brother, at Drum's Saloon. Losing the fight, and thrown to the floor, Wild Bill pulled his gun and shot Privates Jeremiah Lanigan, who eventually recovered, and John Kile, who died the next day; Wild Bill then fled town, escaping from Custer, who hightailed it back to the fort and returned with a bevy of soldiers looking for Hickok.

Perhaps Hickok's most famous gunfight occurred with Phil Coe, who was leading about 50 drunk Texans on a wild spree in Abilene, Kansas on October 5, 1871 when Hickok warned them to behave themselves. Hickok then alerted Deputy Mike Williams about the trouble. Hearing a shot, Hickok investigated and found Coe with a gun in his hand. Coe alleged he had shot at a dog, but Hickok went for his guns as Coe fired at him, hitting his coattails. Wild Bill's bullet hit Coe, standing eight feet away, in the belly. As Coe fell, his gun went off again, the bullet going through Hickok's legs. Meanwhile, Mike Williams, who was scheduled to catch a train 45 minutes later to be with his ailing wife, burst through the crowd of violent cowboys to help Hickok. Hickok, jumpy in the situation, whirled and shot his close friend Williams twice in the head. The deputy died instantly; Coe died three days later. Hickok, upset and distraught, closed down the town and paid the funeral expense for Mike Williams. Ironically, after the death of Williams, Wild Bill Hickok is not known to have ever fired a shot at someone again.

Hickok's eyesight failed and so did his fortunes during his last few years. In 1874 he headed back West from Illinois, where he recovered from a wound. In 1876 he moved to Cheyenne but was arrested on several occasions for vagrancy. A known womanizer who may have married Calamity Jane somewhere along the line but almost definitely fathered a daughter by her, Hickok married Agnes Lake on March 5, 1876 in Cheyenne. He

Wild Bill Hickok   *(Kansas State Historical Society)*

then moved on to Deadwood, a mining boom town where he gambled in the hope of attracting a fortune.

On August 2, 1876 in Deadwood, Dakota Territory at Saloon No. 10, Hickok was in an afternoon poker game with Carl Mann, Charles Rich and Frank Massie. Massie, a Missouri river pilot, was sitting opposite Hickok against the wall; Hickok twice asked to change places, but Massie laughed and joked that no one would shoot him in the back.

Hickok had to borrow $50 from the house—Carl

Mann was one of the saloon's proprietors—after playing for half an hour. At 4:10 P.M. Jack McCall came in and drank a glass of whiskey, then drew an old .45 Colt and walked up behind Hickok. Reportedly, Hickok and McCall were in a card game the previous day and McCall had lost $110 to Wild Bill, although rumors also float that Hickok's enemies had offered McCall $200 to kill the legendary figure. Rich, a gambler, had just dealt a pair of aces, a pair of eights and a queen to Hickok when McCall shot Hickok in the back of his head, the slug coming out under his right cheekbone and ending up in Massie's left forearm.

Hickok died instantly while McCall said, "Take that!" and fled the building. But bartender Anson Tipple climbed the bar to get to McCall, who tried to shoot but the gun misfired. Massie thought Hickok, upset over gambling losses, had shot him, and he ran out into the street shouting, "Wild Bill shot me!" Ironically, it was discovered that the bullet that killed Hickok was the only round not defective in the gun. McCall was later executed. (See also CALAMITY JANE; CODY, BUFFALO BILL; COE, PHIL; MCCALL, BROKEN NOSE JACK; STRAWHIM, SAMUEL; THOMPSON, BEN.)

HIDATSA INDIANS The Hidatsa became famous when artist George Catlin lived with them and painted the tribe in the early 1830s; artist Karl Bodmer also painted them in 1834 when Prince Maximilian visited. In 1837 most of the Hidatsa were wiped out (along with the Mandan) in a smallpox epidemic. Like the Mandan, the Hidatsa hunted the buffalo but were not nomadic; they lived in earth-domed lodges and grew corn. Young warriors formed an important organization, the Dog Society, that gained glory in battle and served as tribal police. A small tribe, also known as the Minnetaree, they were first visited by whites when Lewis and Clark visited during their 1804 expedition.

HIGGINS, PINK (b. John Calhoun Pinckney Higgins near Atlanta, Georgia in 1848; d. Kent County, Texas on December 18, 1914)

Around 1874 in Lampasas County, Texas, rancher Pink Higgins found cowboy Zeke Terrell butchering one of Higgins's cows, which had just been shot. Pink, about 90 yards away, aimed his Winchester rifle at Terrell and killed the cowboy. Then Pink disemboweled the dead cow, stuffed Terrell's corpse inside and rode into town to tell law officers where they could find a miracle taking place—a cow giving birth to a man.

Bad blood had flowed between Higgins and the Horrell brothers at a neighboring ranch. The feud originated when the Horrells killed three law officers—including Pink's son-in-law—in 1873. Around 1875 Pink ran into one of Horrell's cowboys, Ike Lantier, at a waterhole used by both ranchers. Lantier went for his pistol, but Pink put a rifle bullet into the gunman, who dropped out of the saddle and died. Higgins also killed Merritt Horrell—claiming he had tampered with some of Pink's steers—on January 22, 1877 in Lampasas, Texas at the Matador Saloon. On March 26 of that same year, Higgins and some friends ambushed Sam and Mart Horrell

about five miles outside town; the Horrells put up a fight and survived. But on June 14 in Lampasas there was a major shootout. Higgins, top aid Bill Wren and brother-in-law Frank Mitchell faced three Horrells—Mart, Sam and Tom—as well as Bill and Tom Bowen, John Dixon and Bill Crabtree. Mitchell was killed and Wren was seriously wounded in the melee. Meanwhile, in the midst of the fight Higgins slipped out of town and got reinforcements, so the gunfight continued until local citizens convinced both sides to stop fighting.

The next month, Higgins and his 14 cowhands—all armed with Winchesters by Pink—went over to the Horrell Ranch and trapped the brothers and their crew inside the ranch house and bunkhouse. After two days, Higgins's ammunition ran low and he called a retreat. He had only wounded two Horrell men. Finally, the Texas Rangers got Higgins to sign a truce, ending the war with the Horrells.

That was not the last of trouble for Pink Higgins. Around 1884 in Mexico Higgins went to pick up 125 horses he had purchased. When he crossed the Rio Grande, the other man tried to deny the sale, so Higgins killed him. Then he had to make a stand on the river-bank; he did this until dark and then swam back across to Texas.

Pink's final shootout occurred on October 4, 1903 in Kent County, Texas when he ran into an old nemesis, Bill Standifer, as Higgins was returning to his ranch. The two dismounted and began firing their rifles at each other about 60 yards apart; Standifer hit Higgin's horse, but Pink shot Standifer in the heart. By this time Higgins had moved his ranching operation from Lampasas to a spread about 13 miles south of Spur, Texas. Here he died at the age of 66 from a heart attack. (See also HORRELL, BENJAMIN; HORRELL, MARTIN; HORRELL, MERRITT; HORRELL, SAMUEL W.; HORRELL, THOMAS W.)

HIGH CHAPARRAL, THE TV show that starred Leif Erickson as Big John Cannon, Cameron Mitchell as Buck Cannon, Mark Slade as Billy Blue Cannon (1967–70), Henry Darrow as Manolito Montoya, Linda Cristal as Victoria Cannon, Frank Silvera as Don Sebastian Montoya (1967–70), Don Collier as Sam Butler, Ted Markland as Reno (1967–70), Roberto Contreras as Pedro (1967–70), Roubert Hoy as Joe and Rudy Ramos as Wind (19701–71).

The High Chaparral was the ranch owned by the Cannons in Arizona Territory in the 1870s. Big John Cannon, the family patriarch, married Victoria, daughter of Don Sebastian Montoya, a prominent Mexican landowner and rancher. The Cannons, with the help of their Mexican family connections, attempted to tame the Wild West and have a thriving cattle ranch. They did so for four seasons, doing well in Europe as well as the United States despite some consumer objections to the violence they showed. The hour-long shows were filmed in Tucson, Arizona, and the sets can still be seen at the Old Tucson Movie Location Park there. The show aired from September 10, 1967 until September 10, 1971 before going into syndication. It appeared first on NBC's Sunday night lineup and then moved to Friday nights, where it finished its run. The show was created by David Dortort, who also created "Bonanza."

HIGH NOON   Film produced by Stanley Kramer; directed by Fred Zinnemann; screenplay by Carl Foreman (from the story "The Tin Star" by John W. Cunningham); music by Dimitri Tiomkin; released in 1952 by United Artists; 85 minutes in length. Cast: Gary Cooper, Grace Kelly, Thomas Mitchell, Lloyd Bridges, Katy Jurado, Otto Cruger, Lon Chaney, Jr., Henry (Harry) Morgan, Sheb Wooley and Jack Elam.

The action in this film takes place over a period of about 85 minutes, which is the time of the movie itself. It begins on a Sunday morning about 10:40 A.M. when Will and Amy Kane are getting married; she is a pacifist Quaker, so he's agreed to hang up his guns, although he's been the marshal of town. But Frank Miller, an outlaw sent to jail by Kane, is getting out of prison this day, and word arrives he'll be in town around noon. At the station, three of Miller's buddies are waiting. Kane can leave town with his new bride, but a sense of duty compels him to stay. He goes to the townspeople for help, but they all refuse. Further, Kane's bride foresakes him. Throughout the movie, shots of clocks are shown, giving a sense of the impending hour and creating added tension. Finally, the train pulls in and the four outlaws come after Kane. A shootout ensues, and Kane's Quaker wife comes to his rescue—the only one to do so. When Kane emerges victorious, he takes off his badge and throws it down in the dirt; he then rides out of town on a buggy with his bride. The movie won four Academy Awards: Best Actor (Gary Cooper), Best Song ("Do Not Forsake Me, O My Darling," sung by Tex Ritter), Best Score (Dimitri Tiomkin) and Best Editing (Elmo Williams and Harry Gerstad).

HIGH NOON THEME SONG   "Do Not Forsake Me, O My Darling," music by Dimitri Tiomkin; lyrics by Ned Washington; published by Leo Feist, Inc. in 1952.

The song for the movie *High Noon* was not part of the original picture, but after initial screenings for movie executives the producer and director knew the movie needed more than just background music. Dimitri Tiomkin, who composed the music for the movie, came up with the melody and an idea for lyrics to tell the plot at the beginning of the movie; he engaged lyricist Ned Washington to work on the words. Tiomkin and Washington wrote the song and Tiomkin called Tex Ritter, who first refused to do the song but, then relented and sang it for the movie soundtrack off camera. (See also HIGH NOON (movie).)

HIGH PLAINS DRIFTER   Film produced by Robert Daley; directed by Clint Eastwood; screenplay by Ernest Tidyman; released in 1973 by Universal; 105 minutes in length. Cast: Clint Eastwood, Verna Bloom, Mariana Hill, Mitchell Ryan, Jack Ging, Stefan Gierasch, Ted Hartley, Bill Curtis and Geoffrey Lewis.

This was the first movie directed by Clint Eastwood. In this movie, Eastwood is "the Stranger," who is hired by some townfolk to protect them from outlaws. There are some metaphysical flashbacks and pschobabble dreams. In the end, Eastwood destroys the town after renaming it "Hell" while he protects it against the outlaws.

HILL, TOM   (aka Tom Chelson; b. ?; d. Alamo Springs, New Mexico on March 13, 1878)   Tom Hill, sometimes known as Tom Chelson, was the right-hand man of cattle rustler Jesse Evans, who raided the Tunstall and Brewer Ranches in Lincoln County, New Mexico. In September 1877 Dick Brewer and a posse chased the outlaws to a secluded dugout where they forced the outlaws to surrender. But several weeks later the outlaws' cohorts galloped into town and freed them from jail.

Other altercations occurred, but on February 18, 1878 John Tunstall, with four men, was driving a herd of horses. The Lincoln County feud was heating up and Tunstall was supposed to be arrested. Hill and Jesse Evans were in the posse and Hill came up behind Tunstall. The rancher agreed to submit to their custody, but Hill shot the rancher in the back of his head, killing him. Then he killed Tunstall's horse and the posse rode off. This event triggered the Lincoln County War.

On March 13, 1878 Hill and Evans came up to a sheep drivers' camp, stole a horse and mule and rummaged through items in the wagon. The half-blood Cherokee guarding the camp had grabbed a rifle but was shot by Hill and Evans. The Cherokee fled—hit in the leg—but crawled back toward the camp while Hill and Evans continued to rifle the camp. At point-blank range, the Cherokee shot Hill, killing him, and then hit Evans in the wrist, but the outlaw managed to escape. (See also LINCOLN COUNTY WAR; TUNSTALL, JOHN HENRY.)

HINDMAN, GEORGE W.   (b. ?; d. Lincoln, New Mexico on April 1, 1878)   George Hindman was a deputy sheriff and member of the posse that gunned down John Tunstall on February 18, 1878. On April 1, Monday, at 9 in the morning, Hindman and Sheriff William Brady were walking down the middle of the street in Lincoln, New Mexico when they were hit in an ambush by Billy the Kid, Henry Brown, John Middleton, Fred Wait and French. Brady died immediately; Hindman died a few moments later. (See also BILLY THE KID; LINCOLN COUNTY WAR; TUNSTALL, JOHN HENRY.)

HITE, WOOD   (b. Robert Woodson Hite in Kentucky; d. Ray County, Missouri in January 1882)   In 1876 brothers Wood and Clarence Hite—first cousins of Jesse and Frank James—joined the James Gang. But Wood soon left the gang after a few train holdups; his prominent, decaying front teeth made him easily recognizable. In January 1882 Wood and Dick Liddel, a member of Jesse James's gang, were hiding out at the home of Martha Bolton, the widowed sister of Bob Ford, the man who later shot Jesse James. Hite and Liddel were quarreling about Mrs. Bolton after breakfast, and both drew their guns—while still at the table—and began shooting. While they were shooting at each other, Bob Ford drew his pistol, cooly aimed at Hite and shot him in the head. Hite died a short while later, and after dark Bob and Cap Ford wrapped the body in an old horse blanket and buried him in a shallow grave about a mile from the house. (See also FORD, BOB; JAMES, JESSE.)

HOBBLE   Tying a horse's legs together so it can graze but can't wander too far. This can be done with a rope or with a steel (or iron) shackle.

HODGES, THOMAS   See BELL, TOM.

HOLLADAY, BEN   (b. Nicholas County, Kentucky on October 14, 1819; d. Portland, Oregon on July 8, 1887)   A financial baron through his stagecoach line, the Holladay Overland Mail and Express Company, Holladay became a powerful self-made millionaire by putting together a stagecoach company that carried the mail (the U.S. government paid him $650,000 annually to deliver the mail). He also carried passengers with a top line that hired the best drivers, used the best horses and mules and had the best coaches during the 1860s. In 1866 Holladay sold his line, which operated on more than 2,760 miles of western roads, to Wells, Fargo and Company and then formed a steamship company, the Northern Pacific Transportation Company. He bought into railroads in 1868 when he purchased the Oregon Central Railroad company but ran into financial problems in 1873 and was ousted by bond holders who took over the railroad. From this point on, Holladay's life was in decline.

HOLLIDAY, DOC   (b. John Henry Holliday in Griffin, Georgia on August 14, 1851; d. Glenwood Springs, Colorado on November 8, 1887)   Doc Holliday was a

Doc Holliday   *(Western Archives)*

Ben Holladay

dentist, but his fame in the West came from his guns, his friendship with Wyatt Earp and his role in the gunfight at the O.K. Corral in Tombstone, Arizona.

Major John Holliday served for the Confederacy in the Civil War and raised his family in the genteel southern tradition. There is evidence that father and son quarreled, most likely after young John's mother died and his father remarried, and that young John left home about 1867 or 1868. "Doc" graduated from the Pennsylvania College of Dental Surgery in 1872 and practiced briefly in Atlanta (with Dr. Arthur C. Ford) before opening his own office in Griffin, Georgia. But a hacking cough was diagnosed as chronic pulmonary tuberculosis, and the young dentist was advised to try a drier climate; thus, Doc Holliday moved west in late 1872 or early 1873 for his health and to try to save his life. He first went to Dallas, where he practiced dentistry with Dr. John Seegar, but soon developed his gambling skills and spent an increasing amount of time playing poker and faro. After Holliday left Dallas, he made the gambling rounds, to Fort Griffin, Jacksboro, Pueblo, Denver, Cheyenne, Deadwood and then Dodge City, where he met and married a prostitute named Kate Elder (otherwise known as "Big-Nose Kate," real name: Mary Katherine Michael). He practiced dentistry in Dodge City, but mostly he gambled. There, also, his fate as a legendary western gunman was sealed when he befriended Wyatt Earp. Holliday reportedly came to Earp's aid when the lawman was surrounded by rowdy gunmen, and grabbed a cowboy's gun to stop him from shooting Earp in the back. From that point on, Earp and Holliday were friends, although most of Earp's friends did not like Holliday and he later proved to be a political embarrassment to Earp.

It is not known how many men Doc Holliday actually killed, but it is a fact he killed Mike Gordon, a former army scout, on July 19, 1879 in Las Vegas, New Mexico. Here, Holiday and John Joshua Webb ran a saloon where one of the prostitutes was Gordon's girlfriend. Gordon wanted her to quit; when she refused, he decided to shoot up the building. Gordon had fired two shots at the building when Doc stepped outside and fired one shot into him; Gordon died the next day.

Doc's gunfighting prowess is etched in history because of the gunfight at the O.K. Corral on October 26, 1881 in Tombstone, Arizona. The source of the gunfight was a feud between the Clantons and Earps; ironically, Holliday was part of that feud because the Clantons knew he was involved in a stagecoach holdup and was appointed as a sheriff by the Earps anyway. When the shooting began at the corral, Holliday pulled a shotgun from his long overcoat and killed the unarmed Tom McLaury, who was standing behind his horse. Holliday himself was grazed in the side by a shot from Frank McLaury. Holliday blasted McLaury with 12 buckshot under his right arm; Holliday also fired his pistol at Ike Clanton, who escaped into the building next door.

This gunfight led to the death of Morgan Earp, and Holliday was in the group that avenged that death by killing Frank Stilwell in Tucson on March 20, 1882 and Florentino Cruz on March 22, 1882 in Tombstone. That same year Doc and Wyatt Earp fled Tombstone; in Denver Holliday was arrested on trumped-up charges as a ruse for an extradition back to Arizona, but Bat Masterson interceded with the governor and Holliday was not returned. The next year, 1883, Holliday was involved in the Dodge City War.

Doc Holliday knew he was dying; in 1887 his cough was worse, so he went to a health spa in Glenwood Spring, Colorado to recover. He died there at the age of 36. His wife Kate later remarried, opened a boardinghouse in Arizona and wrote about her life with the celebrated Doc Holliday. (See also BIG-NOSED KATE; EARP, WYATT; GUNFIGHT AT THE O.K. CORRAL.)

HOLLISTER, CASH (b. Cassius M. Hollister on December 7, 1845 in Cleveland, Ohio; d. Hunnewell, Kansas on October 18, 1884)   Cash Hollister was a well-known lawman who chased down a number of horse thieves. He had moved to Caldwell, Kansas in 1877 when he was 31 and was elected mayor of Caldwell in 1878. In 1883 he was appointed a deputy U.S. marshal; he also served as deputy sheriff of Sumner County. On October 18, 1884 in Hunnewell, Kansas, Hollister went out with a posse to arrest Bob Cross, the son of a Texas minster who had left his wife to run off with the young daughter of a farmer—and then deserted the girl to return to his wife. When the girl went back to her father, he swore out a warrant for Cross's arrest. Around

3 A.M. the group reached the farm; lawmen ordered Cross to come out, but his wife came out and protested that he wasn't there. When the lawmen kicked open the door, Mrs. Cross offered to let the posse search inside; the posse demanded that a lamp be lit, and the woman quickly went back in the house and shut the door. The lawmen then kicked open the door and two shots were fired; the lawmen backed off and began gathering hay to burn the house. Another shot was fired, and George Davis, the marshal of Hunnewell, looked around and discovered that Hollister was dead. Davis picked Hollister up and tried to put him on the wagon, but the team ran away; finally the team was caught and Hollister's body put into the wagon bed. Cross came out, shielded by his wife, who helped him escape, but he was caught the next day.

HOLSTERS   See SCABBARDS.

HOLT, TIM (b. John Charles Holt, Jr. in Beverly Hills, California on February 5, 1918; d. Shawnee, Oklahoma on February 15, 1973)   Holt's father, Jack Holt, was an actor in Hollywood, and his sister, Jennifer, was a cowgirl in "B" westerns. Between 1940 and 1952 Tim Holt made 47 "B" westerns; his screen debut came in *The Red River Valley* (1928) with this father. He appeared with Barbara Stanwyck in *Stella Dallas* (1938), with Harry Carey in *The Law West of Tombstone* (1938), with George O'Brien in *Renegade Ranger* (1939), and with John Wayne in *Stagecoach* (1939). During World

Tim Holt

War II Holt served with the air force; after the war he appeared in *My Darling Clementine* (1946) and *The Treasure of Sierra Madre* (1948). Holt moved to Denver in 1959 and to Oklahoma in the early 1970s, where he hosted a local TV western film show. (See also MOVIES.)

HOMBRE (term) This can be a term of rugged affection for a friend, but it generally implies a lowlife or man of disreputable character.

HOME ON THE RANGE The poem "A Home on the Range" was first recorded as a song by folk song collector John Lomax in San Antonio, Texas in 1908; the singer was Bill Jack McCurry, a black owner of a beer parlor in the red-light district of that city. It began to appear in sheet music form in 1925 based on McCurry's version, and in 1933 this was a top radio hit. The first printed version of the lyrics appeared in 1873 in a Kansas newspaper; it was written by Dr. Brewster Higley, a frontier physician who lived near Smith Center, Kansas on West Beaver Creek. The tune was sung by Dan Kelley, a patient of Higley's as well as a member of a musical group, who performed the song locally. The song soon spread and became popular. It evolved into "Colorado Home (Prospector's Song)" in the mid-1880s near Leadville, Colorado. The original may have been titled "Oh, Give Me a Home Where the Buffalo Roam" and also printed as "Western Home." This was adopted as the Kansas state song in 1947. Ironically, the origin of this song was uncovered in the 1930s after an Arizona couple, William and Mary Goodwin, filed a copyright infringement suit alleging "Home on the Range" was a copy of "An Arizona Home" they had published in 1904. The Music Publishers Protective Association hired attorney Samuel Moanfeldt to find the source of the song, and he found it in Kansas newspaper archives.

HOMESTEAD ACT The Homestead Act (1862) allowed any United States citizen to claim any unclaimed tract of public land of up to 160 acres and live on it for five years, at which time he or she would obtain title. The settler would have to make some improvement on the land during this time and had to pay the registration fees. Congress first passed the Homestead Act in 1860, but President James Buchanan vetoed it (over the slavery issue). The Homestead Act passed under President Lincoln and was signed by him on May 27, 1862.

HONDA The sliding knot on a rope for a lasso.

HONDO Film produced by Robert Fellows; directed by John Farrow; screenplay by James Edward Grant from a story by Louis L'Amour; released in 1953 by Warner Brothers; 83 minutes in length. Cast: John Wayne, Geraldine Page, Ward Bond, Michael Pate, James Arness, Lee Aaker and Paul Fix.

John Wayne as Hondo Lane walks out of the desert with his saddle, his rifle and his dog, Sam, onto a small spread and meets a boy, Johnny Lowe, chopping wood. The man of the house has left because he's scared of an Apache attack, leaving his wife and son, who are determined to protect their isolated ranch. Hondo Lane is

attracted to her; but when he rides into town the Apache attack. The Apache break off their attack because of the boy's courage in defending his mother, and the chief spares their lives to bring over some braves so she can pick a husband. Meanwhile, back in town, Hondo runs into a stranger and quarrels, and when the stranger tries an ambush, Hondo kills him; he then discovers he's killed Ed Lowe, the rancher. Finally, Hondo, Mrs. Lowe and Johnny head off to California, where Hondo has a ranch.

HONDO TV show that starred Ralph Taeger as Hondo Lane, Kathie Browne as Angie Dow, Buddy Foster as Johnny Dow, Noah Berry, Jr. as Buffalo Baker, Gary Clarke as Captain Richards, Michael Pate as Chief Vittoro and William Bryant as Colonel Crook.

Hondo Lane was an army scout based in Arizona Territory at Fort Lowell just after the Civil War. This action-packed character, with his dog Sam, led an action-packed series, based on the movie *Hondo*, starring John Wayne, which in turn was based on a Louis L'Amour novel. Wayne and his production company, Batjac, produced this series, which was filmed in color at MGM's studios and locations in the Mojave Desert. The show didn't last long—just 17 episodes—premiering on September 8, 1967 and ending on December 29, 1967. The hour-long show aired on ABC on Friday evenings.

HOOLIHAN A rope throw, done quietly and subtly, in which a loop comes from below the waist up over an animal's head. It was often done in the midst of a herd without disturbing the rest of the animals.

HOPALONG CASSIDY TV show that starred William Boyd as Hopalong Cassidy and Edgar Buchanan as Red O'Connors.

The Hopalong Cassidy movies starring William Boyd had peaked by 1948, but the character and actor were rejuvenated by television, just starting to come into its own at this time. In fact, Hopalong Cassidy was the first TV cowboy hero. The major problem was that Boyd was not a young man by the time TV came along (he was 50), so the 40 black-and-white 30-minute shows created for television were not exactly action packed. In fact, the first TV shows were edited versions of his movies, with Boyd adding some narration or a scene or two. Dressed in black and astride his faithful horse, Topper, the TV Hoppy debuted on NBC on June 24, 1949 on Friday nights and continued in that time slot until October 1949; beginning in April 1950, he appeared on NBC on Sunday evenings, and his last network telecast was December 23, 1951. After this time, the Hopalong Cassidy shows went into syndication, enjoying a Saturday morning slot in the 1950s. So popular was Hopalong Cassidy that Hoppy products reportedly brought in $70 million annually. The merchandising included Hopalong Cassidy lunch boxes, pajamas, wallpaper, bicycles (with handlebars shaped like steer horns and a spot for a six-shooter on the frame), cookies, pocket knives, watches, compasses, hair cream, toothpaste, records, guns, hats, chaps, books, belts, candy bars, peanut butter and roller skates with spurs but did *not* include bubble gum because Boyd refused to license it. In 1950 Hopalong Cassidy was seen on 63 TV stations and heard on 152 radio outlets, and 155 newspapers carried his adventures on the comics page. William Boyd got rich from Hopalong Cassidy, a result of his having the wisdom to buy the TV rights to the theatrical films in the 1940s. (See also MULFORD, CLARENCE EDWARD.)

HOPI INDIANS The Hopi live in pueblos of adobe and stone on mesas in northern Arizona high above the desert. Sedentary farmers, the Hopi grow corn, vegetables, fruit and cotton and use irrigation methods to make the desert fertile. Known for their rich artistic heritage, the Hopi make intricately designed pottery and are also engaged in basketry, weaving, carving and silversmithing. Their first contact with whites was in 1540 with Coronado's expedition. Juan de Onate, governor and colonizer of New Mexico, swore the Indians to an oath of fealty to the Spanish crown and attempted to convert them to Christianity in 1598, but the first Catholic mission was not established until 1629. The Pueblo revolt of 1680 ended efforts to Christianize the tribe, although attempts were made in 1692 and 1700 by the Spanish. Because the Hopi lived in such an isolated region, they were unaffected by Anglos moving west until the 1880s; in 1882 the U.S. government set aside a Hopi reservation. There are 10 Hopi settlements in the Southwest, and one of them, Oraibi, may be the oldest continuously inhabited town in the United States.

HORN, TOM (b. Memphis, Missouri on November 21, 1860; d. Cheyenne, Wyoming on November 20, 1903) Tom Horn represents the Old West at its wildest. He was a bounty hunter, Pinkerton detective and Apache scout and worked for big cattlemen during the Wyoming range wars; he was also in the Spanish-American War, competed as a rodeo cowboy and, while in jail waiting to be hung, wrote his autobiography. Horn was a legendary character who did a great many things in his life; ironically, he was hung for a crime he may not have commited.

A $600 price tag was on sheepherder Kels Nickells's head, and on July 18, 1901 a bounty hunter fired two bullets from a Winchester into who he thought was Nickells. Instead, Nickells's 13-year-old son, Willie, was killed—a case of mistaken identity from a killer 300 yards away. Later deputy U. S. marshal Joe LeFors found Tom Horn in a bar in Denver, and the drunken Horn, a braggart, boasted of the Nickells killing. LeFors arranged another meeting with Horn, hired a stenographer (who stayed hidden) and drew out the story of Nickells's killing again. This spelled doom for Horn, who was convicted of the killing and hung. There is speculation he may not have been the actual killer of the boy and that his confession brought to an end a fascinating life story.

Fourteen-year-old Tom Horn supposedly ran away from his Missouri farm home after whipping his father. By 1876 he was working for the army with Al Sieber as civilian chief of scouts and played a major role in the final capture of Geronimo (Horn spoke fluent Spanish and Apache). During the Pleasant Valley War in 1887 in Arizona, he hired himself out as a gunman and later became a deputy sheriff of Yavapai County. In 1890 he joined the Pinkerton Detective Agency in Denver and then became a range detective in 1892 for the Wyoming Cattle Growers' Association, helping recruit gunmen for the association. Somehow, he missed the Johnson County War. He was then hired by the Swan Land and Cattle Company in 1894, reportedly as a killer of rustlers and homesteaders—setting up ambushes and killing with a high-powered rifle for $600 a killing. Horn rejoined the army and went to Cuba in the Spanish-American War (helping with the Rough Riders) and then returned to Wyoming as a hired killer. Horn also enjoyed success as a rodeo cowboy, winning a roping contest in Phoenix.

In 1901 he was employed by rancher John Coble, who owned a large spread near Iron Mountain, north of Laramie. When schoolteacher Glendolene Kimmel's family feuded with neighboring homesteader Kels Nickells, Horn decided to kill him. In the months in jail awaiting his hanging, Horn wrote his autobiography. Neither the tearful pleas of Miss Kimmel (his sometimes girlfriend) nor the lawyers of the big cattlemen ($5,000 was anonymously put up for his defense fund) could stop the hanging.

Horn certainly had a reputation as a killer. On July 8, 1900 on Cold Springs Mountain in Routt County, Colorado he went into Matt Rash's neighborhood and trailed the rustler. Calling himself James Hicks, he hid outside Rash's cabin and, when the rustler came out, shot four times. The rustler crawled back inside and died, while Horn rushed to Denver to establish an alibi. On October 3, 1900 in Routt County, Colorado, Horn (again calling himself James Hicks) killed Nigger Isom Dart, a black cowboy suspected of rustling, with a rifle after the cowboy stepped outside his cabin.

After his conviction for the Nickells killing, Horn and another prisoner pulled a jail break, but he was recognized by a brothel keeper, who hauled him back in. Horn was hung in Cheyenne on November 20, 1903.

HORNER, JOE See CANTON, FRANK.

HORRELL, BENJAMIN (b. Arkansas; d. Lincoln, New Mexico on December 1, 1873) One of the Horrells who was in the notorious Horrell-Higgins feud, Ben Horrell moved from Texas to Lincoln County, New Mexico with his brothers to establish a ranch. On December 1, 1873 Ben and some friends were on a drunken binge, shooting up Lincoln, when Constable Juan Martinez came to arrest Horrell. An exchange of gunfire resulted inthe death of Horrell and two of his buddies, Dave Warner and Jack Gylam, as well as Martinez. After Horrell's death, a thief chopped off his finger to get his gold ring. (See also HIGGINS, PINK.)

HORRELL, MARTIN (b. Arkansas; d. Meridian, Texas on December 15, 1878) The Horrell brothers, Mart, Sam and Tom, built a ranching operation in Lampasas County, Texas, where they became embroiled in the Horrell-Higgins feud. Mart was badly wounded on March 19, 1873 in Lampasas at the Matador Saloon when the Texas State Police attempted to arrest Clint Barkley. After the shootout, Mart's brothers escaped and freed Mart and Jerry Scott from prison in a show of force.

After this, they moved to Lincoln County, New Mexico. There the Horrells shot up a Mexican wedding dance at a private home, killing four Mexicans, after brother Ben had been killed and local authorities refused to act. About a month later the Horrells were in an adobe house when they were surrounded by Lincoln County sheriff Alex Mills and a posse of about 60 Mexicans, but the all-day fight produced no fatalities. Finally, they were run out of the area by vigilantes.

Back in Lampasas in 1877, Mart and Tom Horrell were ambushed by Pink Higgins, which led to more gunfights. On June 14, 1877 there was a gunfight in the Lampasas town square, and in July 1877 Mart and his brothers were pinned down by Pink Higgins and 14 cowboys. But after two days, the Higgins party withdrew.

In late 1878 Mart and Tom Horrell, along with Bill Crabtree, John Dixon and Tom Bowen, were arrested for robbing and murdering a Bosque County merchant. On December 15, 1878, before their trial, some citizens broke into the jail and shot the Horrell brothers to death. (See also HIGGINS, PINK.)

HORRELL, MERRITT (b. Arkansas; d. Lampasas, Texas on January 22, 1877) A member of the Horrell family, and part of the Horrell-Higgins feud, Merritt was in Jerry Scott's saloon warming himself on a cold Monday when Pink Higgins slipped in the back door. Merritt was shot four times by Higgins with a Winchester and died. (See also HIGGINS, PINK.)

HORRELL, SAMUEL W. (b. Arkansas; d. New Mexico c. 1880s) A member of the violent Horrell family, Sam was the only one to survive, leaving Lampasas, Texas in 1880 and moving to New Mexico, where he lived quietly with his family. (See also HIGGINS, PINK.)

HORRELL, THOMAS W. (b. Arkansas; d. Meridian, Bosque County, Texas on December 15, 1878) Tom Horrell and Pink Higgins had a saloon quarrel over a cattle drive the two had organized for Abilene in 1872 that led to the Horrell-Higgins range feud. At this time the Horrells had a big ranch in Lampasas County, Texas, second in size only to that of Pink Higgins. Tom Horrell was killed with his brother Mart when citizens rushed the jail where they were being held for their trial. The brothers were suspected of robbing and murdering a merchant, but the crowd never listened to any evidence; they burst in one night and shot the Horrells to death. (See also HIGGINS, PINK.)

HORSE The Spanish introduced domestic horses to the Americas; the first were brought to the West Indies by Christopher Columbus in 1493. Horses were first brought to Mexico in 1519 by Hernando Cortes; later, Spanish colonists in Mexico introduced cattle and horse ranching in the 16th century. Fossil records show horses were indigenous to the Americas but had disappeared before the Spanish came.

Horses were necessary in the Spaniards' quest to conquer the Native Americans, who were initially afraid of the "big dogs." Horses were also necessary for transportation in the vast lands and for cattle ranching; later when horses became part of the Plains Indian culture, they changed the lives of the Native Americans. First, horses made Indians more mobile; next, they made buffalo hunting easier; third, they provided more leisure time for the males. Horses spread rapidly throughout the plains (a result of Indians trading), so that during the period 1650–1770 all the tribes had acquired horses.

In addition to the Spanish, English settlers brought horses to the new country to be used for work, such as plowing, harvesting and other farmwork. As European settlers pushed westward, they brought horses to do their farmwork and for transportation. Thus the spread of horses in the area now known as the United States is due to several factors: (1) the Spanish, who first brought the horses from Europe and introduced them to the Americas; (2) the Native Americans, who began to acquire horses through the capture of wild horses and through trading; (3) the British colonists, who brought horses to the new land and who pushed westward from the East Coast throughout the 18th and 19th centuries.

Two types of horses emerged in the United States. The riding horse had smaller bones and a trimmer shape; the draft or work horse was much heavier, with a stockier build and heavier bones. The western horses stood between 14 hands and 15 hands two inches at the withers (one hand equals four inches). Horse less than 14 hands are called ponies. A full-grown horse weights 800–1,050 pounds, although a draft horse can weigh more.

Horses in the West were used as pack animals, for trading, to hunt, as transportation (either ridden or pulling a wagon) and sometimes for food. For a cattle drive, a single cowboy would use about 10 horses; at least one would be a good "night" horse with better night vision (all horses can see better at night than humans, but some horses have especially good night vision). During roundup a working cowboy needed two or three good "cutting horses," which would separate cattle in a herd and were trained to help a cowboy who was roping cattle from its back.

A horse was saddle broken when it was four to five years old. The gestation period for a foal is 11-1/2 months. Stallions were preferred by the Spanish and by Indians, who considered mares too effeminate for real men. Later, cowboys often preferred geldings because they were easier to handle, but still male, although mares tended to lose some of their stigma as only fit for women as the 19th century progressed.

HORSES AND THEIR COWBOYS The real working cowboy in the 19th century used a number of horses on a cattle drive because it was hard, strenuous work. The horses were divided into cutting horses and

Horses and their cowboys: Roy Rogers and Trigger

night horses and perhaps a "green broke" horse for daytime, and while a cowboy may have had a "favorite" he was certainly not as attached to it as the movie and TV cowboys. First, the ranch owner usually owned the horses (a working cowboy owned only his saddle), and second, a single horse couldn't do everything required of a working horse, especially with no rest. The first movie cowboy to give his horse co-billing was William S. Hart, whose Fritz was the first horse "star." But the real pioneer was Tom Mix, whose horse Tony (later Tony, Jr.) was trained to do tricks and actually be a co-star. From this point almost every TV and movie cowboy had a horse as a co-star and these horses were often as well-known as the cowboy. Listed are famous horses and their cowboys:

Ace and Tom Tyler; Apache and Bob Baker; Black Eyed Nellie (also called Ringeye) and Smiley Burnette; Black Jack and Allen "Rocky" Lane; Brownie and Bob Steele; Buttermilk and Dale Evans; Cactus and Sunset Carson; Champion and Gene Autry; Chico and Bill Cody; Cyclone and Don "Red" Barry; Diablo and the Cisco Kid (Duncan Renaldo); Duke and John Wayne; Falcon and Buster Crabbe; Flash, Copper, or White Cloud and Eddie Dean; Fritz and William S. Hart; Goldie and Hoot Gibson; Joker and Andy Devine (Jingles); Jubilee and Dale Robertson (on "Tales of Wells Fargo"); Knight and Rod Cameron; Koko and Rex Allen; Lightning and Tim Holt; Loco and Pancho (Leo Carillo); Mike and George O'Brian; Mutt and Hoot Gibson; Pardner and Monte Hale; Raider and Charles Starrett; Rebel and Johnny Mack Brown; Rocky and Kermit Maynard; Rush and Lash LaRue; Rusty and Tom Keene; Scout and Jack Hoxie; Scout and Tonto (Jay Silverheels); Sheik and Tim Holt; Silver and Buck Jones; Silver and The Lone Ranger (Clayton Moore); Silver Bullet and Whip Wilson; Silver King and Wally Wales; Smoke and Dick Foran; Starlight and Bob Livingston; Starlight and Jack Perrin; Starlight or Midnight and Tim McCoy; Sunset and Jimmy Wakely; Tarzan and Ken Maynard; Thunder or Sonny and Wild Bill Elliott; Tony or Tony, Jr. and Tom Mix; Topper and William Boyd (Hopalong Cassidy); Trigger and Roy Rogers; White Flash and Tex Ritter; White Knight and Fred Scott.

HOTEL DE PAREE   TV show that starred Earl Holliman as Sundance, Judi Meredith as Monique, Jeanette Nolan as Annette Deveraux and Strother Martin as Aaron Donager.

The Hotel de Paree was located in Georgetown, Colorado in the rough-and-tumble West. Unfortunately, it was run by two women who preferred to view it in terms of European elegance. Sundance helped them keep law and order there with the help of his silver hatband, which blinded adversaries—a rather far-fetched idea that came along when TV was overrun by westerns and desperate for new gimmicks. Actually, the initial premise was a gimmick: Sundance had served 17 years in prison for killing a man in Georgetown, Colorado. For some reason he returned and found the dead man's relatives running this hotel; they hired him. This show only lasted one season, premiering October 2, 1959 and

ending September 23, 1960. Thirty-three episodes of the 30-minute show were filmed, and they aired on CBS on Friday evenings.

HOUSTON, SAMUEL   (b. in Rockbridge County, Virginia on March 2, 1793; d. near Huntsville, Texas on July 26, 1863)   Before Sam Houston became the greatest figure in the history of Texas, he was one of the greatest figures in the history of Tennessee. He grew up in Tennessee and lived for several years with the Cherokee Indians, who called him "the Raven." He served in Congress from 1823 to 1827 and was elected governor of Tennessee in 1827. He left Tennessee in 1829 while he was governor because his wife left him. Houston lived with the Cherokee in Indian Territory (Oklahoma) and took an Indian wife; he moved to Texas in 1832 after first visiting the area on behalf of President Andrew Jackson to discuss Indian affairs. Houston became commander in chief of the rebel army when Texas revolted against Mexican rule in 1835. After the defeat of American troops at the Alamo on March 6, 1836, Houston organized a force of fewer than 800 men; at the Battle of San Jacinto on April 21, 1836 he surprised a Mexican army of 1,300 who were taking a siesta and defeated them, capturing their General Santa Anna, and declared Texas a free and independent republic. Houston served as first president of the republic from 1836 to 1838 and again from 1841 to 1844. In 1845, when Texas became a state, Houston went to Washington as a senator. In March 1861 Houston, a unionist, refused to take the oath of the Confederacy and resigned from public office. Houston had married for the third time in 1840, and this was a happy and productive marriage. After he left political office, Houston retired to his farm near Huntsville, where he died before the end of the Civil War.

Sam Houston   *(Western Archives)*

HOWARD, OLIVER OTIS (b. Leeds, Maine on November 8, 1830; d. Burlington, Vermont on October 26, 1909) Army general Howard led the pursuit of Chief Joseph and the Nez Perce for over 1,000 miles when the Indians tried to flee to Canada in 1877; the tribe was captured in October 1877 just 30 miles from the Canadian border. Howard provoked this tragedy when he demanded that Chief Joseph move his people from their homeland to a reservation within 30 days because gold had been discovered on the tribe's land. The Nez Perce defeated the First Cavalry in the Battle of White Bird Canyon and then started their long trek. Howard had previously served in the Civil War (losing his right arm in the Battle of Fair Oaks) and then the Southwest, where he patiently negotiated a treaty with Cochise in 1872. In 1894 Howard retired from the army.

HOWDY DOODY TV show hosted by Buffalo Bob Smith.

One of the most popular children's shows of all time, it featured Howdy Doody dressed in western garb. The puppet show, hosted by Buffalo Bob, began on December 27, 1947 and was titled "Puppet Playhouse" and "Puppet Television Theater" during the first few months. The show ran until September 24, 1961 on NBC. From June 16, 1956 on, it was exclusively a Saturday morning show. The show featured live action and marionettes, and was the first television show to complete 1,000 broadcasts, eventually appearing on NBC for 2,343 shows. In 1976 Buffalo Bob Smith attempted to revive the show as "The New Howdy Doody Show," but it was not successful in reaching an appreciative audience.

HOW THE WEST WAS WON Film produced by Bernard Smith; directed by John Ford, Henry Hathaway and George Marshall; screenplay by James R. Webb; released in 1963 by MGM (1962 in London); 165 minutes in length. Cast: Carroll Baker, Lee J. Cobb, Henry Fonda, Carolyn Jones, Karl Malden, Gregory Peck, George Peppard, Robert Preston, Debbie Reynolds, James Stewart, Eli Wallach, John Wayne, Richard Widmark, Brigid Bazlen, Walter Brennan, David Brian, Andy Devine, Raymond Massey, Agnes Moorehead, Harry Morgan, Thelma Ritter, Mickey Shaughnessey, Russ Tamblyn, Lee Van Cleef and Jack Lambert.

This movie was a group effort, with a lineup of superstars and 12,617 extras. Narrated by Spencer Tracy, the movie cost over $14 million and was based on a series of articles from *Life* magazine. A 60-year period (1830–90) in the life of four generations of a pioneer family is divided into five segments: the settlement of the Ohio River area; the California gold rush and the wagons headed west; the Civil War; the railroad reaching across the country, and law and order coming to the West.

HOW THE WEST WAS WON TV show that starred James Arness as Zeb Macahan, Fionnula Flanagan as Aunt Molly Culhane, Bruce Boxleitner as Luke Macahan, Kathryn Holcomb as Laura Macahan, William Kirby Cullen as Josh Macahan and Vicki Schreck as Jessie Macahan.

Originally titled "The Macahans" when it was a pilot and based loosely on the movie of the same title, this TV show featured Zeb Macahan, who returned east to his family in Virginia after 10 years as a loner in the Dakotas. He was helping his brother's family get ready for their trek west when the Civil War broke out; the brother, Tim, and his wife were killed, leaving Zeb with their three children. Aunt Molly came from Boston to help and the group set out. The first season showed the group moving west, and the second season of this series saw them on a ranch in the Tetons, raising Appaloosas. John Mantley, the producer for "Gunsmoke," was the executive producer for this series, which was filmed on location in Arizona, Colorado, Utah and southern California. The hour-long show premiered on February 12, 1978 on Sunday night on ABC. In January 1979 the show moved to Monday nights, where it became a two-hour series until its final episode on April 23, 1979. There are 43 episodes of this show—a result of some of the two-hour shows being edited.

HUD Film produced by Martin Ritt and Irving Ravetch; directed by Martin Ritt; screenplay by Irving Ravetch and Harriet Frank, Jr. (from the novel *Horseman, Pass By* by Larry McMurtry); music by Elmer Bernstein; released in 1963 by Paramount; 112 minutes in length.

General Oliver Howard *(Library of Congress)*

Cast: Paul Newman, Melvyn Douglas, Patricia Neal, Brandon De Wilde, Whit Bissell and John Ashley.

Hud Bannon (Paul Newman) is a cynical, selfish and self-centered cowboy in the 1960s West who wants to sell a herd of cattle with hoof-and-mouth disease to another rancher who doesn't know they have the disease. An old cowboy stops him. The old cowboy is Homer, Hud's uncle, who also stops Hud from drilling for oil on the land. Homer kills the cattle, and a portion of his soul dies with them; after Homer dies, Hud is glad to be alone. It is a movie about an antihero, a man who looks cynically at the New West.

HUGHES, BORDER BOSS   See HUGHES, JOHN REYNOLDS.

HUGHES, JOHN REYNOLDS   (b. John Reynolds Hughes in Cambridge, Illinois on February 11, 1857; d. Austin, Texas on June 3, 1947)   Hughes became a left-handed gunfighter after his right arm was shattered and was so adept that few guessed he was actually right-handed. He had started a small ranch in Texas, but in 1886 six rustlers, led by the Renald brothers, stole a herd of almost 100 horses, with 18 of those horses belonging to Hughes. Hughes set out with $43 in his pocket to track them. After about a week he found their camp, and during the shootout, Hughes's horse was killed, but the six outlaws escaped with the herd. Although the rustlers set some ambushes, Hughes shot his way out and still pursued them. Along

the way, the outlaws found they were unable to sell the horses, and one outlaw quit the band. Finally, on April 15, 1887—almost a year after the horses were stolen—Hughes and Sheriff Frank Swafford, with a deputy, encountered the outlaws, killing three of the rustlers and arresting the other two. In the end Hughes also got his horses back. For this he had traveled 1,200 miles and used up nine mounts in the process, returning with just 76 cents from the original $43 he'd started with.

Hughes was a member of the Texas Rangers for a number of years, retiring after 28 years in 1915. Later, he lived in El Paso and became a bank president. The lifelong bachelor died at the age of 92 in 1947.

HUMAN WILDCAT, THE   See SOTO, JUAN.

HUNT, J. FRANK   (b. ?; d. Caldwell, Kansas on October 11, 1880)   J. Frank Hunt is probably the man who killed George Flatt from an ambush on June 19, 1880 in Caldwell, Kansas. Flatt, who was drunk and disorderly, was going to Louis Segerman's Restaurant for a meal before heading home when a shot rang out, the slug hitting Flatt at the base of his skull and severing his spinal cord. He died instantly. Hunt was killed about five months later in Caldwell as he was sitting at an open window of the notorious Red Light saloon and dance hall. Hunt was drinking and watching the dancers when an unknown assassin crept up behind him and fired a bullet. He died a few hours later. (See also FLATT, GEORGE W.)

I

ILIFF, JOHN WESLEY (b. McLuney, Ohio in 1831; d. Colorado in 1878)   Iliff became known as the "cattle king of the plains" and, at his death, controlled the range along 150 miles of the South Platte River; because Iliff carefully chose water sites to purchase, he actually controlled much more land than he actually owned. Iliff attended Ohio Wesleyan University and then moved to Kansas, where he helped organize the Ohio City Town Company. In 1859 he went to Colorado, where he settled in the Cherry Creek area and bought a small herd of cattle that grew to a herd of over 50,000 by the time of his death.

I'M AN OLD COWHAND   Song written by Johnny Mercer (November 18, 1909–July 25, 1976) and published by Leo Feist in 1936.

Johnny Mercer began as a Tin Pan Alley songwriter in New York. He was a big-band vocalist with the Paul Whiteman Orchestra and went to Hollywood in 1935 as

a songwriter and singer. On a trip from California to Georgia by car to visit relatives, Mercer and his wife drove through Texas, where cowboys dressed in hats and boots with spurs drove cars; this inspired Mercer to write "I'm an Old Cowhand." The melody was based on the old folk song "Westminster Chimes." The song was first sung by Bing Crosby in the 1936 movie *Rhythm on the Range*. In 1941 Gene Autry performed this song in his movie *Back in the Saddle*, and Roy Rogers did it in 1943 in his movie *King of the Cowboys*. Johnny Mercer also wrote "On the Atchison, Topeka and the Santa Fe," "Lazybones," "In the Cool, Cool, Cool of the Evening," "Moon River" and "Days of Wine and Rose." He was one of the founders of Capitol Records.

INDEPENDENCE, MISSOURI   This town, founded in 1827 on the Missouri River, was a center for Mexican and Indian trade before it became a major starting point and outfitting center for emigrants on the

Oregon and California trails. It was also a starting and ending spot for the Santa Fe Trail.

In the 1840s Independence was replaced by Westport, a town farther up the river. Independence came to fame in July 1831 when Mormon leader Joseph Smith announced it was the "New Zion" for his religion; however, in the winter of 1833–34 mobs drove the Mormons out of the area, and thus began a series of hardships that would eventually lead them to the Great Salt Lake in Utah, where they established their community.

INDIAN CHARLEY   See CRUZ, FLORENTINO.

INDIANS   See APACHE INDIANS; ARAPAHO INDIANS; ARIKARA INDIANS; ASSINIBOIN INDIANS; BANNOCK INDIANS; BLACKFOOT INDIANS; CAYUSE INDIANS; CHEYENNE INDIANS; COCHISE; COMANCHE INDIANS; CRAZY HORSE; CROW INDIANS; FIVE CIVILIZED TRIBES; GALL; GERONIMO; GHOST DANCER; HIDATSA INDIANS; HOPI INDIANS; INDIAN SCOUTS; INDIAN TERRITORY; JOSEPH, CHIEF; KANSA INDIANS; KICKING BIRD; KIOWA INDIANS; MANDAN INDIANS; MANGAS COLORADAS; MODOC INDIANS; NAVAJO INDIANS; NEZ PERCE INDIANS; OMAHA INDIANS; OSAGE INDIANS; OURAY, CHIEF; PAIUTE INDIANS; PAWNEE INDIANS; PIMAN INDIANS; PLAINS INDIANS; PUEBLO INDIANS; QUANAH PARKER; RAIN-IN-THE-FACE; RED CLOUD; ROMAN NOSE; SACAJAWEA; SATANTA; SHOSHONI INDIANS; SIOUX INDIANS; SITTING BULL; SUN DANCE; TRAIL OF TEARS; UTE INDIANS; VICTORIO; WASHAKIE, CHIEF; WICHITA INDIANS; YUMAN INDIANS; ZUNI INDIANS.

INDIAN SCOUTS   To a large extent, the Indians of the Old West were defeated by Indian scouts. The Indians willingly served as scouts when the U.S. Army fought their traditional enemies; thus Crow Indians scouted against the Sioux. In the Southwest, Apache were organized in loose bands, so an Apache scout from one band would track Apache from another band. Generals Custer, Crook and Miles used Indian scouts extensively (especially Crow and Arikara) during the Sioux War of 1876–77. The famous Pawnee Battalion of Indian Scouts was formed by Major Frank North and his brother Luther and served on the plains in the 1860s and 1870s.

INDIAN SIGN LANGUAGE   Indians needed sign language because the numerous tribes all spoke different languages. In order to communicate, they develop a set of hand signals. Some examples: "Buffalo" was expressed holding two crooked fingers (representing horns) to the side of the hand; "white man" was indicated by drawing the index finger across the forehead (indicating the brim of a hat); "good" was signaled by putting the right hand, palm down, against the left breast and then pushing the hand away and upward; "bad" was expressed by holding the clenched right fist against the left breast and then pulling downward opening the hand fully.

INDIAN TERRITORY   Now the state of Oklahoma, Indian Territory was the assigned land for the Five Civilized Tribes (Cherokee, Chickasaw, Choctaw, Creek and Seminole) when they were removed from their native lands in North Carolina and Tennessee by President Andrew Jackson in the Indian Removal Act of 1830. From 1803, when the United States purchased the Louisiana Territory from France, until the 1830s, when this land was held in public domain, Indian Territory meant lands west of the state of Missouri and Arkansas Territory. This land was considered out of the way and too remote for white settlement. Removal of Indians to this area became federal policy under Jackson. Sixty thousand people in the Five Civilized Tribes resettled there between 1828 and 1846 from southeastern states. During the Trail of Tears in 1838, the U.S. Army escorted 15,000 Cherokee on a forced march of 800 miles. The government made the Five Tribes give the western part of their lands to Indians from Kansas and other states in 1866. About two million acres in the heart of Indian Territory were purchased from the Creek and Seminole in 1889 and opened for white settlement. In 1890 the United States created the Territory of Oklahoma from this area; statehood for Oklahoma came in 1907.

INDIAN WARS   The primary job of the U.S. Army after the Civil War was to make the West "safe" for settlers; this meant the elimination of the threat of Indians in the West, so the army established reservations, coerced Native Americans to settle on these reservations and, if they would not, waged war against them. It also involved the destruction of the buffalo, because the Indian culture depended so heavily on these animals, as well as the establishment of Indian treaties, which provided land and peace for Indians but were inevitably broken and thus led to more bloodshed.

The period from 1865 to 1890 is the era of the Indian Wars in the West, although the history of warfare against the Indians certainly goes back to the 17th century when English settlers first came to the United States. From 1789 to 1865 there were fights with Indians in the Old Northwest (Indiana and Ohio), and the Battle of Fallen Timbers (August 20, 1794) saw Mad Anthony Wayne lead troops (including Meriwether Lewis and William Clark) in a victory against Indians. In November 1811 William Henry Harrison defeated Tecumseh's village of Tippecanoe; in 1813 Tecumseh was killed at the Battle of the Thames and Andrew Jackson defeated the Creek Indians at Horseshoe Bend in 1814. During the 1820s and 1830s there was a great deal of "Indian removal" from eastern lands, but it was generally peaceful. There was the Black Hawk War of 1832 and the second Seminole War (1835–42) in the East, while in Oregon Territory there was the Rogue River War, Yakima War and the Campaign of 1858 to defeat Indians there. During the Civil War there was the Minnesota Uprising (1862), and the army moved against the Sioux in Dakota Territory. There was also the Sand Creek Massacre (1964) in Colorado, wars in the Southwest and fighting in California. But it was not until after the Civil War that the army turned its full attention to the West and the Native Americans living there. By this time Indians had been virtually removed from all lands east of the Mississippi, and the Great Plains between the Mississippi River and the Rocky Mountains were home to most American Indians.

The Indians Wars were not "wars" in the traditional sense; certainly the methods and reasons of the army's fighting contrasted sharply with the methods and reasons of the Indians' fighting, and herein lies the essential problem in this "war." First, the army was organized for full-scale warfare in which large armies organized and attacked one another; the Indians, on the other hand, did not engage in this type of "warfare." Instead, they used the element of surprise, avoided large-scale confrontations and preferred to hit quickly and then retreat and isolate settlers or soldiers in order to win. For the army it was a "war" that was conducted as a series of small skirmishes; for the Indians it was an attempt at self-preservation as they engaged in "battles" for their homes and lives.

The army had to clear roads into the West so settlers and freighters could pass; the Indians were in the way. Further, the army had to ensure that settlers in the West would be safe from Indian attacks. Thus the first "war" was Red Cloud's War (1866–68), which the army lost; this war involved the Bozeman Trail which went right through Sioux and Cheyenne Territory on the way to the Montana gold fields. This war led to the Fetterman Massacre and Wagon Box Fight and concluded with the Treaty of Fort Laramie when the army agreed to abandon its forts along the Bozeman Trail and the Indians burned them to the ground. But the Indian victory was short lived and, in the long run, almost irrelevant.

During the period from 1865 to 1868 there were fights against the Snake and Paiute Indians in California culminating in the Battle of Infernal Caverns in California (September 26–27, 1867). From 1867 to 1869 there were a number of fights on the Texas plains against the Comanche, Kiowa, Arapaho and Cheyenne Indians. After the Treaty of Medicine Lodge (1867), in which Indians agreed to settle on permanent reservations in Indian Territory, Major General Philip Sheridan planned a winter campaign to punish all renegade Indians; this led to the Battle of the Washita (November 27, 1868), in which General George Armstrong Custer destroyed an Indian village.

On the West Coast, the Modoc War (1972–73) began after the Modoc Indians, under Captain Jack, left the Klamath Reservation and holed up in the Lava Beds in northern California where 50 Indians held off about 400 soldiers before their leaders were captured and hung in October 1873. Meanwhile, in the Southwest General Crook, head of the Department of Arizona, used buffalo soldiers against the Apache. In Texas there was the Red River War, which ended in June 1875 when Quanah Parker surrendered.

In 1876–77 the army organized a campaign against the northern Cheyenne and Sioux to clear the Montana-Wyoming and Black Hills regions. An ultimatum was given in November 1875 for all Indians to remove to reservations, but few complied. This led to a series of military engagements, beginning with a war on the Powder River in March 1876, and in May and June a huge concentration of Indian warriors, led by Sitting Bull and Crazy Horse, gathered in the Bighorn-Yellowstone region. This led to the Battle of the Rosebud (June 17, 1876) and the Battle of the Little Bighorn (June 25, 1876), in which Custer and the Seventh Cavalry were slaughtered. Although this was a major victory for the Indians—and a major defeat for the army—this last battle mobilized public opinion against the Indians and inspired the army, the public and the Congress to wipe out the troublesome Indians once and for all. This resolve led to the final stage of the Indian Wars.

In 1877 the Nez Perce War occurred because Chief Joseph and his people were ordered off their homelands after gold was discovered. Chief Joseph led his people 1,700 miles but was captured about 30 miles from the Canadian border after winning a series of skirmishes against the army. Sitting Bull and Crazy Horse had gone to Canada but came back in May 1877 to the Red Cloud Agency and surrendered.

There was the Bannock War in 1878 in the Oregon-Idaho-Wyoming area; wars against the Ute in Colorado and Utah that led to the Meeker Massacre, and in 1866-86 wars against the Apache in Arizona and New Mexico that ended with the capture of Geronimo. The war in the Southwest was the last major campaign waged by the army against the Indians, but the final "battle" occurred at the end of 1890 with the Wounded Knee Massacre at the Pine Ridge Agency in South Dakota when the army came up against the Sioux after the ghost dance movement caused fear in the United States government, which was afraid the Indians would revolt. (See also ARMY IN THE WEST; CUSTER, GEORGE ARMSTRONG; FETTERMAN MASSACRE; GHOST DANCE; LITTLE BIGHORN, BATTLE OF; ROSEBUD, BATTLE OF THE; SHERIDAN, PHILIP HENRY; WAGON BOX FIGHT.)

INGRAHAM, PRENTISS (b. Adams County, Mississippi on December 22, 1843; d. Beauvoir Confederate Home in Mississippi on August 16, 1904)   Prentiss Ingraham may have been the most prolific dime novelist of all time; he wrote about 1,000 dime novels, and a number of plays, poems and short stories. He was the man most responsible for promoting the career of Buffalo Bill Cody. After Ned Buntline wrote the first story on Buffalo Bill, Ingraham became the chief chronicler of Cody, writing over 200 tales about the scout. Ingraham also served as the press agent for Cody's Wild West show. A well-educated man, Ingraham was a soldier of fortune as well as a writer; after service in the Civil War and then as commander of scouts in the Texas cavalry, he hired out as a soldier in Mexico, Austria, Crete, Africa and Cuba.

INNOCENTS, THE   See PLUMMER, HENRY.

IN OLD ARIZONA   Film directed by Raoul Walsh and Irving Cummings; screenplay by Tom Barry; released by Fox in 1929. Cast: Warner Baxter, Edmund Lowe, Dorothy Burgess, J. Farrell MacDonald, Fred Warren, Henry Armetta, Frank Campeau and Duke Martin.

This is the first outdoor talking western (three other previous westerns had sound effects and music). Director Raoul Walsh set up microphones in trees and under rocks. This is also the first Cisco Kid movie, based on the O. Henry character from the story "The Caballero's Way." Filmed in Zion County, Utah, much of the movie takes place within a cabin. Director Raoul Walsh was going to star in the picture, but one night while driving through the desert a jackrabbit jumped through his car's windshield and Walsh's right eye was injured with the flying glass. Walshthen had to wear a black patch, and Warner Baxter played the lead; Baxter was awarded an Oscar for his performance.

I RIDE AN OLD PAINT   This song, remarkably similar to "Goodbye Old Paint," came from the oral tradition and was learned in Santa Fe by Margaret Larkin and playwright Lynn Riggs, who popularized it. Larkin included the song in a book published in 1931; earlier John Lomax had published both the "Old Paint" songs as "Old Paint (I)" and "Old Paint (II)." Larkin and Riggs produced *Green Grow the Lilacs* in New York, beginning in 1931, which starred Tex Ritter; later this play became the basis for Rodgers and Hammerstein's play *Oklahoma!* (See also GOODBYE OLD PAINT.)

IRON HORSE, THE   Silent film directed by John Ford; released by the Fox Film Corporation in 1924.

This silent movie, directed by John Ford, tells the story of the building of the transcontinental railroad. In the Nevada desert, Ford assembled 3,000 railway workers, 1,000 Chinese laborers, 800 Indians, 2,800 horses, 1,300 buffalo and 10,000 Texas steers for his story, which begins with Abraham Lincoln wanting to see the nation linked by rail. For the 29-year-old Ford, this was his 40th western and 49th film made by him.

IRON HORSE, THE   TV show that starred Dale Robertson as Ben Calhoun, Gary Collins as Dave Tarrant, Bob Random as Barnabas Rogers, Roger Torrey as Nils Torvald (1966–67) and Ellen McRae as Julie Parsons (1967–68).

A gambler wins a railroad in a card game but discovers the track line is only half built and the whole enterprise is near bankruptcy. That was the setting for Ben Calhoun's acquiring the Buffalo Pass, Scalplock and Defiance Railroad (B.P.S. & D.) and the plots for this show as Calhoun forged a railroad west. Most of the location shots were done in Sonora, California, which has plenty of tracks and a vintage train. The show began on September 12, 1966 on ABC on Monday nights. The hour-long show moved to Saturday nights in September 1967, where it finished its run on January 6, 1968.

IVERS, ALICE   See POKER ALICE.

I WANT TO BE A COWBOY'S SWEETHEART
Song writen by Patsy Montana (October 30, 1912–) in 1934 while she was on tour.

Patsy, born Ruby Blevins, had moved to California in 1928 and become part of a girl group, "The Montana Cowgirls," on Stuart Hamblen's radio program. Later, she moved back East and became a member of the WLS "Barn Dance" with the Kentucky Ramblers, who changed their name to the Prairie Ramblers to take advantage of the cowboy craze in the 1930s. Touring with the "Round-up of WLS Radio Stars" with other "Barn Dance" regulars Gene Autry, Smiley Burnette, Max Terhune, Pat Buttram, Lulu Belle and Scotty and others, Patsy wrote this song while she was alone in a hotel room in Illinois because her husband was visiting his mother. The song was first sung on the WLS Barn Dance in Chicago and soon became her theme song. In August 1935 she recorded it for the American Record Company under the direction of Art Satherley. It sold over a million copies, making Patsy Montana the first female country artist to have a best-selling recording. (See also MONTANA, PATSY.)

J

JACKRABBIT   A large rabbit with a black tail, the jackrabbit can move at a speed of up to 40 miles an hour and jump up to 20 feet. Its name comes from "Jackass rabbit," given because of its large ears. The jackrabbit is actually a hare, not a rabbit, and is a rather sturdy creature that often makes good target practice for cowboys or a meal for a hungry cowboy.

JAMES, FRANK   (aka B. J. Woodson; b. Franklin James in Clay County, Missouri on January 10, 1843; d. Clay County, Missouri on February 18, 1915)

Frank James was the eldest son of the notorious James family. His father, Robert James, was a frontier preacher who moved from Kentucky to Missouri, where he pastored a Baptist church. But Robert caught "gold fever" and went to California in 1850; there he fell ill and died. Zerelda James, his widow, soon remarried, but the marriage lasted only a few months; her third marriage occurred in 1855 to Dr. Reuben Samuel. The James boys grew, and during the Civil War Frank and Jesse joined William Quantrill's guerrillas about 1862 and were involved in the massacre at Lawrence, Kansas. After the war, Frank and Jesse, along with the Younger brothers, began robbing banks. When the

Frank James *(Western Archives)*

Pinkerton Detective Agency began trailing the James and Younger gang, a detective, John W. Whicher, was killed on March 10, 1874 near the James family's farm; it was assumed Frank and Jesse did it. Frank married Annie Ralston in 1876, and two years later she bore him a son.

After the Northfield, Minnesota raid in 1876 Frank and Jesse lived in Nashville, Tennessee. In 1881 they moved back to Missouri. About six months later, Jesse was murdered by Bob Ford, on April 3, 1882; Frank then surrendered to Missouri governor Thomas J. Crittendon. After a number of trials and legal moves, as well as pleas for sympathy and leniency, Frank James was acquitted. He was released from custody in 1885 and lived for 30 more years in a number of places, including New Jersey, Texas, Oklahoma and New Orleans and his mother's old farm in Missouri.

Frank James lived an honest existence his final years and had a partnership in a Wild West show (with Cole Younger) in 1903. When Frank James died in 1915, his ashes were kept in a bank vault until 1944, when his wife died. Then their ashes were interred together in a Kansas City cemetery. (See also JAMES, JESSE; NORTHFIELD, MINNESOTA RAID; YOUNGER, COLE.)

JAMES, JESSE (aka "Dingus" and Thomas Howard; b. Jesse Woodson James in Clay County, Missouri on September 5, 1847; d. St. Joseph, Missouri on April 3, 1882)   Jesse James was three when his father died in the gold fields of California; his first stepfather was apparently mean to him and brother Frank, leading to the demise of that marriage. His mother then married a gentle, wealthy man, Dr. Reuben Samuel. Since the James family were slaveholders, they were aligned with the Confederacy, and Frank joined William Quantrill's raiders in 1861 while still a teenager; Quantrill didn't want Jesse in the gang because of his youth, so the younger brother joined Bloody Bill Anderson's guerrillas. With them he learned to loot and kill and was introduced to guerrilla tactics that would serve him well robbing banks and trains. He took part in the Centralia Massacre on September 27, 1864 with Bloody Bill Anderson, in which an ambush was laid for Major A. V. E. Johnson and a federal pursuit force who were chasing the gang after a looting raid. Johnson and 100 of his men were killed, with Jesse getting the credit for killing Johnson. Jesse also reportedly served as a spy while dressed as a woman.

After the war the James brothers, with their cousins the Youngers, formed a gang, and on February 13, 1866

Jesse and Frank James, with mother in the background

Jesse James *(Western Archives)*

they committed their first robbery, as well as the first daylight bank robbery in the country during peacetime when they held up the Clay County Savings Bank in Liberty, Missouri and made off with $60,000. A college student, George Wymore, was killed during this robbery. The gang was always masked, and no bystanders could ever be sure who did the shootings and killings during these robberies. Ironically, after each robbery the James Gang was blamed for, Jesse would publish a letter in which he proclaimed his innocence and established an alibi.

Jesse married Zerelda Mimms, his lifelong sweetheart, on April 23, 1874, and they had a son and daughter, Jesse and Mary, both born in Nashville, Tennessee. Jesse remained a devout Christian during his life as well, baptized into the Baptist Church in 1868. Zerelda had nursed Jesse back to health after he had been shot in the lung by a Federal soldier while carrying a flag of truce after Lee had surrendered.

After their first robbery in 1866 the James gang succeeded in a number of other heists. On March 21, 1868 the gang robbed a bank in Russellville, Kentucky and shot the bank president, Nimrod Long (who had only a slight head wound). In Gallatin, Missouri on December 7, 1869 Jesse and Frank James were transacting business with a banker named John W. Sheets.

The James brothers held a deep grudge against Sheets, a former Civil War officer, and they killed him. They also wounded a clerk as they got away with a bag full of money. Outside one of their horses proved unruly so they had to escape on one horse, stealing a second horse from a farmer along the way. The James brothers were at home on the Clay County farm on December 15, 1869 when Deputy Sheriff John Thomason and a posse came out to capture them and the $3,000 reward on their heads. But the brothers bolted out of the barn on fast horses and escaped. On September 26, 1872 a small girl was wounded in the leg when Jesse and two others came up to a ticket seller at the crowded Kansas City Fair and grabbed the money from his tin box. The outlaws escaped into some nearby woods.

Jesse and his gang continued to rob banks, then trains, which led the Pinkerton Agency to put agents on their trail. Pinkerton agent J. W. Whicher was killed when he set out to arrest the James boys, and Frank and Jesse were widely believed to be the killers. On January 25, 1875 three men—probably Pinkerton operatives—surrounded the Samuels home and threw in a blazing flare; Frank and Jesse weren't there, but their mother, Mrs. Zerelda Samuels, lost her right arm and their nine-year-old stepbrother, Archie Samuels, was killed. This led to a public outrage that put sympathy on

Jesse James on horseback

the side of the James boys. Also contributing sympathy to their cause was the legend that they robbed railroads because the railroads had taken away their home. Certainly, at this time, there was not much public sympathy for the big business railroads.

On September 7, 1876 the gang was decimated in Northfield, Minnesota at the raid on a bank there, although Jesse and Frank James managed to escape. This robbery caused public sympathy to go against Jesse and his gang; after this robbery, the James boys kept a low profile and moved around a bit—mostly living in Nashville, Tennessee—and did not engage in another heist for over three years.

In 1881 Jesse moved to St. Joseph under the name of Thomas Howard and returned to his old occupation of robbery. With a new gang, the James boys robbed the Chicago, Rock Island and Pacific Railroad evening train from Kansas City on July 15, 1881 in Winston, Missouri, and Jesse killed conductor William Westfall; in the ensuing gunfire, passenger Frank McMillan was also killed before the gang escaped with the contents of the safe. This led to a $10,000 reward on the head of Jesse James by Missouri governor Thomas Crittenden. Bob Ford, a member of Jesse's gang, met with Crittenden and agreed to do the dastardly deed for the money.

On the morning of April 3, 1882 Jesse was at his home with his family; gang members were also there, planning another robbery. Jesse knew the hounds were on his trail and suspected Bob Ford and his brother, who were in the living room. But Jesse needed some time to think; he walked to the wall and straightened a picture; as he did this, Bob Ford pulled out a gun and pumped slugs into his head. The legendary outlaw slumped to the floor, dead.

Jesse was buried in the front yard of his mother's home. Mrs. Samuel sold pebbles from the grave for a quarter each—replenishing her supply from a nearby creek—and charged a quarter to visitors for a tour of Jesse's home and grave. She also reportedly purchased a number of old guns and sold them (at hugely inflated prices) to those who wanted a gun owned by Jesse. (Jesse's real guns—a .45 Colt Peacemaker and a .45 Smith and Wesson Schofield—were auctioned off for $15 after his murder. His legendary navy revolvers had probably been sold in the 1870s.) (See also FORD, BOB; JAMES, FRANK; NORTHFIELD, MINNESOTA RAID; PINKERTON'S NATIONAL DETECTIVE AGENCY; YOUNGER, BOB; YOUNGER, COLE; YOUNGER, JAMES; YOUNGER, JOHN.)

JAYHAWKER   During the Kansas-Missouri border war of 1857–59 the issue was slavery: Would Kansas be a slave state or not? The "Jayhawkers" were those who opposed slavery, or wanted a "free state." The term "Jayhawker" originally was a derogatory term meaning "thief." Later, it became a badge of honor, and Kansas adopted the term as its nickname, the Jayhawker State.

JEFFERSON DRUM   TV show that starred Jeff Richards as Jefferson Drum, Cyris Delevanti as Lucius Coin, Eugene Martin as Joey Drum and Robert Stevenson as Big Ed.

Jefferson Drum was a newspaper editor in the fictional town of Jubilee, a mining town set in the West around the 1850s. Drum preferred the pen but took up the gun on occasion. Drum was a widower who lived with his young son, Joey, and was aided in his efforts to establish law and order by his printer, Lucius Coin, and the local bartender, Big Ed. The show premiered on April 25, 1958 on Friday nights on NBC. The half-hour series moved to Thursday evenings in October 1958, where it finished its run on April 23, 1959. Twenty-six episodes were filmed.

JEFFORDS, THOMAS J.   (b. Thomas Jonathan Jeffords in Chautauqua County, New York on January 1, 1832; d. Owls Head, Arizona on February 19, 1914)   Thomas Jeffords is best remembered as the "blood brother" of Cochise after he went alone to the desert to meet with the famed Apache chief; Cochise was so impressed with Jeffords's bravery that he would not let his men kill Jeffords and then agreed to Jeffords's request that the Apache stop attacking the stagecoaches that crossed Apache country. Jeffords was a Great Lakes sailor before he moved west and arrived in Taos, New Mexico in 1859, where he worked as a stage driver on the Butterfield route. In 1860 he became a prospector in the San Juan Mountains; during the Civil War he was in the Battle of Valverde (February 21, 1862). During this time he came to the attention of Union commander Edward R. S. Canby, who entrusted Jeffords with army dispatches. In 1866 Jeffords became conductor and then mail superintendent on the stagecoach route between Tucson and Mesilla; in this position he lost 14 men in 16 months, which prompted him to ride alone to Cochise's camp in the Dragoon Mountains in 1867. Jeffords formed a trading partnership with Elias Brevoort in 1870. In 1872 he escorted General Oliver Otis Howard to Cochise's camp; there, Howard granted the Chiricahua Apache a reservation in southeastern Arizona and, at the insistence of Cochise, made Jeffords the Indian agent. Jeffords treated the Indians well and fairly, but after the death of Cochise the Chiricahua were moved to San Carlos, Arizona, and Jeffords did not remain as Indian agent. In November 1882 Jeffords was deputy sheriff in Tombstone and during the Geronimo campaign of 1886 served for the government.

JEHU   Term used for a stagecoach driver, also known as a "whip." (See also STAGECOACH.)

JEREMIAH JOHNSON   Film produced by Joe Wizan; directed by Sydney Pollack; screenplay by John Milius and Edward Anhalt; released in 1972 by Warner Brothers; 108 minutes in length. Cast: Robert Redford, Will Geer, Stefan Gierasch, Allyn Ann McLerie, Charles Tyner, Delle Bolton and Josh Albee.

The story of a real mountain man ("Liver-Eating" Johnson) revised to be politically correct for the 1970s, this movie was based on two books: a short biography of Johnson by Raymond W. Thorp and Robert Bunker, and a historical novel, *Crow Killer*, by Vardis Fisher. This became one of the first successful ecological films. Ironically, the movie led to the discovery that Johnson was buried near the San Diego Freeway in Los Angeles; his body was dug up and reburied in Wyoming because he had wanted to be buried in the mountains. (See also JOHNSON, LIVER-EATING.)

JESSE JAMES Film produced by Nunnally Johnon; directed by Henry King; screenplay by Nunnally Johnson; music by Louis Silvers; released in 1939 by Twentieth Century–Fox; 105 minutes in length. Cast: Tyrone Power, Henry Fonda, Nancy Kelly, Randolph Scott, Henry Hull, Brian Donlevy, John Carradine, Jane Darwell and Donald Meek.

A fictionalized tale of the James brothers from the Civil War until Jesse is killed by Bob Ford. The theme here is how big business (banks and the railroad) drove Jesse to become an outlaw and kill when he'd rather have been a peaceful man of the land.

JESSE JAMES One of the most popular of all the "outlaw ballads," this song was composed by Billy Garshade, who lived in Clay County, Missouri, the same area where the James brothers were born and grew up and where their mother still lived at the time of Jesse's death. The song was written shortly after Jesse was killed by Bob Ford (April 3, 1882) and tells the story of some of his robberies and his death, including the line "that dirty little coward that shot Mr. Howard/Has laid poor Jesse in his grave" (Jesse was living under the alias "Thomas Howard" at the time he was shot). (See also JAMES, JESSE.)

JESSE JAMES See LEGEND OF JESSE JAMES, THE.

JIM BOWIE See ADVENTURES OF JIM BOWIE, THE.

JIM STINSON TRAIL This trail was pioneered by James Stinson, manager of the New Mexico Land and Livestock Company, in 1882 when he drove 20,000 cattle from west-central Texas to the Estancia Valley in New Mexico. Stinson drove his cattle through some of the driest country imaginable across New Mexico and into Arizona. The trail headed due west from Matador, Texas to Fort Sumner, New Mexico and then past some towns and across the Plains of San Agustin into Arizona to supply military posts and Indian reservations with beef. Stinson had settled in Arizona in 1873 and then moved into Pleasant Valley in the Tonto Basin about 1880, where he became indirectly involved in the Graham-Tewksbury feud. Stinson at one time employed members of both families on his ranch; later, each family accused the other of stealing some of Stinson's cattle. Jim Stinson lived to the age of 93. He died on January 8, 1932 and is buried in Kline, Colorado. (See also PLEASANT VALLEY WAR.)

JINGLE BOB A cow's ear slit completely from tip to base so that the cow looks like it had two ears. This was the earmark used by John Chisum; his crew became known as the "jingle-bob outfit."

JOHNNY-BEHIND-THE-DEUCE (b. Michael or John O'Rourke possibly in April 1861 or 1862; d. Sulphur Springs Valley, Arizona in 1882) There are two rumors about Johnny-behind-the-Deuce that helped make him a legend: One was that Wyatt Earp saved him from a mob lynching, and the other was that he killed Johnny Ringo. Actually, it was probably Virgil Earp, along with Tombstone sheriff John Behan, who saved him from a lynching after O'Rourke had killed Henry Schneider, chief engineer for the Corbin Mill, on January 14, 1881. Some say that Pony Deal, a friend of Ringo's, killed Johnny-behind-the-Deuce after a fight. But this story is clouded by the fact that after O'Rourke escaped from jail in Tucson on April 18, 1881, he disappeared.

JOHNNY RINGO TV show that starred Don Durant as Johnny Ringo, Karen Sharpe as Laura Thomas, Mark Goddard as Cully and Terence de Marney as Case Thomas.

The real-life Johnny Ringo didn't resemble the TV Johnny Ringo except in name. The TV Johnny Ringo was sheriff of Velardi, Arizona in the 1880s and was good, clean and straightforward; the gunfighting past was alluded to but never explored. One of the secrets to the TV Ringo's success was a pistol, a two-barrel type with the bottom barrel shooting a shotgun shell. The show only lasted one season, premiering on October 1, 1959 and ending on September 29, 1960. The half-hour show was filmed in black and white and produced by Aaron Spelling. The 38 episodes were aired on CBS on Thursday evenings.

JOHNSON, LIVER-EATING (b. John Johnston c. 1823; d. Los Angeles, California on January 21, 1900) Liver-Eating Johnson's wife, a Flathead Indian, and unborn child were killed by Crow braves, which caused Johnson to exact revenge on Crow for many years, killing and scalping Crow warriors and, according to legend, eating their livers. During his life he became known as "Crow killer. " There is a story (perhaps true) that Johnson had a load of rotgut whiskey when he was captured by the Blackfeet who intended to trade him over to the Crow; however, the Blackfeet got drunk on the whiskey and Johnson escaped, after severing the leg of his guard, which he used as nourishment until he was back home. Johnson was a mountain man who first went to the Rocky Mountains around 1843 with his partner John L. Hatcher. A member of the Colorado Cavalry during the Civil War, Johnson returned to the West and trapped in the mountains. Johnson's last job was in 1888 as town marshal in Red Lodge, Montana; however, his health soon failed and he died in a veterans' hospital. Johnson's life story served as the basis for the

The cast of the "Johnny Ringo Show" (left to right):
Mark Goddard, Karen Sharpe and Don Durant

movie *Jeremiah Johnson* (1972). (See also JOHNSON, JERE-MIAH.)

JOHNSON, TURKEY CREEK   (b. John Johnson c. 1872; d. ?)   Turkey Creek Johnson was aligned with the Earp clan in Tombstone and helped avenge the death of Morgan Earp in the revenge killings of Frank Stilwell and Florentino Cruz in March 1882. Prior to this, Johnson had been in Deadwood, Dakota Territory to hunt for gold. After a quarrel in a saloon with his two mining partners, the three went out to the cemetery, followed by a large crowd, for a showdown. The two partners grazed Johnson, but he shot them both dead and then paid for their burials. Because it was winter and the ground was frozen, the graves had to be blasted out with dynamite. (See also CRUZ, FLORENTINO; EARP, WYATT; STILWELL, FRANK.)

JOHNSON, WILLIAM H.   (b. Marion County, Ohio; d. near Seven Rivers, New Mexico on August 16, 1878)   Johnson, a former Civil War captain for the Confederacy, was in the Lincoln County War with the Seven Rivers crowd, a result of being married to Henry Beckwith's daughter. Johnson was one of the defenders of the Beckwith ranch when John Chisum and a number of his cowboys, convinced the Beckwiths were stealing stock, attempted to raid the ranch. He was also in the posse that killed Frank McNab and Ab Sander and

captured Frank Coe after the group had dismounted to water their horses. Johnson also served as one of Sheriff William Brady's deputies for a while and survived the Lincoln County hostilities. But on August 16, 1878 Johnson and his father-in-law got into an argument at Beckwith's ranch. Beckwith then grabbed a double-barrel shotgun and killed Johnson. Wallace Olinger shot Beckwith in the face during the fracas, but the rancher survived. (See also LINCOLN COUNTY WAR.)

JOHNSON COUNTY WAR   From the view of the large cattle ranchers and their organization, the Wyoming Stock Growers' Association, the Johnson County War (1892) was an attempt to stop cattle rustling. But viewed from another perspective, this war was an attempt by wealthy cattle barons to drive out homesteaders, who were intent on settling the land with their small herds and parcels of land. Compounding the problem was the fact that a number of these small homesteaders used to work as cowboys for the large ranchers and had decided to set up their own spreads. There were also "grangers" or "nesters"—the terms generally used for small farmers—who were increasingly coming into the West and staking claims, breaking up the cattle country and demanding access to public lands for grazing, a privilege the wealthy cattle barons had reserved for themselves.

The Wyoming Stock Growers' Association was originally formed in 1873 and based in Cheyenne. It controlled political power in the state but did not control juries, who increasingly decided against the big cattlemen in rustling cases. This led the big ranchers to hire range "detectives" and then vigilantes (called "Invaders" or "Regulators"). These hired guns from the cattlemen went to Johnson County and lynched Ella Watson, known as "Cattle Kate," a whore from Kansas who lived on a small settlement south of Johnson County and sometimes accepted cattle as payment for her favors from cowboys. Ella's neighbor and husband (they staked adjoining claims), James Averill, ran a small saloon and store and wrote articles for the *Casper Weekly Mail* accusing cattle baron Albert J. Bothwell (whose ranch adjoined their homesteads) of a variety of misdeeds. Averill denounced the cattle kings with their monopolistic power and greed for land, and in July 1889 Ella and Averill were dragged from their cabins by masked men and hung. The cattlemen, attempting to justify this deed, spread the word that Ella was "Cattle Kate," a notorious rustler.

In 1892 the Northern Wyoming Farmers' and Stock Growers' Association was formed, with the announced intention of holding its own roundup, independent from the Wyoming Stock Growers' Association, and named two foremen for the event. One of the foremen was Nathan ("Nate") Champion, a top cowhand and gunfighter from Texas. Soon, the "Regulators" hired by the cattlemen made an attempt on Champion's life in a cabin on the Powder River, but they were unsuccessful in their ambush and Champion drove them off. Meanwhile, back in Cheyenne at a meeting in the luxurious Cheyenne Club the wealthy cattlemen decided to invade Johnson County (about 250 northwest of Cheyenne) and wipe out all rustlers—both known and suspected. They drew up a death list of 75 names ("nominations" for this list were sent to the associate secretary of the association and approved by the executive committee) and hired some gunfighters to supplement their local group of Regulators, led by Frank Wolcott and Frank Canton. On April 5, 1892 a group of 46 vigilantes, composed of 22 hired gunmen (all from Texas except one from Idaho), 19 cattlemen and five stock detectives, and six observers (including two newspaper reporters) boarded a train for Johnson County. The Union Pacific Railroad provided a special train (three passenger cars and three baggage cars that held horses, wagons and "gear") for the event, a number of prominent politicians knew of the conspiracy and supported it, and the two newspaper reporters, partisan to the cattlemen, were expected to report the story so it could be presented properly to the world.

At Casper, about 100 miles from Johnson County, the group got off the train and rode their horses toward Buffalo, the seat of Johnson County. Along the way, they heard that Nate Champion and some other "rustlers" were only about 12 miles away at the KC Ranch. On April 9, soon after daybreak, the group reached the KC and surrounded the place where Champion and his friend—and another name on the death list—Nick Ray were holed up along with two trappers, who had spent the night there. The trappers were recognized as innocent bystanders when they emerged and made prisoners. But when Nick Ray emerged, the group gunned him down. Champion ran out and managed to drag Ray—still alive—inside under a hail of bullets.

The siege lasted all day, and Champion lay on the floor and returned the fire from his attackers. He also took the time to write an account of the siege. Around three in the afternoon, Jack Flagg rode by. Flagg was also on the death list but managed to escape and get to Buffalo, about 13 miles north, where he sent out an alarm, and a posse of men about 200 strong, headed by Sheriff Red Angus, headed out to the KC. But before the Buffalo group could get there, Nate Champion was killed, felled by 27 bullets as he tried to make a dash for freedom while firing his Winchester. When the smoke had cleared, the attackers found Champion's written account and, after apparently erasing a name in the account, gave it to one of the reporters. It was published in the *Cheyenne Daily Leader* on April 14, 1892.

Warned that angry townsfolk were on their way, the Regulators decided to head for the TA Ranch nearby and barricaded themselves in for a fight. For three days, Red Angus and his group of homesteaders besieged the ranch. Meanwhile, back in Cheyenne, news of the plight reached the political friends of the powerful cattlemen, including acting governor Amos Barber, who contacted Senators Francis E. Warren and Joseph M. Carey, and they began pulling some political strings to get the barricaded men out of their predicament. President Ben-

jamin Harrison in Washington received the plea for help and dispatched some cavalry aid to suppress this insurrection.

Colonel J. J. Van Horn and three troops of the Sixth Cavalry arrived from Fort McKinney just in time to save the group holed up. Two of the Texas mercenaries had suffered accidental wounds and died, but the rest were alive. The group from Buffalo wanted them tried in Johnson County, but they were taken to Cheyenne as prisoners and soon released. There, a group of powerful attorneys, headed by Willis Van Devanter (who would later serve on the United States Supreme Court), mounted a skillful defense, aided by the fact that Johnson County did not have the finances to pay for a lengthy legal battle and the two trappers who witnessed the siege had been whisked out of the state and hidden. As a result, the vigilante group went free.

But although the wealthy cattlemen won this battle, they lost the war they were waging. More than any other event, the Johnson County War symbolized the arrival of the New West, settled by homesteaders, and the end of the Old West, ruled by cattlemen with their huge herds, large ranches, hired gunfighters, and use of public grazing lands for their own. (See also; CANTON, FRANK; CATTLE KATE; CHAMPION, NATE; SHONSEY, MIKE ; SMITH, TOM.)

JONES, BUCK (b. Charles Fredrick Gebhart in Vincennes, Indiana on December 12, 1891; d. Boston, Massachusetts on November 28, 1942) Actor Buck Jones lived a wild life both on-screen and off; one of the top cowboys in the silent era, he died in the famous Coconut Grove fire on Thanksgiving night in Boston. Jones grew up on a ranch in Red Rock, Oklahoma and became an expert horseman. In the army he saw action against Pancho Villa and then served in the Philippines before he was discharged in 1913. Jones then joined the Miller Brothers' 101 Wild West Show and also worked with the the Ringling Brothers Circus. His first movie feature was *The Last Straw* (1919); he was then signed by Fox to make Westerns as their counter to Tom Mix. In nine years, Jones made more than 50 films and reigned with William S. Hart and Mix as the top cowboys during the silent-movie era. In 1931 he signed with Columbia for 27 films and then in 1934 moved to Universal, where he did five serial chapter plays: *Gordon of Ghost City, The Red Rider, Roaring West, The Phantom Rider* and *Riders of Death Valley.* Jones appeared in the Columbia serial *White Eagle* (1941) and starred in the Rough Rider series. At one point his fan club had over four million members. (See also B WESTERN MOVIES; MOVIES.)

JONES, FUZZY Q. See ST. JOHN, FUZZY.

JONES, JOHN (b. Iowa on January 6, 1885; d. Lincoln County, New Mexico on August 29, 1879.) John Jones moved to Lincoln County, New Mexico in 1866 and set up a ranch, which he sold to the Horrell brothers from Texas. He then became involved in the

Buck Jones

Murphy-Dolan gang of rustlers. Jones killed Bob Riley in an argument and on July 15–19 was a member of the 40-man group surrounding the McSween house at the climax of the Lincoln County War. Jones killed rancher John Beckwith on August 26, 1879 in a shootout after an argument over a herd of cattle. A month later Jones ran into lawmen Bob Olinger and Milo Pierce, and Jones shot at Olinger because of, in his words, "those lies I've heard you told about my killing John Beckwith." Olinger then fired three shots into Jones, killing the cowboy. (See also LINCOLN COUNTY WAR; OLINGER, BOB.)

JONES, STAN   (b. Stanley Davis Jones in Douglas, Arizona on June 5, 1914; d. Los Angeles, California on December 13, 1963)   Stan Jones is known as the writer of the song "Ghost Riders in the Sky." He served in the navy during World War II and then received a degree in zoology from the University of California before he went to work as a park ranger in Death Valley in 1949. While acting as a guide for movie scouts filming *Three Godfathers,* Jones sang his song to the Hollywood group; later that year a movie was written for this title starring Gene Autry, with Jones appearing in the movie. Jones also wrote the song "Whirlwind," which became a 1951 movie of the same name also starring Gene Autry. Jones wrote the title song for *The Searchers,* a John Wayne movie, and songs for the movie *Wagonmaster* starring Ward Bond. Jones also wrote a number of songs for Walt Disney movies and TV shows. (See also GHOST RIDERS IN THE SKY (song).)

JOSEPH, CHIEF   (b. c. 1840; d. Nespelim, Washington on September 21, 1904)   Chief Joseph achieved national fame during the Nez Perce War of 1877 and is known for his eloquent speech when he surrendered: "I am tired of fighting. . . . It is cold and we have no blankets. The little children are freezing to death. My people, some of them, have run away to the hills, and have no blankets, no food; no one knows where they are, perhaps freezing to death. . . . Hear me, my chiefs. I am tired. My heart is sick and sad. From where the sun now stands, I will fight no more forever."

Chief Joseph's father, also known as Chief Joseph, was a Christian convert and friend of whites. The Nez

Chief Joseph   *(National Archives)*

Perce had settled on their ancestral lands in the Wal-lowa Valley in Oregon after ceding a large part of their lands to the United States in a treaty in 1855. But gold was discovered on these new lands, so the government wanted to take it away from the Nez Perce and move the tribe to another reservation in Idaho. An ultimatum was delivered by General O. O. Howard: All Nez Perce must leave within 30 days. Although Chief Joseph did not want war—and had always been friendly with whites—he saw no choice at this point but to fight. When the first cavalry column came, it was defeated by the Nez Perce, who then decided to flee to Canada, although they were pursued by a large force led by General Howard. The Nez Perce eventually marched 1,300 miles, fighting—and usually beating—the army in small encounters. The Nez Perce were only about 30 miles from the Canadian border on October 5, 1877, but they were surrounded by fresh army troops. The tribe was cold, hungry and exhausted; so Chief Joseph gave his eloquent speech when he surrendered to Generals Nelson Miles and Howard. After their capture, the Nez Perce were sent to a reservation in Indian Territory. Chief Joseph was sent to the Colville Reservation in Washington State in 1885, where he died years later.

JUDAS STEER   Sometimes a steer is trained to lead the other steers into the slaughterhouse. This was known as a "Judas steer."

JUDSON, EDWARD   See BUNTLINE, NED.

JUNIOR RODEO   Children's TV show hosted by Bob Atcher and featuring games, music and contests. Valerie Alberts also appeared regularly. Originally telecast on WBKB-TV in Chicago in 1951 the 30-minute show was broadcast on ABC from November 15, 1952 to December 13, 1952 on Saturday mornings.

JUSTINS   Cowboy boots, especially those made by Joseph Justin, who started his boot-making business in 1879 in Old Spanish Fort, Texas. The firm still operates in Fort Worth, Texas.

KANSA INDIANS   First discovered by French explorer Father Jacques Marquette in 1673, the Kansa people took special notice of the wind, believing it helped warriors in battle ("Kansa" means "wind people"). They were a semipermanent tribe, living in earth lodges. They engaged in warfare, so warriors could achieve high social position, but did not travel far. The tribe was decimated by smallpox and alcohol, and by 1873 they were on reservations in Indian Territory, the last of their lands captured or purchased. During the 1850s, travelers on the Santa Fe Trail often passed Kansa villages.

KANSAS PACIFIC RAILROAD   The Kansas Pacific Railroad was the reason Texas cattle were driven north to the Kansas cattle towns of Abilene, Ellsworth and Hays. This line then took the cattle east to the beef markets. But this same railroad also brought settlers west, and when the area was settled, the cattle drives were forced to stop using the old trails because of "tick fever" carried by their cattle and because the cattle destroyed crops planted on farms. This railroad began as the Leavenworth, Pawnee and Western Railroad when it was originally chartered in 1855, but not much

rail was laid. In June 1863 General John C. Fremont and Samuel Hallett acquired control and renamed it the Union Pacific, and construction began in earnest. This is the railroad that hired Buffalo Bill Cody to supply buffalo meat to its 1,200 workers; over an 18-month period, he reportedly killed 4,280 buffalo and earned his sobriquet, "Buffalo Bill." The name of the railroad was changed to Kansas Pacific Railroad in April 1869, and tracks to Denver were completed the following year. It merged with the Union Pacific Railroad Company and became part of that vast empire in January 1880.

KEARNY, STEPHEN WATTS   (b. Newark, New Jersey on August 30, 1794; d. St. Louis, Missouri on October 31, 1848)   Kearny spent most of his military life in the West and was commander of the army in the West during the Mexican War (1846–48). He initially served in the War of 1812 and then was assigned duty in the West from about 1819 on. During the Mexican War he was assigned to capture the Mexican territories of New Mexico and California. Kearny left Fort Leavenworth, Kansas with about 2,000 men and first conquered New Mexico, where he was named military governor. Then he marched to California and into San Diego and then Los Angeles, where he played a major role in securing this area for the United States. Kearny's fight on December 7–8, 1846 against Mexicans was inconclusive, but he and Commodore Robert Field Stockton joined forces to occupy Los Angeles on January 10. Here Kearny and John Fremont were engaged in a conflict over who should govern this area; the squabble was decided in favor of Kearny. After leaving Los Angles he marched south to Mexico into Vera Cruz, where he became military governor. He contracted a tropical disease there and returned to the United States to recover, where he died in the home of Meriwether Lewis at the age of 54.

KELLY, ED O. (aka "Red"; b. Harrisonville, Missouri in 1842; d. Oklahoma City, Oklahoma on January 13, 1904) Ed O. Kelly was the man who killed Bob Ford, the "dirty little coward" who shot Jesse James. Kelly killed Ford with a shotgun on June 8, 1892 in Creede, Colorado after being accused of stealing Ford's diamond ring. He was sentenced to life in prison but released in 1900. Kelly kept running into trouble after his release, and on January 13, 1904 in Oklahoma City Kelly was killed by a policeman who was trying to restore order after a brawl. (See also FORD, BOB.)

KENO Keno was a game of chance similar to bingo that was popular in casinos. Numbered balls were placed inside a container mounted on a pivot (called a "goose") and this was spun; the "roller" (who conducted the game) then pushed a lever and a ball dropped out. If a player had bet the number on his keno card (something like a bingo card, purchased from the house), he put a button on that number, and when he had covered five numbers in a row, he won. (See also GAMBLING.)

KENTUCKY JONES TV show that starred Dennis Weaver as Kentucky Jones, Ricky Der as Ike Wong, Harry Morgan as Seldom Jackson, Cherylene Lee as Annie Ng, Arthur Wong as Mr. Ng, Keye Luke as Thomas Wong and Nancy Rennick as Edith Thorncroft.

This program was a contemporary western in which the main character was a veterinarian with a 40-acre ranch in Southern California and a number of regulars came from the Chinese community in California. The show premiered on September 19, 1964 on NBC on Saturday nights; its last telecast was September 11, 1965.

KETCHUM, BLACK JACK (b. Thomas Ketchum in San Saba County, Texas c. October 31, 1863; d. Clayton, New Mexico on April 25, 1901) Black Jack was known as a deadly gunman and for robbing banks, trains and stages. On July 2, 1899 he killed two miners in Camp Verde, Arizona in a saloon during an argument over a card game. Ten days later in Turkey Canyon, New Mexico, Ketchum and two fellow robbers, Elzy Lay and G. W. Franks, were surprised by a posse at dawn. During the all-day battle, three lawmen were killed but the three outlaws escaped—although Black Jack was hit in the shoulder. About a month later, on August 16,

1899 near Folsom, Arizona, Black Jack tried to rob the Colorado and Southern train by himself. He shot it out with conductor Frank Harrington but managed to escape; the next day he was found propped against a tree near the tracks, and doctors had to amputate his arm, which had been shattered by the buckshot from Harrington's shotgun. On the day of his hanging, he ran up the steps of the gallows and said, "I'll be in hell before you start breakfast, boys," and then yelled, "Let 'er rip!" after the hood was put over his head. When the trap door was sprung, Black Jack's head and body came apart. (See also LAY, ELZY.)

KICKING BIRD (b. c. 1810; d. Fort Sill, Oklahoma on May 5, 1875) After Kicking Bird—the grandson of a Crow who was captured and adopted by the Kiowa—signed the Treaty of Medicine Lodge in 1867, which removed the Kiowa to a reservation in Indian Territory, he was taunted by young warriors who challenged his courage. So Kicking Bird led a raiding party through Texas and defeated an army column sent after him. This victory allowed him to remain a chief in the Kiowa, although he was friendly toward whites and counseled his tribe not to wage war against them. Kicking Bird was ordered by the army to select those Kiowa who would go to prison when hostile tribe members were captured. After Kicking Bird selected Mamanti, a medicine man, the Indian vowed vengeance. Kicking Bird died mysteriously from poison a short time later.

KIDDER MASSACRE (June 29, 1867) Lieutenant Lyman Stockwell Kidder of the Second Cavalry, was carrying dispatches from General William Tecumseh Sherman to General George Armstrong Custer during the Indian Wars after the Civil War. Kidder left Fort Sedgwick, Colorado on June 29, 1867 with 10 of his men and Red Bead, a Sioux chief who served as Indian guide, but they never arrived at their destination. General Custer and his troop discovered them all dead and mutilated, with 20–50 arrow shafts in each body.

KING, RICHARD (b. Orange County, New York on July 10, 1825; d. San Antonio, Texas on April 14, 1885) Richard King was the founder of the King Ranch in south Texas, one of the largest ranches in the West. By the end of his life, King owned 1.27 million acres and had 40,000 cattle, 6,600 horses and 1,200 sheep and goats. Known for his progressive breeding practices, King crossed longhorns with British breeds; he also developed the Santa Gertrudis breed, which was 3/8 Brahma and 5/8 shorthorn. Born to immigrant Irish parents, King was apprenticed to a jeweler but at 13 left New York for Mobile, Alabama on a steamer. King then became a Gulf coast river boatman; during the Mexican War King's steamer supported General Zachary Taylor's expedition. After the Mexican War, King and partner Captain Mifflin Kenedy formed the Rio Grande Steamship Company which ran from 1850 to 1874; by the time the firm dissolved they had built or bought over 20 steamers and developed an immense trade in cotton. In fact, during the Civil War the firm

Richard King and Mifflin Kenedy

was the cotton agent for the Confederacy and circumvented the Union blockade.

KIOWA INDIANS The Kiowa and Comanche were among the most hostile tribes toward whites. These two tribes ruled the southern plains in the United States until they were forced onto reservations in Indian Territory in 1868. Even this confinement did not stop their hostilities, and during raids into Texas in 1871 Chiefs Satank, Satanta and Big Tree were finally halted; Satank was killed and the other two were imprisoned. Originally from western Montana, the Kiowa moved to the Black Hills of Dakota, where they established an alliance with the Crow Indians. Under the influence of the Crows, the Kiowa became Plains Indians, living in buffalo-skin tipis, conducting an annual summer sun dance and organizing warrior societies. The Kiowa moved south into western Oklahoma and the panhandle of northern Texas and parts of New Mexico after being forced there by the Sioux; there they established an alliance with the Comanche. The Kiowa are known for the pictographic records, especially in the form of calendar histories.

KIT CARSON See ADVENTURES OF KIT CARSON, THE.

KLONDIKE TV show that starred Ralph Taeger as Mike Halliday, James Coburn as Jeff Durain, Mari Blanchard as Kathy O'Hara and Joi Lansing as Goldie.

The novel *Klondike Fever* by Pierre Benton was the basis of this program about the Alaskan gold rush of 1897–99. The series was based in Skagway, Alaska and featured a good guy and a shyster and the women of each. There were only 18 episodes of this brief series, which ran one season. The program debuted on October 10, 1960, and the last telecast was February 8, 1961. The 30-minute show was broadcast on NBC on Monday nights.

KNIGHT, FUZZY (b. Fairmont, West Virginia on May 9, 1901; d. Hollywood, California on February 23, 1976) Fuzzy Knight was most famous as Johnny Mack Brown's movie sidekick. Knight appeared in more than 100 films over an 18- year period and made his first sidekick appearance with Ken Maynard in 1935–36; he then appeared with Bob Baker before he joined up with Brown for 38 films between 1939 and 1943, beginning with *Desperate Trails* (1939). After he worked with Brown, Knight went to Monogram, where he worked with Tex Ritter, Russell Hayden, Rod Cameron, Eddie Dew and Kirby Grant; later he worked with Jimmy Ellison, Whip Wilson and Wild Bill Elliott and was a regular on "The Adventures of Captain Gallant" with Buster Crabbe. A graduate of the University of West Virginia, Knight starred in vaudeville and on Broadway before coming to Hollywood in 1933 for a Mae West picture, *She Done Him Wrong*.

KOHRS, CONRAD (b. Wewelsfleth, Holstein, Denmark on August 5, 1835; d. Helena, Montana on July 23, 1920) Born in Denmark, Kohrs went to sea and ended up in the United States, where he became a citizen on October 4, 1857 while he lived in Iowa. He joined the gold rush in the late 1850s, going first to California and then to British Columbia before he returned to Iowa. In 1862 he went to Montana as a prospector but got a job in a butcher shop in Bannack, Montana owned by Henry Crawford. Crawford and Henry Plummer had a shootout, and afterward Crawford left town, which left Kohrs with a butcher shop. Kohrs soon expanded into cattle raising and, ever mindful of gold strikes, moved his business to Virginia City after a gold strike there. Kohrs bought out his partner, Ben Peel, in 1866, began to furnish cattle to other butchers and expanded into sheep and hogs. He started a ranch in Deer Lodge, Montana and business grew quickly, owing in large part to a total lack of competition. This monopoly was broken when Texas cattle began to populate the Montana ranges. Deer Lodge became Kohr's permanent headquarters. He was elected to the territorial legislature in 1885 and the Montana Constitutional Convention in 1889 and became state senator in 1902. He nominated Teddy Roosevelt for president in 1904.

KUNG FU TV show that starred David Carradine as Kwai Chang Caine, Keye Luke as Master Po, Philip Ahn as Master Kan, Radames Pera as Caine (as a youth) and Season Hubley as Margit McLean (occasional appearance).

Kwai Chang Caine was a Chinese Buddhist monk

from the Shaolin Temple who accidently killed a member of the royal family and ended up in the Wild West of the 1880s. Caine was a philosopher who used Kung Fu, a type of martial arts, instead of a gun and practiced New Age mysticism in the midst of the dust and violence of the Old West. The show developed a cult following with its philosophy of cosmic oneness and use of martial arts. It premiered on October 14, 1972 on ABC on Saturday night. The hour-long show switched to Thursday nights in January 1973, to Saturday nights in September 1974 and to Friday nights in November 1974 before ending up where it began, on Saturday nights, from January 1975 to its final show on June 28, 1975.

L

L'AMOUR, LOUIS (b. Louis Dearborn L'Amour in Jamestown, North Dakota on March 22, 1908; d. Los Angeles, California on June 10, 1988) The most popular western novelist of all time, Louis L'Amour wrote 86 novels, 14 short-story collections, a book of nonfiction and a memoir—more than 100 books—during his life. L'Amour did not start out to become a western novelist; his first book was a collection of poetry published in 1939, and it was not until 1951, under the pseudonym of Tex Burns (his publishing company gave him this name because it did not feel a western audience would buy books written by someone named "L'Amour"), that he published his first western novel. L'Amour's career as a western novelist began after World War II when a publisher, who wanted some western novels in his catalog and knew that L'Amour came from the West, asked him if he'd try his hand at writing westerns. *Hondo* (1953) was L'Amour's first novel published under his own name. This book sold over 1.5 million copies and was made into a movie starring John Wayne. After this L'Amour began writing paperback western novels, and in 1955 he agreed to a contract with Bantam that required him to write three novels a year. L'Amour wrote five pages a day in order to fulfill his contract. L'Amour's novels were popular with readers but not critics; during his lifetime over 200 million copies of his works in more than 20 languages were sold. Forty-five were made into feature movies or TV movies.

L'Amour never finished high school; he dropped out at 15 and began to travel in the West and did a number of odd jobs, including stints as a longshoreman, lumberjack, prospector, circus roustabout, fruit picker, cattle skinner and professional boxer. In his later life he lectured at a number of universities and received an honorary doctorate from Jamestown College (in his hometown in North Dakota); he was presented the Medal of Freedom, the nation's highest civilian award, by President Ronald Reagan in 1984.

L'Amour's novels generally pit man against nature or against other men in a life-or-death struggle. His novels are known for being accurate historically and geographically; his heroes are intelligent and literate men well versed in survival skills and physically tough.

L'Amour's novels include:

Westward the Tide (1950)
Hondo (1953)
Crossfire Trail (1954)
Heller with a Gun (1954)
Kilkenny (1954)
To Tame a Land (1955)
Guns of the Timberlands (1955)
The Burning Hills (1956)
Silver Canyon (1956)
Last Stand at Papago Wells (1957)
The Tall Stranger (1957)
Sitka (1957)
Radigan (1958)
The First Fast Draw (1959)
Taggart (1959)
Flint (1960)
Shalako (1962)
Killoe (1962)
High Lonesome (1962)
How the West Was Won (1963)
Fallon (1963)
Catlow (1963)
Dark Canyon (1963)
Hanging Woman Creek (1964)
Kiowa Trail (1965)
The High Graders (1965)
The Key-Lock Man (1965)
Kid Rodelo (1966)
Kilrone (1966)
The Broken Gun (1966)
Matagorda (1967)
Down the Long Hills (1968)
Chancy (1968)
Conagher (1969)
The Empty Land (1969)
The Man Called Noon (1970)
Reilly's Luck (1970)
Brionne (1971)
Under the Sweetwater Rim (1971)
Tucker (1971)
North to the Rails (1971)

Callaghen (1972)
The Ferguson Rifle (1973)
The Quick and the Dead (1973)
The Man from Skibbereen (1973)
The Californios (1974)
Rivers West (1975)
Over on the Dry Side (1975)
The Rider of the Lost Creek (1976)
Where the Long Grass Blows (1976)
Borden Chantry (1977)
Fair Blows the Wind (1978)
The Mountain Valley War (1978)
Bendigo Shafter (1978)
The Iron Marshal (1979)
The Proving Trail (1979)
The Warrior's Path (1980)
Comstock Lode (1981)
Milo Talon (1981)
The Cherokee Trail (1982)
The Shadow Riders (1982)
The Lonesome Gods (1983)
Son of a Wanted Man (1984)
The Walking Drum (1984)
Passin' Through (1985)
Last of the Breed (1986)
West of the Pilot Range (1986)
A Trail to the West (1986)
The Haunted Mesa (1987).
The Sackett Family novels include:
The Daybreakers (1960)
Sackett (1961)
Lando (1962)
Mojave Crossing (1964)
The Sackett Brand (1965)
Mustang Man (1966)
The Skyliners (1967)
The Lonely Men (1969)
Galloway (1970)
Ride the Dark Trail (1972)
Treasure Mountain (1972)
Sackett's Land (1974)
The Man from the Broken Hills (1975)
To the Far Blue Mountains (1976)
Sackett's Gold (1977)
The Warrior's Path (1980)
Lonely on the Mountain (1980)
Ride the River (1983)
Jubal Sackett (1985).

Under the pseudonym Tex Burns, L'Amour published a series of Hopalong Cassidy novels, including *Hopalong Cassidy and the Riders of High Rock* (1951), *Hopalong Cassidy and the Rustlers of West Fork* (1951), *Hopalong Cassidy and the Trail to Seven Pines* (1951) and *Hopalong Cassidy: Trouble Shooter* (1952).

Under the pseudonym Jim May, L'Amour published *Showdown at Yellow Butte* (1954) and *Utah Blaine* (1954).

Short-story collections published by L'Amour include *War Party* (1975), *Yondering* (1980), *The Strong Shall Live* (1980), *Buckskin Run* (1981), *Law of the Desert Born* (1983), *Bowdrie* (1983), *The Hills of Homicide* (1984), *Bowdrie's*

Law (1984), *Riding for the Brand* (1986), *Dutchman's Flat* (1986), *The Trail to Crazy Man* (1986) and *Lonigan* (1988).

Other books L'Amour wrote include his collection of poetry, *Smoke from This Altar* (1939), *Frontier* (a collection of essays, 1984), *The Sackett Companion: A Personal Guide to the Sackett Novels* (1988) and *The Education of a Wandering Man* (1989). A collection of quotes, *A Trail of Memories: The Quotations of Louis L'Amour* (1988), was compiled by his daughter Angelique L'Amour.

LANCER   TV show that starred James Stacy as Johnny Madrid Lancer, Wayne Maunder as Scott Lancer, Andrew Duggan as Murdoch Lancer, Elizabeth Baur as Teresa O'Brien and Paul Brinegar as Jelly Hoskins (1969–70).

Murdoch Lancer had two sons who had never met. The setting is the 1870s, and the two brothers grew to respect each other as they hung onto the ranch for several seasons. The boys, from different mothers, were quite different: One was a gunslinger and the other a college-educated Bostonian. But they both came to their father's ranch when he beckoned them. The elder Lancer was about to lose his vast spread and needed help fending off attempts to wrestle the San Joaquin Valley land away from him. The hour-long show premiered on September 24, 1968 on Tuesday evenings on CBS. It was moved to Thursday nights in May 1971 and ended its run on September 9, 1971 after 51 episodes.

LANDON, MICHAEL   (b. Eugene Maurice Orowitz in Forest Hills, Queens, New York on October 31, 1936; d. Malibu, California on July 1, 1991)   Michael Lan-

Michael Landon

don first came to fame as "Little Joe" on "Bonanza" and then as Charles Ingalls on "Little House on the Prairie." Known for producing uplifting programming on television, Landon had a difficult, unhappy childhood. Taunted by anti-Semitic schoolmates, he had a problem with bed-wetting that was exacerbated by his mother, who displayed the sheets to their neighbors. He excelled in javelin throwing but barely survived academically (he graduated 300 in a class of 301) and received an athletic scholarship to the University of California–Los Angeles. Landon left school after a year and took acting lessons at Warner Brothers. He changed his name to Michael Landon (he found the name in a telephone book) and made his movie debut in *These Wilder Years* (1956) and had his first starring role in *I Was a Teenage Werewolf* (1957). Landon's roles in some TV westerns caught the attention of David Dortort, who was casting for "Bonanza." During his "Bonanza" period Landon began writing and directing and eventually wrote over 30 scripts for that show. After "Bonanza" Landon created "Little House on the Prairie" and had complete control over the show as well as the starring role of Charles Ingalls. His autobiographical TV movie "The Loneliest Runner" (about bed-wetting) was broadcast on NBC in December 1976. After "Little House" went off the air (because the children in the series were all grown), Landon created and starred in "Highway to Heaven," which lasted until 1989. Landon planned a new series, "Us," which was scheduled for CBS in 1991–92, when he was diagnosed with cancer of the pancreas and liver. (See also BONANZA; LITTLE HOUSE ON THE PRAIRIE; TELEVISION WESTERNS.)

Allan "Rocky" Lane

LANE, ALLAN "ROCKY" (b. Harry Albershart in Mishawaka, Indiana on September 22, 1904; d. Woodland Hills, California on October 27, 1973)   Rocky Lane was a top athlete at the University of Notre Dame, starring in football, baseball and basketball. His first film was *Not Quite Decent* (1929), and his first western was *The Law West of Tombstone* (1938) with Tim Holt and Harry Carey. Lane signed with Republic in 1940 and filmed three western serials, and in 1944 he began his own western series. He took over the role of Red Ryder from Wild Bill Elliott in 1946. Lane's best-known series for Republic began in 1947 and lasted for 32 films with his horse, Black Jack. In 1953 he made his last "B" western and then toured with circuses and rodeos. Lane's final movie appearance was in *Posse from Hell* (1961), and from 1961–1966 he was the voice of Mr. Ed on television. (See also B WESTERN MOVIES; MOVIES.)

LARAMIE TV show that starred John Smith as Slim Sherman, Robert Fuller as Jess Harper, Hoagy Carmichael as Jonesy (1959–60), Bobby Crawford, Jr. as Andy Sherman (1959–61), Dennis Holmes as Mike Williams (1961–63), Spring Byington as Daisy Cooper (1961–63) and Stuart Randall as Mort Corey (1960–63).

This program was set in Wyoming Territory in the 1870s on a cattle ranch outside Laramie. The central plot was that two brothers, whose father had been gunned down, were trying to save their ranch, so they established a stagecoach relay station there. This accounted for all the odd characters, desperadoes and guest stars appearing on the series each week. The show premiered on September 15, 1959 and ended its run on September 17, 1963. The 124 hour-long shows—some in color as well as black and white—were always shown on NBC on Tuesday nights.

LARAMIE, TREATY OF In an effort to establish peace on the plains, allow emigrant wagon trains to pass safely, and establish boundaries for various Indian tribes, Indian agent Thomas "Broken Hand" Fitzpatrick persuaded Congress to fund the Treaty of Fort Laramie (1851). Fitzpatrick, appointed an Indian agent in 1846, was an excellent agent, trusted by the Indians, and he persuaded nine Indian nations, including Sioux, Snakes, Arapaho, Shoshoni, Crows, and Cheyenne (normally mortal enemies), to gather to discuss a treaty. Fitzpatrick had been alarmed at the destruction caused when about 50,000 gold seekers had gone west in 1850, as well as the deteriorating relations with Indians because of white emigration. In the treaty, the Indians agreed to boundaries for their tribes (something they had never done before), to allow safe passage for wagon trains and to allow the army to build forts in the area. In return, the government agreed to give the Indians $50,000 a year for 50 years (the Senate reduced it to 10 years during ratification). About 10,000 Indians had gathered for the treaty, the largest single gathering of Indians on the plains, and it would be a landmark treaty until the summer of 1854 when the tribes gathered for the distribution of annuities. At this time a Sioux killed a stray cow; the owner complained, and a hotheaded army lieutenant, John L. Grattan, went out to arrest the Indian brave, although he had no jurisdiction to do so (each side agreed to punish its own for improprieties). When the Sioux refused to give up their brave, Grattan ordered a volley fired and a major chief was killed, which caused the Indians to retaliate and kill Grattan and his party of 30. Grattan himself was discovered later with 24 arrows in him. This caused the army and government to renounce the treaty and attempt retaliation to punish the Indians, thus ending the Treaty of Laramie.

LAREDO TV show that starred Neville Brand as Reese Bennett, Peter Brown as Chad Cooper, William Smith as Joe Riley, Philip Carey as Captain Edward Parmalee and Robert Wolders as Erik Hunter (1966–67).

This was a story of post–Civil War Texas and some Texas Rangers with a sense of humor. Not a comedy but full of wit, the show premiered on September 16, 1965 on Thursday nights on NBC. The hour-long series moved to Friday nights in September 1966 and stayed there until its last telecast on September 1, 1967.

LARIAT From the Mexican-Spanish term *la reata,* meaning "rope." Used for catching cattle or horses, the lariat has a loop that can be enlarged or tightened because of a *honda,* or special slip knot, so the noose can be made larger by swinging it and then tighten once the animal is caught.

LARN, JOHN M. (b. Mobile, Alabama on March 1, 1849; d. Albany, Texas on June 22, 1878) John Larn was a former cowboy who had a tendency to run into violence—in 1871 he killed a ranch owner in Colorado, a sheriff in New Mexico and two Mexicans near the Pecos River in Texas—but then attempted to settle down, establish a ranch near Fort Griffin, Texas and raise a family. He was elected sheriff of Shackleford County, Texas and often deputized John Selman, his friend and a noted gunman. Larn had to resign as sheriff on March 7, 1877 because he and Selman were involved in cattle rustling. He also attempted to ambush a local rancher named Treadwell, but the rancher escaped. Finally, he was arrested on his ranch on June 22, 1878 and taken to jail in Albany, but that night he was shot and killed by a masked mob that broke into the jail. (See also SELMAN, JOHN.)

LaRUE, LASH (b. Alfred LaRue in Gretna, Louisiana on June 14, 1917) Film actor known as the "King of the Bullwhip," LaRue got his big break when he played the Cheyenne Kid in *The Song of Old Wyoming* with Eddie Dean, in which his bullwhip abilities attracted a legion of fans. This role led to a starring role in *The Law of the Lash* (1947), a series of "B" westerns and then tours of rodeos and carnivals. Ironically, LaRue was not signed by Warner Brothers because the studio thought he looked too much like star Humphrey Bogart.

LASH OF THE WEST TV show that starred Lash LaRue as Marshal Lash LaRue, Al "Fuzzy" St. John as Deputy Fuzzy Q. Jones, Cliff Taylor as Flapjack and John Martin as Stratton.

This program consisted of fifteen-minute clips of some of Lash LaRue's old movies. The shows were introduced by Lash LaRue in his U.S. marshal's office—while trading quips with Flapjack and Stratton—and presented as stories about the exploits of his grandfather. The grandfather just happened to also be named Lash LaRue, was also a U.S. marshal and looked amazingly like the current Lash LaRue. The show premiered on ABC on January 4, 1953 and ended on April 26, 1953. This show was also on ABC's Saturday morning lineup from March to May 1953. Known as the "King of the Bullwhip," the black-clad Lash was always accompanied by his trusty sidekick, Fuzzy Q. Jones.

LASSO From the Spanish word *lazo,* meaning "noose." To "lasso" a steer means to get the rope on it so it can be controlled. Made of rawhide (from the skin of a buffalo or cow), it is used like a lariat to catch animals with a running noose. "To lasso" a cow or horse means to catch it with a rope—rawhide or grass. In practice, the working cowboy used "rope" as a noun or verb, so he would use his rope to rope a steer.

LAST OF THE MOHICANS See HAWKEYE AND THE LAST OF THE MOHICANS.

LAST ROUND-UP, THE Song written by Billy Hill (July 14, 1899–) and published by Shapiro, Bernstein and Company, New York, 1933.

One of the most popular cowboy songs of all time, this one came out during the Great Depression, first achieving fame in the "Ziegfeld Follies of 1934" when performed by Don Ross, then through radio broadcasts. Songwriter Billy Hill was born in Boston and studied violin; as a teenager he visited the West and worked briefly as a cowboy and miner. During a visit to a Texas ranch in the mid-1920s he and a friend watched a cowboy trampled to death after a fall from his horse; this incident became the inspiration for this song. A professional songwriter who wrote songs for the movies, Hill married DeDette Walker, who was the model for the "Columbia lady" logo of Columbia Pictures. The two moved to New York where Hill struggled to make a living. In 1931 he wrote "The Last Round-Up" when he was penniless. When his wife gave birth to their daughter in an elevator because a hospital refused to admit them without payment in advance, Hill almost sold "The Last Round-Up" for $25 but was advanced $200 by Gene Buck, head of a performing rights organization (ASCAP) just in time. In 1933 Shapiro, Bernstein, and Company, a top New York firm, published the song, and it was first sung by Joe Morrison at the Paramount Theater in New York.

LATIGO Leather strap that connects the saddle to the cinch.

LAW ENFORCEMENT Settlers sought to have law and order when they moved into an area; the era of "lawlessness" was relatively short lived in any town or city and even this period had its sense of justice, albeit one not necessarily compatible with the laws and courts of an established society. When settlers first entered an area, the first "official" agents of law enforcement were generally the army, militia detachments or Indian agents. A sheriff was soon elected, with powers to collect taxes, form a posse and deputize citizens. Jails were usually crude, primitive structures, if they existed at all. Many times judges or justices of the peace did not have legal training; they dispensed rulings based on "common sense" and "frontier justice," although in general they often seemed to be fair and just. These judges (as well as many law officers) were not paid a salary; instead, they received income from fees assessed. The higher court judges were usually circuit riders appointed by federal officials; as an area became more settled, the federal or territorial officials (or state) assumed a greater role than local officials. United States marshals were political appointments and served under the jurisdiction of the federal district courts; generally the deputy United States marshals did the actual work of law enforcement. At the local level, there were sheriffs elected by the populace; they often received a small salary that was supplemented by fees and fines assessed. The major laws that these local authorities had to enforce concerned tax payments, carrying concealed weapons, gambling, prostitution and public drunkenness; in the cattle and mining towns there was the constant problem of men letting off steam, which had to be monitored to avoid senseless killings. As areas grew, the power brokers (cattle associations, railroads and mining interests) increasingly had a say in law enforcement, often hiring their own police force and generally controlling other law enforcement officials. (See also MARSHAL; SHERIFF.)

LAWMAN, THE TV show that starred John Russell as Marshal Dan Troop, Peter Brown as Deputy Johnny McKay, Bek Nelson as Dru Lemp (1958–59), Peggy Castle as Lily Merrill (1959–62) and Dan Sheridan as Jake (1961–62).

Set in Laramie, Wyoming, this was a no-nonsense western whose basic story line was criminals being brought to justice. Marshal Dan Troop often carried a double-barrel shotgun, while Deputy Johnny McKay was lightning fast on the draw. In the second season, the Birdcage Saloon was opened by Lily Merrill, who provided a romantic—as well as humanizing—touch for the marshal. The show premiered on ABC on October 5, 1958 on Sunday evenings; its final show was on October 2, 1962. The half-hour series, shot in black and white, was not actually filmed in Laramie but on Hollywood studio lots.

LAW OF THE PLAINSMAN TV show that starred Michael Ansara as deputy marshal Sam Buckhart, Dayton Lummis as Marshal Andy Morrison, Gina Gillespie as Tess Logan and Nora Marlowe as Martha Commager.

Sam Buckhart was an Apache Indian, educated at Harvard, who returned to Santa Fe to become a deputy marshal. Buckhart was played by Michael Ansara, who regularly played Indian roles although he was actually of Lebanese descent, and the show featured the conflicts of an Indian lawman being accepted (or rejected) by the white community as well as the Indian community. The show premiered on October 1, 1959 on NBC on Thursday evenings. In July 1962 it moved to ABC, where it was shown on Monday evenings and where it ended its run on September 24, 1962. Thirty-four half-hour episodes were filmed, all in black and white.

LAY, ELZY (aka William McGinnis; b. William Ellsworth Lay in McArthur, Ohio on November 25, 1862; d. Los Angeles, California on November 10, 1934)   Elzy Lay was a member of the Wild Bunch and helped Butch Cassidy steal $8,000 from the mining camp at Cattle Gate, Utah in April 1897. Involved in a train robbery with the Ketchum Gang on July 11, 1899, Lay, Tom Ketchum and G. W. Franks camped at Turkey Creek Canyon, New Mexico, about 35 miles from the robbery, but were found by Sheriff Edward Farr. At dawn the lawmen opened fire on Lay when he went to the creek to fill up his canteen. Lay was wounded but helped his partners defend themselves in the day-long battle that saw the three lawmen killed. That night the outlaws managed to escape, but a few days later Ketchum was captured. Lay was captured at an isolated hideout cabin in Eddy County, New Mexico in August 1899. A posse was waiting for him when he walked in the door; Lay pulled his gun and wounded a posse member, but the

John Russell as Marshall Dan Troop and Peter Brown as Deputy John McKay in "The Lawmen"

others jumped him and beat him unconscious. He was sentenced to life at the New Mexico territorial prison but was pardoned on January 10, 1906 after he helped quell a riot. Lay remarried, had two daughters, moved to California and spent his final years as head watermaster of the Imperial Valley Irrigation System. (See also KETCHUM, BLACK JACK.)

LEADVILLE, COLORADO Leadville was a gold boom town originally named Oro City, a gold camp, established in 1860. Located about 120 miles southwest of Denver, the town boomed until 1867 when the gold ran out. But in 1877, extensive silver-lead deposits were discovered, which created a second boom and renamed the town Leadville. Leadville is famous for the Matchless Mine, which made Horace A. W. Tabor a rich man and national figure. Tabor, the first mayor of Leadville and at one time a postmaster, built a beautiful opera house where Oscar Wilde lectured on the "ethics of art" in 1882. About $100 million in gold, silver, lead and other metals came from Leadville mines from 1879 to 1885. Leadville's heydays ended in 1893 when a national depression caused the price of silver to drop and Tabor to lose his huge fortune.

LEDOUX, CHRIS (b. Biloxi, Mississippi on October 2, 1948) Former rodeo cowboy (bareback champion in 1976) LeDoux is known for his recordings by and about rodeo cowboys. LeDoux began riding in rodeos when he was 14 and settled on a ranch in Wyoming. He began to write songs and record them on his own label and then achieved fame when Garth Brooks sang his name in a song. After this LeDoux joined Brooks's label as a recording artist.

LEE, OLIVER MILTON (b. Buffalo Gap, Texas on November 8, 1865; d. Alamogordo, New Mexico on December 15, 1941) Oliver Milton Lee was a prime suspect in the murder of Albert Jennings Fountain and his eight-year-old son. Chased by a posse led by Pat Garrett, Lee and James Gilliland eventually surrendered, were brought to trial in Hillsboro, Texas and acquitted. By this time Lee was a prominent rancher with a prosperous spread called the Dog Canyon Ranch, but his early life was filled with violence. In 1888, after George McDonald, Lee's best friend, was killed, Lee led a vigilante party that resulted in the death of John Good's son. The body was left to rot in the White Sands Desert in New Mexico and was discovered about two weeks later by John Good with some friends and relatives. Riding back to Las Cruces with five others, Good ran into Lee and five other friends and a shootout ensued, although no one was killed. Lee also killed two cowboys on February 12, 1893 near El Paso, Texas on a trail drive. In 1914 Lee sold his ranch and later was elected to the state legislature, becoming involved in a number of business organizations until his death by a stroke in 1941. (See also FOUNTAIN, ALBERT JENNINGS; GARRETT, PAT.)

LEFT-HANDED GUN, THE Film produced by Fred Coe; directed by Arthur Penn; screenplay by Leslie Stevens; released in 1958 by Warner Brothers; 102 minutes in length. Cast: Paul Newman, Lita Milan, John Dehner, Hurd Hatfield, James Congdon, James Best and Denver Pyle.

A story about Billy the Kid based on the assumption that the Kid was left-handed; he wasn't. The basis of this legend is a picture printed backward that shows the right-handed Kid looking like a left-hander; still, the legend persists. Written by Gore Vidal as a play for television, this story makes Billy the Kid a late 1950s juvenile delinquent full of youthful energy and restlessness. Billy becomes famous from his exploits and then, in a story filled with religious mysticism, is killed by his own publicity.

LEGEND OF CUSTER See CUSTER..

LEGEND OF JESSE JAMES, THE TV show that starred Christopher Jones as Jesse James, Allen Case as Frank James, John Milford as Cole Younger, Tim McIntire as Bob Younger, Robert Wilke as Marshal Sam Corbett and Ann Doran as Mrs. James.

The real Jesse and Frank James were not as nice, handsome, lovable and wholesome as portrayed in this TV series. Neither were the Younger brothers, who also appeared in these shows. But TV gave the James boys winning ways and put them in prime time on September 13, 1965 on Monday evenings on ABC. The 26 episodes of this half-hour show ended on September 5, 1966.

LEGEND OF NIGGER CHARLEY, THE Film (changed to *The Legend of Black Charley* when it was released in Atlanta) produced by Larry G. Spangler; directed by Martin Goldman; screenplay by Martin Goldman and Larry G. Spangler, based on a story by James Bellah; released in 1972 by Paramount; 100 minutes in length. Cast: Fred Williamson, D'Urville Martin, Don Pedro Colley, Gertrude Jeanette, Marcia McBroom and Alan Gifford.

Fred Williamson, a former football star, makes his film debut here as a slave who escapes to the West (pursued by slave catchers) and becomes a gunfighter.

LEONARD, BILL (b. William Leonard in New York c. 1850; d. Eureka, New Mexico on June 6, 1881) Bill Leonard was one of the outlaws who robbed the stage from Tombstone on March 15, 1881, which eventually led to the shootout at the O.K. Corral. Leonard, Harry Head and Jim Crane stopped the night stage, with eight passengers and $26,000 in gold, while Luther King held the horses. Driver Budd Philpot was killed, and so was a passenger. The runaway stage was saved by some daring heroics by Wells Fargo agent Bob Paul, who got down on the wagon tongue and retrieved the reins to stop the runaway horses. Luther King was soon caught and named his accomplices, who had "dead or alive" rewards on their heads. Three months later Leonard and Head tried to rob a store owned by Bill and Ike Haslett in Eureka, New Mexico, but in the ensuing gunfight both were shot and killed. (See also HARRY THE KID.)

LESLIE, BUCKSKIN FRANK (b. Nashville Franklin Leslie probably in Galveston, Texas c. 1842; d. possibly in California c. 1922) Buckskin Frank got his nickname because he wore a fringed leather shirt. Leslie was in Tombstone during the time of the fight at the O.K. Corral and later killed Billy Claiborne, who was in the fight at the O.K. Corral but escaped by fleeing into C. S. Fly's photographic studio with Ike Clanton. On November 14, 1882 Claiborne attempted to ambush Leslie when he came out of the Oriental Saloon, but Leslie sneaked out the side door and startled Claiborne, who fired a wild shot before Leslie nailed him. Claiborne died cursing Leslie. Before that, Leslie had killed Mike Killeen over a woman. Leslie and Killeen's wife, May, had been seeing each other, and the jealous husband came gunning for Leslie on June 22, 1880 and a gunfight occurred, with Killeen dying from his wounds five days later. A week after her husband's death, May married Frank Leslie. Leslie used his wife's silhouette for target practice, which led to May becoming known as the "Silhouette Girl." She divorced him after seven years and married someone else but then went through another divorce to remarry Frank. During the time Frank and May were divorced, Frank was living with blond Mollie Williams, who worked at the Bird Cage Saloon. One day a drunken Leslie shot and killed Mollie after a quarrel. Leslie also tried to kill a witness, a ranch hand named Jim Neal. But the wounded Neal managed to escape and testified against Leslie—who thought Neal was dead and had confidently claimed "self-defense" in the killing. Leslie was sentenced to 25 years in the Yuma territorial prison but was pardoned 12 years later. Ironically, a broke, down-and-out Leslie was given a job in a pool room in Oakland, California in 1925 by Jim Neal—35 years after the trial that sent him to prison. Buckskin Frank disappeared after about six months on the job with Neal's pistol; he probably committed suicide. (See also CLAIBORNE, BILLY.)

LEVI'S When Levi Strauss (1829–1902) arrived in San Francisco during the gold rush in 1850, he carried with him some canvas he intended to sell for tents. But he soon found there was a shortage of tough work pants, so he had a tailor make some trousers from the canvas. The canvas pants were soon popular with the miners, so Strauss set up shop in San Francisco making them; soon, he switched to another fabric, cotton that was originally loomed in Nimes, France, called *serge de Nimes*. This material was supplied in a special indigo blue color, which assured unvarying color quality; it was soon called "denim" from "de Nimes." A fabric similar to denim called *genes* was used for pants worn by Genoese sailors; this led to "jeans" being another name for these sturdy pants, which were soon popular with farmers, ranchers, cowboys, railroad workers, lumberjacks and miners. Strauss added copper rivets to strengthen pockets and seams in the late 1860s and was granted a patent for these clothes with copper rivets in 1873.

LEWIS, MERIWETHER (b. near Charlottesville, Virginia on August 18, 1774; d. on Natchez Trace in Tennessee on October 11, 1809) Meriwether was the "Lewis" of the Lewis and Clark Expedition; he was the one who picked William Clark to help with the trip to

Levi Strauss

explore the Louisiana Purchase and sent the first white Americans to the Pacific to bring back a report. Lewis was in the Virginia militia that suppressed the Whiskey Rebellion; he met William Clark when he served under him during General "Mad Anthony" Wayne's Ohio and Indian campaign that culminated in the Battle of Fallen Timbers. Lewis became a captain in the army infantry, learned the Choctaw language while he was stationed in Memphis and then was sent to Detroit in 1801. Thomas Jefferson had wanted to send an expedition to the Pacific to explore the West (and try to find a Northwest Passage to the Pacific) during the time he was in George Washington's cabinet; thus, in 1792, Lewis applied to Jefferson to lead an expedition to the Pacific coast. When Jefferson became president, Lewis became his private secretary. Jefferson still wanted the West explored, so when, in 1803, Congress financed an expedition to the Pacific, Jefferson picked Lewis, who in turn picked Clark. The group left on May 14, 1804, traveling up the Missouri, and on October 26 reached the North Dakota Mandan villages, where they wintered. An educated, scientific man, Lewis added invaluable knowledge and information on this journey; Clark, a more practical man with a talent for management and a working knowledge of

Meriwether Lewis *(Western Archives)*

Indians, provided a good counterbalance. On November 7, 1805 the expedition reached the Pacific coast, where they built Fort Clatsop and wintered; they began their return on March 23, 1806. On their return Lewis and Clark split up, and Lewis took a group north where they crossed the Rockies and reached the upper Missouri on July 7. On the way to join up with Clark, Lewis was accidentally shot through the thighs by Pierre Cruzatte, who thought Lewis was an elk. After the group rejoined, they went back down the Missouri and arrived in St. Louis on September 23, 1806 after an absence of more than two years. In November Lewis and Clark went to Washington, where Lewis resigned from the army and was then appointed by Jefferson to be governor of the Louisiana Territory. But Lewis was not a good politician, temperamentally unsuited for the position, and served only 18 months as an unpopular leader before being called to Washington to explain some irregularities and help publication of the expedition's journals. But on the night of October 11, 1835, at the age of 35, Meriwether Lewis stopped at an inn on the Natchez Trace in southwestern Tennessee. Lewis died this night—but no one knows whether it was murder or suicide.

LEWIS AND CLARK EXPEDITION   (1804–6) Thomas Jefferson had wanted an expedition mounted to explore the West for a long time and first

proposed such a venture in 1792 while he was serving in George Washington's cabinet, although he had promoted this idea since 1783. But the idea did not take root until Jefferson became president in 1801. He persuaded Congress to approve $2,500 and authorize a trip up the Missouri River to its source in the Rocky Mountains, then on to the Pacific. The idea of a Northwest Passage was still prevalent during this time, and many thought there was a water route from the Atlantic to the Pacific in the continental United States. Congress approved the money and expedition in January; by a stroke of fate the United States purchased the Louisiana Territory from France at the end of April, so the venture became an exploration of territory recently purchased. At this point the Louisiana Territory included not only New Orleans (the original point of the negotiations that resulted in the purchase of the territory) and present-day Louisiana but also the area between the Mississippi River and Rocky Mountains. The Pacific Northwest was claimed by four different countries: the United States, England, Spain and Russia.

Jefferson picked Meriwether Lewis, his private secretary and an army captain in the First United States Infantry regiment, to head the expedition, and Lewis requested William Clark to be co-leader. Lewis had served under Clark in the 1790s when both were in the army headed by General "Mad Anthony" Wayne. Clark was managing his family's plantation near present-day Louisville, Kentucky at the time he received Lewis's request.

On July 5, 1803 Lewis left Washington for Pittsburgh, traveled down the Ohio River where he picked up Clark and some others at Louisville and then headed out the mouth of the Ohio and up the Mississippi River to Wood River, Illinois, opposite the mouth of the Missouri River. There they camped for the next five months while they recruited and trained men for the expedition, gathered supplies and equipment and collected whatever information they could from traders and boatmen who had traveled up the Missouri River. Finally, on April 1, 1804 they chose their crew of 27 young unmarried soldiers, an interpreter and half-breed hunter named George Drouilliart, and Clark's black slave, York, for the journey. The "Corps of Discovery" officially began on May 14, 1804 when the crew pushed up the Missouri in a 55-foot keelboat and two canoes, averaging about 15 miles a day. On October 26 they reached the Mandan and Minnetaree Indian villages near the Knife River in present-day North Dakota and set up winter camp. A number of French boatmen, as well as a corporal and five privates, went back East with specimens and records from the first part of the trip.

At their winter quarters the expedition built a log fort and sat through a long, cold winter; they spent their time getting as much information as possible from Indians and making notes. On April 7, 1805 they headed west again, this time with 33 men, including French trapper Toussaint Charbonneau and his Shoshoni squaw Sacajawea, who had an infant son. On August 17 they reached the end of their boat ride on the Missouri; from there they had to get over the Rockies. At this point the group ran into a group of Shoshoni Indians, and Sacajawea, acting as interpreter, discovered they were her family. (Sacajawea had been stolen from the tribe as a young girl and sold as a slave; Charbonneau had won her in a gambling game.) Because of Sacajawea, the expedition obtained horses and crossed the Continental Divide through Lemhi Pass; they then headed north along the Salmon River and down Bitterroot Valley until they reached the mouth of Lolo Creek, near present-day Missoula, Montana. Here they headed west and crossed the Bitterroot range on the most difficult and treacherous part of their journey. On September 22 this part of the journey was complete, so the expedition members left their horses with a friendly Indian tribe and, with five canoes, went down the Clearwater, Snake and Columbia Rivers until they reached the Pacific on November 18, 1805. They erected a post on the south side of the Columbia River, named Fort Clatsop (after a nearby Indian tribe), and settled in for a rainy winter. The expedition gathered and recorded information, kept an eye out for ships to take them back and tried to ward off thieving Indians. On March 23, 1806 they began their eastward journey. In early July on Lolo Creek the group split in two. Lewis took nine men and explored the Marias River and northern Montana as he headed to the Falls of the Missouri; Clark returned to the Three Forks of the Missouri, crossed over to the Yellowstone River and then traveled down that river until August 12, when they were reunited with the rest of their group just below the mouth of the Yellowstone.

The group traveled down the Missouri until they reached the Mandan villages, where they visited before they continued on to St. Louis, where they arrived on September 23, 1806 after having traveled 8,000 miles over a period of two years, four months and nine days. The expedition lost only one man, Sergeant Charles Floyd, whose death was due to a ruptured appendix. The group received a warm welcome in St. Louis and Washington, D.C., where they had been given up as lost, and the accounts of their journey—as well as the invaluable information and specimens—provided much-needed information about a previously unknown country. This trip cost the government about $40,000 but opened up the West to the United States; after this expedition, American trappers and fur traders would begin to work in the Rocky Mountains and Pacific Northwest, providing the first permanent American presence in the West. (See also CLARK, WILLIAM; LEWIS, MERIWETHER; LOUISIANA PURCHASE; SACAJAWEA.)

LIFE AND LEGEND OF WYATT EARP, THE TV show that starred Hugh O'Brian as Wyatt Earp, Mason Alan Dinehart III as Bat Masterson (1955–57), Denver Pyle as Ben Thompson (1955–56), Hal Baylor as Bill Thompson (1955–56), Gloria Talbot as Abbie Crandall (1955–56), Don Haggerty as Marsh Murdock (1955–56), Douglas Fowley as Doc Fabrique (1955–56), Lloyd Corrigan as Ned Buntline, Paul Brinegar as Jim "Dog" Kelly (1956–58), Ralph Sanford as Jim "Dog" Kelly (1958–59), Selmer Jackson as Mayor Hoover (1956–57), William Tannen as Deputy Hal Norton (1957–58), Douglas Fowley as Doc Holliday (1957–61), Myron Healy

as Doc Holiday (temporary: 1959), Carol Stone as Kate Holliday (1957–58), Morgan Woodward as Shotgun Gibbs (1958–61), Dirk London as Morgan Earp (1959–61), John Anderson as Virgil Earp (1959–61), Randy Stuart as Nellie Cashman (1959–60), Trevor Bardette as Old Man Clanton (1959–61), Carol Thurston as Emma Clanton (1959–60), Lash La Rue as Sheriff Johnny Behan (1959), Steve Brodie as Sheriff Johnny Behand (1959–61), William Phipps as Curley Bill Brocious (1959–61), Britt Lomond as Johnny Ringo (1960–61), Stacy Harris as Mayor Club (1960–61) and Damien O'Flynn as Doc Goodfellow (1959–61).

Yes, there was a real Wyatt Earp as well as a real Doc Holliday, Ned Buntline, Clanton Gang, Johnny Ringo, Virgil Earp, Morgan Earp and a number of others who appeared as characters in this series. But the stories were long on legend and short on life as it was actually lived, which was necessary because this extremely popular show filmed 226 half-hour episodes during its six-year run. The show premiered on September 6, 1955 and ended on September 26, 1961, always on ABC on Tuesday evenings. During the first season Wyatt was marshal of Ellsworth, Kansas; the next season he moved on to Dodge City, Kansas, where he patrolled the town on Tuesday evenings while Marshal Dillon took care of the same place on Saturday nights with no conflicts mentioned. Wyatt moved to Tombstone, Arizona during the 1959–60 season, and here he ended the ongoing series with the gunfight at the O.K. Corral, done over a five-week period as the conflict between the Clantons and the Earps, with Doc Holliday, heated up and finally ended with the famous showdown. Author-playwright Frederick Hazlitt Brenman wrote the scripts, which contributed to this being one of the first successful adult westerns and a consistently top-rated show during its run.

LIFE AND TIMES OF GRIZZLY ADAMS, THE TV show that starred Dan Haggerty as James "Grizzly" Adams, Denver Pyle as Mad Jack, Don Shanks as Nakuma and John Bishop as Borrie Cartman.

A man is falsely accused of a crime so he flees civilization, living in the mountains and communing with nature. That was the basic premise of this TV show, based on a movie of the same name and very loosely on a real-life Grizzly Adams who took to the mountains after some personal bankruptcies. Grizzly raised a bear from a cub into a tame friend. Ben the bear was played by Bozo the bear. This show premiered on February 9, 1977 on Wednesday evenings on NBC and ended on July 26, 1978. A good amount of the filming was done in Park City, Utah, near Salt Lake City.

LIFE WITH SNARKY PARKER Children's TV show produced and directed by Yul Brynner; puppeteers: Bil Baird and Cora Baird.

This was a children's program where puppets starred in tales of the Old West. Snarky Parker was the Hot Rock's deputy sheriff who rode a horse named Heathcliffe, fought the local villain, Ronald Rodent, and was in love with the local schoolteacher. Slugger, the Bent Elbow Saloon's piano player, and Paw, the schoolteacher's father, were also regulars in this series produced and directed by Yul Brynner. The show premiered in prime time on January 9, 1950 on CBS on Monday, Tuesday, Thursday and Friday. The 15-minute show was telecast every weekday beginning in April 1950, and it ended its prime-time run on August 30, 1950. After its prime-time run, the show became a weekday afternoon show for a month.

LILLIE, GORDON See PAWNEE BILL.

LINCOLN COUNTY WAR The Lincoln County War (1878–84) is perhaps most famous because Billy the Kid achieved his fame in this struggle. Names like Pat Garrett and John Chisum are also associated with the war, which was actually a battle for economic and political power in a lawless region that ended up costing numerous lives from gun battles involving partisans of the two major warring factions.

Lincoln County was dominated by attorney Lawrence G. Murphy and James J. Dolan, a businessman who operated a general store and engaged in some large-scale ranching and small-town banking. Murphy and Dolan held the government contract to supply the Mescalero Apache Indian Reservation with beef and flour. On intimate terms with Indian agent F. C. Godfroy and officers at nearby Fort Stanton, the businessmen regularly and systematically cheated the Indians and the government. Murphy and Dolan were aligned with Thomas B. Catron, attorney general of New Mexico Territory, president of the First National Bank in Santa Fe and leader of the "Santa Fe Ring," a group who held political control of New Mexico.

The control exerted by the Murphy-Dolan group was challenged by several events. In 1876 cattleman John Chisum moved into the area and set up a large ranching operation on the Pecos River; Chisum's empire would become perhaps the largest cattle ranch in the United States, and he wanted some government contracts to supply beef to the army and Indian reservations. The following year Englishman John Tunstall also moved into the area and set up a ranch and also opened a general store, which competed with Dolan's mercantile monopoly. Both Chisum and Tunstall joined forces with Alexander McSween, an attorney who had formerly worked for Murphy but left the firm after problems arose with the estate of Emil Fritz. Dolan claimed to be a creditor of the deceased and demanded settlement of the account from the $10,000 insurance policy; McSween as executor refused to pay and insisted the claim was fraudulent. Murphy and Dolan in turn accused McSween of being an embezzler. A long legal battle then began that resulted in Murphy-Dolan attaching McSween's property in February 1878, including the general store he owned with Tunstall that competed with Dolan's. Meanwhile, on February 18 a large posse of gunmen went out to Tunstall's ranch, where they ran into the Englishman and shot him down in cold blood. Several of Tunstall's employees, including Billy the Kid, witnessed the slaying before they fled for their lives. Warrants were sworn out for the killers, but Lincoln

sheriff William Brady, an ally of the Murphy-Dolan group, would not serve them. And Governor Axtell, also a Murphy-Dolan partisan who placed full blame on McSween, requested military assistance from President Rutherford Hayes. This resulted in members of the Ninth Cavalry (the buffalo soldiers) coming into Lincoln under Captain George Purington; however, the situation was so confused that Purington pulled his men out.

In March, Dick Brewer, Tunstall's foreman, organized a posse (which included Billy the Kid) and, with warrants issued from the justice of the peace, arrested Frank Baker and William Morton, but both captives were killed before they got to the jail. On April 1 Sheriff Brady and deputy George Hindman were gunned down on the streets of Lincoln by several from the McSween faction (including Billy the Kid), who hid behind Tunstall's store. This led to a search of McSween's home for weapons, and on April 5 a reward of $200 was posted for Brady and Hindman's assassins. This inspired Murphy-Dolan partisan Buckshot Roberts to go out to Blazer's Mill, on the Mescalero Reservation, where he ran into a group that included Dick Brewer, Billy the Kid and others; shooting erupted and Brewer and Roberts were both killed. After this, Billy the Kid became leader of the group Brewer had formerly headed.

A McSween sympathizer, John S. Copeland, was elected sheriff, but Governor Axtell, at the insistence of Murphy-Dolan, removed him from office and appointed George Peppin, a Murphy-Dolan partisan, to the post. Troops were again called in, and N. A. M. Dudley, the rather inept commander of the buffalo soldiers at Fort Stanton, came in and put the army on the side of Murphy-Dolan despite orders from superiors not to put the troops on either side.

On July 15, 1878 Alexander McSween and 41 followers rode into Lincoln and prepared for battle at the attorney's home. When Sheriff Peppin, Dolan and a posse of over 50 men came into Lincoln to serve warrants, they were fired upon as Deputy John Long approached the house. Both sides then dug in during the night for a siege, and in the morning the gun battle began. Finally, the Murphy-Dolan faction set McSween's house on fire and then gunned down four who came out, including McSween. However, several McSween partisans, including Billy the Kid, managed to escape under a hail of gunfire. Tunstall's store was then pillaged by the victors, who carried away merchandise worth thousands of dollars.

On September 30, 1878 Governor Axtell was replaced by General Lew Wallace, who ordered in federal troops and issued a general amnesty for all concerned. But more gun battles erupted (mostly with Billy the Kid), and on February 18, 1879 attorney Chapman was gunned down in front of the Lincoln County Courthouse by the Murphy-Dolan faction. On April 14 a grand jury in Lincoln returned 200 indictments, mostly against the Murphy-Dolan crowd, and a court of inquiry against Dudley resulted in his removal (although he was later exonerated). But the real end of the Lincoln County War came with the deaths of Billy the Kid (1881) and John Chisum (1884). The final murder also occurred in 1884 when

Juan Patron, leader of the Mexican Americans in Lincoln County and a McSween supporter, was gunned down. (See also BECKWITH, JOHN H.; BECKWITH, ROBERT W.; BILLY THE KID; BOWDRE, CHARLIE; BREWER, DICK; BROWN, HENRY NEWTON; CHISUM, JOHN; COE, FRANK; COE, GEORGE WASHINGTON; GARRETT, PAT; HILL, TOM; HINDMAN, GEORGE W.; JOHNSON, WILLIAM H.; JONES, JOHN; LONG, JOHN; MATTHEWS, JACOB; MCNAB, FRANK; MIDDLETON, JOHN; O'FOLLIARD, TOM; OLINGER, BOB; OLINGER, JOHN WALLACE; PICKETT, TOM; ROBERTS, BUCKSHOT; SALAZAR, YGINO; SCURLOCK, DOC, TUNSTALL, JOHN HENRY.)

LINE RIDERS   Cowboys who patrol the boundaries of the ranch they're working for. Originally called *outriders,* these line riders make sure cattle aren't in trouble, that they stay on their home range, that fences are mended and that no trouble is happening.

LITTLE BIG HORN, BATTLE OF   (June 25, 1876)   Just after noon on June 22, 1876 Lieutenant Colonel George Armstrong Custer, astride his sorrel gelding Vic, led the Seventh Cavalry from Rosebud Creek, where it empties into the Yellowstone River, south toward the headwaters of the Rosebud. He was leaving his superior officer, General Alfred H. Terry, and riding toward the Valley of the Little Bighorn. Before he left, Colonel John Gibbon yelled to him, "Now, don't be greedy, Custer, as there are Indians enough for all of us. Wait for us." Custer replied, "No, I-I won't." That day Custer and his Seventh Cavalry covered 12 miles and camped on Rosebud Creek. That night as the 600 soldiers camped, Custer was irritable and tense as he called his officers together for a meeting in his tent. Custer wanted no trumpet calls (except in emergencies), every order had to be cleared with him personally, and he and he alone would decide where they camped and when they broke camp.

It was obvious Custer was under a great deal of pressure. This campaign was part of one instigated by General Philip Sheridan the previous year to annihilate the northern Plains Indians, particularly the Sioux, who were the most numerous and warlike. In 1875, miners had invaded the Black Hills of the Dakotas—home of the Sioux—after Custer had led an expedition there and found gold. The Sioux were understandably angry that their homeland was being ravaged and had joined with the Cheyenne to fight the whites. The Indians had gathered together an imposing force in this war.

Sheridan wanted to trap the Indians in eastern Montana and Wyoming, so he sent General George Crook north from Fort Fetterman, Colonel Gibbon east from Fort Ellis and Custer west from Fort Abraham Lincoln in Dakota Territory. It was believed that any of these three forces could defeat the Indians; all three together were certain to crush the rebellion.

Custer and his wife, Libbie, had gone to New York City in early fall 1875, where they enjoyed a round of parties and dinners. Custer also addressed the Century Society and the New-York Historical Society and was carefully politicking with influential figures such as James Gordon Bennett, publisher of the *New York Herald.*

Custer had gotten into hot water in 1875 when he offered to give evidence against Secretary of War W. W. Belknap, who was scamming army trading posts by overcharging soldiers and Indians. Belknap lined his pockets with these profits. Custer had a run-in at Fort Abraham Lincoln when he complained to Belknap about the trader there overcharging, and the politician decided against Custer. In March 1876 Custer was called to Washington to testify before Congress against Belknap and charged Orville Grant, brother of the president, with receiving payoffs. This testimony incurred the wrath of President Ulysses Grant.

The year 1876 was a presidential election year, and Custer was looking at the political arena. But after the hearings, Grant gave orders that someone other than Custer must lead the Dakota regiment against the Indians, thereby depriving Custer of glory, which the soldier craved. Custer sat outside Grant's office for hours to see Grant and plead his case, but the president would not see him.

Without orders, Custer left Washington and was arrested in Chicago. General William Sherman, commander of the army, would not respond to Custer's pleas, so he pleaded with General Alfred Terry, who was to head the Dakota column. After a meeting in St. Paul, Minnesota (Custer is reported to have shed tears and gotten down on his knees before Terry) the general agreed to intercede. President Grant finally relented to allow Custer to go on the expedition with Terry. But Custer was already hatching more plots: He agreed to let Mark Kellogg, a reporter for the *New York Herald,* march with him, although Sherman had issued specific orders against this.

General Terry took control of Terry's and Custer's column when they met on the Yellowstone. Scouts found a heavy Indian trail going north up Rosebud Creek on June 14. No one would guess that about 12,000 Indians—the largest group ever gathered together—were camped on the Little Bighorn. There were 1,500–2,500 warriors in this group and they had agreed to fight together, an unusual tactic for Indians who preferred individual glory in battle.

Unknown to Terry and Custer, the Indians engaged General Crook on June 17 at the Battle of the Rosebud, and Crook retreated toward Wyoming. Terry divided his forces, with Custer taking the Seventh up the Rosebud while Terry went west and Gibbon headed up the Yellowstone River to the mouth of the Little Bighorn. According to this plan, the Indians at the Little Bighorn would be caught in a trap.

When attacked, Indians usually fled; their style of warfare was hit and run and predicated on surprise. Soldiers expected Indians to flee when attacked; this was a continual source of frustration for the army during the Indian Wars because soldiers wanted a big battle or two to end the Indians' domination of the plains. Custer, especially, was convinced that Indians would not stand and fight but would have to be trapped or chased.

Custer needed a huge success to get himself out of hot water with the army brass, to gain national publicity and fame and to fulfill his own political ambitions. His entire career—whether in the army or in politics—depended on success so spectacular that it would protect him from presidential wrath.

Since the Indians were expected to try to escape, and because the easiest escape route was south to the Big-horn Mountain—where they could divide into smaller groups—Custer's orders were to block the escape route. A vain, greedy man who had abandoned troops and officers in 1868 on the Washita River, Custer had difficulty gaining loyalty and respect from his troops. He surrounded himself with his family—his brother Captain Tom Custer and brother-in-law Lieutenant James Calhoun were part of the regiment, while brother Boston Custer and nephew Armstrong Reed were on the campaign as civilians—and tried to convince his officers to be loyal to him. But his officers were still disdainful of their vain leader.

On June 23 Custer led his Seventh Cavalry on a march that began at 5 A.M. and continued through the heat of the day. This march caused blisters to form and split on men's legs and horses to suffer. The Indian trail was big and clear; it was obvious a large number of them were up ahead. Deserted campsites also made it obvious there were a large number of Indians, and Custer scout Mitch Bouyer warned Custer there were too many Indians to fight.

The Seventh covered about 30 miles on the 23, and about 28 miles on the 24th of June before they stopped to camp on Rosebud Creek. Around 9 P.M. Custer's scouts reported that the huge Indian trail had turned west toward the Valley of the Little Bighorn. These scouts—whites as well as Arikara and Crows—were all reluctant to engage an Indian force so large. Lonesome Charley Reynolds, a favorite scout of Custer's, asked to be relieved twice but had been convinced to stay. Following a trail half a mile wide was not difficult, but convincing Custer to avoid attacking the Indians who made this trail was proving impossible. Custer's favorite scout, an Arikara named Bloody Knife, and another favorite, Lieutenant Charles Varnum, were disturbed and had sung their death songs while riding on this trail.

Custer's major concern was that the Indians would escape and thus his dreams of glory would vanish. Supremely confident of success, he ordered his troops to begin marching at 11 P.M. on the night of June 24. General Terry had ordered him to swing south and then double back, but Custer openly disobeyed those orders and pushed on, hoping to get the victory alone instead of waiting for Terry and Gibbon, who would share the victory in a coordinated move.

The night march covered 10 miles between the Rosebud and Little Bighorn on the Indians' trail. The head of the column stopped at 2 A.M. in a wooded ravine, but Custer had been driving his men so hard that it took several hours before the whole regiment was regrouped. Some sleep followed; then the regiment marched again for 10 more miles. The dust raised from the soldiers had alerted the Sioux scouts, who had been spotted by the soldiers during the march.

Custer was now at a critical junction. Ordered to march south, he could do so and then double back and wait for Terry and Gibbon. Or he could turn off the Rosebud toward the Indians, a turn that meant he had to attack and fight. Custer turned.

Custer had deployed Lieutenant Varnum to a lookout point where they could see the Little Bighorn Valley, and when the sun came up, this group was awed by the Indian encampment they saw. The narrow Little Bighorn ran through a broad valley in horseshoe bends, cutting steep bluffs 80 to 100 feet high on the eastern side while a flat plain lay on the western side. Varnum sent word back to Custer informing him about the huge group of Indians assembled, and Custer came up to see for himself. Custer looked but could not see clearly through the haze; it probably did not matter because he did not care about anything except attacking the Indians and achieving a victory.

Custer had long been known as a lucky man; indeed, he depended on his luck. And he probably felt he was extremely lucky that day to find so many Indians camped in one place; it would provide a glorious victory and incredible fame. After Custer left, Varnum spotted a group of Indians heading back to the main camp after a scouting mission. Fearing the Indians were going to escape, Varnum alerted Custer, who triggered the attack.

Custer led his regiment on a grueling march; around noon they were about 15 miles from the Indian encampment but traveling at a fast trot. Near Ash Creek (later named Reno Creek) Custer stopped and divided his command, assigning one company to guard the pack train, three companies (about 125 men) to Benteen to cover the bluffs to the south of the valley and three companies to Reno to march down the creek and charge the southern end of the Indians. Custer, with five companies (215 men), said he would support Reno, which Reno took to mean that Custer would ride behind and follow up the initial attack. Instead, Custer swung right and rode downstream hidden behind high bluffs.

Fearing only that the Indians would escape, Custer pushed on with horses that had not had any water since the day before (the creeks where he stopped were too alkaloid to drink), and could not eat their oats because of the dryness. With Benteen on the west and Reno on the south, the Indians were held in place for Custer to attack. Several times Custer rode up the bluffs to look at the Indians as his five companies marched; he was apparently elated and thought he'd caught the Indians by surprise. Just before he turned into the Medicine Tail Coulee, Custer sent a message to Benteen to bring more ammunition.

Reno, with his 134 men and 16 scouts, faltered in his command. He crossed the river and attacked the Indians, who fell back toward the encampment. Fearing a trap, and sensing warriors were hidden in a ravine ahead of him, Reno ordered his men to dismount. Ordering every fourth man to take four horses and wait in some timber, Reno with about 80 men formed a line and began to fire at the Indians, who were too far away. This made Reno's tactic ineffective and ultimately led to his disgrace: Some argued that he disobeyed orders and thus left Custer to be slaughtered; others argued that Reno and his troops would have been slaughtered if they had advanced. In a defensive—instead of offensive—position, Reno's group faced Indians attacking on horseback, and the Indians got in back of his troops, trapping the soldiers in a crossfire. As the soldiers pulled in tighter, the Sioux continued to attack until Reno ordered his men to retreat to the woods. But the Sioux kept coming and firing. At this point, the remaining soldiers were primarily concerned with survival. Meanwhile, Indians set fire to the grass and then came through the smoke firing at the soldiers, who fired back frantically .

During a brief lull when the soldiers were confused, scout Bloody Knife was killed by a Sioux warrior and Reno apparently panicked. He mounted his horse and fled the timber, his soldiers following him, and left the wounded for certain death. The Sioux rode after Reno and killed a number of his men as they fled across the river and up a bluff, where Reno finally found some safety. He had lost about a third of his men.

Benteen, meanwhile, traveled west for about an hour and then headed back to the Little Bighorn. When he received Custer's message for ammunition, he knew men were needed and moved forward until he found Reno, unaware that Custer had further divided his forces. Unfortunately, Reno did not know where Custer was and did not obey the basic military dictum to march toward the sound of firing when there were no other orders. Captain Thomas Weir took a company down toward Custer but could not see them; Benteen came to a vantage point and suddenly realized the enormous number of Indians gathered.

Indians saw the soldiers watching and moved toward them, wounding several as the soldiers sought refuge on the bluffs. Here, they held off Indians for about three hours, and when darkness came, the Indians retreated. Later that night, soldiers saw Indians dancing and celebrating by the firelight.

Although no one knows exactly what happened to Custer and his men, most believe he led his men up Medicine Tail Coulee, where he was attacked and then pushed forward to the Little Bighorn until the Indian camp lay directly across the river. In this area the 200 men faced about 1,000 warriors who came across the river as well as up from gullies and ditches. It is possible Custer tried a charge, although it could not have been successful, and they moved to their right to open, high ground. Unfortunately, they were moving against Crazy Horse, a brilliant battle leader who had engineered the Fetterman Massacre 10 years before when he lured William Fetterman to chase him into a trap. Crazy Horse had led his Indians to defeat General Crook at the Battle of the Rosebud about a week earlier, on June 17.

When Custer moved to high ground, the Sioux chief Gall, who was attacking Reno, entered the battle against Custer, attacking him from the rear. Crazy Horse crossed the river and met Custer head on, coming up one side of the same hill Custer was climbing from the other. The Indians got there first, ahead of Custer's retreat, but Custer rallied his men for a final stand. Gall's warriors continued to attack Custer's rear, killing men with bows and arrows, some shot high in the air and landing silently in a soldier's back. Finally, Gall's warriors charged L Company, who stood their ground and fought until all were dead. Higher up the hill, Custer was busy arranging a good defense; unfortunately, the rifles became too hot, and the men were forced to work on jammed guns as smoke, sweat and dust swirled around them.

Custer's I Company was next in line for Gall's warriors,

and he rolled over them on his way to Custer, whose men emptied their pistols and swung their rifles like clubs in frantic fighting. Some saved their last shot for themselves.

Crazy Horse and his warriors came toward Custer and cut them down. A few soldiers broke and ran trying desperately to escape, but there were too many Indians, and all the soldiers were hunted down and killed. Finally, less than an hour after it had begun, an eerie quiet pervaded the battlefield as Custer and all his men lay dead on the battlefield.

The next day, June 26, the Indians struck against Benteen and Reno again and fought until midafternoon when, suddenly, they withdrew, broke camp and moved south. On June 27, General Terry's troops came down from the north and found the 197 dead bodies on the hill. Custer, who had worn a blue flannel shirt, white wide-brimmed hat, high boots and buckskins, with hair newly trimmed and thus not long and flowing as he usually wore it, was found naked, but he was neither scalped nor mutilated. The Indians never knew it was Custer who was killed, or even who killed him.

The Battle of the Little Bighorn was a devastating defeat for the United States Army and appeared at first to be a major victory for the Indians. But this battle ultimately led to the Indians' final defeat because the country rallied to the cause of exterminating the Plains Indians and avenging Custer's death. Custer himself became a hero after his death, and his bones, initially buried at Little Bighorn, were dug up and reinterred at West Point.

There was never another battle between Indians and the U. S. Army on the scale of the Little Bighorn. After this time, the army relentlessly pursued Indians and massacred them in their villages, on reservations and whenever there was any sort of resistance. For the Indians, it was the beginning of the end; for the country it was the end of an era; and for Custer it was the start of a legend that has caused more books to be written about him and this battle than about any other battle in American history.

LITTLE BIG MAN Film produced by Stuart Millar; directed by Arthur Penn; screenplay by Calder Willingham from the novel by Thomas Berger; released in 1970 by NGP; 150 minutes in length. Cast: Dustin Hoffman, Faye Dunaway, Martin Balsam, Richard Mulligan, Chief Dan George, Jeff Corey, Amy Eccles, Kelly Jean Peters, Carol Androsky and Robert Little Star.

This story is narrated by a 121-year-old survivor of Custer's Last Stand. Jack Crabb (Dustin Hoffman) is found in a nursing home by a young reporter. Based on the novel by Thomas Berger, the story is about a man who spent part of his life with Indians and part with whites. A mixture of history and fiction, the story vividly tells of the injustices suffered by the Indians in the West. Jack goes through a number of "periods": his religious phase, as a gunfighter period, a businessman (co-owner of a general store), as a con man with a medicine show, as a drunk, a hermit, and a scout for the cavalry. There were several massacres in the movie; one was based on the November 27, 1868 Battle of Washita, the other on the Battle of the Little Bighorn.

The cast of "Little House on the Prairie" (left to right): Matthew Laborteaux, Melissa Gilbert, Michael Landon, Karen Grassle (seated), Dean Butler, Lindsay Greenbush, Melissa Sue Anderson and Linwood Boomer

LITTLE HOUSE ON THE PRAIRIE

LITTLE HOUSE ON THE PRAIRIE   TV show that starred Michael Landon as Charles Ingalls (1974–82), Karen Grassle as Caroline Ingalls (1974–82), Melissa Gilbert as Laura Ingalls Wilder, Melissa Sue Anderson as Mary Ingalls Kendall (1974–81), Lindsay Greenbush as Carrie Ingalls (alternating: 1974–82), Sidney Greenbush as Carrie Ingalls (alternating 1974–82), Karl Swenson as Lars Hanson (1974–78), Richard Bull as Nels Oleson, Katherine MacGregor as Harriet Oleson, Alison Arngrim as Nellie Oleson Dalton (1974–81), Jonathan Gilbert as Willie Oleson (1975–83), Kevin Hagen as Dr. Baker, Dabbs Greer as the Reverend Robert Alden, Charlotte Stewart as Eva Beadle Simms (1974–78), Victor French as Mr. Isaiah Edwards (1974–77; 1982–83), Ted Gehring as Ebenezer Sprague (1975–86), Bonnie Bartlett as Grace Edwards (1976–87), Merlin Olsen as Jonathan Garvey (1977–81), Patrick Laborteaux as Andy Garvey (1977–81), Linwood Boomer as Adam Kendall (1978–81), Wendy Turnbeaugh as Grace Ingalls (alternating: 1978–82), Brenda Turnbeaugh as Grace Ingalls (alternating: 1978–82), Don "Red" Baker as Larrabee (1978–79), Ketty Lester as Hester Sue Terhune (1978–83), Dean Butler as Almanzo Wilder (1979–83), Lucy Lee Flippin as Eliza Jane Wilder (1979–82), Steve Tracy as Percival Dalton (1980–81), Jason Bateman as James Cooper (1981–82), Missy Francis as Cassandra Cooper (1981–82), Allison Balson as Nancy Oleson (1981–83), Shannen Doherty as Jenny Wilder (1982–83), Stan Ivar as John Carter (1982–83), Pamela Roylance as Sarah Carter (1982–83), Lindsay Kennedy as Jeb Carter (1982–83), Davis Friedman as Jason Carter (1982–83) and Leslie Landon as Etta Plum (1982–83).

Based on the "Little House" series by Laura Ingalls Wilder, a memoir of growing up on the prairie frontier, this show was a classic family show. Instead of the traditional western with good guys, bad guys and lots of gun play, this show centered on the trials and tribulations of family life on the plains. The show lasted nine years. In the beginning the family, led by father Charles Ingalls and mother Caroline Ingalls with children Laura, Mary and Carrie, moved from Plum Creek, Minnesota to Walnut Grove, Kansas in the 1870s to join a growing community. Caroline gave birth to a fourth daughter, Grace (1978), but Mary lost her sight. Sent to a school for the blind, Mary fell in love with her instructor, Adam Kendall, married him and moved to the Dakotas. Walnut Grove fell on hard times, so Charles, his family and a number of other regulars moved to Winoka, where the Ingalls household added Albert, a young orphan. After a spell there, the family moved back to Walnut Grove. Mary, Adam and their newborn son were living in Walnut Grove at this time when the school for the blind caught fire and burned, killing the baby. Meanwhile, Laura became a teacher and married Almanzo Wilder (1980). Nellie Oleson got married too, but then a scandal was uncovered: She'd married a Jew! A pregnancy compounded the problem, which was solved when she had twins—the boy was raised Jewish and the daughter a Christian. Jonathan Garvey, who now lived in Sleepy Eye, and Charles set up a freight business between there and Walnut Grove. Adam, who had miraculously re-gained his sight, went away to law school and then to his father's law firm in New York, where he and Mary joined Nellie and Percival. Orphans James and Cassandra Cooper joined the Ingalls household (1981–82), and Laura gave birth to a daughter, Rose. At the end of 1982, star and executive producer Michael Landon decided to leave the show, so the final season was run under the title "Little House: A New Beginning." Landon appeared briefly now and then, but Laura and Almanzo were now the principals—Charles Ingalls had to move to Burr Oak, Iowa. This series was consistently in the top ten of TV shows during its run, appearing first on September 11, 1974 on Wednesday nights on NBC. In September 1976 the show moved to Monday nights, where it enjoyed its long and fruitful run, ending on March 21, 1983.

LITTLE JOE THE WRANGLER   This song, written by Nathan Howard "Jack" Thorp, is based on a true story. Thorp was born and raised in the East; he then went west and became a cowboy for the Bar W Ranch in New Mexico and began collecting cowboy songs as well as writing some himself. He wrote "Little Joe the Wrangler," to the tune of "Little Old Log Cabin in the Lane," in 1898 while on a trail drive from Chimney Lake, New Mexico to Higgins, Texas. Thorp first sang his song to his trail-driving buddies, then to other trail hands, and the song began to circulate among cowboys through the oral tradition. It was first printed by Thorp in 1908 in *Songs of the Cowboys* and in a larger edition in 1921. The song "Little Joe the Wrangler's Sister Nell" was

Bob Livingston

published by Kenneth S. Clark in 1934 and tells the story of the wrangler's sister coming out to the Circle Bar Ranch looking for him. The cowboys cannot bring themselves to tell her Little Joe had been killed in a stampede, but she realizes it later.

LIVINGSTON, BOB (b. Robert Randall in Quincy, Illinois on December 9, 1890; d. Tarzana, California on March 16, 1988) Livingston played the role of Stoney Brooke, leader of the Three Mesquiteers, in 29 Republic films (1936–41). Livingston moved to California when he was 12 and began working in films in 1929; he starred in *The Lone Ranger Rides Again* and then had the lead in "The Lone Rider" series. Livingston's brother, Jack Randall, was also a western film star; after his acting days, Livingston became a scriptwriter.

LOADED FOR BEAR Phrase used to mean heavily armed and looking for trouble.

LOCO WEED A plant *(Astragalus)* poisonous to cattle and sometimes addictive to horses. It has purple or white flowers, and its appeal stems from its ability to hold large amounts of moisture and thus stay green even in times of drought. It is also known as "crazy weed."

LOGAN, HARVEY See CURRY, KID.

LOGAN, LONIE (b. Rowan County, Kentucky c. 1873; d. Dodson, Missouri on February 29, 1900) Lonie and his brother, Kid Curry, were members of Butch Cassidy's Wild Bunch. In the 1890s Lonie left the gang and opened a saloon in Harlem, Montana, but the law kept pursuing him so he sold the saloon and went back to Missouri. On February 28, 1900 in Dodson, Missouri, Pinkerton detective Bill Sayles and a local posse came up to Logan's aunt's house around eight in the morning. Logan saw them coming and ran out the back door, precipitating a gunfight in the snow for about half an hour. Finally, Logan loaded his guns and made a mad-dash charge toward the posse. He was shot down in a hail of bullets.

LOMAX, JOHN AVERY (b. Goodman, Mississippi on September 23, 1867; d. Greenville, Mississippi on January 26, 1948) John Lomax's first book, *Cowboy Songs and Other Frontier Ballads* (1910), was the first major collection of cowboy ballads published (although N. Howard "Jack" Thorp had published *Songs of the Cowboys* privately in 1908). Lomax also wrote *Songs of the Cattle Trail and Cow Camp* (1919) and helped with *The Book of Texas* (1916, guided by Harry Yandell Benedict). Lomax grew up on a farm near the Chisholm Trail and notated the songs he heard cowboys singing. But Lomax viewed his folk song collecting as a hobby until the Great Depression. He had graduated from the University of Texas and then taught English at Texas A&M before he went to Harvard University on a scholarship; there he was encouraged to take the collection of western ballads seriously. His first book was a result of this research. Lomax worked for the Ex-students Association of the University of Texas and then became vice president of a Dallas banking company, the Repub-

lic National Company, where he worked until 1931 when his wife died, he lost his job and his health failed. Lomax then began to tour the country giving lectures on folk songs, which rejuvenated his interest in folk song collecting and guided the rest of his life. Lomax and his son, Alan, found the black folksinger "Leadbelly" while touring southern penitentiaries; Lomax wrote *Negro Folk Songs As Sung by Lead Belly* (1936) and, with Alan, wrote *American Ballads and Folk Songs* (1934) and *Our Singing Country* (1941). Lomax helped organize the Tennessee Folklore Society and wrote his autobiography, *Adventures of a Ballad Hunter,* which was published in 1947, just before his death.

LONER, THE TV show that starred Lloyd Bridges as William Colton.

"The Loner" lasted one full season, premiering on September 18, 1965 and ending on April 30, 1966. The 26 half-hour episodes, done in black and white, were aired on CBS on Saturday evenings. The plot featured a former Union cavalry officer who wandered the West looking for the meaning of life. His encounters with a wide variety of people served as the essence of this drama, which was created by Rod Sterling of "The Twilight Zone" fame.

LONE RANGER, THE TV show that starred Clayton Moore as the Lone Ranger (1949–52, 1954–57), John Hart as the Lone Ranger (1952–54) and Jay Silverheels as Tonto.

"The Lone Ranger" premiered on ABC on September, 15, 1949. The show had begun filming on June 21, 1949 under the supervision of George W. Trendle, who had created the radio version. Trendle insisted that the Lone Ranger be clean-cut and an example for youth. The guide for writers for the show states:

- The Lone Ranger never makes love on radio, television, in movies, or in cartoons;
- He is a man who can fight great odds, yet takes time to treat a bird with a broken wing;
- The Lone Ranger never smokes, never uses profanity, and never uses intoxicating beverages;
- The Lone Ranger at all times uses precise speech, without slang or dialect. His grammar must be pure;
- The Lone Ranger never shoots to kill. When he has to use guns, he aims to maim as painlessly as possible;
- The Lone Ranger keeps out of saloons. Scenes of gambling and drinking must be played down. When this cannot be avoided, writers must try to make the saloon a cafe, and deal with waiters and food instead of bartenders and liquor.

The first TV show told the essential story of the Lone Ranger: His real name was John Reid, and he and five other Texas Rangers had been ambushed by the Butch Cavendish Gang. Reid had been left for dead but was discovered by an Indian, Tonto, and nursed back to life. Reid buried the other five Rangers (one of whom was his brother, Don Reid) and also dug a sixth grave to fool the

The Lone Ranger and Tonto (Clayton Moore and Jay Silverheels)

The Lone Ranger and Silver *(Western Archives)*

outlaws as well as bury the old John Reid so he could begin life anew as the Lone Ranger. Donning a mask and mounting a trusty white steed, Silver (whom he had captured after Tonto led him to this perfect horse), with his sidekick Tonto on his pinto, Scout, the two roved the West righting all wrongs. The Lone Ranger never accepted any money for his deeds but was supported by a secret silver mine he owned with his brother (the dead Ranger Don) and run by a trusty old miner. It was at the mine that he loaded up on his trademark silver bullets, which he regularly passed out as a calling card.

The TV series was filmed at locations in Utah and in California at Corriganville, Iverson's Ranch, Big Bear and Sonora. The show was produced by Jack Chertok and directed by George B. Seitz; it was sponsored by General Mills. Starring in the series were Clayton Moore, a 34-year-old actor who had appeared in a number of serials, and Jay Silverheels, a full-blooded Mohawk Indian from Canada.

Clayton Moore was the first TV Lone Ranger but was replaced at the end of the 1950 shooting when he demanded more money (he had been receiving approximately $500 for each show). Trendle then hired John Hart to play the masked man, and Hart appeared in 26 episodes. In 1954 producer Chertok auditioned actors for the part again and wisely decided to resign Clayton Moore. The Lone Ranger appeared on ABC network television until September 23, 1961; the 30-minute programs ran regularly on Thursday evenings from September 1949 until September 1957 and also on Friday evenings in the summer of 1950. Since that time the episodes have been syndicated. They appeared on network Saturday morning TV on CBS beginning on June 13, 1953.

The showed stopped filming new episodes in 1956; at that time, Clayton Moore had appeared in 195 episodes, John Hart in 26 and Tonto in all 221 shows.

LONE RANGER, THE The Lone Ranger appeared as a TV cartoon on Saturday mornings from September 10, 1966 until September 6, 1969 in a 30-minute Filmation series.

LONE RANGER TELEVISION MOVIES The following movies consisted of several episodes of the Lone Ranger, which were put together as a "movie." These are the first "made for TV" movies of westerns. The movies, all aired in 1956, are *Champions of Justice, Count the Clues, Justice of the West, The Lawless, Masquerade, More Than Magic, Not Above Suspicion, One Mask Too Many, The Search, Tale of Gold , Trackers, The Truth* and *Vengeance Vow.*

LONESOME DOVE TV show starring Robert Duvall as Gus McCrae, Tommy Lee Jones as Woodrow F. Call, Diane Lane as Lorena Wood, Robert Ulrich as Jake Spoon, Danny Glover as Joshua Deets, Ricky Schroeder as Newt, Frederic Forrest as Blue Duck, Anjelica Huston as Clara Allen.

Based on the Pulitzer Prize–winning novel by Larry McMurtry, this is the story of some old cowboys on a final cattle drive from Lonesome Dove, Texas to Montana. The show is a miniseries consisting of four two-hour shows; it was originally broadcast February 5–8, 1989 on CBS.

LONG, JOHN (aka "Long John"; fl. 1870s) John Long is the man who set the McSween house afire during the Lincoln County War in 1878. Firing at Billy the Kid and others in the McSween house, Long sneaked around back and got into the kitchen, where he soaked the floor with coal oil before being discovered. He ran out of the house and jumped in a privy ditch, where he had to stay until after dark. Long finally soaked several sticks in oil, lit them and threw them into the kitchen, igniting the house and forcing its members out into a hail of gunfire. (See also LINCOLN COUNTY WAR.)

LONG, STEVE (aka "Big Steve"; b. ?; d. Laramie, Wyoming on October 19, 1868) Long was a six-foot-six deputy marshal of Laramie, Wyoming who moonlighted as a thief. On October 18, 1868 Long ambushed

Rollie "Hard Luck" Harrison, a prospector he wanted to rob. Harrison played dead when Long's bullet grazed him, and then he fired a bullet into Long's shoulder when the ambusher appeared. Long hightailed it back to town to his fiancee's house, where she treated his wound. But when she discovered Long was a thief, she told some local vigilantes, who strung him up from a telegraph pole the next day. Long's fiancee then erected a marker to his memory.

LONGABAUGH, HARRY   See SUNDANCE KID, THE.

LONGHORN CATTLE   The breed of cattle in Texas that were driven north after the Civil War by cowboys on trail drives to the Kansas railheads and then shipped east for slaughter. These cattle evolved from Spanish stock first brought to America in the 16th century. Over the years, some cattle escaped from Spanish ranches, the Indians raided other settlements and captured cattle and some cattle were just left to roam when the settlers abandoned ranches and settlements. Thus the longhorn developed over a period of time through natural selection as long, rangy cattle able to withstand long travel, extensive heat and limited water. Its horns were three to five feet across. By the end of the Civil War there were an estimated six million roaming around Texas. Prior to the Civil War these cattle's value was mostly in their hide, not their meat, but when the eastern markets needed beef after the Civil War (the war had depleted the eastern beef) and Texans, broke and desperate, looked around and saw all these longhorns just wandering around, they began to gather them in herds and drive them north to the Kansas railheads. The longhorns were driven about 1,000 miles in herds of 2,500 to 3,000 on an average drive. Although sturdy, these cattle were also skittish and often stampeded. But their sturdiness allowed them to survive the long drives to Kansas and later the northern ranges where they adapted to the hard winters better than eastern cattle. The decline of the longhorn came when the ranges were fenced; at this point ranchers began a breeding process of introducing

Texas longhorn

shorthorns and Herefords to produce fatter cattle and improve the texture and flavor of the beef. The newer breeds were not as fit for travel, but by this time the railroads had reached into the West, so long cattle drives were not necessary. The better beef was welcomed by consumers, but it brought a major change into the cattle business; the longhorns had been sold by the head, but the new cattle were sold by the pound. (See also CATTLE DRIVES; COWBOYS; TRAIL DRIVES.)

LONGLEY, WILD BILL   (b. William Preston Longley in Austin County, Texas on October 16, 1851; d. Giddings, Texas on October 11, 1878)   Known as the "nigger killer" because he directed his violence at so many blacks, Longley was only 15 when he killed his first man, a black soldier in 1867 in Evergreen, Texas. That same year Longley and another cowboy shot up a black street dance in Lexington, Texas, killing two. Then, in December 1868 near his boyhood home in Evergreen, he killed another Negro. Longley had to leave the area and moved to Karenes County, where he worked as a cowboy for John Reagon. But in Yorktown, Texas, Longley killed a soldier who had mistaken him for Charles Taylor, one of the principals in the Sutton-Taylor feud. Longley and Tom Johnson, a horse thief, were on the run when the two were captured at Johnson's house and lynched. But Longley survived the lynching (Johnson didn't) and was cut down after the posse left. Longley then joined Cullen Baker's gang in 1869 but returned to Evergreen when Baker was killed. Longley joined up on a cattle drive to Kansas but soon fell out with the trail boss and killed him; he then hightailed it to Salt Lake City. The next year, 1870, Longley returned to Kansas, where he killed a soldier in a Leavenworth saloon. Trying to escape on a freight train, he was captured in St. Joseph, Missouri and returned to Fort Leavenworth, but he bribed a guard and escaped.

Longley then moved to Camp Brown (which later became Fort Washakie), where he landed a job as a teamster and packmaster. He and a crooked quartermaster cooked up a scheme to embezzle money from the government by miscounting stock and selling the extra animals. The quartermaster discovered that in one sale Longley had lied to him—telling him he'd sold some mules for $300 when he actually received $500. The quartermaster threatened to kill Longley, but the outlaw hid at the post corral and shot down the quartermaster. Three days later, after attempting his escape on a mule, Longley was arrested and sentenced to 30 years in the Iowa state prison. But, again, he escaped before he was transferred from Camp Brown.

In Indian Territory, Longley lived with the Ute and then moved back to his father's farm in Evergreen. On the way to Texas Longley stopped in Parkersville, Kansas where he got into a card game and killed Charles Stuart, whose father posted a $1,500 reward for the killer, who was then traveling under the alias "Tom Jones."

Longley killed another Negro in 1874 in Comanche County, Texas, after learning the man had insulted a white woman. Longley was caught but again bribed his way out of jail. In Bastrop County, Longley went hunting for boyhood friend Wilson Anderson, after learning that Anderson had killed his cousin, Cale Longley. Longley killed Anderson with a shotgun in a field where he was working. This is the murder, on April 1, 1875, that led to Longley's arrest and execution.

In November in Bell County, Texas, Longley, Bill Scrier (whose real name was Lon Sawyer) and a youth were heading toward Scrier's home when Longley drew his gun. Scrier and Longley had grown wary of each other and a gunfight erupted, with Scrier shooting at Longley 18 times but only killing his horse. Longley put 13 bullets into Scrier before a shot in the head killed his foe; Longley always considered Scrier the bravest man he ever fought.

The next year, in Delta County, Texas, Longley killed a minister named Roland Lay at a corral with a shotgun after some differences between the two. After this killing, Wild Bill fled to Louisiana, renting some land near Keatchie in the western part of the state. Two lawmen with shotguns from Nacogdoches went down and arrested Longley, putting him in jail in Giddings, Texas. Longley spent his time in jail complaining to the government that John Wesley Hardin had only received a long prison term instead of hanging. He also wrote long letters to newspapers expressing regret and converted to Catholicism.

Wild Bill Longley was hung five days before he turned 27. He showed courage when he had to be hoisted up and rehung after his knees dragged the ground on the first attempt. (See also BAKER, CULLEN MONTGOMERY.)

LONG, RIDERS

The film produced by Tim Zinneman; directed by Walter Hill; screenplay by Bill Bryden, Steven Philip Smith, Stacy Keach and James Keach; released by United Artists in 1980; 100 minutes in length. Cast: David Carradine, Keith Carradine, Robert Carradine, James Keach, Stacy Keach, Dennis Quaid, Randy Quaid, Kevin Brophy, Harry Carey, Jr., Christopher Guest, Nicholas Guest, Shelby Leverington, Felice Orlandi, Pamela Reed, James Remas, Fran Ryan, Savannah Smith, Amy Stryker and James Whitmore, Jr.

In this story of outlaw brothers, real-life brothers were cast: The Youngers are played by the Carradines; Jesse and Frank James are played by the Keachs; the Miller brothers are played by the Quaids; and the Ford brothers are played by the Guests.

LOST DUTCHMAN'S MINE

A mythical gold mine supposedly located east of Mesa, Arizona in Superstition Mountain. According to legend, the mine was discovered by a Mexican boy in 1840. The "Dutchman" was Jacob Waltz, who was shown the mine by three Mexicans. Waltz killed the Mexicans and took over the mine; he reportedly also killed those who got near the mine. On his deathbed, Waltz handed over a map showing the mine's location, but although many have tried to find the mine, no one ever has.

LOUISIANA PURCHASE

The Louisiana Purchase (1803) gave the United States a "west" on the other side of the Mississippi River. Prior to this purchase, the United States was only on the eastern side of the Mississippi. This purchase also doubled the size of the United States and, with the Treaty of Guadalupe Hidalgo, made the nation into what became the continental United States, extending east to west from Atlantic to Pacific Oceans, and north to south from Canada to Mexico. A total of 828,000 square miles was included in this purchase, and 12 future states were included: all of Nebraska, Kansas, Oklahoma, Arkansas, Missouri and Ohio, most of South Dakota and parts of Colorado, Texas, North Dakota, Minnesota and Louisiana.

Settlers had long wanted to go beyond the Mississippi River and had put pressure on the U.S. government to allow them into this territory, which had been owned by Spain and was now owned by France. However, a more immediate problem for the government was how to assure settlers and traders on the Mississippi that they were protected.

France had obtained the Louisiana Territory from the government of Spain first in the secret Treaty of San Ildefonso on October 1, 1800 and then in the Godoy-Lucien Bonaparte Treaty of March 21, 1801. The French Revolution had ended, and Napoleon Bonaparte had assumed dictatorial powers and was intent on creating an empire. When war in Europe ended in 1802 with the Treaty of Amiens, Napoleon sent troops to occupy New Orleans, the key city for Mississippi River trading. This alarmed President Thomas Jefferson, who first received the news in February 1802; Jefferson responded in April with a letter to French ambassador Robert Livingston telling him to warn France that the United States would align with Great Britain if the French controlled New Orleans. Since France and England were constantly at war, and because the young United States could not really trust either—although it had to alternately trust both at different times—it was in a precarious position. Therefore, Jefferson sent James Monroe to Paris in early 1803 to help Livingston with negotiations for New Orleans.

Meanwhile, developments in Europe indicated that war would soon erupt between France and England, and Napoleon feared the British would capture New Orleans. Livingston and French cabinet minister Talleyrand were negotiating the purchase of New Orleans and the Floridas when Talleyrand suddenly asked if the United States would like to purchase the entire territory. Although he had not been authorized to do so, Livingston quickly agreed, and, unknown to Jefferson, the sale was nearly complete when Monroe finally arrived. The purchase price for the Louisiana Territory was $11,250,000 with the proviso that the U.S. government assume all debts owed by France to U.S. citizens. This debt was $3,750,000, which meant the final purchase price for the Louisiana Territory was $15 million when the sale was concluded on April 30, 1803. Two weeks later (May 15) Great Britain declared war on France, which made this quite a good deal for the French; they didn't have to worry about defending this territory, which would have scattered and thinned their forces, and they had plenty of money to purchase goods and equipment needed in the war effort.

The territory comprised lands west of the Mississippi as far north as Montana; in essence, it was shaped somewhat like a funnel from present-day New Orleans up through what became the midwestern United States and ended at Canada, giving the United States the middle third of its nation. At the time of the purchase a little more than 10,000 people lived in this vast region; about three-fifths were Anglo-American. After the purchase, army captain Amos Stoddard became the civil commandant for the area; he administered Spanish laws and customs and preserved public order. In October 1804 Congress created the District of Louisiana, composed of present-day Louisiana. In March 1805 the remaining area was organized as a territory with Brigadier General James Wilkinson appointed the first governor; in March 1807 Meriwether Lewis was named governor of the territory. In April 1812 the Territory of Orleans became the state of Louisiana, and the rest of the area was renamed the Missouri Territory two months later. In 1821 the state of Missouri was admitted to the Union.

LOVE, NAT (aka "Deadwood Dick"; b. Nashville, Tennessee c. 1877; d. 1907) In 1907 Nat Love published *The Life and Adventures of Nat Love, Better Known in the Cattle Country as "Deadwood Dick"*, in which he claimed to have met Billy the Kid and Pat Garrett; he also claimed to be the "real" Deadwood Dick. Love's claims are probably exaggerated, but his book is significant because it shows a black cowboy as part of the cowboy heritage and western myth. (See also BLACKS IN THE WEST; DEADWOOD DICK .)

LOVING, COCKEYED FRANK (b. Frank Loving c. 1854; d. Trinidad, Colorado in April 1882) In Dodge City, Kansas Cockeyed Frank Loving and Levi Richardson had been quarreling over a woman. On Saturday night, April 5, 1879 at the Long Branch Saloon sometime between eight and nine, Richardson was getting ready to leave when Loving walked in and took a seat at the gambling table. A heated exchange between the two took place, and Richardson drew his gun and fired while Loving drew his and fired back. Neither hit the other—Loving's gun misfired—and Loving then went behind the stove while Richardson pursued him. Richardson shot twice more before Loving began firing at his opponent, who staggered back when he was hit. Richardson fell against a table while still holding his .44, and as he slumped to the floor, bystander William Duffey grabbed his pistol. Loving had only a scratch on his hand; Richardson died a few moments later from wounds in the chest, side and right arm.

Loving continued gambling and moved to Colorado. In April 1882 Loving and Jack Allen, a former citizen of Dodge, got into an argument that led to a gunfight—but none of the 16 shots hit. The next day Allen came into George Hammond's hardware store, where Loving was emptying his revolver, and killed him. Jack Allen later became an evangelist.

LOVING, OLIVER (b. Hopkins County, Kentucky c. 1812; d. Fort Sumner, New Mexico on July 1867) The Goodnight-Loving Trail is named for Oliver Loving, who, with Charles Goodnight, pioneered this cattle trail in 1866 when they drove a herd from Red Fork on the Brazos River in Texas to Fort Sumner, New Mexico and the Bosque Redondo Navajo Reservation. Actually, Loving pioneered three cattle trails. A native of Kentucky, Loving moved to Lamar County, Texas in 1845 and had driven a herd of cattle to Chicago in 1858 and to Denver in 1859 for the gold rushers. During the Civil War he helped furnish beef to the Confederate forces. In 1867 Loving set out for Fort Sumner with Billy Wilson to let purchasers know a herd was coming; unfortunately, Loving and Wilson ran into some hostile Indians, and Loving was shot in the wrist and side. At Loving's insistence, Wilson went for help; Loving went for seven days without food before he was picked up by some Mexicans and taken to Fort Sumner. Gangrene had set into Loving's wounds, and he soon died after requesting to be buried in Texas. He was buried in Greenwood Cemetery in Weatherford, Texas.

LOWE, ROWDY JOE (b. Joseph Lowe In Illinois In 1845 Or 1846; d. Denver, Colorado in February 1899) Rowdy Joe and his wife, Rowdy Kate, ran a combination saloon-whorehouse in several wide-open towns, including Wichita, Ellsworth and Newton, Kansas. On February 19, 1872 Rowdy Joe became incensed at Kate for refusing a customer and slapped her. A. M. Sweet, another customer, took advantage of the situation and got Kate drunk and then bedded down with her at Franny Grey's, a rival establishment. The next morning Rowdy Joe burst into the room and put two bullets into Sweet, killing him.

In Wichita, Kansas on October 27, 1873 Rowdy Joe and Red Beard, who owned a dance hall next door to Rowdy Joe's place, got into an altercation. It began when the drunken Red Beard threatened to shoot Josephine DeMerritt, a prostitute, and then shot at Lowe next door. Red then shot Anne Franklin in the stomach, mistaking her for Josephine. Lowe, also drunk, got to the door in time to fire a shotgun at Beard, who fired back and chased Lowe down the street. Back at the bar, Bill Anderson had collapsed from a bullet in the head; he became blind from this wound. On the bridge over the Arkansas River Rowdy Joe unloaded a round of buckshot into Beard. Beard died from these wounds two weeks later. Rowdy Joe met his end in February 1899 in Denver when, in a drunken state, he began insulting the local policeman and the two men drew; Lowe was killed in the exchange. (See also BEARD, RED.)

LYNCHING When a man or woman was hung without due process of the law. The term comes from Charles Lynch (1737–96), a Virginia farmer who, during the Revolutionary War, hung people who he thought ought to be hung. A lynching was usually done by a group, mob or committee, generally after some version of a trial and fitting somebody's idea of justice.

MACKENZIE, RANALD SLIDELL (b. New York City on July 27, 1840; d. Staten Island, New York on January 19, 1889) Mackenzie led the Fourth Cavalry in the Indian Wars. Acknowledged as a better soldier and Indian fighter than Custer, Mackenzie did not cultivate publicity like his famous counterpart (he never published any articles or his memoirs and would not permit reporters and correspondents to ride with him) and therefore never achieved the fame (or ignominy) of Custer. Mackenzie graduated from West Point in 1862 at the top of his class and served in the Civil War, in which he was wounded six times. He campaigned in Texas in 1871 against the Comanche and Kiowa and found the winter camp of the Comanche, Kiowa and Cheyenne at Palo Duro Canyon on the Staked Plains in September 1874. Mackenzie led a surprise attack, killed over 1,000 horses and burned the village, winter stores and other supplies, forcing the Indians to surrender. He was part of the pursuit of the Sioux and Cheyenne on the northern plains after Custer's death at the Little Bighorn and defeated the northern Cheyenne, led by Dull Knife, in November 1876. Mackenzie was ruthless, disciplined, dedicated to the army and a tireless campaigner. He drove his men to become the best cavalry regiment in the army and drove himself to become one of the most effective Indian fighters in the army. Mackenzie retired as brigadier general in March 1884 but went insane before he died at 48.

MACKENZIE'S RAIDERS TV show that starred Richard Carlson as Colonel Ranald S. Mackenzie.

Based on the book *The Mackenzie Raid* by Colonel Russell Reeder, this show featured the exploits of the real-life Ranald Mackenzie, the commander of the U.S. Fourth Cavalry stationed at Fort Clark, Texas in 1873. Mackenzie was given secret orders by President Ulysses S. Grant and General William Sheridan to chase Mexicans and Apache out of Texas and across the Rio Grande in Mexico to protect Texas citizens. The problem: If caught, the government would deny he was acting on its behalf; if successful, there would be no medals or honors. This was a desperate, illegal tactic and could have caused an international furor if the United States was caught. Mackenzie did his job. The show premiered in October 1958, produced by ZIV Television, the same group that produced "The Cisco Kid." Thirty-nine episodes of the half-hour series were produced in 1958 and 1959 and were syndicated to various stations; the program was never part of the regular prime-time schedule of any network.

MADISON, GUY (b. Robert Moseley in Bakersfield, California on January 19, 1922) Guy Madison starred as "Wild Bill Hickok" in the popular TV series. A handsome romantic lead, Madison came to Hollywood after serving in the navy in World War II and debuted in *Since You Went Away* (1944). He also appeared in *Till the End of Time* (1946), *The Charge at Feather River* (1953), *The Command* (1954), *The Last Frontier* (1956), *Gunmen of the Rio Grande* (1965), and *Where's Willie* (1978). (See also ADVENTURES OF WILD BILL HICKOK, THE.)

MADSEN, CHRISTIAN (b. Schleswig-Holstein, Denmark on February 25, 1851; d. Guthrie, Oklahoma on January 9, 1944) Madsen was a member of Teddy Roosevelt's Rough Riders, was present when Buffalo Bill Cody scalped Cheyenne warrior Yellow Hand and helped bury the bodies of Seventh Cavalry members after the Battle of the Little Bighorn. He was also part of the "Three Guardsmen," a trio of lawmen in Oklahoma, with Bill Tilghman and Heck Thomas. Prior to moving to the United States, he had fought in the Danish army against

Guy Madison

Christian Madsen *(Oklahoma Historical Society)*

the Germans, been part of the French Foreign Legion when the Franco-Prussian War broke out and fought at the Battle of Sedan before arriving in New York in 1871. Madsen was an active Indian fighter through 1890 and then became deputy United States marshal in El Reno, Oklahoma and Guthrie, Oklahoma. He was appointed U.S. marshal for Oklahoma in 1911 and was special investigator for Oklahoma governor J. B. A. Robertson from 1918 to 1922. He tried to enlist in World War I but was turned down because he was too old. A legendary, though often underestimated, figure in the Old West, Madsen had the bravery and coolness that so many others claimed. He died at the age of 93 at the Masonic Home in Guthrie. (See also THOMAS, HECK; THREE GUARDS-MEN, THE; TILGHMAN, BILL .)

MAGNIFICENT SEVEN, THE   Film produced and directed by John Sturges; screenplay by William

Roberts (from the movie *Seven Samurai* by Akira Kurosawa); music by Elmer Bernstein; released in 1960 by United Artists; 126 minutes in length. Cast: Yul Brynner, Eli Wallach, Steve McQueen, Horst Buchholz, Charles Bronson, Robert Vaughn, Brad Dexter and James Coburn.

What happens when the Wild West ends but a man is still trying to make a living with his guns? Well, he hires himself out to a Mexican village that's trying to save itself from a gang of bandits. There are different motives for each of the gunmen, although the pay is small and the prestige almost nonexistent. The seven gunmen train the Mexican peasants to defend themslves, and in the showdown the townspeople win. The music in this film was so vibrant and exciting that Marlboro cigarettes used it as their theme song. Because this movie was so successful, a string of sequels followed, including *The Return of the Seven* (United Artists, 1966), *Guns of the Magnificent Seven* (United Artists, 1968) and *The Magnificent Seven Ride Again* (United Artists, 1972).

MAHAN, LARRY   (b. Salem, Oregon on November 21, 1943)   Mahan won six All-Around Cowboy titles, more than any other rodeo cowboy, and acquired the title "King of the Rodeo." Mahan parlayed his success in rodeo to create a line of clothing, boots and hats, embark on a recording career, become a TV announcer for rodeo, star in a movie, *The Great American Cowboy* that won the Academy Award as Best Documentary Feature in 1973, and author a book, *Fundamentals of Rodeo Riding: A Mental and Physical Approach to Success.*

Mahan grew up in Brooks, Oregon and entered his first Youth Rodeo in Redmond, Oregon at 12, winning $6 for the calf ride event. In 1962 he moved to Phoenix to attend Arizona State University; however, he was still eligible to compete in high school events during his first year and won the Arizona High School All-Around Cowboy title. Mahan competed in a number of amateur rodeos in the Southwest in 1962 and 1963 and then turned professional in 1963. In 1965 he won his first World Championship in bull riding and the following year won the first of five consecutive All-Around Cowboy titles, competing in bareback, saddle bronc and bull-riding events. In 1971 and 1972 he was sidelined with injuries but in 1973 came back to win a record-setting sixth All-Around title. In 1977 Mahan retired from active rodeo competition; by that time he had competed in over 1,200 rodeos (sometimes as many as 150 a year), ridden more than 6,000 bulls and broncs and earned over half a million dollars in the rodeo arena. (See also RODEO.)

MAJOR ADAMS, TRAILMASTER   Syndicated title for the TV show "Wagon Train."

Under the "Major Adams, Trailmaster" title, the original "Wagon Train" show appeared on ABC in the weekday daytime lineup from September 1963 until September 1965 and then on Sunday afternoons from January 1963 to May 1964. (See also WAGON TRAIN.)

MAJORS, ALEXANDER   See RUSSELL, MAJORS AND WADDELL.

MAN AND BOY Film produced by Marvin Miller; directed by E. W. Swackhamer; screenplay by Harry Essex and Oscar Saul; released in 1971 by Levitt- Pickman; 98 minutes in length. Cast: Bill Cosby, Gloria Foster, Leif Erickson, George Spell, Douglas Turner Ward and Dub Taylor.

This movie marked the film debut of Bill Cosby, who plays a former cavalryman with a wife, son, 14-acre farm and horse. When the horse is stolen by a black outlaw headed for Mexico, the father and son set out to retrieve it.

MAN CALLED SHENANDOAH, A TV show that starred Robert Horton as Shenandoah.

Shenandoah was a man suffering from amnesia who roamed the West trying to find somebody who knew who he was. He had been found unconscious by two buffalo hunters who carried him back to town, figuring he was an outlaw with a bounty on his head. He wasn't—but when he recovered, he discovered he couldn't remember a thing about his past, including his name. So he took the name Shenandoah and began his adventures. The show only lasted one season—34 episodes—and premiered on September 13, 1965 on Monday evenings on ABC. The half-hour series ended its run on September 5, 1966.

MANDAN INDIANS The Mandan became famous in the early 19th century because artists George Catlin and Karl Bodmer both painted them. However, in 1837 the tribe was decimated by an outbreak of smallpox, which reduced their number from about 1,600 to 150. The Mandan lived on the Missouri River in North Dakota and were primarily a sedentary tribe, living in circular earth-covered lodges about 40 feet wide and 20 feet tall. They grew maize, beans, gourds and sunflowers, hunted buffalo for clothing and food and fished. The Mandan were extremely friendly to whites and were first "discovered" by Lewis and Clark in 1804. This tribe spent much time on sports and games, although they had an important ceremony related to the Sun Dance that used self-inflicted torture and amputation.

MAN FROM BLACKHAWK, THE TV show that starred Robert Rockwell as Sam Logan.

An insurance agent in the Wild West? A man who dressed in a suit and tie (albeit a string tie) and didn't carry a gun in a TV western? Yes to all of this. Sam Logan represented the Blackhawk Insurance Agency in Chicago and went west to investigate claims of insurance fraud as well as take care of the company's policyholders. The show lasted one season, filming 37 episodes. The half-hour show premiered on October 9, 1959 and ended September 23, 1960, appearing on Friday nights at 8:30 on ABC.

MANGAS COLORADAS (b. c. 1790; d. 1863) Mangas Coloradas hated whites and fought them with a vengeance. His hatred of whites was well founded: An American trapper, James Johnson, invited the chief and his people, the Mimbrenos Apache to Santa Rita del Cobre, a Mexican village, for a feast but then slaughtered about 400 with a concealed cannon to collect bounties for Apache scalps offered by the Mexican government. The chief was also beaten by gold miners in 1851 when he visited their camp alone. White settlers paid for these atrocities with their own lives. Mangas Coloradas, whose name meant "Red Sleeves" in Spanish from the red flannel shirt he wore at one time, was six feet six inches tall. He allied himself with Cochise, chief of the Chiricahua Apache, and they terrorized whites in the Southwest. During the Battle of Apache Pass in 1862 Mangas Coloradas was wounded by the California volunteers under General James Henry Carleton. The chief was captured by U.S. soldiers in January 1863, and guards jabbed him with red-hot bayonets and then shot him dead. The soldiers claimed he was trying to escape.

MANIFEST DESTINY The term "Manifest Destiny" was first used in the *Democratic Review* in July 1845 by editor John L. O'Sullivan to support the annexation of Texas; however, the idea of manifest destiny was an essential part of the eastern United States as citizens pushed westward. The notion of territorial expansion, the acquisition of Oregon, purchase of California and acquisition of the Southwest—indeed, the very idea that the United States should extend from the Atlantic Ocean to the Pacific—was the inherent belief in manifest destiny. This idea said, in essence, that Americans were destined through Divine Guidance to expand their national domain, to acquire land and improve lives. This self-confidence came from a feeling of superiority; Americans felt a moral superiority that led to a special mission to exercise power, control and influence over land and people.

MANNING, JAMES (b. near Huntsville or Mobile, Alabama c. 1839; d. Los Angeles, California on May 27, 1915) Jim Manning killed lawman Dallas Stoudenmire in El Paso and then killed Stoudenmire's brother-in-law, Doc Cummings. The feud started when the Manning brothers ran a rustling outfit and Stoudenmire was a law officer. Manning had gotten into a fight (reluctantly) on February 14, 1882 when a drunken Cummings provoked him. Manning and bartender David Kling then shot the belligerent Cummings in the Coliseum Variety Theater. Jim's brother was involved in a gunfight with lawman Dallas Stoudenmire on September 18, 1882 in El Paso in which both men were wounded. They were still wrestling when Jim came up with a .45 and hit Stoudenmire just behind the left ear; the lawman was dead when he hit the ground. Manning, however, lived a long life, dying of cancer more than 30 years after this incident. (See also CUMMINGS, DOC; STOUDENMIRE, DALLAS.)

MAN WHO SHOT LIBERTY VALANCE, THE Film produced by Willis Goldbeck; directed by John Ford; screenplay by James Warner Bellah and Willis Goldbeck; released in 1962 by Paramount; 123 minutes in length. Cast: John Wayne, James Stewart, Vera Miles, Lee Marvin, Edmond O'Brien, Andy Devine, Woody Strode, Lee Van Cleef, Strother Martin, John Carradine, Denver Pyle and Eva Novak.

This movie begins with the funeral of Tom Doniphan (John Wayne) in a western town. When Senator Ranse

Stoddard (James Stewart) is asked why he has come all the way from Washington for this funeral, he tells the story of Doniphan, which produces a long flashback. The senator is famous as the "man who shot Liberty Valance" (Lee Marvin), an outlaw who killed for hire. Stoddard faced Valance as an eastern lawyer in the West but, despite the odds against him, supposedly killed Valance, which led to his successful political career. However, in reality it was Doniphan—hidden in the shadows—who killed Valance with his rifle. Doniphan then loses his girl (who becomes Stoddard's wife) and becomes an obscure part of western history while Stoddard's star rises. When Stoddard has finished telling this story to a newspaperman, correcting the version that has come down through the years, the writer states the famous line "This is the West, sir. When the legend becomes fact, print the legend."

The theme song, "The Man Who Shot Liberty Valance," was written by Hal David and Burt Bacharach and was a top-five pop hit for Gene Pitney in 1962.

MAN WITHOUT A GUN   TV show that starred Rex Reason as Adam MacLean, Mort Mills as Marshal Frank Tallman, Harry Harvey, Sr. as Mayor George Dixon and Forrest Taylor as Doc Brannon.

Adam MacLean was editor of the *Yellowstone Sentinel* in Dakota Territory during the 1880s. Believing the pen was mightier than the sword, MacLean crusaded with his paper and let the town's youngsters use his office for a schoolroom. The show was syndicated and never a regular part of network programming. The 52 episodes of the half-hour show were produced from 1957 to 1959 and originally released in the fall of 1958.

MAN WITHOUT A STAR   Film produced by Aaron Rosenberg; directed by King Vidor; screenplay by Borden Chase and D. D. Beauchamp (based on a story by Dee Linford); released in 1955 by Universal-International; 89 minutes in length. Cast: Kirk Douglas, Jeanne Craine, Claire Trevor, William Campbell, Jay C. Flippen, Myrna Hansen, Mara Corday, Richard Boone, Eddy C. Waller, Sheb Wooley and Mark Hanna.

A rowdy cowboy (Kirk Douglas) runs into a cattle baroness, who is terrorizing the small nesters in her desire to control the open range. Later, this movie was remade as *A Man Called Gannon* (1969).

MARLOW, BOONE   (b. 1865; d. near Fort Sill, Oklahoma on January 24, 1889)   Outlaw Boone Marlow was killed by bounty hunters Martin Beavers, J. E. Direkson and G. E. Harboldt for a $1,700 reward. Marlow was apparently poisoned on Hell Creek, about 20 miles east of fort Sill, Oklahoma, and the body was delivered to the Fort on January 28, 1889 to collect the reward. Previously, Boone Marlow had killed a man in Wilbarger County, Texas in 1886 but fought arrest, killing Deputy Sheriff Tom Wallace in the process. His four brothers were arrested but sawed their way out of jail and then stood down a mob ready to lynch them. But while being transferred to another jail, a mob fired upon the four Marlow brothers, and two of the brothers—Alf and Epp— were killed,along with a lawman.

Meanwhile George and Charley Marlow were wounded and shackled to a dead brother but fought back hard and killed three in the mob. George and Charley survived to become old men.

MARQUIS DE MORES   (b. Antoine Amedee Marie Vincent Manca de Vellombrosa in France in 1858; d. North Africa in 1896)   In 1883 the Marquis de Mores with his American wife, Medora, moved to the Dakota badlands with $3 million (mostly from his father-in-law) and purchased a 45,000-acre ranch and formed a town, which he named Medora. He also built a slaughterhouse and formed the Northern Pacific Refrigerator Car Company to establish a western business of slaughtering beef and sending it back East. Three years later he expanded into retail and set up shops in New York City, but the butchers there organized against him, and in 1887, after the disastrous winter of 1886–87 that decimated the cattle industry on the northern ranges, the Marquis abandoned this enterprise. He also abandoned several other enterprises, including a freight line and a business shipping salmon from the Northwest to New York City. Finally, he moved out of the West after losing $1–2 million.

The Marquis, a French nobleman, was an interesting inhabitant of the plains who built a 28-room mansion filled with fine furniture and servants. A neighbor of Theodore Roosevelt, the Marquis lived a lavish life on the barren plains. He was a colorful character as well and killed one man and wounded two others after they cut some fence wire on his land; he was acquitted following a long trial.

After the Marquis left the West he traveled to India for a tiger hunt and then was involved in an attempt to build a railroad through French Indochina to China. In France he became a leader in anti-Semitic attacks and promoted socialism and public housing. In 1896 he was in Northern Africa and involved in a colonial war when he was assassinated by anticolonialists.

MARSHAL   There were several kinds of "marshals" in the Old West; the federal marshal was a political appointment and had jurisdictions that corresponded to those of the district courts of the United States. The actual work of investigations and arrests was actually done by deputy marshals; the marshal was actually a lawyer, politician or merchant who received this position as a political payoff. The town marshal was elected or appointed by a town council or group of citizens and was in charge of law enforcement for the town; these marshals are equivalent to the contemporary chief of police, whose job it is to keep order in a city or town.

MARSHAL DILLON   TV Show.

"Gunsmoke" was originally a 30-minute show. When it became a 60-minute show, during the 1961 season, the original half-hour shows were seen on Tuesday evenings as "Marshal Dillon." (See GUNSMOKE.)

MARSHAL OF GUNSIGHT PASS, THE   TV show that starred Russell "Lucky" Hayden as the marshal (March), Eddie Dean as Marshal Eddie Dean

(March–September), Rosco Ates as Deputy Rosco and Jane Adrian as Ruth.

A short run—only six months— and a number of cast changes make this show a rather obscure footnote in early television. The show was performed live on a stage set, which destroyed any possibility of authenticity. It premiered on March 12, 1950 on ABC on Saturday evenings. On September 30, 1950 the 30-minute series was over. The only notable part of this series is that it attempted to resurrect the singing cowboy, with Andy Parker and the Plainsmen providing some musical interludes and Eddie Dean singing some songs.

MASTERSON, BAT (b. William Bartholomew Masterson (later changed his name to William Barclay Masterson) in County Rouville, Quebec, Canada on November 26, 1853; d. New York City on October 25, 1921) Bat Masterson was the most famous of the Masterson's seven children, but his claims as a gunfighter were exaggerated. In fact, his brother Jim engaged in more gunfights than Bat, who was involved in only three. He possibly killed three men but may have killed just one man.

The Masterson family lived in Canada, New York and Illinois before they moved to Wichita, Kansas in 1867. Bat and his older brother, Ed, moved to Dodge City in 1872, where Bat became a buffalo hunter for a while. Bat was engaged in the Battle of Adobe Walls in the Texas panhandle when Quanah Parker led an Indian attack. After this, Bat served as a army scout for General Nelson A. Miles.

The only man positively killed by Bat Masterson was a member of the Fourth Cavalry named Corporal Melvin A. King in January 1876. The fight was over a woman, Molly Brennan, a dance hall girl who was courted by both Masterson and King. According to stories, Bat and Mollie Brennan were together in a saloon when King came in, in a jealous rage. King shot both Molly and Bat before Bat drew his gun and shot King. Both Molly and King died, and Bat, according to legend, had to adopt his trademark cane after this gunfight. Bat may have gotten his nickname from this cane, although he may also have gotten it from "Battling," a rather common nickname for those who got into many scraps. He could have also gotten it from "Bartholomew," his middle name before he changed it to "Barclay."

Bat moved back to Dodge City in 1877 and opened a saloon. He became deputy sheriff of Ford County and worked alongside his brother Ed, who was a policeman in Dodge City. Bat was elected sheriff of Ford County (by three votes) in November 1877. On April 9, 1878 Bat's brother, city marshal Ed Masterson, was in an altercation with Jack Wagner and Alf Walker outside the Lady Gay Dance Hall and Saloon. Bat was about 20 paces away when the gun went off into Ed's belly, setting the lawman's clothes on fire. Ed staggered away and died 30 minutes later. One story says that Bat's guns blazed at Wagner and Walker; Wagner died 24 hours later while Walker lingered on for a month. Ed's murder did have a great effect on Bat, though, and he remained in Dodge City as a lawman.

Bat Masterson *(Western Archives)*

Bat was appointed deputy U.S. marshal in January 1879 and then hired out as a gunman to the Atchison, Topeka and Santa Fe Railroad. He was defeated in the election for sheriff in 1879 and then went to Colorado, New Mexico, Nebraska, and Kansas City. He moved to Tombstone, Arizona in 1881 to join friends Wyatt Earp and Luke Short. Bat was involved in the "Dodge City War" in 1883 in which Luke Short was reestablished in that town as a lawman.

Probably the most famous gunfight in Bat's career occurred on April 16, 1881 when he stepped off the train in Dodge City from Tombstone. Bat had come in response to a telegram from his brother Jim for help with a disagreement with Al Updegraff and A. J. Peacock. Peacock and Jim Masterson were partners in the Lady Gay Dance Hall and Saloon, and Peacock had hired Updegraff as a bartender; Jim Masterson and Peacock's relationship had deteriorated to the point of animosity. Bat's train arrived at 11:50 A.M and as soon as he left the train, he saw Peacock and Updegraff in the crowded street walking together. Bat headed straight for the two, and when he was about 20 feet away, he yelled, "I have come over a thousand miles to settle this. I know you are heeled—now fight!" The three drew guns and began shooting. Peacock and Updegraff went around the corner of the city jail while Bat ducked behind the rail bed,

Actor Gene Barry played Bat Masterson in the
long-running series

and then some others in the nearby saloon also began shooting. Bat got some dirt in his mouth from a shot that hit nearby, and Updegraff took a bullet in his lung. When the shooters stopped to reload, Mayor A. B. Webster and Sheriff Fred Singer came out with shotguns and ordered all parties to stop. Bat had to pay a small fine and board the evening train out of Dodge—four hours after he'd arrived.

Bat continued to wander throughout the West even though he lived in Denver; still, as a gambler and friend of gamblers, he tried his luck at a number of tables. In 1891 he became manager of Ed Chase's Palace theater; that same year he married Emma Walters. But liquor was an increasing problem for him, and in 1902 he was asked to leave Denver, so he and Emma moved to New York City. There, President Theodore Roosevelt appointed him marshal of the southern district of New York State; he was removed from this office by President William Howard Taft. Masterson achieved fame when newspaperman Alfred Henry Lewis wrote stories about him and featured him in a novel, *The Sunset Trail.* Masterson himself wrote a series of articles for *Human Life* magazine about his gunfighter friends Wyatt Earp, Luke Short, Doc Holliday, Bill Tilghman, Ben Thompson and William F. Cody.

The last 15 years of Masterson's life were spent writing about sports for the *New York Morning Telegraph,* for which he served as sports editor and wrote a column. Masterson, who had experience promoting fights in Denver, became an expert on boxing but generally hacked out the sports news of the day. He became a man who outlived his time; the days of the Old West were gone and far behind, but people still came wanting a remnant; Masterson reportedly bought guns at hock shops and carved notches in the butts and then handed them out to satisfy curiosity seekers and celebrity demands. Masterson died, ironically, at his desk at the newspaper; he suffered a heart attack while writing his sports column. (See also MASTERSON, EDWARD J.; MASTERSON, JAMES P.; SHORT, LUKE L.)

MASTERSON, EDWARD J. (b. Henryville, Canada on September 22, 1852; d. in Dodge City, Kansas on April 9, 1878.) Ed was Bat Masterson's oldest brother. Ed and Bat left home after the Civil War; Ed was appointed deputy marshal of Dodge in June 1877 and promoted to city marshal in January 1878. During the evening of April 9, 1878 in Dodge City, Masterson and Deputy Nat Haywood had tried to calm some cowboys at the Lady Gay Dance Hall and Saloon. Masterson disarmed Jack Wagner, one of the rowdy cowboys, about 10 P.M. that night and gave the pistol to Wagner's boss, A. M. Walker. Walker gave the pistol back to Wagner, and the two drunken cowboys both went after Masterson, who got in a fight with Wagner for the gun. Deputy Haywood tried to help Masterson, but some cowboys drew their guns and forced him back; then Wagner—who had shot at Haywood but the gun misfired—shot Masterson. The gun was so close to Masterson that it set the lawman's clothes on fire. The bullet went through Masterson's stomach and out his back, but he managed to pull his gun and hit Wagner with one shot and Walker with three. Wagner died the next day but Walker recovered. Masterson walked into George Hoover's saloon, about 200 yards away, before he gasped, "I'm shot," and fell to the floor. He was carried to brother Bat's room, where he died about half an hour later. (See also MASTERSON, BAT; MASTERSON, JAMES P.)

MASTERSON, JAMES P. (b. Iroquois County, Illinois in 1855; d. Guthrie, Oklahoma on March 31, 1895) Younger brother of Ed and Bat Masterson, Jim joined his brothers in Dodge City and became a law officer. Jim Masterson became city marshal of Dodge in November 1879, about a year and a half after his brother's death. He became one of the first settlers in Guthrie, Oklahoma after being part of the Oklahoma land rush of 1889 and was appointed deputy U.S. marshal there in 1893. During his life Jim Masterson was involved in some memorable gunfights. On July 26, 1878 in Dodge City, about three and a half months after his brother Ed's death, Jim Masterson and Wyatt Earp killed a cowboy (actually the cowboy died four weeks later of an infection from the wound) after a group of cowboys had shot up a saloon. A few years later Jim solicited help from brother Bat over a dispute with Lady Gay Dance Hall and Saloon bartender Al Updegraff. Jim Masterson and A. J. Peacock owned the saloon, and Updegraff and Masterson just didn't get along. On April 16, 1881 Bat stepped off the noon train in Dodge and immediately saw Peacock and Updegraff and yelled a challenge; soon others joined in the gunfight and Updegraff was killed. The Mastersons left town after Bat paid a small fine. One of the more interesting Old West confrontations occurred on January 14, 1889 in Cimarron, Kansas when Jim Masterson, Bill Tilghman, Fred Singer, Neal Brown, Billy Ainsworth, Ed Brooks and Ben Daniels went to the courthouse to remove the town's records. The town of Ingalls hired the Dodge City gunmen, swearing them in as deputy sheriffs, to go to Cimarron, where the county records were held, because Cimarron and Ingalls, about six miles apart, both wanted to be the seat of Gray County. Some gunfire was exchanged and some Cimarron citizens were killed. At the courthouse, Masterson, Singer, Ainsworth and Watson were pinned inside by the gunfire. The next day they surrendered to the county sheriff, who, because he was an Ingalls sympathizer, released them immediately after leaving Cimarron. Jim Masterson was also in the gunfight with the Doolin Gang on September 1, 1893 in Ingalls, where Arkansas Tom Daugherty surrendered. James Masterson died of "galloping consumption" in Guthrie in 1895. (See also MASTERSON, BAT; MASTERSON, EDWARD J.)

MATHER, DAVE. H. (aka "Mysterious Dave"; b. Connecticut in 1845; d. ?)   Mysterious Dave may have been a descendant of Cotton Mather, although his genealogy and details of his life are unclear. What is known is that he was a horse thief and robber and ran with outlaw Dutch Henry Born. He was also a law officer and worked as a constable in Las Vegas, New Mexico, deputy city marshal of Dodge City, deputy sheriff of Ford County and city marshal of New Kiowa, Kansas.

Mysterious Dave ran into trouble in Dodge City; he was accused of being a bully and in cahoots with criminals. He and Tom Nixon, who replaced Mather as assistant city marshal of Dodge, had a running feud, and on July 18, 1884 outside the Opera House in Dodge City around 9 P.M. Nixon and Mather got into a quarrel. Nixon shot at Mather but the fight ended quickly. Three days later, on July 21, around 10 P.M. Mather came up to Nixon, who was standing at the corner of a busy street, and shot him down, pumping three bullets into his body after he lay on the street. In fact, one of Mather's bullets passed through Nixon and hit an innocent bystander. After another shooting incident in Dodge in which one man was killed and two others wounded, Dave and his brother jumped bail and hightailed it out of Dodge. From here his trail goes to Kansas, where he was marshal of New Kiowa, Barber County and then Long Pine, Nebraska, before it vanishes.

MATTHEWS, JACOB B.   (b. Woodbury, Tennessee on May 5, 1847; d. Roswell, New Mexico on June 3, 1904)   Jacob Matthews was involved in the Lincoln County War; he led the posse that assassinated John Tunstall and was in the gunfight that killed Sheriff William Brady and his deputy George Hindman. In this fight Matthews wounded Billy the Kid, who was trying to get Brady's and Hindman's Winchesters after the two

were lying dead in the street. Matthews also killed lawyer H. J. Chapman, though he was later acquitted, and was in the four-day shootout at the McSween house, firing at Billy the Kid and others inside the house.

Matthews had moved to New Mexico after the Civil War (he fought in the Confederacy for Company M of the Fifth Tennessee Cavalry) and in 1873 was a circuit court clerk. (See also BILLY THE KID; HINDMAN, GEORGE W.; LINCOLN COUNTY WAR.)

MAVERICK   The term, meaning an unbranded calf, came from Samuel A. Maverick, an attorney who moved to Matagorda County, Texas in 1835 and farmed and ranched between 1844–1847. A neighbor owed Maverick $1,200; reluctantly Maverick agreed to accept 400 cattle, in exchange for the money, and they were placed under the care of a black family. Many were not branded, and soon all residents of the area began to refer to unbranded cattle as "one of Maverick's." Maverick sold his cattle to A. Toutant Beauregard in 1856, and Beauregard's cowboys gathered up all the unbranded cattle they found, claiming them as "Maverick's." By 1857 people in areas south of San Antonio referred to all unbranded cattle as "Maverick's," although it was not until after the Civil War that the term came into widespread use in Texas.

MAVERICK   TV show that starred James Garner as Bret Maverick (1957–60), Jack Kelly as Bart Maverick, Diane Brewster as Samantha Crawford (1958–59), Roger Moore as Cousin Beauregard Maverick (1960–61) and Robert Colbert as Brent Maverick (1961).

This western replaced the "hero" with a "character" and introduced a healthy dose of humor into a straight western series. The key to it all was James Garner, who played Bret Maverick as a straight character until about the third episode, when his flair for comedy took over while shooting an episode. From this point on, Bret Maverick was fun to watch. A card shark always in search of a poker game, Bret preferred to slip out of town quietly rather than face a showdown at high noon. He was joined by his brother, Bart, in the first season, and cousin Beauregard Maverick joined for the 1960–61 season; brother Brent Maverick, who had fought in the Civil War and then moved to England for a while, came on during spring 1961. Brent joined because James Garner had left the series over a contract dispute with Warner Brothers. Garner never returned to the series, although he starred later in another series, "Bret Maverick," and was seen in reruns inserted during the final season. The show was number one in TV ratings in 1959 and won an Emmy that year as "Best Western Program." It premiered on September 22, 1957 on ABC on Sunday nights. The final show was telecast on July 8, 1962; by that time the one-hour show had filmed 124 episodes.

MAYNARD, KEN   (b. Mission, Texas on July 21, 1895; d. Los Angeles, California on March 23, 1973)   Ken Maynard was one of the top cowboy stars in the 1920s and 1930s and helped the transition to "talking" westerns by providing the first singing westerns. May-

Ken Maynard

nard's early talkies featured some singing, and he built one movie *(The Strawberry Roan)* around a song. Maynard played and sang in his movies (and even recorded some records), but his lack of singing talent led movie executives to hire Gene Autry to sing in Maynard's film *In Old Santa Fe,* which first introduced Autry to moviegoers. On Maynard's next film, *Mystery Mountain,* Maynard's drinking problem got the best of him; he was a difficult man to work with, often argumentative and belligerent, and the producers decided to fire him after this movie and use Autry in the following serial, *Phantom Empire,* which launched Autry's career as a singing-cowboy star. Maynard was an excellent horseman who began his show business career with a traveling medicine show and then rodeos; he joined the Ringling Brothers Circus, and his first screen role was *Janice Meredith* (1924). His first western was *$50,000 Reward* for Davis Studios, and he then starred in a series of silent westerns. In 1929 he signed with Universal, then Tiffany, World Wide and back to Universal. Movie executives recognized Maynard's talent (he usually wrote, directed and starred in his movies). In the late 1930s he worked for Columbia, Grand National and then Colony. He starred in the "Trail Blazer" series at Monogram in 1943, and his last western was *Harmony Trail* in 1944, although it was not released until 1947. After movies Maynard toured with the Cole Brothers Circus and made rodeo appearances before he retired in Los Angeles. (See also AUTRY, GENE; B WESTERN MOVIES; MOVIES; SINGING COWBOYS.)

McCABE AND MRS. MILLER   Film produced by David Foster and Mitchell Brower; directed by Robert Altman; screenplay by Robert Altman and Brian McKay (from the novel *McCabe* by Edmond Naughton); music by Leonard Cohen; released in 1971 by Warner Brothers; 121 minutes in length. Cast: Warren Beatty as John McCabe, Julie Christie as Constance Miller, Rene Auberjonois as Sheehan, Hugh Millais as Dog Butler, Shelley Duvall as Ida Coyle and Michael Murphy as Sears.

A wandering gambler comes to a small town and sets up shop—a saloon and whorehouse. John McCabe (Warren Beatty) is helped by Mrs. Miller (Julie Christie), who is a Cockney madam, and business is so good that a corporation wants to buy him out. When McCabe refuses, the corporation hires killers to wipe him out. Canadian singer-songwriter Leonard Cohen did the songs in the picture.

McCALL, BROKEN NOSE JACK   (aka Buffalo Curly and Bill Sutherland; b. John McCall in Jefferson County, Kentucky in 1850 or 1851; d. Yankton, Dakota Territory on March 1, 1877)   Jack McCall is the man who killed Wild Bill Hickok by shooting him in the back of the head on August 2, 1876 in Saloon No. 10 in Deadwood, Colorado. When asked later why he didn't shoot him from the front like a man, McCall replied, "I didn't want to commit suicide." McCall had gone into the saloon and ordered a drink at the bar before walking over to Wild Bill, who was engaged in a poker game. McCall ran out of the saloon after shooting Wild Bill and trying to shoot bartender Anson Tipple, who had jumped the bar and tried to stop him. (Later, it was revealed that the gun had five defective cartridges and only one good one—the one that killed Hickok). McCall jumped on a horse while being chased by Harry Young, but the saddle cinch broke and McCall landed in the dust. He was captured when he tried to hide in a butcher's shop. At his trial, McCall was acquitted after lying that he was the brother of Samuel Strawhim, killed in 1869 in Hays City by Hickok. McCall had been using the alias "Bill Sutherland" in Deadwood. In Cheyenne, McCall was arrested by a deputy U.S. marshal, who overheard the drunken McCall bragging about the lie that brought the acquittal. McCall was tried again in the federal court of Yankton, Dakota Territory and hung at 10:15 A.M. on March 1, 1877 gasping, "Oh, God," just before dropping through the trapdoor to his death. (See also HICKOK, WILD BILL; STRAWHIM, SAMUEL.)

McCARTY, HENRY   See BILLY THE KID.

McCARTY, TOM   (b. Utah c. 1855; d. Montana c. 1900)   Tom, along with his brothers Bill and George McCarty, was associated with Butch Cassidy's Wild Bunch, although George was never involved in any of the robbing. Bill and Tom, along with the Mormon Kid, held up the Roslyn Bank in Roslyn, Washington c. 1892 and the Farmers and Merchants Bank of Delta in Delta, Colorado on September 7, 1893. During this Colorado robbery Tom's brother Bill and nephew Fred were both killed, but Tom never stopped riding. He moved to

Montana and became a sheepherder but around 1900 got into a hot argument and was killed after an altercation. (See also MORMON KID, THE.)

McCLUSKIE, ARTHUR (b. ?; d. Medicine Lodge, Kansas in June 1873) Arthur McCluskie set out to avenge his brother Mike's death. He confronted Mike's killer, Texan Hugh Anderson, in June 1873 in Medicine Lodge, Kansas, where Anderson was working as a bartender for the trading post. McCluskie challenged him to a duel and Anderson accepted, choosing pistols over knives. In late afternoon, about 70 people watched as the two stood 20 paces apart, facing away from each other. When the starter fired a shot in the air, the two turned and fired but neither of the first shots hit; McCluskie's second shot broke Anderson's arm. Anderson fired back and hit McCluskie in the mouth. McCluskie— blood all over his face and screaming with pain and rage—charged Anderson, who pumped bullets into McCluskie as he came. Finally, McCluskie collapsed but suddenly raised himself up—though everyone thought the fight was over—and fired a slug into Anderson's belly, who crumpled. McCluskie then grabbed his knife and crawled toward Anderson. Although a few in the crowd wanted to stop the carnage, others insisted the fight be fought to its finish. Anderson managed to sit up, draw his knife and slash McCluskie in the neck as he crawled on him. McCluskie stuck his knife into Anderson's side before both men collapsed in death. (See also ANDERSON, HUGH; MCCLUSKIE, MIKE; NEWTON MASSACRE.)

McCLUSKIE, MIKE (aka Arthur Delaney; b. ?; d. Newton, Kansas on August 20, 1871) McCluskie was head of a railroad crew for the Atchison, Topeka and Santa Fe Railroad and had been in Newton, Kansas a few weeks when a special election was held on August 11, 1871. William Bailey— whose real name was Bill Wilson—was hired by the town as election deputy. But Bailey became drunk and obnoxious during the election and was given a tongue-lashing by McCluskie when the two clashed. Around 8 that night at the Red Front Saloon, Bailey ordered McCluskie to buy the house a round of drinks. McCluskie refused and a fight started; the big McCluskie sent Bailey through the saloon's swinging doors with a punch. McCluskie followed him outside and saw Bailey leaning on a hitching rail with a six-gun; McCluskie grabbed his own gun and killed Bailey and then hightailed it out of town. Eight days later—on August 19, 1871—McCluskie went back into Newton to Perry Tuttle's dance hall. About one in the morning Hugh Anderson, a friend of Bailey's, came to the faro table where McCluskie was sitting, pulled a pistol and shot him in the neck. McCluskie rose, blood spurting from his throat, and shot at Anderson; meanwhile, Anderson kept firing at McCluskie. Other cowboys also opened fire—three others were hit and one died—before a young friend of McCluskie's, Jim Riley, locked the door behind him and fired his gun at the Texas cowboys until no bullets were left in the chambers. When the shooting stopped, four others had been

hit and two would die. McCluskie was carried to his hotel room, where he died around 8 in the morning. (See also ANDERSON, HUGH; MCCLUSKIE, ARTHUR; NEWTON MASSACRE.)

McCONNELL, ANDREW (b. Massachusetts.c. 1835; d . ?) McConnell killed Bear River Tom Smith, marshal of Abilene. McConnell had come from Massachusetts to homestead in Kansas, just outside Abilene. On October 23, 1870 he killed a neighbor, John Shea, who was driving a herd of cattle across his land. On November 2, 1870 some of Shea's neighbors swore out a warrant for McConnell's arrest. After a county officer was driven away, Marshal Tom Smith and his deputy, J. H. McDonald, rode out to McConnell's dugout. McConnell was with Moses Miles, whose testimony had freed McConnell, and while Smith stood and read the warrant, he was shot by McConnell in the chest. Smith shot back and hit McConnell and the two began wrestling. Miles and McDonald then fired at each other; Miles was hit but McDonald fled. Miles then helped McConnell beat Smith and hauled him out in the yard, where Miles grabbed an axe and chopped Smith's head almost off his body. Miles received a term of 16 years in the state penitentiary, and McConnell got a 12-year sentence. (See also SMITH, BEAR RIVER TOM.)

McCOY, JOSEPH GEATING (b. Sangamon County, Illinois on December 21, 1837; d. Kansas City, Missouri on October 19, 1915) More than any other single individual, Joseph McCoy was responsible for creating the *business* of the cattle drives by going to Abilene, Kansas, a small collection of buildings that called itself a town in June 1867, and purchasing 250 acres for $2,400. McCoy built stockyards, holding pens and the Drover's Cottage, a hotel for cattlemen. Next he worked out an arrangement with the railroad to ship the beef east and then spread the word in Texas that Abilene was the place where cattlemen could sell the beef they drove up the Chisholm Trail. He thus created the first great cattle town as well as the huge business of cattle drives; by the end of 1867 over 35,000 cattle had come to Abilene to be shipped east. McCoy's venture was profitable for himself, the cattle ranchers, Abilene and the railroad, but the railroad reneged on its arrangement to pay McCoy, and he had to sue to receive the $200,000 due him. In 1871 McCoy was elected mayor of Abilene and two weeks later hired Wild Bill Hickok as town marshal. Abilene remained the principal cattle town until the quarantine line was moved west and Wichita, Kansas became the major cattle town; McCoy then followed the cattle trade to Wichita. Later McCoy served as an Indian agent before he went into politics. In 1874 he published *Historical Sketches of the Cattle Trade of the West and Southwest,* which detailed his efforts in the cattle business and is a standard work for those studying cowboys and the cowboy culture.

McCOY, TIM (b. Timothy John Fitzgerald McCoy in Saginaw, Michigan on April 10, 1891; d. Nogales, Arizona on January 29, 1978) Tim McCoy had a distinguished career before he began work in the movies; he was a top expert on Indian lore and worked as an Indian agent in Wyoming before his first contact with the movie industry, which came when he served as technical adviser for *The Covered Wagon* (1923). McCoy served in World War II, then went to Hollywood and became a cowboy star in the silent era; his first supporting role came in *The Thundering Herd* (1925), and his first sound western was *The Indians Are Coming* (1930). McCoy made 24 films for Columbia from 1931 to 1935 and then joined the Ringling Brothers–Barnum and Bailey Circus before he formed his own Wild West show in 1938. McCoy worked for a number of movie studios and launched the "Rough Riders" series with Buck Jones and Raymond Hattin in 1941. In 1942 McCoy ran for the United States Senate but lost; he then reenlisted in the armed services and received a Bronze Star in Europe. After the war he toured with circuses and Wild West shows until the 1960s; his last film appearance was in *Requiem for a Gunfighter* (1965). (See also MOVIES.)

McCREA, JOEL (b. Joel Albert McCrea in South Pasadena, California on November 5, 1905; d. Woodland Hills, California on October 20, 1990) McCrea grew up around Hollywood and worked as an extra whenever possible. He first appeared in *The Jazz Age* (1929) and during the 1930s had key roles in *Wells Fargo* (1937; his first western) and *Union Pacific* (1939). McCrea's heyday as a star occurred in the 1930s and early 1940s, when he gained the reputation as a solid actor. From the mid-1940s on, Joel McCrea appeared

Joel McCrea

almost exclusively in westerns; his final role was in *Ride the High Country* (1962) with another western acting legend, Randolph Scott. McCrea and his son, Joel McCrea, Jr., starred in the TV series "Wichita Town" and together in the movie *Cry Blood, Apache* (1970). In addition to the movies mentioned, McCrea also had roles in the following westerns:

Buffalo Bill (1944)
The Virginian (1946)
Four Faces West (1948)
Colorado Territory (1949)
The Outriders (1950)
Saddle Tramp (1950)
Cattle Drive (1951)
The Lone Hand (1953)
Rough Shoot (1953)
Black Horse Canyon (1954)
Wichita (1955)
The First Texan (1956)
Cattle Empire (1957)
Gunfight Ridge (1957)
The Oklahoman (1957)
The Gunfight at Dodge City (1959)
Great American Cowboy (1973)
Mustang Country (1976)

McLAURY, FRANK (b. Iowa in late 1851 or 1852; d. Tombstone, Arizona on October 26, 1881) Frank McLaury was killed in the gunfight at the O.K. Corral by

Tim McCoy

Wyatt Earp. There had been trouble in town the previous night, so before noon Frank McLaury and Billy Clanton rode into town. Frank went into a store, and when he came out, he saw Wyatt Earp pulling McLaury's horse's bit. McLaury confronted Earp, and heated words were exchanged. McLaury was asked to give up his guns by Sheriff John Behan but refused to surrender his six-shooter. Behan was trying to head off trouble and walked with Frank toward the O.K. Corral, where Behan asked the Clanton-McLaury group to give up their guns. Frank declined again; at this point the Earp brothers and Doc Holliday appeared coming towards them. Shooting began, and Frank was one of the first hit. Wyatt said later he went for Frank first because "he had the reputation of being a good shot and a dangerous man." Frank, despite his wound, and Billy Clanton then wounded Morgan and Virgil Earp and Doc Holliday, but Frank was killed by a bullet from Morgan Earp, who yelled, "I got him," after the slug hit Frank beneath his right ear. McLaury was dead when he hit the dust. (See also EARP, WYATT; GUNFIGHT AT THE O.K. CORRAL.)

McLAURY, THOMAS (b. Iowa after 1852; d. Tombstone, Arizona on October 26, 1881)   Tom McLaury was killed by a shotgun blast from Doc Holliday at the O.K. Corral in the famous gunfight on October 26, 1881. The Clantons and McLaurys were engaged in rustling, and the McLaurys testified against Doc Holliday concerning a stage robbery in March 1881. Holliday was acquitted but swore revenge. Tom McLaury and Ike Clanton had come into Tombstone the afternoon of October 25, 1881, and the next morning Wyatt Earp pistol-whipped Tom McLaury with his Buntline Special after Tom refused to fight Earp. Tom McLaury did all he could to avoid a fight with the Earps—he turned over his revolver and gun belt to a local saloon keeper, Andy Mehan, about an hour before the gunfight at the O.K. Corral. Tom pointed out that he was unarmed when the Earps and Doc Holliday approached, but that did not stop the lawmen from opening fire. Tom was standing by his horse—there was a rifle in the scabbard—when Doc Holliday opened fire with a shotgun he had pulled from under his long overcoat. The horse had jumped away from Tom when the gunfire erupted, leaving Tom exposed when Holliday fired at him. Twelve buckshot came into his right side. He was carried into a nearby house—with Billy Clanton—and died soon afterward, unable to utter a last word. (See also GUNFIGHT AT THE O.K. CORRAL; HOLLIDAY, DOC.)

McNAB, FRANK (b. ?; d. near Lincoln, New Mexico on April 30, 1878)   McNab worked for rancher John Chisum and was in the Lincoln County War on the side of the "Regulators," the group that included Billy the Kid. He became a leader of the "Regulators" after the death of Dick Brewer and played a part in the revenge murders of Frank Baker, Billy Morton and William McCloskey. On April 30, 1878 McNab went to Ab Sanders's ranch with fellow Regulators Frank Coe and Ab Sanders. At a stream getting a drink the group was jumped by a posse of about 24. McNab and Sanders

were off their horses and McNab was hit. He tried to crawl away but was hunted down; then his body was filled with buckshot and he was left to rot. Later his friends found his body and buried him where he lay. (See also LINCOLN COUNTY WAR.)

McNELLY'S BULLDOG   See ARMSTRONG, JOHN BARCLAY.

McQUEEN, STEVE (b. Terrence Steven McQueen in Beech Grove, Indiana on March 24, 1930; d. Juarez, Mexico on November 7, 1980.)   Steve McQueen received his first fame in the TV series "Wanted: Dead or Alive" (1958–60) and then became a major actor in movies. After McQueen left the Marine Corps, he drifted a bit and then enrolled in the Neighborhood Playhouse in New York in 1951. Along the way, McQueen developed the alienated but "cool" loner as a character. In addition to his starring TV role as Josh Randall, McQueen also starred in such western movies as *The Magnificent Seven* (1960), *Nevada Smith* (1966) and *Tom Horn* (1980). (See also TELEVISION WESTERNS.)

MEAGHER, MICHAEL (b. County Cavar, Ireland in 1843; d. Caldwell, Kansas on December 17, 1881) Michael and his brother, John, fought in the Civil War after moving to the United States from Ireland. After the war they went west to Kansas, where Mike was a distinguished law officer in two wide-open cattle towns, Wichita and Caldwell. Meagher was elected mayor of

Steve McQueen in "Wanted Dead or Alive"

Caldwell in 1880 and became city marshal the next year. On a Friday night drunken cowboy Jim Talbot was raising a ruckus and had a run-in with Meagher. A series of arrests ensued, with Texas cowboys Talbot, Bob Bigtree, Dick Eddleman, Tom Love, Jim Martin, Bob Munson and George Speers against city marshal John Wilson and Meagher. The next day, December 17, 1881, on the sidewalk in front of the Opera House, Talbot began firing at Wilson and Meagher with a Winchester and hit Meagher with a slug that went through the lawman's right arm and both his lungs, then out the other side. Some friends helped Meagher get inside a barbershop, where he died about 30 minutes later after saying, "Tell my wife I have got it at last." (See also TALBOT, JIM.)

MEDICINE LODGE, TREATY OF
In the summer of 1867 the Comanche, Kiowa and Kiowa-Apache engaged in negotiations with the United States government that gave them a reservation in Indian Territory between the Washita and Red Rivers; it covered about three million acres. The Cheyenne and Arapaho received about four million acres immediately north. As part of the deal, the government agreed to provide the Native Americans with plenty of food, clothing and other supplies; the Indians retained the right to hunt buffalo anywhere south of the Arkansas River. This treaty was enacted just after Congress established the Indian Peace Commission and ended warfare on the central plains.

MEEK, JOE
(b. Joseph Lafayette Meek in Virginia on February 7, 1810; d. Oregon on June 20, 1875)
Joe Meek was a jovial, well-humored mountain man who trapped with Jim Bridger and Kit Carson. He became a farmer in the Oregon country in the 1840s after the trapping business declined and was elected to the legislature. He became famous in Washington, D.C. when he arrived there in 1848 as "Envoy Extraordinary and Minister Plenipotentiary from the Republic of Oregon to the Court of the United States" to request protection from the U.S. government against the British for settlers in the Oregon area. Later Congress created an Oregon Territory, and Meek served there as a United States marshal.

MEEKER MASSACRE
(September 29, 1879)
The Ute Indians rebelled against Indian agent Nathan C. Meeker of the White River Agency in Colorado because he tried to turn the nomadic tribe into farmers. Meeker, aware of the danger of the Indian uprising, sent for military aid, and Major T. T. Thornburgh arrived with 150 soldiers, but they were stopped by the Ute about 25 miles from the White River Agency at Milk Creek. There, the soldiers were pinned down for six days. On the same day the soldiers were stopped, a group of Ute killed Meeker and his staff of eight and carried off three women (including Meeker's wife and daughter) and raped them. Eventually, Ute chief Ouray brought an end to the conflict and the women were returned. But the government exacted its revenge on the Ute, whose actions just three years after the Custer massacre kept the hostilities toward Indians at fever pitch. For their actions, all treaty rights with the Ute were canceled, they were removed from their tribal homelands (12 million acres of rich land coveted by white settlers) and were relocated on a barren reservation in Utah.

MELDRUM, BOB
(b. New York in 1865; d, ?)
Bob Meldrum worked with a man named Wilkinson as a harness maker in Dixon, Wyoming. One day the two men went to the post office, where Meldrum received a notice for a reward on Wilkinson—dead or alive. Meldrum quickly put the notice in his pocket, and the two men walked outside, across a field, where Meldrum pulled out a .44 Colt and plugged Wilkinson in the back of the head, later collecting the reward.

MEN FROM SHILOH, THE
During the last season of the TV show "The Virginian" (1970–71), it was retitled "The Men from Shiloh," and Colonel Alan MacKenzie took over ownership of the Shiloh Ranch. James Drury starred as the Virginian, with Lee Majors as Roy Tate and John McLiam as Parker. This was the eighth, and last, year for "The Virginian" show, which remained a 90-minute series. The final show aired on September 8, 1971 still in its time slot on Wednesdays on CBS. (See VIRGINIAN, THE [TV show].)

MESA
An area of land that is flat; a plateau.

MESQUITE
A tree with a short trunk, often with a V fork and low branches. It has thorns and thick twigs that are eaten by cattle. The tree flowers several times: in April after the winter, in June and July and sometimes in the fall. The tree belongs to the locust family.

MEXICAN WAR, THE
In the early 1800s Mexico extended into what is now the western United States, including Texas, Arizona, New Mexico, California, Kansas, Oklahoma, Wyoming, Colorado, Nevada and Utah. In the area that is now Texas a number of settlers from the United States arrived and began establishing homesteads. In 1835 the American settlers revolted against the Mexican government; basically, they wanted Texas to become part of the United States.

Mexican general Antonio Lopez de Santa Anna marched his army north in March 1936 and at the Battle of the Alamo defeated the Texas forces. However, the Texans organized an army and inspired by cries of "Remember the Alamo" defeated Santa Anna in August in San Jacinto near present-day Houston. The army, led by Sam Houston, won the battle against superior forces in 18 minutes when it caught the Spanish force taking an afternoon siesta. Santa Anna was captured disguised as a pauper and released with the agreement that he would accept Texas as a republic. At this point "Texas" included the present area of Texas as well as Colorado, Kansas, New Mexico, Oklahoma and Wyoming. Meanwhile the Mexican government in Mexico City refused to recognize Santa Anna's treaty and removed him from office.

President James Polk had declared that he would like to see Texas as part of the United States, despite Mexican objections and threats of war if the United States chose to annex the area. Texas became part of the United States in 1845 without a war, but there were still border disputes—the United States wanted the Rio Grande to be the border, whereas Mexico wanted the border farther north at the Nueces River. Americans were also upset at the loss of land and property in Texas because of revolutions in Mexico and wanted Mexico to pay these debts. Further, Americans had begun to believe in "Manifest Destiny," the idea that it was their right to extend the nation from sea to sea and that Americans were destined to settle the West as they had settled the East. This climate led to the Mexican War, which began in April 1846 when American and Mexican forces clashed.

The Mexican War made a hero of General Zachary Taylor and led him to become president of the United States in the next election. Taylor took his forces from the Nueces River to the Rio Grande in April 1846, prompting the Mexican army to stop him. Back in Washington, President Polk had already decided to declare war on Mexico and just needed a reason for doing so; the defeat of a small U.S. cavalry unit by the Mexicans gave him that excuse, saying Mexico had invaded United States territory and shed American blood on American soil—even though Mexico had as much claim to the territory in question as the United States did.

The United States wanted to use its superior power to force Mexico's hand on several issues, the most important of which was the acquisition of land claimed by Mexico in what is now the southwestern United States. Brigadier General Stephen W. Kearny led a revolt in California after he had taken control of New Mexico. California declared its independence from Mexico in 1846 after U.S. naval forces, under Commodore John D. Sloat, occupied San Francisco after capturing Monterey; Kearny defeated the Mexicans near San Diego at the Battle of San Pasqual; and the Battle of San Gabriel, near Los Angeles, was won in January 1847 by Kearny and Commodore Robert F. Stockton.

Meanwhile, in Texas General Taylor occupied Matamoros after two battles there. He then marched his army south and occupied Monterey, then Saltillo and Victoria after battles, but the Mexicans refused to negotiate because their government was divided, and each side feared political reprisals for "caving in" to American demands.

The breakthrough in the war occurred when Polk decided to put American troops under the command of General Winfield Scott, send them to Veracruz and march toward Mexico City. President Santa Anna commanded the Mexican army and was badly defeated. In the Battle of Chapultepec a number of young boys in military school threw themselves over a cliff to their deaths rather than surrender. A monument to the boy heroes now stands outside Mexico City at the foot of Chapultepec Hill in their honor.

The Mexican War ended with the Treaty of Guadalupe Hidalgo, which was signed in February 1848. At first, Mexico would not negotiate with the Americans, even after American troops occupied Mexico City, but Mexico finally established a new government after Santa Anna resigned.

With the treaty the United States acquired California, Nevada, Utah, Arizona and parts of Colorado, New Mexico and Wyoming. In addition, Mexico recognized Texas as part of the United States, and the Rio Grande as its southern border. For this the United States gave Mexico $15 million. In 1853 the United States paid Mexico $10 million for the Gadsden Purchase, which included southern Arizona and New Mexico and established the southern and western borders of the United States.

The Mexican War had another significant impact on the United States: the territory acquired during the War led to the inevitable question of slavery in new states. Southern legislators felt they would lose their power and influence—and that slavery would be abolished and cause economic ruin in their area—if future states were non-slave states. Abolitionist territory here would also upset the balance of power in Congress. In political compromises, they agreed to "popular sovereignty," which meant each state could decide whether to be a slave state or not. But popular sovereignty led to bitter disagreements—especially during the Kansas-Nebraska conflict—which ultimately led to the Civil War.

It was also during the Mexican War that military leaders who would later be the leaders during the Civil War were tried and tested. Among those who served in the Mexican War who later played a major role in the Civil War were Ulysses S. Grant, Robert E. Lee, Jefferson Davis, William Tecumseh Sherman, George Gordon Meade, George B. McClellan and Thomas "Stonewall" Jackson. (See also GADSDEN PURCHASE; GUADALUPE HIDALGO, TREATY OF; MEXICO; SANTA ANNA.)

MEXICO   At one time Mexico owned most of the western United States. This area included the Southwest and what is now California, Texas, New Mexico, Arizona, Colorado, Nevada, Utah and the Louisiana Purchase area. The area of the Louisiana Purchase, encompassing most of the middle of the country, was ceded by Spain to France with the agreement that France would not sell it to the United States. However, Napoleon, short on money from his European wars, reneged on this agreement and sold this area in 1803.

The contemporary history of Mexico generally begins in 1519 when the Spanish conqueror Hernando Cortes defeated large native armies after he landed with a contingent of 650 Spaniards and conquered the territory for Spain. He called the area "New Spain." However, there were people living in Mexico ("Indians" and unknown tribes) more than 10,000 years before this invasion, and the people Cortes conquered, the Aztecs, had a great empire at the time.

Actually, there were several great empires established by natives before the Spaniards arrived. Between 1200 B.C. and 400 B.C. the Olmec Indians developed a calendar and a counting system. The "classic period" of Mexican Indians occurred about A.D. 300–900, when the Maya Indians constructed beautiful temples, pyramids and houses and developed a kind of picture writing to record their history and events. This period was followed by an empire established by the Toltec Indians, fierce warriors who made their capital just north of present Mexico City.

In the 1400s the Aztec Indians established the last—and greatest—Indian empire. These people were highly skilled artisans and made great advances in poetry, music and medicine. The Aztecs believed in human sacrifice, and each year a number of prisoners captured in wars were sacrificed to their gods. Their capital was Tenochtitlan, which was established during the mid-1300s on an island in the middle of Lake Texoco, at the site of the present-day Mexico City. About 100,000 people were living in this city in 1519 when the Spaniards arrived—more people in a city than the Spaniards had ever seen.

The Spaniards had established a colony in Cuba in 1511. In 1517 the governor of Cuba, Diego Velazquez, sent ships west under Francisco Fernandez de Cordoba to look for treasure. Cordoba discovered the Yucantan Peninsula and reported large cities in Mexico. In 1518 Juan de Grijalva was sent to explore the Mexican coast.

The Aztec emperor, Montezuma II (sometimes known as "Moctezuma" II), heard reports of the Spanish explorers with their guns and horses and soldiers dressed in armor. When Cortes landed in 1519, he defeated Aztec armies with horses and cannons, which the Aztecs had never seen. Montezuma sent rich gifts to Cortes, but Cortes marched on the capital, joined by numerous tribal enemies of the Aztecs. Fearing Cortes was a god, Montezuma did not oppose him, and thus the Spanish captured the country despite overwhelming numbers against them. Montezuma was then held hostage by Cortes.

Cortes first conquered Tenochtitlan in November 1519; in June 1520 the Aztecs revolted and drove the Spaniards out. But in May 1521 Cortes attacked the city, nearly destroyed it completely and killed thousands of Aztecs. The city surrendered in August 1521, and from that point the Aztecs never threatened the Spanish again.

The Spanish king, Charles I, granted huge estates to Cortes and other military conquerors, a Spanish tradition that led to Central and South America being dominated by a few rich people holding vast tracts of land over a very large class of poor people. This basic economic structure still survives in a number of Spanish-language countries today.

Cortes was named governor and captain general of New Spain in 1522; however the king did not trust Cortes and sought to limit his powers, appointing a Council of the Indies in 1524 to make laws for the Spanish colonies and establishing a court of judges in 1527 to govern the country. In 1535 the first viceroy, or king's representative, was sent to head the government of New Spain. This Spanish nobleman was Antonio de Mendoza.

During this period the political power was held in Spain, and those born in Spain were the ruling class. The "Creoles" were people of Spanish ancestry born in the New World; they could hold government or church posts, but not very important ones. The "mestizos," or people of mixed Spanish and Indian ancestry, were the laborers, farmers and craft workers while the Indians or natives either lived in their own villages or worked on estates as slaves. In addition, a number of black slaves were brought from Africa.

The Spanish were Roman Catholics, and as early as the 1520s there were priests establishing missions, building churches and converting the native population to Catholicism. In fact, it was the Catholic priests who first established missions in advance of settlers in what is now California, Texas, Arizona and the rest of the Southwest.

New Spain lived in relative peace for almost 300 years, or until 1810, when a revolt, fueled by the ideas of the French and American Revolutions and the political instability in Europe (France had invaded Spain in 1808), occurred. The Mexican War of Independence began late at night on September 15, 1810 when Miguel Hidalgo y Costilla, a Creole priest, demanded independence from Spanish rule after calling Indians and mestizos into church in the town of Dolores. The next day, armed with clubs, knives, axes and anything else they could get their hands on, the untrained followers marched across estates and cities until Father Hidalgo controlled much of New Spain. However, the Spanish troops captured Hidalgo and executed him in 1811. Then another priest, Jose Maria Morelos y Pavon, took up the struggle and organized a trained army that captured Acapulco in 1813 and declared Mexico an independent nation and organized a government.

Morelos outlined a series of reforms that included breaking up the large estates; however, many of Morelos's followers turned against him, and the Spanish forces won some important victories in 1814. In 1815 Morelos was captured and shot while most of the nation swore allegiance to the king of Spain, Ferdinand VII. However, September 15 and 16 are considered "Independence Days" for Mexico, and today the Mexican president rings the "Liberty Bell" late at night on September 15, and Independence Day celebrations are held on September 16.

There was a revolt in Spain in 1520 that caused Ferdinand to accept a constitution that limited his powers. The idea that reforms would be enacted caused the wealthy landowners and other conservatives to develop a plan for independence that would allow them to keep their positions and privileges. In February 1821 Mexico was created as an independent nation after revolutionary leader Vicente Guerrero and Spanish military leader Agustin de Iturbide joined forces to form a new government. There was now a division within the new government: Liberals wanted a republic, but the conservatives wanted a king from a member of Spain's royal family. Instead, Iturbide seized power and was declared Emperor Agustin I in 1822. Iturbide was driven from power in 1823 by General Antonio Lopez de Santa Anna, a former army officer, who eventually headed the government several times.

Mexico officially became a republic when a federalist constitution was completed in 1824, and a two-house Congress was established. Guadalupe Victoria was elected to be the first president of Mexico. But power struggles dominated Mexican government throughout the mid-1800s, and Santa Anna became the leading political figure by switching his loyalty from one group to another. Finally, he assumed the powers of a dictator.

In 1846 the United States waged war on Mexico over a border dispute. Mexico was finally defeated when U.S. forces captured Mexico City. At this time Mexico ceded what is now the southwest area of the U.S. to the U.S. government.

After the Mexican War there was a period of turmoil. Santa Anna gained power again before being ousted a final time in 1855, when liberal reforms ended his dictatorship, created a new constitution for a federal system of government and promoted the private ownership of land. The liberals were headed by Benito Juarez, who became president during the War of the Reform, a civil war between conservatives and liberals. The war left Mexico broke, and it consequently stopped payments for debts to France, Great Britain and Spain. As a result, the three nations sent troops to occupy Veracruz in 1862. The British and Spanish soon left, but the French army, under Emperor Napoleon III, invaded and conquered Mexico during this time. Napoleon then named Maximilian, brother of the Austrian emperor, to be emperor of Mexico in 1864.

Because the United States was involved in its own civil war during this time, it offered no help. However, after the Civil War the United States pressured France to leave Mexico. Pressure from the United States and the situation in Europe—Napoleon feared war was inevitable between France and Prussia and needed his troops in Europe—caused the French troops to leave Mexico in 1867. Without protection of the French soldiers, Maximilian was captured and shot by Juarez's forces, and Mexico united behind the liberals. Juarez died in 1872, at which time his Reform Laws became part of the constitution.

Political instability followed, and after the 1876 election a mestizo general, Porfirio Diaz, led a revolt that established a dictatorship. Diaz held office until 1911, with no opposition to his "elections," although opposition to his rule began around 1900. Diaz was responsible for Mexico's economy improving, and a number of mines, oil wells and railroads were built. But most Mexicans were kept in poverty and ignorance; the benefits of the economic gains went primarily to large landowners, businessmen and foreign investors.

In 1910 a liberal landowner, Francisco Madero, ran against Diaz; Diaz had his opponent thrown in jail. Diaz "won" the election and Madero fled to the United States; however, in November 1910 Madero called for a revolution. Guerrilla bands defeated federal troops, attacked towns and estates and destroyed railroads. Finally, in May 1911 Diaz was forced to resign and leave Mexico as Madero became president. The new president only lasted until 1913, when he was shot after General Victoriano Huerta seized power.

Huerta established a dictatorship that United States president Woodrow Wilson refused to recognize. Instead, Wilson sided with Venustiana Carranza, a landowner who attracted Madero's followers. In 1914 the United States forces seized Veracruz after some American sailors were arrested. Later that year Huerta was forced to leave the country, and Carranza's forces occupied Mexico City. But dissension among the victors caused a split that saw Francisco "Pancho" Villa and Emiliana Zapata challenge Carranza's rule. Pancho Villa raided Columbus, New Mexico in 1916 and killed 16 Americans, after the United States stopped the export of guns to Carranza's enemies. This led President Wilson to send General John J. Pershing to Mexico to capture Villa, but he failed to apprehend the Mexican revolutionary.

Carranza, like Madero, was killed during a revolt led by an army leader. This happened in 1920 when General Alvaro Obregon led a revolt; later he would become president. (See also LOUISIANA PURCHASE; MEXICAN WAR; SANTA ANNA.)

MIDDLETON, JOHN (b. ?; d. May 1885)
Middleton was in the Lincoln County War in New Mexico in 1878. He had been hired by John Tunstall and was near the rancher when a posse killed him. Along with Billy the Kid, Middleton was part of the "Regulators," the group aligned with Alexander McSween, who killed Frank Baker, Billy Morton and William McCloskey and, with Billy the Kid, was one of the ambushers who killed Sheriff William Brady and Deputy George Hindman. At the shootout at Blazer's Mill, Middleton was wounded. Later he was involved with Belle Starr in Oklahoma but was killed in the spring of 1885 by an ambush. (See also LINCOLN COUNTY WAR; STARR, BELLE.)

MILES, NELSON APPLETON (b. near Westminster, Massachusetts, on August 8, 1839; d. Washington, D.C. on May 25, 1925). General Nelson Miles was a relentless, aggressive, effective Indian fighter during the Indian Wars in the 1870s and 1880s. Miles had gone west as head of the Fifth Infantry after serving in the Civil War. His column of infantry and cavalry defeated the Comanche, Kiowa and Cheyenne in the Red River War of 1874–75. In 1876 he helped quell the Sioux nation in Montana after the Custer massacre, and the following year he chased the Nez Perce in the northwest and forced Chief Joseph to surrender just 30 miles from the Canadian border. Miles became commander of the Department of Arizona, succeeding General George Crook, and began his pursuit of Geronimo and his renegade Apache, who surrendered to Miles on September 4, 1886 in Skeleton Canyon, Arizona. During the ghost dance controversy, Miles was commander of field operations when the Sioux were slaughtered at Wounded Knee in December 1890. Convinced his officers committed a major blunder in killing women and children, Miles ordered a court of inquiry. Miles became commanding general of the army in 1895, his life's ambition. He died at the age of 86.

MILLER, ALFRED JACOB See ART.

MILLER, CLELLAND (b. Lincoln County, Missouri on December 16, 1849; d. Northfield, Minnesota on September 7, 1876.) Clell Miller was in the James

General Nelson Miles (*Library of Congress*)

boys rode with Quantrill) and because Miller and the James boys lived fairly close. Miller probably took part in robberies in Otterville, Missouri and Corydon, Iowa before he was killed in Minnesota. (See also JAMES, FRANK; JAMES, JESSE; NORTHFIELD, MINNESOTA RAID; YOUNGER, COLE.)

MILLER, HENRY (b. Heinrich Kreiser in Brackenheim, Wurttemberg, Germany on July 21, 1827; d. San Francisco on October 14, 1916)   Henry Miller became the largest landowner and cattle rancher in northern California in the 19th century. Miller was widely known as an unscrupulous businessman, unpleasant and interested solely in himself and his holdings. He had moved to the United States in 1847 and first worked as a butcher in New York; in 1850 he changed his name to Miller and moved to San Francisco, where he operated a butcher business until 1857. With Charlie Lux, another butcher, Miller went into the cattle business in 1857, and in 1863 the two purchased a ranch in the San Joaquin Valley of California; eventually Miller would control more than 15 ranches, covering over 800,000 acres in the Pacific area. With these ranches and others in Oregon and Nevada, Miller had over 80,000 cattle and 100,000 sheep. After Lux died in 1887, Miller was involved in a 20-year court battle with his heirs. Miller incorporated as the Pacific Livestock Company and controlled a million cattle with this company. He also built irrigation systems and storage dams in the San Joaquin Valley and farmed about 500,000 acres there.

MILLER, KILLIN' JIM   (aka "Killer Miller" and "Deacon "; b. James B. Miller in Van Buren, Arkansas on October 24, 1866; d. Ada, Oklahoma on April 19, 1909)   Killin' Jim Miller was one of the most ruthless, cold-blooded killers in the history of the West; he is the man who shot Pat Garrett in the back. A church deacon who served as a gun for hire, Miller finally met his match when he ran up against an angry necktie party. Killin' Jim started killing early: When he was eight, his grandparents were murdered, and he was arrested, but never prosecuted, for the crime. He had been sent to live with them after the death of his parents. Miller was then sent to live with his sister and her husband, J. E. Coop, and killed Coop at 17 while he was asleep on his porch. Miller was found guilty but was released on a legal technicality.

Miller worked for Manny Clements and ambushed Clements's killer. In 1891 he married Manny's daughter, Sallie Clements, and became a devout Methodist, earning the nickname Deacon Jim. Miller had been a deputy sheriff of Reeves County and then town marshal of Pecos. Pecos sheriff Bud Frazer and Miller had a feud over a pair of mules Miller stole. Frazer tried to kill Miller twice, but Miller was saved by a steel plate he wore on his chest. Finally Miller murdered Frazer but was acquitted; he then killed Joe Earp in an ambush because Earp had testified against him. The district attorney who prosecuted Miller, Judge Stanley, died mysteriously in Memphis, Texas, and it was suspected that Miller had put arsenic in his food. Miller joined the Texas Rangers; in 1900 he moved to Fort Worth, where he became

Gang and was killed in the Northfield, Minnesota robbery on September 7, 1876. Miller and Cole Younger were outside the First National Bank when Miller moved to close the bank door during the robbery. But this alerted J. S. Allen, owner of the hardware store. Miller ordered Allen to get away from the bank, and Allen left yelling, "Get your guns, boys! They're robbing the bank!" Shooting then began inside the bank as citizens outside the bank, who had heard the warning, also began firing. Miller managed to get on his horse despite being hit in the face with birdshot from citizen Elias Stacy but was killed when young medical student Henry Wheeler shot him out of the saddle from a second-story window. Miller probably knew the James brothers from his days as a Civil War guerrilla fighter with Bloody Bill Anderson (the James widely known as a killer for hire who charged $150 per victim. In between killings he spoke at prayer meetings. Killin' Jim killed many men—but seldom face to face.

Lubbock lawyer James Jarrott was "the hardest damn man to kill [he] ever tackled" said Miller. Jarrott had won several cases on behalf of local nesters, so Miller was hired by cattlemen to kill the attorney for $500. As usual, Miller ambushed his victim while Jarrott was watering his horses. The first rifle shot hit Jarrott in the chest, but the attorney managed to get on his hands and knees, and Miller then shot him in the neck and shoulder—but it would take two more shots before Miller was sure Jarrott was killed. Miller also killed U.S. deputy marshal Ben Collins in an ambush after the lawman had shot and partially paralyzed Port Pruit. The Pruitt family had hired Miller for revenge.

Miller's most famous killing was Sheriff Pat Garrett, who was urinating at the time. The event occurred February 29, 1908 about four miles outside Las Cruces, New Mexico while rancher Garrett was with two neighboring ranchers, Wayne Brazel and Carl Adamson. When Garrett stepped out of the buggy to relieve himself, Miller ambushed him with a .45 bullet in the back of his head and then another shot in the belly when the former lawman turned around. For some reason Brazel confessed to the killing—although he had probably been the one who hired Miller.

The end for Miller came over a hired killing in Ada, Oklahoma. Three cattlemen hired Miller to kill rancher Gus Bobbitt; Miller hid near Bobbitt's house and then killed Bobbitt with a shotgun when he drove up in a supply wagon. Miller—who always hightailed it after a killing to create an alibi, once even galloping all night to cover 100 miles—went to Fort Worth but was extradited. Miller and the three cattlemen were hung in an Ada livery stable two months after the killing, on April 19. Just before being hung, Miller calmly asked to have his hat placed on his head. (See also FRAZER, BUD; GARRETT, PAT; HARDIN, JOHN WESLEY.)

MILLER BROTHERS' 101 RANCH AND WILD WEST SHOW
The 101 Ranch was founded near Ponca City, Oklahoma by George W. Miller in 1892. At the Jamestown Exposition of 1907 it presented its "Wild West" show and developed into a traveling rodeo that featured such stars as champion woman rider Tad Lucas; Suicide Ted Elder, who rode two horses standing while they leaped over an automobile, and Bill Pickett, the black cowboy who "invented" bulldogging. During the 1920s a tremendous surge in the popularity of rodeos provided a comeback for the Miller Brothers' show which, like most Wild West shows, had declined after World War I. The show folded in 1931, although Zack Miller, the last surviving brother, attempted to revive the show later.

MILLHOUSE, FROG   See BURNETTE, SMILEY.

MILNER, MOSES   See CALIFORNIA JOE.

MINNESOTA MASSACRE   (1862)   The Santee Sioux had ceded their lands to the federal government in exchange for government annuities, supplies and other benefits. But the provisions somehow did not always arrive. When the hungry Santee Sioux pleaded with Indian agent Andrew Myrick for food, he replied, "Let them eat grass or their own dung." This caused the tribe, led by Chief Little Crow, to go on the warpath, loot the agency store and kill Myrick and then stuff his mouth with grass. The Indians then spread out to the surrounding settlements and killed 644 whites. The Indians killed 757 soldiers when the army came against them before they were subdued, and 30 Indians were hanged in December 1862 in the town of Mankato. Little Crow escaped this hanging but was killed by a white settler on July 3, 1863. Because of this uprising, the government moved the Santee Sioux to a reservation in Dakota Territory and confiscated all the Indians' annuities and lands.

MISSISSIPPI RIVER   The Mississippi River is the natural division between "East" and "West" in the United States. This great river begins at Lake Itasca in northern Minnesota and flows for almost 2,500 miles to the Gulf of Mexico. Approximately 250 tributaries flow into the river; the four principal ones are the Missouri, the Arkansas, the Red and the Ohio Rivers. The first white person to "discover" the Mississippi was Spanish explorer Hernando de Soto in 1541 near Memphis, Tennessee. De Soto was buried in the Mississippi. French explorers Father Jacques Marquette and Louis Jolliet traveled down the river in canoes to the mouth of the Arkansas River in 1673, and Rene LaSalle, another French explorer, traveled the river from Illinois to the Gulf of Mexico. Henry R. Schoolcraft discovered the origin of the Mississippi River in 1832.

MISSOURI RIVER   Known as the "Big Muddy" because its powerful currents carry so much dirt and silt (the river was characterized by early immigrants to the West as being "too thick to drink, too thin to plow"), the Missouri River was the water highway to the West. The longest river in the United States (2,700 miles), the river begins in Montana in the Rocky Mountains at the confluence of the Jefferson, Madison and Gallatin Rivers. First explored by whites when Frenchmen Jacques Marquette and Louis Joliet explored the Mississippi in 1673, the Missouri is the principal reason St. Louis became the center of the fur trade. The first whites to explore the upper parts of the Missouri were Merriwether Lewis and William Clark during their 1804–6 expedition.

MITCHELL, WADDIE   (b. Elko, Nevada on August 22, 1950)   Waddie Mitchell began writing cowboy poetry as a teenager and continued while he worked on a 3,600-acre ranch. In 1984 he and Hal Cannon began the Elko Cowboy Poetry Gathering, which has become a major event for cowboy poets; later he became emcee for Michael Martin Murphey's "West Fests." Mitchell's first book, *Waddie Mitchell's Christmas Poems*, was published in 1987, followed by *The Cowboy's Night before Christmas* in 1991. In addition he recorded several several albums for Warner Brothers, including "Buckaroo Poet and "Lone Driftin' Rider." Mitchell was an

Waddie Mitchell *(GM Records)*

turned to touring, creating the Tom Mix Circus. Mix's last film role was in *The Miracle Ride,* a serial from Mascot. He continued to tour in personal appearances and in 1938 merged his circus with the Sells-Floto Circus. Mix was killed in a car crash on U.S. Highway 80 after a performance in Tucson.

MOCCASIN Indian shoes that came in a wide variety of designs—from tall boots to smaller slipperlike shoes and from plain deerskin to some ornately designed. Moccasins were preferred by a number of white mountain men because they protected the feet from frostbite better, especially when stuffed with deer hide and dried leaves.

MODOC INDIANS Originally from northern California, the Modoc are interesting because they were slave traders, capturing the Digger Indians from the deserts in California and Nevada and selling them as slaves to the wealthy northwestern tribes. The Modoc were moved to the Klamath Indian reservation in Oregon in 1864 after reluctantly ceding their lands to the federal government. This led to the Modoc War (1872–73) when their leader Captain Jack ("Kintpuash" or "Kientpoos") led them off the reservation because of conflicts with the Klamath tribe. The army was called in to force them back, but Captain Jack and his followers took refuge in

original inductee into the Cowboy Poets and Singers Hall of Fame.

MIX, TOM (b. Thomas Edwin Mix in Mix Run, Pennsylvania on January 6, 1881; d. near Tucson, Arizona on October 12, 1940) A genuine movie legend, Tom Mix, more than any other early cowboy star, brought glitz and glamour to the movie cowboy and became the major cowboy star of the silent era. He did this through his good looks, his sharp, fancy clothes and his horses Tony and Tony, Jr., which were trained to do a variety of tricks and were as well attired as Tom. Mix studied at Virginia Military Institute and was in the Spanish-American War; he also served in the Philippines, China and South Africa, where he trained horses for the British during the Boer War. He worked for the Miller Brothers' 101 Ranch in Oklahoma beginning in 1909 and competed in rodeos; in 1909 and 1911 he won the National Riding Championship in Prescott, Arizona. In 1910 Mix made his first movie appearance in *Ranch Life in the Great Southwest* and then made short one- and two-reel films for the next seven years for Selig. In 1918 he signed a contract with Fox, for which he created action-packed adventure in his cowboy movies and did his own stunt work; by 1921 Mix's fan club had two million members, and he replaced William S. Hart as the top cowboy star. The end of the silent era almost ended Tom Mix's career; in 1929 he left the movies and starred in the Sells-Floto Circus and Wild West Show. But he returned to Universal in 1932 for a series of westerns, beginning with *Destry Rides Again.* After nine features, he again re-

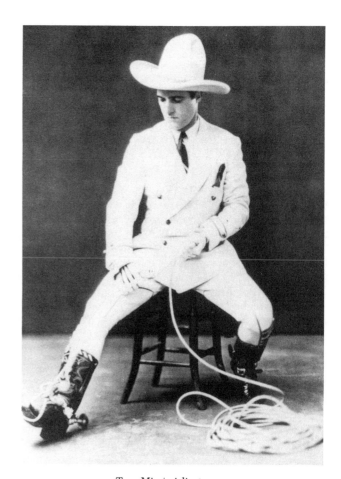

Tom Mix twirling rope

the Lava Beds on the Oregon-California border. These beds, full of caves and natural trenches, proved almost impregnable for months. Finally, after their surrender, Captain Jack and four others were hung on October 3, 1873 at Fort Klamath, and the rest of the tribe was sent to an Indian Territory (Oklahoma) reservation.

MONROES, THE   TV show that starred Michael Anderson, Jr. as Clayt Monroe, Barbara Hershey as Kathy Monroe, Keith Schultz as Jefferson Monroe, Kevin Schultz as Fennimore Monroe, Tammy Locke as Amy Monroe, Liam Sullivan as Major Mapoy, Ron Soble as Dirty Jim, Ben Johnson as Sleeve, Jim Westmoreland as Ruel Jaxon, Robert Middleton as Barney Wales and Buck Taylor as John Bradford ("Brad").

After their parents drowned, these five Monroe orphans (ages 6–18) attempted to establish a homestead in Wyoming Territory in 1876. With their dog Snow and an unlikely ally in the character of renegade Indian Dirty Jim, they fought the efforts of British cattle baron Major Mapoy to run them off their land. The series, which was filmed on location in Grand Teton National Park in Wyoming, debuted on September 7, 1966 on Wednesday evenings on ABC. The hour-long show was last telecast on August 30, 1967.

MONTANA, PATSY   (b. Ruby Blevins near Hot Springs, Arkansas on October 30, 1912)   Patsy Montana is most famous for writing and recording "I Want to Be a Cowboy's Sweetheart," which became the first song to sell over a million copies by a country female artist. The Blevins family had 10 boys and one girl; the girl, Ruby, taught herself to play guitar and moved to California in 1928, where she became enchanted with cowboy music and began performing as "Rubye Blevins, the Yodeling Cowgirl from San Antone" on KMTR in Hollywood. She moved to KMIC in nearby Inglewood in 1930 to join two other girls, Lorraine McIntire and Ruthy DeMondrum, as part of Stuart Hamblen's group. The three girls were called "The Montana Cowgirls," and Rubye changed her name to Patsy to avoid confusion with Ruthy. In 1933 Patsy went back to Arkansas for a

Patsy Montana and Prairie Rose

visit and while there auditioned for the Kentucky Ramblers, members of the WLS "National Barn Dance," who needed a female vocalist. To capitalize on the growing popularity of cowboys and cowboy music, the group changed its name to the Prairie Ramblers. Patsy's theme song was "Montana Plains," written by Stuart Hamblen as "Texas Plains," who did not like anyone tampering with his lyrics. So Patsy wrote "I Want to Be a Cowboy's Sweetheart" for her theme song. She first sang the song on the WLS "Barn Dance," and it soon became popular. Patsy recorded the song in 1935 in New York. (See also I WANT TO BE A COWBOY'S SWEETHEART.)

MONTANA TRAIL   See Texas-Montana Trail.

MONTE   Monte, or "three-card monte," was more sleight of hand than an actual game. It was derived from the shell game of three walnut shells and a pea; the shells were manipulated until the shuffler slipped the pea out. Three-card monte was played with two insignificant cards along with a face card or ace, called a "baby." A professional gambler would put the three cards facedown and move them around and then bet the onlooker he could not pick the "baby." Of course, the gambler had slipped the "baby" out and replaced it with another card. (See also GAMBLING.)

MONUMENT VALLEY   Although this area has no particular importance in the history of the West, it has become famous because it was the location for a number of movies, particularly those directed by John Ford. These movies include *Stagecoach, My Darling Clementine, She Wore a Yellow Ribbon, The Searchers, How the West Was Won* and *Cheyenne Autumn.* Monument Valley is located on the Arizona-Utah border and is part of the Navajo Indian reservation.

MOORE, CLAYTON   (b. Chicago, Illinois on September 14, 1914)   Clayton Moore starred as TV's "Lone Ranger" from 1949 to 1956 in 221 half-hour episodes, except for one brief season (26 episodes) when he was replaced by John Hart. (Moore left the role because of a contract dispute; he had a weekly salary of less than $500 per show, and the producer would not raise it.) Moore had starred in several Republic series during the 1940s, including *Perils of Nyoka* (1942), *The Crimson Ghost* (1946), *Jesse James Rides Again* (1947), *The Adventures of Frank and Jesse James* (1948) and *G-Men Never Forget* (1948).

Born and raised in Chicago, Moore worked as a model after high school and then became part of a flying-trapeze act in a traveling circus. He moved to Hollywood in 1938 and worked odd jobs while trying to get work in the movies. During World War II Moore was a pilot in the air force. After the war he worked as a stuntman and extra and played the "heavy" in films starring Gene Autry, Roy Rogers and Charles Starrett; he also appeared as a trapeze artist in the Rex Allen film *Down Laredo Way* (1953). After "The Lone Ranger" TV series ended, Moore remained under contract to appear as the Lone Ranger, starring in Dodge commercials. In 1979 a court ordered him to make no more appearances as the

Clayton Moore

Lone Ranger, and he had to wear special sunglasses instead of a mask at personal appearances. Western movies Clayton Moore appeared in include:

Kit Carson (1940)
Along the Oregon Trail (1947)
The Cowboy and the Indians (1949)
Riders of the Whistling Pines (1949)
The Ghost of Zorro (1949)
Montana (1950)
Cyclone Fury (1951)
Buffalo Bill in Tomahawk Territory (1952)
Night Stage to Galveston (1952)
Montana Territory (1952)
Barbed Wire (1952)
Son of Geronimo (1952)
Hawk of Wild River (1952)
Kansas Pacific (1953)
Down Laredo Way (1953)
Black Dakotas (1954)
Gunfighters of the Northwest (1954)
The Lone Ranger (1956)
The Lone Ranger and the Lost City of Gold (1958)

(See also LONE RANGER, THE (TV SHOW); SILVERHEELS, JAY; TELEVISION WESTERNS.)

MOOSE   The largest deer in North America, the moose *(Alces americanus)* grows to seven feet tall at the shoulders and weighs 900–1,500 pounds; a bull moose's horns spread to six feet. Moose feed on twigs, and the term "moose" comes from the Algonquian word meaning "twig eater." An excellent swimmer, the moose prefers water plants in summer, which it eats while standing partially submerged in water, and eats tree bark in winter. It can be hostile and aggressive if cornered or bothered at the wrong time. Indians ground up moose antlers and horns for medicines. The nickname "Moose" was often applied to large men in the West.

MORAN, THOMAS   See ART.

MORCO, HAPPY JACK   (b. John Morco; d. Ellsworth, Kansas on September 4, 1873)   Happy Jack killed four unarmed men who had come to his wife's aid after her screams attracted the men's attention. A drunken Happy Jack was beating Mrs. Morco at the time. Happy Jack then fled to Ellsworth, Kansas, where he became a lawman. Here, Morco got in a fight with brothers Ben and Billy Thompson on August 15, 1873 that ended in the death of Sheriff C. B. Whitney. Because Morco failed to appear the next morning to press charges against the Thompsons, he was dismissed from his job by a motion from the town council but promptly rehired by the next motion. However, two weeks later he was fired permanently and left town with a pair of expensive six-shooters that didn't belong to him. After being relieved of the guns in nearby Salina, Morco returned to Ellsworth, where he was approached by policeman Charlie Brown who ordered him to surrender his gun. Morco went for his pistol instead, but Brown drilled him in the head and heart. (See also THOMPSON, BEN; THOMPSON, TEXAS BILLY; WHITNEY, CAP.)

MORES, MARQUIS DE   See MARQUIS DE MORES

MORGAN   A type of horse developed by Justin Morgan (1747–98) of Massachusetts. These horses were crossed with mustangs and Spanish horses to produce a sturdy, lively breed.

MORMON KID, THE   (aka Matt Warner; b. Willard Erastus Christianson in Ephraim, Utah in 1864; d. Price, Utah on December 21, 1938)   Christianson, known as Matt Warner, came to Utah with his parents as Mormon converts. In 1878 he fell in with some rustlers and became known as the Morman Kid, operating out of Robber's Roost, where he joined up with Butch Cassidy. He served time in the Utah state prison because of a shooting incident in 1896 but was released for good behavior in 1900. He settled in Carbon County, Utah, where he was elected justice of the peace and served as deputy sheriff. He died peacefully at the age of 74.

MORMONS   Religious group that played an integral role in settling the West when its members established Salt Lake City and proved the Great Basin could support a settlement.

The religion, known officially as the Church of Jesus Christ of Latter-Day Saints, began on April 6, 1830 under the leadership of Joseph Smith, Jr. in Fayette, New York. Smith claimed to have received revelations beginning in 1820 including a direct revelation from the angel Moroni in 1827 to translate some plates of gold. This translation was completed in 1829, and the Book of Mormon was published in 1830. The term "Mormon" is the name of a prophet who completed his people's (the Nephites) 1,000-year history.

A year after Smith organized his church in New York, he moved to Kirtland Mills, in the Western Reserve of Ohio, with several hundred followers. Smith intended to establish a spiritual community and moved to Independence, Missouri to do so, although church headquarters initially remained at Kirtland Mills. In Missouri, Smith and the Mormons ran into problems because of their economic unity and success, alien religious practices that included polygamy, and anti-slavery beliefs. Driven from Missouri after he was imprisoned for six months, Smith and his followers built a city north of Quincy, Illinois in 1839 called Nauvoo after the Hebrew word for "beautiful." The church and community grew and thrived, although anti-Mormon feeling also continued to grow, based primarily on opposition to practices of polygamy. Smith was imprisoned in Carthage, Illinois, and on June 27, 1844 a mob broke into the prison and murdered him and his brother Hyrum.

Before Smith's death, the Mormon founder believed the future for the Mormons lay in the unsettled West. When Brigham Young followed Joseph Smith as leader of the Mormon Church, he acted on this vision, and after Nauvoo was bombed and burned by mobs in the winter of 1846, Young and his followers headed west to a temporary settlement near Omaha, Nebraska. After the winter there Young led a group of wagons to the Salt Lake Valley in July 1847 and claimed the site for the Mormons. Originally under Mexican rule, this region became part of the United States when the Treaty of Guadalupe Hidalgo was signed the next year.

The Great Basin, where Salt Lake City is located, is situated in a large valley near the Great Salt Lake. The area was initially considered a wasteland, but Young and his followers began to irrigate the land and plant crops. Young laid out Great Salt Lake City from a plan developed by Joseph Smith in 1833 for a "City of Zion." The streets were 88 feet wide and ran north, east, south and west. There were 10 acres in each block, and a "Temple Block" was designated as the center point.

During the first two years the Mormons suffered, but the gold rush of 1849 brought a number of people through en route to the gold fields. Merchandise and commodities sold well at inflated prices to prospectors, and this set the city on firm economic footing.

A Mormon theocracy was established, and Brigham Young named the area the State of Deseret and petitioned the United States for statehood. The petition was rejected, but the area was given territorial status under the name "Utah." In 1851 Brigham Young was appointed governor of the territory. Young wanted to encourage Mormon settlement in the area and in 1849 set up the Perpetual Emigration Fund to help Mormons relocate. A large number of Mormons came into the region pulling handcarts that held their goods. The

Brigham Young *(Latter-Day Saints)*

emigration program worked well; in 1849 there were only 6,000 settled in the Great Basin, but by 1852 there were over 100,000.

In 1852 the Mormons publicly announced that polygamy was part of their religion; previously they had denied that members engaged in polygamy. Public opposition to the Mormons had centered on their practice of polygamy. Opposition to this practice, and fears that Mormon leaders had too much influence over the citizens, led to the Mormon War (sometimes called the Utah War) from 1857 to 1859. The war began when President James Buchanan removed Brigham Young from his office of governor and sent United States troops to Utah. Mormons believed the troops had come to annihilate them; this led to the Mountain Meadows Massacre. The Mormons cut off supplies to the troops, burned the trading posts at Fort Bridger and Fort Supply, destroyed military supply trains and destroyed forage around the troops. Finally, Mormons evacuated Salt Lake City and were prepared to destroy it, but a reconciliation and pardon from the federal government were accepted by Young on June 12, 1858.

Utah's isolation ended in 1869 when the railroad arrived. This led to a mining boom as more developers settled in the area. By this time, the Mormons were firmly established in the area, and consequently the Gentiles (or non-Mormons) were not a political threat. Mormon polygamy continued unabated until the Supreme Court ruled against it in 1872. The conflict continued, and Utah was not admitted as a state because of the Mormon control. In 1877 Brigham Young died, and in 1882 Congress passed laws against polygamy. At first Mormon leaders continued to argue for polygamy but in 1890 issued a manifesto against it, which led to Utah's admission as a state in 1896. (See also MOUNTAIN MEADOWS MASSACRE; YOUNG, BRIGHAM.)

MORMON WAGON A covered wagon that was used by the Mormons on their trek west to Utah. A bit lighter than a Conestoga, it was sturdy and strong and often had a Morgan brake, an extra log that dropped and provided extra drag when going down a steep hill.

MORSE, HARRY N. (b. New York City on February 22, 1835; d. Oakland, California on January 11, 1912) Harry Morse is the man who captured the outlaw Black Bart. Morse had originally gone to California with the forty-niners to search for gold but did not last long in the gold fields. As a law officer he developed a reputation for tracking killers and then, in 1878, opened a detective agency in San Francisco. He also killed the "Human Wildcat" Juan Soto in Sausalito Valley, California in 1871 after a fierce gunfight. (See also BLACK BART; SOTO, JUAN.)

MOSES, PHOEBE ANN See OAKLEY, ANNIE.

MOSSMAN, BURT (aka "Cap"; b. Burton Mossman near Aurora, Illinois on April 30, 1867; d. Roswell, New Mexico on September 5, 1956) Burt Mossman was the first captain of the Arizona Rangers, formed in 1901 to bring law and order to the southwest territory. Mossman had gone to New Mexico when he was 16 and became manager of a large ranch the Hashknife outfit in 1897. Mossman resigned from the Rangers in 1902 after he caught the Mexican murderer Augustino Chacon, who reportedly killed 52 men (37 of whom were Mexicans). Chacon was captured in Sonoro and brought back across the border and was hung at Solomonville on November 21, 1902. Mossman later turned to ranching and owned the Diamond A Ranch.

MOUNTAIN GOAT Also called a Rocky Mountain goat, goat antelope or antelope goat, the mountain goat (*Oreamnos americanus*) is not really a goat but a relative of the chamois. It stands four feet tall at the shoulder and weighs up to 300 pounds with a long, white shaggy coat (year round) and small horns that stick straight up and curve backward. These animals live in the mountains above the timberline.

MOUNTAIN LION Also called a puma, panther or cougar, the mountain lion (*Felis concolor*) is a large carnivorous cat. It can have a body length of five feet and weigh 100–175 pounds. The mountain lion feeds on deer, elk, bighorn sheep, cattle, horses and other domestic livestock and can leap 25 feet to capture its victim. The high rocky country is the preferred habitat for this short-haired cat. Usually it will not attack humans unprovoked.

MOUNTAIN MEADOWS MASSACRE (September 11, 1857) The Fancher party, a group of 140 settlers from Missouri, was traveling west when they were attacked by Mormons and Indians while crossing southern Utah, and all but 17 small children were killed. These "Missouri Wild Cats" had provoked the Mormons by trampling crops, insulting Mormon women, killing Mormons' chickens and bragging about taking part in the massacre of Mormons 20 years previously in Missouri. The wagon train was first attacked by Indians (at the instigation of Mormons) on September 7; on September 11 John D. Lee led a group of Mormons who approached the group and offered safe passage through the area if the group would give up its weapons. The settlers did so, but the Mormons and Indians then attacked the unarmed party. In 1875 the Mormons brought John Lee to trial and executed him in 1877 on the site of the Mountain Meadows Massacre.

MOUNTAIN MEN The term "mountain men" generally refers to the men who lived in the Rocky Mountains from 1820 to 1840 as trappers and hunters, rugged individuals who trapped beaver and then sold the hides to fur companies. The earliest mountain men were French who actually purchased furs from Indians; later, the British Hudson's Bay Company hired trappers for regular salaries, a method used by the Missouri River entrepreneurs until William H. Ashley revolutionized the fur trade by employing men who would be paid for the furs on an individual basis. Instead of a regular fort, Ashley established a "rendezvous" where the trappers would meet to sell their furs to the highest bidder. The mountain men trapped beavers in streams; once caught, the beaver drowned because he was unable to escape, thus preserving his skin. The trapper skinned the animal and then stretched the fur over a frame, dried and scraped it and then bundled it up in a square with 10 or 20 other skins. Mountain men usually made about $130 a year for trapping. The trapping season was spring and fall, the rendezvous was in the summer, and in the winter the trappers holed up in winter quarters. The mountain man learned to live on his own by himself or with Indians and often married an Indian woman. At the "rendezvous" every year (usually at the Green River in Wyoming) the mountain men would gather for a week-long celebration of drinking and gambling. They would bring their hides to sell to the highest-bidding fur company representative, who would load them up and carry them back East (usually to St. Louis), where the beaver pelts would be sold for hats. Around the 1840s the Rocky Mountain trapping died out because of the drop in demand for beaver hats. Later, many of these mountain men became scouts for the army and guides for settlers. Some of the most famous mountain men are Jim Bridger, Tom "Broken Hand" Fitzpatrick, Caleb Greenwood, Kit Carson, Joe Walker, Jim Beckwourth, Jed Smith, the Sublette Brothers and Joe Meek.

MOUNTAIN SHEEP See BIGHORN SHEEP.

MOVIES The first "feature" movie was a western, The *Great Train Robbery*, filmed in 1903 by Edwin S.

Porter. This movie ran approximately 10 minutes and was filmed on the Delaware and Lackawanna Railroad in New Jersey for Thomas Edison's movie company. Prior to this feature, movies were "shorts" consisting of single scenes. In 1898 there was a three- to four-minute short, *Cripple Creek Bar-Room,* which consisted of some cowboy actors in a saloon, re-creating a vintage western scene. In the 1890s there were also films of Annie Oakley shooting and Buffalo Bill and others with his Wild West shows.

The first person to create a series of western films was Broncho Billy Anderson, who also created the first western hero/character, Broncho Billy. The Broncho Billy films began in 1908 and were finished by 1920. But Billy Anderson did two very important things for westerns: He created the first serial hero, and he moved the western filmmaking business to California when his Essanay Productions began filming in Niles, California, near San Francisco.

The first important director for movies was D. W. Griffith, who is best known for the first movie "classic," *The Birth of a Nation* (1915). Griffith created a number of early breakthroughs in movie making, including the use of closeups, cutaways and editing techniques, with westerns such as *The Last Drop of Water* (1911) and *The Battle of Elderbush Gulch* (1913).

Hollywood, California was established as a center for movie making with the tremendous success of *The Squaw Man,* directed by Cecil B. DeMille, a western released in 1913.

An important early movie executive was Thomas Ince, who created the idea of the movie company and organized movie making and developed a star system. Ince sponsored William S. Hart in a number of influential and popular westerns, and Hart emerged as the first authentic western movie star.

Hart dominated western movies from 1915 to 1925. During this period a number of other actors and directors who would become influential with western films first became involved in the movie industry, including Pete Morrison, Tom Mix, William Duncan, Harry Carey and Roy Stewart. Major movie studios during this time were Essanay, Selig, Triangle, Universal, Biograph, and American.

The movies of William S. Hart were sentimental and romantic but extremely popular with audiences. In fact, westerns in general were popular during the silent era of the 1920s, when they came of age. This is the period of such early classics as the first epic western, *The Covered Wagon* (Famous Players Lasky, 1923); *The Iron Horse* (Fox, 1924), directed by John Ford; *Three Badmen* (Fox, 1926); and *North of '36* (Paramount, 1924).

Also during this period the movie industry began versions of popular western author Zane Grey's books. These movies included *To the Last Man* (Paramount, 1923), *Riders of the Purple Sage* (Fox, 1925), *The Vanishing American* (Paramount, 1925), *The Thundering Herd* (Paramount, 1925), and *Wild Horse Mesa* (Paramount, 1925). Other important movies during this period include *The Pony Express* (Paramount, 1925), *The Flaming Frontier* (Universal, 1926) *Jesse James* (Para-

mount, 1927), *Red Raiders* (First National, 1927), and *The Mysterious Rider* (Paramount, 1927).

After William S. Hart, the next major cowboy star was Tom Mix, who introduced flashy clothes to the silver-screen cowboy's image. While Hart insisted on realism, Mix introduced escapism and the elements of the mythic cowboy: the loner who was clean living and fun loving and who always did the right thing. Although Hart was the first to list his horse (Fritz) in the screen credits, Mix made his horse (Tony) a star. Tony was a talented, unique horse who did a number of fancy tricks in Mix's movies.

Other major stars during this period were Ken Maynard, Harry Carey, Fred Thomson, Tim McCoy, Buck Jones and Hoot Gibson. Female stars included Allene Ray and Ruth Roland.

During the 1920s, as the movies became a major industry, several different types evolved. First were the "feature" or "A" movies, which featured top budgets and top stars. These usually played in major cities and in the best movie houses. Next were "B" movies, which could stand for "budget" or simply a notch below "A." These movies had restricted budgets and often lesser-known actors and actresses. They often played in rural areas and "second-line" movie houses. Finally, there were the "serials," which consisted of a number of chapters with each chapter usually ending in suspense. These serials were shown on Saturdays, with westerns and science fiction working best for this type.

The period 1927–32 was one of transition for the western. First, westerns had suffered a decline in 1926, a result of too many cheap ones being produced. Second, the coming of sound with *The Jazz Singer* in 1927 marked a new era for the movies. At this time, most of the major studios stopped making westerns, and a new group of small, independent studios, called "poverty row" studios or "Gower Gulch," became the dominant makers of westerns.

The first "sound" western was *In Old Arizona* (1929), a Cisco Kid movie starring Warren Baxter. This movie is significant for two reasons: Sound engineers had previously thought it was impossible to record sound for westerns in the wide outdoors; and Baxter won an Academy Award for his role. Other important sound westerns were *The Virginian* (1929), starring Gary Cooper, and *Cimarron* (1931), which won the Academy Award for Best Picture in 1931 and was the most successful western financially during this time.

The sound western did not truly emerge until after 1932, when most of the technical problems had been solved by the sound engineers and movie makers and the movie theaters in the country had all been wired for it. At this point the country was in the grips of the Great Depression, although Hollywood, because of the tremendous success of the movies, seemed immune to these hard times. The Depression hit the South hardest, and that's where the main audience for westerns was. In 1929–31, most westerns were basically silent movies with sound effects added. Also during this period some westerns were released in two versions: one silent and the other with sound.

In addition to the previously mentioned movies, other important films during the 1929–31 period were *The Spoilers* (Paramount, 1930), starring Gary Cooper; *The Big Trail* (Fox, 1930), directed by Raoul Walsh and featuring John Wayne in his first starring role; *Billy the Kid* (MGM, 1930), directed by King Vidor; *The Squaw Man* (MGM, 1931), directed by Cecil B. DeMille; and *Law and Order* (Universal ,1931).

Between 1928 and 1932 the "B" western and the serial were developed and played an increasing role in western movie releases. The "B" features and serials would be the backbone of the western genre for the next 25 years. Indeed, for theatergoers and fans of the western, these "B" westerns and serials had a greater impact than the "A" features simply because there were more of them; thus there was a constant exposure in movie theaters.

In the early 1930s Ken Maynard may have been the most popular cowboy star. His horse, Tarzan, did more amazing tricks and stunts than Tom Mix's "Tony." Hoot Gibson was also extremely popular during this time, as was George O'Brien, Buck Jones, Bob Steele, Tim McCoy and Tom Mix.

The period from 1933 to 1937 has been called the "boom years" for the western because they provided a welcome relief from daily life during the Great Depression. "B" westerns were escapist entertainment, creating a West that never was. Westerns of this period moved from an attempt at realism with the William Hart silents to the pure escapist entertainment of Gene Autry and other singing cowboys.

During the "boom years" about 530 western features were released, and almost 500 of them were "B" movies. In addition, 17 serials were released, accounting for 220 chapters. For fans of the traditional western the big star was Buck Jones, who rode his horse, Silver, in 10 releases for Columbia, 22 features for Universal and four Universal serials. Tom Mix and Ken Maynard made the transition from silents to sound westerns, and Johnny Mack Brown got his start in western features. One company, Mascot, was formed by Nat Levine just to produce western serials. In 1935, through a series of mergers, Mascot became Republic, and this studio would dominate western filmmaking for the next 20 years.

In addition to Buck Jones, "B" western serial stars included Tim McCoy (Columbia), Randolph Scott (Paramount), George O'Brien (Fox), Charles Starrett (Columbia), William Boyd (Paramount), Ken Maynard (Columbia, Universal and World Wide), and Gene Autry (Republic). Other major cowboy stars of this era include Harry Carey, Hoot Gibson, Tom Mix and John Wayne.

The most interesting phenomenon of this period was the development of the singing western, with Gene Autry becoming the most popular movie cowboy of this era. With his sidekick, Smiley Burnette, Autry pioneered several areas: the extensive use of music in westerns; the increasing emphasis on escapism through gaudy costumes no real cowboy could ever wear on the range; filming of the contemporary West in traditional plots; and the use of the "fool" sidekick who caused as many problems as the outlaws.

Autry's first feature was *Tumbling Tumbleweeds* (1935), and after the huge success of this musical western, other singing cowboys followed, including Roy Rogers, Tex Ritter, Rex Allen and others (see SINGING COWBOYS).

The Hopalong Cassidy hero was also created during this period. The character was based on the novels of Clarence Mulford and played by actor William Boyd, and the "Hopalong" series was created by Harry "Pop" Sherman, a producer who arranged for the films to be released through Paramount. The Lone Ranger also became popular during this period with two features, *The Lone Ranger* (1938) and *The Lone Ranger Rides Again* (1939).

Another popular series was the Three Mesquiteers, originally played by Ray Corrigan, Robert Livingston and Max Terhune. Buster Crabbe starred in a popular Billy the Kid western series before leaving his cowboy clothes to star in the Flash Gordon series at Universal.

Among the actresses who were popular in the "boom year" westerns were Claire Rochelle, Louise Stanley, Lois January, Beth Marion, Eleanor Stewart, Lucille Browne, Joan Barclay, Dorothy Revier, Marion Shilling, Polly Ann Young and Allene Ray.

Major features during this period were *The Plainsmen* (1936), starring Gary Cooper; *Sutter's Gold* (1936), *Three Godfathers* (1936), *and Wells Fargo* (1937) starring Joel McCrea. This period is not known for its major features; instead, this period was dominated by "B" westerns, singing cowboys, and western serials.

The period from 1938 until the outbreak of World War II (1941) constituted the peak years for westerns, with over 700 films released, or an average of 3.4 per week. During this period the popularity of the singing cowboys, the "B" westerns and the serials continued, but major features were also produced that helped define the genre and the period. Perhaps the best example is *Stagecoach* (1939); directed by John Ford and starring John Wayne, this film became a classic and was nominated for an Academy Award for Best Picture.

Other great movies of this era include *Union Pacific* (1939), directed by Cecil B. DeMille and starring Joel McCrea and Barbara Stanwyck; *Frontier Marshal* (1939), starring Randolph Scott; *The Oklahoma Kid* (1939), starring James Cagney and Humphrey Bogart; *Jesse James* (1939), starring Tyrone Power and Henry Fonda; *The Westerner* (1940), starring Gary Cooper and Walter Brennan; *The Return of Frank James* (1940), starring Henry Fonda; and *Western Union* (1941), starring Randolph Scott.

Also popular during this time was one of the earliest successful western spoofs, *Destry Rides Again* (1939), starring James Stewart and Marlene Dietrich. There were other western comedies during this period as well, including the all-black western *Harlem Rides the Range* (1939); *My Little Chickadee* (1940), starring W. C. Fields and Mae West; and *Buck Benny Rides Again (1940)*, starring Jack Benny.

The number one money-making movie cowboy of the 1938–41 period was undeniably Gene Autry, ranking fourth among all Hollywood stars in popularity in 1940 and sixth in 1941. Roy Rogers also emerged in this period at Republic with singing-cowboy movies; he remained third, behind Autry and William Boyd, in popularity among western stars.

During the 1942–46 period almost 500 "B" western movies and 11 serials were released. The major features of the era are *They Died with Their Boots On* (1942), starring Erroll Flynn as General George Custer; *The Spoilers* (1942); *The Shepherd of the Hills* (1942); *The Ox-Bow Incident* (1943); *Buffalo Bill* (1944); *The Outlaw* (1945); *San Antonio* (1945); and *My Darling Clementine* (1946). In these features can be seen the future of westerns after World War II: the increasing use of sex in *The Outlaw*, the character study and psychological western in *The Ox-Bow Incident*, and the emergence of John Wayne as the major dramatic actor in cowboy movies such as *My Darling Clementine, The Spoilers* and *The Shepherd of the Hills.*

The "B" market was dominated by Republic, despite losing Gene Autry to the air force for the war. Still, Roy Rogers, the Three Mesquiteers, Sunset Carson, Rocky Lane, Monte Hale, Wild Bill Elliott and others continued to film successful westerns for the studio, which developed the best assembly-line staff and method for making western "B's." Its major competition came from two other small studios: PRC and Monogram. Most of Monogram's westerns starred Johnny Mack Brown and Jimmy Wakely, and its most successful series was The Cisco Kid, which began in 1944 starring Duncan Renaldo.

After the war, major studios began producing large-scale westerns. The most significant of these were released in 1948: *Duel in the Sun*, starring Jennifer Jones and Gregory Peck; *Red River*, directed by Howard Hawks and starring John Wayne; *Three Godfathers*, directed by John Ford; *Treasure of the Sierra Madre*, a "fringe" western starring Tim Holt, Humphrey Bogart and Walter Huston and directed by John Huston; and *Fort Apache*, the first of John Ford's cavalry trilogy that starred John Wayne and Henry Fonda. The cavalry trilogy was completed with *She Wore a Yellow Ribbon* (1949) and *Rio Grande* (1950).

Other important films in the postwar period include *Angel and the Badman* (1947), starring John Wayne; *Trail Street* (1947), starring Randolph Scott; and *Ramrod* (1947), starring Joel McCrea. These three actors, Wayne, Scott and McCrea, also emerged as the three major stars of dramatic westerns during this period.

The most important western in the early fifties was *High Noon* (1952), starring Gary Cooper. For this movie, Cooper won an Oscar as Best Actor, and the theme song, "Do Not Forsake Me" sung by Tex Ritter, also won an Oscar.

The early fifties saw the sale of a number of the earlier "B" western movies to television, which was emerging as America's favorite entertainment medium. Television also ended the serials: Roy Rogers serials were canceled by Republic in 1952, while Gene Autry's serials at Columbia lasted until 1953. After this, these cowboys would ride across the TV screen. The Hopalong Cassidy films and serials were also adapted to television, with

Hoppie becoming the first TV cowboy. The Lone Ranger quickly followed (see TELEVISION WESTERNS).

During the period 1953–57 the "B" western audience watched TV fill the former role of movies as serials became weekly series and "B" movies became, in essence, hour-long TV shows. The western movies of this period increasingly appealed to an adult audience, whereas TV westerns catered to children. Psychological or "mature" westerns emerged, of which *Shane* (1953) and *The Searchers* (1956) are prime examples. Randolph Scott, John Wayne, Joel McCrea and Audie Murphy were the major stars of dramatic western movies.

The 1958–62 period is characterized as a time of "realism" in westerns, when the glamour and heroes of the Old West were discarded for gritty antiheroes. Sex and violence were increasingly prevalent in westerns as the mythological Old West of the 1930s and 1940s lost its appeal and was replaced by a West in which heroes and civilization weren't what they seemed. The West lost its appeal not only artistically but economically as well: Only 23 westerns were released in 1961 and 16 in 1962. Significant features of this era include a number of John Wayne westerns, such as *Rio Bravo* (1959), *The Horse Soldiers* (1959), *The Alamo* (1960), *North to Alaska* (1960), *The Comancheros* (1961) and *The Man Who Shot Liberty Valance* (1962). Other important films in this era include *Ride the High Country* (1962), directed by Sam Peckinpah and starring Randolph Scott in his last movie; *The Big Country* (1958), *The Magnificent Seven* (1960), *Cimarron* (1960), *Two Rode Together* (1961), and *Lonely Are The Brave* (1962).

The years 1963 to 1967 saw the West lose even more of its luster as the antihero became the dominant character. The western has always adapted itself to reflect the prevailing public mood, and this period in the United States, beset with the civil rights struggle, the Vietnam War and other social upheavals, left the West in a quandary: No longer could movies be made that were just escapist entertainment, they had to reflect or promote some social issue or address some injustice.

Significant films during this period are *How the West Was Won* (1963), *Cheyenne Autumn* (1964), *The Sons of Katie Elder* (1965) and *El Dorado* (1967). Humor was important during this time, as proved by *Cat Ballou* (1965), *The Hallelujah Trail* (1965) and *The Rounders* (1965), but these also starred an antihero. Perhaps the greatest antihero to emerge was Clint Eastwood in the "spaghetti" westerns produced by Serge Leone in Italy: *A Fistful of Dollars* (1967), *For a Few Dollars More* (1967) and *The Good, the Bad and the Ugly* (1968).

The period from 1968 to 1972 represented a cynicism in westerns, reflecting the cynicism Americans were feeling toward the Vietnam War. Movies like *Little Big Man* (1971), in which Custer was a buffoon, and *Dirty Little Billy* (1972), in which the once hero outlaw was shown as a punk killer, were reflective of this period. In general, violence was prevalent as filmmakers sought to bring unvarnished truth in candid, direct terms to the screen.

This period produced the most successful commercial western up to this point, *Butch Cassidy and the*

Sundance Kid (1969), and *True Grit* (1969), the movie for which John Wayne won his first Academy Award. Also in this period were movies such as *Will Penny* (1968), Sam Peckinpah's *The Wild Bunch* (1969), *A Man Called Horse* (1970), *McCabe and Mrs. Miller* (1971), *Billy Jack* (1971), *The Great Northfield Minnesota Raid* (1972), *The Culpepper Cattle Company* (1972), *The Life and Times of Judge Roy Bean* (1972), *Jeremiah Johnson* (1972), and *Junior Bonner* (1972).

Clint Eastwood emerged as a full-fledged western star during this period, with *Hang 'Em High* (1968) and *High Plains Drifter* (1973).

The 1973–77 period saw the final films of John Wayne: *Cahill, United States Marshal* (1973), *The Train Robbers* (1973), *Rooster Cogburn* (1975) and his final film, *The Shootist* (1976). Although fewer westerns were now being produced by Hollywood, they reflected a wide variety of themes. Significant films of this era include *High Plains Drifter* (1973), *Pat Garrett and Billy the Kid* (1973), *The Trial of Billy Jack* (1974), perhaps the ultimate western spoof, *Blazing Saddles* (1974), *The Missouri Breaks* (1976), *Macintosh and T.J.* (1976), and *The Outlaw Josey Wales* (1976). This was also a period of black exploitation films as well as an era when the African American's role in history was reexamined. In westerns this reexamination was evident in films such as *The Soul of Nigger Charley* (1973), *Boss Nigger* (1974), *Adios Amigo* (1975) and *Joshua* (1977).

The period from 1980 to 1990 was rather dry for westerns. With the move away from action and toward "psychological" drama, the western lost its essential appeal; it was replaced by science fiction epics such as *Star Wars* and by "action" films such as *The Terminator*.

Perhaps the decline of the western during this period is best told in the story of *Heaven's Gate* (1980), a movie about the Johnson County War that epitomized all that was wrong with Hollywood when it became a financial fiasco, costing over $40 million, and an organizational nightmare, nearly causing a studio to fold. But Westerns such as *The Long Riders* (1980), *Bronco Billy* (1980), *Cattle Annie and Little Britches* (1981), *Rustlers' Rhapsody* (1985), *Silverado* (1985), and *Young Guns* (1988) as well as the phenomenally successful *Dances with Wolves* (1991), which won the Academy Award for Best Picture, proved that westerns were still alive. After the success of *Unforgiven* (1992) Hollywood rediscovered that quality westerns have a timeless appeal and a large audience. The history of the movies shows that westerns will never die, although Hollywood will periodically ignore the western. But the genre is too strong and enduring to ever pass away.

MULE   The mule was more valuable than a horse for hauling wagons, stagecoaches and other heavy objects because it is stronger and generally has more endurance. It can also survive in rougher areas and on rougher fare than a horse. Mules are faster than oxen, though not as sturdy. Freighters especially liked mules for "wheelers," or the team hitched closest to the wagon. A hybrid between a jackass and a horse, the mule (usually sterile) was brought to America by George Washington in the 1780s when he imported asses from Spain and Malta. A mule is the product of a male jackass and female horse; the hybrid from a male horse (stallion) and female ass is technically called a "hinny," although the term "mule" is often applied to both.

MULESKINNER   The driver of a mule-team wagon. Also called a skinner, the muleskinner rode on the wagon; bullwhackers walked.

MULFORD, CLARENCE EDWARD   (b. Streator, Illinois on February 3, 1883; d. Fryeburg, Maine on May 10, 1956)   Mulford is the author of the Bar 20 novels that featured Hopalong Cassidy. Mulford moved to Brooklyn with his family when he was six, and he later entered the civil service. He read a number of western novels and was influenced by *The Virginian* by Owen Wister. Mulford entered a Western short story contest for *Metropolitan* magazine and won first prize; he then wrote a series of stories for *Outing*, which were collected and published as *Bar 20* (1907), his first novel. Mulford's next novel, *The Orphan* (1908), was patterned after *The Virginian* and led to Fox Pictures making a movie from the book called *The Deadwood Coach* (1924), starring Tom Mix. For the next several years Mulford wrote about the West and used a cast of characters on the Bar 20 ranch that included owner Buck Peters and three cowboys: Hopalong Cassidy, Red Connors, and Johnny Nelson. In these books Hoppy was a red-haired cowboy who swore, smoked, drank, and was rough and tough but ethical. His real name was Bill Cassidy but his right leg was injured in a gun fight, which caused him to limp, hence the moniker "Hopalong." Other novels by Mulford included *Hopalong Cassidy* (1910), in which the cowboy married Mary Meeker; *Bar 20 Days* (1911), *Buck Peters, Ranchman* (1912); *The Coming Of Cassidy* (1913), which told of the gun fight that gave Cassidy his permanent limp and the name "Hopalong"; *The Man from Bar 20* (1918); *Johnny Nelson* (1920); *The Bar 20 Three* (1921); *Tex* (1922); *Bring Me His Ears* (1923); *Black Buttes* (1923); *Rustlers' Valley* (1924); *Hopalong Cassidy Returns* (1924), in which Hoppy loses his wife and child; *Cottonwood Gulch* (1925); *Hopalong Cassidy's Protege* (1926); *Corson of the JC* (1927); *Mesquite Jenkins* (1928); and *Hopalong Cassidy and the Eagle's Brood* (1931). Mulford did not take his first trip West until 1924 at the age of 41. Mulford preferred to live and work in the East; in 1926 he settled permanently in Fryeburg, Maine and vacationed at Bridgeport, Connecticut.

In 1935 Mulford was contacted by movie producer Harry "Pop" Sherman about producing the Bar 20 novels and they met and agreed on a contract that gave Mulford 5% of the gross, which made him a rich man. The movies were produced by Paramount and starred William Boyd, after several actors (including David Niven) turned down the part. Ironically, William Boyd, who was afraid of horses, broke his leg from a fall from his horse during the first movie, *Hop-A-Long Cassidy*, and this was worked into the plot to explain his name.

However, during the rest of the movies Hoppy never limped and no explanation was ever given.

Mulford wrote his last Hoppy novel, *Hopalong Cassidy Serves a Writ*, in 1941. He died after his character had become an American hero on TV.

MURPHEY, MICHAEL MARTIN   (b. Oak Cliff, Texas on March 14, 1945)   Murphey organized the first West Fest in 1986 in Copper Mountain, Colorado and popularized traditional cowboy music with his 1990 album "Cowboy Songs." A native Texan, Murphey studied Greek at North Texas State University and then transferred to the University of California–Los Angeles, where he majored in creative writing. In Los Angeles he wrote songs for Screen Gems; he then moved to Austin, Texas in 1971 and joined the alternative music scene, writing "Geronimo's Cadillac" and "Cosmic Cowboy." Murphey moved to Colorado in 1974 and to Taos, New Mexico in 1979. A talented performer, Murphey is also known as an organizer and a contemporary artist with a social conscience; he is involved in Native American issues in addition to his work with preserving cowboy songs.

MURPHY, AUDIE   (b. Audie Leon Murphy near Kingston, Texas on June 20, 1924; d. near Roanoke, Virginia on May 28, 1971)   The most decorated soldier in World War II became a Hollywood movie star after the war, starring in 33 westerns (out of 44 films he did). Murphy was well known as a "B" western star and was voted the top western box office attraction in 1955. Murphy was one of nine children born to sharecroppers; in 1939 his father left, and at 15 Audie quit school to help support his family. At 17 Audie's mother died, and he tried to enlist in the Marine Corps. Turned down because he was too young, Audie, with his older sister Corrine, falsified papers and was thus accepted into the National Guard; his unit was activated as a unit of the Third Army and served in Italy and Sicily. Audie won a field commission as second lieutenant and then fought in France and Austria; by the end of the war he had won 24 citations including the Congressional Medal of Honor and had killed approximately 240 Germans in combat. Unable to fulfill his dream of entering West Point, Murphy obtained a screen test in Hollywood and first appeared in *Beyond Glory* (1948). Murphy had his service pension sent home to help his brothers and sisters in a Texas orphanage, so his first years in Hollywood were spent in poverty. He wrote his autobiography, *To Hell and Back*, and in 1951 starred in *The Red Badge of Courage*, directed by John Huston; he then starred in the movie version of *To Hell and Back* (1955). In 1961 he starred in a TV series "Whispering Smith," which was denounced by a congressional committee for excessive violence. Meanwhile, Murphy's personal life was in turmoil; his two marriages were unhappy, and so was his life in general. Murphy was a poor, uneducated young man who knew he had no talent but continued to make movies; he made over $2.5 million in Hollywood but by the end of the 1960s was broke and suffered from bad publicity. He died with five other men when their plane crashed after leaving Atlanta, Georgia; it was found in the woods outside Roanoke, Virginia. There is an eight-foot bronze statue of Audie Murphy outside the Audie L. Murphy Memorial Veterans' Hospital in San Antonio, and all his World War II medals are displayed in a room inside this institution. Murphy's western movies include:

> *The Kid from Texas* (1950)
> *Sierra* (1950)
> *Kansas Raiders* (1950)
> *The Cimarron Kid* (1951)
> *The Duel at Silver Creek* (1952)
> *Gunsmoke* (1953)
> *Column South* (1953)
> *Tumbleweed* (1953)
> *Ride Clear of Diablo* (1954)
> *Drums across the River* (1954)
> *Destry* (1954)
> *Walk the Proud Land* (1956)
> *The Guns of Fort Petticoat* (1957)
> *Night Passage* (1957)
> *Ride a Crooked Trail* (1958)
> *No Name on the Bullet* (1959)
> *Cast a Long Shadow* (1959)
> *The Unforgiven* (1960)
> *Hell Bent for Leather* (1960)
> *Seven Ways from Sundown* (1960)
> *Posse From Hell* (1961)
> *Six Black Horses* (1962)
> *Showdown* (1963)
> *Gunfight at Comanche Creek* (1963)
> *The Quick Gun* (1964)
> *Bullet for a Badman* (1964)
> *Apache Rifles* (1964)
> *Gunpoint* (1966)
> *The Texican* (1966)
> *Arizona Raiders* (1965)
> *40 Guns to Apache Pass* (1967)
> *A Time For Dying* (1971)

(See also B WESTERN MOVIES; MOVIES; WHISPERING SMITH.)

MUSTANG   A wild horse, descended from the original Spanish stock brought into Mexico. These horses either escaped or were stolen by Indians or their riders died. Mustangs run wild in herds of mares with a stallion and lead mare. Inbreeding made them small, multicolored, durable, hardy and able to find food in adverse conditions. When bred with eastern stock, they produced quarter horses, excellent for cutting cattle. Mustangs are difficult to catch and, when caught, are often killed or crippled while trying to get away. In the Old West the biggest and best mustangs tended to get away; the ones that were caught and broken often had their spirit broken as well—and their hearts went out of them, making them indifferent animals. *Mustangers* earned their living capturing mustangs by laying traps at water holes or appealing to the mustang's curiosity, dropping a noose over them when they were unaware. Some were run down or stampeded into a pen at the end of a narrowing lane of men, brush or stakes. Mustangs generally had an established range, which they stuck to. The hierarchy of the herd generally meant a stallion, a wise older mare, some mules or geldings, and about six to 20 younger mares. The term "mustang" comes from the Spanish *mestenos*, which means horses that have escaped a group of stock raisers, known as *mesta*.

MY DARLING CLEMENTINE   Film produced by Samuel G. Engel; directed by John Ford; screenplay by Samuel G. Engel and Winston Miller, from the book *Wyatt Earp, Frontier Marshal* by Stuart Lake; released in 1946 by Twentieth Century–Fox; 97 minutes in length. Cast: Henry Fonda, Victor Mature, Linda Darnell, Walter Brennan, Tim Holt, Cathy Downs, Ward Bond, Alan Mowbray, John Ireland, Roy Roberts and Francis Ford.

This was the third film inspired by Stuart Lake's biography of Wyatt Earp, and the central story in this movie is the gunfight at the O.K. Corral. The story begins with the Earps driving cattle into Tombstone; James, the youngest Earp, is left to tend the cattle while the rest of the brothers go into town. Wyatt runs into a drunken Indian and runs him out of town and is thereby offered the job as marshal. When the Earps go back to their cattle, they find their youngest brother dead and the cattle gone, so the Earps go back and Wyatt accepts the job as marshal. The Clantons had killed James and rustled the cattle and so they must be faced; this is done at the O.K. Corral. The "Clementine" in the film is Clementine Carter, a young lady from the East who is Wyatt's love interest. She brings a civilizing influence to the wild and woolly Tombstone.

MY FRIEND FLICKA   TV show that starred Gene Evans as Rob McLaughlin, Anita Louise as Nell McLaughlin, Johnny Washbrook as Ken McLaughlin, Frank Ferguson as Gus Broeberg and Pamela Beaird as Hildy Broeberg (1956).

The McLaughlin family was trying to make a living on a ranch in Montana, but problems kept arising from neighbors, friends, strangers and the weather. Young Ken's best friend was his horse Flicka, and this show, set around the turn of the century, was about family. Flicka was owned by Ralph McCutcheon and trained by Les Hilton. The program premiered on February 10, 1956 on CBS on Friday nights. In March 1957 it moved to Saturdays and in April 1957 moved to Sunday evenings before being shifted to Wednesday evenings in June 1957. The show then moved to NBC, where it was seen on Sundays from September 1957 until June 1958. It later moved to ABC in the afternoons and was also on Saturday mornings for a while. There were 39 episodes of the half-hour show, which was based on the 1943 movie, which had in turn been based on Mary O'Hara's stories.

MYSTERIOUS DAVE   See MATHER, DAVE H.

N

NATION, CARRY   (b. Carry Amelia Moore in Garrard County, Kentucky on November 25, 1846; d. Leavenworth, Kansas on June 9, 1911)   Carry Nation was famous as a crusader against liquor; she achieved notoriety by attacking saloons with a hatchet and for fiery speeches on temperance. This temperance movement led to the Prohibition amendment in 1920.

Carrie Nation knew the problems of men's drinking firsthand. Her first husband, Dr. Charlie Gloyd, would not give up drinking or his membership in the Masons sc Carrie left him; after he died, she married David Nation, a teetotaler. But Carrie separated from her husband now and then and ran some small hotels. A religious conversion in Richmond, Texas led her to become an evangelist; her husband became a Disciples of Christ minister in Medicine Lodge, Kansas, and she joined him there, where she decided that liquor was a problem that must be abolished. Although Kansas was a dry state at the time, Carry stormed into the Medicine Lodge drug store and destroyed a keg containing "medicinal" whiskey; she then continued her antiliquor crusade by breaking up three saloons in Kansas, which brought her much publicity. As her fame grew, so did her antics; the first time she used a hatchet to bust up a saloon was in Topeka, Kansas, and her "hatchetations" soon became legendary. In 1901 she divorced her husband and began to travel and lecture all over the country; the lectures were often accompanied by "hatchetations," which were covered by the press, who often followed her into the saloons. Nation wrote an autobiography, *The Use and Need of the Life of Carry A. Nation,* and spent her final years in Alpena Pass and Eureka Springs, Arkansas.

NATIONAL CATTLE TRAIL   This trail was developed in 1885 by a group of cattlemen who met in Dallas to discuss the problems of driving cattle north after Kansas had closed its borders to Texas cattle. There was still a demand for Texas cattle on the northern ranges—as well as government contracts at army forts and Indian reservations—so the cattlemen needed a route to get their cattle north. The cattlemen agreed that trails should follow the Western Trail northward from southern Texas, across the Red River into the Texas panhandle, then up Coldwater River to Buffalo Springs and then across "No Man's Land" or the Neutral Strip (now the Oklahoma panhandle) and the Cimarron River area into Colorado. This trail, roughly three miles wide, then followed the eastern border of Colorado (just west of Kansas) up to the Canadian border at Montana.

NAVAJO INDIANS The Navajo (also spelled Navaho) were a nomadic, warring tribe, related to the Apache, who preyed on the more docile Pueblo Indians. Later, they attacked Spanish, then English, settlements in their native New Mexico and Arizona area. Because the Navajo were considered a threat to settlers, the federal government decided to confine them to a reservation and teach them agriculture in order to become placid farmers. For this, the government enlisted Kit Carson to round them up in 1863 and put them on the Bosque Redondo Reservation in New Mexico. Carson was ruthless in his pursuit of the Navajo, killing their sheep and horses and destroying their corn and peach orchards until the tribe was starved into surrendering. The United States signed a treaty with the Navajo in 1868 that allowed them to return to their reservation, where they began to become known as silversmiths, weavers and shepherds. The Navajo are now the most prosperous of Native American tribes and have the largest Indian reservation, covering 24,000 square miles, in the United States .

NED BLESSING: THE STORY OF MY LIFE AND TIMES TV show starring Brad Johnson as Ned Blessing, Luis Avalos as Crecencio, Tim Scott as Sticks Packwood, Wes Studi as One Horse, Brenda Bakke as the Wren, Bill McKinney as Verlon Borgers, Rob Campbell as Roby Borgers, Richard Riehle as Judge Longley, Rusty Schwimmer as Big Emma and Jeremy Roberts as Hugh Bell.

Ned Blessing was a notorious outlaw who came back to visit his father in Plum Creek, Texas and discovered the town had been taken over by bullies. Blessing then renounces his outlaw past and becomes the lawman of Plum Creek. The show, set in the post–Civil War West, is actually a series of flashbacks for Blessing, an old man, whose reminiscences constitute the show's segments. the show premiered on Wednesday, August 18, 1993 on CBS.

NELLYBELLE This is the jeep that Pat Brady drove as the comic sidekick to Roy Rogers on the TV series "The Roy Rogers Show." The jeep was introduced in the movie *The Golden Stallion* (1949) and was built and rigged by Rogers himself, who tinkered with an old army jeep to create a "character" after these jeeps became popular in World War II. (See also BRADY, PAT; ROGERS, ROY; ROY ROGERS SHOW, THE.)

NEWCOMB, BITTER CREEK (aka "Slaughter's Kid"; b. George Newcomb in Fort Scott, Kansas c. 1867; d. at the Dunn Ranch on the Cimarron River in Oklahoma on May 1, 1895) Bitter Creek got his name from an old cowboy song he used to sing, "I'm a wild wolf from Bitter Creek / And it's my night to howl." He worked for rancher John Slaughter and earned another nickname, "Slaughter's Kid." A member of the Dalton and Doolin Gangs, Newcomb was in the big shootout at Ingalls, Oklahoma on September 1, 1893 and, indeed, precipitated the shooting when a lawman asked a local youth who the rider of a particular horse was. The youth replied, "Bitter Creek Newcomb," alerting one and all to the Doolin Gang's presence. Newcomb, sensing danger, had left a poker game, gone outside the saloon and gotten on his horse. Posse member Dick Speed shot at Newcomb, wounding him, and Newcomb shot back before his gun jammed. Newcomb's life was saved when Arkansas Tom Jones killed Speed from an upstairs window at a hotel. Newcomb was in the shootout in spring 1895 near Dover, Oklahoma in which Tulsa Jack Blake was killed. This was the incident in which gang member Red Buck's horse had been killed during the getaway, so he stole a horse and then shot the owner. Newcomb had given Buck a ride to help him escape the posse. Newcomb's end came on May 2, 1895 on the ranch of his wife's family. Newcomb was married to Rosa Dunn, and she became famous as the "Rose of Cimarron." Newcomb and another outlaw, Charley Pierce, went to the Dunn ranch so Newcomb could see his wife and because her brothers owed him $900. But there was a $5,000 reward on Bitter Creek's head, prompting her brothers to shoot the two outlaws when they rode up. The next day the Dunn brothers threw the bodies into a wagon to take them into Guthrie and collect their reward. Surprisingly, the supposedly dead Newcomb muttered a request for water, prompting the Dunn brothers to shoot him again, this time fatally. (See also ARKANSAS TOM JONES; BLAKE, TULSA JACK; DOOLIN, BILL; SLAUGHTER, TEXAS JOHN.)

NEW LAND, THE TV show that starred Bonnie Bedelia as Anna Larsen, Scott Thomas as Christian Larsen, Todd Lookinland as Tuliff Larsen, Debbie Lytton as Anneliese Larsen, Kurt Russell as Bo, Donald Moffatt as Reverend Lundstrom, Gwen Arner as Molly Lundstrom and Lou Frizzel as Murdock.

In 1858 some Scandinavian immigrants came to Solna, Minnesota to carve out a home in the wilderness. Based loosely on two Swedish movies, *The Emigrants* (1972) and *The New Land* (1973), the series lasted only six weeks. The hour-long show debuted on September 14, 1974 on Saturday nights on ABC and was last telecast on October 19, 1974.

NEWTON, KANSAS Newton was a wild cattle town whose heyday lasted from July 1871, when the Atchison, Topeka and Santa Fe Railroad reached it (the town was founded just four months before, in March), until 1873, when Wichita replaced it as the terminus for cattle drives. Newton was notorious for its "Hide Park," an area for sporting houses catering to wild Texas cowboys, and for the Newton Massacre on August 20, 1871. (See also NEWTON MASSACRE.)

NEWTON MASSACRE (August 20, 1871)   The roots of the Newton Massacre were in a special election held in Newton on August 11, 1871. William Bailey was hired as election deputy by the town, but he became drunk and obnoxious during the election. Bailey, whose real name was Bill Wilson, clashed with Mike Mc-Cluskie, also known as Arthur Delaney, and Bailey was dressed down verbally by McCluskie. That night around eight at the Red Front Saloon, McCluskie was ordered by Bailey to buy the house a round of drinks. McCluskie refused and a brawl began; the burly McCluskie landed a punch that sent Bailey crashing through the saloon's swinging doors. McCluskie then pushed through the saloon doors and followed Bailey outside. When Mc-Cluskie went outside, he saw Bailey leaning against a hitching rail with a six-gun; McCluskie pulled his own gun and killed Bailey and then left town. On August 19, 1871—eight days later—McCluskie went back into Newton to Perry Tuttle's dance hall. Around one in the morning Hugh Anderson, a friend of Bailey's, came up to McCluskie, who was sitting at the faro table. Anderson pulled a pistol and shot McCluskie in the neck. With blood spurting from his throat, McCluskie rose and shot at Anderson; meanwhile, Anderson kept pumping lead at McCluskie. Others in the saloon quickly drew their guns and opened fire. Three others were hit and one died. At this point Jim Riley, a frail consumptive who looked up to McCluskie and who had been watching from the door, closed and locked the saloon door and began firing and did not stop until his gun's chamber was empty. He killed two and wounded one man. McCluskie was carried to his hotel room where he died around eight in the morning. Later, in June 1873, McCluskie's brother, Arthur, would fight a bloody duel with Hugh Anderson in Medicine Lodge, Kansas. The two shot each other and then, covered with blood and crawling on the ground, stabbed each other on the ground until both were dead. (See also MCCLUSKIE, ARTHUR; MCCLUSKIE, MIKE.)

NEZ PERCE INDIANS   Named by French fur trappers, the Nez Perce (the term means "pierced nose") lived in the northwestern United States as fishermen until they acquired horses and became buffalo hunters. The Nez Perce became excellent horse breeders and developed the famed Appaloosa horses. This tribe befriended Lewis and Clark in 1805 during their expedition and remained friendly with whites until 1877. The Nez Perce had ceded their lands to the United States in 1855 and settled in Oregon and Idaho; however, when gold was discovered on their lands, the government ordered the Nez Perce to move to a reservation at Lapwai, Idaho. The Nez Perce of Wallowa Valley in Oregon were given 30 days to comply but they refused, which led to the Nez Perce War (1877). Led by their great leader, Chief Joseph, the Nez Perce defeated soldiers at White Bird Canyon and then began a journey to flee the United

States for Canada. The army pursued the Nez Perce for 1,300 miles until October 1977, when the cold, starving Indians were surrounded by cavalry and surrendered. At this point they were about 30 miles from the Canadian border. The army sent the Nez Perce to Indian Territory, but in 1885 Chief Joseph and most of his tribe were moved to a reservation in Washington State.

NICHOLS   TV show that starred James Garner as Nichols, Neva Patterson as Ma Ketcham, John Beck as Ketcham, Stuart Margolin as Mitch, Margot Kidder as Ruth and Alice Ghostley as Bertha.

This show was changed to "James Garner as Nichols" a month after it began, but it lasted only one season despite its popular star. In this 1914-era western, Nichols had mustered out of the army after 18 years and returned to Nichols, Arizona, the town named after his family, only to discover it had been taken over by Ma Ketchum, a dominant matriarch, and her bully son Ketchum. Ma made Nichols—who never had a first name—the sheriff, a job he abhorred. Nichols never carried a gun and drove an old car and motorcycle. In the last episode Nichols was killed, with his twin brother James Nichols (also played by James Garner) set to avenge him. The hope was that a more masculine, macho hero would help the ratings for the next season, but the series was canceled. The show premiered September 16, 1971 on Thursday nights on NBC. In November 1971 it moved to Tuesday nights. Twenty-six episodes of the hour-long show were filmed; it ended on August 1, 1972.

NIGHT GUARD   Cowboys assigned to watch the cattle at night. The night guard generally consisted of two cowboys circling the herd from opposite directions so they passed each other twice around the herd. These night guards often sang or whistled to calm the cattle as well as to let each other know their location. The night guard rode a night horse, which, when trained well, could circle the cattle while the cowboy caught a catnap in the saddle. A quiet, steady animal, this horse was the most reliable of the cowboy's mounts, able to keep calm around the cattle and avoid spooking them and, during a stampede, willing to run after wild cattle in the pitch-dark night.

NOLAN, BOB   (b. Robert Clarence Nobles in New Brunswick, Canada on April 1, 1908; d. Los Angeles, California on June 16, 1980)   One of the greatest songwriters in the history of western music, Nolan penned "Cool Water" and "Tumbling Tumbleweeds," perhaps the two best-known western songs of all time. He also was one of the founding members of the Sons of the Pioneers, and his distinctive lead vocals were the signature sound for this group during its heyday, 1938 to 1949.

Born in Canada, Nolan moved to Boston to attend school and lived with his aunts. His father, Harry Nobles, joined the United States Army during World War I and then, after the war, retired to Tucson, Arizona, where he changed his name to "Nolan" because it sounded more "American." When he was 14, Bob joined his father in Tucson, and the southwestern landscape had an immediate and profound impact on him. For the rest of his life, Nolan was captivated by the desert and the themes of deserts, and the southwestern landscape would dominate his writing.

Nolan attended the University of Arizona, where he began to compose poems seriously, influenced by 19th-century poets Keats, Shelley and Byron as well as Scottish poet Robert Burns. It was there that he wrote the poem that eventually became the song "Cool Water." After college Nolan traveled a bit before moving to California, where he joined his father in 1929, who had moved there earlier. In the Los Angeles area Nolan joined a Chautauqua troupe and began to write songs and perform, and he soon was infected with the show business bug. He was working as a lifeguard when he read an advertisement in the newspaper for a singer who could yodel and answered it. The ad was placed by Leonard Slye—later to become Roy Rogers—and the two formed a singing duo who performed with the Rocky Mountaineers. They soon realized they needed another voice, and Nolan suggest his old friend, Bill "Slumber" Nichols, who joined the group. Nolan dropped out in mid-1932 and landed a job as a golf caddy at the prestigious Bel Air Country Club. It was during this period of time, while home at his apartment one day, that he wrote "Tumbling Leaves," which later became "Tumbling Tumbleweeds."

Nolan was replaced in the trio by Tim Spencer, but after a disastrous southwestern tour from June to September 1933, the group, known then as the O-Bar-O Cowboys, disbanded. Slye joined Jack and His Texas Outlaws but still wanted a trio. He and Spencer convinced Nolan to try a trio again, and after several weeks of rehearsal the group joined Jack and His Texas Outlaws, appearing under the name "The Pioneers." The name became the "Sons of the Pioneers" when a radio announcer introduced them as that one day, explaining later that they all looked too young to be "pioneers." At this time the group also appeared under the name "The Gold Star Rangers."

From the beginning, Nolan's songs were so distinctive that the group decided to develop a "western" image and sing "western" songs. He wrote a number of songs for movies, first writing out what he wanted to say in the song and then working on the lyrics and, finally, the music.

Nolan was an integral part of the Sons of the Pioneers until he retired in 1949. In fact, during the 1940s the group was known as "Bob Nolan and the Sons of the Pioneers" because of his good looks, his distinctive vocals and his immense songwriting talents. Nolan also appeared in a number of western movies, often with the Sons of the Pioneers in Roy Rogers movies. After his retirement, he came back to sing with the Sons of the Pioneers in 1955–57 when they recorded for RCA Victor. He spent his last years living in Studio City, near Republic Studio. During his final years he was frustrated because he thought he would never see his music widely accepted during his lifetime. At his death, he requested his ashes be scattered across the Nevada desert. (See also COOL WATER; ROGERS, ROY; SONS OF THE PIONEERS; SPENCER, TIM; TUMBLING TUMBLEWEEDS.)

NO MAN'S LAND   Originally, this was the area known today as the Oklahoma panhandle, which was not part of any state; later it came to mean any area that was dangerous and forbidding.

NORTH, FRANK JOSHUA   (b. Ludlowville, New York on March 10, 1840; d. Columbus, Nebraska on March 14, 1885)

If Frank North had been more verbose, the world might never have known Buffalo Bill Cody. According to reports, dime novelist Ned Buntline, in the West in search of characters and story plots, approached Frank North to discuss the frontiersman's exploits. North demurred and pointed out a young scout sleeping under a wagon. He told Buntline that young Bill Cody was the cowboy to talk to. Buntline soon engaged Cody in telling wild stories, starting Cody on his road to fame and show business. North certainly deserved to be a western hero. He had grown up in Nebraska and learned the Pawnee language as well as Indian sign language. He formed the Pawnee Scouts during the Civil War to fight Indians and then re-formed them in 1867 to protect the Union Pacific Railroad's construction crews. In January 1865 North engaged his Pawnee Scouts against the Cheyenne and Arapaho. When North organized the battalion of four Pawnee companies in 1867, his brother, Luther North, became captain of one of the companies. North killed Tall Bull, a Cheyenne chief, at the Battle of Summit Springs on July 11, 1869—a feat that Buffalo Bill sometimes took credit for. After the Pawnee battalion was disbanded in April 1877, North and Buffalo Bill became partners in a Nebraska ranch; later North joined Cody's Wild West show. Frank North died from injuries he suffered in the summer of 1884 when he fell from his horse during a performance in Hartford, Connecticut and was trampled on.

NORTHER   A wind from the north, often carrying cold, wet air. A really strong one was called a blue norther.

NORTHERN PACIFIC RAILROAD   The first railroad line to cross the northern plains of the United States, linking Lake Superior to the Pacific Ocean. It was authorized by Congress in 1864 to be built from Lake Superior to Puget Sound, and construction began in July 1870 near Duluth, Minnesota after it was financed by Jay Cooke and Company. Construction made it to Bismark, North Dakota in 1873 before a financial panic brought ruin to Cooke and Company and thus bankruptcy to the railroad. Construction would not resume for five years. In 1881 Henry Villard, head of the Oregon Railway and Navigation Company, purchased control of the company. As president of the railroad, Villard faced the problem of acute labor and material shortages in 1882 but solved the problem by bringing in 15,000 Chinese coolies to work on the railroad. He imported steel from England and France, solving the material shortage, and on September 8, 1883 at Gold Creek in

Montana Territory, President Ulysses Grant drove in the ceremonial spike connecting tracks from the east and west.

NORTHFIELD, MINNESOTA RAID
The Northfield, Minnesota raid led to the breakup of the original James Gang, with the Younger brothers all being caught while Jesse and Frank James escaped. The robbery began when the James brothers, the Younger brothers, and their gang—a total of eight armed men—rode into Northfield, Minnesota on September 7, 1876 and entered the First National Bank to rob it. Cashier Joseph L. Heywood refused to open the safe after being ordered to do so by the robbers; one outlaw then slashed Haywood's throat while another shot him. Teller A. E. Bunker received a shoulder wound as he ran from the building.

The gunfire attracted local citizens, who were soon shooting it out with the outlaws. Townsman Nicholas Gustavson was killed. Among the outlaws, Clell Miller and William Stiles were both killed and Bob Younger was severely wounded. When Cole and Jim Younger would not abandon their brother, Jesse and Frank James split from the group and raced away. The Younger brothers were all taken into custody, and another gang member, Charlie Pitts, was killed a few days later. (See also JAMES FRANK; JAMES, JESSE; MILLER, CLELLAND; STILES, WILLIAM LARKIN; YOUNGER, BOB; YOUNGER, COLE; YOUNGER, JAMES; YOUNGER JOHN.)

NORTHWEST PASSAGE
TV show that starred Keith Larsen as Major Robert Rogers, Buddy Ebsen as Sergeant Hunk Marriner, Don Burnett as Ensign Langdon Towne and Philip Tonge as General Amherst.

Set during the French and Indian War of 1754–59, this show featured the exploits of Rogers's Rangers to find the mythical waterway across America. Upstate New York and eastern Canada were the "West" at this time, and the show featured the attempts of men to explore and map the frontier. The show premiered on September 14, 1958 on NBC and played on Sunday evenings. In January 1959 it moved to Friday nights and remained there until July 1959, when it switched to Tuesdays. The half-hour series ended there on September 8, 1959 after 26 episodes, all shot in color.

NUBBINS COLT
See BARNES, SEABORN.

OAKLEY, ANNIE
(b. Phoebe Ann Moses in Darke County, Ohio on August 13, 1860; d. Pinehurst, North Carolina on November 3, 1926) One of the most famous women connected by legend to the Old West never traveled farther west than the Mississippi River. But through her appearances with Buffalo Bill's Wild West show, which allowed her to demonstrate her astounding ability as a sharpshooter, Annie Oakley achieved international fame.

Ann Moses' father, Jacob, died when she was four, and her mother, Susan, sent their eight children to various friends, relatives and institutions. Annie was abused by one foster family and, after two years, ran away to her mother, who had remarried and was looking for her. By age 12, she was working and paying the family's mortgage by shooting quail and selling them to customers. At 15, Annie challenged 25-year-old sharpshooter Frank Butler in a match arranged by one of her customers, Charlie Katzenberger. The match was held in Cincinnati just after Thanksgiving, 1875. Annie won the match on the last shot—shooting clay pigeons, which she had never shot before—and a year later she and Butler married. Frank Butler was a well-known sharpshooter who appeared in theaters; after their marriage Annie joined him first as stagehand and then

Annie Oakley (*Annie Oakley Museum*)

Annie Oakley, Little Sure Shot *(Annie Oakley Museum)*

partner to the star before Frank began managing her. She changed her name to Oakley, after a Cincinnati neighborhood. In New Orleans at the World's Industrial and Cotton Exposition, Buffalo Bill's Rocky Mountain and Prairie Exhibition was appearing. The show was near bankruptcy when Annie auditioned in the pouring rain. Standing in mud, Annie shot glass balls in the air, a cigarette from her husband's lips and dimes from his hand.

When Cody renamed his show Buffalo Bill's Wild West, Annie became the top attraction. She acquired her nickname, "Little Sure Shot," from Sioux chief Sitting Bull, who was amazed at her skill. Among her legendary tricks: She would slice a playing card held up sideways by her husband at 30 paces; she could hit coins thrown into the air, shoot a cigarette out of her husband's lips (in Europe she shot a cigarette from the lips of Kaiser William II, who was German crown prince at the time), hit a small target behind her by using a hand mirror, and break glass balls thrown into the air. She could also shoot accurately from the back of a running horse. Annie Oakley was a major feature of Buffalo Bill's shows for 17 years. In 1897 she was challenged by Grand Duke Michael of Russia while on a tour of Britain. Although Cody tried to convince her to throw the match, Annie refused and defeated the Duke, leading her to international fame.

On October 28, 1901 the train carrying the Wild West show collided with another train near Lexington, Kentucky. Annie was carried from the twisted wreckage by Frank and awoke 17 hours later with her left side partially paralyzed, in intense pain from internal injuries, and her auburn hair now snow white. She managed to walk again—after two years and five operations—and perform her shooting, but she was never the same. Annie was in an automobile accident in 1922; it was so severe that she never walked or fired a gun again. A few years later she died in her sleep; her husband died three weeks later. After her death she was immortalized in Irving Berlin's musical *Annie Get Your Gun.*

O'BRIEN, GEORGE (b. San Francisco, California on April 19, 1900; d. Broken Arrow, Oklahoma on September 4, 1985)   A cowboy movie star, O'Brien starred in 40 "B" westerns for Fox and RKO from 1930 to 1940. O'Brien's father was a policeman and was assigned to escort Tom Mix around San Francisco in 1922; through Mix, George got a job at Fox. O'Brien had been an excellent high school athlete, served in the navy during World War I and while there won the Light Heavyweight Boxing Championship. After the service, O'Brien entered Santa Clara State College, where he became involved in drama. In 1924 O'Brien landed the lead role in *The Iron Horse,* directed by John Ford; when the silent era ended, O'Brien became a star in the talkies. His first "B" was in 1930, *The Lone Star Ranger,* and he stayed with Fox until 1935, when he went to RKO. His first film at RKO was *Daniel Boone* (1936). During World War II, O'Brien reenlisted in the navy and was sent to the Pacific. Back in Hollywood in 1946, he landed some small parts and then appeared in *Fort Apache* (1948) and *She Wore a Yellow Ribbon* (1949) with John Wayne. His last film role was in *Cheyenne Autumn* in 1964, directed by John Ford, who had given him his first starring role. (See also B WESTERN MOVIES; MOVIES.)

O'BRIEN, HUGH (b. Hugh J. Krampe in Rochester, New York on April 19, 1925)   Actor Hugh O'Brien starred as Wyatt Earp in the popular TV series "The Life and Legend of Wyatt Earp." O'Brian served in the Marine Corps during World War II and became a drill instructor at the age of 18. After the war O'Brian intended to study law but ended up in Hollywood, where he made his television debut in 1948 and appeared in "Fireside Theater" and "The Loretta Young Show" before he landed the role of Wyatt Earp in 1955. In 1972–73 O'Brian starred in an adventure series, "Search," as Hugh Lockwood.

O BURY ME NOT ON THE LONE PRAIRIE
This song is based on an old sea song in which sailors requested listeners to "bury me not" at sea. The lyrics for the cowboy version came primarily from a poem, "The Ocean-Buried," written by a Boston Universalist clergyman, Edwin Hubbell Chapin, in 1839 and published in the *Southern Literary Messenger.* Another poem, "O, Bury Me Not" by E. B. Hale of Putnam, Ohio, was also

George O'Brien

tobacco (or perhaps because he suspected danger) as the group passed the old post hospital when Garrett shouted, "Halt!" O'Folliard went for his gun and was shot just below his heart; the outlaws rode away and O'Folliard attempted to follow them, but after a short while he reined in his horse, walked back to the posse and said, "Don't shoot, Garrett. I'm killed." The lawmen helped him down off his horse and put him inside the old hospital, where he died less than an hour later. He was buried in the Fort Sumner cemetery. Later, two other gang members, Charles Bowdre and Billy the Kid, were buried near him. (See also BILLY THE KID; GARRETT, PAT; LINCOLN COUNTY WAR.)

O'KEEFFE, GEORGIA See ART.

OKLAHOMA LAND RUSH At noon on April 22, 1889 a pistol was fired to signal the start of a stampede of about 10,000 people lined up to grab land in the north-central region of the Oklahoma Territory, known as the Unassigned Lands. A claimant was allowed to claim 160 acres for a filing fee of $15. Although army troops were strategically stationed to ward off cheaters, a number of people snuck in early and staked a claim; these were known as "sooners." Following this initial land rush, there was another held on September 22, 1891 in central Oklahoma, one on April 16, 1892 in western Oklahoma, one on September 16, 1893 in the

published in the *Southern Literary Messenger* (1845), and in 1857 another poem, "Oh, Bury Me Not" by poet W. F. Wightman, was published in the same magazine. In 1850 a ballad, "The Ocean Burial," was rewritten by George N. Allen, based on the old song "Hind Horn." Some folklorists believe that young Canadian and New England men carried these songs west with them and altered the lyrics. Several westerners have been credited with composing the song: H. Clemons of Deadwood, South Dakota, Venice and Sam Gentry from Texas, and others, but there is probably no single author and the true authors will most likely never be known. The first complete version of the lyrics were printed in the *Journal of Folklore* in 1901 by Annie Laurie Ellis of Uvalde, Texas. This song was incredibly popular with cowboys in the West—most knew it—and it inspired the later song by songwriter Carson Robison, "Carry Me Back to the Lone Prairie," written in 1934.

O'FOLLIARD, TOM (b. Uvalde, Texas in 1858; d. Fort Sumner, New Mexico on December 19, 1880) O'Folliard was a friend and member of the gang of Billy the Kid. Involved in the Lincoln County War, O'Folliard managed to escape the burning McSween house in July 1878. On December 19, 1889 O'Folliard was riding into Fort Sumner with the Kid, Charlie Bowdre, Tom Pickett, Dave Rudabaugh and Billy Wilson for some entertainment and did not realize a posse headed by Pat Garrett waited for them. The Kid and O'Folliard were in front of the group, but Billy dropped back to get a chaw of

Hugh O'Brien

Cherokee Strip in northwestern Oklahoma and a final one on May 23, 1895 in the center of the territory.

OKY DOKY RANCH See ADVENTURES OF OKY DOKY.

OLD CHISHOLM TRAIL, THE This is a true folk song, changing with each singer. The couplets are easily made up, and often coarse lyrics were sung by cowboys; the refrain remains the same, but outside a handful of verses the song has a number of different variants. Perhaps the original tune belonged to the old Stephen Foster song "Old Uncle Ned" or perhaps the old railroad song "Drill, Ye Tarriers, Drill."

OLINGER, BOB (aka the "Big Indian"; b. Robert A. Olinger in Ohio c. 1841; d. Lincoln, New Mexico on April 28, 1881) While Billy the Kid was in the Lincoln jail waiting to be hung, Deputy Sheriff Olinger constantly tormented and bullied him. On April 28 Olinger left with some other prisoners for an evening meal around 6 P.M. The Kid got a gun and killed J. W. Bell, who was guarding him, and Olinger raced out in the street after hearing the shots. The Kid aimed the shotgun out a second-story window, said, "Hello Bob," and then blasted Olinger, who was dead in the dirt. The Kid then escaped from the town. (See also BILLY THE KID; LINCOLN COUNTY WAR.)

OLINGER, JOHN WALLACE The Olinger brothers were involved in the Lincoln County War against McSween and the Regulators. During the war John Olinger was present when John Tunstall was murdered, and Olinger's brother, Bob, was killed by Billy the Kid during a jail break. John Olinger shot rancher Henry Beckwith in the cheek and nose after Beckwith had killed his own son-in-law, William H. Johnson, and almost killed his son, John Beckwith, after a bitter family quarrel. When Henry Beckwith recovered, charges against John Olinger were dropped. (See also LINCOLN COUNTY WAR.)

OLIVE, PRINT (b. Isom Prentice Olive in Louisiana on February 7, 1840; d. Trail City, Colorado on August 16, 1886) Print Olive was a wild character of the Old West, and his story is filled with examples of violence, frontier justice, and revenge for those who wronged him. Olive and his family moved to Williamson County, Texas when he was a boy; during the Civil War he joined the Confederate army and fought at Shiloh, was captured at Vicksburg, paroled and then went to Galveston, Texas for the rest of the war. Olive was known for throwing a wide loop when he went into ranching. He reportedly shot a stock rustler, Rob Murday, who was after Print's stock, and then nursed him back to health and hired him. Olive set up the "Olive Pens" on 20 acres near Taylor, Texas and sent herds north up the trails from there. He was reputed to chase rustlers with guns blazing, and he never shied away from violence. Olive killed Dave Fream in a horseback duel in 1870 and was

wounded badly in a saloon gunfight with Jim Kennedy. Print and his brother, Jay, ambushed rustler W. H. McDonald, and Print was responsible for the deaths of rustlers James H. Crow and Turk Turner in March 1876. On the night of August 1-2, 1876 Print and his brother Jay were in a gunfight, and Jay died about three weeks later. Soon afterward the man responsible was killed by Print. When brothers Ira and Bob were killed by Ami Ketchum and Luther Mitchell, Print avenged their deaths by lynching both men, then shooting Mitchell for shooting Bob and, afterward, burned both the bodies. For this he was sentenced to life in prison but after a new trial was freed. Print moved into Kansas, where he established a ranch and a home in Dodge City. There he opened a saloon, stable and wagon yard in Coolidge, Kansas and hired Joe Sparrow; later Sparrow opened his own saloon and dance hall in direct competition, which led to a gunfight in which Print Olive was killed by Sparrow.

OLIVER, DEAN (b. Dennis Dean Oliver in Dodge City, Kansas on November 17, 1929) Dean Oliver won eight calf-roping championships (1955, 1958, 1960–1964, and 1969) during 25 years of rodeo competition with earnings of $527,000, a record for its time. Oliver also won three All-Around Championships (1963, 1964 and 1965) through his winnings in calf roping and his second event, steer wrestling. Oliver's family moved to Idaho when he was a boy, and his father, a commercial pilot, was killed in a plane crash when Dean was 10. Unsuccessful in school, Oliver dropped out in the 10th grade and began working. A trip to a rodeo inspired him to become a calf roper, and he practiced on the calves at a dairy farm where he worked. In 1951 Oliver entered his first rodeo and soon began winning; a turning point came when he purchased a top roping horse, Mickey, which led to calf-roping championships from 1960 to 1964. Oliver would have also won the calf-roping championship in 1966 but during the National Finals his rope broke after he had roped his calf. (See also RODEO.)

OMAHA INDIANS Originally from Ohio, the Omaha Indians moved to South Dakota, where they lived in houses of earth and sod and used the tipi when they traveled to hunt. The Omaha were always friendly to whites and were visited by Lewis and Clark in 1804. The tribe had been greatly reduced by a smallpox epidemic in 1802. The Omaha ceded all their lands to the United States in 1854 and moved to a reservation in northeastern Nebraska in 1856.

OMOHUNDRO, TEXAS JACK (b. John Burwell Omohundro, Jr. near Palmyra, Virginia on July 26, 1846; d. Leadville, Colorado on June 28, 1880) Texas Jack was a showman with Buffalo Bill Cody, starring with Cody in the play *Scouts of the Plains*, which was the first venture into show business for them and for their third costar, Wild Bill Hickok. Omohundro served as a civilian orderly in the Confederacy during the Civil War;

Wild Bill Hickok, Texas Jack Omohundro
and Buffalo Bill Cody

a livestock newspaper, *Horn and Hoof.* In 1886 he became a probate judge and in 1888 was elected sheriff of Yavapai County; he ran for Congress twice and was defeated but was elected mayor of Prescott in 1897. In a famous Old West incident, O'Neill and a posse pursued for over 600 miles four cowboys who robbed a train in Arizona, engaged them in a shootout, captured them and then took them to jail in Kanab, Utah.

OPEN RANGE The range for common use, which legally had no controls put upon it. However, big-time cattlemen and ranchers often took possession of this range simply by inhabiting it and running their herds on it.

OREGON TRAIL The most famous emigrant trail of all time was originally used by fur trappers in the West from Spain, Great Britain, Russia and the United States, which all held competing claims for the territory at various times. For the United States, the first settlers were missionaries, and, through them, American citizens received their first information about the Pacific Northwest. The area was quickly labeled a paradise for agriculture. In 1841 the Wilkes Expedition reported on the area; in 1843 John C. Fremont explored the region for the army and gave it another major boost.

The first emigrants to travel to Oregon left Independence, Missouri in May 1841 and went along the Platte River through South Pass and then to the Columbia River; this soon became known as the origin of the Oregon Trail. The trail soon became well known and well worn; it went from Missouri to Fort Kearny on the Platte River, then forded the river and went on to Fort Laramie, where the emigrants would stop and rest after traveling about 670 miles from Missouri. They would also trade in their livestock for fresh stock there, get new supplies and repair their wagons before leaving Fort Laramie and heading north to the mouth of the Sweetwater River's tributary across present-day Wyoming. From there they traveled to South Pass, at which time they had covered about 950 miles from Missouri. The emigrants then crossed the Green River valley and headed to Fort Bridger, about 1,000 miles from their point of origin, and then northwest to Fort Hall on the Snake River, about 1,300 miles from where they started. The emigrants traveled along the Snake River past Fort Boise and across the Blue Mountains to missionary Marcus Whitman's compound on the Columbia River. From there, the settlers made boats to get down the Columbia River to the mouth of the Willamette River; they then headed south to the Willamette Valley, a journey that took about four to six months and covered around 2,000 miles.

In 1842 Dr. Elijah White led 100 people and 18 wagons to Oregon Territory, where he was to establish a new post as Indian agent. He brought with him the news that the Presbyterian missions were to be discontinued in the Pacific Northwest, which caused Marcus Whitman to travel back East and get the decision reversed. Whitman's return to Oregon in 1843 led the Great Migration, a result of an economic depression in

he then enlisted and became a courier and scout during the Shenandoah campaign. After the war he briefly taught school in Florida and then moved to Texas, where he took the name Texas Jack for Wild West show work. Omohundro served as a scout with Cody and Hickok before they jointly began their show business career in Chicago. Omohundro continued in show business and married leading actress Giuseppina Morlacchi. He was featured in some of Ned Buntline's dime novels and worked on stage with Cody until 1875; after this time he organized his own company and worked with his wife.

O'NEILL, BUCKEY (b. William Owen O'Neill in Ireland on February 2, 1860; d. Santiago, Cuba on July 1, 1898) Buckey O'Neill became one of Teddy Roosevelt's Rough Riders and was named captain of A Troop, First U.S. Volunteer Cavalry; he was killed by a sniper in Cuba and buried there during the Spanish-American War; his remains were moved to Arlington National Cemetery on May 2, 1899.

O'Neill got his nickname because of his love for faro, a game in which players "buck the tiger." He moved from St. Louis to Phoenix in 1879 and edited the *Arizona Gazette;* he then moved to Prescott, where he operated the country as well as continuing news of the potential of the area.

On one trip in 1843 Peter H. Burnett led 1,000 men, women and children in more than 100 wagons to Oregon. In 1844 a wet spring caused late starts, and fewer traveled the trail than in the previous years, but in 1845 about 3,000 emigrants went over the Oregon Trail, generally in small groups of 12 to 24 wagons. An estimated 4,000–5,000 traveled the trail in 1847. In 1882–84 the Union Pacific Railroad constructed a short line from Granger, Wyoming to Portland, Oregon, and settlers could then use the railroad for the last leg of their journey. Although the Oregon Trail is most famous for its use by settlers to get to the West, it was also used as the route for cattle and sheep; in 1880 about 200,000 cattle went over the trail into the Great Plains, and in 1885–90 a number of herds of sheep went from Omaha to Kansas City over the trail.

A pattern developed for emigrants using the Oregon Trail. The departure was timed in the spring so that livestock could feed off the rich grass; if the start was too late, grass would be scarce. Belongings were kept to a minimum, and family treasures were often abandoned en route. Oxen were preferred over horses because they were stronger and sturdier, did not need grain and were less appealing to Indians. At night the wagons were drawn into a circle to create a stockade for the animals. Families generally planned the next day's travel, and leaders made key decisions. The emigrants traveled in constant fear of Indians, and guards were always posted, although Indians seldom attacked large groups and most of the Indians encountered were either curious or hungry.

OREGON TRAIL, THE　TV show that starred Rod Taylor as Evan Thorpe, Darleen Carr as Margaret Devlin, Charles Napier as Luther Sprague, Andrew Stevens as Andrew Thorpe, Tony Becker as William Thorpe and Gina Maria Smika as Rachel Thorpe

Widower Evan Thorpe left Illinois in 1852 with his three children and headed west to Oregon Territory with a wagon train. Elected captain because of the unreliability of the original captain, Thorpe found a love interest in fellow traveler Margaret Devlin as the group faced the difficulties of moving west by wagon train in pre-Civil War America. The show debuted on September 21, 1977 on Wednesday nights on NBC. The hour-long show ended on October 26, 1977.

O'ROURKE, JOHN　See JOHNNY-BEHIND-THE-DEUCE.

OSAGE INDIANS　The Osage Indians were very tall, the males averaging from six feet to six and a half feet in height. Originally from the Missouri River area, the Osage migrated to Kansas around 1820. General George Custer used Osage scouts at the Battle of Washita in 1868. The Osage were removed to Oklahoma Territory in 1870 and became the richest tribe in the country when oil was discovered on their land in 1920.

OURAY, CHIEF　(b. c. 1830; d. 1880)　A chief of the Ute Indians and close of friend of Kit Carson and other whites, Chief Ouray went to Washington, D.C. in

1868 and negotiated a treaty. He spoke Spanish and English and never used tobacco or alcohol. Because he was not present at the White River Agency in September 1879, he was unable to prevent the Meeker Massacre. (See also MEEKER MASSACRE.)

OUTCASTS, THE　TV show that starred Don Murray as Earl Corey and Otis Young as Jemal David.

"The Outcasts" was an attempt to show an interracial western. Jemal David was a former slave, and Earl Corey was a former Virginia aristocrat; the two teamed (albeit with numerous difficulties and differences) as bounty hunters. The show began on September 23, 1968 and was last telecast on September 15, 1969. Only 26 episodes of the hour-long show were filmed, which were shown on Mondays on ABC.

OUTFIT　The term "outfit" can mean a group of cowboys belonging to a specific ranch or on a particular mission (such as a roundup), or smaller groups within a ranch divided up for a particular job—for example, gathering cattle from a particular range or branding. The term can also mean an individual's clothes and belongings.

OUTLAW　A man or beast; if a man, it was someone who had broken the law and was wanted for justice. When applied to a horse or cow, it generally meant one that was unmanageable.

OUTLAW, BASS　(b. Baz Outlaw in Georgia c. 1865; d. El Paso, Texas on April 5, 1894)　Well educated and from a good family, Bass Outlaw had a drinking problem that kept him in trouble. A member of the Texas Rangers, he had to resign after being caught drunk on duty. On April 5, 1895 Outlaw was drunk and fired a shot into a sporting house in El Paso, Texas. When Constable John Selman and Texas Ranger Joe McKidrict confronted him, Outlaw killed McKidrict and hit Selman several times. But Selman put a slug in Outlaw's chest, which caused Outlaw to surrender to Texas Ranger Frank McMahon, who took him to a saloon. On a prostitute's bed, Bass Outlaw died about four hours after the shooting. (See also SELMAN, JOHN.)

OUTLAW, THE　Film produced and directed by Howard Hughes; screenplay by Jules Furtham; released by Howard Hughes Productions in 1943; 123 minutes in length. Cast: Jack Buetel, Jane Russell, Thomas Mitchell and Walter Houston.

This film was supposedly based on Billy the Kid but was in fact created for Jane Russell to expose her assets and attributes. The poses struck by Jane Russell to promote this film are still famous. The film has Billy the Kid, Pat Garrett and Doc Holliday all in the same film (historically, they were never together), but the central character is actually Rio, played by Miss Russell, and she and Billy will ride off together. For this film Howard Hughes invented a special pneumatic bra to show off Russell's heaving cleavage. There was also some erotic dallying between the Kid and Rio. In the end, what

Jane Russell in *The Outlaw*

makes this a memorable picture is Russell's anatomy and the conflicts with the censors at the Hays Office.

OUTLAWS TV show that starred Rod Taylor as John Grail, William Lucking as Harland Pike, Charles Napier as Wolfson "Wolf" Lucas, Richard Roundtree as Isaiah "Ice" McAdams, Patrick Houser as Billy Pike and Christine Belford as Lieutenant Maggie Randall.

Science fiction met a western and became a detective drama in this show. Sheriff John Grail was leading a posse after his old gang in 1899 when they were all caught in an electrical storm and in the resulting time warp found themselves in contemporary Texas. The whole group then reconciled their differences, bought a ranch (the Double Eagle) and opened the Double Eagle Detective Agency, dispensing old-fashioned justice in and around Houston. The show premiered on December 26, 1986 on CBS on Sunday nights. After a two-hour pilot, the show became a one-hour series beginning in January 1987 on Saturday nights on CBS before its final telecast on May 30, 1987.

OUTLAWS, THE TV show that starred Barton MacLane as U.S. marshall Frank Caine (1960–61), Don Collier as Deputy Marshal Will Forman, Jock Gaynor as Deputy Marshal Heck Martin (1960–61), Bruce Yarnell as Deputy Marshal Chalk Breeson (1961–62), Slim Pickens as Slim (1961–62) and Judy Lewis as Connie Masters (1961–62).

Set in Stillwater, in what became Oklahoma, in the 1890s, this series was on the air for two seasons: During the first season the shows were done from the perspec-

tive of the outlaws being pursued; in the second season the shows were from the perspective of the lawmen. Some cast changes occurred as well. The show debuted on September 29, 1960 and finished on September 13, 1962. The hour-long series was shown on Thursday nights on NBC and, after the first show—done in black and white—was shot in color. Fifty episodes were filmed.

OVERLAND TRAIL, THE TV show that starred William Bendix as Frederick Thomas Kelly and Doug McClure as Frank "Flip" Flippen.

Before the railroads linked America, the stagecoach carried passengers from coast to coast. The Overland Trail was one of the major roads for stagecoaches, and this series was about opening this trail and keeping it open. The show premiered on February 7, 1960 on Sunday nights at 7 on NBC. The hour-long series was gone after 17 episodes, with the last telecast on September 11, 1960.

OWENS, COMMODORE PERRY (b. east Tennessee on July 29, 1852; d. Seligman, Arizona on May 10, 1919) Owens's parents named him after the hero of the War of 1812. Owens moved to Arizona, where he was known for his long hair and his guns, which included a pair of .45s and two rifles. He became sheriff of Apache County, but after an 1887 gunfight he cut his locks, got married and settled into the life of a family man.

The most famous gunfight for Owens occurred on a Sunday afternoon, September 4, 1887 in Holbrook, Arizona. Owens was looking for Andy Blevins, who used the alias Andy Cooper and whose father and brother had recently been killed in the Pleasant Valley War. Owens went to the home of Mrs. Blevins and saw Andy looking out through the window. Both men fired and Owens hit Andy, who died in his mother's arms. A brother, John Blevins, then fired at Owens, but the lawman shot him in the shoulder. Owens killed Mose Roberts, a Blevins brother-in-law from Texas, at the side of the house and then killed 16-year-old Sam Houston Blevins, Andy's youngest brother, with a bullet in the heart. After firing a few more shots through the walls of the house, Owens quit firing. At this point only John Blevins, his mother and two other women were left alive in the house. (See also COOPER, ANDY; PLEASANT VALLEY WAR.)

OX-BOW INCIDENT, THE Film produced by Lamar Trotti; directed by William Wellman; screenplay by Lamar Trotti (from the novel by Walter Van Tilburg Clark); music by Cyril J. Mockridge; released in 1943 by Twentieth Century–Fox; 77 minutes in length. Cast: Henry Fonda, Dana Andrews, Mary Beth Hughes, Anthony Quinn, William Eythe, Henry Morgan, Jane Darwell and Matt Briggs.

Based on the Walter Van Tilburg Clark novel, this haunting movie was about a lynch mob who lynches the wrong men for the wrong reason. Told from the point of view of two cowboys who saw the whole thing, the story concerns three men who are accused of killing a rancher and stealing his cattle by a former Confederate officer leading a group of townsfolk. The lynch mob hangs the three men but then discovers the rancher is still alive and had sold the cattle.

PAINT HORSE Another name for a pinto. (See also PINTO.)

PAIUTE INDIANS The Paiute are the "Digger Indians," a nomadic group who wandered through Nevada, Oregon, California, Utah and Arizona in a constant quest for food. These Indians, described by mountain man Jedediah Smith in 1827 as "the most miserable objects in creation," hunted small game, mice, snakes and other reptiles, edible roots and insects. These Indians lived in wickiups. In 1860 they fought the Battle of Pyramid Lake (Nevada) in the first skirmish of the Paiute War; however, by the end of 1861 the Paiute were scattered and defeated. A Paiute prophet, Wovoka, began to preach the ghost dance, which ultimately ended in tragedy in December 1890 at Wounded Knee, South Dakota. (See also GHOST DANCE; WOUNDED KNEE MASSACRE.)

PALL MALL PLAYHOUSE This was a summer TV series of dramatic westerns that had been pilots for TV shows but were never developed. The show's first telecast was July 20, 1955, and the last was on September 7, 1955. The half-hour show was broadcast on ABC on Wednesday nights.

PALOMINO A golden-color horse that is large, strong and sturdy and descended from Spanish-Mexican stock.

PALO VERDE A yellow-flowered plant (*Cercidium microphyllus*) found in the Southwest, particularly Arizona. It blooms in April and May, causing fields to be covered with yellow and attracting bees to its nectar. Found in desert areas, it is mostly leafless when not in bloom and is generally located where water settles.

PANNING Filling a pan with water from a stream and then sloshing it around so the dirt and sand are washed away and gold is left. This was a popular and inexpensive way to look for gold in rivers and streams.

PANTHER See MOUNTAIN LION.

PAPOOSE An Indian child carried on the back of his or her mother; sometimes it just meant an Indian child.

PARADISE TV show that starred Lee Horsley as Ethan Allen Cord, Sigrid Thornton as Amelia Lawson, Dehl Berti as John Taylor, John Cittendon as Deputy Charlie, Nicholas Surovy as Marshal P. J. Breckenhous, Jenny Beck as Claire, Matthew Newmark as Joseph, Brian Lando as Ben and Michael Patrick Carter as George.

A lone gunslinger ends up with his sister's four chil-dren when she dies. Additionally, he is asked to help bring some law and order to the town of Paradise now and then. The show premiered on October 27, 1988 on Saturday nights. It did not appear during fall 1990 but reappeared on January 4, 1991 as "Guns of Paradise." It was last shown on June 14, 1991 after 57 episodes.

PARKER, FESS (b. Fort Worth, Texas on August 16, 1926) Fess Parker's fame began when he starred as Davy Crockett in the Walt Disney series in the 1950s, which set off a Crocket-mania craze. Parker recorded a version of "The Ballad of Davy Crockett," which was a huge hit in 1955; later, he starred in the TV series "Daniel Boone." Parker grew up around San Angelo, Texas and graduated from the University of Texas. During World War II he served aboard a minesweeper and went to Hollywood in 1943 while he was with the navy; after the war he studied dramatics at the University of Southern California. (See also DANIEL BOONE; DAVY CROCKETT: KING OF THE WILD FRONTIER; TELEVISION WESTERNS; WALT DISNEY PRESENTS.)

Fess Parker

Judge Isaac Parker *(Western Archives)*

PARKER, JUDGE ISAAC CHARLES (b. near Barnesville, Ohio on October 15, 1838; d. Fort Smith, Arkansas on November 17, 1896) Parker is the famous "hanging judge" who held court at Fort Smith, Arkansas. A no-nonsense, stern Methodist who stood six feet tall and weighed 200 pounds, Parker presided over Indian Territory, a particularly ruthless area and hideout for criminals of all types. During the 21 years Parker served as federal judge, 65 deputy marshals were killed. Parker was a hard worker; his court convened each morning at 8:30, and he often worked until dark, six days a week. During this time he tried 13,490 cases, sentenced 172 men to death and hung 79. Appointed in May 1875, he soon built a gallows in Fort Smith that would hold 12 men, and in September 1875 he had six men hung for public view. During the first 14 years of Parker's rule, there was no appeal for any of his convictions.

PARKER, QUANAH See QUANAH PARKER.

PARKER, ROBERT LEROY See CASSIDY, BUTCH.

PARKHURST, CHARLEY (aka "Cockeyed Charley"; b. Charlotte Darkey Parkhurst in Lebanon, New Hampshire in 1812; d. near Watsonville, California on December 29, 1879) Everybody thought Charley Parkhurst was a man until he died; that's when they discovered that one of the most prominent and able stagecoach drivers in California was a woman who dressed as a man. Charley was abandoned by her parents and then ran away from an orphanage in boys' clothes. She met stabler Ebenezer Balch in Worcester, Massachusetts, and he taught Charley how to drive a team of six horses. She moved with Balch to Providence, Rhode Island and then on to Georgia and California, where she lived as a man. She voted in an election in Santa Cruz in 1868, which makes her the first woman to cast a vote in the United States. Charley chewed tobacco, smoked cigars and wore a patch over her left eye to cover an injury suffered when a horse kicked her. About five feet seven inches tall, she raised stock and worked as a logger when she wasn't driving stagecoaches. After she died of cancer, an autopsy uncovered her secret; the autopsy also disclosed she had once given birth to a child.

PARKMAN, FRANCIS (b. Boston, Massachusetts on September 16, 1823; d. Jamaica Plain, Massachusetts on November 8, 1893) Francis Parkman is most famous as the author of *The Oregon Trail*, published in 1849 after he had visited the Great Plains Indian country. This book later became part of Parkman's nine-volume series *France and England in North America*, published in 1892. The son of a Unitarian minister, Francis Parkman inherited a good deal of money, which made him financially independent. He graduated from Harvard University in 1844 as a Phi Beta Kappa.

Parkman made his life work the study of the struggle between France and Britain for America. He decided to spend a summer on the plains in 1846 with mountain man Henri Chatillon in order to understand Iroquois society of the colonial era. In April of that year, Parkman set out on a journey on the Oregon Trail to study Indians; he lived with a band of Sioux briefly in an attempt to study a primitive lifestyle. At the end of his life Parkman was going blind and for five years could neither concentrate nor see to write for more than a few minutes at a time; still he published a series of major historical works; these works, as well as *The Oregon Trail*, made him one of America's greatest historians.

PAT GARRETT AND BILLY THE KID Film produced by Gordon Carroll; directed by Sam Peckinpah; screenplay by Rudolph Wurlitzer; released in 1973 by MGM; 106 minutes in length. Cast: James Coburn, Kris Kristofferson, Richard Jaeckel, Katy Jurado, Chill Wills, Jason Robards, Bob Dylan, R. G. Armstrong, Luke Askew, John Beck, Rita Coolidge, Jack Elam, L. Q. Jones, Slim Pickens and Dub Taylor.

The story of Billy the Kid and the man who killed him is retold by director Sam Peckinpah. Notable is the fact that Bob Dylan appears in his film debut (as a character named "Alias") and composed the score for the movie, which included the hit single "Knockin' on Heaven's Door." Peckinpah tells the story of big business killing off individualism when Garrett, who sold out to Santa Fe businessmen, guns down the Kid. But the film was chopped up, and the version released has important sections missing that tie the story together.

PAWNEE BILL (b. Gordon William Lillie in Bloomington, Illinois on February 14, 1860; d. Pawnee, Oklahoma on February 3, 1942) Pawnee Bill (Gordon W. Lillie) had a Wild West show that competed with Buffalo Bill Cody's; the two joined forces from 1908 to 1913, when the partnership was dissolved. Lillie learned the Pawnee language while he was a teacher in the industrial school at the Pawnee Agency in Indian Territory. Major Frank North, head of the Pawnee Scouts, intro-

Pawnee Bill

duced Lillie to Buffalo Bill Cody, and Cody used Lillie as an interpreter for the Pawnee in his Wild West show in 1888. After this season, Lillie left Buffalo Bill and formed his own Wild West show, which soon folded; in 1890 he tried again, and this time he prospered with a Wild West show that toured for 20 years, including some stints in Europe. Because of Cody's financial troubles, he merged his show with Lillie's in 1908 and they toured until 1913, when they dissolved their partnership. At this time Lillie moved to his 2,000-acre ranch near Pawnee, Oklahoma, where he established Old Town, the Indian Trading Post and Pawnee Bill's Buffalo Ranch, where he helped preserve buffalo. Lillie became vice president of the Fern Oil Company, wrote several books and helped establish the Wichita Wildlife Refuge.

PAWNEE INDIANS A powerful, advanced tribe of Indians, the Pawnee were a seminomadic group that occupied the area that is now Nebraska. The rich Platte River area allowed the Pawnee to grow corn, beans, pumpkins, melons and squashes in their earth-lodge villages. But for part of the year they went to the southwest plains and hunted buffalo. Skilled artisans and very religious, the Pawnee were hit especially hard by smallpox in 1831, which killed about half their people, and by cholera in 1849, which killed about 1,200 of their tribe. The Pawnee never fought the whites but often helped whites fight other tribes. They ceded all their land to the government and in 1876 were placed on a reservation in Indian Territory.

PEACEMAKER Any gun could be called a Peacemaker, but the true Peacemaker was the Colt revolver Model 1873 that used .44 ammunition.

PEACE PIPE A pipe smoked by Indians as part of a ceremony to seal an agreement or as part of bargaining. The peace pipe symbolized the end of battles between warring factions.

PECKINPAH, SAM (b. Samuel David Peckinpah in Fresno, California on February 21, 1925; d. Inglewood, California on December 28, 1984) Sam Peckinpah was director of some of the most violent westerns ever filmed, bringing a gritty realism to films such as *Ride the High Country* (1962), *The Wild Bunch* (1969) and *Pat Garrett and Billy the Kid* (1973). Peckinpah grew up in California and attended the University of Southern California, where he received an M.A. in drama. In the mid-1950s Peckinpah worked under director Donald Siegel, and during the late 1950s he became a TV writer for shows such as "Gunsmoke," "The Rifleman" and "Broken Arrow." Peckinpah's first western as a director was *The Deadly Companions* (1961), and his next was *Ride the High Country* (1962), which brought together Randolph Scott and Joel McCrea. He followed this with *Major Dundee* (1965), *The Wild Bunch* (1969)—considered to be his best film—then *The Ballad of Cable Hogue* (1970), *Straw Dogs* (1971), *Junior Bonner* (1972), *The Getaway* (1972), *Pat Garrett and Billy the Kid* (1973), *Bring Me the Head of Alfredo Garcia* (1974), *The Killer Elite* (1975), *Convoy* (1978) and *The Osterman Weekend* (1983).

PECOS BILL The first Pecos Bill stories were told in 1870s; they were the western version of stories about the larger-than-life Paul Bunyon figure. The stories were originally oral tales, passed from cowboy to cowboy. The first written version of the Pecos Bill stories appeared in *Century* magazine in October 1923. Other deeds were published, and in 1948 Walt Disney produced a cartoon version of Pecos Bill. According to these cowboy folk tales, Pecos Bill was raised by coyotes and was a grown man before he saw another human. Joining the Hell's Gate Gulch outfit, Bill rode a cougar with a 12-foot snake for a lariat. He could drink a gallon of boiling coffee with a gulp and wipe his mouth with cactus. After joining the outfit, Pecos Bill taught the cowboys how to brand cattle, throw a lasso and yell "yippeee." The horse he rode was raised on nitroglycerin and dynamite; when another cowboy tried to ride his mount, Bill had to lasso him from the top of Pike's Peak. Pecos Bill rode an Oklahoma cyclone, and when the storm couldn't throw him, it rained enough to create the Grand Canyon. Death Valley was formed by Pecos Bill's rear end when the ride ended.

PEMMICAN Food preserved and carried by Indians and mountain men. Pemmican was either buffalo or deer meat cut into strips and dried (either in the sun or in the smoke of a wood fire) until it was hard and then beaten between stones into a powder that was mixed with animal fat. The result was a paste, sometimes seasoned with berries; it was put into a skin bag, carried and used on long journeys or during winter months.

PETRIFIED FOREST Located in northern Arizona in the Painted Desert, the Petrified Forest is an area of trees that have turned to stone. The petrification process began when the trees were buried in mud, sand and volcanic ash and unable to rot or decay because of lack of oxygen. Water with silica penetrated the wood. The water then evaporated leaving the silica, which turned to quartz in the form of the wood tissues.

PEYOTE A spineless cactus used to make mescal, a hallucinatory drug. This gray-green plant looks like the tops of carrots; when these "buttons" or tops are peeled and chewed, chewers often experience a trancelike state accompanied by visions. Tea is often made from the roots, which are even more potent. The plant is mostly found in southern Texas in the Rio Grande valley.

PHILLIPS, PORTUGEE (aka John Phillips; b. Manuel Felipe Cardoso in the Azores near Terra, Pico Island on April 8, 1832; d. Cheyenne, Wyoming on November 18, 1883) Portugee Phillips is the mountain man who traveled 200 miles in freezing snow on the back of a mule to deliver the news of the Fetterman Massacre at Fort Phil Kearny, and also to bring relief to the fort, which was surrounded by Indians. Phillips rode from Fort Phil Kearny (Wyoming) to Fort Laramie after the December 21, 1866 massacre of Captain Fetterman and 80 men by Chief Red Cloud and the Sioux. Phillips and another "citizen carrier," Dan Dixon, were hired by Colonel Henry Carrington, the commander of Fort Phil Kearny, for $300 each to travel through hostile Indian Territory to Horseshoe Station, then 40 miles farther to Fort Laramie. Phillips arrived on Christmas about 11 P.M. during a Christmas night dance. Legend has it that Phillips rode Colonel Carrington's Kentucky thoroughbred "Grey Eagle" and that the horse dropped dead after the ride, but there is no proof this actually happened. Phillips changed his name from Manuel Felipe Cardoso around 1850 when he went to California during the gold rush. He spent a number of years mining and prospecting and was wintering at Fort Phil Kearny when the Fetterman Massacre occurred.

PICKENS, SLIM (b. Louis Bert Lindley, Jr. in Kingsburg, California on June 29, 1919; d. Modesto, California on December 8, 1983. Louis Lindley changed his name to "Slim Pickens" because his father did not like him riding in rodeos—and "Slim" wanted to keep on but didn't want his father to find out. Pickens began riding in rodeos at 14 and, while mending from some rodeo injuries, did a screen test for Warner Brothers; his first movie appearance was in *Smoky* (1945) with Fred MacMurray. He was in *Rocky Mountain* with Erroll Flynn before joining Republic in 1951 as the sidekick for Rex Allen, taking over from Buddy Ebson. Pickens appeared in a number of westerns, including *The Big Country* with Gregory Peck, *Blazing Saddles* (1974) and the country music movie, *Honeysuckle Rose* (1980) and was a regular in two TV series, "The Outlaws"

Slim Pickens

and "Custer." Later, he appeared as host of "The Nashville Palace" and as a regular on "Hee Haw." Pickens's most famous role was as Major King Kong in *Dr. Strangelove* (1964), in which he rode a nuclear bomb like a bucking bronco. Pickens was inducted into the National Cowboy Hall of Fame in Oklahoma City.

PICKETT, BILL (b. near Taylor, Texas c. 1860; d. near Guthrie, Oklahoma on April 2, 1932) Bill Pickett invented "bulldogging," or steer wrestling. Son of a Choctaw mother and mulatto father, Pickett was hired as a cowboy in 1880 by George Miller of the 101 Ranch in Oklahoma. Here, Pickett "bulldogged" his first steer by wrestling the steer to the ground and then biting the steer's upper lip. The pain on the sensitive area of the lip kept the steer from moving. Pickett had seen bulldogs do the same thing, hence the term "bulldogging." When the 101 Ranch began to produce a Wild West show, Pickett was part of the performances, demonstrating his bulldogging technique first at the Arkansas Valley Fair in Rocky Ford, Colorado in 1900 and then traveling throughout the country. Pickett, along with Tom Mix and Will Rogers, was the star attraction of the 101 show. In Mexico Pickett bulldogged a bull-fighting bull; he also appeared in Madison Square Garden and in England. Pickett had retired and purchased land near Chandler, Oklahoma but returned to the 101 to help Zack Miller when he was injured by an unbroken horse and died 11 days later. Miller arranged a lavish funeral for the black the early 1890s. After the gangs split, Pierce joined up with Bitter Creek Newcomb, and on May 2 the two went to the Dunn Ranch, where Newcomb's wife, the "Rose of Cimarron," lived. Dunn's brothers also owed Newcomb $900. But there was a $5,000 reward on the outlaws' heads, and the Dunn brothers shot them both when they rode up to the house. When Pierce made a groaning noise after hitting the ground, the Dunn brothers shot him again, this time finishing the job. (See also NEWCOMB, BITTER CREEK.)

PIERCE, SHANGHAI (b. Abel Head Pierce in Little Compton, Rhode Island on June 29, 1834; d. Matagorda County, Texas on December 26, 1900.) Shanghai Pierce was a legendary Old West cattleman who built an empire by throwing a wide loop. Never a modest man, Pierce had a larger-than-life-size sculpture of himself done by Ed Teich as a monument for his grave, which is where it now stands. Pierce first got to Port Lavaca, Texas when he stowed away aboard a schooner; once in Texas he worked on a ranch and then joined the Confederate cavalry during the Civil War. With his brother he established the Rancho Grande on the Trespalacios River by 1871 and then left Wharton County, Texas for Kansas for two years to avoid being lynched. When he returned to Texas, Pierce acquired a 250,000-acre ranch, which he fenced. When he and his brother split, Shanghai took the northern half of the ranch and his brother took the southern half. Pierce sent a number of longhorns up the cattle trails to Kansas and imported Brahma cattle to improve his stock.

PIERRE'S HOLE, THE FIGHT AT (July 18, 1832) This fight, between mountain men and the Gros Ventre Indians, occurred on July 18, 1832 in the Teton Mountains in eastern Idaho. The trappers and some accompanying Indians were attacked by the Gros Ventre, who built a log fortification during the fight. The following morning, at sunrise, the trappers rushed the stockade but discovered that the Indians had abandoned their fort during the night. Killed during the fight were five trappers, and seven Indians with the trappers, and about a dozen were wounded, including mountain man Bill Sublette. The Gros Ventre left nine dead warriors and about 30 dead horses.

PIKE, ZEBULON M. (b. Lamington, New Jersey on January 5, 1779; d. York, Ontario on April 27, 1813) Pike discovered Pike's Peak during an expedition in Colorado in 1806–7. Previously, he had led an expedition in 1805–6 to the upper Mississippi. Pike published *An Account of Expeditions to the Sources of the Mississippi and through the Western Parts of Louisiana*, a book about his explorations. In it, he opined that the Great Plains were uninhabitable and a great desert; this would deter settlement there for a number of years. Pike was killed in Toronto (then York) during the War of 1812 as he led an assault on the British fort there.

Bill Pickett with rope *(Oklahoma Historical Society)*

cowboy. (See also BLACKS IN THE WEST; MILLER BROTHERS' 101 RANCH AND WILD WEST SHOW; RODEO.)

PICKETT, TOM (b. in Camp Throckmorton, Texas c. 1856; d. Pinetop, Arizona on May 14, 1934) Pickett was in Billy the Kid's gang during the Lincoln County War. He was captured with the Kid by Pat Garrett at a rock cabin in Stinking Springs but released on bail. Pickett then moved to northern Arizona, where he joined the Hashknife outfit and was part of the Graham-Tewksbury feud. Pickett had a number of odd jobs during the years—cowboy, gold prospector, gambler—and was appointed deputy U.S. marshal by President Woodrow Wilson. He died at age 76 in Pinetop, Arizona. (See also LINCOLN COUNTY WAR; PLEASANT VALLEY WAR.)

PIERCE, CHARLEY (b. in Texas; d. Dunn Ranch on Cimarron River, Oklahoma on May 2, 1895) Pierce was a member of the Dalton and Doolin Gangs in

PIKE'S PEAK Pike's Peak was the symbolic destination for thousands of miners during the Pike's Peak gold rush, which began in 1858, although the gold was actually discovered about 70 miles away on Cherry Creek. Although Zebulon Pike "discovered" the peak (height: 14,110 feet) in 1806, the peak was first climbed by Dr. Edwin James in 1820 and named "James' Peak." But trappers and traders continued to refer to the mountain as Pike's Peak, and eventually the name became official. The view from Pike's Peak inspired poet Katherine Lee Bates to compose the words to "America, The Beautiful" when she visited there in 1893.

PIMAN INDIANS The Piman and Papago Indians lived in the hot desert areas in southern Arizona. The Piman lived along the Gila River in flat-roofed houses constructed from cactus sticks and brush and covered with adobe to cool them. Wearing few clothes, the Piman grew cotton and crops and were skilled makers of baskets and pottery. The Papago lived south of the Piman and were known for raising mesquite beans. The lands of the Pima and Papago were acquired by the United States in the Gadsden Purchase (1853).

PINION A dwarf pine with edible nuts.

PINKERTON, ALLAN (b. Glasgow, Scotland on August 25, 1819; d. Chicago, Illinois on July 1, 1884) Allan Pinkerton became the first detective for the Chicago police force after he moved to the United States from Scotland in 1842. He opened a private detective

Allan Pinkerton

agency in Chicago in 1850 and during the Civil War served under the alias "Major E. J. Allan" as General George McClellan's intelligence officer. Pinkerton also helped stop an assassination attempt on President-elect Abraham Lincoln. Pinkerton opened branches of his agency in Philadelphia and New York after the war. In the history of the West, he is known for his pursuit of outlaws Jesse James and Butch Cassidy and for his strong anti-Union activities, working for big companies to put down labor movements. At his death, his sons Robert and William A. Pinkerton took over the agency.

PINKERTON'S NATIONAL DETECTIVE AGENCY The Pinkerton Agency was the 19th-century equivalent of the modern-day FBI. Pinkerton agents roamed throughout the West investigating crimes, tracking criminals and providing a national law enforcement network. Their logo was a large wide-awake eye, and their slogan was "We Never Sleep," which in part led to the term "private eye" being linked with detectives. Famous outlaws pursued by the Pinkerton agents included the Reno Brothers, Sam Bass, Rube Burrows, Butch Cassidy and the Wild Bunch and Jesse James. The greatest negative publicity for the agency came in 1875 when Pinkerton detectives threw a "flare" in the home of the James family in Missouri, believing Jesse and Frank James were there. They weren't and the device exploded, killing Jesse's nine-year-old half brother and severing the arm of Jesse's mother. This incident brought a great deal of national sympathy for Jesse James and his gang; eventually three Pinkerton agents would be killed by the James Gang. The agency was run by founder Allan Pinkerton until 1884, when he died, and sons William and Robert continued it. Famous Pinkerton agents include Charles Siringo and Tom Horn. The Pinkerton Agency was hired by big businesses in the late 19th and early 20th century as Union busters, and this hostility to labor eventually led to bad publicity. (See also PINKERTON, ALLAN)

PINTO A multicolored horse with large patches. Indians liked pintos but cowboys didn't, believing solid-colored horses were better and stronger and had more stamina. There was a bit of logic behind this: The pintos came from mixed mustang stock, where inbreeding was a common occurrence.

PIONEERS, THE This is a rerun of the popular TV show "Death Valley Days" with Will Rogers, Jr. as host. (See DEATH VALLEY DAYS)

PISTOLS 'N PETTICOATS TV show that starred Ann Sheridan as Henrietta Hanks, Douglas Fowley as Grandpa, Ruth McDevitt as Grandma, Carole Wells as Lucy Hanks, Gary Vinson as Sheriff Harold Sikes, Robert Lowery as Buss Courtney, Lon Chaney, Jr. as Chief Eagle Shadow, Marc Cavell as Gray Hawk and Alex Henteloff as Little Bear.

A western situation comedy, this series told the story of the Hanks family in the town of Wretched, Colorado in the 1870s. Their household pet was a wolf named Bowser, and gunslingers far and near were amazed at the toughness of this family: All three generations—both male and female—could outdraw and outshoot the meanest young whippersnappers around. The show was first telecast on September 17, 1966 on CBS on Saturday evenings; its last telecast was August 19, 1967.

PLAINS INDIANS The Plains Indians were actually a number of different tribes who lived in the area from the Mississippi River to the Rocky Mountains, from northern Texas to southern Canada. They were bound together by two things: the buffalo and the horse. However, although all Plains Indians hunted buffalo and saw it as an animal with religious significance, some tribes were nomadic while others were seminomadic. The nomadic tribes, such as the Arapaho, Blackfoot, Cheyenne, Comanche, Crows, Kiowa and Sioux, were strictly hunters who lived in tipis made from buffalo skins. Their villages were temporary, capable of being taken down quickly and transported via travois to another site where their village would be reestablished. The seminomadic Indians, such as the Arikara, Hidatsa, Kansa, Mandan, Omaha, Osage and Pawnee, spent part of their lives hunting buffalo and living in tipis, but they spent the rest of their time in permanent villages made of earthen or grass-covered lodges. Before the Spanish introduced the horse to the plains, the Indian tribes hunted buffalo on foot. However, once Indians began to capture and tame wild horses on a large scale (generally the 17th century), they became adept horsemen and their range increased dramatically. The end of the buffalo, from the buffalo hunters and railroads, signaled the end of the Plains Indians. When there were no buffalo left, their means of sustenance, as well as a sense of purpose, was gone from their lives. Another common denominator in Plains Indian culture was the sun dance, a sacred ritual usually performed in conjunction with a buffalo hunt. Most of the tribes were warrior tribes, and the highest honors belonged to the warriors who "counted coup," or touched an enemy in battle with a "coup stick" and lived to tell. Consequently, a number of tribal wars were constantly pursued so warriors could have social standing and honors. (See also APACHE INDIANS; ARAPAHO INDIANS; ARIKARA INDIANS; ASSINIBOIN INDIANS; BANNOCK INDIANS; BLACKFOOT INDIANS; CAYUSE INDIANS; CHEYENNE INDIANS; COMANCHE INDIANS; CROW INDIANS; HIDATSA INDIANS; HOPI INDIANS; KANSA INDIANS; KICKING BIRD; KIOWA INDIANS; MANDAN INDIANS; MANGAS COLORADAS; MODOC INDIANS; NAVAJO INDIANS; NEZ PERCE INDIANS; OMAHA INDIANS; OSAGE INDIANS; PAIUTE INDIANS; PAWNEE INDIANS; PIMAN INDIANS; PUEBLO INDIANS; SHOSHONI INDIANS; SIOUX INDIANS; UTE INDIANS; WICHITA INDIANS; YUMAN INDIANS; ZUNI INDIANS.)

PLAINSMAN, THE Film produced and directed by Cecil B. DeMille; screenplay by Waldemar Young, Harold Lamb and Lynn Riggs, based on the book by Frank J. Wilstach; released by Paramount in 1936; 115 minutes in length. Cast: Gary Cooper, Jean Arthur, James Ellison, Charles Bickford, Helen Burgess, Porter Hall, Paul Harvey, George Hayes, Pat Moriarty, John MiljanFuzzy Knight and Anthony Quinn.

A western epic by Cecil B. DeMille, this movie features all of the legends of the West, from Abraham Lincoln to Wild Bill Hickok (Gary Cooper), Calamity Jane (Jean Arthur), Buffalo Bill Cody (James Ellison), Mrs. Buffalo Bill (Helen Burgess) and General George Armstrong Custer (John Miljan). Another version of this movie was released by Universal in 1966 (92 minutes); it was produced by Richard Lyons and Jack Leewood and directed by David Lowell, with the screenplay by Michael Blankfort. The cast included Don Murray, Guy Stockwell, Abby Dalton, Bradford Dillman, Henry Silva, Simon Oakland, Leslie Nielsen and Emily Banks.

PLAINS RIFLE The plains rifle was actually a number of rifles that evolved from the long Kentucky rifle. Shorter than the Kentucky rifle and more powerful (with a larger bore, usually .45 to .55 caliber), the plains rifle was accurate up to 350 yards. The first popular plains rifle was made in St. Louis by the Hawken family. Muzzle loaded and fired from the percussion system of ignition, it was used extensively by mountain men in the first half of the 19th century.

PLEASANT VALLEY WAR John D. Tewksbury was of Irish stock, his wife American Indian; the family, including sons Edwin, James and John, Jr., moved into the Pleasant Valley area of Arizona in 1880. This area was well watered and a number of ranchers lived there. The three Tewksbury brothers and three sons of Samuel Graham (Tom, John and William) joined forces to build a herd with a branding iron used on cattlemen's stock. The deal agreed on was that the cattle would graze on the Graham land until the Tewksburys wanted their share, at which point they could just cut them out. Unknown to the Tewksburys, the Grahams registered the brand under their own name, so when the Tewksburys came for their cattle, the Grahams informed them in no uncertain terms that they had no claim on the cattle. Thus the Pleasant Valley War, or Graham-Tewksbury feud, began.

Knowing how much cattlemen hated sheep, the Tewksburys set about becoming sheep ranchers and invited the Daggs brothers to bring their flocks over in the fall of 1886; the general idea was that the sheep would graze the grass so short that the cattle couldn't eat. This incident moved the Graham-Tewksbury feud into a classic cattlemen-sheepherders' feud.

The first victim of the "war" was a Navajo sheepherder who was killed by an ambusher in February 1887. Later that year, in July, Mart Blevins disappeared, and then on August 10 at the Middleton Ranch, Hampton Blevins and John Paine were killed and Bob Charrington, Tom Tucker and Bob Glasspie were wounded by the Tewksbury brothers. A week later, 18-year-old William Graham (the youngest of the Graham brothers) was killed in a shootout with sheepman James Houck, who was also serving as a deputy sheriff of Apache County at the time.

On September 2, 1887 the Grahams (Tom and John), along with Andy, Charles and John Blevins, ambushed Ed and John Tewksbury and Bill Jacobs near their sheep camp one morning. John Tewksbury and Bill

Jacobs were both killed when they went outside, and the rest of the Tewksburys were under siege in the hut. The group in the hut escaped that night, but hogs ate the corpses of John Tewksbury and Bill Jacobs.

Two days later Sheriff Commodore Perry Owens killed Andy and Sam Houston Blevins and Mose Roberts; John Blevins was seriously wounded. On September 17, cowboy Harry Middleton was killed and Joe Underwood wounded badly by the Grahams.

On September 21, a posse of 16 men, led by Sheriff William Mulvenon of Yavapai County and Sheriff Commodore Perry Owens of Apache County, came to Pleasant Valley to clear up the feud, and by the day's end John Graham and Charlie Blevins were dead.

This did not end the conflict, which continued to rage for several more years. In August 1888 three cowboys were hanged by some Tewksbury supporters; on November 1 Al Rose, on the Graham side, was killed in an ambush. In September 1891 George Newton, on the Tewksbury side, was killed in an ambush. On August 2, 1892 Tom Graham, who had posted rewards for the death of sheepmen, was ambushed while he was driving a wagon of grain into Tempe. Before he died the next day, Graham revealed Ed Tewksbury and John Rhodes as the names of his assailants. The two were arrested and held for two and a half years in jail but were finally acquitted. By this time there were 19 men dead, five wounded and two missing as a result of this war. (See also COOPER, ANDY; OWENS, COMMODORE PERRY; TEWKSBURY, EDWIN; TEWKSBURY, JIM.)

PLUMMER, HENRY (b. near Houlton, Maine on July 6, 1837; d. Bannack, Montana on January 10, 1864)   Henry Plummer was hung on the gallows he had erected. Before he was hung, he had managed to work both ends of the law game. At 19 he served as marshal of Nevada City, California, but within a year of his election he had killed a man—his lover's husband. He managed a pardon and did not serve the 10-year sentence but instead opened a bakery. He murdered several more men, including an Oregon sheriff, and was involved with several more women, including a prostitute and a married woman in Walla Walla, Washington. In Lewiston, Idaho Plummer organized a secret band of thieves, then joined the vigilante group organized to catch the thieves and arranged to have one of the vigilante leaders killed. In Bannack, Montana Plummer's gang, who called themselves the Innocents, identified themselves by secret handshakes and special neckerchief knots. They also marked secret code symbols in stagecoaches to signify which would be robbed. Plummer became city marshal of Bannack but was uncovered as the leader of the secret gang in 1863 when he shot Jack Cleveland, a criminal who wanted a cut of the action. Before his death, Cleveland told butcher Hank Crawford—who carried the dying outlaw to his home—that Plummer was the secret leader. Crawford became marshal of Bannack and Plummer tried to ambush him. Several attempts later, Plummer was shot by Frank Ray, one of Crawford's friends, who plugged Plummer in the right arm, causing Plummer to become

a left-handed gunman. A short while later Crawford moved back to his native Wisconsin. Plummer then moved to Virginia City, Montana when it was booming and became city marshal, but citizen Nathaniel Langford stopped Plummer from being appointed deputy U.S. marshal and pursued Plummer and his gang. During the first five weeks of 1864 a vigilante group hung or shot 20 of Plummer's gang members. Finally, Plummer was caught and brought to the gallows he had built. With two associates, he was hung—left to strangle to death when the rope didn't snap his neck—after he had pleaded for mercy.

POINT   The position at the front of the herd during a trail drive, responsible for directing the cattle on a drive. There were two point riders, one on each side of the herd, and these were the best, most trusted cowboys in the outfit.

POKER ALICE   (b. Alice Ivers in Sudbury, England in 1851; d. Sturgis, South Dakota in 1930.)   Poker Alice's fame came as a legendary poker dealer; she smoked cigars, carried a .45, dealt poker in Colorado and Deadwood and collected several husbands. Educated in England, she moved with her family to Colorado, where she married a mining engineer named Duffield, who soon left her a widow. Alice then began to haunt gambling saloons, where she became a professional poker dealer and made good money. She moved to Deadwood for a while and then back to Creede, Colorado, where she dealt in Bob Ford's saloon; she moved back to Deadwood in the 1890s where she married a professional gambler named Tubbs. Alice lived on a chicken farm until 1910 when, once again a widow, she returned to gambling and opened her own gambling hall between Fort Meade and Sturgis, South Dakota. Her last husband was a gambler named George Huckert.

PONDEROSA   This TV program consisted of reruns of "Bonanza" and aired during the summer of 1972 on Tuesday evenings. The shows were from the 1967–70 period. Current episodes of "Bonanza" were running on Sundays at this time. (See BONANZA.)

PONY EXPRESS   From the very beginning the Pony Express captured the imagination and attention of the American public; but it was also doomed to financial disaster. The Pony Express existed for a period of 18 months in 1860–62, and only ran for 14 months because of a four-month war with the Paiute Indians. The Pony Express was the brainchild of William H. Russell of the freighting firm Russell, Majors and Waddell and was enmeshed in politics from the beginning. The problem started when the southern forces in Congress behind Secretary of War Jefferson Davis chose a southern route for mail delivery to the West Coast. This southern route looked like an oxbow, stretching from Missouri down through Texas, through El Paso and into southern California and then northward to San Francisco. A number of people were opposed to the southern route, preferring the more direct central route, but southerners argued that the route would be closed by snow during the winter. The other political problem involved Russell, Majors and Waddell's freighting during the Mormon War (1857–58) for the United States Army. The firm carried a great deal of freight during the war, but the government then reneged on payments, saying there was no official contract, so the firm lost $493,000. Russell's partners were conservative and wanted to earn the amount back over the long period, but Russell was a financial adventurer and wanted to get it back quickly. He entered into an illegal agreement with Secretary of War John Floyd in which Floyd signed credit vouchers for $400,000 so Russell could secure loans.

The first Pony Express trip was on April 3, 1860. There were riders in St. Joseph, Missouri and San Francisco, and they each mounted and rode toward each other until they met in Salt Lake City; they then exchanged bags of mail and rode in the opposite direction. There were almost 2,000 miles between St. Joseph and San Francisco, and the Pony Express could make it in 10 days, much quicker than the three or more weeks it took Butterfield's Overland Stage to carry the mail. There was also the $600,000 Butterfield received from the government for the mail route that Russell wanted. The St. Joseph rider, Johnny Fry, carried 49 letters, some eastern newspapers, five private telegrams and some telegraphic dispatches in a specially built mochila, or leather mail patch that fit over the saddle, which was constructed by Israel Landis, a well-known St. Joseph saddle maker. The cost for a letter on the Pony Express was $5 per half ounce, and Fry carried less than 15 pounds on this first trip. In San Francisco, James Randall headed east on the first trip.

The Pony Express was necessary because telegraph wires had not been strung between Fort Kearney, Nebraska and Carson City, Nevada, a distance of about 1,600 miles. Although there were telegraph wires between St. Joseph and Fort Kearney, Russell decided to make St. Joseph the headquarters for the Pony Express because the railroad's western terminus ended there and because the city made some major concessions to have the Pony Express there. Russell bought about 500 horses at an average of $200 each for his operation and set up 190 stations; these were mostly converted from stagecoach stations from a previous venture he had, which were divided into 25 "home" stations where riders were changed and 165 "swing" stations where horses were changed. The Pony Express preferred young men (about 20) who were skinny (about 125 pounds) and preferably orphans for the work; they received $50 a month plus board and keep. Initially, 80 riders were hired and 40 more would serve. They were supposed to carry a rifle and two revolvers, but this proved too heavy and cumbersome; instead, they carried a knife and a revolver and depended on their horses' speed to save them. Actually, their horses' speed was their best defense; their grain-fed horses could simply outrun and outlast the grass-fed horses of the Indians.

The first Pony Express riders met in Salt Lake City on the evening of April 9, 1860; they exchanged mo-

chilas and headed back, and on April 13, two hours less than 10 days, Alexander Hamilton rode into St. Joseph to complete the first Pony Express delivery. But the empire of William H. Russell was already crumbling as the Pony Express took off. On the verge of bankruptcy, Russell went to Washington and made an agreement with Godard Bailey, a law clerk in the Interior Department in charge of bonds for Indians, and Bailey lent Russell the bonds in order to secure bank loans; this was illegal, and on December 24, 1860 Russell was arrested in his New York office and brought to Washington to face a congressional hearing. Meanwhile, Floyd resigned from the Department of War and fled to Virginia and the Confederacy. Because of legal maneuvering and the distraction of the Civil War, the case against Russell was finally dismissed on a technicality, but it was the end of Russell and his financial empire. At first things looked bright because Congress agreed that the central route was preferable to the southern route, but it added an amendment to the bill that required the existing company, Butterfield, to switch routes and eliminated competitive bidding for the account (which would be $1 million annually), thus freezing out Russell and the Pony Express. Actually, Congress also froze out Butterfield, who had been ousted from his company because of debts, and the company had been taken over by Wells, Fargo and Company which was the firm that benefited the most. In March 1861 the Pony Express got a brief reprieve when the Overland company arranged for some mail to be delivered by Pony Express (and thus the government footed the bills), but Russell was ousted by his board of directors and the company was turned over to attorney Bela M. Hughes. Hughes was a close friend and a business associate of stagecoach entrepreneur Ben Holladay, who gave credit to the Pony Express and then through some legal maneuvers took it over. The real end of the Pony Express came on October 24, 1861 when telegraph lines from east and west were joined in Salt Lake City; these lines eliminated the need for the Pony riders, although a few short rides were still made, the last on November 20, 1861. By this time the Pony Express was $300,000 to $500,000 in debt; it had carried 35,000 pieces of mail and received about $3 per letter, but the actual cost, when everything was tallied up, was about $16 per letter. The Pony Express provided an exciting, through brief, chapter in the history of the West. It proved the superiority of the central route, and when the railroad spanned the country, it used this route.

POWELL, SYLVESTER (b. ?; d. Wichita, Kansas on January 1, 1877)   Sylvester Powell tried to kill Wichita marshal Mike Meagher when the lawman was in the outhouse. Powell was known to be violent when drinking and on New Year's Day was in that condition. He had a confrontation with E. R. Dennison, who turned him in to Marshal Meagher, who took him to the city jail. Powell was released that evening and immediately went in search of Meagher. A little after nine o'clock that night Powell found Meagher in the outhouse behind Jim

Hooper's saloon and fired several bullets, hitting the marshal in the calf and hand and putting a hole in his coat. Meagher fired at Powell and then pursued him. When he saw Powell on the street in front of the drug store, Meagher put a bullet into his heart. (See also MEAGHER, MICHAEL.)

PRAIRIE CHICKEN   A plump game bird *(Tympanuchus americanus)* related to the grouse. The sage grouse, greater prairie chicken, lesser prairie chicken and sharp-tailed grouse provided pioneers and early settlers with an important source of food.

PRAIRIE CLIPPER   Large covered wagon, generally used for hauling freight for trade.

PRAIRIE DOG   A burrowing rodent, the prairie dog *(Cynomys ludovicianusis)* is a member of the squirrel family and lives underground in communities. Ranging from 11 to 14 inches long, the prairie dog emits a barking yap, hence its name. The prairie dog was regarded as a pest, nuisance and scourge by cowboys because of the dangers that prairie dog holes posed to riders on horses.

PRAIRIE OYSTERS   Also called mountain oysters, they are the testicles of a bull fried for eating.

PRAIRIES   At one time, the primary ecosystem in the United States was prairies, which extended from the Rocky Mountains eastward to the western area of Indiana, southward to the deserts of the Southwest, and covered the vast area between Texas and Canada. Prairies also included areas on the western side of the Rockies, including the Palouse area of Washington State and the great valley of California. Prairies are dominated by grasses, which need less rain than trees, and hot, dry summers. Trees are located along rivers or in groves, with cottonwoods *(Populus deltoides* var. *occidentalis)*, a form of poplar, in the north and dwarf oaks *(Quercus macrocarpa* var. *depressa)* dominating the south. There are forests along the eastern edge of the prairie. Buffalo country was in the area east of the Rocky Mountains, with major grasses only a few inches high; the buffalo may have determined the boundary of the prairies. (See also GRASSES.)

PRAIRIE SCHOONER   Wagons whose design was based on the original Conestogas that carried settlers and freight in the West. Like the Conestogas, these wagons were shaped like boats with a flared-out body and wheels turned outward and bowed wood (usually hickory) that held a canvas or tarpaulin covering (usually white) to keep the people or goods inside dry. These four-wheeled wagons had front wheels smaller than the rear wheels for easier pulling; there were iron reinforcements in the wheels, but iron was kept to a minimum to keep the weight as light as possible. In the dry areas, the wagon wheels often shrank and had to be swollen with water and tightened with wedges. Unlike smaller wagons, the prairie schooner had brakes, and, when going downhill, the wheels could be chain locked or a heavy log would be dragged to anchor it. Sometimes a rope would be tied to the wagon and around a tree to ease the wagon down a steep grade. Unlike freight wagons, the prairie schooners had a driver's seat with springs; the seat was located on the right side so the driver could reach the hand brake. These wagons could carry about three-fourths of a ton and might cost as much as $1,500. The wagon box was usually nine to 10 feet long and four feet wide; the sides were usually about two feet high, and sometimes supplies were stored under a false floor. After the 1870s the railroads replaced the wagons for hauling people and freight out West. (See also CONESTOGA WAGON.)

PRONGHORN   See ANTELOPE.

PROSPECTOR   A person who searched for gold and other minerals. A true prospector either worked alone or with a partner or two, using burros as pack animals. Prospectors were different from gold hunters, who were mostly inexperienced men trying to get rich quick and were attracted by news of a gold strike.

PUEBLO INDIANS   The Pueblo Indians are actually two different tribes, the Hopi and Zuni. Named by the Spanish because *pueblo* meant "town," the two tribes are similar because both live in highly organized permanent villages of stone and adobe built on high, steep-sided flat-topped rock formations. These Indians were skillful farmers, growing corn, vegetables and fruits in arid deserts and mesas by irrigation. Living in New Mexico (Zuni) and Arizona (Hopi), the Pueblo were placed under Spanish rule beginning in the 16th century. However, in 1680 a rebellion drove the Spanish out, and the Spanish did not return until 1692. The area containing the Pueblo Indians was acquired by the United States from Mexico in 1848.

PUMA   See MOUNTAIN LION.

QUANAH PARKER (b. c. 1845; d. Cache, Oklahoma on February 23, 1911) Quanah Parker was the son of a Comanche chief and a Texas white woman, Cynthia Ann Parker. Parker, the daughter of a prominent Texas family, was captured in 1836 when she was nine. A contingent of Texas Rangers "rescued" her in 1860, but by that time she had three children and was the wife of a chief. Distraught and unhappy with the life of whites, Cynthia tried to escape and return to the Comanche but her family stopped her. She eventually starved herself to death. Quanah, meanwhile, grew up with dark skin but blue eyes; he and his band refused to sign the Medicine Lodge Treaty in 1867 and continued to hunt buffalo and raid white settlements. In June 1874, angry over buffalo hunters killing off the beasts, Quanah and his band fought 30 buffalo hunters in the second Battle of Adobe Walls. Even though the Indians numbered 700, they were defeated by the fortifications at Adobe Walls and by the buffalo hunters' rifles, which killed Quanah's horse from under him. In the summer of 1875 Quanah finally surrendered and entered into a life between the Indian and white worlds. He became a prosperous businessman, built a large home in Indian Territory and became the leader of the Comanche, Kiowa and Apache federation.

QUANTRILL, WILLIAM C. (b.Canal Dover, Ohio on July 31, 1837; d. Taylorsville, Kentucky on June 6, 1865) Quantrill was the leader of a group of Confederate guerrillas in Missouri during the Civil War who raided antislavery towns. Among those in Quantrill's group were Frank and Jesse James and two of the Younger brothers. Quantrill's most famous raid took place on August 21, 1863 when he slaughtered all the citizens of Lawrence, Kansas and then looted the town. Quantrill died from wounds suffered during a raid in Kentucky in May 1865 when federal forces (who had declared Quantrill and his group outlaws) attacked him.

QUARANTINE LINE The Texas longhorn carried a dangerous tick north that infected other cattle and led to their death, although the longhorn was immune. Kansas enacted a series of "quarantine lines" that no Texas cattle could cross in order to keep the local herds safe from disease. This line was moved farther west during the 1870s and 1880s until Texas cattle were forbidden in Kansas. This quarantine line was established by the Kansas legislature to protect Kansas farmers and settlers.

QUARTER HORSE The quarter horse received its name because it was so successful in quarter-mile races

in Virginia and the Carolinas, where it was developed during the colonial period. Characterized by a large rump and powerful back legs, quarter horses are popular with cowboys because the horse has "cow sense" and its quick speed is essential when working with cattle.

QUEST, THE TV show that starred Kurt Russell as Morgan Beaudine and Tim Matheson as Quentin Beaudine.

The central plot for "The Quest" involved two brothers searching for their long-lost sister. One of the brothers—Morgan Beaudine—and his sister, Patricia, had been captured by the Cheyenne. Somehow they had become separated along the way. Morgan was raised by the Cheyenne and understood Indian ways and language; his brother was a San Francisco–educated doctor. The show was set in the 1890s and was an attempt by the

William Quantrill *(Western Archives)*

networks to bring back westerns, which had not been seen on prime-time TV for a number of years. "The Quest" premiered on September 22, 1976, and its last telecast was December 29, 1976, all on NBC on Wednesday nights. The first show was a 90-minute drama, but the other episodes were an hour in length.

R

RAGTIME COWBOY JOE   Song written by Grant Clarke (May 14, 1891–May 16, 1931); music by Lewis F. Muir (May 30, 1883–December 3, 1915) and Maurice Abrahams (March 18, 1883–April 13, 1931); published in 1912 by F. A. Mills, New York.

This song was written by three Tin Pan Alley writers, inspired by composer Maurice Abrahams's four-year-old nephew, Joseph Abrahams, who liked to dress up in cowboy clothes. Grant Clarke wrote the lyrics about an adult "ragtime cowboy Joe" (the name Abrahams called his nephew) and convinced Lewis Muir and Abrahams the next day to compose a melody. Ironically, Clarke had been turned down as a songwriter by the Tin Pan Alley publisher the same day he composed these lyrics. That same publisher accepted the song the next day from Muir (Clarke was across the street), which led to an apocryphal story about the musical tastes of Tin Pan Alley publishers. This song was a hit when it was originally published partly because of the success of "ragtime" music ("Alexander's Ragtime Band" was the biggest hit of this era) and received a second life in 1943 when it was sung by Alice Fay in the movie *Hello, Frisco, Hello*. In 1945 the song was sung by Betty Hutton in the movie *Incendiary Blonde*.

RAIDLER, LITTLE BILL   (b. William F. Raidler in 1865; d. Yale, Oklahoma c. 1905)   Little Bill Raidler was shot so many times that his last years were spent as a cripple. A member of the Doolin Gang, Raidler escaped in the gunfight in which Tulsa Jack Blake was killed. Later, Raidler was hit in the hand by the bullet of a .45-90 Winchester from Heck Thomas near Bartlesville, Oklahoma in July 1895, but the outlaw hacked off two of his fingers, then hid in a tree and escaped. On September 6, 1895 Raidler was hiding at a ranch near Elgin, Kansas when he was ambushed by Bill Tilghman and two other lawmen. Raidler was hit in the right wrist, then Deputy W. C. Smith plugged the outlaw with a shotgun and wounded him in both sides, his neck and head. Raidler survived all these wounds and was sent to prison in Ohio, where he received a parole later through the help of Tilghman. (See also THOMAS, HECK; TILGHMAN, BILL; DOOLIN, BILL)

RAILROADS   See CENTRAL PACIFIC RAILROAD; GOLDEN SPIKE; GREAT NORTHERN RAILWAY; KANSAS PACIFIC RAILROAD; NORTHERN PACIFIC RAILROAD; SOUTHERN PACIFIC RAILROAD; UNION PACIFIC RAILROAD.

RAIN-IN-THE-FACE   (b. c. 1835; d. Standing Rock, South Dakota on September 14, 1905)   A Hunkpapa Sioux chief, Rain-in-the-Face joined Buffalo Bill's Wild West show and is thought to have killed General George Armstrong Custer at the Battle of the Little Bighorn. No one can verify that fact; however, he was arrested in 1875 by General Custer's brother, Tom. Rain-in-the-Face supposedly swore revenge on Tom Custer after the chief escaped from jail and, at the Little Bighorn, cut out Tom Custer's heart and ate it.

RANCH   A western cattle-raising enterprise. Although there are sheep ranches, and large farms may be called ranches, for a cowboy a ranch means a place for raising cattle. The ranch has grazing lands, a home, some barns, corrals, loading pens and a bunkhouse. A ranch in the California of Spanish West was called a ranchero, and the concept of cattle-raising ranches comes from early Spanish settlers in northern Mexico.

RANGE   The land used for grazing by cattle or sheep. For a cattleman his range was his "spread"—whether he had legal title or not. A range had grass, not crops.

RANGE RIDER, THE   TV show that starred Jock Mahoney as the Range Rider and Dick Jones as Dick West.

Jock Mahoney was a legendary stuntman before being cast in this show, so there are plenty of action-packed scenes in which Mahoney does his own stunts. The show was never a network show; it was produced by Gene Autry's Flying A Productions. The 78 black-and-white 30-minute episodes were filmed in 1951–52 with the shows first released in fall 1952. The show appeared originally on CBS, sponsored by Table Talk pies. Reruns appeared on ABC on Sunday afternoons in fall 1965. The Rider rode his trusty mount, Rawhide, along with sidekick Dick West, who rode his trusty mount, Lucky, on Saturday mornings as well as in 23 issues of *The Range Rider* comic book.

RANGO   TV show that starred Tim Conway as Rango, Guy Marks as Pink Cloud and Norman Alden as Captain Horton.

This is the story of Rango, the inept Texas Ranger whose father happened to head the organization. This western comedy featured Pink Cloud, an Indian who preferred to spend days in bed reading a good book rather than roaming the great outdoors as a brave Indian warrior, as Rango's assistant in the post supply room at Deep Wells Ranger Station. The show premiered on January 13, 1967 on Friday nights on ABC. The half-hour series was last telecast on September 1, 1967.

RATTLESNAKE A poisonous snake that can grow to well over six feet long with a big diamond pattern on its back. A rattler's bite can be lethal, and this snake is one of the most feared creatures on the range (in fact, the rattlesnake, from the pit viper subfamily, is unique to the Americas). The "rattle," on the tail, is made of interlocking horny segments that emit the sound of a "rattle" when the snake is agitated. Easily heard 15–20 yards away, the "rattle" serves as a clear warning to steer clear, but it is not a warning the snake is ready to bite because the rattler will usually remain silent when ready to strike its prey. A rather sluggish ground dweller, a rattlesnake rarely attacks unless provoked. The bigger the rattler, the more dangerous, and the biggest can be about six feet long and weigh about 15 pounds. The rattler strikes with its jaws open. Its fangs sink into its victim with the venom injected through the hollow fangs. There about 30 species, all venomous; the most dangerous are the western diamondback, the timber rattlesnake, the Mojave rattlesnake and the western rattlesnake. The three most common types are the western diamondback, in the prairies and deserts; the prairie rattlesnake; and the sidewinder, generally found in southwestern deserts.

RAWHIDE Hide from cattle (usually) that was untreated. It was used for nearly everything—ropes, clothing, whips. When damp it expanded and when dry it contracted. It could be very tough once hardened.

RAWHIDE Film produced by Samuel C. Engel; directed by Henry Hathaway; screenplay by Dudley Nichols; released in 1951 by Twentieth Century–Fox; 86 minutes in length. Cast: Tyrone Power, Susan Hayward, Hugh Marlowe, Dean Jagger, Edgar Buchanan, Jack Elam, Jeff Corey and George Tobias.

This movie takes place mostly inside a stagecoach station during one 24-hour period. A group of outlaws takes over the station and holds the station attendant (Tyrone Power), a woman passenger (Susan Hayward) and a child hostage. The outlaws want to hold up an incoming stage with gold; the hostages want to warn the stage of the trouble. Another movie with the same title was released in 1938 starring Smith Ballew and Lou Gehrig, but it is not the same story.

RAWHIDE TV show that starred Clint Eastwood as Rowdy Yates, Eric Fleming as Gil Favor (1959–65), Sheb Wooley as Pete Nolan (1959–65), Paul Brinegar as the cook Wishbone, Steve Raines as Jim Quince, Rocky Shahan as Joe Scarlett (1959–64), James Murdock as Harkness "Mushy" Mushgrove (1959–65), Robert Cabal

Eric Flemint and Clint Eastwood in "Rawhide"

as Hey Soos Patines (1961–64), Charles Gray as Clay Forrester (1962–63), David Watson as Ian Cabot (1965–66), John Ireland as Jed Colby (1965–66) and Raymond St. Jacques as Solomon King (1965–66).

"Rawhide" was about the cattle drives in which cowboys took a herd—in many cases a herd assembled from several ranches—to a railhead for shipment back East. Trail boss Gil Favor and his right-hand man, Rowdy Yates, led the way, and they were met along the way by an assortment of characters, situations, disasters and problems that gave the shows the plots. There were 144 episodes of the hour-long black-and-white shows, which premiered on January 9, 1959 on Friday nights on CBS. The show enjoyed its longest run on Fridays but later appeared on Thursday and then Tuesday evenings; the final telecast was on January 4, 1966. In its last season, Rowdy Yates took over as trail boss before the show was canceled in midseason. "Rawhide" has become an immortal series for two major reasons: After Clint Eastwood left his Rowdy Yates role, he went to Spain for his first spaghetti western and, from there, on to movie superstardom; and the theme song, "Rawhide," sung by Frankie Laine, became a hit song that was resurrected by John Belushi and Dan Ackroyd in the movie *The Blues Brothers*. "Rawhide" won a Western Heritage Award.

RAZORBACKS Wild hogs that are extremely dangerous when cornered. An unsung hero of the West, these hogs had hide and meat that were useful.

REACH FOR THE SKY   Phrase used to order someone to put his hands straight up in the air.

REAGAN, RONALD   (b. Tampico, Illinois on February 6, 1911)   Ronald Reagan was a radio announcer before he went to Hollywood in 1937 and signed with Warner Brothers. He performed in over 50 films, mostly "B" movies, and his greatest impact on the Hollywood industry came as president of the Screen Actor's Guild (1947–52 and 1962). Among the western movies Reagan appeared in were *Cowboy from Brooklyn* (1938), *An Angel from Texas* (1940), *The Santa Fe Trail* (1940), *Law and Order* (1953) and *Cattle Queen of Montana* (1954). Reagan also hosted two television show, "Death Valley Days" and "General Electric Theater."

REATA   A rope made of rawhide (as opposed to grass) and braided in four, six or eight strands. The reata would last longer than a grass rope but was not as strong. The term "lariat" comes from this word.

REBEL, THE   TV show that starred Nick Adams as Johnny Yuma.

After the Civil War, former Confederate soldier Johnny Yuma roamed through the West, possessing high principles and morals as he dispensed justice, with the help of a sawed-off shotgun strapped to his leg. Although Yuma was the only regular character, General Robert E. Lee was sometimes played by actor George MacCready, and Ulysses S. Grant was sometimes played by William Bryant; actors Tex Ritter and Bob Steele also held key roles. "The Rebel" was first telecast on October 4, 1959 on ABC on Sundays. In June 1962 it switched to NBC, where it aired on Wednesdays and ended its run on September 12, 1962. Seventy-six black-and-white episodes of the half-hour series were shown, and each opened and closed with Johnny Cash singing the theme song.

RED BUCK   (b. George Weightman or Waightman in Texas; d. Arapaho, Oklahoma on March 4, 1896)   Red Buck—the name came from his flaming red hair—served three years in prison after being arrested by Heck Thomas for horse stealing. A dangerous man, he reportedly killed for hire, charging $50 per head. When he got out, he joined Bill Doolin's gang but was thrown out of the gang when he killed an old preacher after stealing the man's horse during a getaway near Dover, Oklahoma. Red Buck was killed by lawmen in a shootout in Arapaho, Oklahoma after they found him in his hideout, a dugout. (See also DOOLIN, BILL.)

RED CLOUD   (b. Makhpiya-luta in 1822; d. Pine Ridge, South Dakota on December 10, 1909)   Red Cloud, an Oglala chief, was the only Indian to defeat the United States government. Red Cloud's War (1866–67) occurred when the government built forts along the Bozeman Trail to protect settlers and prospectors who used the trail to travel through Wyoming's Powder River country—Indian hunting grounds—to get to the gold fields in Montana. Red Cloud's first victory came in the summer of 1865 when he captured some troops and held them captive when they began work on the forts. Red Cloud at first refused to meet with government commissioners; he did attend a peace council in June 1866 at Fort Laramie but walked out of the meeting when he learned the army intended to build forts along the trail used by whites. Red Cloud harassed the three forts built along the trail—Fort Phil Kearny, Fort Reno and Fort C. F. Smith—but concentrated his efforts on Fort Phil Kearny, which he kept under constant siege. In December 1866 Red Cloud and his tribe were responsible for the Fetterman Massacre when Captain Fetterman and 80 men attempted to rescue a wood-cutting party. Finally, the government agreed to abandon the forts, and Red Cloud burned them to the ground before he would sign the Fort Laramie Treaty of 1868, which created the Great Sioux Reservation. Red Cloud kept his part of the treaty and did not engage in the Sioux hostilities of the 1870s, although he continued to speak out against the government and its Indian agents. One agent, Dr. McGillycuddy, was the subject of Red Cloud's ire, and the agent had the chief deposed in 1881.

REDIGO   TV show that starred Richard Egan as Jim Redigo, Roger Davis as Mike, Rudy Solari as Frank Martinez, Elena Verdugo as Gerry and Mina Martinez as Linda Martinez.

When "Empire" left the air after the 1962–63 season, the lead character, Garret ranch foreman Redigo, emerged with a series of his own, in which he played the owner and operator of his own small ranch in the same area. This series told the stories of trying to make a ranch run smoothly and profitably. The show began on September 24 and was last telecast December 31, 1963. The half-hour series aired on NBC on Tuesday evenings.

RED LIGHT DISTRICT   The area in a town where prostitutes lived and conducted their business. The term originated in Dodge City, Kansas, where a sporting house called the Red Light had red glass in its front door, giving off a red light. In Abilene the area for prostitutes was known as the "Beer Garden" or "McCoy's addition," in Ellsworth it was known as "Nauchville" or "Scragtown" and in Newton this area was known as "Hide Park."

RED RIVER   There are two Red Rivers, but the most important to cowboys is the one that forms the boundary between Texas and Oklahoma. This river begins in the Texas panhandle and flows 1,300 miles southeast to join the Mississippi about 250 miles north of New Orleans. It was one of the major rivers cattle had to cross during the famous cattle drives from Texas to the Kansas cattle towns. The two most popular crossings were Doan's Crossing and Red River Station, where a sandbar allowed cattle to almost walk across the river when it was running low. The other Red River (known as the Red River of the North) provides the boundary line between North Dakota and Minnesota.

RED RIVER   Film produced and directed by Howard Hawks; screenplay by Borden Chase and Charles Schnee (from the story "The Chisholm Trail" by Borden

Chase); music by Dimitri Tiomkin; released in 1948 by United Artists; 125 minutes in length. Cast: John Wayne, Montgomery Clift, Joanne Dru, Walter Brennan, Coleen Gray, John Ireland, Noah Beery, Jr., Chief Yowlachie, Harry Carey, Sr. and Harry Carey, Jr.

This is the movie that made John Wayne a star. Based on a *Saturday Evening Post* story, "The Chisholm Trail" written by Borden Chase, the story involves Tom Dunson, a rugged individualist (Wayne's favorite character) who does what is right for himself, which means it is right for the country. Dunson heads some cattle north on a drive and faces Indian attacks, a swollen river and a mutiny led by his adopted son. During the cattle drive, Dunson becomes a bit too belligerent and hard driving, and so for the good of the drive and Dunson himself, Garth takes the cattle to Abilene. In Abilene, the two meet up again and engage in a knock-down, drag-out fistfight—stopped by a young lady—before they reconcile and agree to join forces with a new brand. This new brand was put on a belt buckle by director Howard Hawks and given to Wayne, who wore it in several other films.

RED RIVER VALLEY   Although this song is generally accepted to be about the Red River valley in Texas, it was originally a Canadian song about the northern Red River. The song may have originally been a poem written by Jethro de la Roche, a young man who gave the poem to his love, Amaryllis Milligan, after she had refused to marry him when it was discovered she had contracted tuberculosis. Roche, according to this story, gave the poem to his sweetheart in Ontario before he left. The song is associated with the 1869 Red River Rebellion in the Northwest Territories. The tune was apparently set to Roche's words later, and other verses were added in the West. Significantly, the first versions were heard in the northern plains of the United States. The first recording of this song was in 1925 by Carl T. Sprague and called "Cowboy Love Song." Jules Verne Allen, another Texas cowboy singer, recorded it in 1929, and this version was the one to achieve greatest national popularity.

RED RYDER   TV show that starred Rocky Lane as Red Ryder and Louis Letteri as Little Beaver.

A Saturday morning cowboy series about lawman Red Ryder, this 30-minute program was syndicated beginning in 1956.

REED, CHARLIE   (b, ?; d. Ogallala, Nebraska c. 1883)   Ogallala, Nebraska was a wild cattle town and Charlie Reed was a wild cowboy. He had been involved with a rustler ring headed by John Selman and John Larn in the 1870s around Fort Griffin, Texas. On January 17, 1877 at the Beehive Saloon and Dance Hall in Fort Griffin, Reed and another rustler, Billy Bland, were raising a drunken ruckus. A gunfight erupted and Reed killed Dan Barron, a young lawyer. He fled Texas and headed to Nebraska, where sometime around 1883 he got into a quarrel with a man named Dumas in a saloon and killed him. A mob quickly hung Reed for the deed.

REED, JIM   (b. Rich Hill, Missouri in 1844; d. near Paris, Texas on August 6, 1874)   Teenager Jim Reed courted 13-year-old Belle Starr (then she was named Myra Belle Shirley), which led to a bloodless gunfight with her father, John Shirley. After serving in the Civil War with a group of guerrilla raiders in Missouri, Reed was reunited with Belle in Texas, who now had a daughter, Pearl, fathered by Cole Younger. Belle and Reed moved in together and she bore him a son, Eddie, in Dallas. Reed, Belle and another outlaw named Dan Evans went to the home of Watt Grayson, a Creek Indian chief, who handled the government subsidies for his tribe, and tortured Grayson until he revealed where $30,000 could be found. This episode caused Reed to be pursued by the law, so he had to leave Belle. Rewards totaling $4,000 were put on Reed's head after he robbed a stagecoach near Blanco, Texas on April 7, 1874. Four months later, on August 6 near Paris, Texas, Reed and Deputy Sheriff John T. Morris stopped at a farmhouse for a meal. Morris was a friend who knew Reed's true identity. The two left their guns outside so the lady of the house would not be afraid. But during the meal Morris decided the money was greater than the friendship and slipped out and got his pistol. Back inside he told Reed he was under arrest, and the two men began wrestling. Finally, Morris shot Reed in the stomach and within minutes the outlaw was dead. (See also STARR, BELLE.)

REGULATORS   See VIGILANCE COMMITTEES.

REMINGTON   This was the gun named after Eliphalet Remington of Ilion, New York, who made his first flint-lock muzzle loader in 1816 and by 1828 had a thriving business. He produced standard arms for the army in 1845 in large batches; both sides in the Civil War used his rifles, although he manufactured exclusively for the North.

REMINGTON, FREDERIC   (b. Frederic Sackrider Remington on October 4, 1861 in Canton, New York; d. Ridgefield, Connecticut on December 26, 1909)   During his time, Frederic Remington was the most renowned western artist in America, and since his death he has emerged as one of the two (the other is Charles Russell) western artists whose work virtually defines the genre.

Remington was an easterner, son of a Civil War hero, who loved horses and studied them. He showed his talent in painting portraits at 15 when he entered the Highland Military Academy in Massachusetts and painted other cadets. Remington's father, Pierre, was a journalist who wanted his son to pursue journalism; however, Frederic loved drawing too much. In 1878 he enrolled at Yale University in the School of Fine Arts. Significantly, these were the first classes of this sort ever offered by Yale. Remington played on the Yale football team and drew a battered football player, which was published in The *Yale Courant*, his first published drawing.

In February 1880 Remington dropped out of Yale after the death of his father and began working in the

New York governor's office as a clerk. In the summer of 1881, at the age of 19, he took a vacation out West. This trip would change him and western art forever.

Remington camped out in Montana and quickly realized he was witnessing a vanishing scene: The wild cowboys and big empty land would soon be gone. He returned to Albany but could not stop thinking about the West. On October 4, 1882—his 21st birthday—Remington went to a ranch in Kansas, living there on his small inheritance. He painted at night while spending his days working on the ranch. He sent some drawings back East, and his first publication appeared in *Harper's Weekly* with a drawing entitled "Cowboys of Arizona" on February 26, 1882.

Remington continued to sell his drawings to magazines in the East and returned to Canton, New York in 1884 to marry Eve Caten. He had met her in 1879 and wanted to marry her since, but her father had refused to give his blessing. The couple moved to Kansas City for two years, but Eve never liked living in the West, so they moved back to Brooklyn, New York. Here, Remington enrolled in the Art Students League.

Remington studied art formally at Yale and in New York—a marked contrast to Charles Russell, who used only his own primitive genius for his works. Remington spent most of his life in the East, close to the magazines and book publishers who commissioned work for illustrators. Although Remington would live in New York the rest of his life, he would continue to make trips to the West. He even joined troopers searching for Geronimo in the Apache badlands.

Remington's big break came when *Harper's Weekly* used his illustration, "The Apache War—Indian Scouts on Geronimo's Trail," on the cover of their January 9, 1886 edition. In December of that year he did his first illustrations for *Outing* magazine and over the next several years did a number of illustrations for magazines.

Remington began writing as well as painting by the end of the 1880s, a time when he was one of the most famous illustrators in the nation. In 1889 he traveled with the Mexican army and painted their skirmishes with Indians. In 1890 he went to the Little Bighorn, just missing the Wounded Knee Massacre.

Remington began sculpting in 1895. At first he sculpted with clay and then in August he finished his first bronze cast, *The Bronco Buster*. In 1902 he completed *Coming through the Rye*, his famous sculpture of four cowboys riding horses and shooting their guns. (This sculpture was seen at the World's Fair and may now be seen at the National Cowboy Hall of Fame in Oklahoma City.)

Remington's fame was such that Theodore Roosevelt wanted him as illustrator for his western memoirs. He also illustrated the re-releases of Francis Parkman's *The Oregon Trail* and Henry Wadsworth Longfellow's *Song of Hiawatha.*

As Remington's fame grew, so did his fortune. By 1892 he had a studio and stable for his horses in New Rochelle, New York. In his studio he surrounded himself with western artifacts. He also had an apartment near

Frederic Remington   *(Frederic Remington Art Gallery)*

Central Park. Remington kept a vigorous working schedule, rising at 6 A.M. and working until midafternoon, then taking a long walk or riding horses. In the evening he went back to his studio to plan improvements and revisions of his work.

In 1909 the painter moved to Ridgefield, Connecticut, where he had built a large house with a studio. That summer he completed some of most famous paintings, including *The Stampede, Among the Led Horses, The Buffalo Runners* and *The Outlier*. In December he had his finest hour: an exhibition at New York's Knoedler Gallery with praise from both critics and the public. By this time he had completed nearly 3,000 works of art.

Remington began suffering severe abdominal pains just before Christmas, 1909 and died the day after Christmas at the age of 48 following an emergency appendectomy.

Frederic Remington is buried in the Evergreen Cemetery in Canton, New York. The grave is about 12 miles from the Frederic Remington Museum in Ogdensburg, New York. (See also ART; RUSSELL, C.M.)

REMITTANCE MAN   During the late 19th century a number of rich British families had "second sons" or "n'er do wells" who were sent to the American West, where they received a stipend or "remittance." These young men, mostly British, were known as "remittance men."

REMUDA   The group of saddle horses used on a trail drive or at the ranch. A large group of saddle horses was needed because trail driving was a hard, demanding job and horses needed rest. A wrangler—usually a younger, less experienced cowboy—was in charge of the remuda. Later, this term came to signify the horses owned by a particular cowboy.

RENALDO, DUNCAN (b. Rumania on April 23, 1904, d. Golita, California on September 30, 1980) Forever known as "The Cisco Kid" to TV cowboy fans, Renaldo first played this character in *The Cisco Kid Returns* (1945); the series had begun in 1929 with Warner Baxter in *In Old Arizona*. Renaldo first became involved in the theater in New York; his screen debut was in *The Devil's Skipper* (1928), and he then got a role in *Trader Horn* (1930). Renaldo had problems with the U. S. Immigration Service, which claimed he was an illegal immigrant; after this was cleared up, he became part of the Three Mesquiteers beginning in 1939. In 1945 he signed with Monogram, for which he made three Cisco Kid features; then Gilbert Roland took the role in 1946. United Artists revived the Cisco series in 1949, and Renaldo got the role with Leo Carrillo as Pancho. In 1949 and 1950 they made five films. "The Cisco Kid" TV series began in the early 1950s; in 1955 the last episodes were filmed. (See also CISCO KID, THE.)

RENO, MARCUS ALBERT (b. Carrollton, Illinois on November 15, 1834; d. Washington, D.C. on April 1, 1889) Reno's fame rests with his actions during the Battle of the Little Bighorn, June 25, 1876, when he was deployed by General George Custer to attack the Indian village with the belief that Custer would support him. Reno, however, found himself outnumbered and in the retreat panicked and scrambled back to some bluffs overlooking the river, where he was attacked by Indians; in all 49 of Reno's men were killed and 46 wounded before John Gibbon and Alfred Terry arrived to help on June 26. This was Reno's first experience fighting Indians and resulted in charges that he was "cowardly" and that his actions caused the slaughter of Custer. In 1877 Reno was court-martialed, and in 1879 he requested an official inquiry into the Little Bighorn action. He was dismissed from the military in 1880 after a series of charges and spent the rest of his life trying to have his name cleared. Initially Reno was buried in an unmarked grave in Glenwood Cemetery in Washington, D.C., but in 1967 he was reburied at the Custer Battlefield in Montana and the 19th-century charges were dismissed.

RENO BROTHERS The first train robbery occurred on October 6, 1866 just outside Seymour, Indiana when the Reno brothers robbed a car of the Adams Express Company on the Ohio and Mississippi Railroad of $10,000. The four brothers—John, Frank, William and Simeon—led a band of outlaws that robbed trains and banks in Indiana, Illinois, Iowa and Missouri. Pursued by the Pinkerton Agency, and Allan Pinkerton himself, the lawmen finally arrested John Reno and sentenced him to 40 years in prison. But the other Reno brothers continued to steal and rob until the Pinkertons apprehended them in New Albany, Indiana. The Renos were in jail on December 13, 1868 when a vigilante mob burst in, overtook the sheriff and his staff and hung Frank, William and Simeon Reno.

REPUBLIC PICTURES The major producer of "B" westerns in the 1930s and 1940s, this studio was responsible for singing cowboys Gene Autry and Roy Rogers, for the early success of John Wayne and for popular western serials.

Republic Pictures was founded by Herbert J. Yates in 1935. Yates had entered the movie business in 1915 with Hedwig Laboratories, a film-processing company; in 1918 he put up the money for Republic Laboratories, and then he consolidated several processing plants into Consolidated Film Laboratories in 1924. Meanwhile, Mascot Pictures had been founded by Nat Levine, and the studio was known for producing serials; the bankroll for Mascot was provided by Consolidated Film, owned by Yates. Mascot had good serials, but the western program and feature films were not doing well, so Yates approached Levine in 1935 about joining forces; they joined with W. Ray Johnston and Trem Carr, both of Monogram Pictures, and other independents to form Republic Pictures Corporation with headquarters in North Hollywood on Ventura Boulevard at Colfax and Radford Avenue in the old Mac Sennett studios. Within 18 months Levine left the organization to join Metro-Goldwyn-Mayer, and within two years Johnston and Carr left; Johnston then revived Monogram Pictures.

Republic produced 22 movies its first year and soon

Duncan Renaldo

The logo of Republic Studios

established its market; the studio made "B" movies, which were needed to supplement "A" movies as a second feature (see B WESTERN MOVIES). The major markets were the South, Midwest and Southwest, and the movies were sold in groups to exhibitors who bought them in packages of six to eight movies. The westerns were escapist and appealed to children; they were shown at Saturday matinees and consisted of serials or features. Republic's strength was that it made good movies quickly and relatively inexpensively; it had top technical facilities and technicians and provided a great deal of action and good music in scores or through its singing cowboys. The studio was quite popular and profitable until the 1950s when TV took over the Saturday matinee habits of American children. Republic went into serious decline during the 1950s; first, its audience was increasingly lost to television, and then it sold its movies to TV; finally, Herbert Yates insisted on financing large production movies for his wife, Vera Ralston, and these consistently flopped. Republic produced a total of 386 "B" westerns during its time. Its top stars included Gene Autry, Roy Rogers and John Wayne, and among its most successful series

was the Three Mesquiteers series (1936–43). On July 1, 1959 Yates finally yielded control of Republic, and the studio died. An excellent businessman throughout most of the history of Republic, Herbert Yates ruled the studio with an iron hand and assured audiences that good quality pictures would be made effectively and efficiently; however, his love for his wife blinded him in his final years and led to his decline as a studio executive.

RESTLESS GUN, THE   TV show that starred John Payne as Vint Bonner.

This western was about a loner who wandered through the West—via the back lots of Hollywood—trying to avoid trouble but always ending up in the middle of it. The show premiered on September 23, 1957 on NBC on Monday nights and stayed in that slot for its entire run of 77 episodes (all in black and white) before ending on September 14, 1959. Later it appeared on ABC, from October 1959 to September 1960, and was part of Saturday morning programs from November 1959 to March 1960.

REYNOLDS, LONESOME CHARLEY   (b. c. 1842; d. Little Bighorn, Montana on June 25, 1876)

Lonesome Charley was killed at the Battle of the Little Bighorn. A scout assigned to Major Marcus Reno's battalion, he died while trying to cover Reno's rear as the major, panicked and confused, led his troops across the river to safety. Reynolds's horse had been killed, and the scout apparently used the dead animal as a cover and fought a good, long fight before his death. Reynolds had served in the Civil War, then as a buffalo hunter, before he joined up with General George Custer in 1873. Custer admired and respected Reynolds, and the scout played a major role in leading Custer's foray into the Black Hills in 1874.

RIDERS IN THE SKY   This humorous western

singing group is composed of Doug Green (b. March 20, 1946), Fred LaBour (b. June 3, 1948) and Woody Paul Chrisman (b. August 23, 1949). As Ranger Doug, Idol of American Youth, Too Slim LaBour and Woody Paul, King of the Cowboy Fiddlers, the group has recorded a number of albums and appeared on a Saturday morning children's show on CBS and a syndicated program on National Public Radio.

RIDERS OF THE PURPLE SAGE   Film directed

by Hamilton McFadden; released in 1931 by Fox; 59 minutes in length. Cast: George O'Brien, Marguerite Churchill, Noah Beery, Frank McGlynn, Yvonne Pelletier and James Todd.

Based on the novel by Zane Grey, the movie was first made in 1925 as a silent starring Tom Mix. Set against the Graham-Tewksbury feud (the Pleasant Valley War) in the Tonto basin in Arizona (1886–92), the story centers on Jim Lassiter, who searches for the man who wrecked his sister's life. The 1941 version, released by Twentieth Century–Fox (56 minutes) was produced by Sol Wurtzel and directed by James Tinling, and the screenplay was by William Buckner and Robert Metzler. The cast included George Montgomery, Mary Howard, Robert Barrat, Lynne Roberts, Kane Richmond, Patsy Patterson, Richard Lane and Oscar O'Shea.

RIDE THE HIGH COUNTRY   Film produced by

Richard Lyons; directed by Sam Peckinpah; screenplay by N. B. Stone, Jr. and Sam Peckinpah; music by George Bassman; released in 1962 by MGM; 93 minutes in length. Cast: Randolph Scott, Joel McCrea, Ronald Starr, Mariette Hartley, James Drury, R. G. Armstrong and Edgar Buchanan.

This story about the ending of the Old West (there are both horses and cars on the roads in this turn-of-the-century movie) shows two old cowboys—Randolph Scott and Joel McCrea—who have been friends for years. Steve Judd (McCrea) rides into town in the midst of a car race; he's there for a job as guard for a gold shipment. He hunts up his old pal Gil Westrum (Scott) because he's afraid he might be a bit old for this job. Both Judd and Westrum were heroes in the Old West, but they have outlived their time. There's a twist in the plot when Westrum and a young buddy, Heck Longtree, plan to steal the gold. Along the way the group finds a young

woman who is planning to marry Billy Hammond, but the Hammond family are a bunch of no-accounts, so the two aging gunmen whisk her away and the family begins their pursuit. Judd catches Westrum and Longtree trying to steal the gold and is going to turn them in, but Westrum escapes. But when the Hammond family attacks, Westrum returns and helps Judd defeat the Hammonds in a shootout. However, Judd is fatally wounded; Westrum then vows to deliver the gold and does.

RIDING LINE, OR RIDING THE LINE   See LINE RIDERS.

RIFLEMAN, THE   TV show that starred Chuck

Connors as Lucas McCain, Johnny Crawford as Mark McCain, Paul Fix as Marshal Micah Torrance, Joan Taylor as Miss Milly Scott (1960–62), Patricia Blair as Lou Mallory (1962–63), Bill Quinn as Sweeney, the bartender, and Hope Summers as Hattie Denton.

This classic western featured Lucas McCain with a modified Winchester enabling him to shoot as he cocked—reportedly firing off his first round in three-tenths of a second. Lucas had a small homestead in New Mexico Territory, just outside the town of North Fork, which he shared with his motherless son, Mark. Trouble came because North Fork's marshal was a little past his prime and gunfighters kept messing up the town, which caused Lucas McCain to be constantly involved in helping straighten things out as well as raise his son to be a

Johnny Crawford and Chuck Connors in "The Rifleman"

real man. The show premiered on ABC on September 30, 1958 on Tuesday nights; it finished its run on Monday nights. The final telecast was July 1, 1963, at which time the half-hour program began a long series of reruns.

RIGGS, BARNEY (b. ?; d. Fort Stockton, Texas c. 1900) Barney Riggs was sentenced to the Yuma territorial prison after killing his employer over a mutual sweetheart. In October 1887 Riggs saved the life of prison superintendent Thomas Gates—shooting a convict who had wounded Gates during an attempted prison break—and won a pardon. Riggs then moved back to Texas, married Bud Frazer's sister and became involved in the Sheriff Frazer–Killin' Jim Miller feud. Riggs killed two of Miller's men in 1897 in Pecos, Texas when they tried to kill him. Later, Riggs was shot and killed by his stepgrandson in Fort Stockton after a family quarrel. (See also FRAZER, BUD; MILLER, KILLIN' JIM.)

RILEY, JIM (b. 1853; d. ?) Riley was the 18-year-old cowboy who closed and locked the saloon doors in Newton, Kansas when his friend, Mike McCluskie, was shot, and then proceeded to fire at the Texas cowboys in the Newton Massacre (August 19, 1871). At Perry Tuttle's Place about one in the morning McCluskie was at a faro table when Hugh Anderson came in and shot McCluskie in the neck. McCluskie and Anderson then got into a gun battle, which other Texas cowboys joined, that left two others dead, one wounded and McCluskie killed. At this point Riley, a frail consumptive who looked up to McCluskie and who had been watching from the door, closed and locked the saloon door and began firing. He killed two and wounded one—Anderson—before the firing stopped. (See also ANDERSON, HUGH; MCCLUSKIE, ARTHUR; MCCLUSKIE, MIKE; NEWTON MASSACRE.)

RINGO, JOHN (b. Green Fork, Wayne County, Indiana on May 3, 1850; d. Turkey Creek Canyon, Arizona on July 13, 1882) Some say Ringo's real name was Ringgold and that he was probably born in the early 1850s in New Jersey or Missouri. Others say his real name was Ringo and that he was one of the deadliest gunfighters of all time. But Ringo's life is too shrouded in mystery to ascertain where fiction stops and fact begins. It is known he was involved in the Sutton-Taylor feud in Texas, along with John Wesley Hardin, Bill Taylor and Mannen Clements. He then went to New Mexico, then Tombstone. Ringo was well educated—he attended William and Jewell College in Liberty, Missouri—and liked to quote Shakespeare. But he was addicted to the bottle. He was friends with the Clantons and McClaurys in Tombstone and rustled some cattle around there. Ringo died a mysterious death. In fact, there are two stories of his death. The first says that in the summer of 1882 Ringo and Buckskin Frank Leslie went on a two-week drinking binge, and afterward Ringo was found dead from a bullet in his head in Turkey Creek Canyon. Ringo had his rifle and both six-guns—all fully loaded—with him and had been scalped. Billy Claiborne claimed Leslie had killed Ringo, while Pony Deal claimed Johnny-Behind-the-Deuce (Johnny

O'Rourke) did it. A little while later Pony Deal killed O'Rourke to avenge Ringo's death. The second story says that cowboy John Yoast, hauling wood for B. F. (Sorghum) Smith, saw a man lying in a group of oaks near Smith's ranch house. When Yoast came over—believing the man was asleep—he discovered it was Ringo dead. There were some suspicious clues—a cartridge belt was buckled on upside down—but the death was ruled a suicide.

RIN TIN TIN The original Rin Tin Tin was one of six young dogs discovered in an abandoned German infantry trench in Fleury, France on September 13, 1918. Pilot Lee Duncan found the brood and kept two: a female he named Nanette and a male he named Rin Tin Tin, taking the names from a story about two lovers who survived a German attack on a railway station when everyone else was killed. The female died, but Rin Tin Tin survived and appeared in 22 movies as well as numerous vaudeville dates before his death on August 10, 1932. The original Rin Tin Tin (1916–32) was the first important animal star in Hollywood and was the most financially successful actor for Warner Brothers during the 1920s. His first movie was *The Man from Hell's River*. The movie *The Return of Rin Tin Tin* appeared in 1947 starring Rin Tin Tin III, grandson of the original, and father of the TV Rin Tin Tin. The TV dogs were owned by Billy Duncan and trained by Frank Barnes.

RIN TIN TIN See ADVENTURES OF RIN TIN TIN, THE.

RIO BRAVO Film produced and directed by Howard Hawks; screenplay by Jules Furthman and Leigh Brackett (from a B. H. McCampbell story); music by Dimitri Tiomkin; released in 1959 by Warner Brothers; 141 minutes in length. Cast: John Wayne, Dean Martin, Ricky Nelson, Angie Dickinson, Walter Brennan, Ward Bond, John Russell, Claude Akins, Harry Carey, Jr. and Bob Steele.

Rio Bravo was John Wayne's answer to *High Noon*, a movie he never liked because he didn't believe a marshal would ask for help from townspeople in a gunfight and that townsfolk, many of whom had seen service in the Civil War, would back down so easily. In *Rio Bravo* Wayne, as Sheriff John T. Chance, fights a gang of outlaws with some pals. He refuses the help offered by townsfolk and captures a killer and puts him in jail. The killer's brother, a wealthy rancher, comes to town with a bunch of ruffians. Wayne, his deputy Stumpy (Walter Brennan), a former deputy, Dude (Dean Martin), and Colorado Ryan (Ricky Nelson) confront them. There's some singing provided by Dean Martin and Ricky Nelson in the long movie, and finally Wayne and his cohorts emerge victorious. This movie bears an amazing resemblance to *El Dorado* and *Rio Lobo*, which also star Wayne and are directed by Howard Hawks. The films form a trio (all written by Leigh Brackett) whose theme is that a group of professionals with group loyalty will beat a bunch of rowdy amateurs any day.

RIO GRANDE The Rio Grande (called "Rio Bravo" by Mexicans) is the river that divides Texas and Mexico.

This border was the dispute that led to the Mexican War; the United States wanted the Rio Grande to divide the countries, but the Mexicans insisted on the Nueces River, farther north. The dispute was settled by the Treaty of Guadalupe Hidalgo (1848) after the Mexican War. The Rio Grande flows 1,800 miles, from the San Juan Mountains in Colorado through New Mexico and then southeast to the Gulf of Mexico.

RIO GRANDE   Film produced by John Ford and Merian C. Cooper; directed by John Ford; screenplay by James Kevin McGuinness from a story in the *Saturday Evening Post* by James Warner Bellah; released in 1950 by Argosy/Republic; 105 minutes in length. Cast: John Wayne, Maureen O'Hara, Claude Jarman, Jr., Ben Johnson, Harry Carey, Jr., Chill Wills, J. Carol Naish, Victor McLaglen, Grant Withers, Stan Jones and the Sons of the Pioneers.

The third part of John Ford's cavalry trilogy (the first two were *Fort Apache* and *She Wore a Yellow Ribbon*), this film features John Wayne as Lieutenant Colonel Kirby Yorke—the same character he played in *Fort Apache*—who is frustrated at being unable to stop Indian raids across the Rio Grande. He hasn't seen his wife and son in 16 years, but they both arrive on the scene; his son is a new recruit and his wife is there to get her son discharged. The son proves himself as a soldier, the husband and wife reunite and the Indians get defeated.

RIO LOBO   Film produced by Howard Hawks and Jody McCrea; directed by Howard Hawks; screenplay by Burton Wohl, Leigh Brackett and Sean MacGregor; released in 1970 by National General; 114 minutes in length. Cast: John Wayne, Jorge Rivero, Jennifer O'Neill, Jack Elam, Christopher Mitchum, Victor French, Susana Dosmantes, David Huddleston, Sherry Lansing, George Plimpton and Bob Steele.

This is the last film directed by Howard Hawks—his 44th and his fifth with John Wayne. For Wayne, this was his 144th film. It begins during the Civil War when a group of Confederates steal some gold from a Union army train. Cord McNally (Wayne) is knocked unconscious into a stream when he chases the crooks; they make him a prisoner and establish a rapport. McNally knows somebody in his outfit is betraying him, telling the Confederates about the gold shipments, but he doesn't know who. After the war, McNally and the two Rebels meet again, and the Rebels let him know there were two Union traitors, who coincidentally are also involved in a land dispute with the Rebels and McNally. One of the traitors ends up in jail and must be held until the cavalry arrives.

RITTER, TEX   (b. Woodward Maurice Ritter in Panola County, Texas; d. Nashville, Tennessee on January 2, 1974)   Tex Ritter starred in 58 singing-cowboy movies between 1936 and 1945—more than any other actor in that genre except Gene Autry and Roy Rogers. His first singing-cowboy movie, *Song of the Gringo*, came out a few months after Gene Autry's first feature film, *Tumbling Tumbleweeds*, and he remained in Autry's and Rogers's shadow through his entire career, a victim of

Tex Ritter

third- and fourth-rate productions. If he had been with Republic, like Autry and Rogers, instead of Grand National, Monogram and PRC, he might have risen to greater heights because he was a true singing artist; instead, he was never any great competition at the box office for Autry and Rogers, although he appeared seven out of these nine years in the Top Money-Making Western Stars poll of exhibitors.

Ritter was born in Texas and was a pre-law student at the University of Texas, where he met several people who would greatly influence him: J. Frank Dobie, noted western folklorist; Oscar J. Fox, his voice teacher as well as composer and arranger of western songs; and John A. Lomax, legendary collector of cowboy songs. Forced to leave school because of finances, Ritter went to New York, where he landed a job singing four western songs in the Broadway show *Green Grow the Lilacs*. While on Broadway, he obtained a spot on radio station WOR with "The Lone Star Rangers," as well as a children's program, "Cowboy Tom's Roundup." Later, he moved to WHN and had "Tex Ritter's Campfire" and in 1934 was a featured performer on the "WHN Barn Dance."

Ritter signed a contract with Edward Finney, and the producer-agent negotiated roles with movie studios. Ritter never really had major starring roles alone in movies; usually he was paired with others who often dominated the picture. Ritter's first film featured Fuzzy Knight as his sidekick, and later he starred with Johnny Mack Brown in a series of westerns at Universal. In these

Tex Ritter with his horse

films, the Jimmy Wakely Trio provided most of the music.

Ritter recorded for Decca Records and then for Capitol from its inception in 1942. Among the hits songs he recorded were "There's a New Moon over My Shoulder," "Rye Whiskey," "Boll Weevil," "Deck of Cards," "You Two-Timed Me One Time Too Often" and "Do Not Forsake Me, O My Darling" (theme from *High Noon*), which won an Academy Award in 1952. In the 1950s Ritter was a regular performer on the "Town Hall Party," a popular West Coast TV show, and hosted his own syndicated TV show, "Tex Ritter's Ranch Party" in the 1957–58 season. He was elected to the Country Music Hall of Fame in 1964 and joined the Grand Ole Opry in 1965, the same year he moved from California to Nashville.

Listed are the movies in which Ritter had a starring role:

Song of the Gringo (1936)
Headin' for the Rio Grande (1936)
Arizona Days (1937)
Trouble in Texas (1937),
Hittin' the Trail (1937)
Sing, Cowboy, Sing (1937)
Riders of the Rockies (1937)
Mystery of the Hooded Horsemen (1937)
Tex Rides with the Boy Scouts (1938)
Frontier Town (1938)
Rollin' Plains (1938)
Utah Trail (1938)
Starlight over Texas (1938)
Where the Buffalo Roam (1938)
Song of the Buckaroo (1938)
Sundown on the Prairie (1938)
Rollin' Westward (1939)
Down the Wyoming Trail (1939)
The Man from Texas (1939)
Riders of the Frontier (1939)
Roll, Wagons, Roll (1939)
Westbound Stage (1939)

Rhythm of the Rio Grande (1940)
Pals of the Silver Sage (1940)
Cowboy from Sundown (1940)
The Golden Trail (1940)
Rainbow over the Range (1940)
Arizona Frontier (1940)
Take Me Back to Oklahoma (1940)
Rollin' Home to Texas (1940)
Ridin' the Cherokee Trail (1941)
The Pioneers (1941)
King of Dodge City (1941)
Long Star Vigilantes (1942)
Bullets for Bandits (1942)
North of the Rockies (1942)
Devil's Trail (1942)
Prairie Gunsmoke (1942)
Vengeance of the West (1942)
Deep in the Heart of Texas (1942)
Little Joe, the Wrangler (1942)
The Old Chisholm Trail (1942)
Tenting Tonight on the Old Campground (1943)
Cheyenne Roundup (1943)
Raiders of the San Joaquin (1943)
The Lone Star Trail (1943)
Arizona Trail (1943)
Marshall of Gunsmoke (1943)
Oklahoma Raiders (1943)
Gangsters of the Frontier (1944)
Dead or Alive (1944)
Whispering Skull (1944)
Marked for Murder (1945)
Enemy of the Law (1945)
Three in the Saddle (1945)
Frontier Fugitives (1945)
Flaming Bullets (1945)

RIVERBOAT TV show that starred Darren McGavin as Grey Holden, Burt Reynolds as Ben Frazer (1959–60), William D. Gordon as Travis (1959–60), Richard Wessell as Carney, Jack Lambert as Joshua, Mike McGreevey as Chip (1959–60) Jack Mitchum as Pickalong (1959–60), Bart Patten as Terry Blake (1959–60) and Noah Beery, Jr. as Bill Blake (1960–61).

In this TV show set in the 1840s, the 100-foot-long *Enterprise* was a riverboat won in a poker game by Grey Holden. It traveled up and down the Mississippi and Ohio Rivers (actually floating on the lake in Universal's back lot). The show, which changed some key cast members during its first season, premiered on September 13, 1959 on Sunday nights on NBC. In February 1960 it was moved to Monday nights, where it ended its run on January 16, 1961. Forty-four episodes of the hour-long show were done.

ROAD AGENT'S SPIN Also called a Curly Bill spin, it means to hand over a gun while the forefinger is kept on the trigger guard so the gun can be spun back into the hand ready to shoot. Named for "Curly Bill" Brocius (or Graham).

ROADRUNNER Part of the cuckoo family, the roadrunner (*Geococcyx californianus*) can fly but prefers to run, reaching speeds of up to 17 miles an hour. Its large tail is stuck straight up as a wind brake at the end of a run. The roadrunner eats small rodents, birds, snakes and lizards and is eaten by coyotes and bobcats. A large bird, nearly two feet long, it is primarily found in the Southwest.

ROAD WEST, THE TV show that starred Barry Sullivan as Benjamin Pride, Andrew Prine as Timothy Pride, Brenda Scott as Midge Pride, Kelly Corcoran as Kip Pride, Charles Seel as Grandpa Pride, Glenn Corbett as Chance Reynolds and Kathryn Hays as Elizabeth Reynolds.

Moving to Kansas Territory from Ohio after the Civil War, widower Benjamin Pride and his children, his second wife and her children attempt to make a life as pioneers on the frontier. This show debuted on September, 12, 1966 on Monday nights on NBC. The hour-long show was last telecast on August 28, 1967.

ROAR OF THE RAILS, THE Sponsored by the A. C. Gilbert Company, manufacturer of American Flyer model trains, this TV series told of events in railroad history. Model trains were used for dramatizations, and veteran railroad men talked about their jobs and life. The show premiered on October 26, 1948 on CBS on Tuesday evenings. The 15-minute show was moved to Mondays in October 1949, and its last telecast was on December 12, 1949.

ROBERTS, BUCKSHOT (b. Andrew L. Roberts; d. Blazer's Mill, New Mexico on April 4, 1878) Buckshot Roberts was killed by the "Regulators" led by Dick Brewer and Billy the Kid during the Lincoln County War. Buckshot had been wounded earlier in his life, and he limped and shot his rifle from the hip because he couldn't get it above his waist. There was a $200 reward on the head of those who had killed Sheriff William Brady, and Roberts wanted it. At Blazer's Mill, owned by a retired dentist, Dr. J. H. Blazer, this group of Regulators—who had killed Brady—stopped for a meal. In the group were Billy the Kid, Dick Brewer, Charlie Bowdre, Frank and George Coe, Henry Brown and John Middleton. Roberts walked in with a Winchester and two six-shooters. Frank Coe, a former friend of Roberts, tried to talk him into a surrender, but Roberts would hear none of it. Then Dick Brewer— head of the Regulators and foreman for rancher John Tunstall, who had been killed by a posse that included Roberts—decided to arrest Roberts. Frank Coe and Roberts were outside talking; Charlie Bowdre, Henry Brown and George Coe came to take Roberts in. Roberts and Bowdre fired at each other; the shot ricocheted off Bowdre's cartridge belt and hit George Coe in his right hand, cutting off his trigger finger. Roberts shot three more times, knocking off Billy the Kid's hat and hitting John Middleton in the chest. Roberts then got inside Blazer's bedroom, positioned himself by the lone window and got Blazer's buffalo gun for added support. Brewer shot at Roberts and maneuvered to shoot again,

but Roberts blew the top off Brewer's head with the buffalo gun. Blazer then came into the room with Roberts and the outlaw said, "I'm killed." Blazer confirmed this, and the Regulators left to get help for Middleton and Coe. When Roberts died, about an hour later, Blazer buried him beside Dick Brewer behind the mill. (See also BILLY THE KID; BREWER, DICK; LINCOLN COUNTY WAR.)

ROBERTS, JIM (b. Bevier, Macon County, Missouri in 1858; d. Clarkdale, Arizona on January 8, 1934) When Jim Roberts was 70 years old, he spotted some thieves in a car trying to make a getaway after robbing a bank in Clarkdale, Arizona. Roberts pulled out his Colt revolver and killed one of the bandits, which caused the car to crash. Roberts then held his gun on the other bandit until help arrived. About 40 years before this Roberts was involved in the Pleasant Valley War in Arizona on the side of the Tewksbury clan. Roberts died in the street at the age of 75 from a heart attack. (See also PLEASANT VALLEY WAR.)

ROBERTSON, BEN F. (See WHEELER, BEN.)

ROBERTSON, DALE (b. Harrah, Oklahoma on July 14, 1923) Dale Robertson starred in the TV series "Tales of Wells Fargo" and "Iron Horse" and was host and star on "Death Valley Days." A star school athlete in

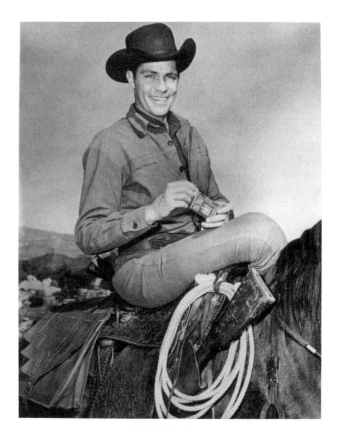

Dale Robertson

Oklahoma (boxing and football), Robertson attended Oklahoma Military College and worked as a cowboy near Tulsa during the summers. During World War II he served in the army and afterward studied drama in college. He moved to Hollywood and signed with Twentieth Century–Fox, appearing in films such as *Call Me Mister* (1951), *Golden Girl* (1951), *The Outcasts of Poker Flat* (1952), *The Farmer Takes a Wife* (1953), *City of Bad Men* (1953) and *The Gambler from Natchez* (1954). "Tales of Wells Fargo" ran for six and a half years and made him a star; afterward he studied filmmaking at Southern California University and learned the business of movie making. He also learned about horse raising and developed a quarter horse ranch in Yukon, Oklahoma (Haymaker Farms), where he breeds and trains horses. Western films he appeared in include:

> *Fighting Man of the Plains* (1949)
> *The Cariboo Trail* (1950)
> *Two Flags West* (1950)
> *Golden Girl* (1951)
> *Return of the Texan* (1952)
> *The Silver Whip* (1953)
> *City of Bad Men* (1953)
> *Devil's Canyon* (1953)
> *The Gambler from Natchez* (1954)
> *Sitting Bull* (1954)
> *Dakota Incident* (1956)
> *A Day of Fury* (1956)
> *Hell Canyon Outlaws* (1957)
> *Law of the Lawless* (1964)
> *Blood on the Arrow* (1964)
> *The Man from Button Willow* (1965)

(See also TALES OF WELLS FARGO; TELEVISION WESTERNS.)

ROCKY MOUNTAINS The Rocky Mountains extend from Alaska to New Mexico, achieving their highest points in Colorado, where there are more than 50 peaks over 14,000 feet high. The Rockies divide the continental United States; all rivers to the west of them flow to the Pacific, and all rivers to the east flow toward the Mississippi. The Rockies consist of a series of ranges: the Coeur d'Alene in Montana, the Bighorn Mountains in Wyoming and Montana; the Tetons in Wyoming and Idaho; the Bitterroot Range in Montana and Idaho; the Wasatch Range and Unita Mountains in Utah; the Sawatch and Front Ranges in Colorado; the Sangre de Cristo Mountains in New Mexico and Colorado; and the San Juan Range in New Mexico and Colorado. Early explorers of the Rockies include Lewis and Clark (1804–6), Zebulon M. Pike (1806–7) and John C. Fremont (1840s). The Rockies were rich in beaver, attracting trappers and mountain men in the first half of the 19th century; the rich deposits of gold, silver and other minerals led to gold rushes and mining in the latter half of the 19th century.

RODEO Rodeo is the sport of cowboys. The word "rodeo" appears to be derived from the Spanish word *rodear*, which means "to surround" or "to encircle" and could also mean "to gather" or "a gathering" as cowboys got together and formed an area where these contests could take place. The major organization for rodeo cowboys is the Professional Rodeo Cowboys Association (PRCA), headquartered in Colorado Springs, Colorado. The headquarters are adjacent to the ProRodeo Hall of Fame and Museum of the American Cowboy. There is also a Rodeo Hall of Fame in the Cowboy Hall of Fame in Oklahoma City. The PRCA began as the Cowboys' Turtle Association in 1936 (because they were "slow as turtles" getting organized); in 1954 the name was changed to the Rodeo Cowboys Association and then to the Professional Rodeo Cowboys Association in 1975. In 1929 the management of several leading rodeos had formed the Rodeo Association of America.

The PRCA is the major sanctioning body in professional rodeo and in 1992 sanctioned approximately 750 rodeos (out of approximately several thousand held) in the United States and Canada. In those 750 rodeos about 5,500 rodeo cowboys competed for prize money totaling approximately $18 million. Each year in December the PRCA holds the National Finals Rodeo, in which the top 15 cowboys in each event compete for almost $3 million in prize money. The first National Finals Rodeo was held in 1959 in Dallas, where it remained until 1962, when it moved to Los Angeles. In 1965 it moved to Oklahoma City for 20 years and in 1985 moved to Las Vegas, Nevada.

In order to become a member of the PRCA a rodeo cowboy must first become a "permit cardholder" and compete in smaller association-sanctioned rodeos until he has earned $2,500, at which time he may become a PRCA member. Cowboys earn prize money in rodeos and each dollar represents a "point"; at the end of the year, the total number of dollars won or "points" are added up and the top 15 rodeo cowboys in each event compete in their respective events in the National Finals. The "All-Around Champion" (also called "All-Around Cowboy") is the top honor for a rodeo cowboy; the winner of this honor is the rodeo athlete who wins the most prize money in two or more events in a single year.

The history of rodeo can be traced back to two major sources: the gatherings of working cowboys and the Wild West show. What became known later as "rodeos" were probably informal affairs in which cowboys would place wagers on who could ride a particular bronc or who could rope better or faster. This competition then extended to neighboring outfits, especially during roundups in the spring and fall when several outfits might get together to join forces to gather cattle, sort them out and brand them. On holidays such as the Fourth of July cowboys gathered together for a good party and had contests in roping and riding.

The first recorded mention of a rodeolike contest was in Santa Fe in 1847. There were some bronc-riding contests between rival outfits in Deer Trail, Colorado in 1869, so this town lays claim to the earliest rodeo; in 1872 there was a day of Texas steer riding and bronc riding. Actually, these early events were called "frontier days," "stampedes," "roundups" and "celebrations"; it was the Wild West show that first used the term "rodeo" for its "cowboy fun" segment.

Possibly the first "rodeo" in Texas occurred in Pecos on July 4, 1883; this city boasts of the first organized event and the oldest continuously run rodeo. In Payson, Arizona there were "races" in the early 1880s, and in 1884 the community sponsored a rodeo; Prescott, Arizona claims to have given the first rodeo in which a trophy was awarded and admission was charged when they organized their Prescott Frontier Days Celebration on July 4, 1888.

The first real "rodeo" as entertainment came in North Platte, North Dakota on July 4, 1882 when Buffalo Bill Cody organized the "Old Glory Blowout" at the request of town officials. Cody persuaded some merchants to put up prizes for contests in which cowboys would shoot, ride, rope, and bust some broncs; he expected about 100 cowboys to show up and was surprised to find about 1,000 vying for the prizes. This was the real beginning of the Wild West show, which Cody organized and took on the road the next year. This show did a great deal to make the cowboy a romantic hero; in fact, Buck Taylor, one of Cody's performers, was dubbed "King of the Cowboys" and was the model for heroes in dime novels. In this show cowboys performed trick riding and roping tricks and also rode wild Texas steers.

The Wild West show dominated cowboy entertainment until World War I; in addition to Cody's show there were shows on the road organized by Pawnee Bill, the Miller Brothers' 101 Ranch and about 80 others. The Miller Brothers' show is especially significant because black cowboy Bill Pickett introduced "bulldogging," an act developed for the Wild West show that was later incorporated into rodeo performances as "steer wrestling." In the show, Pickett on his horse would chase a steer, drop down on it and then get the steer's lips in his teeth, which immobilized the animal because of pressure on this sensitive area. The term "bulldogging" arose because Pickett had seen bulldogs control steers this way; as this activity became a rodeo sport, the practice of paralyzing the steer by the cowboy biting the steer's lip was replaced with the cowboy throwing the steer until its legs were straight up.

The rodeo as performed today emerged in the period 1915–25 as the Wild West show died; the last Wild West show to close was that of the Miller Brothers, which ended in 1931; by that time Buffalo Bill Cody had been dead about 15 years. By the early 1930s, several rodeos were well established; the Cheyenne Frontier Days had been going continuously since 1897. But it is significant to note that the Cheyenne celebration was patterned after a Wild West show with its mock battles, stagecoach holdups, Pony Express rides and other entertainments in addition to the cowboy contests. In addition to Cheyenne, two other rodeos with a long history are the Pendleton Roundup in Oregon, which began in 1911, and the Calgary Stampede in Alberta, Canada, which began in 1912.

There are six major established events in a rodeo: saddle bronc riding, bareback bronc riding, bull riding, steer wrestling, calf roping and team roping. In addition, steer roping is sometimes included; barrel racing is the only rodeo event in which females may participate. The exclusion of women from rodeos occurred after the 1930s; prior to this time women could and did participate in rodeos, particularly from 1910 to 1930. Women did trick riding and roping as well as bronc riding, and such cowgirls as Florence Randolph, Fannie Sperry Steele, Mabel Strickland, Tad Lucas, Lucille Mulhall, Prairie Lillie Aline, Fox Wilson, Bertha Blancett and Prairie Rose Henderson became rodeo stars during these early years. In 1948 the Girls Rodeo Association was formed, and they put on a few all-cowgirl shows each year.

The rodeo that has emerged has two basic kinds of events: the events that come directly from work done on ranches by cowboys, and events that were created especially for the rodeo. Bull riding and steer wrestling are examples of the latter; bronc riding and the roping events are examples of events that come directly from the activities of the working cowboy.

Most of the cowboys in the riding events are young— late teens and early 20s—and many haven't worked on ranches. These are athletic contests, and rodeo schools have developed in order to help athletic men become involved in these activities. The roping contestants are often older, and they're working cowboys; it takes the special skills developed on a ranch to be a good roper, and a ranch is needed to train and develop a roping horse. There is less skill involved for bull and bronc riders; it's mostly a matter of climbing on and hanging on.

The rodeo is held in a large oval-shaped area; at one end are the chutes and gates for the roping events, and on one side of the oval are the chutes for the broncs and bulls in the bucking contests. These animals are kept in a pen behind the chutes and driven into the chute, where the cowboy mounts the animal (the chutes are narrow so the animal cannot move around); when the gate is opened, the animal bucks out into the ring. Across the oval from the chutes are the grandstands; above the grandstands are the announcer, timers and scorekeepers.

In the saddle bronc-riding contest, the horse bucks and the cowboy must begin his ride with his feet over the horse's shoulders; he is judged on how well he rides (half his score) and how well the bronc bucks (the other half of his score). The cowboy should be in rhythm with the horse, and judges look for a cowboy whose spur strokes are smooth from the horse's neck back to the saddle cantle; the feet of the cowboy should be straight out in front when the bronc's front feet are on the ground, and when the horse bucks up, the cowboy's feet should strike the back of the saddle, knees bent. The ride must last eight seconds; at the end of that time a pickup rider comes up, loosens the bucking strap on the rear flank of the horse (which causes him to buck) and helps the cowboy off. In bareback bronc riding, a cowboy only has a leather rigging to hold; this leather is held in place by a cinch. The bareback rider should lie back on the bucking animal and spur from the horse's neck to the top of its withers. He must stay on for eight seconds, and half the points come from his ride, the other half from how well the bronc bucks. (In the earliest rodeos a cowboy had to mount a bronc in the open field and then ride him until he stopped bucking.) In bull riding, the final event of the evening for rodeo because it is the most exciting and dangerous, a rider just tries to stay on for eight seconds. The cowboy only has a flat-braided rope to hold, which is tied around the bull's middle just behind his front legs. Spurring gets a cowboy extra points, but basically he's judged on whether he manages to stay on or not.

For calf roping, a calf is released from a chute and it runs into the arena; after giving the calf a predesignated head start, the rider begins the chase, swinging his rope. As the roper throws his loop over the calf's head, his horse is trained to stop and keep the rope taut; then the cowboy dismounts, runs to the calf, throws it to the ground and ties any three legs of the calf with a "piggin' string" (a rope about six feet long); when the roper throws up his hands after tying the calf, the clock, which began when the calf was released from the chute, stops. The cowboy who ropes and ties the calf in the shortest time wins, but there is one proviso: The calf must stay tied for six seconds after the cowboy remounts his horse to prove the cowboy has made a good tie. In team roping, two cowboys go after a released steer (bigger than a calf); the first roper, or "header," throws his rope and catches the steer's horns or head and then dallies his rope around his saddle horn, which causes the steer to turn away and allows the second partner, called the "heeler," to throw his loop, which catches the steer around the hind legs. This causes the steer to fall; the horses then keep the ropes taut. The clock is stopped when both horses face the steer and the ropes are taut. In steer roping (not an event in all rodeos) a 750-pound steer is released and the cowboy must rope him around the horns; then the slack rope drops down over the steer's right hip while the cowboy rides to the left; this causes the rope to trip the steer. With the steer down, the rider dismounts, ties up any three legs and throws up his hands, which stops the clock. The steer must remain tied for six seconds. There are two reasons why steer roping is not an event in all rodeos: (1) Some states have outlawed it because it can kill or injure a steer, and (2) it must be performed in a larger arena, and not all rodeos are big enough. With roping events, the actions of the calf or steer determine to a large extent a cowboy's success; if a calf dips and dodges or stops and starts, the cowboy loses valuable time chasing it down.

In steer wrestling, a steer is released from the end chutes, and two cowboys—one on each side—give chase after a short head start. One cowboy is the "hazer," and his job is to run alongside the steer and keep it going straight; the other cowboy pulls up to the side of the steer and slides off the saddle and down on top of the steer with his arms around the steer's horns while his legs are straight out, boots digging into the ground to stop the steer. The cowboy turns the steer's head by lifting up with his right hand and pushing down with

his left until the steer's head twists and the steer tumbles onto the ground. This is a timed event, and the clock stops when the steer's legs are off the ground.

Animals for the riding and roping contests are supplied by a stock contractor, who negotiates with a rodeo committee for animals and services. Since a cowboy riding a bronc is judged half by the animal's performance and half by his own, it is imperative that good bucking animals are used. The stock contractor does not provide horses ridden by ropers; these horses are trained and developed by the ropers themselves, since a well-trained horse is about 75% responsible for a roper's success.

Each rodeo is organized by a local committee that plans the promotion and production of the rodeo; some rodeos are sponsored by volunteer organizations, whereas others have professional promoters. These committees arrange insurance, deal with the stock contractors, arrange for prize money and entry fees and get a crowd in the stands. Obviously the rodeos with the largest prize money attract the top competitors.

In addition to the regular events scheduled for a rodeo, there is usually a barrel-racing contest. This is a timed event in which a woman on a horse comes out and has to ride around three barrels in a clover pattern and then race back to the starting gate; the fastest time wins.

Since rodeo is an entertainment event as well as a sport, there are generally "acts" that fill in the time between events. These acts might include trick riders, trick ropers and other speciality acts, all generally with a western theme. The announcer is particularly important at a rodeo because he announces the performers and events, banters with the clowns, puts words into the mouths of animals and keeps up a lively patter from his "crow's nest" that informs and entertains the rodeo crowd.

In the arena with the contestants for the riding events are two judges; one gives points for the rider, and the other gives points for the animal—both based on the personal assessment of the judge. In the roping and steer-wresting events there are also two judges, or flagmen, in the arena; one judge watches to see if the animal gets a proper head start (and the cowboy is penalized 10 seconds if not), and this first flagman starts the timekeeper's clock; the other flagman drops his flag to stop the clock. The timekeeper, who sits with the announcer, works every event. In addition to these judges and timekeepers, the other essential rodeo performers in the arena with the contestant are the clowns for the bull-riding events. Brahma bulls weigh over a ton and are wild, vicious animals; they will gore a cowboy with its horns, and rodeo contestants have been severely injured or killed by bulls after a ride. The clown engages the bull after the ride and diverts its attention from the cowboy; the clown provides humor with an assortment of barrels and other props in addition to providing a lifesaving service to the cowboy.

Other "contract personnel" in addition to the announcers, clowns, judges, specialty-act stock contractors, and timekeepers are laborers, secretaries and photographers. These are all hired and paid by the rodeo committee putting on the event. The rodeo cowboy must pay an entry fee for each event he enters, and if he doesn't finish "in the money," he does not receive any money at all. Rodeo cowboys pride themselves on their individualism and independence; there are no guarantees and no salaries, just winnings or empty pockets. The cowboy incurs all his own expenses (travel, hotels, food, entry fees) and keeps all his money; there are no teams, managers or coaches, although some sponsors such as hat companies and tobacco or beer companies may pay rodeo cowboys for endorsements. Competing in various rodeos is known as "going down the road" to the rodeo cowboys.

There are several levels of rodeo contestants. Some contestants are full-time rodeo cowboys traveling coast to coast; others are working or "ranch" cowboys who compete on the weekend. A great number of rodeo contestants compete in "circuits" that consist of rodeos in a specific area; for example, the Texas Prorodeo Circuit consists of the state of Texas; the Turquoise Prorodeo Circuit includes the states of Arizona and New Mexico; the Prairie Prorodeo Circuit includes the states of Oklahoma, Kansas and Nebraska. In all there are 12 circuits. In addition to these professional rodeo circuits, sanctioned by the PRCA, there is another organization, the International Rodeo Association, which also sanctions events. There are also high school, college and 4-H rodeos as well as local and amateur events held all over the West each year.

ROGERS, ROY (b. Leonard Franklin Slye in Cincinnati, Ohio on November 5, 1911)   When young Leonard Slye was two, his family moved to Portsmouth, Ohio, where they lived on the Ohio River in a houseboat. They then bought a farm around 1918 in Duck Run, Ohio but lost that when the Depression hit. Later they moved back to Cincinnati, where young Leonard took a job at the United Shoe Company working alongside his father. This was the late 1920s, and two things had deeply affected the young Slye: First, he was a fan of country singer Jimmie Rodgers and his blue yodel, and second, he had heard a German singer on an early cylinder on his family's Edison phonograph. Slye was intrigued with yodeling and found he had a knack for it; he kept practicing and working at it and soon developed fancy yodeling tricks as he practiced at home.

The Slye family's daughter, Mary, had married and moved to California, and she invited her family to come for a visit. It didn't take much persuading for young Leonard and the rest of the family to visit Mary in Lawndale, California, and in the summer of 1930 they piled in their car and headed there. The family returned to Ohio but Leonard wanted to go back, so the next year he and Mary's father-in-law went out to visit and Leonard stayed.

Slye's first job was driving a sand and gravel truck; unfortunately, the truck's owner missed some payments and the truck was repossessed, so Leonard lost his job. His next job was working as a migratory farmworker, picking peaches for Del Monte. But by mid-1931 he was back in Los Angeles, where he entered an ama-

Roy Rogers

teur program with his cousin Stanley, singing and playing banjo and mandolin. After they appeared on the "Midnight Frolic" on radio station KMCS in Inglewood, Ebb Bowen of the Rocky Mountaineers invited young Slye to join the group, which was appearing on radio station KGER. The Rocky Mountaineers were an instrumental group who hired Slye to sing. Wanting harmonies, Slye convinced them to try a duet and then ran an advertisement in the *Los Angeles Herald* on September 30, 1931 for a "Yodeler . . . Tenor preferred." Several things are obvious here: Slye was not comfortable singing alone because he loved harmonies, and he already knew he wanted someone else who could yodel. The cowboy yodel would be an integral sound for Roy Rogers and the Sons of the Pioneers.

The ad was answered by a number of singers, one of whom was Bob Nolan. Nolan got the job and the two began to rehearse. It was soon obvious the group needed a third voice, and Nolan recommended a friend, Bill "Slumber" Nichols. This trio of Slye, Nolan and Nichols debuted in December, 1931 on KGER in Long Beach.

During the audition Slye was particularly impressed with Nolan's ability to yodel—indeed, that was what Slye was looking for. Later, he told biographer Ken Griffis: "Nolan apparently had done little yodeling prior to joining me. He was a good yodeler, but was not able to do any of the fancy yodeling. From the beginning I could do a variety of yodeling, both fast and slow, and created my own style, which made my yodels much more adaptable to western and country songs. Jimmie Rodgers had some impact on my desire to make yodeling a strong part of my singing. By taking these yodels, changing the rhythm and breaks, I created a yodeling style all my own. I think Bob, Slumber and I were the first to do trio yodeling, at least I had never heard any before."

Nolan left the group in late summer 1932, and Slye put another advertisement in the *Los Angeles Herald* for a "Harmony yodeler." Although Tim Spencer had never really yodeled, he answered the ad and was hired in mid-August. The trio of Slye, Nichols and Spencer worked with the Rocky Mountaineers for a few weeks and then left to join Benny Nawahi's International Cowboys, where they played live gigs and appeared on radio stations KGER and KRKD in Los Angeles. In June, calling themselves the O-Bar-O Cowboys, the trio left for what would be a disastrous tour of the Southwest. The money was next to nothing and the shows were ragged, but Slye did meet his future wife, Arleen Wilkins, in Roswell, New Mexico, and Spencer met his future wife in Texas. The group returned to Los Angeles in September 1933 and broke up.

Back in Los Angeles, Slye joined Jack and His Texas Outlaws, but he still dreamed of a trio. He contacted Tim Spencer, who agreed to give it another shot, and the two drove out to the Bel Air Country Club and convinced a very reluctant Bob Nolan to give it another shot. Nolan finally relented, and the two began rehearsals at a boardinghouse in Hollywood at Carlton and Bronson. Within a few weeks the trio joined Jack and His Texas Outlaws and called themselves The Pioneer Trio. They were put on the staff at KFWB and performed a morning show from eight to nine; they then performed another show from 5 to 6 P.M. as the Gold Star Rangers. In the evenings, they often appeared with the Jack Joy Orchestra.

The name "Sons of the Pioneers" came from announcer Harry Hall, who explained to the surprised and disgruntled group after their morning show that they looked too young for "pioneers," hence "Sons of the Pioneers." The name stuck and became official in March 1934.

It quickly became obvious that the sound of harmony yodeling and trick yodeling developed by Slye and the songs of Bob Nolan fit together well. Nolan was an extremely talented songwriter, and by the time he joined Slye and Spencer he had already written "Way Out There" and "Tumbling Tumbleweeds," which the group performed. This gave the group their distinctive sound, and they were soon popular in the Los Angeles area. They performed on radio station KFWB from 1934 to 1936 and then moved to KHJ, where they were part of Peter Potter's Barn Dance with the Four Squires and Stafford Sisters. They were signed to appear in a series of western movies starring Charles Starrett, but Len only appeared in the first two. By this time he was seeking to establish himself as a singing cowboy, inspired by the tremendous success of Gene Autry at Republic and then Tex Ritter and Dick Foran.

In mid-1937 Slye, then going by the professional name "Dick Weston," learned that auditions for a singing cowboy were being held at Republic. The reason: Republic's star Gene Autry was threatening to walk off the set over a contract dispute. Slye went to the audition

Roy Rogers and Trigger

but the guard refused to let him enter. Slye decided to walk in with the workers; the guard yelled for him to stop just as producer Sol Siegle came by. Siegle knew Slye and rescued him from the awkward situation. Slye auditioned, after going back to his car for his guitar, doing "Hadie Brown" with a fast yodel and some other songs. Siegle liked Slye but waited until Autry walked before deciding to sign the young singer. On October 13, 1937 Slye signed with Republic and was immediately cast in *Under Western Stars*, a movie written originally for Autry. Slye's name was then changed to "Roy Rogers" by studio executives Sol and Moe Siegle and Herbert J. Yates. Slye did not legally change his name to Roy Rogers until 1942.

Autry's contract dispute was soon settled and the star returned to the studio, but he and Rogers continued to make films for Republic. There were some essential differences, though. Autry's films generally had five to eight songs in each 70-minute film. Autry always played a character named "Gene Autry," and the films were generally contemporary westerns, with planes, cars and other modern technology around, although Autry wore six-shooters and rode his horse Champion. Rogers's westerns were generally historical, set in the post–Civil War to 1880s period with Rogers playing a character such as Billy the Kid, Wild Bill Hickok or Buffalo Bill. There was always music, but never as much as Autry used; there were generally two or three songs in a Roy Rogers movie.

Republic Pictures decided to give Roy Rogers a major

publicity and promotional campaign during World War II when Autry joined the armed services. Rogers received a deferment because he had two children and was over 30.

Rogers was killed by Republicas "King of the Cowboys," and a movie by that title starring Rogers was soon released. He began to play a character named "Roy Rogers" and more songs were included in his films, making them more like Autry's. Rogers also began wearing gaudier, less authentic cowboy clothing and developed a supporting cast of his horse, Trigger; his dog, Bullet; a female lead, Dale Evans; and a sidekick, Pat Brady, with his jeep Nellybelle. Lavish production numbers were incorporated into the films because studio head Herbert J. Yates had seen the musical *Oklahoma* in New York. In effect, Rogers's pictures became western musicals instead of cowboy movies with some singing.

The budget for the Roy Rogers movies was increased during the war years, and the movies were marketed to the "A" theaters in major cities, particularly in the South and Midwest, rather than the "B" movie houses that were primarily in small towns and rural areas.

Dale Evans first appeared with Roy Rogers in 1944 in *The Cowboy and the Senorita*. This would be the first of 20 consecutive films together. In November 1946 Rogers's wife died after giving birth to their third child. A little over a year later, on December 31, 1947, Roy Rogers and Dale Evans married.

On November 21, 1944 Roy Rogers began his own network radio program,"The Roy Rogers Show" sponsored by Goodyear, which appeared on the Mutual network on Tuesday evenings. The show costarred Bob Nolan and the Sons of the Pioneers, female vocalist Pat Friday, Perry Botkin and his band, and announcer Vern Smith. The showed ended in late spring 1945, when Goodyear did not pick up the option. Rogers's next radio show began in 1946 and was on the NBC network on Saturday nights sponsored by Miles Laboratories. This show featured Bob Nolan and the Sons of the Pioneers, Gabby Hayes, Dale Evans, Pat Buttram and Country Washburn and his Orchestra. This show was also canceled at the end of the season. Rogers's third radio program, sponsored by Quaker Oats, began in fall 1948 on the Mutual Broadcasting System on Sunday evenings. This shasted for three years, until the summer of 1951. In the fall of 1951 "The Roy Rogers Show" was broadcast on NBC on Friday nights the first year, on Thursdays afterward. Sponsored by General Foods and then, for the last year, Dodge Motors, the show continued until 1954. These radio shows consisted of Roy and Dale singing ballads or westerns songs, comedy by Gabby Hayes, Pat Brady or Pat Buttram and about a 10-minute drama. In general, the radio shows were patterned after Autry's successful "Melody Ranch" radio program.

Rogers's contract with Republic was up in 1951, and Rogers wanted the TV rights to his movies. Yates refused and, instead, cut them up and made them available to TV himself. "The Roy Rogers Show," a regular 30-minute TV series from Rogers, premiered on NBC on December 30, 1951 on Sunday evenings sponsored by Post Cereals.

In 1964 Roy and Dale moved to Apple Valley, California and then in 1976 to Victorville, where they have a museum. Trigger died in 1965 at the age of 33; he had been retired in 1957 at the age of 25 after the TV series had ended.

Roy Rogers appeared in the following films as a member of The Sons of the Pioneers:

The Old Homestead (1935)
Slightly Static (1935)
Tumbling Tumbleweeds (1935)
Way Up Thar (1935)
Gallant Defender (1935)
The Mysterious Avenger (1936)
Rhythm on the Range (1936)
The Big Show (1936)
The Old Corral (1936)
The Old Wyoming Trail (1937)
Wild Horse Rodeo (1937)
The Old Barn Dance (1938)

He appeared in these films as a star himself:

Under Western Stars (1938)
Billy the Kid Returns (1938)
Come On, Rangers (1938)
Shine On, Harvest Moon (1938)
Rough Riders' Roundup (1939)
Frontier Pony Express (1939)
Southward Ho (1939)
In Old Caliente (1939)
Wall Street Cowboy (1939)
The Arizona Kid (1939)
Jeepers Creepers (1939)
Saga of Death Valley (1939)
Days of Jesse James (1939)
Young Buffalo Bill (1940)
The Dark Command (1940)
The Carson City Kid (1940)
The Ranger and the Lady (1940)
Colorado (1940)
Young Bill Hickok (1940)
The Border Legion (1940)
Robin Hood of the Pecos (1941)
Arkansas Judge (1941)
In Old Cheyenne (1941)
Sheriff of Tombstone (1941)
Nevada City (1941)
Bad Man of Deadwood (1941)
Jesse James at Bay (1941)
Red River Valley (1941)
Man from Cheyenne (1942)
South of Santa Fe (1942)
Sunset on the Desert (1942)
Romance on the Range (1942)
Sons of the Pioneers (1942)
Sunset Serenade (1942)
Heart of the Golden West (1942)

Ridin' down the Canyon (1942)
Idaho (1943)
King of the Cowboys (1943)
Song of Texas (1943)
Silver Spurs (1943)
Man from Music Mountain (1943)
Hands Across the Border (1943)
The Cowboy and the Senorita (1944)
The Yellow Rose of Texas (1944)
Song of Nevada (1944)
San Fernando Valley (1944)
Lights of Old Santa Fe (1944)
Brazil (1944)
Lake Placid Serenade (1944)
Hollywood Canteen (1944)
Utah (1945)
Bells of Rosarita (1945)
The Man from Oklahoma (1945)
Sunset in El Dorado (1945)
Don't Fence Me In (1945)
Along the Navajo Trail (1945)
Song of Arizona (1946)
Rainbow over Texas (1946)
My Pal Trigger (1946)
Under Nevada Skies (1946)
Roll On Texas Moon (1946)
Home in Oklahoma (1946)
Out California Way (1946)
Heldorado (1946)
Apache Rose (1947)
Hit Parade of 1947 (1947)
Bells of San Angelo (1947)
Springtime in the Sierras (1947)
On the Old Spanish Trail (1947)
The Gay Ranchero (1948)
Under California Skies (1948)
Eyes of Texas (1948)
Melody Time (1948)
Night Time in Nevada (1948)
Grand Canyon Trail (1948)
The Far Frontier (1948)
Susanna Pass (1949)
Down Dakota Way (1949)
The Golden Stallion (1949)
Bells of Coronado (1950)
Twilight in the Sierras (1950)
Trigger, Jr. (1950)
Sunset in the West (1950)
North of the Great Divide (1950)
Trail of Robin Hood (1950)
Spoilers of the Plains (1951)
Heart of the Rockies (1951)
In Old Amarillo (1951)
South of Caliente (1951)
Pals of the Golden West (1951)
Son of Paleface (1952)
Alias Jesse James (1959)
MacKintosh and T.J. (1975)

(See also B WESTERN MOVIES; EVANS, DALE; MOVIES; NOLAN, BOB; REPUBLIC STUDIO; ROY ROGERS AND DALE EVANS SHOW, THE; ROY ROGERS SHOW, THE; SINGING COWBOYS; SONS OF THE PIONEERS; SPENCER, TIM.)

ROGERS, WILL (b. William Penn Adair Rogers in Oolagah, Oklahoma on November 4, 1879; d. Point Barrow, Alaska on August 15, 1935)   Will Rogers was one of the most famous Americans during the late 1920s and early 1930s through his movies, newspaper columns and personal appearances. Known as the "Cowboy Philosopher," Rogers possessed wit and wisdom that enlightened and amused a nation trying to figure out the Roaring Twenties and then the Great Depression. The son of a rancher, Rogers learned to rope and became an expert trick roper, performing in Wild West shows and then vaudeville shows. Rebelling against his father, a powerful, wealthy rancher in Oklahoma, Will ran away and became a cowboy on the Texas panhandle. He sailed to Argentina in 1902 and then caught a ship to South Africa, where he began to appear in Texas Jack's Wild West Circus as "The Cherokee Kid" rope artist and bronco buster. Rogers returned to the United States in 1904 after a tour of Australia and appeared at

Will Rogers

the St. Louis World's Fair. He received his first national fame at Madison Square Garden in 1905 as a member of Zach Mulhall's show. Rogers readily adapted to show business, first performing rope tricks and then adding comments and wisecracks in his western drawl to enhance the act. He appeared with the Ziegfeld Follies in 1916–18, 1922 and 1924–25 and then moved to Hollywood and became a star. Rogers's daily newspaper column was syndicated to 350 outlets; he wrote political commentary gleaned from his travels around the country and meetings with politicians. Rogers died in an airplane crash with Wiley Post in Point Barrow, Alaska as they were heading toward Russia for a tour there.

ROMAN NOSE (b. c. 1830; d. Beecher's Island, Colorado on September 17, 1868) Roman Nose was a fierce warrior and leader of the Cheyenne. He owned a special war bonnet given to him by medicine man White Bull. The bonnet was supposed to protect Roman Nose from his enemies if he engaged in a strict purification rite before battles. This protection worked in September 1865 when Roman Nose's pony was killed from under him in the Powder River country during a fight with soldiers but he was unscathed. During the fight at Beecher Island, Roman Nose violated one of the purification taboos; however, the other warriors shamed the reluctant warrior into fighting against the soldiers. On the first charge against the soldiers, Roman Nose was killed. (See also BEECHER ISLAND, BATTLE OF.)

ROOSEVELT, THEODORE (b. New York City on October 27, 1858; d. Sagamore Hill, Oyster Bay, Long Island on January 6, 1919) Teddy Roosevelt brought publicity and fame to the Old West and cowboys when he became president in 1901. Known as the "Cowboy President," Roosevelt had lived in Dakota Territory in the 1880s and raised cattle on a ranch there. The Old West made a deep impression on Roosevelt and affected his life. Born to a wealthy, influential family in New York City, the sickly, weak boy worked hard at physical activities to overcome his defective eyesight and asthma. He graduated in 1880 from Harvard University and entered politics. He first visited the badlands of the Dakotas in 1883 when he went to hunt buffalo and purchased the Maltese Cross Ranch at this time. Roosevelt was elected to the New York State Assembly in November 1883, but the following February his wife and mother both died, leaving him with an infant daughter. Roosevelt moved to his ranch in the West and then bought another ranch, the Elkhorn, and began raising cattle, which numbered about 1,600 head by August 1885. Roosevelt worked the ranch from his horse and participated actively in the cowboy life, earning the respect and friendship of the cowboys. Roosevelt suffered great financial loss when his cattle were wiped out in the 1886–87 winter. At this point he returned to New York and politics. Among the books Roosevelt wrote were *Hunting Trips of a Ranchman* (1885), *Ranch Life and the Hunting Trail* (1888) and *The Winning of the West* (1889), a book about western expansion in America. Roosevelt raised the "Rough Riders," the First U.S. Vol-

Teddy Roosevelt

unteer Cavalry for the Spanish-American War in 1898, and achieved military glory in Cuba and returned a national hero. Roosevelt was William McKinley's vice president when he was elected in 1900; after McKinley was assassinated, Roosevelt became president in 1901; he was reelected in 1904.

ROOSTER COGBURN Film produced by Hal B. Wallis; directed by Stuart Millar; screenplay by Martin Julien (Martha Hyer; based on the character from the novel *True Grit* by Charles Portis); released in 1975 by Universal; 107 minutes in length. Cast: John Wayne and Katharine Hepburn.

In *True Grit* (1969) John Wayne played a character named "Rooster Cogburn," a role so successful that it earned Wayne an Academy Award. This movie, six years later, has Wayne reprise his character and star with Katharine Hepburn. The plot is similiar: to find the killers of a woman's father. But in *True Grit* it was a young girl; in *Rooster Cogburn* it is an old spinster. Wayne and Hepburn are excellent together in this humorous film and of course get the outlaws.

ROPE There were two types of rope used by 19th-century cowboys: reata, or braided rawhide, and the grass rope, which was twisted (not braided) and made of manila hemp and maguey in the early days but later sisal and cotton. The grass rope was cheaper and stronger than the rawhide, although the reata could last longer than a grass rope. There were a number of uses for a rope: catching cattle or horses, as a whip, to construct a fence or corral, pull bogged-down cows out to safety, haul in some firewood, help in pulling a wagon, rescuing men in a river, killing snakes, making a hackamore, or dispensing justice for a horse thief.

ROPING Catching an animal with a rope by forming a loop and throwing it so the animal's head or legs are caught. Cowboys used two basic kinds of roping techniques: The hard and fast meant the rope was tied to the saddle horn. The dally method meant the rope was looped around the saddle horn when a cow (or other object) was caught. Skill in roping was the most important attribute a cowboy could have. TV shows and movies tend to emphasize a cowboy's skill with a gun, but his skill with a rope was much more valuable and the source of pride for most top cowboys.

ROSE, DELLA See BULLION, LAURA.

ROSEBUD, BATTLE OF THE (June 17, 1876) Just before the Battle of the Little Bighorn, a number of soldiers were killed in the Battle of the Rosebud, which served as a preview of the big battle about to occur. The Battle of the Rosebud marked the first time that a large number of Indians, from several different tribes, united to fight whites. Previously, each tribe fought its own battle. The Rosebud was a creek in Montana where 1,500 Sioux and Cheyenne were gathered on June 17, 1876. General George Crook led a column of about 1,000 troops and 300 friendly Indians, mostly Crow and Shoshoni, into a battle that lasted six hours and had a battle line that extended about three miles. Neither side actually won the battle, although Crook and his troops were stunned that they were unable to gain a victory. Eight days later some of these same Indians slaughtered the Seventh Cavalry troops led by Custer at the Battle of the Little Bighorn.

ROUGH RIDERS, THE TV show that starred Kent Taylor as Captain Jim Flagg, Jan Merlin as Lieutenant Kirby and Peter Whitney as Sergeant Buck Sinclair.

Three Civil War veterans—two Union and one Confederate—unite to travel west. The result was a series of adventures detailed in this series, which had nothing to do with Teddy Roosevelt's group from the Spanish-American War. The show premiered on October 2, 1958 on ABC on Thursday nights. There were 39 episodes of the half-hour show, which was last telecast on September 24, 1959.

ROUNDERS, THE TV show that starred Ron Hayes as Ben Jones, Patrick Wayne as Howdy Lewis, Chill Wills as Jim Ed Love, Bobbi Jordan as Ada, Janis Hansen as Sally, Jason Wingreen as Shorty Dawes, Walker Edmiston as Regan and J. Pat O'Malley as Vince.

This was a contemporary western comedy about a rich ranch owner, Jim Ed Love, and the two ranch hands who were deeply in debt to him. Jim Ed dressed in a custom-tailored white cowboy suit and drove a fancy station wagon, while the cowboys had a cantankerous horse named Old Fooler. They partied in the nearby town of Hi Low, hung out at the Longhorn Cafe and had some lovely girlfriends. Originally a novel by Max Evans and then a movie in 1965 starring Chill Wills, the show debuted on September 6, 1966 on Tuesday evenings on ABC. The half-hour show was last telecast on January 3, 1967.

ROUNDUP In a general sense, a gathering of cattle or other animals. Originating in east Texas, roundups were originally called "cow hunts," in which cowboys went out and found unbranded cattle and drove them into a central point. Sometimes several ranches would band together on these roundups. In larger roundups, a well-organized group of ranchers would gather up cattle under a roundup boss, who laid down the law and made decisions about branding mavericks. In Wyoming and Montana the cattle associations organized the roundups. In Wyoming during the 1880s there were district roundups organized by the associations that demanded that mavericks be sold every 10 days. The most important part of the roundup was branding the calves. Generally, there were two cattle roundups a years—one in the spring for branding calves, and the other in the fall to gather beef. Other beef were rounded up in the middle of the year for a trail drive to market.

ROUSTERS, THE TV show that starred Chad Everett as Wyatt Earp III, Jim Varney as Evan Earp, Maxine Stuart as Amanda Earp, Timothy Gibbs as Michael Earp, Hoyt Axton as Cactus Jack Slade and Mimi Rogers as Ellen Slade.

Wyatt Earp III was the great-grandson of the legendary Wyatt Earp. The young Earp worked for a traveling carnival show in Cactus Jack's Sladetown Carnival and was the only sane member in a cast of misfits. The show, set in the contemporary Southwest, debuted on October 1, 1983 on Saturday nights on NBC; it ended its run on July 21, 1984.

ROYAL CANADIAN MOUNTED POLICE TV show that starred Gilles Pelletier as Corporal Jacques Gagnier, John Perkins as Constable Scott and Don Franks as Constable Mitchell.

This show, popular on Saturday mornings, was a 30-minute series about the Canadian police in the northwest. It was syndicated beginning in 1956.

ROY ROGERS AND DALE EVANS SHOW, THE TV show whose regulars were Roy Rogers, Pat Brady, Sons of the Pioneers, Kirby Buchanon, Kathy Taylor, Cliff Arquette (as Charley Weaver) and the Ralph Carmichael Orchestra.

This was a musical variety show from the King of the Cowboys and his singing partner. The show debuted on September 29 and the final telecast was December 29, 1962. The one-hour show aired on Saturday evenings on ABC.

ROY ROGERS SHOW, THE

TV show that starred Roy Rogers, Dale Evans and Pat Brady.

Roy Rogers lived on the Double R Bar Ranch, just outside Mineral City, where Dale Evans owned the cafe. He imposed law and order with the help of his Palomino horse, Trigger; German shepherd dog, Bullet, and trusty sidekick, Pat Brady, who drove a cantankerous jeep, Nellybelle. Sometimes Dale hopped on her horse, Buttermilk, to help. Dale also helped in another way: She wrote the theme song, "Happy Trails to You." Roy's old group, the Sons of the Pioneers, sometimes appeared on the show as well. The TV show premiered on December 30, 1951 on NBC on Sunday evenings. It held that same slot until its final telecast on June 23, 1957 (except for July 1952). The show appeared on Saturday mornings on CBS in January 1961 and ran there until September 1964. The 104 episodes were purchased by Rogers from NBC in the 1950s and then syndicated.

RUDABAUGH, DAVE

(b. Illinois on July 14, 1854; d. Parral, Mexico on February 18, 1886) One of the most notorious scoundrels in the West, Dave Rudabaugh led a gang of thieves and rustlers in Texas in the 1870s; he then moved on to Kansas and train holdups. He was caught and arrested by Bat Masterson and a posse but gained release by ratting on his gang members. After this Rudabaugh went to New Mexico, where he robbed stagecoaches and trains around Las Vegas, New Mexico and then pulled some thievery and confidence games in town. Rudabaugh's gang was helped by city marshal John Joshua Webb, who was in Bat Masterson's posse and who had arrested Rudabaugh several years before. These scams came to an end when Webb was arrested for murder in March 1880. Webb was scheduled to hang and Rudabaugh tried to free him; instead a lawman was killed. Rudabaugh then joined Billy the Kid's gang and was in the ranch house near White Oaks, New Mexico on November 30, 1881 when the gang held lawman James Carlyle hostage. Carlyle was killed early the next morning and the gang fled. A couple of weeks later Rudabaugh was with the Kid and other gang members when they were ambushed by Pat Garrett and a posse at Fort Sumner. Gang member Tom O'Folliard was killed on this cold Sunday but the others got away, although Rudabaugh's horse was killed and he had to hitch a ride with Billy Wilson. Rudabaugh was with the Kid's gang a few days later, holed up in a rock cabin near Stinking Springs, when Garrett and a posse found them and forced them to surrender. In September 1881 in Las Vegas, New Mexico, Rudabaugh—sentenced to death—was in a jail cell with his old buddy John Joshua Webb when they attempted a jailbreak. This break failed, but a couple of months later the group dug themselves out, using a pick, an iron poker and a knife, to escape under the wall one night. The end for Rudabaugh came in Parral, Mexico, where he was foreman of a ranch owned by the governor of Chihuahua. During a card game on February 18, 1886 a quarrel developed, and Rudabaugh killed a Mexican who was in the game and then another Mexican who tried to help. Rudabaugh then tried to escape but his horse was gone,

so he returned to the cantina where, in the dark, somebody cut off his head. Rudabaugh's head was then put on a pike and paraded through the streets. (See also BILLY THE KID; MASTERSON, BAT; O'FOLLIARD, TOM; WEBB, JOHN JOSHUA.)

RUNNING IRON

A plain iron that could alter brands on a cow. In the 1870s and 1880s, a man caught with a running iron was automatically considered a cattle thief. The running iron was used legally as well to give a temporary brand for a calf with no brand.

RUSSELL, C. M.

(b. Charles Marion Russell in Oak Hill, Missouri on March 19, 1864; d. Great Falls, Montana on October 24, 1926) Charlie Russell was the second son of six children of Charlie Silas and Mary Elizabeth Mead Russell, a prominent family in Missouri. Russell's father graduated from Yale University and helped manage the family-owned mining business. Among Russell's ancestors were William Bent, a great-uncle who built the first trading post on the Arkansas River in 1832, and Silas Bent, chief surveyor of the Louisiana Territory and later chief justice of the supreme court of Missouri Territory.

From an early age Charlie Russell had two abiding interests: the Wild West and art. He did not like school and by age 16 had finished all the schooling he would ever acquire. His parents, convinced that the only cure for their son was a taste of the real Wild West, arranged for him to visit Montana with a family friend, Pike Miller, who had a sheep ranch on the Judith River. On this trip Charlie Russell found his home; he would never again live in "civilized" society.

"Kid" Russell, as he was called by those who knew him in the West, disdained the conventions of society and ignored personal hygiene, preferring shaggy hair, dirty clothes and the like. His first job was working with Miller on the sheep ranch, a job he did not particularly care for, so at the first opportunity he moved in with a trapper, Jake Hoover. He stayed with the trapper for two years before going back to St. Louis to visit his family. In addition to trapping, Russell also drew and sketched extensively on whatever material he could find. He did this for his own pleasure.

Back in Montana, Charlie joined a "cow outfit" as a guard for the cowboys' horses at night. Later, his job was to watch the cattle at night. Russell joined this group as they were heading out on a two-month cattle drive with 75 riders and 400 horses; he remained a cowboy helping with cattle for 11 years.

Russell also painted and drew. He did his first famous drawing in the winter of 1886–87 when an extremely harsh winter almost wiped out the cattle industry in Montana. Russell was helping to tend a herd owned by two ranchers. When one of the ranchers sent a letter inquiring about the condition of the cattle, Russell answered with a sketch, *Waiting for a Chinook*, later called *Last of the 5000*. In this picture, an old steer is standing in blinding snow, its ribs showing. It summed up the condition of cattle all over the Montana range that winter.

Russell had begun using oils in 1885 and often sold his paintings and sketches in saloons for whatever he could get—$5 or $10 at the most but usually swapping them for food, whiskey or other provisions and often giving them away to whoever expressed admiration. By the early 1890s, a number of his sketches were hanging in the homes of wealthy Montanans. Russell's first formal commission came from a saloon keeper in Utica, who wanted a painting to hang behind the bar. Russell painted *Utica* on a large slab of wood.

In 1888, Russell spent the summer in Canada; returning to Montana, he met Chief Black Eagle of the Bloods and the cowboy went home with the Indian, living with the Bloods for six months until the snow melted in March. This time spent with the Indians gave Russell a deep understanding and appreciation for Indians and their way of life; it also helped him portray them realistically in his paintings.

In 1891 Russell went to the World's Fair in Chicago and then to St. Louis, where he visited William Niedringhaus, who commissioned several paintings. This commission gave him confidence and some financial security; he was allowed to paint whatever he wanted, and from this time forward he gave up cow herding and devoted himself to painting.

In 1895 Russell met Nancy Cooper when visiting his friend Ben Roberts. He was 31 and she was 17; they married in September 1896. Nancy encouraged him with his art and helped manage his affairs; she began negotiating higher prices for Russell's pictures and inspired him to keep regular working hours and give discipline to his art.

Russell had always spurned financial help from his family; earlier they had offered to set him up on a large ranch. But after his marriage to Nancy, Russell accepted his father's offer to build the couple a home in Great Falls.

Russell had been sending some illustrations to magazines in New York. After his marriage, Nancy encouraged him to write some stories, which he also sent. In 1897 the popular magazine *Recreation* published his first story with three of his illustrations.

In the fall of 1903, Russell went to St. Louis, where one of his paintings was accepted for exhibition at the World's Fair, then Chicago and New York. There he met a number of artists, such as western painter Charles Schreyvogel, and celebrities like Will Rogers. In 1903 the first one-man show of his paintings was held by the Noonan-Kocian Galleries in St. Louis.

In 1904 Russell illustrated two books, *My Sixty Years on the Plains* by W. T. Hamilton and *Chip of the Flying U* by B. M. Bower, as well as several magazine articles for *McClure's* and *Leslie's Illustrated Weekly*. Additionally, *Outing* magazine chose him to write and illustrate a series of short stories, called "Line Camp Yarns." Charlie Russell had finally arrived as an artist well known and respected by the eastern establishment as well as by the cattlemen and cowboys of the West.

In 1909 there was an exhibition of Russell's work in Brooklyn, New York, and in 1911 the prestigious Folsom Galleries presented a major Russell show, which the *New York Times* covered with a review. In 1911 Russell was commissioned by Montana to paint a mural to hang behind the Speaker's station in the House of Representatives in the state capital. For this Russell painted the historic meeting of Lewis and Clark with the Ootlashoot Indians. This work is considered one of Russell's masterpieces.

In 1912 Russell exhibited his work in Canada at the Calgary Stampede; in 1913 he prepared a special show for the Prince of Wales in Saskatchewan where the prince purchased one of his works. In 1914 Russell exhibited his work at the Dore Galleries in London. During the tour, Russell sent humorous, illustrated letters to his friends to tell of his adventures; these became valued additions to Russell collections.

In 1925 Russell had exhibitions in every major city, from Los Angeles to New York to Washington; that same year the University of Montana awarded him the honorary degree of Doctor of Law.

Charlie Russell's art is authentic because he was authentic; he had the rare ability to combine his innate talent for art with his love for the Wild West. His authenticity was a result of his work as a cowboy, the time he spent with the Plains Indians and most of all his arrival in the West in 1880 and his 30-year residence there at the height of its Wild West glory.

Charles Russell is buried in Great Falls, Montana, where the C. M. Russell Museum is located. (See also ART; REMINGTON, FREDERIC.)

RUSSELL, MAJORS AND WADDELL William H. Russell, Alexander Majors and William Waddell formed a freighting company in January 1855 with a large government contract for all military freight west of the Missouri River. The firm actually began when the government decided that army trains and personnel were inefficient for supplying posts in New Mexico Territory after the Mexican War. So the government began awarding contracts to civilian firms to transport supplies to the army posts; in 1854 the army decided to award a contract to supply all the posts for a two-year period, instead of a contract for each post and each trip. Russell, Majors and Waddell was formed for this purpose.

William Hepburn Russell (1812–72) was born in Burlington, Vermont; he moved west to Missouri and met William B. Waddell about 1840. A born promoter, Russell formed a number of partnerships and in 1847 entered the freighting business along the Santa Fe Trail. Russell and Waddell became partners in 1852 in their mercantile business; they also transported military supplies to Santa Fe. In 1854 Alexander Majors joined them.

Alexander Majors (1814–1900) was born near Franklin, Kentucky; he entered the freighting business in 1848 with six wagons carrying goods along the Santa Fe Trail. Soon, Majors was transporting military supplies for the government. A strict disciplinarian who made his men pledge not to swear, drink, gamble, mistreat animals or travel on Sundays, Majors oversaw the field operations of the firm. William Bradford Waddell (1807–

72) was born in Fauquier County, Virginia and moved to Kentucky, then Illinois. A cautious businessman, Waddell was in charge of the day-to-day operations in the firm's office.

The firm overextended itself to deliver supplies to Utah during the Mormon War (1857). Russell also entered the stagecoach business and then the Pony Express, although Waddell tried unsuccessfully to keep Russell from further overextending himself. In order to pay their mounting debts, Russell persuaded Secretary of War John B. Floyd to issue drafts on the War Department for previous or future services; Russell then used these drafts as security for Indian Trust Fund bonds,

held by the Interior Department, for cash. The whole affair collapsed and became public, becoming a major scandal; Floyd had to resign and Russell was indicted, causing the firm to fold in 1862. Majors continued in the freighting business until 1866 and then worked for the Union Pacific Railroad; he died in Chicago, Illinois. Waddell never attempted business again; the Civil War postponed the trial of Russell, who attempted to enter several business enterprises in New York, none of which succeeded. He died bankrupt. (See also PONY EXPRESS.)

RUSSELL, WILLIAM H. (See RUSSELL, MAJORS AND WADDELL.)

S

SACAJAWEA (b. Bird Woman c. 1790; d. 1812 or 1884) This was the young Indian woman with an infant son who accompanied Lewis and Clark on their expedition and proved invaluable as a guide and translator, especially when the explorers reached her native Shoshoni country. Sacajawea was captured by the Hidatsa Tribe when she was 12 and then sold to Toussaint Charbonneau, a French Canadian fur trader, who married her according to Indian rites. Lewis and Clark hired Charbonneau as a guide and interpreter, but his wife proved even more valuable. She gave birth to a boy at the Mandan village in February 1805 while Lewis and Clark wintered there and accompanied the expedition when they left in March. On the journey, Sacajawea found her brother, Cameahwait, in the Rocky Mountains, and through this reunion the tribe was persuaded to sell horses to the explorers so they could cross the mountains. Sacajawea elected to stay with the explorers and traveled to the Pacific, then back to the Mandan country, where she lived with her husband. Nobody knows for sure when Sacajawea died: Some say she died of childbirth fever in 1812, whereas others say she died on a reservation in Wyoming in 1884.

SADDLE PAL CLUB This TV show consisted of old western movies and serials, which began airing in December 1951 on ABC on Saturday evenings. In May 1952 this show was extended to an hour; it lasted until August 1952.

SADDLES A wooden and leather seat for cowboys on horseback. The styles of saddles vary according to the way they are used, from riding in flat country to riding broncs, and are defined by the number of cinches used and where they are placed. The single-rigged (one-cinch) saddle came directly from the Mexican vaquero's

saddle. In the vaquero's saddle, the cinch was placed directly under the pommel while the lance was used when working cattle, but when the rope became dominant and was tied around the horn, one cinch under the pommel became unstable, so the cinch was moved to the center under the saddle (center-fire rig). This saddle worked fine if a long rope was used, but if a cowboy used a shorter rope tied to the saddle horn, then two cinches—one at the front and one at the rear of the saddle—were needed. The Mother Hubbard saddle was a Mexican saddle with a heavy tree, but the horn was a bit smaller and the straps were narrow; it was covered with a mochila to make a one-piece saddle and developed around 1868. The plains saddle was generally double-rigged. John S. and Gilbert M. Collins receive most of the credit for the development of the plains saddle; the two brothers had saddle-making shops in Cheyenne, Omaha, Billings and Great Falls during the late 19th century. The components of the saddle include the wooden tree, over which the leather seat is stretched. The horn or pommel is in the front of the saddle and sits atop the "fork." The cantle rises from the back of the seat. The stirrup holds the foot, and the fender protects the leg from the horse's sweat. The skirt is in the back of the saddle, and the ties are leather strips used to fasten things like bedrolls.

SAGA OF ANDY BURNETT, THE See WALT DISNEY PRESENTS.

SAGEBRUSH PHILOSOPHER A wise old cowboy who could philosophize and ruminate.

SAGUARO CACTUS Cactus plants (*Carnegiea gigantea*) found in Arizona and northern Mexico that grow 40–50 feet tall and live 150–200 years. During rainy weather, this cactus can absorb up to a ton of water; desert inhabitants and travelers learned water was stored in this plant and could be drunk when necessary. The white blossom in the spring becomes fruit, which the Piman Indians ate.

SALAZAR, YGINO (b. New Mexico on February 14, 1863; d. Lincoln, New Mexico on January 7, 1936) Fifteen-year-old Ygino Salazar was involved in the Lincoln County War with the McSween faction, miraculously surviving the siege at the McSween home. Salazar had bolted from the burning house and been cut down by three bullets. When he regained consciousness, he realized his enemies were walking among the bodies; two talked of putting a final slug into Salazar but decided against it because he was already dead. After they left, Salazar crawled to the river to drink and then to his brother's house, where he collapsed and had two of the three bullets removed by a surgeon. Later Salazar gave Billy the Kid a file and some other tools, which allowed the outlaw to escape from the Lincoln jail. After the Lincoln County War, Salazar became a rancher in the area and died peacefully at the age of 72. (See also BILLY THE KID; LINCOLN COUNTY WAR.)

SALOON Place where liquor is sold. Saloons in the West varied widely; some were rough, primitive places— a plank across some barrels—but others were lavish and opulent. They were open 24 hours a day in trail towns when the cowboys hit town. Many also served as dance halls, whorehouses and places to gamble. Most required cowboys to hang their guns up when inside the saloon. No respectable woman would ever enter a saloon, although saloons often served as a social center where town leaders might gather and talk over public affairs.

SALT LAKE CITY This is the city designed by Brigham Young before the advance party of Mormons had arrived. Founded in 1847, it is in the Valley of the Great Salt Lake, at the base of the Wasatch Mountains. In 1869 the railroad arrived, assuring the city's future and bringing numerous Mormon converts directly there. The major structure in the city is the Tabernacle, a great dome with no interior supports, capable of seating 5,000, completed in 1870. The spiritual center of the Mormon religion is the Salt Lake Temple, which was begun in 1853 and finished in 1893.

SAM BASS This "outlaw ballad" tells the story of Texas outlaw Sam Bass. The lyrics were probably written by John Denton of Gainesville, Texas in 1879, shortly after the death of Bass after a robbery attempt in Round Rock, Texas. The tune was probably written by Jim Fisk, and the song and its variants were soon known by a number of cowboys in the West. Sam Bass was widely loved as an outlaw, the sort of "outlaw hero" the West was fond of, and this song is an example of the respect westerners accorded him. (See also BASS, SAM.)

SAND CREEK MASSACRE (November 29, 1864) Colonel J. M. Chivington was a Methodist minister who wanted to be governor of Colorado. He possessed an intense hatred for Indians. When Indians had raided the area in eastern Colorado because the Civil War caused a shortage of troops in the West, Chivington raised a large Colorado militia. On November 29, 1864 the group went to Sand Creek, where a group of Cheyenne and Arapaho were camped. At the tipi of Cheyenne chief Black Kettle the American flag was flying. Black Kettle and his camp were peaceful, and the American flag indicated the camp was protected by the U.S. government—at least that is what Black Kettle believed. But Chivington and his men stormed the area and slaughtered 150–500 Indians indiscriminately, mostly women and children. Although military leaders deplored the situation and spoke against it, Chivington was never brought to trial.

SAN FRANCISCO This city was named "San Francisco" on January 30, 1847 after the Mission San Francisco de Asis (Mission Dolores), which was founded by the Spanish in 1776. Originally known as Yerba Buena (good herb) after a wild plant in the area, this port city was taken by the Americans on July 10, 1846 during the Mexican War when they raised the flag over it. It is located on San Francisco Bay, a body of water about 50 miles long and 13 miles at its widest point, which is connected to the Pacific Ocean by a narrow channel, the Golden Gate, named by John C. Fremont. The city had a population of 459 in 1847 but became a major port during the 1848 gold rush. Because so many arrived in San Francisco for the gold fields, the city grew quickly and by 1852 had 35,000 people. Lawlessness reigned in those early days, particularly on the Barbary Coast, an area of saloons, sporting and gaming houses on the waterfront. The city's wooden buildings burned several times, but the city was always rebuilt, and by 1870 it was the most important city in the western United States, with 150,000 inhabitants. In 1906 the city was almost entirely destroyed by an earthquake and resulting fires but again rebuilt itself.

SAN JACINTO, BATTLE OF (April 21, 1836) This is the battle in which Texans gained their freedom from Mexico. The battle occurred two months after the fall of the Alamo, and Texans ran into the battle yelling "Remember the Alamo." The Mexican troops were led by General Antonio Lopez de Santa Anna—the victor at the Alamo—who had about 1,400 troops under his command. The Texans were led by General Sam Houston, who had about 700 under his command. The Mexicans and Texans met near Houston where the Buffalo Bayou and San Jacinto River come together. When the Texans did not attack as expected in the morning, General Santa Anna let his troops take an afternoon siesta; meanwhile, he enjoyed the comforts of a young lady in his tent. At just this moment, Houston led his troops against the Mexicans, who were caught by surprise and quickly routed. General Santa Anna was captured while trying to escape disguised as a peasant, but he was set free by Houston. The battle occurred on April 21, 1836 and lasted only a few moments. Only seven Texans died, but more than 600 Mexicans were killed. (See also YELLOW ROSE OF TEXAS, THE.)

SANTA ANNA (b. Antonio Lopez de Santa Anna in Jalapa, Vera Cruz, Mexico on February 21, 1792; d. Mexico on June 21, 1876) For 40 years Santa Anna played a major role in Mexican politics; in the history of the American West he is known as the man who led the Mexican forces at the Battle of the Alamo in 1836 and then lost Texas at the Battle of San Jacinto less than two months later. He is also responsible for selling the United States the southern area of Arizona and New Mexico, known as the Gadsden Purchase, for $10 million. Santa Anna first became president of Mexico in 1833; later, in 1845, he was banished from Mexico during a revolution. But during the Mexican War, Santa Anna was brought back to assume the presidency and lead the army. However, in September 1847, after the Americans had captured Mexico City, he went to Venezuela and into exile. In 1848 he returned but was again forced to leave. Santa Anna returned to Mexico for his last time in 1874; two years later he died there in poverty and ignominy.

SANTA FE TRAIL The Santa Fe Trail extended 800 miles from Independence, Missouri to Franklin and was established by William Becknell in 1822 after Mexico achieved independence from Spain. Prior to 1821 (when Mexico gained its independence) traders were imprisoned and their goods confiscated if they were caught in the Spanish West. Becknell originally established the route from Franklin, Missouri, about 100 miles east of Independence, in the summer of 1822 when he took three wagons west to Council Grove, then across the Arkansas River and then over 60 dry miles of the Cimarron Cutoff to the Cimarron River. The trail then went southwest across the Canadian River to San Miguel del Vado on the Pecos River and over the Glorieta Pass into Santa Fe. Another route avoided Comanche and Kiowa Indians but was longer. This route went west from the Arkansas River to Bent's Fort, then south over the Raton Pass into Santa Fe.

Wagons carrying goods to Santa Fe averaged 10–15 miles a day and the trip took two to three months, although returning wagons could make the trip in half the time. Goods were sold at enormous profits, which enticed traders and freighters to use the Santa Fe Trail.

Prior to the Santa Fe Trail from Missouri, the residents of that city received their goods from the Chihuahua Trail, which was actually the northern tip of the Camino Real, or "Royal Road," from Mexico City to Santa Fe. Since it was 1,600 miles from Mexico City to Santa Fe, the city's residents were in constant need of goods, which were more readily provided by traders from Missouri.

The Mexican government imposed tariffs on goods from American traders to Santa Fe until 1846, when General Stephen Watts Kearny claimed the city for the United States during the Mexican War. The army then constructed forts along the route for protection, and

stagecoach and mail service was inaugurated. In 1878 the Santa Fe Railroad completed its segment through the Raton Pass, and by 1880 the old Santa Fe Trail ceased to exist, replaced by the railroad. (See also BECKNELL, WILLIAM.)

SARA TV show that starred Brenda Vaccaro as Sara Yarnell, Bert Kramer as Emmet Ferguson, Albert Stratton as Martin Pope, William Phipps as Claude Barstow, William Wintersole as George Bailey, Mariclare Costello as Julia Bailey, Louise Latham as Martha Higgins, Kraig Metzinger as Georgie Bailey, Debbie Lytton as Debbie Higgins and Hallie Morgan as Emma Higgins.

This is the story of a schoolteacher who left the East and moved to Independence, Colorado in the 1870s and battled the school board, townspeople, parents and children to bring education and feminism to the West. The show premiered on February 13, 1976 on Friday nights on CBS. The one-hour program was last telecast on July 30, 1976.

SATANTA (b. c. 1830; d. Jacksboro, Texas on October 11, 1878) Known as the "Orator of the Plains," Satanta warned a Texas court where he was tried for murder, "If you kill me, it will be like a spark on the prairie. It will make a big fire—a terrible fire." The jury convicted him but the Texas governor paroled him. Satanta, also known as "White Bear," was a Kiowa chief who led a number of raids against white settlers in Texas and the Southwest. In June 1874 he took part in the Battle of Adobe Walls. Pursued by the military, Satanta finally surrendered in October, 1874 and was imprisoned. However, in prison Satanta sang his death song and then dove out a high window of the prison hospital head first, killing himself.

SATURDAY PLAYHOUSE This TV show consisted of reruns of the Schlitz Playhouse shown on Saturday mornings. This program premiered on September 28, 1957 and ran until June 28, 1958 on CBS.

SATURDAY ROUNDUP TV show with Kermit Maynard.

This was a western anthology of James Oliver Curwood stories that starred Kermit Maynard. Maynard, a rodeo champion and younger brother of cowboy star Ken Maynard, played different characters in the shows, which varied from week to week. The one-hour show premiered on June 10 and was last telecast on September 1, 1951, airing on Saturday nights on NBC.

SAWBONES A term used for a doctor, especially a surgeon, probably derived from the fact that so many wounded limbs were amputated.

SCABBARDS In the Old West, scabbards could be a gun holster, a sheath for knives or swords, or a boot for rifles. The gun holsters in the post–Civil War period generally had a flap over the gun to hold it in; by 1875 or so these flaps had mostly been discarded. The cutaway—designed so a man could get his finger on the trigger while the gun was still in the scabbard—came in the mid 1870s. For cowboys who used the cross draw, the scabbard was always worn high; for the side draw, the scabbard hung at an angle to the body. By the 1880s and 1890s there were hand-tooled scabbards with hide-aways worn under the left armpit strapped on by a shoulder harness. Since guns dictated shape—and the cap and ball pistol was not a quick-draw type—it was not until the Colt Peacemaker that a scabbard was designed for the quick draw. Some gunslingers had their scabbards specially built to their tastes. One type of gun scabbard pivoted so the holster actually moved to shoot without the gun being removed. Most trail cowboys had a deep scabbard with the gun tucked in so the gun wouldn't come out while riding. Rifle scabbards covered the whole barrel and stock—with only the butt exposed. The reason was that dust was everywhere and a gun had to stay relatively clean. The solid-leather scabbards were used around 1885. Some cowboys hung the scabbard over the horn with the barrel secured under the rider's leg. Some riders put the scabbard under their saddles or under their legs between the saddle and the horse, but doing so could rub a horse raw. Fast-draw holsters were developed by Tio Sam Myers for Cherokee Tom Threepersons. These consisted of a holster of hard, thick leather that left hammer, trigger and butt outside the leather, with the scabbard tilting slightly forward. When molded wet to the gun for which it was made, it didn't lose its form.

SCALPING   To scalp someone meant to cut the skin around the crown of a dead enemy's head and pull it off. The scalp became a cherished prize, and when cleaned and dried and stretched over a small hoop or fixed to a pole, it was a trophy. The practice dates from the ancient Scythians, Franks and Visigoths. The eastern tribes of the Iroquois and Muskhogean scalped their enemies at the time the first settlers arrived, but the Plains Indians did not. The practice of scalping was actually promoted by whites. Colonial authorities paid for enemy scalps, and during the French and Indian War (1754–63) the French and British each paid for scalps of the other. Mexican and United States authorities paid bounties for Apache scalps late in the 19th century. Sometimes people were scalped alive, and this was not always fatal.

SCARBOROUGH, GEORGE W.   (b. Louisiana on October 2, 1859; d. Deming, New Mexico on April 6, 1900)   George Scarborough is the man who killed famed lawman (and gunman) John Selman. The dispute went back to the death of Martin Morose, who was killed on June 21, 1891 in El Paso, Texas. Scarborough was with Morose that night when they crossed the bridge over the Rio Grande. Morose had been lured over the bridge when he was shot down by Texas Ranger Frank McMahon, Scarborough's brother-in-law, and deputy U.S. marshal Jeff Milton. Selman accused Scarborough of stealing money from Morose's body. The two ran into each other at 4 in the morning, Easter Sunday, April 5, 1896 at the Wigwam Saloon in El Paso, where Selman was drinking heavily. The two went out to an alley to talk when suddenly Scarborough pulled his gun out and shot the 56-year-old lawman, who died the next day.

Although Selman never pulled his gun, Scarborough was acquitted of murder. Exactly four years later—April 6, 1900—Scarborough met his death near San Simon, Arizona while working as a detective for a cattleman's association. Scarborough and a rancher, Walter Birch-field, tracked a group of rustlers connected with Butch Cassidy's Wild Bunch to a canyon on April 5. Gang member Harvey Logan fired a rifle bullet through Scarborough's leg. The shot killed Scarborough's horse, and he lay there while Birchfield got a wagon and took Scarborough to the railroad station, where they caught a train to Deming. In Deming, doctors amputated Scarborough's leg, but he died. (See also SELMAN, JOHN.)

SCATTERGUN   See SHOTGUN.

SCHLITZ PLAYHOUSE OF STARS   Sponsored by the Schlitz Brewing Company, this TV show was on the air for eight years. Beginning as a live show in 1951, it developed into an all-film series in the summer of 1953. At first the producers acquired top scripts but gradually began showing potboilers. The anthology consisted of a wide variety of shows—mysteries, dramas and westerns. Two shows from the 1956–57 series became regular series: "The Restless Gun" starring John Payne, and "Tales of Well Fargo" starring Dale Robertson. This show was telecast from October 5, 1951 to March 27, 1959 on CBS. Originally the show was an hour-long broadcast on Friday nights but became a half-hour show in April 1952. From October 1955 to March 1959 it was broadcast on Friday nights.

SCORPION   A scorpion generally cannot kill a healthy person, but its poisonous sting may prove fatal to a sickly one and it always causes great pain. Nocturnal animals, scorpions are dangerous because they hide in cowboys' boots and clothing. The scorpion's stinger is in the tip of its tail, which also serves as a poison fang connected to the gland at the base of its tail. The scorpion poisons its prey by first clasping it with its front claws and then curving its tail over its head and plunging the stinger into its victim. The scorpion is located mainly in the Southwest, although it may be found all over the United States and Mexico.

SCOTT, RANDOLPH   (b. Randolph Crane in Orange County, California on January 23, 1898; d. Los Angeles, California on March 2, 1987)   One of the most popular western actors went off to World War I when he was 14 years old after lying about his age. He then attended Georgia Tech and the University of North Carolina, where he received a degree in engineering. He served as Gary Cooper's dialogue coach in *The Virginian* (1929) and then attended the Pasadena Community Playhouse and signed with Paramount, where he starred in a series of nine westerns based on Zane Grey's stories (1932–35). Scott's big break came when he starred as Hawkeye in *The Last of the Mohicans* (1936). Scott became a full-fledged star of "A" movies with *Western Union* (1941) after doing combat films in World War II. After the war Scott's career as an actor in westerns shifted into high gear; he made 45 films, 42 of

Randolph Scott

Return of the Bad Men (1948)
Fighting Man of the Plains (1948)
Colt .45 (1950)
Shoot-Out at Medicine Bend (1957)

SCOTT, WALTER EDWARD   See DEATH VALLEY SCOTTY.

SCOUT   Someone who serves with either the army, a wagon train, explorers or other travelers as a guide. Scouts could be either whites or Indians and had to have a good knowledge of the country as well as the ability to read trails, hunt game, minister to the sick, dress wounds and find herbs, roots, berries and other edible or medicinal plant life. A scout was probably the major pathfinder for a trip, had to find food and water, served as a courier for messages and had to be a diplomat when dealing with army officers or expedition leaders who were strong willed and sometimes obstinate. A number of mountain men became scouts when their trapping days were over, and Indian scouts were often used by the government and army against other Indian tribes who were hostile to the tribes of the Indian scouts. For example, the Arikara and Crow scouts were recruited by General George Custer to fight against the Sioux, Cheyenne and Arapaho; the Pawnee organized under Major Frank North were scouts against the Sioux. Famous scouts include Jim Bridger, Tom Horn, Major Frank North, Bill Williams, Al Sieber. Thomas "Broken Hand" Fitzpatrick, Caleb Greenwood, Elisha Stevens, Isaac Hitchcock, Stephen Hall, Joe Meek, Buffalo Bill Cody, Kit Carson, Tom Tobin, Jim Beckwourth, Mariano Medina and Jim Baker.

SCURLOCK, DOC   (b. Josiah G. Scurlock in Talaposa, Alabama on January 11, 1849; d. Potter County, Texas on July 25, 1929)   Doc Scurlock was part of Billy the Kid's gang of rustlers in New Mexico. Scurlock had worked for John Chisum and then joined the McSween faction during the Lincoln County War. He was at Blazer's Mill when Dick Brewer and Buckshot Roberts were killed. Scurlock survived the Lincoln County War and returned to Texas in 1879 where he farmed, wrote poetry and was a member of the Theosophical Society. (See also LINCOLN COUNTY WAR.)

SEARCHERS, THE   Film produced by Merian C. Cooper and C. V. Whitney; directed by John Ford; screenplay by Frank S. Nugent from a novel by Alan LeMay; released in 1956 by C.V. Whitney/Warner Brothers; 119 minutes in length. Cast: John Wayne, Jeffrey Hunter, Vera Miles, Ward Bond, Natalie Wood, John Qualen, Olive Carey, Ken Curtis, Harry Carey, Jr., Lana Wood, Dorothy Jordan, Pat Wayne and Chief Thunder Cloud.

Ethan Edwards (John Wayne) shoots out the eyes of dead Indians so they'll be blind in the next world. The film begins when Edwards returns to his Texas ranch after the Civil War, but the ranch has been attacked by Comanche during his absence. The Indians killed everybody at the ranch (including Ethan's brother) except two girls; Ethan and a buddy, Martin Pawley, set out to

which were westerns—more than any other star. Scott and Harry Joe Brown formed Ranown as a production company and collaborated with director Budd Boetticher for *Seven Men from Now* (1956), *The Tall T* (1957), *Decision at Sundown* (1957), *Buchanan Rides Alone* (1958) and *Comanche Station* (1960). Scott's last movie was *Ride the High Country* (1962) for director Sam Peckinpah, in which he starred as an over-the-hill former lawman with Joel McCrea. Other western movies starring Scott include:

Heritage of the Desert (1932)
Wild Horse Mesa (1932)
Sunset Pass (1933)
The Thundering Herd (1933)
To the Last Man (1933)
The Last Round-Up (1934)
Wagon Wheels (1934)
Go West, Young Man (1936)
The Texans (1938)
Frontier Marshal (1939)
Jesse James (1939)
Virginia City (1940)
When the Daltons Rode (1940)
Belle Starr (1941)
Western Union (1941)
The Desperadoes (1943)
Abilene Town (1946)
Gunfighters (1947)
Trail Street (1947)

hunt the two girls. They find one dead but track the other for five years; they find her and discover she has become an Indian.

SECRET EMPIRE, THE

TV show that starred Geoffrey Scott as Marshal Jim Donner, Tiger Williams as Billy, Carlene Watkins as Millie, Peter Breck as Jess Keller, Pamela Brull as Maya, Diane Markoff as Princess Tara (February–April), Stephanie Kramer as Princess Tara (April–May), Mark Lenard as Emperor Thorval, Peter Tomarken as Roe, David Opatoshu as Hator and Sean Garrison as Yannuck.

Cowboys meet aliens and the Old West meets outer space in this series, which was a combination western and science fiction show. Above ground it was Cheyenne in the 1880s, but in a secret cave discovered by Marshal Jim Donner while chasing some desperadoes was Chimera, inhabited by aliens from outer space. Each episode ended in suspense; unfortunately, the last episode had the marshal chased into the generator room just before a power load explosion while "To Be Continued" appeared on the screen. Apparently the network didn't care to find out what happened next because the series was canceled, with all questions about what happened left unanswered. This show premiered on February 27 and the last telecast was May 1, 1979. The 20-minute program was shown on Tuesday evenings on NBC as one of three serials aired under the title "Cliff Hangers."

SEE THE ELEPHANT

Expression used to mean that a cowboy intended to have a raucous time combined with an enlightening experience, sometimes at considerable cost. To see the elephant meant to see the bright lights of the city and gather up some experiences of the sinful nature.

SELMAN, JOHN

(b. Madison County, Arkansas on November 16, 1839; d. El Paso, Texas on April 6, 1896) John Selman is the man who killed John Wesley Hardin and Bass Outlaw. In his relatively long and varied life, he came into contact with a who's who of the West, including Wyatt Earp, Bat Masterson, Doc Holliday, Killin' Jim Miller, Jesse Evans, John Larn and Pat Garrett.

Selman and his family moved to Texas in 1858. During the Civil War he joined the Confederacy; he then deserted and moved back to Texas with his family. He married in 1865 and in 1869 moved to Colfax County, New Mexico, where Indians stole all of their cattle, and then back to Fort Griffin, Texas, where local prostitute Hurricane Minnie Martin became his mistress. Selman also became close friends with John Larn, a rustler and business partner of Selman's. Larn was sheriff of Shackleford County for a while and often deputized Selman. In 1876 Selman killed a deaf man wanted by the law who kept walking when Larn ordered him to stop. Selman hid and watched a mob kill Larn on June 22, 1878. He then fled the country—there was a warrant for his arrest—and during the time he was gone, his wife died carrying their fifth child. Selman and his brother Tom went to Lincoln County, New Mexico in 1878 and robbed stores and rustled cattle. The gang became known as

"Selman's Scouts" after Selman killed the former leader, a gunman named Hart, while he ate. Selman also killed a gang member after an argument during a poker game. The gang broke up, and the Selmans moved back to Texas and rustled cattle there until Selman caught smallpox. After he recovered, Selman organized another gang of rustlers and robbers and terrorized the Fort Davis–Fort Stockton area. There John's brother, Tom, was lynched by a mob, but John bribed his jailers and escaped.

Selman had married again but his second wife died. He moved to El Paso, Texas and in 1892 was elected city constable. In 1893 the 53-year-old Selman married a 16-year-old girl. Around 5 P. M. on April 5, 1894 a drunk deputy U. S. marshal Bass Outlaw shot his pistol in Tillie Howard's whorehouse. Texas Ranger Joe McKidrict confronted Outlaw and the lawman promptly killed the Ranger. Selman then went for his gun but was blinded by powder burns from Outlaw's gun. Selman was hit in the right leg by Outlaw, but Selman got the marshal in the chest. Outlaw died, but Selman developed a limp and from this time on had to use a cane.

John Selman killed John Wesley Hardin on August 19, 1895 in El Paso at the Acme Saloon. Hardin was sitting at the bar drinking and Selman came in, guns blazing at Hardin's back. The disagreement was traced back to two related sources: Hardin's girlfriend was Mrs. Beulah Morose, wife of cattle rustler Martin Morose and a former prostitute. Mrs. Morose had been arrested drunk and disorderly by John Selman, Jr. a couple weeks before. The other possible source of the argument was the money taken from the body of Martin Morose about two months earlier when Texas Rangers had killed the cattle rustler. Supposedly Hardin had secretly agreed to split the large sum of money with Selman but later reneged.

Selman met his death at the age of 56 on Easter Sunday, April 5, 1896, about four in the morning. He was drunk at the Wigwam Saloon when George Scarborough came in, and the two men had words. Apparently Selman had spread word around town that Hardin had split Morose's money with Scarborough, who had been with Morose the night the rustler was murdered. Out in the alley, Scarborough pulled his gun and fired it at Selman, hitting him in the neck. Selman hit the ground without drawing his gun and then took three more slugs while lying on the ground. Selman told the crowd that gathered, "Boys, you know I am not afraid of any man; but I never drew my gun." Selman died the next day; Scarborough was acquitted. (See also HARDIN, JOHN WESLEY; LARN, JOHN M.; OUTLAW, BASS; SCARBOROUGH, GEORGE W.)

SERGEANT PRESTON OF THE YUKON

TV show that starred Richard Simmons as Sergeant Preston.

With his malamute dog Yukon King and riding his beautiful black horse Rex, Sergeant Preston of the Royal Northwest Mounted Police patrolled the Yukon Territory in northern Canada during the turn-of-the century gold rush days. The final 26 shows were shot in color—the first 78 were in black and white—and all were done in the mountains of Colorado and California, which provided a splendid backdrop. The show premiered on September 29, 1955 on CBS and ran on Thursday evenings. The half-hour show ended on September 25, 1958, although it also spent time on Saturday morning TV after this, sponsored by Quaker Oats and Mother's Oats. The show was created by George W. Trendle and Fran Striker, who had also created "The Lone Ranger" and "The Green Hornet." Originally a radio show that premiered in 1947, "Sergeant Preston" ended its radio run in 1955, the same year it premiered on TV.

SEVEN BRIDES FOR SEVEN BROTHERS
TV show that starred Richard Dean Anderson as Adam McFadden, Roger Wilson as Daniel McFadden, Peter Horton as Crane McFadden, Drake Hogestyn as Brian McFadden, Bryan Utman as Ford McFadden, Tim Topper as Evan McFadden, River Phoenix as Guthrie McFadden, Terri Treas as Hannah McFadden and Joan Kjar as Marie. Jimmy Webb supplied original music.

Originally a 1954 movie, this was brought to television and updated to contemporary times. The setting was a ranch in northern California, where a family of boys sans parents tries to get along. One boy found a bride during the lone season this show ran, but none of the others did despite all being a lot of fun with their singing, dancing and rowdy ways. Interestingly, pop composer Jimmy Webb provided original music for this show. It premiered on September 19, 1982 on Sunday nights on CBS. The half-hour series was expanded to a full hour after the first show and moved to Wednesday nights; in the summer of 1983, it was moved to Saturday nights, where it ended its run on July 2, 1983.

SEVEN CITIES OF CIBOLA   The "Seven Cities of Gold" was an old folktale in Spain; in the Spanish West these seven cities were believed to be located north of the Rio Grande in present-day New Mexico. The belief in the seven cities was part of the reason Spain explored large areas of the West; reports of the seven cities of gold were widely believed after 1536 when Alvar Nunez Cabez de Vaca and his slave Estevanico were found in the desert. Their expedition had begun eight years before and ended up wandering through much of the Southwest; they told of seeing the seven cities. In 1539 Friar Marcos de Niza and Estevanico traveled north to find the seven cities and returned with reports confirming their existence. In fact, the friar had seen seven adobe Zuni pueblos or villages in the sunlight. In 1540 an army of conquistatores under Francisco Vasquez de Coronado discovered the Zuni villages when they went north to pillage the cities of gold.

SHANE   Film produced by George Stevens; associate producer, Ivan Moffatt; directed by George Stevens; screenplay by A. B. Guthrie, Jr., with additional dialogue by Jack Sher (from the novel by Jack Schaefer); music by Victor Young; released in 1953 by Paramount; 118 minutes in length. Cast: Alan Ladd, Jean Arthur, Van Heflin, Brandon De Wilde, Jack Palance, Ben Johnson and Edgar Buchanan.

The film shows two recurring 1950s themes: Gunfighters are lonely souls who can't escape their past, and good guys win. The story is about a gunfighter, Shane, who rides onto the small farm of the Starrett family. He strikes up a friendship with the boy, Joey, and helps the father clear the land. But the powerful cattlemen want the nesters off (elements of the real Johnson County War are here), and Shane has to put his gun back on and face the cattle baron's hired killer. After Shane wins, he rides off.

SHANE   TV show that starred David Carradine as Shane, Jill Ireland as Marian Starett, Tom Tully as Tom Starett, Christopher Shea as Joey Starett, Bert Freed as Rufe Ryker and Sam Gilman as Sam Grafton.

This was a brief TV series based on the novel and movie by the same name. The show dealt with the conflicts between cattle barons and farmers with the loner Shane helping the settlers. Only 17 episodes of this series were shot. The hour-long show began on September 10, 1966 on Saturday nights on ABC and was last telecast on December 31, 1966.

SHARPS RIFLE   A brand of rifle; about 40 different models were made between the 1840s and 1881. It is often associated with buffalo hunters (and was the first popular "buffalo gun") and was developed because the Henry and Spencer rifles couldn't penetrate a buffalo's hide. The Big Fifty .50–90 (.50 caliber and 90 powder weight) was the most famous Sharps buffalo rifle.

SHAWNEE TRAIL   An early cattle trail that followed an Indian road to Sedalia, Missouri until Missouri officials blocked the border because of Texas fever. This trail started in Texas, crossed the Red River around present-day Terral, Oklahoma and traveled through Indian Territory until it entered Kansas between the Smoky Hill and Arkansas Rivers. The trail ended in Abilene.

SHEEP   The conflict between cattle and sheep ranchers occurred in the West after the Civil War because (1) cattle ranchers wanted control of the ranges; (2) it was believed that sheep ate grass too short, making it impossible for cattle to graze the same range; (3) cattlemen believed sheep ruined water holes for cattle; (4) it was widely believed that cattle would not live on land grazed by sheep because of the smell; and (5) many cowboys felt it was "beneath" them to look after sheep. In truth, sheep ranchers were often discriminated against because of ethnic or racial reasons (many shepherds were Basques and Mexicans) and because the cattle culture deemed cattle to be the major animal of the West and sheep were a nuisance. Too, cattle were looked after on a horse whereas sheep were watched on foot, and the cowboy culture was closely linked to the horse, which put him in a position to look down on mortals on foot.

There were certain areas of the West that were better suited to sheep than to cattle; for example, the southwest region of Arizona and New Mexico often did better with sheep ranching than with cattle because cattle required so much grassland for each cow. Sheep multiplied more rapidly, could live in extremes of climate, could live in mountainous areas and land with sparse grass, and the prices for mutton and wool remained relatively stable throughout the 19th century. All of these reasons gave ranchers a reason to keep sheep.

The first sheep arrived in what is now New Mexico in 1598 when Juan de Ornate and a group of colonizers brought about 1,000 sheep; along with cattle and goats these soon became profitable and a major export. The Spanish missionaries raised sheep and taught Indians to do so. But for most Anglo-Americans, it was degrading to raise sheep and they refused to eat mutton; they also held the shepherds in contempt. By 1800 the quality of sheep had dropped dramatically, and by 1900 about two dozen New Mexican families controlled about 80% of the sheep in the territory. The New Mexicans led in the development of better breeds of sheep with more wool and better meat; the American Merino breed was crossed with the Chaurro in 1859 for a heavier, tougher animal, and new strains, like the Cotswold, Southdown, Shropshire, Lincoln and Rambouillet, were introduced in the 19th century.

In addition to cattle drives there were also sheep drives to get animals to settlers in a region, particularly miners in the gold rushes. By the 1880s sheep ranching had proved more lucrative than cattle or horse ranching, but the sheep had to be more closely watched. By 1900 there were approximately 30 million sheep in the West, but the sheepherder did not become a romantic hero like the cowboy, and since sheepherders did not ride horses but used dogs, there was little appeal for the cowboys.

SHEPHERD, OLIVER   (b. ?; d. Jackson County, Missouri in April 1868)   Shepherd was a member of the James-Younger Gang and helped them pull the first daylight bank robbery in the United States on February 13, 1866 in Liberty, Missouri. Shepherd was also part of the bank robbery in Russellville, Kentucky on March 21, 1868 and after this robbery was chased by posses in Kentucky and Missouri. A Kentucky posse captured Oliver's cousin, George Shepherd, but Oliver made it back to Jackson County, Missouri, where he was cornered by another posse. He tried to shoot his way out, but a hail of gunfire put 20 bullets into his body. (See also JAMES, JESSE.)

SHERIDAN, PHILIP HENRY   (b. possibly in Ireland, or at sea or perhaps in Boston, Massachusetts or Somerset, Ohio or Albany, New York on March 6, 1831; d. Nonquitt, Massachusetts on August 5, 1888)
Sheridan is the man responsible for the phrase "The only good Indian is a dead Indian." (Actually, what he said was, "The only good Indians I ever saw were dead.") Sheridan graduated from West Point in 1853 and fought Indians along the Rio Grande and then in the Northwest. During the Civil War he achieved high honors and rank and was known for burning the Shenandoah Valley to wipe out the South's food supply and hasten the end to the Confederacy. After the war Sheridan became military governor of Texas and Louisiana but, because of his harsh and repressive measures, was removed by Presi-

Philip Sheridan

dent Andrew Johnson. In March 1869 he replaced Sherman as commander of the Military Division of Missouri and from that position waged war against the Plains Indians. Sheridan was ruthless and brutal in his war against the Indians; he also encouraged the slaughter of buffalo because the extermination of the buffalo meant the end of the Plains Indian life. Sheridan became commanding general of the army in 1884, again succeeding Sherman, and in June 1888 was made general, two months before his death.

SHERIFF   An elected official in charge of law enforcement in an area; this jurisdiction could be a city, town or county, but the key factor is that the public elected a sheriff, as opposed to a federal marshal, who was a political appointment, or a town marshal, who was either appointed or elected by a town council. The sheriff was also usually charged with collecting taxes as well as keeping order.

SHERIFF OF COCHISE, THE   TV show that starred John Bromfield as Sheriff/Marshal Frank Morgan, Stan Jones as Deputy Olson (1956–58), Robert Brubaker as Deputy Blake (1958) and James Griffith as Deputy Tom Ferguson (1959–60).

In this police drama set in the contemporary West, the plot centered on Cochise County, Arizona, where there were cops and robbers and car chases. The filming was actually done in Bisbee, Arizona, in Cochise County, and the creator of the series, Stan Jones, was a native of the area. This syndicated show was produced by Desilu Productions and released in fall 1956. There were 156 episodes filmed of the half-hour show. "The Sheriff of Cochise" changed its name to "U.S. Marshal" in 1958 when some characters changed: Deputy Olson dropped out, and Frank Morgan was promoted from sheriff to marshal, in charge of the whole state.

SHERMAN, WILLIAM TECUMSEH (b. Lancaster, Ohio on February 8, 1820; d. New York City on February 14, 1891) Sherman said, "War is hell," and he lived that creed. During the Civil War he burned a 60-mile-wide path through Georgia; after the Civil War he was first commander of the Military Division of Missouri, then commanding general of the army. In these posts he fought the Indians brutally, viewing them as savages who were impediments to the march of civilization. A graduate of West Point (1840), Sherman served in the Mexican War (1846–48) and achieved fame and notoriety in the Civil War (1861–65) before entering the western theater after the war. Sherman believed in total war: He waged war against civilians and destroyed crops, goods and public buildings if they were aligned with the "enemy." Sherman could have been killed by Kiowa warriors in May 1871 when he traveled by coach across the Texas, but the warriors decided to let this single coach go and wait for bigger bounty; they found it when a wagon train followed.

William Tecumseh Sherman *(Library of Congress)*

SHE WORE A YELLOW RIBBON Film produced by John Ford and Merian C. Cooper; directed by John Ford; screenplay by Frank Nugent and Laurence Stallings from a story by James Warner Bellah; released in 1949 by Argos/RKO; 104 minutes in length. Cast: John Wayne, Joanne Dru, John Agar, Ben Johnson, Harry Carey, Jr., Victor McLaglen, Mildred Natwick, George O'Brien, Arthur Shields, Chief John Big Tree, Tom Tyler and Francis Ford.

This is part of John Ford's cavalry trilogy (*Fort Apache, She Wore a Yellow Ribbon,* and *Rio Grande*) and is set in 1876 just after the Little Bighorn massacre when Custer met his doom. Captain Nathan Brittles (Wayne) has only six days left before his retirement, but during this time he stops an Indian war by stampeding their horses. As he rides away, he is stopped and told he's been appointed chief of scouts.

SHINDIG A party and dance and whopping good time.

SHIRLEY, MYRA BELLE See STARR, BELLE.

SHIRT-TAIL OUTFIT Small cattle-ranching operation.

SHONSEY, MIKE (b. Mike Shaughnessy in Canada c. 1867; d. Council Bluffs, Iowa on August 6, 1954) Mike Shonsey became one of the last surviving members of the Johnson County War. Shonsey hired out to the rich cattlemen and alerted the Regulators to rustlers at the KC Ranch. On April 9, 1892 the Regulators surrounded Nate Champion's cabin on the KC Ranch. After Champion's cabin had been set afire, the homesteader made a run for it and headed for a gulch behind the cabin. Unfortunately, Shonsey and five others were hiding there and Champion was cut down by 28 slugs when he ran toward them. A little over a year later Shonsey killed Dudley Champion, Nate's twin brother. This killing—many suspected murder though Shonsey claimed self-defense—led Shonsey to leave Wyoming for Nebraska, where he lived most of the rest of his life. (See also CHAMPION, NATE; JOHNSON COUNTY WAR.)

SHOOTIST, THE Film produced by M. J. Frankovich; directed by Don Siegel; screenplay by Miles Hood Swarthout and Scott Hale from the story by Glen Swarthout; released in 1976 by Paramount; 100 minutes in length. Cast: John Wayne, Lauren Bacall, Ron Howard, James Stewart, Richard Boone, Hugh O'Brian, Bill McKinney, Harry Morgan, John Carradine, Sheree North, Richard Lenz, Scatman Crothers, Gregg Palmer, Dick Winslow, Alfred Dennis, Melody Thomas and Kathleen O'Malley.

This is John Wayne's last movie, and it is the movie in which he said good-bye in his own way. Wayne plays J. B. Books, who has cancer and is dying (Wayne also had cancer at the time of the filming). Books is urged to take his own life but decides he wants to go out in a blaze of glory. The movie begins with a series of flashbacks—culled from a number of Wayne's early movies—to show him as a legendary gunman. The actual plot covers from

January 22, 1901, when he rides into town, until one week later, January 29, which is coincidentally Books's birthday, when he dies in a shootout. There's a great deal of talk in this movie—Wayne wanted his views known, his code expressed and his legend solid—but the end is a violent gun battle.

SHORT, LUKE L. (b. Mississippi in 1854; d. in Geuda Springs, Kansas on September 8, 1893) Luke Short, Wyatt Earp and Doc Holliday were the "Dodge City Gang." Short owned part of the Long Branch Saloon in Dodge City and became embroiled in the "Dodge City War" with Holliday and Earp. Short was also part of the Dodge City "Peace Commission," which included Wyatt Earp and Bat Masterson. Short visited a number of hot towns in the West, including Leadville, Cheyenne, Deadwood, Laramie and Dodge City, where he returned after he killed gambler Charles Storms at the Oriental Saloon in Tombstone on February 25, 1881, although Bat Masterson tried to stop the fight. There, Short purchased the Long Branch with partner W. H. Harris but was forced to leave town when the new mayor, L. E. Deger, passed resolutions against prostitution, gambling and other assorted activities in which Short made his living. After Short left Dodge City, he moved to Fort Worth, where he bought a one-third interest in the White Elephant Saloon. Longhaired Jim Courtright had a detective agency and local protection racket and approached Short to demand payment for "protection." Courtright tried to shake down Short, even after Short sold his interest in the saloon. Accompanied by Bat Masterson, Short met with Courtright, who pulled a pistol on Short. Courtright's hammer caught on Short's watch chain, blocking the shot and giving Short time to draw his revolver and drill Courtright, who died a few moments later.

Short was very small (five foot six and 125 pounds) and always a natty dresser, who had custom-tailored suits with a right pants pocket cut extra long and lined with leather for his gun. Short died before he was 40 at a mineral spa in Geuda Springs, Kansas; he succumbed to dropsy. (See also COURTRIGHT, LONGHAIRED JIM; EARP, WYATT; MASTERSON, BAT.)

SHOSHONI INDIANS Originally from the basin between the Rocky Mountains and the Sierra Nevada chain, the Shoshoni (also spelled Shoshone) moved east and became a Plains Indian tribe around the year 1500. But the tribe split, a result of hostile tribes attacking them, into a northern group, located in western Montana and then in the area west of the Snake River in Idaho to Nevada. The Buffalo Shoshoni in the north lived in tipis and hunted; in the south they lived in brush shelters, and some were known as "Digger Indians" because they dug for roots and berries and "Walkers" because they were too poor to have horses. Important Shoshoni include Sacajawea, the female guide in Lewis and Clark's expedition, and Chief Washakie, who was helpful and friendly to white emmigrants moving west.

SHOTGUN There were a variety of shotguns (also called scatterguns): muzzle and breech loaders, single and double barrel, full barrel and sawed off. The shotgun was especially lethal and devastating at close range because the buckshot scattered when shot. Different shotgun gauges reflect the number of balls to the pound for the barrel. For example, 12 balls to the pound was a 12-gauge or 12-bore, the diameter of which was .729 inches. These guns can can also be loaded with nails or scrap metal as ammunition.

SHOTGUN SLADE TV show that starred Scott Brady as Shotgun Slade.

Shotgun Slade, so named because of the double-barrel shotgun he preferred, was a detective in the Old West who hired out to banks, insurance companies, Wells Fargo, saloon owners or anyone else who wanted a case solved. A healthy dose of jazz on the soundtrack and a variety of country singers, sports heroes and other celebrities as guest stars gave this show a unique look and sound. The pilot for the show aired on the Schlitz Playhouse on March 27, 1959. The half-hour show was released in November 1959, and the 78 episodes were produced from 1959 to 1961. Since this was a syndicated show sold to various TV stations, it never had a regular prime-time slot on the network.

SHOULDERS, JIM (b. Tulsa, Oklahoma on May 13, 1928) Shoulders won 16 world titles in rodeo—more than any other rodeo performer. He won the All-Around Cowboy Championship five times (1949, 1956–59), the bareback bronc-riding championship four times (1950, 1956–58) and the bull-riding championship seven times (1951, 1954–59). Shoulders came from a city background; he grew up in Tulsa, where his father owned an auto body repair shop and did not live on a ranch until he purchased one with his rodeo earnings when he was 26. Shoulders became involved in rodeo by following his older brother, Marvin, who was competing. Jim entered his first rodeo in Oiltown, Oklahoma at the age of 14 and won $18. He turned professional between his junior and senior years in high school and after graduation in 1946 began to compete full-time year-round. Shoulders was one of the first to win big money in rodeo by competing full-time. After he stopped competing in rodeos, Shoulders formed a stock contracting company to supply bucking horses and bulls to rodeos, and opened a rodeo school where he teaches the rudiments of rodeo riding. He became nationally famous during the 1970s and 1980s with appearances in Miller Beer commercials, appearing with Billy Martin, Dick Butkus and other former athletes. (See also RODEO.)

SIDEKICK A partner, companion and friend.

SIEBER, AL (b. Mingolsheim, near Heidelberg, Germany on February 29, 1844; d. near Roosevelt Dam, Arizona on February 19, 1907) Sieber was a famous Indian scout who spoke the Apache language and played a major role in tracking down Geronimo. He immigrated to America as an infant and grew up in Pennsylvania. A Union veteran in the Civil War (he fought at Gettysburg), he moved west after the war and prospected in Nevada and California before he became a ranch foreman in Arizona. A noted Indian fighter who received 29 wounds from bullets and arrows and who reportedly killed approximately 50 Indians, Sieber was hired by General George Crook to form a group of Apache scouts to track hostiles. Sieber worked with the Apache until his final days; he was killed in a construction accident (though some insist the boulder that rolled down on him while working near the Roosevelt Dam was no accident) while he was in charge of a work gang composed of Indians.

SIERRA NEVADA   The mountain range known as the Sierra Nevada (the term means "Snowy Range" in Spanish) was the great barrier between California and settlers traveling west. This historic range is where gold was discovered in 1849, which led to the gold rush, and where the Donner party was trapped in 1846–47. This range was also formidable for railroad builders and crews from the Central Pacific Railroad, who needed three years (1865–68) to get through the mountains and meet the Union Pacific in Utah.

SILVERHEELS, JAY   (b. Six Nations Indian Reservation, Ontario, Canada; d. Woodland Hills, California on March 5, 1980)   Jay Silverheels was "Tonto" on "The Lone Ranger" TV series. A full-blooded Mohawk Indian, Silverheels was a top lacrosse player in the 1930s and a Golden Gloves boxer; he moved to the United States in 1938, and the first film he appeared in was *Captain from Castile* (1947). He also appeared in

Jay Silverheels

Key Largo (1948), *Yellow Sky* (1949) and *The Cowboy and the Indians* (1949). During the time he appeared in "The Lone Ranger" he also had appearances in the movies *Broken Arrow* (1950), *Red Mountain* (1952), *Saskatchewan* (1954) and *Walk the Proud Land* (1956). (See also LONE RANGER, THE; MOORE, CLAYTON.)

SINGING COWBOYS   Singing cowboys is the term used to describe the movie actors who sang in western films, beginning in the 1930s and extending to the 1950s. The most popular of these were Gene Autry and Roy Rogers, but a number of other singing cowboys made their name and fame in these movies, which were often escapist fare with a western theme.

The first actor to appear as a singing cowboy was veteran cowboy star Ken Maynard. Maynard was a popular star of silent westerns in the 1920s and, when sound was introduced to film in 1927 with *The Jazz Singer,* decided to use singing in his movies. Ken first sang in *Wagon Master* (1929) and then played fiddle and sang "The Drunken Hiccough" in *Voice of Hollywood,* a short Tiffany film released on April 1, 1930. In *The Fighting Legion* released by Universal in April 1930, two versions were released—a silent version and one with sound. In this movie the trio of Les Bates, Bill Nestel and Slim Whitaker sang a saloon song. In 1930 Maynard starred in *Song of the Caballero* and *Sons of the Saddle,* in which he sang and accompanied himself on the fiddle and banjo. He sang "Down the Home Trail with You" in *Sons of the Saddle* and recorded eight songs for Columbia Records.

Maynard sang in *Fiddlin' Buckaroo* (1933) and in *The Trail Drive* (1933); he wrote the theme song and also sang it in the latter movie. The following movie, *The Strawberry Roan,* was based on a song, and this is the first time a song dominated a movie. In 1935 Maynard wrote the theme song for *Wheels of Destiny* and sang "She's Only a Bird in a Gilded Cage" and "Buffalo Gals" for *Honor of the Range.*

When Ken Maynard left Universal Pictures and signed with Mascot Pictures, owner Nat Levine hired Gene Autry to sing. Maynard wanted singing in his pictures and Levine agreed, but Maynard wasn't a particularly strong singer, whereas Autry, who had been performing on WLS in Chicago, was an established singer with hit records to his credit.

The first picture for Mascot was *In Old Santa Fe,* which starred Ken Maynard and in which Gene Autry sang. The next was a serial, *Mystery Mountain,* which again starred Maynard and in which Autry only said one line. The next movie was also a serial, *Phantom Empire,* but Levine fired Maynard after *Mystery Mountain* and was forced to cast Gene Autry in the starring role. There were no great plans to make Gene Autry a star at this time, or even plans for a long career in movies, so they cast him under his own name because it was believed his success as a recording artist, especially in the South and Midwest, would help lure customers to the movies. But this series was a resounding success and launched Autry on his career—starring in movies under his own name beginning with *Tumbling Tumbleweeds* in 1935.

Autry's success inspired a number of other studios to try singing cowboys. This move was made because Autry's pictures were so financially successful but also because songs breathed new life into the old westerns, a genre that had been popular for a long time but needed some new, fresh ideas. Singing cowboys were also considered "safe" from the Legion of Decency and Hayes Office in Hollywood, which sought to control moral content in films and restricted gangster violence and romantic passion on the big screen.

After Autry, the next successful singing cowboy was Tex Ritter, who starred for Grand National, although Dick Foran also starred as a singing cowboy in several pictures beginning in 1935. Others who played singing cowboys included Fred Scott, Smith Ballew, Jack Randall, Tex Fletcher and John "Dusty" King. Later came George Houston, James Newall and Bob Baker. Even John Wayne appeared as "Singin' Sandy," with Monte Hale dubbing in the singing voice when Wayne warbled. The next major singing-cowboy star was Roy Rogers.

Leonard Slye (Roy Roger's real name) was a founding member of the Sons of the Pioneers in the early 1930s, and this popular western singing group had appeared in several movies, including Autry's *Tumbling Tumbleweeds*. In fact, one of the other founding members of the Sons of the Pioneers, Bob Nolan, had written the song "Tumbling Tumbleweeds" as well as "Cool Water." Slye, who had changed his name to Dick Weston, went to Republic Pictures to audition in 1937 for the role of a singing cowboy after Autry had threatened to walk off over a contract dispute. The studio wanted another singing cowboy in the wings as a way to keep Autry in line. Slye passed the audition, and when Autry made good his threat and left, he was cast in *Under Western Stars* (1937), a movie written for Autry. Before the filming, the studio executives changed Slye's name to Roy Rogers.

Roy Rogers soon became a singing-cowboy star and continued making pictures for Republic after Autry and Republic settled their differences and Autry returned. The two continued making successful singing-cowboy movies—although Autry was always the bigger star—until World War II, when Autry joined the armed forces. Because Rogers was married with three children, he received a deferment and stayed in Hollywood making movies during the war. With Autry unable to make movies, Republic decided at this time to make Rogers a major star and billed him as *King of the Cowboys*. A major promotion was launched, a movie titled "King of the Cowboys" was released and Roy Rogers soon eclipsed Gene Autry as the top singing cowboy.

There were several essential differences between the movies of Gene Autry and those of Roy Rogers. First, Autry's period of major stardom was 1935 to 1942, when he entered the service, while Roger's heyday was 1943 to 1947, while Autry was in the service. Rogers tended to appear in many historical westerns, playing such characters as Billy the Kid, and did not appear under his own name until after Autry left. Autry always appeared under his own name, and his movies were often

"contemporary" westerns with planes, cars and other modern technology written into the plots.

After the war, Autry returned to Republic but then signed with Columbia Pictures in 1947. The years 1946 to 1953 were the final ones for the movie singing cowboy, a period that lasted roughly from 1935 to 1955. The last singing cowboy signed by Republic was Rex Allen, who starred in a number of pictures. The last musical western was produced by Republic in 1953. But television was replacing movies as the choice of entertainment for Americans, and Autry and Rogers soon signed agreements to have TV shows. At first, the two artists recycled old movies, but they quickly began action series for the TV shows with a limited amount of singing.

SIOUX INDIANS The Sioux were the most numerous of the Plains Indians, and their three major divisions inhabited a large area in the West. The name "Sioux" comes from the Algonquian word *Nadowis-sue*, which meant "enemy" or "snake." The Sioux called themselves the Dakota, or Lakota or Nakota, depending on the dialect. The largest group of Sioux were the Teton or Western Sioux, and they inhabited the high plains from the Dakotas westward. The Eastern or Santee Sioux lived in the area that is now Minnesota, and the Middle or Wiciyela Sioux inhabited the eastern area of present-day South Dakota. The Eastern Sioux were responsible for the Minnesota Massacre, but the Teton Sioux, divided into the tribes of Oglala, Brule, Sans Arcs, Minnekonjou, Two Kettle, Hunkpapa and Blackfeet, were most important in the history of the Old West. Great Chiefs Red Cloud and Crazy Horse were Oglala Sioux; Sitting Bull was from the Hunkpapa. Red Cloud and his warriors were responsible for the Fetterman Massacre in 1866. Both Sitting Bull and Crazy Horse played important roles in the defeat of General George Custer at the Battle of the Little Bighorn in 1876, but this great battle victory ultimately led to the defeat of the Sioux nation. The final subjugation of the Sioux came in 1890 when Big Foot and his tribe were massacred at Wounded Knee, South Dakota after taking part in the ghost dance movement. (See also Crazy Horse; Fetterman Massacre; Little Bighorn, Battle of; Red Cloud; Sitting Bull; Wounded Knee Massacre.)

SIRINGO, CHARLES (b. Matagorda County, Texas on February 7, 1855; d. Hollywood, California on October 19, 1928) Siringo worked for the Pinkerton Detective Agency for 22 years and infiltrated the Hole in the Wall Gang. Siringo wrote several important books, including *A Texas Cowboy, or Fifteen Years on the Hurricane Deck of a Spanish Pony* (1885), *A Cowboy Detective* (1912) and *Riata and Spurs* (1927). Siringo thus became the first authentic cowboy to publish an autobiography.

SITTING BULL (b. Grand River, South Dakota in March 1834; d. Standing Rock, South Dakota on December 15, 1890) Sitting Bull was a medicine man with the Hunkpapa Sioux. During the Battle of the Little Bighorn, he was in his tent "making medicine." The victory in this battle was foretold in a dream to Sitting

Bull when he saw a number of army soldiers falling from the sky upside down; he received this vision after engaging in a self-torture ritual, the sun dance. Sitting Bull was always hostile to whites and refused to be confined to a reservation. After the June 1876 defeat of Custer, Sitting Bull took his people north to Canada, where he remained until July 1881. At this time he returned to the United States and surrendered at Fort Buford in Montana. Sitting Bull was part of Buffalo Bill's Wild West show for a year and gave Annie Oakley her nickname, "Little Miss Sure Shot." Sitting Bull continually argued with Indian agent James McLaughlin at the Standing Rock Reservation in South Dakota where he was confined. McLaughlin ordered Sitting Bull's arrest in 1890 when the ghost dance movement was causing excitement among the Indians. When military policemen came to arrest Sitting Bull, a scuffle broke out with his followers; somehow Sitting Bull was shot "trying to escape" by policemen Red Tomahawk and Bull Head.

SIX-SHOOTER A revolver with six bullets in the chamber.

SKUNK A member of the weasel family, the skunk (*Mephitis mephitica*) is famous for the stinking liquid it shoots at its enemies, which comes from two glands under its tail. Early trappers hunted it for its black-and-white fur, which was purified by heat.

SKY KING TV show that starred Kirby Grant as Sky King, Gloria Winters as his niece Penny and Ron Hagerty as Clipper.

Schuyler "Sky" King was a unique cowboy: Instead of chasing down crooks with a horse, he did it in his plane. Sky, his niece Penny and nephew Clipper lived at the Flying Crown Ranch near Grover, Arizona. At times Grover's sheriff, played by actor Ewing Mitchell, needed help, so Sky left the ranch under the watchful eye of the ranch foreman, played by actor James Bell, and jumped in his twin-engine plane, the *Songbird* (a Cessna 310-B), to help bring justice to the West. This show was originally a radio show on CBS from 1946 to 1954 and was popular on Saturday morning TV. It made its prime-time debut on September 21, 1953 on Mondays on ABC. The last prime-time telecast for the 30-minute show was September 12, 1954. "Sky King" was seen on NBC on Sunday afternoons from 1951 to 1952, on ABC on Saturday afternoons from 1952 to 1953 and then from 1959 to 1966 on CBS on Saturday afternoons. The show was originally sponsored by Peter Pan peanut butter and then by the Nabisco Company. The show was filmed in Apple Valley, near Victorville, Arizona with interior shots done on Hollywood sound stages. Over 130 episodes were filmed but only 72 remain, because a fire broke out where the films were stored.

SLADE, JACK (b. Joseph Alfred Slade in Carlyle, Illinois in 1829; d. Virginia City, Montana on March 10, 1864) Slade had killed Jules Reni near Cold Springs, Colorado in 1859 rather brutally. He had Reni bound to a fence post and shot at him between gulps of whiskey. After inflicting a number of wounds, Slade put his pistol in Reni's mouth and pulled the trigger and then sliced off Reni's ears. The problems with the two went back about a year, when Reni stole some horses from the Pike's Peak Express Company, which employed Slade. Reni had shot Slade five times in Julesburg, Colorado and then ordered that Slade be buried. But the crowd chased Reni out of town and Slade miraculously recovered. Slade was eventually hung after a drunken saloon quarrel because the town considered him a dangerous nuisance and he refused to mend his rowdy ways.

After Jack Slade was hung in Virginia City, Montana, his wife wanted to transport the body back to his native Illinois for burial. She had a tin coffin made, filled it with the body and raw alcohol and sealed it. But the whole thing stunk so much that the body was buried in Salt Lake City. The alcohol was only one reason for the odor; by the time the body was buried, it had been dead four months in spring and summer heat.

SLAUGHTER, C. C. (b. Christopher Columbus Slaughter in Sabine County, Texas on February 9, 1837; d. Dallas, Texas on January 26, 1919) Slaughter was a pioneer in settling west Texas and at one time had over a million acres there on his Long S Ranch. Slaughter started young; when he was 12, he went on his first cattle drive and by 18 owned over 70 head of cattle. He went to west Texas in 1885 with his father, George Webb Slaughter, and settled in Palo Pinto County; the following year he established another ranch 300 miles away and drove 1,500 cattle there, where he sold beef to Fort Belknap and Indian agents. Slaughter was captain in a ranger company and was involved in the capture of Cynthia Parker, mother of Quanah Parker. When settlers in west Texas left the frontier because of problems from Indians and rustlers, Slaughter bought their cattle; later he upgraded his herds with shorthorn and Hereford bulls. Slaughter helped organize the Northwest Texas Cattle Raisers Association and became a civic leader in Dallas.

SLAUGHTER, TEXAS JOHN (aka "Don Juan"; b. John Horton Slaughter in Sabine Parish, Louisiana on October 2, 1841; d. Douglas, Arizona on February 15, 1922) Texas John Slaughter is the kind of man the West celebrated; in his life he was a lawman, cattleman, gambler, gunman, pioneer, politician and empire builder. He established a ranch in Texas in Atascosa and Frio Counties, bossed a number of trail drives but then decided to relocate to Arizona. He purchased the 65,000-acre San Bernardino Grant in 1879 (which had acreage in both New Mexico and Arizona) and eventually employed over 20 cowboys and 30 families and built dams and irrigation canals.

He was elected sheriff of Cochise County in 1886, a county that had Tombstone and Galeyville in its boundary. Slaughter was a tough, effective sheriff but not a cold-blooded killer; in fact, he was known to prefer arresting men to killing them. However, he did kill some men in his time. In 1876 he killed drunken rustler Barney Gallagher on John Chisum's South Spring Ranch in New Mexico. In May 1888 in Cochise County,

Arizona, Slaughter killed bandit Guadalupe Robes, and he wounded an outlaw named Manuel on June 7, 1888. He fired the first shot into outlaw Peg-Leg Finney on September 19, 1898 at the San Bernardino Ranch in Arizona, and then his men pumped two more shots into Finney, who died where he was found. Slaughter also killed gambler Little Bob Stevens around 1900 at the San Bernardino Ranch in Arizona after the thief held up a roulette game and ran off with the money.

Trail driver George Lang, who owned the Bato Rico Ranch next to Slaughter's spread, and Slaughter formed a partnership in 1886. Slaughter bought out Lang in 1890; by this time they had been trailing beef to California and had a slaughterhouse in Los Angeles. In 1895 Slaughter was appointed deputy sheriff and held this commission until his death. He won a seat in the Arizona territorial assembly in 1906 but after one term gave it up. A prominent citizen, he purchased two butcher shops in Bisbee in 1910 and was one of the founders of the Bank of Douglas. Texas John Slaughter died peacefully in his sleep at the age of 80 in Douglas, Arizona, a town he helped found. (See also NEWCOMB, BITTER CREEK.)

SLAUGHTER'S KID   See NEWCOMB, BITTER CREEK.

SLICKER   Raincoat, usually oilskin, carried by cowboys who tied it to the back of their saddle. A *slicker roll* was the bedroll wrapped in a slicker and a *slicker-broke* horse is one that wouldn't spook or kick when the slicker was dropped off the left side. Also called a *fish*.

SMITH, BEAR RIVER TOM   (b. Thomas James Smith in New York City on June 12, 1840; d. near Abilene on November 2, 1870)   Bear River Tom got his nickname from Bear River City, a boom town for the Union Pacific Railroad near present-day Evanston, Wyoming. A tough, fearless man, Smith developed a reputation for fistfighting and was hired as a law officer in the Bear River City camp. Before moving west, Smith had been on the New York City police force, and he continued his career in law enforcement, moving to Greeley, Colorado as a law officer after leaving Bear River City. On June 4, 1870 he became marshal of Abilene and made it an offense to carry guns, which led to several assassination attempts. On November 2 of that year Smith went to a settlement about 10 miles from Abilene to arrest Andrew McConnell, but McConnell shot Smith. McConnell's partner, Moses Miles, then finished killing Smith with an axe. (See also MCCONNELL, ANDREW.)

SMITH, JEDEDIAH   (b. Bainbridge, New York on January 6, 1799; d. Santa Fe Trail on May 27, 1831)   A famed mountain man and trapper, Jedediah Smith was also a noted explorer who became the first American to travel overland all the way to California. In the early 1820s Smith joined William Ashley's company and discovered the South Pass through the Rockies in 1824 while hunting for beaver. Mauled by a grizzly bear, Smith is one of the few men to survive such a tragedy. Smith and two partners purchased William Ashley's fur business in 1826; in August of that year Smith and some other trappers went from the Great Salt Lake to California and the San Gabriel mission near Los Angeles, traveling over the Mojave Desert and San Bernardino Mountains. Smith and his group crossed the Sierra Nevada on their return. Smith retraced his route in 1827, but 10 of the 18 members of the party were killed by Indians, and when the rest reached the mission, Smith was arrested and put into jail by Mexican authorities. Smith entered the Santa Fe trade in 1830 after selling his interest in his fur company. He was killed on the Santa Fe Trail by Comanche Indians.

SMITH, PEG LEG   (b. Thomas Smith in Garrard County, Kentucky on October 10, 1801; d. near San Francisco on October 15, 1866)   In the fall of 1827, while trapping in southeastern Colorado, Smith was wounded in his left leg by Indians; he amputated his foot (with the help of Milton Sublette) and recovered. He was fitted with a wooden leg during the winter while on the Green River and thereafter became known as "Peg Leg" Smith. A legendary horse thief, Smith was also a mountain man who trapped with Antoine Robidoux; he then moved to Taos in 1824 and trapped by himself. Smith stole 300 horses in Los Angeles in early 1829 and drove them to Taos; this set a pattern for Smith, who continued to steal horses from southern California (in 1839 he helped steal 3,000). Smith is also famous for "Peg Leg Smith Gold," which he supposedly found by accident on top of a hill in the California desert during a trip from Colorado to the coast. A number of gold seekers looked for it later, but Smith apparently was not one of them.

SMITH, SOAPY   (b. Jefferson Randolph Smith in Georgia in 1860; d. Skagway, Alaska on July 8, 1898)   One of the all-time great confidence (or "con") men of the West, Smith bilked the naive, the unsuspecting and the gullible out of thousands. He worked a variety of games in Texas, New Mexico, Colorado, Kansas and Old Mexico, including the old "hidden pea" game in which he used three shells and fancy finger work. Smith "found" a 10-foot statue of prehistoric man secretly buried and charged people money to see it. He also sold bars of soap for $5 after claiming that somebody would find a $20 bill wrapped around his or her purchase (none did). Smith apparently met his match in 1897 during the Alaska gold rush when he fleeced thousands and then had to face a group opposed to him. Smith crashed a vigilante meeting, and a shootout ensued between him and city engineer Frank Reid; when the smoke cleared, Smith was dead; Reid hung on for another 12 days before he died.

SMITH, TOM   (b. Texas; d. near Gainesville, Texas on November 5, 1892)   Tom Smith was hired by the Wyoming Stock Growers' Association to recruit Texas gunfighters for the Johnson County War. Smith hired 26 in and around Paris, Texas, offering $5 per day and expenses, a $3,000 accident policy and a bonus of $50 for each enemy shot or hung by a gunman. The group headed to Wyoming, where they were joined by a group recruited by Frank Canton. The head of the expedition was Major Frank Wolcott. These "Regulators" intended to destroy the homesteaders, and the first order of business was to go to Buffalo, Wyoming and kill Sheriff Red Angus and 70 other troublemakers. But on their way to Buffalo they learned two others on their list, Nate Champion and Nick Ray, were at the nearby KC Ranch. The Regulators surrounded the ranch house, but Champion held out all day, which allowed citizens to be alerted. Champion and Ray were killed, but the Regulators were trapped and arrested in Buffalo, where, owing to strings pulled by the influential cattle growers, the Regulators were released. Smith went back to Texas, but in the summer of 1893 near Gainesville he ran into a Negro on a train bound for Guthrie, Oklahoma. Words were exchanged and Smith was killed. (See also CHAMPION, NATE; JOHNSON COUNTY WAR.)

SMITH AND WESSON Guns made by Horace Smith and Daniel B. Wesson, which were popular with Wells Fargo's guards and with Wild Bill Hickok, who carried Smith and Wessons after years of using navy Colts. The revolvers, manufactured in Springfield, Massachussets, were the first to fire a metallic cartridge.

SOD HOUSES On the treeless plains, people constructed homes from sod. The first were built in Kansas in the 1850s, and after the Civil War, when homesteaders moved west, this was a popular type of house. Generally built into the side of a hill or ravine, the "dugout" or "sod house" usually had one room about 16 by 20 feet; about half an acre of ground was needed for the sod "bricks," which were cut from furrows. Each brick was usually about three feet long and several inches thick and, in building the homes, were laid as regular bricks for the walls. Wooden frames for doors and windows (there was usually only one window in a sod house) were set into the walls, and sod was put around them, with cracks filled in by clay or dirt. The walls were usually reinforced with stems, and the roof often consisted of brush placed on wooden rafters, followed by a layer of prairie grass and then one of sod. If a settler could afford tar paper, this was placed over the sod roof. The inside walls of the house were covered with plaster if possible or perhaps smoothed by a shovel; a room divider, such as a quilt or rug, could create the effect of two rooms. During heavy rain the roof leaked—often for days—and it was possible that the roof would cave in if it took too much water. There were constant problems with bugs and rodents falling out of the roof, and homemakers often used a cheesecloth on the ceiling to catch falling bugs, especially over the table where the family ate. The houses were generally cool in the summer and warm in the winter and lasted five to seven years.

SOLD HIS SADDLE Said of a cowboy who had bottomed out, fallen on hard times or given up.

SON-OF-A-BITCH STEW The most famous of all cowboy dishes (and called son-of-a-gun stew in polite society) , this delicacy varied from cook to cook, but the basis of the stew was veal, mainly because calves were most expendable on a trail drive. Ingredients might include half a calf heart, liver, brains, marrow gut, hot sauce, sweetbreads and kidneys; perhaps onions or chilies were added as well as flour to thicken it.

SONS OF THE PIONEERS The singing group the Sons of the Pioneers was formed from the group The Rocky Mountaineers when vocalist Leonard Slye (later known as Roy Rogers) wanted to add more vocalists and form a group that sang harmony. Slye came to the attention of the Mountaineers after he entered an amateur talent contest on radio station KMCS in Inglewood, California with his cousin in 1931. Rogers was their first vocalist. Wanting harmony and feeling more confident singing with others, Rogers ran an ad in the *Los Angeles Examiner* for a vocalist who could yodel. Bob Nolan answered the ad and was hired. The group soon realized it needed a third voice, and Nolan's friend Bill "Slumber" Nichols was hired to round out the trio. At this point the Mountaineers were appearing on a Long Beach, California radio station.

In 1932 Bob Nolan quit the group and became a caddy at the Bel Air Country Club, so Slye ran another ad in August 1932 in the *Examiner*. This ad was answered by Tim Spencer, who was hired. This group had shows on KFAC and KGER; part of the time they sang with the Rocky Mountaineers and the rest of the time with Benny Nawahi's International Cowboys, whom they joined in December 1932.

Taking the name "O-Bar-O Cowboys," the trio of Slye,

Sons of the Pioneers

Spencer and Nichols had a tour of the Southwest from June to September 1933. When they returned, the group disbanded and Slye joined Jack and His Texas Outlaws. Because Slye still wanted a trio, he contacted Spencer, who agreed to try again, and the two then went to the Bel Air Country Club and convinced a reluctant Bob Nolan to give it another shot. They spent several weeks in intense rehearsal at a boardinghouse in Hollywood at Carlton and Bronson. Feeling they had developed a strong sound—the trio harmony was always important, and Slye insisted they do trio yodeling—the group joined Jack and His Texas Outlaws on KFWB. They took the name "The Pioneer Trio" when they joined this group at the end of 1933. They also worked under the name "The Gold Star Rangers" and were on the KFWB staff.

At the beginning of 1934, the trio of singers added an instrumentalist, fiddler Hugh Farr. Also in early 1934 they were introduced on the radio by announcer Harry Hall as "The Sons of the Pioneers." The group was upset with Hall, who told them the new name was more appropriate because they were all so young that they looked more like "sons" than "pioneers." The name stuck, and by March 1934 it was official.

A year later, in March 1935, the group signed with Decca Records. They also recorded a number of transcriptions for Standard Radio, which were shipped to radio stations all over the country to play. In mid-1935 they added another member, guitarist Karl Farr (Hugh's brother), and this is the group known as the "original" Sons of the Pioneers.

Also in mid-1935 the group was offered their first part in a movie: *The Old Homestead* for Liberty Pictures, released in August 1935. In this film they were known by a name they continued to use, The Gold Star Rangers. They also appeared in *Slightly Static*, an MGM short, and *Way Up Thar* with Joan Davis, also in late 1935. They then appeared in two pictures for Columbia with cowboy star Charles Starrett.

By this time the songwriting skills of Bob Nolan and Tim Spencer were widely recognized. Nolan had written "Tumbling Tumbleweeds" in 1932 while he was at the Bel Air Country Club, and the song was used as a theme song for the group. In high school he had written a poem that later became the basis of "Cool Water." The combination of the trio harmonies, the trio yodeling introduced by Slye and the strong western songs of Bob Nolan (and later, Tim Spencer) gave the group a unique, enduring appeal.

The Sons of the Pioneers continued to record for Decca and appear in movies, including *Rhythm of the Range,* starring Bing Crosby, and *The Big Show,* starring singing cowboy Gene Autry.

In 1936 Tim Spencer left the group and was replaced briefly by Charlie Quirk, then by Lloyd Perryman, who would remain in this group for over 40 years, longer than any other member. In 1937 Leonard Slye left the group to audition for the role of a singing cowboy at Republic Pictures. Republic wanted another singing cowboy to keep Gene Autry in line; the star had threatened to walk off, the set over a contract dispute. Autry

did walk off, and Slye was cast in the starring role in *Under Western Skies* in 1937; for his newfound role, his name was changed to Roy Rogers.

The group continued to be popular through recordings, radio appearances, radio transcriptions and appearances in movies, and Glenn Spencer began to direct their music and business activities. By late 1936 they had joined Peter Potter's "Hollywood Barn Dance" and had a regular spot on KFOX in Long Beach, on KRKD in Los Angles and, as the Gold Star Rangers, on KMTR before they settled on KHJ in Los Angeles.

When Rogers left the trio, he was replaced by Bob O'Brady, who soon became Pat Brady. Brady's vocals did not work out as hoped, but he remained with the group as bass fiddle and comedian. Tim Spencer then rejoined the group as they recorded with Decca except for 31 sides cut for Art Satherley at Columbia. For the Columbia sides, the trio was Rogers, Nolan and Perryman.

In 1938 the Sons of the Pioneers began a syndicated radio show, "Sunshine Ranch," over KNX and the Mutual Broadcasting System. At this point the group consisted of Nolan, Spencer, Perryman, Brady and the Farr Brothers. They also continued appearing in Starrett movies through early 1941 and wrote a number of songs for western films.

In 1940 the Sons of the Pioneers went to Chicago, where they stayed for a year, and returned to Los Angeles in September 1941, when they joined the Camel Caravan for a tour of military bases on the West Coast. In October 1941 they appeared in a Roy Rogers movie for Republic, *Red River Valley*. Also in 1941 the group signed to do a series of transcriptions for Dr. Pepper with singers Dick Foran and Martha Mears. These programs were broadcast over the Mutual System and lasted until the end of World War II.

During World War II, Pioneers Lloyd Perryman and Pat Brady joined the service; Perryman served in Asia and Brady served in Europe with Patton's Third Army. Perryman was replaced by Ken Carson, and Shug Fisher replaced Pat Brady, after Deuce Spriggens had filled in briefly. Thus the Sons of the Pioneers during World War II consisted of the trio of Spencer, Nolan and Carson, with Shug Fisher and the Farr Brothers. The group also worked extensively with Roy Rogers, appearing in over 40 westerns with the singing cowboy.

In 1945 Lloyd Perryman and Pat Brady returned from the war and rejoined the group. They signed a recording contract with RCA, and the name became "Bob Nolan and the Sons of the Pioneers" because of Nolan's distinctive vocals and strong songs, which dominated the group.

Tim Spencer retired from the Pioneers in early 1949; a few months later Nolan also retired. Ken Curtis replaced Spencer, and Tommy "Spike" Doss replaced Nolan. Lloyd Perryman assumed leadership of the group, which had a further change when Pat Brady left to join Roy Rogers as a sidekick in movies and on television.

In 1950 the Sons of the Pioneers began a radio program, the Lucky U Ranch with George Putnam as announcer. Both Nolan and Spencer made appearances on the show. The group sang in the movie classic *Wagons West,* which later became the basis for the popular TV show "Wagon Train."

In February 1953 Shug Fisher and Ken Curtis left the group and began the Lucky U Radio and TV program. Dale Warren then joined the group and Deuce Spriggens replaced Fisher. Also in 1953, the Pioneers left RCA after eight years, but the label signed Bob Nolan. The group then signed with Decca in 1954 before returning to Victor in February 1955 with the old trio of Spencer, Nolan and Perryman at the record label's insistence. This meant Doss and Warren were left out, although Ken Curtis was brought back to sing for Spencer, with Spencer running the day-to-day activities of the group. Pat Brady was also brought back to replace Deuce Spriggens; this is the group that recorded for Victor from 1955 to 1957.

During the mid-fifties the trio of Perryman, Doss and Warren made a large number of transcriptions for the government. But there were a number of musical changes, as fiddler Hugh Farr left the group in 1958 and accordionist George Bamby was added in 1959. In 1960 Bamby left the group and Wade Ray joined. In September 1961 Karl Farr suffered a heart attack while performing with the Pioneers and died. He was replaced by Roy Lanham on guitar. Tommy Doss, whose lead vocals sounded incredibly like Bob Nolan's, left in 1967 after being with the group since 1963. Rusty Richards then joined the group, as well as fiddler Billy Armstrong, and from September 1967 to March 1968 Bob Mensor was part of the trio, replaced by Luther Nallie when he left. In 1972 Armstrong left, and Nallie left in 1974, replaced by Rusty Richards. Also in 1974 accordionist Billy Liebert was added.

In May 1977 longtime member Lloyd Perryman died and Rome Johnson was added to the group. Tim Spencer had died in 1974 and Bob Nolan died in 1980. (See also Nolan, Bob; Rogers, Roy; Singing Cowboys; Spencer, Tim.)

SONS OF THE SAN JOAQUIN　　This western singing group is composed of Joe, Jack and Lon Hannah. Influenced strongly by the Sons of the Pioneers, the group originated with brothers Joe and Jack, who learned early Sons of the Pioneers songs from their father, a native of Missouri who moved his family to California in 1935. Later Lon, the son of Joe, convinced his father and uncle to join him in a trio, and the group began performing.

SOONER　　This term came from the opening up of Indian Territory to white settlers, which led, ultimately, to this area's becoming the state of Oklahoma. A land rush was organized and a time set for people to line up and, at the sound of a gun, race westward into the territory and claim a spot of land. It was discovered later that some had gone into the territory earlier and staked a claim before the official start. These people were known as "sooners" because they got there sooner.

SOTO, JUAN　　(aka the "Human Wildcat"; b. ?; d. Sausalito Valley, California in 1871)　　A large man, Soto was part Indian and part Mexican. On January 10, 1971 he robbed a store in Sunol, California, killed the clerk and then shot into the apartment at the rear of the store where a family lived. This incident led to a manhunt headed by Sheriff Harry Morse and a posse. The outlaw and his band were tracked to the Sausalito Valley in the Panoche Mountains; there Sheriff Morse and a deputy named Walker went into an adobe building and discovered Soto seated with a number of other men and women. Morse bravely drew his pistol in the midst of this crowd, ordered Soto to put his hands up and told the deputy to handcuff Soto. But the deputy fled the building when those gathered began to pull out their weapons. Meanwhile, a man and woman grabbed Morse. Morse broke out of the grasp of the Mexicans as Soto jumped up from the table; the sheriff shot a hole in Soto's hat, but the outlaw answered with four bullets in Morse's direction. Morse got out of the building and headed toward the rifle in his horse's scabbard. On the way, the sheriff fired back at Soto and the bullet struck Soto's six-shooter, jamming the gun. Soto ran back inside for more weapons—a pistol in his belt and one in each hand—before heading out for a horse. But Soto's horse spooked and the outlaw was left on foot, so he headed for the mountains. Morse shot the outlaw in the shoulder at about 150 yards, which made the Human Wildcat furious, so he turned and charged the sheriff. Morse then aimed and fired again; this time the bullet hit Soto in the head and killed the outlaw. (See also MORSE, HARRY N.)

SOUTHERN PACIFIC RAILROAD　　Ultimately the Southern Pacific would purchase a number of railroads, including the Central Pacific, for a huge network of rails. The line was originally chartered by the California legislature to run from San Francisco to San Diego and then eastward to connect with another railroad. Plans changed, though, and it took about 12 years (1865 to 1877) before the line reached Yuma, Arizona. When it connected with the Texas and Pacific Railroad east of El Paso, it established a transcontinental route from San Francisco to New Orleans.

SPANISH IN THE WEST　　See MEXICO.

SPENCER　　A rifle made by Christopher Spencer's Spencer Repeating Rifle Company. This was a repeating carbine that had a lever action and was developed during the Civil War for the Union.

SPENCER, TIM　　(b. Vernon Spencer in Webb City, Missouri on July 13, 1908; d. Apple Valley, California on April 26, 1974)　　One of the founding members of the singing group the Sons of the Pioneers, along with Bob Nolan and Leonard Slye (Roy Rogers), Spencer wrote "The Timber Trail," "The Everlasting Hills of Oklahoma," "Silent Trails," "Sagebrush Symphony," "It's a Cowboy's Life for Me," "By a Campfire on the Trail," "Down the Trail," "A Cowboy's Sweetheart," "Moonlight on the Trail" and other western greats, mostly for singing-cowboy movies. Spencer's family moved to New Mexico when he was a child and then to Oklahoma, where he became involved in school musicals and purchased a banjo ukulele. This launched his music career as he began entertaining in and around Tulsa, Oklahoma. After school, Spencer moved to Los Angeles to try to break into the movies. He landed a job at a Safeway warehouse, where he was working when he saw an advertisement in the newspaper in August 1932 for a singer who could yodel. The ad was placed by Leonard Slye, who needed to replace Bob Nolan, who had just quit the singing trio with the Rocky Mountaineers. Spencer auditioned and was accepted, and soon the group was part of Benny Nawai and the International Cowboys. The group then adopted the name "O-Bar-O Cowboys" and went on a tour of the Southwest from June to September 1933. Although the trip was musically a disaster, Spencer met his future wife, Velma Blanton, in Lubbock, Texas during this tour.

The group disbanded when they returned to Los Angeles, but because Slye still wanted a trio, he contacted Spencer, who agreed to try again, and the two then convinced Bob Nolan to give it another shot. The group rehearsed for several weeks and then joined Jack and His Texas Outlaws. Calling themselves the Pioneer Trio, the group was heard on radio station KFWB, where one day the announcer introduced them as the "Sons of the Pioneers," explaining later they looked too young to be "Pioneers."

In 1936 Spencer left the group and was replaced by Lloyd Perryman. He returned in 1938, after Slye had left to become singing star Roy Rogers, and remained with the group until 1949, when he retired. He rejoined as a singer in 1955 when they re-signed with RCA Victor but never toured with them as a singer after his retirement.

Spencer was the driving force behind the Sons of the Pioneers during most of the time with the group. An outgoing person, he conducted the day-to-day activities and business affairs of the group and helped produce their recording sessions through 1957.

Later in his life Spencer formed a religious publishing company, Manna Music, and published the gospel standard "How Great Thou Art." (See also COOL WATER; NOLAN, BOB; ROGERS, ROY; SONS OF THE PIONEERS; TUMBLING TUMBLEWEEDS.)

SPOILERS, THE   There were a number of versions of this movie: 1914, 1923, 1930, 1942 and 1956. The 1914 and 1923 movies were silents. The 1930 version (Paramount) was the first sound version, produced and directed by Edward Carewe with screenplay by Bartlett Cormack; the cast included Gary Cooper, Kay Johnson, Betty Compson, William "Stage" Boyd and Charles K. French. The 1942 version (Universal, 87 minutes) was produced by Frank Lloyd and directed by Ray Enright, with screenplay by Tom Reed and a cast that included Marlene Dietrich, Randolph Scott, John Wayne, Margaret Lindsay, Harry Carey and William Farnum. The 1956 version (Universal-International, 84 minutes) was produced by Ross Hunter and directed by Jesse Hibbs, with screenplay by Oscar Brodney and Charles Hoffman, the cast included Anne Baxter, Jeff Chandler, Rory Calhoun, Ray Danton, Barbara Britton, John McIntire and Wallace Ford.

This film was originally a novel by Rex Stout based on the life of Alexander McKenzie, a politician from North Dakota who pulls some shady deals in Alaska, and each version concludes with a huge, heroic fistfight.

SPRAGUE, CARL   (b. Alvin, Texas on May 10, 1895; d. Bryan, Texas on February 19, 1979)   In August 1925 Carl Sprague traveled to New York, where he recorded 10 songs for Victor, making him the first to record cowboy songs. His first release was "When the Work's All Done This Fall," and he recorded additional cowboy material in 1926, 1927 and 1928. Sprague sang cowboy songs while a student at Texas A&M and later settled in Bryan, Texas.

Sprague grew up on his family's ranch where he originally heard old cowboy songs. He entered Texas A&M in 1915 and joined the campus band. Sprague also played on the campus radio station. He recorded about 30 songs for Victor but never made music a career; in 1930 he joined Texas A&M as athletic trainer, although he continued to appear locally on occasion as a singer.

SPRINGFIELD   A rifle the army used in the Plains Indian wars. Erskine H. Allin developed this gun in 1866 as a faster-loading rifle.

SPUR RANCH   A west Texas ranch begun by Jim Hall in 1878 when he drove 1,900 head of cattle from the Gulf coast. The Spur Ranch eventually became a 439,972-acre spread, which was sold in 1882. The ranch continued to grow and was purchased by S. M. Swenson and Son in 1906, who continued to operate it until 1942, when the Swensons and the John J. Emery family sold the rest. Portions had previously been sold to settlers during the years.

SPURS   Metal apparatus worn on the heel of a cowboy's boot. A spur is composed of four parts: the metal heel band and shank; the rowel attached to the end of the shank; the heel chain that goes under the boot, and the leather strap that fastens on the spur over the instep. The spur serves two important purposes: It can encourage a horse, and it was high fashion for the cowboys, who had a wide array of rowels that they liked to hear jingle when they walked.

SQUAW   A derogatory term whites applied to Indian women.

SQUAWMAN   A white man married to or living with an Indian woman.

SQUAW MAN, THE   Film produced and directed by Cecil B. DeMille; screenplay by Lucien Hubbard and Lenore Coffee; released by MGM in 1931; 12 reels. Cast: Warner Baxter, Lupe Velez, Eleanor Boardman, Paul Cavanagh and Lawrence Grant.

Several versions of this movie were filmed; this 1931 version is the first talking version. Based on a play by the same title written by Edwin Milton Royle, this story is about a white man married to an Indian woman. In a previous silent version, this movie has two distinctions: It featured William S. Hart in his first starring role, and it was the first feature film made in Hollywood. Thus, the first cowboy star in the movies and the Hollywood movie industry both began with this story.

STAGECOACH   Film produced by Walter Wanger; directed by John Ford; screenplay by Dudley Nichols (from Ernest Haycox's story "The Stage to Lordsburg"); music by Richard Hageman, W. Franke Harling, John Leipold, Leo Shuken and Louis Gruenberg; released in 1939 by United Artists; 97 minutes in length. Cast: Claire Trevor, John Wayne, Thomas Mitchell, John Carradine, Berton Churchill, Donald Meek, George Bancroft, Andy Devine, Louise Platt, Tim Holt, Tom Tyler and Chris Pin Martin.

This movie marked the first time John Ford used Monument Valley as a shooting site in his films. A group of people are thrown together in the small space of a stagecoach and faced with a common danger. The Overland Stage is going from Tonto to Lordsburg, and the group is a disparate bunch: a drunken doctor, a whiskey salesman, a prostitute run out of town, a pregnant wife going to join her army officer husband, a gambler, a banker who has embezzled from his bank, the stage driver, his shotgun rider and the Ringo Kid. The stunts were performed by Yakima Canutt, who pioneered such stunts as falling between the horses and letting the stagecoach roll over him. The musical score is composed of American folk songs.

Stagecoach was nominated for an Academy Award for Best Picture; unfortunately it competed against *Gone with the Wind, The Wizard of Oz, Mr. Smith Goes to Washington, Wuthering Heights, Goodbye, Mr. Chips,* and *Ninotchka.* However, Thomas Mitchell did win an Oscar for Best Supporting Actor as Dr. Josiah Boone, the drunken doctor. The version remade in 1966 was produced by Martin Rackin and directed by Gordon Douglas, with the screenplay by Joseph Landon from the original screenplay. The role of the Ringo Kid was played by Alex Cord; others in the cast included Ann-Margret, Red Buttons, Michael Connors, Alex Cord, Bing Crosby, Robert Cum-

Stagecoach

mings, Van Heflin, Slim Pickens, Stefanie Powers, Keenan Wynn, Brad Weston and Joseph Hoover. This version was released by Twentieth Century–Fox (114 minutes).

STAGECOACH The stagecoach was the primary means for mail and passenger service in the West from 1850 to 1870, when it was replaced by the railroads. There were usually six horses hitched to the stagecoach in three teams. There were no horse collars; the breast straps and traces dangled loosely, and the pole that ran from the coach between the horses swung freely to allow "give" if obstacles were hit by the front wheel. To drive a stagecoach, a "jehu" or driver arranged the reins of his leaders (the team farthest from him) between the fore and middle fingers of each hand; the middle (wing) team's reins were between the middle and third fingers, and the wheelers (those closest to him) were between the third and little fingers. The right hand's reins (controlling the "off" horses) had reins that dangled down, but the left hand's reins (guiding the "near" horses) were looped over the left thumb. The driver controlled the horses by "climbing," which meant he alternately gathered the reins with his fingers and then let them slip out the desired amount. Along with the foot brake and whip, a good driver could control all six horses and the coach itself. (See also ABBOT-DOWNING COMPANY; CONCORD COACH.)

STAGECOACH WEST TV show that starred Wayne Rogers as Luke Perry, Robert Bray as Simon Kane and Richard Eyer as David Kane.

The Timberline Stage Line ran from Tipton, Missouri to San Francisco, California. The drivers were Luke Perry and Simon Kane; David Kane, son of Richard, was their small assistant and cohort in adventures. This show is one of the few westerns that dealt with stagecoach drivers in the Wild West before railroads made them obsolete. The show premiered on October 4, 1960 and ended on September 26, 1961. There were 38 episodes of this hour-long series, which ran on Tuesday nights on ABC.

STALLION A male horse. Early Spanish settlers and Indians preferred stallions rather than mares, which were considered effeminate and "unmanly." Geldings, males that had been castrated, came to be preferred by cowboys.

STAMPEDE From the Spanish *estampidea*. For cattle, the term means a herd that is spooked and takes off en masse. Stampedes were a problem on trail drives where cattle were held in unknown territory. Longhorns were a particular problem because they were, by nature, jumpy and skittish and more prone to stampede than domesticated cattle. Longhorns could be provoked to stampede by just about anything—a storm or gunshots could certainly provoke a stampede, but a broken twig, a pot dropped by the cook or a sneeze by a cowboy could cause one as well. They were also more likely to stampede on very dark nights than on moonlit nights.

When longhorns stampeded, the cowboys used several tactics. The most common was to get to the head of the herd and turn them to the right (no cattle naturally turn to the left when running) and get them milling, or

running in a tight circle. The circle would be increasingly tightened until the cattle stopped. Another tactic was just to let them run, the theory being they would "run themselves out" and eventually stop. The herd generally did not separate when stampeding; unlike domestic cattle, which would often scatter when spooked or scared, the longhorns generally stayed together. Stampedes were dangerous for men and cattle. If the herd were of mixed ages, they were liable to run over the smaller and slower ones (although some cattlemen thought that calves were good to have along because they steadied a mother cow and the calves' bleating calmed the herd). Some thought that cattle would not run over a man— even when stampeding—but would divide when they came to him. This is *mostly* true, but if a cowboy got caught in the midst of a particularly violent stampede, he could easily get trampled. The most dangerous aspect of a stampede for the cowboy was riding full speed in the dead of night. Unable to see anything, a horse could step in a prairie dog hole, fall and injure or kill the cowboy, or knock him off his horse while his foot stayed stuck in the stirrup and thus drag him to death.

Although stampedes are generally associated with longhorns, there were also buffalo stampedes, which were even more dangerous because a buffalo ran blind. Since the buffalo's eyes are on either side of its head, it cannot see straight ahead and it just charges forward. Indians sometimes stampeded buffalo off cliffs or into dead-end canyons to kill them, and there were some cases of buffalo running into trains and knocking them off their tracks. A buffalo stampede was generally much more dangerous than even a longhorn stampede because the buffalo could not be stopped and because there would be more of them on a stampede. A longhorn stampede might involve 500–1,000 cattle, but a buffalo stampede might mean that 5,000–10,000 wild buffalo had gone crazy and were on a dead run.

STANWYCK, BARBARA (b. Ruby Stevens in Brooklyn, New York on July 16, 1907; d. Santa Monica, California on January 20, 1990) Barbara Stanwyck was not primarily an actress in westerns, but she starred in several memorable western movies as well as the television series "The Big Valley." Born Ruby Stevens, she was an orphan at four and was boarded out to families after one of her sisters became a chorus girl. She became one too at the age of 15 at the Club Anatole in New York. When Stanwyck's first husband, Frank Fay, was signed to Warner Brothers, she went to Hollywood with him. One of her first movies was a western, *Mexicali Rose* (1929), and she starred in *Annie Oakley* (1935) and *Union Pacific* (1939). Other memorable westerns include *Cattle Queen of Montana* (1955), *The Maverick Queen* (1956) and *Forty Guns* (1957). Barbara Stanwyck starred in 83 movies and received four Oscar nominations.

STARR, BELLE (b. Myra Belle Shirley in Carthage, Missouri on February 3, 1846; d. Oklahoma on February 3, 1889) Daughter of prominent businessman John Shirley, Belle Starr became a woman outlaw, famous for her robberies and sexual appetite. A woman who defied sexual traditions and norms, Belle took as her first lover Cole Younger of the Younger brothers, who rode with Jesse James. Belle's daughter, Pearl, was probably fathered by Cole. She then had a son, Ed, by outlaw Jim Reed while living with him as his common-law wife. She married a Cherokee Indian, Sam Starr, in 1880 and took the name Belle Starr. Belle had an affair with John Middleton, who was killed by the jealous Sam Starr in 1885; Sam probably also killed another lover of Belle's, Indian outlaw Blue Duck, in July 1886. Six months later Sam was killed in a gunfight. Belle's last lover was another Indian, Jim July.

Known as the "Bandit Queen" from dime novels written about her, Belle Starr deserved the reputation as an outlaw; with her first husband, Jim Reed, she helped his band rob train in Texas and California, and she later led a band of horse and cattle thieves after Reed was killed. She served time in prison in Detroit for stealing horses with Sam Starr (and became the first female ever sentenced by Judge Isaac Parker) and after her release joined her outlaw-lovers in a variety of crimes, usually robberies or horse stealing. Belle accompanied her young Creek Indian lover, Jim July, part of the way to Fort Smith, where he was scheduled to face larceny charges; on the way back to her home in Indian Territory (now Oklahoma) she was ambushed while riding alone, shot in the back and killed by an unknown assailant. Suspects included a neighbor named Watson and her own son, Ed Reed, but no one ever found out for sure and no one was ever convicted of her murder.

STARR, HENRY (aka "the Bearcat"; b. Fort Gibson, Indian Territory on December 2, 1873; d. Harrison, Arkansas on February 22, 1921)

Henry Starr was one of the most notorious bank robbers of all time. For Starr, being a holdup man was a high calling, and he wrote in his autobiography: "[It] all came to me in a flash. There was the road for me; it stretched out before me, and I could see its turnings, its high and low places, and, in a dim sort of way, its ending, and I knew it was what I had been long for and I took to it right gladly, feeling the spirit of exultation and freedom surge within me as my resolve was made. It was to answer the voice of the prairies and the mountains, and the blood of my ancestors was to have full play at last." Starr served 18 years of his life behind bars, always a model prisoner, reading the classics and the law. He began by robbing stores and in 1893 robbed his first bank at Caney, Kansas. Just prior to this bank robbery, Starr killed his first (and probably only) man, a detective named Floyd Wilson who had tracked him down for some robberies. With a gang of six, Starr held up a train in Oklahoma and a bank in Bentonville, Arkansas and then fled to Colorado, where he was caught. Starr was sentenced to hang by the "hanging judge," Isaac Parker, but a new trial was ordered; the second trial, also before Judge Parker, again resulted in a death sentence, but an appeal again resulted in a new trial. Finally, Starr plea-bargained and was sentenced to three years, but his mother appealed to President Theodore Roosevelt, who pardoned him be-

cause one of Starr's relatives had been a Rough Rider. Starr went straight for several years, married, and named his first child Theodore Roosevelt Starr, but when Arkansas requested his extradition for a robbery 14 years previously, Starr teamed up with his old partner Kid Wilson and the two went on a bank-robbing spree, hitting banks in Tyro, Kansas and Amity, Colorado before he was caught in Arizona and sentenced to prison. After serving four years in prison, he was released and robbed about 14 more banks before he settled down in Tulsa, where he felt he should top off his career by robbing two banks at once. On March 27, 1915 Starr and a gang of six went into Stroud, Oklahoma to rob two banks, but 17-year-old Paul Curry wounded Starr and he was captured and again went to prison. After he was released from prison, Starr decided to try his luck with motion pictures and filmed a movie of the attempted double robbery; Paul Curry reenacted his role for this movie. In 1920 Starr went back to robbing banks but met his match in Harrison, Arkansas on February 18, 1921 when he attempted to rob the People's National Bank. Former president and large stockholder W. J. Myers had hidden a shotgun in a specially installed back door in the bank vault; when Starr was inside the vault gathering up money, the president blasted him with the shotgun. Four days later Starr died.

STARRETT, CHARLES (b. Athol, Massachusetts on March 28, 1904; d. Borrego Springs, California on March 22, 1986) Charles Starrett appeared in more

Charles Starrett

"B" westerns than anyone else; in all, he made 131 westerns for Columbia between 1935 and 1952, and in over 60 films he starred as the Durango Kid, a masked avenger. Starrett graduated from Dartmouth College and made his first movie appearance in *The Quarterback* (1926); he studied at the American Academy of Dramatic Arts and appeared in four Broadway plays in 1929 before going to Hollywood. Starrett's debut film was *Fast and Loose* (1930). Columbia then signed him in 1935 to replace top cowboy star Tim McCoy, who had quit; Starrett's first western for Columbia was *The Gallant Defender* (1935). Starrett's leading lady for 18 films was Iris Meredith; in his earliest films he didn't have a sidekick but later worked with Ukulele Ike, Cliff Edwards, Stringbean Arthur Hunnicutt, Russ Hayden, Cannonball Taylor, Tex Harding and, for 56 films, Smiley Burnette. Starrett's last "B" western was released in 1952. Starrett, with 17 other film actors, helped found the Screen Actors Guild. (See also B WESTERN MOVIES; MOVIES.)

STARR REVOLVER   A revolver, eclipsed only by the Colt and the Remington, made by Eben T. Starr of the Starr Arms Company of New York. Popular with the army in the West, it wasn't as attractive as the Colt or the Remington but was a very efficient gun.

STATE TROOPER   TV show that starred Rod Cameron as Rod Blake.

Based on case histories from the Nevada State Police and shot on location at Virginia City, Nevada and Palmdale, California, this series combined the old and the new, with cars used to chase criminals sometimes and horses at others, depending upon the terrain. The show began as an episode on "Star Stage," an anthology, and appeared in February 1956. The show was produced by Universal Studio's company, MCA, and syndicated beginning in January 1957. Production ended in 1959 when there were 104 episodes of the half-hour series.

STEAGALL, RED   (b. Russell Steagall in Gainesville, Texas on December 22, 1938)   After Steagall graduated from West Texas State University with a degree in animal science and agronomy, he spent eight years as a music industry executive in Hollywood and songwriter before he moved to Nashville. There he became a recording artist with songs such as "Lone Star Beer and Bob Wills Music" and "I Gave Up Good Morning Darling" and began to appear on the rodeo and cowboy circuit. Steagall is a major organizer for the annual Cowboy Gathering each fall in Fort Worth.

STEELE, BOB   (b. Robert North Bradbury, Jr. in Pendleton, Oregon on January 26, 1906; d. Burbank, California on December 21, 1988)   Bob Steele starred in almost 100 "B" westerns between 1930 and 1946. One of twin sons of director R. N. Bradbury, Steele made his first appearance with his twin Bill in *The Adventures of Bill and Bob,* a series; they also appeared in vaudeville. Steele attended Glendale High School and was a classmate of John Wayne's; he began making films for his father at Sunset Films in 1926 and then changed

Red Steagall   *(Warner Brothers)*

his name from Bradbury to Steele in 1927 when he went to FBO, where his first release was *The Mojave Kid.* Steele signed with producer A. W. Hackel in 1934 and made a series of "B" movies—the first 15 under Supreme and the last 16 by Republic. Steele began the Billy the Kid series in late 1940 and then returned to Republic as one of the Three Mesquiteers (he played Tucson Smith) and made 19 Mesquiteer films from 1940 to 1963. Steele also worked on the Trail Blazers series with Hoot Gibson and Ken Maynard and later appeared on TV in "F Troop." (See also B WESTERN MOVIES; F TROOP; MOVIES.)

STEER   Castrated male cattle; those not castrated are bulls, and cows are generally female cattle. However, all cattle were called "cows" in the presence of women, in accordance with the notion that referring to masculine things—especially when it implied castration—was impolite. Steers had longer horns than bulls, were more manageable—because the male sex drive was gone—and generally had more tender meat. Most cattle raised for market were steers, who were castrated very young and raised for this purpose. These steers were generally called beeves.

STEER WRESTLING   Also called "bulldogging," this is when a man grabs a steer and wrestles it to the ground. In rodeo contests, the man starts out of the chute on horseback and runs alongside the steer; he then drops down on the running steer and grabs the horns, sticks out his feet to stop the steer and twists the animal's neck so the nose points to the sky in order to throw the steer to the ground. The cowboy is timed to see how long it takes from the opening of the chute gate

Bob Steele

until the steer is thrown; the winner is the cowboy who does it the quickest.

ST. ELMO'S FIRE Also called foxfire, a phosphorescent light, often seen on the tips of cattle's horns and on the ears of horses during stormy nights or when electricity is in the air.

STETSON, JOHN B. (b. Orange, New Jersey on May 5, 1830; d. DeLand, Florida on February 18, 1906) John B. Stetson designed and developed the famous "Stetson" hat, which became the trademark western hat and defined the "look" of the cowboy for years. Stetson came from a family of hatters and first went west for health reasons; in 1865 he opened a one-man hat factory in Philadelphia, but lack of sales forced him to design his own hats rather than copy styles. Another trip west for health reasons, this time to Colorado, led him to design a western hat after he observed the distinctive hats worn by westerners. He returned to Philadelphia and his firm began to manufacture cowboy hats; it grew and by 1906 was producing two million hats a year. A philanthropist who gave a great deal of money to Baptist churches and causes, Stetson became interested in the DeLand Academy; he gave it money and buildings and it changed its name to John B. Stetson University. At his death he left a fortune of $5 million.

STEVE DONOVAN, WESTERN RANGER TV show that starred Douglas Kennedy as Texas Ranger Steve Donovan and Eddy Waller as Ranger Rusty.

This was a syndicated children's show that premiered in 1951. The 30-minute shows were popular on Saturday mornings, and the 39 episodes were resyndicated in 1955 as "Steve Donovan, Western Marshal."

STEWART, JAMES (b. Indiana, Pennsylvania on May 20, 1908) Although Jimmy Stewart's most famous movie role was probably in *It's a Wonderful Life,* that bumbling, awkward yet sincere character who represents the best in people is essentially the character he played in a number of movies, including a number of westerns in the 1950s and 1960s. These roles altered his image of a light romantic lead and made it tougher and more cynical. Gossip columnist Hedda Hopper "discovered" him, which led to MGM's signing him. His pre–World War II work included *You Can't Take It with You* (1938) and *Mr. Smith Goes to Washington* (1939; for which he received an Oscar nomination). Stewart worked with his old friend Henry Fonda in two westerns, *Firecreek* (1967) and *The Cheyenne Social Club* (1970). Other major westerns Stewart starred in include *Broken Arrow* (1950), *Winchester '73* (1950), *The Far Country* (1955), *The Man from Laramie* (1955), *How the West Was Won* (1962), *The Man Who Shot Liberty Valance* (1962), *Cheyenne Autumn* (1964), *Shenandoah* (1965), *The Rare Breed* (1966), *Bandolero!* (1968) and *The Shootist* (1976).

STILES, WILLIAM LARKIN (b. ?; d. Nevada in January 1908) Some say that Billy Stiles was just 12 years old when he killed his own father. But it is a known

James Stewart

fact that Billy Stiles was killed by a 12-year-old boy after Stiles had killed that boy's father. Stiles was a member of the train-robbing gang organized by Arizona marshal Burt Alvord and his assistant, Jeff Milton; the gang also included Three-Fingered Jack Dunlap, George and Louis Owens, Bravo Juan Yoas and Bob Brown. Stiles fled to China after Alvord was exposed and arrested but came back and worked as a deputy sheriff in Nevada under the name "William Larkin." In January 1908 Stiles killed a man he tried to arrest. When he rode back to the victim's home where the killing had occurred, he was killed by a shotgun blast fired by the dead man's 12-year-old son. (See also ALVORD, BURT.)

STILWELL, FRANK C. (b. Texas in 1855; d. Tucson, Arizona on March 20, 1882) Stilwell was one of the men responsible for shooting Morgan Earp in the back; he was later killed by the Earp faction in Tucson just after Virgil Earp had been put on a train to California. Stilwell was part of Old Man Clanton's rustling ring and ran into trouble with Wyatt Earp. After the O.K. Corral gunfight, both Morgan and Virgil Earp were ambushed and Stilwell was the main suspect. Ike Clanton and Stilwell were in Tucson when the Earps came to send Virgil back to the family in California; as the train pulled out, the Earps spotted Stilwell and followed him. Wyatt and Warren Earp, Doc Holliday, Sherman McMasters and Turkey Creek Jack Johnson cornered Stilwell and pumped buckshot and bullets into him until he was dead. (See also EARP, MORGAN; EARP, WYATT; HOLLIDAY, DOC.)

STIRRUP The part of the saddle where the cowboy puts his foot. Initially made of wood, and later of iron, the stirrup is held to the saddle by the stirrup leather, the broad piece of leather hanging down each side of the saddle that supports the stirrup and protects the cowboy's leg from the horse.

ST. JOHN, FUZZY (b. Al St. John in Santa Ana, California on September 10, 1892; d. Vidalia, Georgia on January 31, 1963) A comic sidekick for movie cowboys Buster Crabbe, Lash LaRue and Fred Scott, St. John was a master at slapstick. He appeared in over 100 films, including 35 films with Buster Crabbe (1941–46), including the Billy the Kid/Billy Carson series, and he first developed the character Fuzzy Q. Jones when he costarred with singing cowboy Fred Scott. St. John began his cowboy career in *Law of the 45s* (1935), which introduced the Three Mesquiteers. St. John's parents were in vaudeville, and his first movie appearances were in the Keystone Cops films. From 1930 to 1951 he appeared in western films, working as a sidekick for Tom Mix, Bob Steele, Bob Cuter, Bill Cody, Big Boy Williams, William Boyd, John Wayne, Tom Tyler, Rex Bell, Johnny Mack Brown, Tex Ritter, Jack Randall and Buster Crabbe.

ST. JOSEPH, MISSOURI A small but extremely important town, St. Joseph was originally a trading post established in 1826; it was incorporated in 1845. Because of its strategic position on the east bank of the

Al "Fuzzy" St. John

Missouri River, it became a center for transportation—both passenger and freight—and communications, such as the telegraph, railroad and Pony Express. During the 1840s and 1850s, when a number of wagon trains headed west to Oregon and California, St. Joseph was the starting point and staging area where settlers were outfitted for their journey. The Pony Express made this town its eastern terminus in April 1860.

ST. LEON, ERNEST See DIAMOND DICK.

ST. LOUIS, MISSOURI Because of its strategic location on the Mississippi River, near the Missouri and Ohio Rivers, St. Louis became the major center for the fur trade in the early 19th century. Established by French trappers in 1764, St. Louis became the "Gateway to the West." Here transportation and communication systems and lines came together to become the country's hub, the city that separated the East from the West. Supplies, outfits and materials were purchased by trappers and settlers in St. Louis and taken by steamboat up the Missouri to the Kansas border. A manufacturing center as well, St. Louis produced ploughs, wagons, firearms and stoves. The city adapted to changes through the years and became the flour-milling center for western plains wheat during the 1880s.

STONEY BURKE TV show that starred Jack Lord as Stoney Burke, Robert Dowdell as Cody Bristol, Bruce Dern as E. J. Stocker, Warren Oates as Ves Painter and Bill Hart as Red.

Stoney Burke was a rodeo cowboy chasing the elusive Gold Buckle, which would signify him as saddle bronc champion. Interestingly, real-life rodeo champ Casey Tibbs was technical adviser for the show and did some of the riding. The show lasted only one season, premiering on October 1, 1962 and finishing on September 2, 1963, with all episodes of the one-hour show broadcast on ABC on Monday night.

STORIES OF THE CENTURY   TV show that starred Jim Davis as Matt Clark, Kristine Miller as Jonesy Jones and Mary Castle as Frankie Adams.

Thirty-nine episodes of this series were produced by Republic Pictures for television. The half-hour series, filmed in black and white, used some of Republic's stock footage as well as contract actors for the series, which told of an Old West detective working on a case involving real historical figures, such as Doc Holliday or Billy the Kid. This show, filmed in 1955, was never a network program but was syndicated to various stations around the country.

STORY, NELSON   (b. Meigs County, Ohio on April 4, 1838; d. Los Angeles, California on March 10, 1926) Nelson Story was the first to drive a herd of cattle from Texas into the northern ranges. In 1866 he took some cattle from Fort Worth north to Fort Leavenworth and then west along the Platte River to Fort Laramie, across Indian country over the Bozeman Trail to the Yellowstone River. He made a handsome profit when he reached the site of present-day Livingston, Montana and sold most of his beef to gold miners at Alder Gulch. Story had first gone west when he was 20 and had done some gold mining in Alder Gulch before going to Texas for cattle. He kept some of the breeding stock from the herd he drove up the trail and became the leading stockman in Montana within four years. Story settled around Bozeman and fought Indians in addition to raising cattle. Later, he operated a fleet of steamboats on the Missouri River between Montana and St. Louis and then moved on to horse raising. Later he became involved in finance and business and became a millionaire with mansions in Bozeman and Los Angeles.

STOUDENMIRE, DALLAS   (b. Aberfoil, Alabama on December 11, 1845; d. El Paso, Texas on September 18, 1882)   Stoudenmire once said, "I don't believe the bullet was ever molded that will kill me." That statement is proof that a man can be dead wrong. Stoudenmire served in the Confederacy during the Civil War, with the Texas Rangers afterward, and then worked as a carpenter, wheelwright and sheep rancher before he became city marshal of El Paso on April 10, 1881. Four days later Stoudenmire was eating lunch at the Globe Restaurant when trouble arrived. Some men were upset over the deaths of two Mexicans and shouted at a crowd. Constable Gus Krempkau was accused of being a friend of the Mexicans by a drunk, John Hale, who then shot the lawman. Stoudenmire ran into the street and shot at Hale, but the bullet hit a Mexican bystander instead, who died the next day. Stoudenmire's second shot drilled Hale in the head, and the drunk died. George

Campbell, who had been drinking with Hale, sobered up quickly when he saw death and wanted out of the fight, but Krempkau emptied his revolver at Campbell. Stoudenmire also fired at Campbell, hitting him in the stomach. He died the next day. The following Sunday night, Stoudenmire and his brother-in-law, Doc Cummings, were ambushed by Bill Johnson, a friend of Campbell's and Hale's, as they walked the street. Stoudenmire and Cummings killed Johnson with their revolvers, the last shot cutting off Johnson's testicles, and Stoudenmire chased away some other ambushers hiding on the other side of the street. Stoudenmire was the victim of another ambush attempt, on December 16, 1881 in El Paso, but survived this one too. Stoudenmire had a severe drinking problem, and he openly ran around on his wife, causing public opinion to turn against him. Liable to shoot his guns in the dead of night while drunk, and apt to disappear for periods of time while drinking, Stoudenmire had to resign after about a year as marshal. But in July 1882 he was appointed deputy U.S. marshal. Two months later he had a fatal run-in with the Manning brothers, his old enemies. On September 18, 1882 at the Manning's saloon Stoudenmire and Doc Manning started a verbal sparring, which erupted into a gunfight; Manning slugged Stoudenmire first and then charged the big lawman. The two wrestled, and Stoudenmire managed to shoot Manning with a small pistol before Jim Manning came up with a .45 and, on the second shot, plugged Stoudenmire in the head behind the left ear. The dead Stoudenmire was then pistol-whipped by a raging Doc Manning until law officer Jim Gillett pulled him away. (See also CUMMINGS, DOC; MANNING, JAMES.)

STOVE-UP COWBOY   A cowboy who is nursing poor health or an injury.

STRAIT, GEORGE   (b. Pearsall, Texas on May 18, 1952)   Strait is a contemporary country music singer with a strong Texas cowboy background. Raised on a ranch, Strait joined the army and was stationed in Hawaii, where he sang with a country music band. After his service Strait finished his degree at Southwest Texas University in San Marcos and formed a band there. He played locally for several years before he signed with MCA Records and released his first single, "Unwound," in 1981. A series of country hits followed, including "Amarillo by Morning," "Does Fort Worth Ever Cross Your Mind," "The Cowboy Rides Again," "All My Ex's Live in Texas" and the old Bob Wills hit "Right or Wrong." Strait starred in the movie *Pure Country* and sang on the soundtrack.

STRANGLERS   In 1884 a group of powerful Montana cattlemen organized themselves into vigilante groups, led by Granville Stuart, to rid the area of cattle thieves. These vigilantes conducted a number of hangings, which led to them being called "stranglers."

STRAWBERRY ROAN, THE   Originally a poem by rodeo rider Curley Fletcher, this was first published as "The Outlaw Bronc" in the Globe *Arizona Record* in December 1915. Soon a tune was added, and the song

George Strait

moved into the oral tradition, passed along from cowboy to cowboy. Fletcher included this poem, now titled "The Strawberry Roan," in a 1917 book entitled *Rhymes of the Roundup.*

STRAWHIM, SAMUEL   (b. Illinois in 1841 or 1842; d. Hays City, Kansas on September 27, 1869)   Strawhim was killed by Wild Bill Hickok. Some years later, when Wild Bill had been killed by Jack McCall, McCall argued at the trial that he was Strawhim's brother and Hickok's death avenged this murder, which allowed the court to set him free. But when this ruse was exposed, McCall was tried again and hung. Strawhim was a hard case who had been ordered out of Hays City, Kansas by vigilante committee leader A. B. Webster. On September 27, 1869 Strawhim and his buddies were on a drunken binge when they began to tear up a saloon. Hickok and a deputy came over to try to quiet things down, but Strawhim led a charge at the lawmen. Hickock shot him dead in the head and quelled the riot. (See also HICKOK, WILD BILL; MCCALL, BROKEN NOSE JACK.)

STREETS OF LAREDO   See COWBOY'S LAMENT, THE.

STUART, GRANVILLE   (b. Clarksburg (present-day West Virginia) on August 27, 1834; d. Montana on October 2, 1918)   Granville Stuart was one of the founders of and pioneers in Montana and is famous for his writings as well as his involvement with vigilante justice that ended cattle rustling in the Judith Basin. Granville and his older brother, James, moved first to Iowa and

then to Montana, where James is credited with starting the gold rush after he wrote to another brother, Thomas, who was prospecting in Colorado, and told him to come to Montana because there were gold nuggets aplenty. Word soon got around, prompting a stampede to Montana by gold miners. Granville and James were close, but Granville did not share his brother's thirst for gold or prospecting adventures. In 1867 Granville settled in Deer Lodge, where he opened a store and lumberyard and became involved in public affairs. Twice he was elected to the territorial council and was the president of this council in 1883.

Granville and James Stuart pioneered the cattle industry in Montana when they bought 60 head from settlers on the Oregon Trail in 1860; in 1879 they formed a partnership with three others to purchase 2,000 head of cattle in central Montana, and Stuart settled in the Judith Basin near present-day Lewistown. A number of cattle were lost to Indian raids and white rustlers, which prompted the organization of vigilante committees in 1883. Granville Stuart was the leader of this group, which attacked a group of rustlers on July 8, 1884 and killed about 16; although the merits of this activity have been debated, and justice may not have been perfectly served, the fact remains that it did pretty much eliminate major rustling in the area. The winter of 1886–87 virtually devastated the northern cattle industry, including Stuart's spread. In 1891 Stuart was appointed to the state land agency and in 1894 was named ambassador to Uruguay and Paraguay by President Grover Cleveland. He served in this capacity until 1899 and then moved back to Montana, where in 1904 he was named librarian of the Butte Public Library. Stuart wrote several important works about early Montana, including *Montana As It Is* (1865), *Diary and Sketchbook of a Journey to "America"* (1866) and *Forty Years on the Frontier* (2 vols; 1925).

SUBLETTE, WILLIAM LEWIS   (b. near Stanford, Kentucky on September 21, 1799; d. Pittsburgh, Pennsylvania on July 23, 1845)   The Sublette brothers—William, Milton, Solomon, Pinkney—were all engaged in the fur trade. William was a major partner in the Rocky Mountain Fur Company in the 1820s; he was part of the 1823 fur expedition led by William H. Ashley and led his own expedition in 1828. Sublette and partners Jedediah Smith and David Jackson were the first to take wagons to the Rocky Mountains. After selling the Rocky Mountain Fur Company, Sublette formed a fur trading company with Robert Campbell in December 1832, a few months after he was wounded in the fight at Pierre's Hole, and this company lasted until 1842. Sublette ran for Congress from Missouri after his fur-trapping days had ended.

SUGARFOOT   TV show that starred Will Hutchins as Tom "Sugarfoot" Brewster.

Tom Brewster was working on his law degree via correspondence courses while roaming the West for adventures. The cowboys he encountered quickly noted that Brewster was more despicable than a "tenderfoot";

Will Hutchins as Tom "Sugarfoot" Brewster

he was a "sugarfoot," as evidenced by the fact he ordered sarsaparilla in saloons. But though Brewster was naive, he did manage to help people out of jams, charm pretty girls with his boyishness and provide some legal help along the way. His chief nemesis was the Canary Kid—a character also played by actor Will Hutchins—who terrorized him from time to time. "Sugarfoot" was part of the Warner Brothers–produced trio of shows that included "Cheyenne" and "Bronco," and it alternated with "Cheyenne" from week to week from 1957 to 1959 and then with "Bronco" ((1959–60) before becoming part of a series that rotated with the "Cheyenne" series during the final season (1960–61). The show premiered on September 17, 1957 on Tuesday nights on ABC. In its final season (October 1960–July 1961) it was seen on Monday nights on ABC. Sixty-nine episodes of the hour-long show were filmed before its last telecast on July 3, 1961.

SUN DANCE There were different versions of the sun dance by the different Plains Indians tribes, but all involved secret rituals, fasting, self-torture and dancing for up to eight days. The term comes from the Sioux version because dancers stared at the sun during their ritual. The dance usually took place in the summer and involved wooden pins or skewers attached to the breast's muscles or skin; the pins were then attached by ropes to a pole, and participants pulled against the ropes (some hung from the poles) until their skin tore away. This ritual demonstrated physical endurance and induced visions.

SUDANCE KID, THE   (b. Harry Longabaugh in Mont Clare, Pennsylvania c. 1861; d. San Vicente, Bolivia in 1908)   Harry Longabaugh went west to Wyoming when he was a teenager and served time in the Sundance jail (August 1887–February 1889) for horse stealing, picking up his famous nickname. Sundance had been involved in a number of robberies (in Wyoming, Montana and South Dakota) before he met Butch Cassidy in Hole in the Wall country in 1900, when the outlaws had used Robbers' Roost as a hideout. The two ran into each other again at the Bar FS Ranch in Wyoming, and Sundance joined the Wild Bunch, a group of outlaws Cassidy was forming. The Wild Bunch pulled off a host of robberies, and Sundance was involved in all of them, including hauls from the Union Pacific train in Tipton, Wyoming, the First National Bank in Winnemucca, Nevada and the Great Northern train near Wagner, Montana. His girlfriend was Etta Place, a prostitute, and the two, along with Cassidy, went to South America in 1902, where they ranched for a while before returning to their outlaw ways. In 1907 Sundance took Etta to Denver after she had developed appendicitis, but he returned to South America and Cassidy, where the two worked for a mining company and robbed banks. In 1908 Cassidy and Sundance robbed a mule train on a jungle trail in Bolivia that had the company's payroll. The duo went into a restaurant to eat in San Vicente and tied the mules in the plaza; a local youth recognized the mules and contacted the police, who called in a cavalry troop camped outside town. Sundance and Cassidy found themselves surrounded, but Sundance shot the commander and the duo barricaded themselves inside the restaurant. Unfortunately, their rifles and ammunition were on the pack mules. Sundance made a mad dash across the plaza after dark to get the rifles and ammo but was severely wounded. Cassidy also received wounds when he pulled Sundance inside. Cassidy supposedly put a bullet in Sundance's head before he escaped into the night. Although Sundance probably died in Bolivia during this siege, another story says he returned to the United States and that Longabaugh actually died on August 28, 1957 in Casper, Wyoming. (See also CASSIDY, BUTCH.)

SUTTER, JOHN   (b. Johann August Suter in Germany in February 1803; d. Lititz, Pennsylvania on June 18, 1880)   Sutter is famous because it was on his California property that gold was discovered in 1849, precipitating the gold rush. Sutter immigrated to America in 1834 and settled in the Sacramento Valley near the confluence of the Sacramento and American Rivers. At this time this area was part of Mexico, and the Mexican government granted him a large tract of land, where he constructed Sutter's Fort in 1841 and established Neuva Helvetia (New Switzerland), a pioneer colony, which later became the city of Sacramento. When John Marshall discovered gold at a sawmill being constructed for Sutter in January 1848, Sutter made him swear to secrecy, fearing a resulting gold rush would ruin him. The secret was soon out and the gold rush did indeed ruin him. California became a U.S. territory nine days after the gold was discovered, a result of the Mexican War, and consequently Sutter's title was quickly disputed. Because he could not protect his land, it was overrun by prospectors and others; by 1852 the once prosperous Sutter was bankrupt. After years of appealing to state and federal authorities, he was finally given a pension of $250 a month in 1864 by the California legislature. This pension ended in 1878 and Suter died two years later.

SUTTON, WILLIAM E. (b. Fayette County, Texas on October 20, 1846; d. Indianola, Texas on March 11, 1874) One of the principals in the Sutton-Taylor feud, Sutton led a band of "Regulators" that included Shanghai Pierce, Old Joe Tumblinson and Jack Helm. On the side of the Taylors were the Clements brothers and their cousin, John Wesley Hardin. There were a number of bloody confrontations between the two clans before Bill Sutton and Jim Taylor were both killed. Sutton had killed Charley Taylor for stealing horses and then, on Christmas Eve, 1868 in Clinton, Texas, had killed Buck Taylor and Dick Chisholm, which caused the feud to explode. Bill Sutton was finally killed on March 11, 1874 in Indianola, Texas after he had boarded a steamboat bound for New Orleans with his young wife and child. Jim and Bill Taylor came up, opened fire on Sutton and put slugs into his head and heart while the young wife watched in horror. (See also SUTTON-TAYLOR FEUD.)

SUTTON-TAYLOR FEUD The Sutton-Taylor feud actually started in the Carolinas 20 years before the two families became neighbors in DeWitt County, Texas in the 1860s. William E. Sutton killed Charley Taylor for stealing horses and then, on Christmas Eve, 1868, killed Buck Taylor and a buddy, Dick Chisholm. The feud finally ended on March 11, 1874 when William E. Sutton and Gabriel Slaughter were killed by James and William Taylor on a steamboat getting ready to sail for New Orleans. This conflict lasted over five years, killed more than 40 men and involved over 400 people, including such Old West notables as John Wesley Hardin, Shanghai Pierce and Jack Helm. (See also HARDIN, JOHN WESLEY; HELM, JACK; SUTTON, WILLIAM E.; TAYLOR, BILL; TAYLOR, DOBOY; TAYLOR, JIM.)

SWAMP FOX, THE TV show that starred Leslie Nielsen as Francis Marion (the Swamp Fox) and Myron Healey as Major Horrey.

This was part of "Walt Disney Presents" and one of that series' best efforts. Based on the real-life exploits of Colonel Francis Marion during the Revolutionary War, these eight episodes dealt with one of America's first guerrilla fighters, a man who pulled together some fellow fighters and harassed British general Cornwallis and his army in the South around Charleston, South Carolina. Marion was successful in terrorizing the British, hitting them by surprise and quickly escaping into the swamps, and it distracted the invaders from their mission and allowed the Continental army to regroup and have some breathing room before the final encounter in Yorktown, Virginia. The show appeared in fall 1960.

SWING RIDERS The cowboys who rode behind the point men and in front of the flank riders on a trail drive.

T

TAILING To ride up behind the left side of a cow, grab the tail and veer off to the left so the cow is pulled to the ground. Sometimes the cow's tail would be looped around the saddle horn, and sometimes the cowboy would take his foot out of the saddle and use his leg to pull the cow down. This maneuver could be used for throwing cattle for branding but was usually a sport and leisure activity, although it could hurt a cow badly. Cowboys could also be injured if pulled from their saddle.

TALBOT, JIM (b. James D. Sherman; d. Ukiah, California in August 1896) Talbot killed former Caldwell, Kansas marshal Mike Meagher on December 17, 1881 after a heavy drinking spree with a bunch of other cowboys. A mob of citizens shot one of the cowboys dead on the street, but the rest made it out of town into Indian Territory, where they hid in a dugout. When the posse found them, the fugitives killed one of the posse members and then escaped after dark. Talbot moved to California and lived free for 14 years but in 1895 went back to Kansas to stand trial for Meagher's murder. Talbot was acquitted of the murder and returned to California, where he discovered his wife had taken a lover. In August 1896 Talbot was ambushed by an assassin with a shotgun as Talbot came up to his house. Talbot was probably killed by his wife's lover, although some say John Meagher killed him to avenge his brother's death. (See also MEAGHER, MICHAEL.)

TALES OF THE TEXAS RANGERS   TV show that starred Willard Parker as Ranger Jace Pearson and Harry Lauter as Ranger Clay Morgan.

This show premiered on December 22, 1958 on Monday nights on ABC and finished its prime-time run on May 25, 1959. The show had originally been a radio series with Ranger Pearson played by Joel McCrea. When it moved to television, it was first a daytime show, appearing on CBS on Saturday afternoons from September 1955 until May 1957, when it moved to Sunday afternoons on the ABC network. It stayed on ABC's afternoon schedule from September 1957 until June 1958, when it moved to Thursday afternoons on the same network before switching to prime time. The show was unusual in that the setting alternated between the Old West around 1830 and the contemporary West, with the Rangers riding horses one week and driving autos the next. This was an attempt to show the history of the Rangers as well as give a new "twist" to the numerous westerns competing for viewers in the late 1950s.

TALES OF WELLS FARGO   TV show that starred Dale Robertson as Jim Hardie, Jack Ging as Beau McCloud (1961–62), William Demarest as Jeb Gaine (1961–62), Virginia Christine as Ovie (1961–62), Mary Jane Saunders as Mary Gee (1961–62), and Lory Patrick as Tina (1961–62).

This show was set in the gold rush days of the 1850s, and the story line consisted of trying to get the Wells Fargo stage line running despite a series of obstacles, including outlaws, natural disasters and guileful women. This job fell to Wells Fargo detective Jim Hardie, who, on his horse Jubilee, rode in all of the 167 episodes from March 18, 1957, when the program premiered on the NBC network on Monday nights, until the last show on September 8, 1962, still on the NBC network but now telecast on Saturday evenings. The show began as a pilot for the "Schlitz Playhouse" on December 14, 1956. Originally a 30-minute show, it beat out the Arthur Godfrey Talent Scouts Show on its first evening and eventually became the number two rated show on TV during its first years, behind the venerable "Gunsmoke." Robertson had originally been approached by producer Nat Holt and writer Frank Gruber with a script in 1955 but had turned them down. First, he had a chance to be Perry Mason and was also in contention for an aviation series; second, he felt there were already too many westerns on TV. However, a few months later he agreed to do the show.

Robertson was one of the few left-handed gunslingers on TV. During the last season, his character, Jim Hardie, owned a ranch outside San Francisco; the ranch next to his was owned by Widow Ovie and her two daughters, Mary Gee and Tina. The show was produced by Overland Productions and Revue Productions, which was the TV division of Universal.

TALIAFERRO, HAL   See WALES, WALLY.

TALL MAN, THE   TV show that starred Clu Gulager as Billy the Kid and Barry Sullivan as Deputy Sheriff Pat Garrett.t

The real Pat Garrett was a lawman; he knew Billy the Kid and was, in fact, friends of sorts with the outlaw. But the real Pat Garrett eventually killed the real Billy the Kid— shot him in the dark, as a matter of fact. However, this final showdown between these two was not part of this series, which featured the honest, forthright Pat Garrett befriending the young, impetuous, hotheaded Billy with overtones of an imminent showdown in the making. Set in Lincoln County in New Mexico Territory in the 1870s, the series premiered on September 10, 1960 on Saturday night on NBC. The 30-minute show finished its run in the same time slot on the same network on September 1, 1962.

TAPADEROS   Also call taps, a covering for a stirrup, usually made of leather, which protected a man's feet when riding through brush country. Attached to the front of the stirrup, it also prevented a man's foot from going all the way through a stirrup.

TARP   Short for tarpaulin, a water-resistant covering used on the back of a chuck wagon as a windbreaker and shelter. It was also used underneath bedrolls for protection against the damp ground and as a cover against rain.

TATE   TV show that starred David McLean as Tate.

Tate's left arm had been shot up and rendered useless at Vicksburg during the Civil War. He'd lost his wife and child during the war as well. Unable to find respectable work because of his crippled arm—encased on a black leather rawhide casing stitched from his fingertips to above his elbow—he became a gunslinger, to be hired by anyone needing his services. A summer replacement for the second half hour of "The Perry Como Show," the series debuted on June 8, 1960 on NBC on Wednesday nights and ended on September 28, 1960. The show was created by Harry Julian Fink, a western screenwriter who was formerly a New York tuxedo salesman and camera store clerk, and based loosely on a Gerte opera, *The Man with the Silver Arm*.

TAYLOR, BILL   (b. ?; d. ?)   Bill Taylor became a major player in the Sutton-Taylor feud in DeWitt County, Texas on April 1, 1873 after his father, Pitkin Taylor, died from gun wounds suffered about six months before. Jim was the leader of the Taylor family, but Bill played an important part in the feud, and the two brothers were together when Jim killed Old Man Sutton in front of his young wife and child aboard a steamboat. Later, Bill was thrown into jail for the killing, but on September 15, 1875 a storm hit and Bill escaped during the turmoil, although he reportedly rescued several people from the Gulf coastal waters before fleeing. Bill Taylor was supposedly killed in Indian Territory while serving as a law officer. (See also SUTTON-TAYLOR FEUD.)

TAYLOR, BUCK   (b. William Levi Taylor in Fredericksburg, Texas in November 1857; d. Downingtown, Pennsylvania in 1924)   Buck Taylor was the first to really bring "glamour" to the image of the cowboy. Billed as the "King of the Cowboys" in Buffalo Bill's Wild West show, he was the model for the hero in novels by Prentiss Ingraham beginning in the late 1880s. Taylor had worked for Cody at the entertainer's Nebraska ranch before he joined the show. In 1887 Taylor broke his leg in London; in 1890 he bought a ranch in the Sweetwater Valley of Wyoming. Taylor organized his own Wild West show but it failed in 1894.

TAYLOR, DOBOY (b. Phillip Taylor; d. Kerrville, Texas in November 1871) The Sutton-Taylor feud began with the Taylor brothers, Creed, Pitkin, William, Josiah and Rufus. But it was their sons who fought the bloodiest parts of this feud with the Suttons. Doboy was the son of Creed Taylor, a veteran of the Texas Revolution. Doboy's brother, Hays, had been killed on August 23, 1869 by a group of Sutton "Regulators" led by Jack Helm. Ironically, Doboy was not killed in the Sutton-Taylor feud but by a man named Sim Holstein, who had a job Doboy wanted. Taylor attempted to kill Holstein but was killed instead after being shot four times. Taylor died cursing Holstein six hours after being wounded. (See also SUTTON-TAYLOR FEUD.)

TAYLOR, DUB "CANNONBALL" (b. Walter Taylor in Richmond, Virginia in 1908) Dub Taylor was a popular comic sidekick in westerns, specializing in a slapstick style of comedy. A musician (xylophone and harmonica), Taylor grew up in Oklahoma City and played the vaudeville circuit before he went to Hollywood, where his first movie role was in *You Can't Take It with You* (1938). His first western series was with Wild Bill Elliott in 1939–41; he then appeared in nine films with Tex Ritter (1942–44) and starred in a Charles Starrett series before appearing with Jimmy Wakely in a singing-cowboy series of 15 films (1947–49). Taylor appeared in the TV series "Casey Jones" and "Please Don't Eat the Daisies" and in the movies *Bonnie and Clyde* (1967), *A Man Called Horse* (1970), *Support Your Local Gunfighter* (1971) and *The Hallelujah Trail* (1967). Taylor also starred in Hubba-Bubby Bubblegum and Ryder Truck commercials. Taylor became known as "Cannonball" in *Taming of the West* (1939) in the Wild Bill Elliott series.

TAYLOR, JIM (b. Texas in 1852; d. Clinton, Texas on December 27, 1875) Jim's father, Pitkin Taylor, was gunned down outside his home by some ambushers from the Sutton clan in summer 1872 and died from his wounds about six months later. This incident ignited the Sutton-Taylor feud, and brothers Jim and Bill Taylor, along with other relatives, vowed revenge on Old Bill Sutton. Jim Taylor killed three Sutton men, including lawman Jack Helm, and twice tried to kill Bill Sutton during the following two months. Wiley Pridge, a Taylor ally, was killed at the end of 1873, and the Taylors and Suttons squared off in Cuero for a day and night. On March 11, 1874 Jim Taylor finally managed to kill Bill Sutton, gunning him down in front of his young wife and child aboard a steamboat bound for New Orleans. The Suttons lynched Scrap Taylor, Jim White and Kute Tuggle on June 20, 1874 in Clinton as retaliation. Bill Taylor was caught and put in the Indianola jail but escaped. The Suttons' new leader, Rube Brown, marshal of Cuero, was assassinated. The feud subsided and finally petered out on December 27, 1875 when Jim Taylor was killed by a Sutton posse in Clinton, Texas. (See also SUTTON-TAYLOR FEUD.)

TAYLOR-SUTTON FEUD See SUTTON-TAYLOR FEUD.

TEEPEE See TIPI.

TELEVISION WESTERNS When television was introduced to the American public in 1946, the networks had sporadic programming; no one was sure if people would watch TV in the morning or during the day, so there was virtually no daytime programming. And there was limited viewing in the evenings. Still, westerns played an important part in the first programming. In the first prime-time schedules of 1946 a "western movie" was featured on Sunday evenings at 8 on the DuMont network; the next year the "western movie" appeared on Tuesday evenings at 8. Many of these "movies" were the "B" westerns produced by Republic in the 1940s. At this point, radio was still the dominant broadcast medium, and the networks had not yet committed themselves fully to television. But beginning in 1948, four networks

Dub "Cannonball" Taylor

began programming in prime time: ABC, NBC, CBS and DuMont. During this year western movies were seen occasionally, but TV had not yet really caught on in America: There were only 325,000 home sets in use in 1948.

In 1949 "Hopalong Cassidy" and "The Lone Ranger" became regular network programs (although old Hopalong Cassidy movies were shown regularly on TV the previous year). These were the first two regularly scheduled network westerns, and they were popular; during the 1950–51 season "The Lone Ranger" was rated seventh and "Hopalong Cassidy" ninth in the overall ratings.

Television caught on with the American public in 1950–51. In 1950, sales of televisions leaped to 3.8 million, which meant that 9% of American homes had one; in 1951 that figure jumped to 10.3 million homes, or 23.5% of the American households with a television set. Clearly, the age of radio was fading quickly and the era of TV was coming on strong.

In 1951 Gene Autry began his regular network TV series on Sunday nights at 7, but during the 1951–53 period there were only two westerns on network prime time: "The Gene Autry Show" and "The Lone Ranger." In 1953 "Sky King" was added, and in 1954 "The Adventures of Rin Tin Tin" became part of regular prime-time network programming.

Television westerns began to blossom in 1955 when "Gunsmoke" and "The Life and Legend of Wyatt Earp" were introduced; they joined other westerns—"The Lone Ranger," "Sergeant Preston of the Yukon," "The Adventures of Rin Tin Tin" and "The Gene Autry Show"—on regular network programming. In 1956 "Broken Arrow," "The Adventures of Jim Bowie," "My Friend Flicka" and "Dick Powell's Zane Grey Theater" were added. The top western shows during the 1956–57 season were "Gunsmoke," which finished seventh, and "The Life and Legend of Wyatt Earp," which finished at 18 in the overall TV ratings.

The heyday for the network television westerns in prime time began in 1957–58; during this season the overall TV ratings showed "Gunsmoke" at number one, "Tales of Wells Fargo" at three, "Have Gun, Will Travel" at four; "The Life and Legend of Wyatt Earp" at six; "The Restless Gun" at eight; "Cheyenne" at 12; "Dick Powell's Zane Grey Theater" at 21; and "Wagon Train" and "Sugarfoot" tied at number 23. Clearly, the western began to dominate TV during the 1957–58 season. During this season, "Maverick" was on Sunday nights; "Restless Gun" and "Tales of Wells Fargo" on Mondays; "Cheyenne"/"Sugarfoot" (they alternated), "The Life and Legend of Wyatt Earp," "Broken Arrow" and "The Californian" on Tuesday nights. On Wednesdays there was "Wagon Train" and "Tombstone Territory"; "Zorro" and "Sergeant Preston" were on Thursdays; on Friday nights there was "The Adventures of Rin Tin Tin," "Adventures of Jim Bowie," "Colt .45" and "Dick Powell's Zane Grey Theater." Finishing the week on Saturday nights was "Have Gun, Will Travel," followed by "Gunsmoke."

The success of television westerns continued during the 1958 season, when, in the overall ratings, "Gunsmoke" was number one; "Wagon Train" was two; "Have Gun, Will Travel" was three; "The Rifleman" was four; "Maverick" was six; "Tales of Wells Fargo" was seven; "The Life and Legend of Wyatt Earp" was 10; "Dick Powell's Zane Grey Theater" was 13; "The Texan" was 15; "Wanted: Dead or Alive" was 16; "Cheyenne" was 18; and "Sugarfoot" finished at number 21.

There was a veritable feast of westerns on the tube this year: On Sundays there was "Maverick," "The Lawman," "Colt .45" and "Northwest Passage" (a "western" in terms of the Revolutionary War). On Mondays there was "The Texan," "Restless Gun" and "Tales of Wells Fargo"; on Tuesdays, "Cheyenne"/"Sugarfoot," "Wyatt Earp," "The Rifleman," and "The Californians." On Wednesdays there was "Wagon Train" and "Bat Masterson"; on Thursdays there was "Zorro," "Rough Riders," "Yancy Derringer" and "Dick Powell's Zane Grey Theater." On Fridays there was "Rin Tin Tin" and "Buckskin," and the week closed on Saturday night with "Wanted: Dead or Alive," "Cimarron City," "Have Gun, Will Travel" and "Gunsmoke."

In 1959, westerns on the networks in prime time included "Colt .45," "Maverick," "The Lawman," "The Rebel," "The Alaskans," "Riverboat," "Cheyenne," "The Texan," "Tales of Wells Fargo," "Sugarfoot"/"Bronco," "Life and Legend of Wyatt Earp," "The Rifleman," "Laramie," "Wagon Train," "Johnny Ringo," "Dick Powell's Zane Grey Theater," "Law of the Plainsman," "Bat Masterson," "Black Saddle," "Rawhide," "Hotel de Paree," "Wanted: Dead or Alive," "Have Gun, Will Travel," "Gunsmoke" and "Bonanza." During the 1959–60 TV season, in overall TV ratings "Gunsmoke" and "Wagon Train" were tied at two; "Have Gun, Will Travel" was three; "Wanted: Dead or Alive" was nine; "The Rifleman" was 13; "The Lawman" was 15; "Cheyenne" was 17; "Rawhide" was 18; "Wyatt Earp" was 20; and the "Zane Grey Theater" was 21.

During the 1960–61 season and the 1961–62 season, western shows took the top three spots in the overall ratings: "Gunsmoke," "Wagon Train" and "Have Gun, Will Travel" in 1960–61, and "Wagon Train," "Bonanza" and "Rawhide" in 1961-62. In addition, "Rawhide" and "Bonanza" finished in the top 20 in 1960–61, and "Rawhide" finished in the top 20 in 1961–62. In the 1962–63 season no western finished in the top three, but "Bonanza" finished fourth, "Gunsmoke" was 10th, "Rawhide" was 22d and "Wagon Train" was 25th. This is significant because the 1962–63 season marked the end of the heyday for the TV western, although one western ("Bonanza") would consistently be rated at number one or in the top 10 throughout the 1960s. However, beginning in 1963 a handful of westerns dominated the genre; fewer new ones were introduced until the 1980s, when the western virtually disappeared from television as a prime-time series.

The period 1955–63 was the era of the TV western, but the network shows were only part of that. In addition to the network fare, there were syndicated shows such as "The Cisco Kid," "Annie Oakley," "Tales of the Texas Rangers," "The Sheriff of Cochise," "The Range Rider,"

"Buffalo Bill, Jr.," "The Adventures of Champion," "Pony Express," "Union Pacific," "Brave Eagle" and numerous others. Perhaps the key to understanding the influence and success of TV westerns during this time period is to look at the westerns that appeared on Saturday morning TV. This list includes "Acrobat Ranch," "Adventures of Champion," "Adventures of Kit Carson," "Rin Tin Tin," "Annie Oakley," "Broken Arrow," "Buffalo Bill Jr.," "The Cisco Kid," "Cowboy Theater (old western moves)," "Fury," "Gene Autry Show," "Howdy Doody," "Hopalong Cassidy," "Junior Rodeo," "Lash of the West," "The Lone Ranger," "Red Ryder," "The Rough Riders," "The Roy Rogers Show," "Sergeant Preston of the Yukon," "Steve Donovan, Western Ranger," "Tales of the Texas Rangers," "Tim McCoy," "Wild Bill Hickok" and "Yancy Derringer." Although some of these shows were also shown in prime time on the networks or on independent stations, the fact that all of these shows appeared on Saturday mornings indicates their appeal to kids. Children are a key to understanding the appeal of TV westerns.

In the 1930s and 1940s kids went to the theaters on Saturdays to watch a series of movies: serials, features and "B" movies. In the 1950s, kids watched television. The westerns were not the only shows on television—there were action/adventure shows as well—but the Saturday morning TV fare was actually an extension of the Saturday movie-watching habits for most Americans. The westerns that attracted these younger viewers were escapist fare, so the westerns that emerged were filled with clear delineations of good guys versus bad guys, lots of action (horse chases, fights and shooting), little realistic violence and handsome (or pretty) stars who looked like heroes. In short, the Saturday morning western (indeed, the TV western of the 1955–63 period) was about heroes and role models, or in terms of Hollywood, "stars." And such "stars" as the Lone Ranger, Gene Autry, Wild Bill Hickok, Red Ryder, Roy Rogers, Fury, Rin Tin Tin and others became heroes to these young children.

The 1963–70 period saw a handful of westerns dominate the genre, specifically "Bonanza," "Gunsmoke," "The Virginian" and "Rawhide." High-quality westerns consistently did well: Bonanza finished either first or second in overall ratings from 1963 to 1967; during the 1967–68 season it dropped to fourth. Other top-rated shows during this period included "The Virginian," "Gunsmoke," "Branded," "Daniel Boone" and "Wild, Wild West." Other westerns had been introduced: "Kentucky Jones," "Legend of Jesse James," "A Man Called Shenandoah," "The Big Valley," "Laredo," "Iron Horse," "Road West," "The Monroes," "Pistols 'n' Petticoats," "Shane," "Daniel Boone," "Cowboy in Africa," "Legend of Custer," "Cimarron Strip," "Hondo," and "Guns of Will Sonnett," but none achieved the lasting success of "Bonanza" or "Gunsmoke."

The 1967–68 season was the last one in which viewers could watch a TV western on the networks during prime time almost every single night of the week: On Sundays there was "Bonanza" and "High Chaparral" on Mondays there was "Cowboy in Africa," "The Big Valley"

and "Gunsmoke"; on Wednesdays there was "Legend of Custer" and "The Virginian"; on Thursdays there was "Cimarron Strip" and "Daniel Boone"; on Fridays three was "Hondo," "Guns of Will Sonnett" and "Wild Wild West" and on Saturdays there was "Iron Horse." Only on Tuesdays did the western fan have to go to bed unfulfilled with his nightly dose of shoot-'em-ups.

During the 1968–69 season there were six westerns on the networks during prime time, and four of them finished high in the ratings: "Bonanza" finished at three; "Gunsmoke" at six; "The Virginian" at 17; and "Daniel Boone" at 21; only "Lancer" and "High Chaparral" did not score high in the ratings. During the 1969–70 season "Gunsmoke" finished second and "Bonanza" third in the overall ratings, but they were almost the only westerns on network TV during prime time. The only other network western series were "Men from Shiloh" and "High Chaparral."

The 1970s were dominated by a few western series, but these were high quality and did well in the ratings. "Bonanza" and "Gunsmoke" dominated the genre until "Little House on the Prairie" was introduced in 1974; after this point, "Little House" would be the top-rated western on TV. In fact, during the 1975–76 season, "Little House on the Prairie" was the only western TV series on the networks during prime time. For the rest of the 1970s, few westerns were introduced by the networks on prime time, and none survived.

The western was not totally absent from TV during the 1963–80 period; the weekly network TV series was basically replaced by the "made-for-TV" western movie. There were made-for-TV western movies before 1964 (see LONE RANGER TELEVISION MOVIES), but that was the year the genre found its major TV outlet with such shows as "The Pathfinder and the Mohican" and "The Redman and the Renegades." Made-for-TV westerns began with "Scalplock" (1966); after this offering, over 160 western movies were made for TV, about half the number made for movie theaters during the 1965–90 period. A significant year was 1976, when the United States celebrated its 200th birthday; that year a number of westerns were made for TV: "The Oregon Trail," "The Macahans," "Young Pioneers," "Law of the Land," "Banjo Hackett: Roamin' Free," "The Quest," "The Call of the Wild," "The New Daughters of Joshua Cabe," "The Invasion of Johnson County," "Bridger," "Wanted: The Sundance Woman" and "Young Pioneers' Christmas."

There was an attempt to bring the western back to prime-time network TV in the 1980–81 season; shows on the air were "Little House on the Prairie," "Father Murphy," "Bret Maverick" and "Best of the West." In the 1981–82 season "Seven Brides for Seven Brothers" (in an updated contemporary version of the old western movie) was added while "Best of the West" and "Bret Maverick" were dropped. Except for "Little House on the Prairie," which did consistently well, westerns did not seem to fit the 1980s as a network series during prime time. Still, a number of made-for-TV western movies aired throughout the 1980s. It would not be until the end of the 1980s that Hollywood again began to develop quality westerns for prime time on network TV. In 1988

"Paradise" (later renamed "Guns of Paradise") was introduced, and in 1989 "Young Riders" debuted. Both of these shows confronted network executives with the major dilemma of TV westerns: They do not do well in major urban areas, especially the big ratings markets of New York and Los Angeles, but they do extremely well throughout the rest of the country. Then, in the 1990s, the western seemed to find new life. Led by the movie success of "Dances with Wolves" and "Unforgiven," CBS successfully introduced "Dr. Quinn, Medicine Woman."

Through the years television audiences had never lost their love for quality western series, even though some TV executives thought them passe; in the 1990s a number of old westerns, such as "Gunsmoke," "Bonanza," "Wagon Train," "Rin Tin Tin," "The Rifleman" and others, were doing well in syndication or on cable TV stations. Indeed, it seems that cable TV rescued the western series and did a great service for western fans by proving that there's always a demand for high-quality western TV series.

TEMPLE HOUSTON   TV show that starred Jeffrey Hunter as Temple Houston and Jack Elam as George Taggart.

The real Temple Houston was an attorney and the son of Sam Houston, just like the TV Temple Houston. In the TV series Houston traveled around the circuit court in the 1880s with George Taggart, a gnarled old gunfighter who sometimes sided with those the attorney was trying to convict. Executive producer for the show was Jack Webb of "Dragnet" fame. The show ran one season—26 episodes; and the first telecast was September 19, 1963 on Thursday night on NBC. The last telecast for the hour-long show was September 10, 1964.

TENDERFOOT   A greenhorn, pilgrim or Easterner un-schooled in the ways of the West. The term probably was originally applied to Eastern cattle, whose feet were more tender than the feral Longhorns. Later it was applied to humans.

TENDERLOIN   Refers to beef, but by extension the term was used by cowboys for prostitutes or, sometimes, young females in general.

TEN-GALLON HAT   Usually a Stetson, but always a cowboy hat with a high crown and wide brim. Originally created for Buffalo Bill Cody, who wanted a larger-than-life hat for his show, the hat could not really hold 10 gallons.

TERHUNE, MAX   (aka "Lullabye"; b. Robert Max Terhune in Franklin, Indiana on February 12, 1891; d. Cottonwood, Arizona on June 5, 1973)   Terhune was a ventriloquist who started in Chicago on WLS, where he met Gene Autry and Smiley Burnette on the National Barn Dance. A former baseball player in the American Association and later a performer on the vaudeville circuit and with the Hoosier Hot Shots, Terhune was brought to Hollywood by Autry, and his first film was *Ride, Ranger, Ride* (1936) with Autry and Burnette. Terhune then starred in *The Three Mesquiteers* with

Max Terhune and dummy

Robert Livingston and Ray "Crash" Corrigan when he replaced Syd Saylor from the original series; he would make 21 films with the Mesquiteers. He starred in a series with John Wayne and then in The Range Busters series, in which he played the character "Alibi" (his Mesquiteers character was "Lullabye"). Terhune's dummy was "Elmer Sneezewood" (it was "Skully Null" on the vaudeville circuit). Terhune starred in some movies with Johnny Mack Brown and then appeared in *Giant, Gunfight at the O.K. Corral,* and *Rawhide.*

TEWKSBURY, EDWIN   (b. perhaps in Humboldt County, California c. 1852; d. Globe, Arizona on April 4, 1904)   Ed Tewksbury was involved in the Graham-Tewksbury feud, or Pleasant Valley War. He was the son of John D. Tewksbury and the brother of James and John, Jr. The Tewksburys were sheep ranchers when the feud began in 1887. The feud had supposedly ended by 1892, but on August 2 of that year John Graham was killed while he drove a load of grain into Tempe. Before he died, Graham implicated Ed Tewksbury and John Rhodes in the shooting, and both men were arrested. Ed was in jail two and a half years before he was acquitted in 1896. He later served as a constable of Globe, Arizona and deputy sheriff of Gila County, where he died in 1904. (See also PLEASANT VALLEY WAR.)

TEWKSBURY, JIM   (b. Humboldt County, California; d. Globe, Arizona on December 4, 1888)   Involved in the Graham-Tewksbury feud, Jim survived the gun battles but died of consumption at his sister's home in 1888. He went to Globe, Arizona with his family in 1879 and settled in Pleasant Valley and obtained work with the Grahams, which he resigned after learning of their rustling activities. (See also PLEASANT VALLEY WAR.)

TEWKSBURY-GRAHAM FEUD   See PLEASANT VALLEY WAR.

TEXAN, THE   TV show that starred Rory Calhoun as Bill Longley.

Heck Thomas *(Oklahoma Historical Society)*

Bill Longley was a real person in the Old West, although not the roving lawman destined to do right in the guise of actor Rory Calhoun. Somehow, the discrepancies were glossed over, and the series never showed the real Bill Longley's death, which was by hanging. The show premiered on September 29, 1958 on CBS on Monday nights. It ended its run in the same time slot on September 12, 1960 after 78 half-hour episodes, all filmed in black and white.

TEXAS CATTLE TRAIL   See WESTERN TRAIL, THE.

TEXAS FEVER   A sickness in cattle that caused death. The origin of the sickness was longhorns from Texas; when driven into Missouri and Kansas, they caused the native stock to become infected. Later, it was discovered that the disease was spread by the Texas tick, to which the longhorns were immune but which infected other cattle by sucking infected blood from longhorns and depositing it in other cattle. Texas fever created problems for cattle drivers before the Civil War when Kansas farmers attempted to stop cattle drives into their state. In Missouri, state laws were passed in 1866—and grievances date from 1859—because Texas fever was decimating local herds. Kansas vigilantes had formed as early as 1855 to stop Texas cattle drives, which led to some ugly armed conflicts. The quarantine statutes were enacted in 1866 to forbid Texas cattle in eastern Kansas, resulting in the emergence of western Kansas towns such as Dodge City becoming cattle towns for a while. (See also QUARANTINE LINE.)

TEXAS JOHN SLAUGHTER   See WALT DISNEY PRESENTS.

TEXAS-MONTANA TRAIL   During the period 1866–96 a number of Texas cattle were driven north to Wyoming and Montana to supply those ranges with beef. The Texas-Montana Trail began in southern Texas and took a northwestern course across the Red River through Indian Territory, to Dodge City and Ogallala, Nebraska, then west to the Judith Basin and Blackfoot Agency in northwestern Montana. A branch of the trail headed north to Fort Robinson and Deadwood and then west along the Belle Fourche River until it connected to the main trail. Beginning in 1884 the northern trails from south Texas were blocked with barbed wire at the Oklahoma border by Cherokee Strip cattlemen, and in 1885 Kansas closed its borders to Texas cattle because of Texas fever carried by longhorns. This meant that after this time drovers had to go west on the Red River past Doan's store to a point south of the Kansas-Oklahoma-Colorado boundary and then up the Neutral Strip ("No Man's Land") into Colorado, where the trail led north and entered Wyoming through Pine Bluffs. In northeastern Wyoming the trail branched off to the Dakotas, Montana and the Canadian border. This 1,700-mile trail was also known as the Montana Trail.

TEXAS RANGERS   The first "rangers" in Texas were formed by Stephen Austin, who put 20–30 men in charge of protecting settlers against Indians and Mexicans. The Texas Rangers were officially created in 1835 by a resolution; these 25 men were charged with guarding the frontier between the Brazos and Trinity Rivers and protecting settlers. This group was loosely organized; they had no uniforms and no flag and furnished their own horses and arms. A major problem was protecting settlers against Indians. During the 1836–45 period when Texas first became a republic and established itself as a nation, the Texas Rangers were the most important military force in Texas. At this time Rangers such as Ben McCulloch, "Big Foot" Wallace and John Coffee Hays became prominent. The Rangers also played a key role in the Mexican War (1846–48), but after statehood, the Rangers' role decreased until after the Civil War, when they were revived again as settlers streamed into Texas. The Rangers had to guard the border with Mexico and fight Indians, cattle thieves, robbers, outlaws and others who threatened law and order in Texas. The Rangers played a major role in the capture of outlaws Sam Bass, King Fisher and John Wesley Hardin. The Texas Rangers are still part of Texas law enforcement, and since 1890, a staff of 62 Rangers have played a major role in criminal investigations in the state.

TEXAS RANGERS, THE   One of the oldest cowboy songs, it tells about a fight between the Rangers and Indians, although no specific date or battle is noted in the song. The lyrics first appeared in print in 1884 in a book by A. J. Sowell, who had joined the Texas Rangers in 1870. The melody may be traced back to "Nancy of Yarmouth," a British ballad, and the battle could have been a pre–Civil War battle near Fort Belknap on the Brazos River. Folklorist Myra E. Hull collected this song from a cowboy who said he heard it in 1876 in Colorado. It was widely circulated in 1891 when New York printer Henry J. Wehman published the lyrics after receiving them from Nelson Forsyth of Groesbeck, Texas.

TEXAS RODEO   TV show with Paul Crutchfield as commentator. This show was filmed at rodeos in Texas and the Southwest, with all the rodeo events shown as well as special events such as barrel racing and wild-cow milking. The show premiered on April 30, 1959 on Thursdays on NBC. The half-hour series ended on July 2, 1959.

THEY DIED WITH THEIR BOOTS ON   Film; executive producer, Hal B. Wallis; associate producer, Robert Fellows; directed by Raoul Walsh; screenplay by Wally Kine and Aeneas MacKenzie; music by Max Steiner; released in 1941 by Warner Brothers. Cast: Errol Flynn, Olivia De Havilland, Arthur Kennedy, Charley Grapewin, Gene Lockhart, Anthony Quinn, Stanley Ridges and John Litel.

The movie told the story of George Armstrong Custer from his West Point days until the Little Bighorn.

THOMAS, HECK   (b. Henry Andrew Thomas in Oxford, Georgia on January 6, 1850; d. Lawton, Oklahoma on August 11, 1912)   Heck Thomas was a lawman of the highest order; he did not work both sides of the law like so many others. He was one of the "Three Guardsmen" (with Bill Tilghman and Chris Madsen) who tamed Perry, Oklahoma, "Hell's Half Acre" that consisted of 110 saloons and 25,000 citizens. He had learned law enforcement in Fort Worth under Longhaired Jim Courtright after serving in the Civil War under Stonewall Jackson and working as a guard for the Texas Express Company. Thomas worked under the "hanging judge," Isaac Parker, in Fort Smith, Arkansas and covered the Indian Territory. Between 1893 and 1896 he arrested over 300 wanted men.

Thomas foiled the Sam Bass Gang's holdup attempt on March 18, 1878, when he hid $25,000 in a stove and put some decoy packages in the safe; the outlaws rode off with $89 in actual cash and the rest in fake money and false packages. In this robbery, Thomas was wounded. Thomas was instrumental in the near-capture of Ned Christie near Tahlequah in 1889. Thomas set the house on fire and hit the Indian with a shot, but Christie escaped and set up a new fort. Heck Thomas led the posse that intercepted Bill Doolin on August 25, 1896 in Lawson, Oklahoma as Doolin walked down a road on a moonlit night toward his father-in-law's ranch. Doolin tried to shoot his way out but was killed by buckshot from shotguns fired by Thomas and Bill

Dunn. Thomas helped trail and capture both the Doolin and Dalton Gangs.

The last job for Thomas was as chief of police in Lawton, Oklahoma, but he lost this post in 1909 because his health began to fail. Thomas died peacefully at the age of 62 three years later. (See also BASS, SAM; CHRISTIE, NED; PARKER, JUDGE ISAAC CHARLES; THREE GUARDSMEN, THE; TILGHMAN, BILL.)

THOMPSON, BEN   (b. Knottingley, England on November 11, 1842; d. San Antonio, Texas on March 11, 1884)   Ben Thompson owned the famous Bull's Head Saloon with Phil Coe in Abilene, where Wild Bill Hickok killed Coe. The problem centered on the bull's private parts, shown in the picture of the bull above the saloon. Some townsfolk found it offensive and wanted the parts removed; when Thompson and Coe refused, Wild Bill hired some men to paint the offending portion. Coe got upset, and that led to his fatal showdown with Wild Bill. Thompson was a gambler who drank heavily by the end of his life. He spent a good deal of time getting his brother, Billy, out of various scraps, usually after Billy had killed somebody. Ben Thompson's death may have been a revenge killing. Thompson had killed Jack Harris, one of the owners of the Vaudeville Theater and Gambling Saloon in San Antonio, on July 11, 1882. Harris had attempted to shoot Thompson through the window with a shotgun, but Thompson hit Harris instead and the saloon owner died later that night. Thompson went back to this home in Austin and resigned as marshal. Almost two years later, on March 11, 1884, Thompson had met up with King Fisher in Austin, and Thompson decided to catch a train with him back to San Antonio to see a play (Fisher was going to Uvalde, where he was deputy sheriff). After the play Thompson and Fisher went over to the Variety Theater, where Thompson had killed Harris, and ran into Billy Simms and Joe Foster Harris's two partners. In an upstairs box Thompson and Fisher, who had been drinking heavily all day, were with Simms, Foster, and bouncer Jacob Coy. The subject of the Harris killing came up and Fisher wanted to leave. But Thompson pushed on; he then slapped Foster and jammed a gun in his mouth. Suddenly shooting erupted and Thompson and Fisher soon lay dead. Fisher had never drawn his gun and Thompson had shot once, but their bodies had nine and 13 wounds, respectively. It was widely believed that some shots may have been fired by gambler Canada Bill, a bartender named McLaughlin and vaudevillian Harry Tremaine, who were in the next box, after being alerted by Foster. (See also COE, PHIL; FISHER, JOHN KING; HICKOK, WILD BILL; THOMPSON, TEXAS BILLY; WHITNEY, CAP.)

THOMPSON, TEXAS BILLY   (b. William Thompson in Knottingley, England c. 1845; d. Laredo, Texas c. 1888)   Texas Billy had some bad luck with women. One of his girlfiends, a prostitute named Emma Williams, took up with Wild Bill Hickok, and another, Molly Brennan, was later romanced by Bat Masterson and killed in a gunfight between Masterson and another suitor. Billy, the younger brother of Ben Thompson, ran into quite a bit of trouble during his time; the worst was when he killed his good friend Ellsworth sheriff Cap Whitney with a shotgun while drunk. This incident happened on August 15, 1873 when Billy tried to help his brother, Ben, who had been challenged by some armed gamblers during a card game. Whitman and brother Ben were trying to convince Billy to put the shotgun away—it had already gone off accidentally once and nearly hit two bystanders—but the two gamblers appeared and a gunfight started. Sheriff Whitney ran to the door; the drunk Billy ran behind him and then let loose a blast that killed Whitney. The night Ben was killed in San Antonio, Billy was just a few doors away but, since he was unarmed, did nothing. Very little is known of Texas Billy's final years, although some say he was killed in Laredo sometime around 1888. (See also MORCO, HAPPY JACK; THOMPSON, BEN; WHITNEY, CAP.)

THREE-CARD MONTE See MONTE.

THREE GUARDSMEN, THE
These were three lawmen—Chris Madsen, Heck Thomas and Bill Tilghman—who worked in Oklahoma (Indian Territory) at the end of the 19th century and beginning of 20th centuries and helped bring law and order to the area. (See also MADSEN, CHRISTIAN; THOMAS, HECK; TILGHMAN, BILL.)

TIBBS, CASEY
(b. near Fort Pierre, South Dakota on March 5, 1929; d. Ramona, California on January 28, 1990)   In front of the Rodeo Hall of Fame in Colorado Springs is a larger than life bronze statue called *The Champ*, a cowboy riding a bucking bronc. The cowboy is Casey Tibbs on Necktie. Tibbs was the most famous bronco rider of all time, the "Babe Ruth" of rodeo who brought attention to the sport through his own fame. Tibbs grew up on a ranch in South Dakota and entered his first rodeo before he was 14; when he was 20, he won his first saddle bronc championship. During his rodeo career, Tibbs won six saddle bronc championships (1949, 1951– 1959), two All-Around Cowboy championships (1951 and 1955), and one bareback riding championship (1955).

Tibbs was a colorful personality in rodeo; he was featured in a *Life* magazine cover story in 1951, and fans knew him for his love of purple: He wore purple shirts, rode in a purple saddle and drove a purple Cadillac. In 1958 he starred in the American Wild West Show and Rodeo and performed at the World's Fair in Brussels; he also produced rodeos in Japan in the 1950s. In 1964 he retired from rodeo to concentrate on TV and movie roles but returned briefly in 1969. In 1967 he produced the documentary film *Born to Buck*, which presents his theory that bucking broncs can't be trained but are genetically disposed to buck. Tibbs was a pioneer in bucking horse breeding programs. Outside rodeo circles Tibbs was well known for his flashy clothes and personality; inside rodeo he was known for introducing the idea of balance and rhythm in riding bucking broncs. Before Tibbs, bronc riders generally relied on brute strength to stay on a horse, but Tibbs, a small, slight man, adapted a style whereby he got into the rhythm of a horse and stayed on through balance. (See also RODEO.)

TILGHMAN, BILL
(b. William Matthew Tilghman, Jr. in Fort Dodge, Iowa on July 4, 1854; d. Cromwell, Oklahoma on November 1, 1924)   Bill Tilghman was one of the most famous lawmen of the West. He died at the age of 70 with his badge on while he tried to do what he did so many other times—arrest a rowdy drunk and get him to jail. Actually, Tilghman did not start out on the side of the law. In his early days he was arrested for theft. But he was appointed city marshal in Dodge in 1884 and wore a badge made from a pair of $20 gold pieces.

Tilghman was involved in capturing Jennie "Little Britches" Stevens and Cattle Annie McDougal in 1894 near Pawnee, Oklahoma. Little Britches fired at Tilghman with her Winchester and the lawman responded by killing her horse. But she threw dirt in his face, clawed, bit him, and tried to pull a pistol on him. He finally manhandled her and gave her a spanking.

Tilghman joined the Oklahoma land rush of 1889 and staked a claim near Guthrie. He lived in Oklahoma the rest of his life, spending the next 20 years cleaning up the area; he was elected to the state senate in 1910 and joined the Oklahoma City police force in 1911. He also supervised the production of a movie, *The Passing of the Oklahoma Outlaws* (released in 1915). Tilghman retired but in August 1924 was persuaded by citizens to become city marshal of Cromwell, an oil boomtown. A few months later, on November 1, 1924, Tilghman was eating in Murphy's Restaurant when outside a shot was fired by Wiley Lynn, a drunken probation officer who had clashed with Tilghman before. As Tilghman led Lynn toward jail, the drunk pulled out a small automatic and drilled the lawman, who died within 15 minutes. (See also MADSEN, CHRISTIAN; THOMAS, HECK; THREE GUARDSMEN, THE.)

Bill Tilghman   *(Oklahoma Historical Society)*

TIM MCCOY   TV show that starred Tim McCoy.

These 15-minute westerns featured movie cowboy Tim McCoy introducing each film. The show was originally a live program on KTLA-TV in Los Angeles, where it premiered on February 17, 1950. There were 39 of these programs, which were syndicated beginning in 1955 and popular on Saturday mornings.

TIOMKIN, DIMITRI   (b. St. Petersburg, Russia on May 10, 1899; d. London, England on November 11, 1979)   Dimitri Tiomkin composed the theme for the film *High Noon* ("Do Not Forsake Me, O My Darling") as well as the scores for countless movies. A graduate of the St. Petersburg Conservatory of Music in Russia, Tiomkin immigrated to the United States in 1925 and became a citizen in 1937. He began writing film scores and scored a number of movies for directors Frank Capra, Alfred Hitchcock and Howard Hawks. Tiomkin won four Oscars for his work. Although he scored music for a variety of movies, he worked on a significant number of westerns. Some of the westerns Tiomkin scored were *The Westerner* (1940), *Duel in the Sun* (1947), *Red River* (1948), *Canadian Pacific* (1948), *The Dude Goes West* (1948), *The Big Sky* (1952), *Giant* (1956), *Gunfight at the O.K. Corral* (1957), *Rio Bravo* (1959), *Last Train from Gun Hill* (1959), *The Alamo* (1960), *The Guns of Navarone* (1961), *Town without Pity* (1961), *The War Wagon* (1967) and *MacKenna's Gold* (1969). (See also HIGH NOON THEME SONG; WASHINGTON, NED.)

TIPI   The housing for most Plains Indians, the tipi (sometimes spelled teepee) consists of buffalo skins sewed together and erected on poles tied together at the top. The tipi is a cone-like structure with a door flap for entering and leaving and an opening at the top to let out smoke.

TOMAHAWK   An Indian hatchet. The term came from the Algonquian word for hatchet and was eventually used throughout the West; "to tomahawk" meant to use a hatchet on someone.

TOMBSTONE, ARIZONA   Deep in Apache territory in southeastern Arizona, prospector Ed Schieffin began on April 1, 1878 to dig for ore. The army warned him that all he would find would be his "tombstone," so when Schiefflin, clothes tattered and down to his last pennies, discovered silver there in October, he set off a rush and the creation of a boomtown. The town was aptly named "Tombstone." The town quickly attracted miners as well as prostitutes, gamblers and a virtual who's who of Wild West characters, including Buckskin Frank Leslie, Curly Bill Brocius, Johnny-Behind-the-Deuce, Johnny Ringo, Bat Masterson, Luke Short, Doc Holliday and the Earp family—Wyatt, Morgan, Virgil, Warren and Jim. Soon the town had 7,000 inhabitants and 110 places to buy liquor, including such notorious establishments as the Oriental and Crystal Palace, which operated 24 hours a day. Church and schools also thrived, supported by a heavy gambling tax, and Schiefflin Hall featured theatrical plays. There were also newspapers, the most prominent of which was the *Epitaph*,

started by editor John P. Clum, who announced that "every Tombstone needed an *Epitaph*." And, of course, there was also a Boot Hill (a cemetery).

The town prospered, and about $80 million in silver was mined from 1878 to 1886—the town's heyday. Production was halted in the 1890s when the mines were flooded. Known as "the town too tough to die," Tombstone became famous as the site of the shootout at the O.K. Corral in October 1881. In fact, the town became so infamous that President Chester Arthur threatened to impose martial law in 1882 if law and order did not prevail. It did prevail, a result of law officers as well as citizens cracking down on law breakers.

Although the town could find no more silver and gold in its hills during the 20th century, it increasingly found gold and silver from tourists and in 1929 began an annual "Helldorado" celebration. Renovation and restoration continued through this century, and the town remains a major tourist attraction. (See also GUNFIGHT AT THE O.K. CORRAL.)

TOMBSTONE TERRITORY   TV show that starred Pat Conway as Sheriff Clay Hollister, Richard Eastham as Harris Claibourne and Gil Rankin as Deputy Riggs (1957).

"The town too tough to die" was the theme for this show, which featured the narration of newspaper editor Harris Claibourne and the troubles of fictional sheriff Clay Hollister, who tried to clean up the town, although the business interests preferred it wild and woolly. The half-hour show premiered on October 16, 1957 on ABC on Wednesdays; later it moved to Fridays, where it concluded its network run on October 9, 1959. Ninety-one black-and-white episodes were shot, but the last season's worth were done for syndication and never appeared on the network.

TONTO BASIN WAR   See PLEASANT VALLEY WAR.

TOP HAND   A very skilled cowboy, one of the best in the outfit; also called a top waddy.

TOTEM POLE   A totem pole was generally made of cedar and contained a chief's family history, achievements and great events in his life; these poles served as prestige and social standing, proclaiming the wealth, culture and bravery of its owner. Totem poles were carved by Indians of the northwest Pacific coast, specifically the Haida, Tlingit, Tsimshian and Kwakiutl. Other Indian tribes throughout the United States generally did not have totem poles.

TOWERLY, WILLIAM   (b. c. 1870; d. near Atoka, Indian Territory in December 1887)   Towerly killed Frank Dalton, the oldest of the Dalton brothers, whose siblings later formed the Dalton Gang. Lawmen Dalton and James Cole approached Towerly, Dave Smith, Lee Dixon and Dixon's wife when the four were camped on the Arkansas River in Indian Territory on Sunday morning, November 29, 1887. Smith immediately shot Dalton in the chest, and the group opened fire on Cole. Towerly ran toward Dalton, who was hurt and moaning, and fired his Winchester into Dalton's mouth; he reloaded and shot again, killing him. Towerly was killed about a month later when he visited his family near Atoka, in Indian Territory. Lawmen Ed Stokley and Bill Moody set an ambush and hit the outlaw with several slugs, but Towerly managed to get his pistol and kill Stokley. Moody then was jumped by the outlaw's mother and sister, who pulled him into the cabin and locked the door, but the lawman managed to break a window and kill Towerly. (See also DALTON GANG, THE.)

TRACKDOWN   TV show that starred Robert Culp as Hoby Gilman.

The Texas Rangers gave their official approval to this show, which featured fictional Texas Ranger Hoby Gilman wandering throughout Texas in the 1870s trying to clean up the place. The stories were based on actual files from the Texas Rangers, although the show was filmed by Four Star Productions on the back lots in Hollywood. It premiered on October 4, 1957 and was last telecast on September 23, 1959. The half-hour show first aired on CBS on Friday evenings and concluded its run on Wednesdays after 71 black-and-white episodes.

TRADING POST   A store or place of business where goods were sold or exchanged between whites and Indians. Trading posts began as army forts for frontier defense.

TRAIL BOSS   The cowboy in charge of the trail drive and trail herd.

TRAIL DRIVES   Trail drives from Texas north to Kansas usually began in the spring so that cattle could feed on new grass as they moved along; for drives into the northern ranges, it was essential that the cattle arrive at their destinations before hard (and early) winters set in. In addition, spring drives usually avoided flooding rivers; if a herd left at the right time, most of the rivers would be shallow and fordable, whereas a late-starting drive could cause problems as winter snows fed the rivers and caused them to swell. A herd of steers could move about 10–12 miles a day—a drover's favorite speed—although at the start the cowboys might cover 20–25 miles a day in order to get the herds trail-broken and get the drive off to a good start. But herds moved at different speeds. A herd of steers moved faster but was more likely to be spooked; a mixed herd with cows and calves was slower but less likely to stampede.

During a trail drive, the herd was supposed to drift along rather than be driven. The cattle started a little after daybreak after the cowboys had eaten their breakfast and were driven about five hours or until around 11 A.M. when the cowboys would stop for dinner. (Cowboys did not have "lunch"; they had breakfast, dinner and supper.) After breakfast, the cook would pack up the chuck wagon and go ahead to find a spot for the noon meal; the trail boss would also go out ahead to look for a spot to bed down for the night. During the noon dinner the cattle would graze until about 1 P.M. then they would be herded again. The bedding ground had good grass and water so the herd would be well fed and watered before settling for night.

A herd of about 3,000 head would take 10–15 drovers; this included the trail boss, wrangler and cook. Men worked in pairs so two-man watches could be made, and a cowboy's status was determined by his position on the trail drive. The top hands were the "pointers" who rode at the head of the herd and guided them; next came the swing riders about a third of the way back, then the flankers about two-thirds back, and finally in the rear of the herd were the "drag" riders. Pointers kept their posts for the entire drives; others might change positions, although absolutely no one wanted to ride "drag" and eat all that dust from the herd and have to deal with the slow or sickly cattle. At night cowboys would take turns, working in teams for about two hours each; they would often sing to the cattle to keep them calm or sing to themselves to stay awake and let the other rider know their whereabouts. These "night hawks" generally each circled the cattle from a different direction so they would pass each other twice on each circle.

In the best trail outfits each cowboy had eight to 10 horses in the remuda, or group of horses on the trail drive. Each cowboy needed at least one good swimming horse and one that was good for a hard run. A night horse, one that could see especially well in the dark and was surefooted and confident, was also a necessity. In charge of the remuda was a wrangler or remudero, who was usually a young and inexperienced hand (most experienced cowboys got their first experience on trail drives as a wrangler). The wrangler had to know each horse and to whom it belonged. (See also CATTLE DRIVES; CATTLE TOWNS; CATTLE TRAILS; COWBOYS; LONGHORN CATTLE.)

TRAILMASTER   This TV show is the original "Wagon Train" series, syndicated first as "Major Adams—Trailmaster" and later as "Trailmaster." (See WAGON TRAIN.)

TRAIL OF TEARS (1838–39)   In 1830 President Andrew Jackson signed the Indian Removal Act, which said, in essence, that Indians could be removed from lands if whites wanted the lands. In 1835 the Treaty of New Echota was signed, which gave all the land owned by the Cherokee to the United States in exchange for land in Indian Territory, now Oklahoma, located beyond the Mississippi River. The treaty was signed by a minority of the Cherokee tribe, and most Cherokee fought against it. At this time the Cherokee were one of the five civilized tribes (with the Chickasaw, Chickamauga, Seminole and Creek) and had established their own communities patterned after whites, with courts, schools, governments and even slaves. They occupied the area in the Southeast, particularly North and South Carolina, Virginia, Tennessee, Georgia and Alabama. But the army, under General Winfield Scott, expelled the 15,000 Cherokee from their homes and their lands in October and November 1838 and forced them to march 800 miles to their new lands. Approximately 4,000 Indians died on the way from hunger, disease and cold weather. This forced march of the Cherokee by the U.S. Army is called the Trail of Tears.

TRAILS WEST   This TV Show is a rerun of the popular series "Death Valley Days" with Ray Milland as host. (See DEATH VALLEY DAYS).

TRAVELS OF JAIMIE MCPHEETERS, THE
TV show that starred Dan O'Herlihy as "Doc" Sardius McPheeters, Kurt Russell as Jaimie McPheeters, James Westerfield as John Murrel, Sandy Kenyon as Shep Baggott, Donna Anderson as Jenny, Mark Allen as Matt Kissel, Meg Wyllie as Mrs. Kissel, the Osmond brothers as the Kissel brothers, Hedley Mattingly as Henry T. Coe, Vernett Allen III as Othello, Michael Witney as Buck Coulter (1963) and Charles Bronson as Linc Murdock.

Based on Robert Lewis Taylor's 1958 novel of the same name (which won the Pulitzer Prize), this show told the story of a 12-year-old boy on a wagon train headed west in 1849. He was accompanied by a colorful but motley crew of characters, including his scalawag father. This show premiered on September 15, 1963 on Sunday nights on ABC. The hour-long show was last telecast on March 15, 1964.

TRAVIS, WILLIAM BARRET   (b. Edgefield District, South Carolina on August 9, 1809; d. at the Alamo in San Antonio, Texas on March 6, 1836)   Travis and Jim Bowie commanded the forces at the Alamo; however, because of discord, the command was divided with Travis in charge of the regulars and Bowie commanding the volunteers. Travis emerged as the main commander before the final surge by Santa Anna because Bowie was confined to his bed ill. Travis moved to San Felipe, Texas (then the colony's capital), in 1832 from Alabama where he taught school and studied law. Travis established a law practice in Anahuac and became involved in the Texas independence movement. In 1835 he raised a company of 25 volunteers and captured Mexican captain Antonio Tenorio at Anahuac. Afterward he joined the Texas army, and in December 1835 Texas commander in chief Sam Houston named him major of artillery; on December 24 Travis was commissioned lieutenant colonel of cavalry. In January 1836 Travis and 30 army regulars were ordered to Bexar (now San Antonio) to join 120 others there. This group organized a defense against Santa Anna's Mexican army at the Alamo. On February 24, Travis began sending out messages for help, but no reinforcements arrived. Colonel Travis was apparently killed during the early stages of the final assault on the morning of March 6. (See also ALAMO, BATTLE OF; BOWIE, JAMES.)

TRAVOIS   Used by the Plains Indians to transport possessions and children, the travois consisted of two long poles, one on each side of a horse or dog, that came back and joined in a "V." Across the poles were skins or a platform secured to hold the goods and belongings or children of Indians while moving. Whites adopted the travois as a wheelless mode of transportation, sometimes used to carry a wounded man.

TREASURE OF THE SIERRA MADRE, THE
Film produced by Henry Blanke, directed by John Huston; screenplay by John Huston from the novel by B. Traven; released by Warner Brothers–First National in 1948; 126 minutes in length. Cast: Humphrey Bogart, Walter Huston, Tim Holt, Bruce Bennett, Barton MacLane, Alfonso Bedoya and John Huston.

In Tampico, Mexico in February 1925, three men team up to look for gold. The men are honest and helpful when the digging starts, but then "gold fever" sets in and greed, distrust and paranoia take over. Filmed in the Sierra Madre, the film was directed by John Huston, whose father, Walter, starred as the old prospector and won an Oscar for Best Supporting Actor. Huston won Oscars for director and screenplay.

TRUE GRIT   Film produced by Hal Wallis; directed by Henry Hathaway; screenplay by Marguerite Roberts (from the novel *True Grit* by Charles Portis); music by Elmer Bernstein; released in 1969 by Paramount; 128 minutes in length. Cast: John Wayne, Kim Darby, Glen Campbell, Jeremy Slate, Robert Duvall, Dennis Hopper and Strother Martin.

John Wayne was 62 when he made this movie, 30 years after *Stagecoach*, and for his role as Rooster Cogburn he won an Oscar. The book, written by Charles Portis, was written with Wayne in mind, and Portis sent Wayne galleys to read. The story involves a 14-year-old girl, Mattie Ross (Kim Darby), who goes after Tom Chaney (Jeff Corey), a hired hand who killed her father. She goes to Judge Isaac Parker's (the "hanging judge") court and asks the sheriff to help; he turns her down but recommends Rooster Cogburn. Cogburn agrees to help the girl track down the killer; actually, he wants to track down Ned Pepper, the only villain to escape him, and believes Chaney is in Pepper's gang. A Texas Ranger named La Boeuf (Glen Campbell) joins them, chasing Chaney for another crime. The trio of Cogburn, La Boeuf and Mattie don't get along but go along anyway. Cogburn runs into Pepper and his gang, and a gunfight ensues with Cogburn charging the four outlaws like a knight. He kills three but his horse is killed, pinning him under it. Finally, the other outlaw is killed too. Cogburn then takes Mattie home, where she offers him a grave beside her own. The sequel was *Rooster Cogburn* in 1975, also starring John Wayne.

TUBB, ERNEST   (b. Ernest Dale Tubb in Crisp, Texas on February 9, 1914; d. Nashville, Tennessee on September 6, 1984)   Ernest Tubb brought the honky-tonk sound from Texas to the Grand Ole Opry when he joined it in 1943, following the success of his recording "I'm Walking the Floor over You." Tubb grew up wanting to be a movie cowboy and appeared in four Hollywood cowboy movies: *Fightin' Buckaroos* (1943), *Ridin' West* (1943), *Jamboree* (1944) and *Hollywood Barn Dance* (1947). Tubb presented a "cowboy" image on the Grand Ole Opry with his cowboy hats and boots, a legacy of his Texas heritage. Tubb's boyhood hero was Jimmie Rodgers, and his first recordings for RCA were "The Passing of Jimmie Rodgers" and "Jimmie Rodgers' Last

Ernest Tubb

Thoughts." He began on KONO in San Antonio and then moved to KGKO in Fort Worth in 1940, when he joined Decca Records, with which he recorded his major hits. Sponsored by Gold Chain Flour, he began the Gold Chain Troubadours and later named his band the Texas Troubadours. Tubb opened a record shop in Nashville in 1947, a pioneering move that allowed consumers to purchase country albums by mail. He headlined the first country music show at Carnegie Hall and was the sixth member elected to the Country Music Hall of Fame.

TUMBLEWEED A number of varieties of bushes that break off when dry and roll with the wind. Thick, matted bushes sometimes gather and pile up on each other. These herbaceous plants, whose stems snaps at the ground during dry times, can spook cattle and clog up farm machinery. Although tumbleweeds often appear to easterners to be romantic images of the West, in truth these thistle-filled bushes can be a major nuisance when they blow about.

TUMBLEWEEDS Film produced by William S. Hart; directed by King Baggott and William S. Hart; screenplay by C. Gardner Sullvian (from a story by Hal G. Evarts); released in 1928 by United Artists; 81 minutes in length. Cast: William S. Hart, Barbara Bedford, J. Gordon Russell, Richard R. Neill, Lucien Littlefield and Jack Murphy.

This is William S. Hart's last film—and one of the first major western "talkies." The story involves the shift in

the West from a wild frontier to a civilized society, set against the backdrop of the 1889 Oklahoma land rush. The Box K Ranch is getting ready for its final cattle drive, moving the cattle from the Cherokee Strip, where settlers will soon rush in. Don Carver (Hart) rides into town with his sidekick, Kentucky Rose (Lucien Littlefield), and falls in love with Molly Lassiter (Barbara Bedford). The villains want land and the girl; Hart gets the girl and foils the attempt to steal the land. Part of the plot involves a horse race that Hart wins.

TUMBLING TUMBLEWEEDS Song written by Bob Nolan (April 1, 1908–June 16, 1980) and published by Williamson Music Company 1934.

One of the most popular western songs of all time was written by a golf caddy during a rainy day in November 1932 in his apartment in Los Angeles. As Bob Nolan stood at his window watching the wind and rain, he was inspired to write a song called "Tumbling Leaves." Nolan had been a member of the Rocky Mountaineers with Leonard Slye (Roy Rogers) and Tim Spencer, but he had left the group after an ill-fated southwestern tour. Later, the three would reunite and become the Sons of the Pioneers and Slye would become Roy Rogers. When the Sons of the Pioneers were first formed, they performed this song on the radio; however, listeners thought they were singing "Tumbling Weeds," and Nolan rewrote the song a bit so it became "Tumbling Tumbleweeds." Ironically, the famous opening line, "I'm a roaming cowboy, riding all day long," was written by the publisher to replace Nolan's original "Days may be dreary, Still I'm not weary" opening. The song proved so popular that a movie starring Gene Autry was named after it. (See also NOLAN, BOB; SONS OF THE PIONEERS.)

TUNSTALL, JOHN HENRY (b. Dalston, Middlesex, England on March 6, 1853; d. on the road to Lincoln, New Mexico on February 18, 1878) When rancher John Tunstall was killed in cold blood outside his ranch, the Lincoln County War began in earnest. Tunstall was an Englishman who wanted to invest in a ranch in the United States; he met attorney Alexander McSween and was persuaded to inspect Lincoln County. Tunstall first saw the area in November 1876 and soon bought a ranch in the area. But first he turned down some property offered by Lawrence Murphy and James Dolan because McSween warned him there were problems with the title. Tunstall and McSween also opened a general store that competed with Dolan, and this increased the animosity. When McSween's property was attached in a court action, Tunstall's property was also threatened because he was a partner with McSween in some ventures. Tunstall was riding into Lincoln from his ranch on February 18, 1878 when he ran into a posse who first assured him he would not be harmed but then killed him. Several of Tunstall's employees—including Billy the Kid—witnessed the event and fled for their lives. Tunstall was killed by William Morton, who fired his rifle into Tunstall's chest, and Jesse Evans, who then grabbed Tunstall's pistol and shot the rancher in his head and then killed his horse. (See also BILLY THE KID; LINCOLN COUNTY WAR.)

TURNER, FREDERICK JACKSON (b. Portage, Wisconsin on November 12, 1861; d. San Marino, California on March 14, 1932) Turner is famous for his "frontier thesis," a paper he delivered to the American Historical Association in Chicago at its 1893 meeting. The paper, "The Significance of the Frontier in American History," presented the theory that the American character is different from the European because the lure of free land led to a basic democratic spirit that created a self-reliant, practical and pragmatic people. It was the open land that stripped away the cultural, social and political restrictions that hemmed in Europeans; in 1890, it was declared there was no more "frontier," and thus a major chapter in America's history was closed. Turner's paper was first published in *Proceedings of the State Historical Society of Wisconsin* in 1894 and then reprinted in *Annual Report of the American Historical Association.* His first book was *The Rise of the New West* (1906), and he also published two collections of essays, *The Frontier in American History* (1920) and *The Significance of Sections in American History* (1932). Another book, *The United States, 1830–1850: The Nation and Its Sections,* was posthumously published (1935). Turner graduated from the University of Wisconsin in 1884, worked for a while as a newspaper correspondent and then finished his master's degree at Wisconsin before going on to the Johns Hopkins University for his doctorate. He joined the faculty at the University of Wisconsin in 1889 and stayed until 1910; he then became president of the American Historical Association and moved to Harvard University. In 1924 he retired from teaching and in 1927 became a research associate at the Huntington Library of San Marino, California.

TV WESTERNS See TELEVISION WESTERNS.

TWAIN, MARK (b. Samuel Langhorne Clemens in Florida, Missouri on November 30, 1835; d. Redding, Connecticut on April 21, 1910) During his life, Samuel Clemens, who wrote under the name of Mark Twain, was America's most popular humorist and certainly one of the nation's greatest writers. Twain got his start as a writer in the West, working for a newspaper in Virginia City, Nevada. Twain met Artemus Ward and Bret Harte in the West and wrote "Jumping Frog of Calaveras County," his first major humorous piece, which appeared in a New York newspaper in 1865 and was soon reprinted all over the country. This tale was later printed in Twain's book, *The Celebrated Jumping Frog of Calaveras County, and Other Sketches* (1867). Another book, *Roughing It,* is the story of his life out West, where he and his brother went in 1861 to get rich mining gold; Twain lasted only moments in the diggings. Since Twain had worked as a riverboat pilot on the Mississippi for two and a half years before he went west, after he returned he wrote a series of boys' books, beginning with *Life on the Mississippi* (1883), that made him internationally famous.

Mark Twain

26 MEN TV show that starred Tris Coffin as Captain Tom Rynning and Kelo Henderson as Ranger Clint Travis. This is the story of the Arizona Rangers who, like the Texas Rangers, were formed to protect a territory before it became a state. The Rangers were formed in 1901 and consisted of 26 men: a captain, a lieutenant, four sergeants and 20 privates. The show was filmed entirely on location in Arizona, primarily at the Cudia City Studios in Phoenix, and some of the original Rangers served as advisers and had bit spots in the series. The half-hour show was never part of the network prime time schedule, but its 78 episodes were syndicated beginning in October 1957, when it was first released. The show was produced from 1957 to 1959.

TWO FACES WEST TV show that starred Charles Bateman as Rick and Ben January and June Blair as Julie Greer.

In Gunnison, Colorado around 1860 identical twin brothers were reunited: Rick January was a gunslinger and Ben was a frontier physician. The two had been separated 25 years before during an Indian raid and had grown miles apart. They'd run into each other at

Tom Tyler

the Gunnison Hotel, run by Julie Greer, who had a love interest in both. The brothers were played by actor Charles Bateman with some tricky camera work. The program was a syndicated show that premiered in the fall of 1960. There were 39 episodes of the half-hour series, which were seen on a number of stations, but the program was never a regular prime-time network show.

TYLER, TOM (b. Vincent Markowski in Port Henry, New York on August 9, 1903; d. Detroit on May 1, 1954) Tyler was offered a movie contract in 1925 for westerns because of a salary dispute between the studio (FBO) and its top cowboy star, Fred Thompson; Tyler had been working in the film industry since 1924 as an extra, stuntman and roper. His first starring film was *Galloping Gallagher* (1925); he starred in 23 more before leaving the studio in 1929 at the beginning of the sound era. Tyler signed to make the serial *The Phantom of the West* (1930) and then starred in a series of "B" westerns. During the 1930s he appeared in *Powdersmoke Range* (1935) and *The Last Outlaw* (1936). In 1939 he had parts in three classics, *Stagecoach, Gone with the Wind* and *Drums along the Mohawk*. Tyler was in the *Three Mesquiteers* and appeared in the final 13 films of that series, but this was the end of his career: An arthritic condition ended his work, so he moved back to his native Detroit after some final roles in 1940s.

UNFORGIVEN Film produced by Clint Eastwood and David Valdes; directed by Clint Eastwood; released in 1992 by Warner Brothers; 131 minutes in length. Cast: Clint Eastwood, Gene Hackman, Morgan Freeman and Richard Harris.

This is the story of a former gunfighter who kills again in response to a bounty provided by some prostitutes, one of whom had been disfigured by a local cowboy. This film captured the violence of the West in graphic terms and earned Eastwood an Oscar for Best Director.

UNION PACIFIC TV show that starred Jeff Morrow as Bart McClelland, Judson Pratt as Billy Kincaid and Susan Cummings as Georgia.

This show concerned itself with the building of the railroad in the West. Never a prime-time series, it appeared on NBC's daytime programming in 1958. Thirty half-hour shows were filmed in black and white.

UNION PACIFIC RAILROAD One of the great railroads in this country got off to a rather inauspicious start: Ground was first broken at Omaha, Nebraska on December 2, 1863, but because of financial problems, the first rail was not laid until July 10, 1865. The company was incorporated by Congress and authorized to build a line over the central route and join the Central Pacific Railroad, building east from Sacramento, to give the nation its first transcontinental railroad. When the Union Pacific was reorganized under financiers Oakes Ames and his brother Oliver, engineer General Grenville M. Dodge and construction boss Jack Casement, progress came quickly. Although the railroad crews were under constant threat of attack from Indians, Casement drove his workers—mostly Irish immigrants who had served in the Civil War— until 40 miles of rails had been laid by the end of 1865, 250 miles added in 1866 and 245 more miles in 1867, when the railroad reached the

Rocky Mountains. In the next year and a half the line moved another 550 miles until it joined with the Central Pacific at Promontory Point, Utah on May 10, 1869. From this time, when the railroad consisted of just a single line extending over 1,000 miles, the railroad began acquiring other lines until it owned 7,682 miles of track by 1893. But that same year the railroad was forced into bankruptcy. It emerged in 1897 as the Union Pacific Railroad Company under E. H. Harriman.

URBAN COWBOY Film produced by Robert Evans and Irving Azoff; directed by James Bridges; released in 1980 by Paramount; 132 minutes in length. Cast: John Travolta, Debra Winger, Scott Glenn, Madolyn Smith and the Charlie Daniels Band.

This story concerns blue-collar workers who frequent Gilley's bar in Pasadena, Texas (outside Houston) and ride the mechanical bull. This movie was responsible for the "cowboy craze" in the early 1980s and the soundtrack features the Eagles, Mickey Gilley, and Johnny Lee.

U.S. MARSHAL TV show originally titled "The Sheriff of Cochise," the TV show changed its name in 1958 after two seasons because the sheriff was promoted to marshal and the actor playing the deputy left the show. The change was created because the sponsor,

Anheuser-Busch (makers of Budweiser beer), approached the production company, Desilu, about changing the title of the show while keeping the character the same. Since the sponsor was so powerful, the studio acquiesced, and the deed was done in the show as Sheriff Frank Morgan took Arizona's most wanted federal prisoner to Tucson to hand him over to the U.S. marshal. Some men had been sent to kill the prisoner, and they did it when he stepped from the train, as well as mortally wounding the marshal, whose deathbed wish was for Frank Morgan to become marshal and exact revenge on the killers. (See SHERIFF OF COCHISE, THE).

UTE INDIANS The Ute empire comprised the Mouache, Capote, Weeminuche, Yampa, Umcompahgre and Uintah tribes, who lived in the Rocky Mountain areas of Colorado, Utah and New Mexico. These Indians were perhaps the first "Indian nation" to use stone forts north of Mexico. The Ute were Plains Indians, living in tipis, riding horses and hunting buffalo. In an 1849 treaty, the Ute ceded a large amount of their land to the United States in exchange for a large reservation in western Colorado; however, in 1879 the Ute rebelled against Indian agent Nathan Meeker's forcible attempts to make them farmers, and the Meeker Massacre caused the death of Meeker and his associates; the Ute were then forced off their reservation in retaliation.

VAQUERO The Mexican or Spanish term for "cowboy."

VESTS See CLOTHING, COWBOY.

VICTORIO (b. in southwest New Mexico c. 1825; d. near Chihuahua, Mexico on October 15, 1880) A fierce Apache warrior, Victorio led a band of 150 warriors from an Arizona reservation in 1877 into the Candelaria Mountains in Mexico near the border; there he killed a 15-man Mexican posse and then another posse of 14 Mexicans. A bounty of $3,000 was put on his head as he continued his border raids. Finally a group of Mexican irregulars cornered Victorio on October 15, 1880 in the Tres Castillos Mountains where 80 Apache—including Victorio—died in the shootout.

VIGILANCE COMMITTEES Also called vigilantes or regulators, committees composed of citizens with no official recognition of the law; they were determined to impose law and order without benefit of law officers. Vigilance committees defended areas of the West and protected society; these groups were used against horse

thieves, cattle thieves, rowdies and killers. Sometimes these groups became the implements of power and privilege and included some of the most respected members of the community. Illegal but often effective, vigilance committees dispensed a system of justice that seemed necessary and justified in harsh, lawless conditions. Texas was known for having the greatest number of these committees, and Montana (in 1884) and San Francisco (in 1856) had vigilance committees that played an important role in their history.

Although there was need for frontier justice in the early days of the West, in fact the vigilantes were often lawless elements themselves, concerned with evening a score or exercising power from a single individual or group of individuals. As law officers, and the law itself, came into town, vigilantes were viewed more and more as lawless elements, hindering justice rather than enforcing it.

VIGILANTES See VIGILANCE COMMITTEES.

VILLA, PANCHO (b. Doroteo Arango in Chihuahua, Mexico on June 6, 1878; d. Parral, Mexico on July 20, 1923)

Pancho Villa is most famous for leading a band of Mexican revolutionaries across the U.S. border and raiding the town of Columbus, New Mexico on March 9, 1916, killing eight soldiers and 10 civilians. Although President Wilson sent an expedition of 10,000 men led by General Pershing into Mexico to apprehend Villa, the Mexican revolutionary remained free. Villa took his name from a Mexican band, Francisco Villa. Although a bandit, Villa was also a leader in the Mexican Revolution (1910–20), but the United States supported his rival, Carranza, prompting Villa's raid in New Mexico. The Mexican government offered Villa a large pension and big estate if he would retire; Villa accepted. He was assassinated by gunmen while in his car.

VIRGINIA CITY, NEVADA   When the Comstock Lode produced its bonanza of silver in Nevada, Virginia City was founded as the central mining town in the area. Established in 1859, the town rose to a population of 25,000 in 1876 before declining after 1890 into a ghost town. Before it did, however, about $400 million in gold and silver was mined from 1859 until 1882, and the town had five newspapers—including one on which young Mark Twain served as a reporter—a Millionaires Row of homes, a stock exchange, churches and banks. It was the territorial capital of Nevada from 1865 to 1875.

VIRGINIAN, THE   Film produced by Louis D. Lightow; directed by Victor Fleming; assistant director, was Henry Hathaway; screenplay by Howard Estabrook from the novel by Owen Wister; released by Paramount in 1929. Cast: Gary Cooper, Walter Huston, Mary Brian and Richard Arlen.

Directed by Victor Fleming, who would direct *Gone with the Wind* 10 years later, this is the first talking version of this movie, which is set against the Johnson County War. The Virginian must help lynch his buddy Steve, who is caught stealing cattle from the Box H Ranch, where the Virginian is foreman. Later, the Virginian and Trampas shoot it out. The 1946 version from Paramount was 90 minutes long and starred Joel McCrea, Brian Donlevy, Sonny Tufts, Barbara Britton, Fay Bainter, Tom Tully and William Frawley.

VIRGINIAN, THE   TV show that starred Lee J. Cobb as Judge Henry Garth (1962–66), James Drury as the Virginian, Doug McClure as Trampas, Gary Clarke as Steve (1962–64), Pippa Scott as Molly Wood (1962–63), Roberta Shore as Betsy (1962–65), Randy Boone as Randy (1963–66), Clu Gulager as Emmett Ryker (1964–66, 1967–68), L. Q. Jones as Belden (1964–67), Diane Roter as Jennifer (1965–66), Charles Bickford as John Grainger (1966–67), Don Quine as Stacy Grainger (1966–68), Sara Lane as Elizabeth Grainger (1966–67), Ross Elliott as Sheriff Abbott (1967–70), John McIntire as Clay Grainger (1967–68), Jeanette Nolan as Holly Grainger (1967–68), David Hartman as David Sutton (1968–69), Tim Matheson as Jim Horn (1969–70), Stewart Granger as Colonel Alan MacKenzie (1970–71), Lee Majors as Roy Tate (1970–71) and John McLiam as Parker (1970–71).

"The Virginian" was actually a minimovie each week, the first western series to show 90-minute episodes, and lasted eight years on the same network in the same prime-time slot—a remarkable achievement. The series, whose setting was the Shiloh Ranch in Wyoming in the 1890s, was based on the novel *The Virginian* by Owen Wister published in 1902 (there were also three movies made from the novel). James Drury starred as the Virginian, who was never known by any other name. and Lee J. Cobb played Judge Garth. A who's who of Hollywood stars appeared on the show, and several actors stayed for a year or two in regular roles. There was quite a bit of turnover during the long run with the result that the Shiloh Ranch changed ownership several times to account for new characters. After Judge Garth, John and Clay Grainger owned the spread, followed by Colonel Alan MacKenzie in the last season, when the program was retitled "The Men from Shiloh." The program premiered on NBC on September 19, 1962 and ran on Wednesday nights until its final show on September 8, 1971.

WADDELL, WILLIAM B.   See RUSSELL, MAJORS AND WADDELL.

WADDY   Also called a cow waddy, a cowhand, or sometimes extra help hired during a roundup.

WAGON BOSS   The head or captain of a wagon train. The term could also refer to the head of a cattle roundup.

WAGON BOX FIGHT   (August 2, 1867)   Outside Fort Phil Kearny in Wyoming, a group of civilians, escorted by the army's Company C of the 27th Infantry headed by Captain James W. Powell, were out cutting wood when they were attacked by several thousand Sioux and Cheyenne. This attack was part of Red Cloud's War against the army and the Bozeman Trail. Some wagons, used for hauling wood, had their running gear removed and formed a corral around the campsite for the men, mules and supplies. When the Indians attacked, Powell, his men and the civilians took refuge behind this wagon box corral. For the next four and a half hours the army fought off the Indians. They were saved by the Springfield breech-loading rifle that had just been issued to replace the slow muzzle loaders. Finally, a relief group with a howitzer arrived from Fort Phil Kearny and drove off the Indians. About 60 Indians were killed and 120 wounded; five soldiers were killed and two wounded. Nobody recorded civilian casualties.

WAGONMASTER, THE Film produced by John Ford and Merian C. Cooper; directed by John Ford; screenplay by Frank Nugent and Patrick Ford; released in 1950 by Argosy/RKO; 86 minutes in length. Cast: Ben Johnson, Harry Carey, Jr., Joanne Dru, Ward Bond, Charles Kemper, Alan Mobray, Jan Darwell, James Arness, Francis Ford and Jim Thorpe.

This is the movie that led to the TV series "Wagon Train." Like the series, the movie starred Ward Bond as the wagon master. In the wagon train a group of Mormons are headed to Utah, and two horse traders are hired as guides. The group is joined by some outlaws and some traveling actors.

WAGONS Wagons were used for hauling people and goods to the West. Most were based on the original Conestoga wagon developed by the Pennsylvania Dutch and modified for western use. Wagons were essential to haul freight on the Santa Fe Trail in the 1830s and 1840s. These wagons, usually drawn by oxen, stood high off the ground and had watertight wagon boxes for river crossings; the wheels were usually five inches wide to stop bogging and sinking. The freight haulers often used large wagons pulled by 10 or 12 teams of oxen; these wagons were about 14 feet long and four feet wide. Settlers generally used smaller wagons and thus smaller teams. (See also CONESTOGA WAGONS; PRAIRIE SCHOONER.)

WAGON TEAMS The animals used to pull wagons; the animals used depended on the weight of the wagon or the number of wagons, the length of journey and the nature of the terrain. On the Santa Fe Trail, merchants preferred oxen because they could live well on grass and were less likely to be stolen by Indians; the disadvantage was that oxen were slow. Mules were good for pulling in hard country where the use of a jerk-line team was popular. Mules were also used by many cow outfits for trail drives. Horses were more susceptible to disease than oxen or mules, had less strength and endurance but were faster; they were also more likely to be stolen by Indians. When oxen pulled heavy wagons, there were four to eight teams (eight to 16 animals); smaller wagons often had only one span (two animals). For mules, the most common alignment was two or three teams (four or six animals), although the legendary "20-mule teams" pulled the borax wagons out of Death Valley.

WAGON TRAIN TV show that starred Ward Bond as Major Seth Adams (1957–61), Robert Horton as Flint McCullough (1957–62), Terry Wilson as Bill Hawks, Frank McGrath as Charlie Wooster, Scott Miller as Duke Shannon (1961–64), John McIntire as Christopher Hale (1961–65), Michael Burns as Barnaby West (1963–65) and Robert Fuller as Cooper Smith (1963–65).

"Wagon Train" became the number one TV show in the 1961–62 season, replacing "Gunsmoke," which it had trailed for three years. The hour-long show premiered on September 18, 1957 on NBC on Wednesday evenings. When the September 1962 season began, the show moved to ABC in the same time slot. It stayed with ABC and moved to Monday evenings, when it became a 90-minute western shot in color (the previous episodes were black and white) and finished its run on September 5, 1965 on ABC on Sunday nights, having filmed 138 episodes.

The show was set in the post–Civil War days when families were moving west. Each season the show began with the wagon train leaving St. Joseph, Missouri and ended when the settlers reached California. The rest of the episodes consisted of encounters with settlers, drifters, mother nature, scoundrels, Indians and others along the wagon trail. The wagon master was Seth Adams, played by Ward Bond, who starred until 1961, when he died. He was replaced by John McIntyre, playing Chris Hale. Lead wagon driver Bill Hawks (played by Terry Wilson) and trail cook Charlie Wooster (played by Frank McGrath) appeared during the whole series. The major appeal for the show was the "character studies" done on the people drifting into the show for each episode. The characters were often played by top Hollywood actors and actresses (Rhonda Fleming, Jock Mahoney, Mickey Rooney, Ernest Borgnine, Raymond Massey, Linda Darnell, Barbara Stanwyck, George Montgomery and others appeared on the show), and each show tended to revolve around this "star" with the regulars on "Wagon Train" serving in supporting roles. The show has been syndicated under its original title as well as "Major Adams—Trailmaster."

WAIT, DASH (aka Dash Waite; b. Frederick T. Wait in Indian Territory in 1853; d. Indian Territory on September 24, 1895) Wait rode with Billy the Kid during the early skirmishes of the Lincoln County War and then went with the Kid to the Texas panhandle for some rustling. Wait was part of the ambush that killed Sheriff William Brady in Lincoln and, like the Kid, was slightly wounded in the shooting. On the Texas panhandle, a posse almost hung Wait, but the outlaw escaped by flashing the secret distress signal of a Freemason. When the Kid decided to return to New Mexico from the panhandle, Wait went back to Indian Territory, where he worked as a tax collector and died at the age of 42. (See also BILLY THE KID; LINCOLN COUNTY WAR.)

WAKELY, JIMMY (b. Mineola, Arkansas on February 16, 1914; d. Mission Hills, California on September 23, 1982) Jimmy Wakely was a successful singer before he became a film star, and he capitalized on the demand for singing cowboys by Hollywood in the 1930s and 1940s. Wakely grew up in Oklahoma and formed the Jimmy Wakely Trio in 1937 with Johnny Bond and Scotty Harrell. They moved to the "National Barn Dance" on WLS in Chicago and began recording for Decca in 1938. Wakely's film debut came in the Roy Rogers movie *The Saga of Death Valley* (1939). The Wakely Trio appeared as regulars on Gene Autry's "Melody Ranch" radio program and began appearing in Autry's films; they also appeared in the films of Tex Ritter and Charles Starrett. Wakely was signed to star in his own series of musical westerns by Monogram in 1944; the first was *Song of the Range.* Between 1944 and 1949 Wakely made 28 films for Monogram. Wakely had several hit records; the biggest were "Slipping Around" and "One Has My Name, the Other Has My Heart," written by fellow singing-cowboy star Eddie Dean. (See also AUTRY, GENE; BOND, JOHNNY; SINGING COWBOYS.)

WALES, WALLY (b. Floyd Taliaferro Alderson in Sheridan, Wyoming on November 13, 1895; d. Sheridan, Wyoming on February 12, 1980) Floyd Alderson was raised on a ranch and first worked in some Tom Mix westerns as an extra in 1916; in World War I he served in France, and he then returned to Hollywood and was signed by Pathe in 1924. The studio changed his name to Wally Wales for his first film, *Tearing Loose.* During the silent years, Wales was a major box office attraction for Pathe. Wales's first sound film was *Canyon Hawks.* He signed with Imperial Pictures in 1934 and starred in

Wally Wales (Hal Taliaferro)

Jimmy Wakely

some movies with his horse, Silver King, which had formerly belonged to silent movie cowboy star Fred Thompson. In 1936 Wales changed his name to Hal Taliaferro and starred in the Republic serial "The Lone Ranger" (1937).

WALKER A gun, also known as a Walker Colt. Captain Samuel Walker of the Texas Rangers took Samuel Colt's original five-shot revolver and went to Colt's factory where he helped develop improvements in the original; he then persuaded President Polk to place an order for 1,000 units. This order enabled Samuel Colt to get out of financial trouble and back into the gun-manufacturing business.

WALKER, CLINT (b. Norman Eugene Walker in Hartford, Illinois on May 30, 1927) Best known for his starring role in the TV series "Cheyenne," Walker grew up in Mississippi River towns. He held a wide variety of jobs, including deputy sheriff in Las Vegas, Nevada, an insurance agent, a vacuum cleaner salesman and a lumberman before he became an actor. Walker walked off the "Cheyenne" show in 1958 because of disagreements with Warner Brothers studio. Walker sat out the 1958–59 season legally forbidden to work for anyone else but returned in 1959.

WALKER, JOE (b. Texas c. 1850; d. near Thompson, Utah in May 1898) Walker rode with Butch Cassidy and the Wild Bunch. Prior to his death, Walker had problems with the Whitmore family in Carbon County, Utah. George and Tobe Whitmore were prominent bank-

Clint Walker

ers and ranchers in Utah; their father was Walker's uncle (his mother's brother), who had managed the Walker cattle after Walker's father died, when the boy was an infant. Whitmore combined the herd and moved to Arizona, where he was killed by Indians. His widow and sons then moved to Utah. When Walker's mother died, he went to Utah to settle up with the property, but the Whitmores denied any claims or relationship. When Walker began to run with some outlaws at Robbers Roost (located nearby), he often stole stock from the Whitmores. On April 21, 1897 Walker was in the Wild Bunch when they pulled off an $8,000 robbery from the Castle Gate payroll. Walker stole some Whitmore livestock in 1898 and was chased by a nine-man posse. With cowboy Johnny Herring, Walker bedded down for the night. When the posse found them early the next morning, it mistakenly believed them to be Cassidy and Sundance. They surrounded the two sleeping men and pumped the bodies full of lead. The two men died in their bedrolls.

WALKER, JOSEPH R.　　(b. Joseph Reddeford Walker in Tennessee on December 13, 1798; d. Contra Costa County, California on November 13, 1876)

A big (six feet tall, 200 pounds) powerful mountain man and trail blazer, Joseph Walker helped establish the Santa Fe Trail, discovered Walker Pass, the gap in the Sierra Nevada, and was the first white to find the Yosemite Valley in California. Walker spent about 12 years as a trapper in the Far West; he had long hair and a full beard and always had a number of Indian women to keep him company. After trapping, Walker became the first sheriff of Jackson County, Missouri but headed west again with Captain Benjamin Bonneville to lead an expedition to California. This group left Green River in Wyoming in July 1833 and arrived on the Pacific coast in November of that year. They spent the winter in California and in February 1834 headed back and arrived at the Bear River rendezvous in Utah in July. Walker also served as John Fremont's guide on his expedition in 1845. Later, Walker served as an army scout and prospected for gold.

WALKER, TEXAS RANGER　　TV show starring Chuck Norris as Cordell Walker, Clarence Gilyard as Jimmy Trivette, Sheree J. Wilson as Alex Cahill, Noble Willingham as C. D. Parker and Floyd Red Crow Westerman as Uncle Ray.

This is a contemporary drama with "Old West" justice. Cordell Walker (Chuck Norris) is a modern-day Texas Ranger who believes in old-fashioned justice. His partner, Jimmy Trivette (Clarence Gilyard), serves as a contrast by believing in modern law enforcement and the criminal justice system. The two-hour premiere was originally broadcast on April 21, 1993 on CBS and then rebroadcast on Saturday night, September 28. The series appeared on Saturday night after "Dr. Quinn" and "Harts of the West," giving CBS a Saturday night lineup of westerns in 1993–94.

WALLACE, BIGFOOT　　(b. William Alexander Anderson Wallace in Lexington, Virginia on April 3, 1817; d. Frio County, Texas on January 7, 1899)　　A Texas Ranger of renown, Bigfoot Wallace (his shoe size was a 12, he stood six feet two inches and weighed 240 pounds) served under John Coffee Hays around the San Antonio area, fighting Indians and outlaws. He served with the Texas Mounted Rifle Volunteers in the Mexican War and was given command of his own company of Rangers in 1850. Bigfoot survived a number of fights with Indians, the most notable one when he confronted alone 40 Indians who had stolen horses. Bigfoot had put hickory nuts inside his clothing like a sheet of armor and tied the arms and legs, and the Indian arrows could not hurt him. The Indians fled when they realized he was immune to their arrows.

WALSH, RAOUL　　(b. New York City on March 11, 1887; d. Hollywood, California on December 31, 1981) Raoul Walsh directed *In Old Arizona* (1929), the first major sound western, which won an Oscar for Warner Baxter, who starred as the Cisco Kid. Walsh was supposed to star in the movie, but a traffic accident before filming put out his right eye, and he wore a trademark black eye patch for the rest of his life. Walsh directed films for 50 years and finished his career with a western, *A Distant Trumpet* (1954). Walsh came from a wealthy family but ran off to Texas to become a cowboy; in 1909 he began working in movies and was an assistant director for D. W. Griffith in 1912 and starred in *The Birth of a Nation* (1915) as John Wilkes Booth. Walsh cast John

Bigfoot Wallace *(Western Archives)*

Wayne in his first starring role, in *The Big Trail* (1930). Other westerns that Walsh directed include *Dark Command* (1940), *They Died with Their Boots On* (1941), *Cheyenne* (1947), *Colorado Territory* (1949), *Gun Fury* (1953), *The Lawless Breed* (1953) and *The Sheriff of Fractured Jaw* (1958).

WALT DISNEY PRESENTS   In the history of television, "Walt Disney" holds several distinctions. First, it is the longest-running prime-time series in network history, premiering in October 1954. Next, it was the first attempt by a major Hollywood studio to enter the television market. Prior to Disney's show, the movie studios looked at TV as an enemy to be shunned, avoided or fought; Disney embraced the new medium. Because Disney led the way—lured by the fledgling ABC network and a major coup for its programming—TV received the benefit from current major productions. Previously, TV audiences saw a number of "live" shows and old "B" movies from the 1930s instead of contemporary shows. Part of the deal hammered by Disney was that ABC would help finance a proposed amusement park in Anaheim, California. ABC agreed (CBS and NBC would not) to pay Disney $500,000 plus $50,000 per program—an unheard-of sum in those days. But the theme park and TV show, "Disneyland," were big hits, with the show providing ABC with its first major hit

series. The "Disneyland" show was a variety show of sorts, all from Walt Disney, and featured cartoons, nature stories, documentaries and four rotating segments from the proposed theme park areas: Frontierland, Fantasyland, Tomorrowland and Adventureland. Two months after the two premiered in 1954, Disney aired the three-part series on Davy Crockett, which took the country by storm and led to Crockett-mania breaking out in America (see DAVY CROCKETT: KING OF THE WILD FRONTIER). Disney followed up with more western stories: "The Saga of Andy Burnett" starring Jerome Courtland appeared in 1958, "The Nine Lives of Elfego Baca" set in Tombstone, Arizona and starring Robert Loggia, "Texas John Slaughter" starring Tom Tryon and "Swamp Fox" starring Leslie Nielsen as Francis Marion (see SWAMP FOX, THE) all in 1958. Fess Parker starred in "Westward Ho! The Wagons," another western series. The original title of the series was "Disneyland" but was changed to "Walt Disney Presents" in 1958 and then, in 1961, to "Walt Disney's Wonderful World of Color." Originally the hour-long show aired on Wednesday nights, but from September 1958 to September 1959 it was aired on Friday nights. It enjoyed its longest run on Sunday nights after it shifted to NBC in 1961 and remained there until NBC canceled it in 1981, at which time it was picked up by CBS and broadcast until September 1983. In February 1986 the show returned to ABC, its original home, on Sunday nights.

WANTED: DEAD OR ALIVE   TV show that starred Steve McQueen as Josh Randall and Wright King as Jason Nichols (1960).

A spin-off of the series "Trackdown," also done by Four Star Productions, this show featured bounty hunter Josh Randall, who carried a sawed-off .30-.40 rifle strapped to his leg and brought in desperadoes from all over the West. The pilot was shown as part of "Trackdown" in March 1958, and the show premiered on CBS on September 6, 1958 on Saturday nights; later, it moved to Wednesday evenings. The last show was telecast on March 29, 1961. The 94 half-hour shows were filmed in black and white, though later colorized. Perhaps the greatest significance of this show is that it launched actor Steve McQueen, a virtual unknown when the series began, into a movie superstar after the series had ended.

WARNER, MATT   See MORMON KID, THE.

WAR WAGON, THE   Film produced by Marvin Schwartz; directed by Burt Kennedy; screenplay by Clair Huffaker; released in 1967 by Marvin Schwartz/Batjac/Universal; 101 minutes in length. Cast: John Wayne, Kirk Douglas, Howard Keel, Robert Walker, Jr., Keenan Wynn, Bruce Cabot, Valora Noland, Gene Evans, Bruce Dern and Sheb Wooley.

The plot of this classic John Wayne movie centers on Wayne getting out of prison after being cheated by his land and framed by Bruce Cabot. Wayne gets revenge by knocking off Cabot's supposedly impenetrable gold shipmen (or war wagon), with 33 guards, 28 outriders and five guards in the coach. Wayne's costar is Kirk

Douglas; the two don't trust each other, although they have a great deal of fun together (Douglas had originally been hired by Cabot to kill Wayne but abandoned this mission when Wayne offered more money to rob Cabot's wagon). Of course, the wagon is defeated by Wayne's crew.

WASHAKIE, CHIEF (b. c. 1804; d. Fort Bridger, Wyoming on February 20, 1900)   A Shoshoni chief whose tribe was in eastern Wyoming, Washakie gained fame because of his friendliness and cooperation with whites. Because of this cooperation, he was rewarded with a reservation in the Wind River country of Wyoming in 1868. Washakie is also known for his answer to the charge by young braves that he had lost his courage: He went on a lone adventure and returned with seven enemy scalps. He is buried in Fort Washakie, Wyoming

WASHINGTON, NED (b. Edward M. Washington in Scranton, Pennsylvania on August 15, 1901; d. Beverly Hills, California on December 20, 1976)   Ned Washington composed the lyrics for the theme song for the movie *High Noon* ("Do Not Forsake Me, O My Darling"). He also wrote "The Marshal of Wichita," "The Man from Laramie," "Gunfight at the O.K. Corral," "The 3:10 to Yuma," "Broken Arrow" and "Rawhide" for the TV show by that name.

WASHITA, BATTLE OF THE   (November 27, 1868) On a bitterly cold day, General Custer led his Seventh Cavalry against a Cheyenne Indian village in Indian Territory (Oklahoma) on the Washita River. The attack was ordered by General Philip Sheridan to punish the Indians for various offenses. Custer attacked Black Kettle's village and destroyed their winter food supplies, tipis and buffalo robes. Custer's troops killed about 100 Indians and about 800 horses just before the hard winter set in. The Indians were caught by surprise by the dawn attack but regrouped and fought valiantly. During the battle Custer learned that there was a series of villages along the Washita, including those of Cheyenne, Kiowa, Comanche and Arapaho. Custer feigned an attack on the other villages but, under cover of night, retreated.

WATSON, ELLA   See CATTLE KATE.

WAYNE, JOHN (b. Marion Robert Morrison in Winterset, Iowa on May 26, 1907; d. Westwood, California on June 11, 1979) John Wayne personifies the movie cowboy better than any other actor who played in westerns. The first movie Wayne starred in *(The Big Trail)*, the movie that made him a star *(Stagecoach)*, the movie that Wayne claimed made him an "actor" *(Red River)*, the movie for which he won his only Academy Award *(True Grit)* and his final movie *(The Shootist)* were all westerns. During his career of almost 50 years, about half the movies he starred in were westerns; these movies accounted for $800 million at the box office and meant that for 20 years (1949–68) John Wayne reached the top 10 in box office polls every year except one (1958).

Young Marion Morrison moved with his family from

John Wayne in *True Grit*

Iowa to California because of his father's health. The boy picked up the nickname "Duke" because he had a pet Airedale by that name. An excellent athlete, Morrison received a football scholarship for the University of Southern California; his athletic career ended because of a shoulder injury incurred while surfing.

As a college student, Morrison worked in the prop department at Fox Studio; there, in 1926, he became friends with young John Ford, who would eventually direct Wayne in 31 films. Ford gave Wayne bit parts in films, beginning with *Hangman's House* (1928) and *Mother Machree* (1928). Wayne's first starring role came in *The Big Trail* (1929) directed by Raoul Walsh. According to legend, when Walsh could not obtain the services of Gary Cooper—his first choice—he cast about for another actor. In one story, John Ford recommended Wayne to Walsh; another said Walsh liked the way Wayne walked when he saw the prop boy on the Fox lot. This movie would change Wayne's life because at this time he ceased being Duke Morrison and became "John Wayne," a name created by director Edmund Goulding and Walsh.

Wayne lost his major studio contract because of a personality conflict with the studio head and then worked in a number of low-budget westerns produced by Mascot, Monogram and Republic. He even became a singing cowboy during the heyday of the singing cowboy. (Wayne starred as "Singing Sandy" Saunders in a serial; his singing voice and guitar playing was dubbed by Smith Ballew.) Wayne's first "B" movie were *Ride Him*

Cowboy (1932), in which he and his horse "Duke" were introduced. At Monogram he made 16 westerns produced by Paul Malvern's Lone Star Productions (these are generally called Lone Star westerns) before he signed with Republic and made eight Three Mesquiteer films.

The film that made him a star was *Stagecoach* (1939), in which he played the Ringo Kid in John Ford's classic. Wayne then starred in 14 other movies directed by Ford, including *She Wore a Yellow Ribbon,* (1949), *The Searchers* (1956) and *The Man Who Shot Liberty Valance* (1962).

As the years passed and screen credits rolled up, Wayne increasingly played the character of John Wayne, the on-screen presence matching the offscreen persona of a man's man, who was tough and independent, suiting a conservative image of "rugged individualism." In addition to his acting, Wayne produced a number of movies, including *Angel and the Badman* (1947), *The Fighting Kentuckian* (1949), *Hondo* (1953), *The High and the Mighty* (1954), *Blood Alley* (1955) and *The Alamo* (1960).

Wayne won one Oscar for Best Actor as Rooster Cogburn in *True Grit* (1969). Wayne's last film was *The Shootist,* about an aging gunfighter facing his last days. Here audiences got a look at Wayne's past through a series of clips from previous films—ostensibly to show the development of the character—and then the old gunfighter passed along to a young man his philosophy and code of the West.

John Wayne is probably the most popular western actor ever. After his death, a congressional medal was made in his likeness, a rare honor for an actor. His old films have been reformatted as videos and sell well; the actor himself was a classic who made the films he starred in—especially during his last 20 years—a "John Wayne film" no matter what the subject.

The major westerns starring John Wayne are:

The Big Trail (1929)
Stagecoach (1939)
Allegheny Uprising (1939)
The Dark Command (1940)
Three Faces West (1940)
The Spoilers (1942)
In Old California (1942)
A Lady Takes a Chance (1943)
In Old Oklahoma (1944)
Tall in the Saddle (1944)
Flame of the Barbary Coast (1945)
Dakota (1945)
Angel and the Badman (1947)
Fort Apache (1948)
Red River (1948)
Three Godfathers (1948)
The Fighting Kentuckian (1949)
She Wore a Yellow Ribbon (1949)
Rio Grande (1950)
Hondo (1953)
The Conqueror (1956)
The Searchers (1956)
Rio Bravo (1959)

The Horse Soldiers (1959)
The Alamo (1960)
North to Alaska (1960)
The Comancheros (1961)
The Man Who Shot Liberty Valance (1962)
How the West Was Won (1963)
McLintock (1963)
Circus World (1964)
The Sons of Katie Elder (1965)
El Dorado (1967)
The War Wagon (1967)
True Grit (1969)
The Undefeated (1969)
Chisum (1970)
Rio Lobo (1971)
Big Jake (1971)
The Cowboys (1972)
The Train Robbers (1973)
Cahill: U.S. Marshal (1973)
Rooster Cogburn (1975)
The Shootist (1976)

WEAVER, DENNIS   (b. Joplin, Missouri on June 4, 1924)   Dennis Weaver first achieved national fame as Chester Goode on "Gunsmoke" ("Mr. Dillon! You know what, Mr. Dillon?"), who had a stiff-legged limp but was always law abiding. After he left "Gunsmoke," Weaver starred in another TV series, "Kentucky Jones," and then "McCloud." Weaver was a good athlete growing up, starring in track and field and football. After a year at Joplin Junior College he entered the U.S. Naval Reserve and starred on the navy's track-and-field team; after the navy he enrolled in the University of Oklahoma and starred on its track-and-field team, which led to a tryout for the 1948 Olympics. Weaver attended the Actors' Studio in New York after he graduated from the University of Oklahoma and made his Broadway debut in *Come Back, Little Sheba* in 1951; later he appeared in *A Streetcar Named Desire.* He was signed to Universal-International movie studio and appeared in a number of westerns, including *The Raiders* (1952), *The Lawless Breed* (1952), *Law and Order* (1953), *The Man from the Alamo* (1953), *The Nebraskan* (1953) and *War Arrow* (1953). Just before he received the part of Chester in "Gunsmoke" he appeared in four major movies: *Dragnet, The Bridges at Toko-Ri, Ten Wanted Men* and *Seven Angry Men.* (See also GUNSMOKE.)

WEBB, JOHN JOSHUA   (aka Samuel King; b. Keokuk County, Iowa on February 13, 1847; d. Winslow, Arkansas on April 12, 1882)   Webb arrested Dave Rudabaugh in 1878; later the two would become close friends and break out of jail together. In 1880 Webb became city marshal of Las Vegas but was also part of a band of thieves and con men known as the "Dodge City Gang" headed by justice of the peace Hoodoo Brown (real name: Hyman Neill), who, like Judge Roy Bean, held court in a saloon. Webb was arrested for murder in March 1880 when he killed Michael Kelliher during an argument. Webb was supposed to be hung when Dave Rudabaugh tried to spring him. It didn't work, but

Webb's sentence was commuted to life. When Rudabaugh was thrown in the jail with Webb, the two managed to escape on December 3, 1881 by digging out under the jail wall and went to Texas and Mexico, where Rudabaugh was killed. Webb took the alias "Samuel King" when he returned to Texas; he then moved on to Arkansas. He supposedly died of smallpox. (See also RUDABAUGH, DAVE.)

WEIGHTMAN, GEORGE   See RED BUCK.

WELLS, HENRY   See WELLS, FARGO AND COMPANY.

WELLS, SAMUEL   (aka Charlie Pitts; b. Independence, Missouri; d. near Madelia, Minnesota on September 21, 1876)   Wells was a member of the James-Younger Gang. After the train robbery in July 1876 at Rocky Cut, Missouri, he jilted his sweetheart, Lillian Beamer, to marry another girl. Miss Beamer then told authorities about Wells. Wells took part in the Northfield, Minnesota holdup; he shot teller A. E. Bunker and then killed bank president Joseph L. Heywood. Wells went with the Younger brothers when the Youngers and James boys split to avoid posses after the Minnesota holdup. On September 21, 1876 the outlaws were camped on the Watonwan River near Madelia when a posse came after them. A shootout occurred and the Youngers surrendered, but Wells was killed in the battle. (See also NORTHFIELD, MINNESOTA RAID.)

WELLS, FARGO AND COMPANY   In 1852 Henry Wells and William G. Fargo opened an office in San Francisco to serve the gold rush prospectors who needed to send their gold east. The company grew rapidly and established a network of offices throughout the West; by 1870 it was the major power in East-West express transportation and communications. Known for its beautiful Concord coaches and the green-painted strongbox with money and other valuables under the driver's seat and guarded with a company guard carrying a shotgun, Wells Fargo emerged as the most powerful transportation company in the West, especially after it purchased the Holladay Overland Mail and Express Company in 1866. The importance and necessity of the stagecoach declined when railroads linked the West, so Wells Fargo acquired railroad rights as it cut back its stagecoach operations. It lost its lucrative mail contract in 1895 when the federal government took over all mail services.

The company was established in New York as a joint stock association to take advantage of the gold bonanza in the West. When Adams and Company failed in 1855, Wells, Fargo and Company became the dominant express carrier. Wells, Fargo also engaged in banking, buying and selling gold as well as general banking. During the California banking crisis of 1855, Wells Fargo held on, despite large losses, and emerged as a dominant bank because of the failure of so many others.

Founder Henry Wells (1805–78) was born in Thetford, Vermont and raised in New York State. He began working in transportation in 1836 with Erie Canal companies, then in Pennsylvania with railroad lines. The originator of the express business, William F. Harnden, had hired Wells to work as an agent in Albany; Wells soon formed a partnership with George Pomeroy and Crawford Livingston to operate another express business and then formed another partnership with James W. Hale.

William George Fargo (1818–81) was born in Pompey, New York and in 1840 became an agent for the Auburn and Syracuse Railroad. He then became a messenger for Livingston, Wells and Pomeroy and later an agent; in 1844 he became a partner, with Henry Wells and Daniel Dunning, in Wells and Company, an express firm. Wells and Fargo formed Western Express in 1844 but sold out in 1846. Wells served as president of the American Express Company for 18 years, beginning in 1850, when that company was created by merging three other firms. Wells died in Glasgow, Scotland. Fargo became president of the American Express Company in 1868 (then known as the American Merchants Union Express Company) and was president of Wells, Fargo and Company from 1870 to 1872. Active in Buffalo, New York politics, Fargo was twice elected mayor.

WELLS FARGO   Film produced and directed by Frank Lloyd; screenplay by Paul Schoefield, Gerald Geraghty and Frederick Jackson from the story by Stuart N. Lake; released by Paramount in 1937; 115 minutes in length. Cast: Joel McCrea, Bob Burns, Frances Dee, Lloyd Nolan and Johnny Mack Brown.

This is Joel McCrea's first western. It is the story of 25 years in the history of the company, Wells Fargo, beginning with the decision to transport passengers coast to coast.

WELLS FARGO   See TALES OF WELLS FARGO.

WESTERNER, THE   Film produced by Samuel Goldwyn; directed by William Wyler; screenplay by Niven Busch and Jo Swerling; music by Dimitri Tiomkin; released in 1940 by United Artists; 100 minutes in length. Cast: Gary Cooper, Walter Brennan, Doris Davenport, Fred Stone, Paul Hurst, Chill Wills, Charles Halton, Forrest Tucker, Tom Tyler and Lillian Bond.

Based on the story by Stuart N. Lake (whose biography of Wyatt Earp was the major instrument used to establish that lawman's legend), this is the story of Judge Roy Bean. Bean, known as "the law west of the Pecos," basically made up the law as he went along, holding court in his saloon. But Bean's big weakness was his infatuation with the actress Lily Langtry. When a cowhand (Gary Cooper) is brought before Bean (Walter Brennan) falsely accused of stealing a horse, it looks like the judge's mean-spirited dispensation of justice will prevail; however, the cowboy plays to Bean's devotion to Miss Langtry, intimating he knows her. Promising Bean a lock of Miss Langry's hair, the cowboy escapes but then returns to help some local homesteaders in their fight against Bean and the cattlemen. Before he dies, Bean gets to meet Miss Langtry in an empty theater where Miss Langtry is performing (Bean has purchased all of the seats). It is here that Cooper and Brennan engage in their shootout.

WESTERNER, THE TV show that starred Brian Keith as Dave Blassingame and John Dehner as Burgundy Smith.

"The Westerner" didn't last long. It began on September 30, 1960 and ended on December 30 of the same year, shown on NBC on Friday nights. Created by Sam Peckinpah, a movie director noted for his depictions of violence on screen, the show was predictably violent. Dave Blassingame, with his dog Brown (the same dog that played "Old Yellar" in the Disney movie) wanted to settle down on a ranch and raise horses but kept running into problems that needed his gun for correction. The other constant in the show was Burgundy Smith, a con man always trying to weasel money from some townsfolk.

WESTERNERS, THE This TV show consisted of episodes of "Black Saddle," "Johnny Ringo," "The Law of the Plainsman" and "The Westerners" packaged as a single series and syndicated.

WESTERN HOUR, THE This was the title for a syndicated TV show in which "The Rifleman" and "Dick Powell's Zane Grey Theater" were packaged as an hour-long show.

WESTERN STAR THEATER This is a rerun of the popular "Death Valley Days" TV show with Rory Calhoun as host. (See DEATH VALLEY DAYS).

WESTERN TRAIL, THE This cattle trail led to Dodge City in western Kansas and was blazed after eastern Kansas was declared off-limits to Texas cattle. The trail began in southern Texas around San Antonio, then moved up to Fort Griffin, crossed the Red River at Doan's Store and then headed north through Indian country across the Washita, Canadian and Cimarron Rivers. From Dodge City, the trail then headed north to Colby, Kansas and then Ogallala, Nebraska, where the first cattle pens and loading chutes were constructed by the Union Pacific Railroad in 1874. This trail served Ogallala, which was the cowboy capital of Nebraska from 1874 to 1888, and the miners in the Black Hills. After Ogallala, the trail turned west through South Dakota, through the Badlands, and then headed toward one of several markets: the miners at Deadwood or, heading north, the soldiers at Fort Union and Fort Buford in North Dakota near the Canadian border. The trail was also known as the Texas Cattle Trail and Fort Griffin–Fort Dodge Trail.

WESTERN UNION Film produced by Harry Joe Brown; directed by Fritz Land; screenplay by Robert Carson from a story by Zane Grey; released by Twentieth Century–Fox in 1941, 94 minutes in length. Cast: Robert Young, Randolph Scott, Dean Jagger, Virginia Gilmore, John Carradine, Slim Summerville, Chill Wills, Russell Hicks, Chief Big Tree and Chief Thunder Cloud.

There is a controversy over whether Zane Grey actually finished the novel *Western Union* himself before he died or whether some ghostwriter finished it for him. At any rate, the story involves an outlaw who falls in love with the sister of a train engineer. But the sister likes another man. When some outlaws disguised as Indians raid the telegraph company, the feud between the outlaw and engineer comes to a boil.

WESTWARD HO! THE WAGONS See WALT DISNEY PRESENTS.

WHEELER, BEN (b. Ben F. Robertson in Rockdale, Milam County, Texas in 1854; d. Medicine Lodge, Kansas on April 30, 1884) Ben Wheeler was involved in one of the West's most notorious and bizarre bank robberies when he and Henry Brown—law officers and prominent citizens of Caldwell, Kansas—were caught robbing the bank at Medicine Lodge, about 40 miles away. Wheeler had a checkered past before the robbery. He abandoned his wife and four children in Texas and moved to Cheyenne, then, using the alias Ben F. Burton, he moved to Indianola, Nebraska and married again, but he abandoned this wife and a child and moved to Caldwell, Kansas. In Caldwell, he was appointed deputy by Marshal Henry Brown in December 1882. On April 30, 1884 Brown and Wheeler told town officials they were going to look for a murderer; instead they went to Medicine Lodge with two other associates to rob the bank. They arrived about midmorning in a driving rain and went inside the bank, but something went wrong and bank president E. W. Payne and cashier George Geppert were both killed. A posse chased the outlaws and cornered them in a box canyon, and they were taken back to town and locked up. A mob burst in around 9 that night, and in the ensuing chaos Brown was shot dead. Wheeler ran for his life, but his vest caught fire from a gun flash and he was gunned down in the dark. Still alive, Wheeler was taken to a tree where, after pleading for mercy, he was strung up with his two other confederates. (See also BROWN, HENRY NEWTON.)

WHEN THE WORK'S ALL DONE THIS FALL The original lyrics to this song, written by cowboy D. J. O'Malley and published in the *Stock Growers' Journal* of Miles City, Montana in 1893, were sung to the tune of the popular song "After the Ball," written by Charles K. Harris. This western song was supposedly based on the death of cowboy Charlie Rutledge in 1891 (O'Malley also wrote a poem about Rutledge's death in 1891, and this song is known as "Charlie Rutledge.") O'Malley was born in New York in 1867, and after his father's death, his mother married Charlie White, so O'Malley took the name "White" when the family moved west. He worked as a cowboy in Montana and wrote a number of cowboy poems during this time. This song first came to national attention in 1929 when the the F. B. Haviland Music Company of New York published it in sheet music and credited it to R. O. Mack; however, John Lomax had already published a version of this song in his 1910 book *Cowboy Songs*. After the Haviland company published this song, O'Malley wrote a letter to *Western Story* magazine, a popular pulp, in 1932 and told the true story of the origin of this song; his letter was popularized by John I. White, who was known as the "Lonesome Cowboy" on "Death Valley Days," an NBC radio show.

WHIPLASH TV show that starred Peter Graves as Christopher Cobb and Anthony Wickert as Dan.

This Australian western was set in the 1850s "Down Under" and filmed there as well. The story involved an American, Chris Cobb, attempting to establish Cobb and Company, the first stagecoach line in Australia. As Cobb fought the bad guys with whips and boomerangs, the show attempted to show the indomitable American spirit—and American characters—in an Australian setting. The show was filmed in 1960 but released in the United States in 1961. The 34 episodes of the half-hour series were syndicated and never part of regular network programming.

WHIRLYBIRDS, THE TV show that starred Ken Tobey as Chuck Martin, Craig Hill as Pete (P. T.) Moore, Sandra Spence as Janet Culver (1956–57) and Nancy Hale as Helen Carter (1957–59).

The contemporary West of southern California was the setting for this show, in which the heroes rode choppers instead of horses. The 30-minute program was produced in 1956–59 with the first program released in January 1957. The 111 episodes were syndicated and never part of regular network prime-time schedules.

WHISPERING SMITH TV show that starred Audie Murphy as Detective Tom "Whispering" Smith, Guy Mitchell as Detective George Romack and Sam Buffington as Chief John Richards.

"Whispering Smith" was originally a movie from 1949 starring Alan Ladd. The TV series served as a vehicle for movie cowboy Audie Murphy. It got off to a rather rough start and things turned worse as it progressed. First, Murphy was unhappy with NBC and made his views known publicly. The series began filming in September 1959, and after seven episodes costar Guy Mitchell suffered a broken arm when he was thrown from his horse, so shooting stopped. Then actor Sam Buffington, who played detective Chief John Richards, committed suicide during the filming. The story was set in Denver in the 1870s, and Whispering Smith was a railroad detective using the progressive methods of criminology to solve his cases. The show premiered on May 15, 1961 and ended on September 18, 1961. Twenty-six half-hour episodes were shot in black and white, but only a few were shown, all on NBC on Monday evenings. But even the telecasts caused trouble: The first episode, "The Grudge," was condemned for being excessively violent by the Senate Juvenile Delinquency Committee.

WHITLEY, RAY (b. Georgia on December 5, 1901; d. Mexico on February 21, 1979)

Ray Whitley wrote the original version of the classic "Back in the Saddle Again;" later, Gene Autry rewrote the song and used it as his theme song, so his name now appears as co-writer. Whitley was a handsome, talented singing cowboy who never became a star. He and his Six Bar Cowboys singing group were signed to RKO in 1937, and he made about 24 15-minute music shorts and then five films with George O'Brien, beginning in 1938, and, in 1940, a dozen pictures with Tim Holt. But despite his good looks, charisma and talent, Whitley never rose

Ray Whitley

above supporting roles. (See also AUTRY, GENE; BACK IN THE SADDLE AGAIN.)

WHITMAN, MARCUS (b. Rushville, New York on September 4, 1802; d. near Walla Walla, Washington on November 29, 1847) One of the first white settlers in Oregon Territory, medical doctor Marcus Whitman first went to the area in 1835 as a missionary. Whitman had applied to the American Board of Commissioners for Foreign Missions to establish a mission with the Indians; the board agreed and sent Whitman and the Reverend Samuel Parker there in 1835 to select mission sites. Whitman returned and recruited mission workers William Gray, Narcissa Prentiss and the Reverend Henry Spalding and his wife Eliza. In February 1836 Marcus and Narcissa Prentiss married, and on March 31 the group headed out over the Oregon Trail; Narcissa and Eliza became the first two women to cross that trail. At Waiilatpu, near present-day Walla Walla, Washington, Whitman established his mission with the Cayuse Indians; Spalding worked about 110 miles east at Lapwai with the Nez Perce. The Indians were rather indifferent to Christianity, and the mission board ordered the missions closed; however, Whitman returned east in 1843 and pleaded with the board to let the missions remain open; the church relented. On the return trip over the Oregon Trail, Dr. Whitman joined a wagon train on the Great Migration and helped settlers with his guidance and medical skills. Great tragedy occurred in 1847 when settlers brought measles to the Indians, who had no resistance, and the disease killed about half the tribe. The Cayuse then attacked the mission, killed the Whitmans and about a dozen others and destroyed all the buildings. (See also WHITMAN MASSACRE.)

WHITMAN MASSACRE (November 29, 1847) Between November 29 and December 6, 1847, the Cayuse Indians at the Waiilatpu Mission, headed by Dr. Marcus Whitman and his wife, Narcissa, in northern Oregon, instigated a series of killings. The mission had been established in 1836, but in the summer of 1847 about half the Indians died from an outbreak of measles and dysentery, brought by white settlers entering Oregon Territory. The Indians believed that Dr. Whitman was the cause of this curse, and on Monday, November 29, 1847 subchiefs Tomahas, Tilaukait and Tamsucky led a group into Whitman's home and killed the doctor and his wife. The following week a number of others were killed or taken prisoner. The siege ended when the Indians received $500 in trade goods and released their prisoners.

WHITNEY, CAP (b. Chauncey Belden Whitney in New York State on March 31, 1842; d. Ellsworth, Kansas on August 18, 1873) Whitney was killed by Billy Thompson, whom he was trying to help. Billy and his brother Ben were armed because of a challenge to Ben from Happy Jack Morco and John Sterling during a card game. Billy was drunk and, while Ben appreciated his brother's help, wanted him not to do any unnecessary damage in his inebriated condition. Whitney and John DeLong came over to the Thompsons and invited them to have a drink. In the saloon, Ben and Whitney both attempted to persuade Billy to put down the shotgun, but he refused. When Morco and Sterling came toward the group with their guns drawn, Ben shot and Whitney came toward the men. Billy, who was behind Whitney, fired his shotgun in the general direction of the ruckus and blasted Whitney, who died three days later. Whitney had been one of the earliest settlers of Ellsworth, was the town's first constable, built the first jail and served as city marshal, deputy sheriff and county sheriff. Whitney also fought at the Battle of Beecher Island. He was 31 when he died. (See also MORCO, HAPPY JACK; THOMPSON, BEN; THOMPSON, BILLY.)

WICHITA, KANSAS Wichita was the major Kansas cattle town for Texas cattle from 1872, when the railroad reached there, until 1875, when Dodge City took over the title. In 1874 there were 200,000 cattle shipped from there, and about 2,000 cowboys enjoyed the town. Originally a trading post for the Wichita Indians in 1864, the area developed into a white settlement after the Indians were removed in 1867. After the boom years of the cattle drives Wichita developed into an agricultural and industrial center.

WICHITA INDIANS Originally "discovered" by Coronado in 1541 living on the Arkansas River in Kansas, the Wichita later moved to the Red River in Oklahoma and then to Kansas and the present-day site of Wichita. The Wichita lived in grass huts, constructed of a circle of poles bent at the top and joined to form a domelike structure. Then long grass was tied together in thick thatches and layered on the house in a beehive fashion. Elm bark was used to tie together the grass. The Wichita were also known for their tattoos and the scalp lock on the men. They grew corn, beans and melons and hunted buffalo.

WICHITA TOWN TV show that starred Joel McCrea as Marshal Mike Dunbar, Jody McCrea as Ben Matheson, Carlos Romero as Rico Rodriguez, George Neise as Dr. Nat Wyndham, Bob Anderson as Aeneas MacLinahan and Robert Foulk as Joe Kingston.

This TV series was based on the 1955 movie *Wichita*, in which Joel McCrea had played Wyatt Earp. The setting for the show was the early years of the cattle town when trail drives ended there. The leading citizen, Mike Dunbar, was a cattle driver who arrived in Wichita and decided to stay. The 30-minute show only lasted one season, premiering on September 30, 1959 and ending on September 23, 1960.

WICKIUP A shelter constructed quickly, usually of brush and saplings; the term was often used by Indians to describe their nontipi dwellings.

WIDE COUNTRY, THE TV show that starred Earl Holliman as Mitch Guthrie and Andrew Prine as Andy Guthrie.

This show was about rodeo cowboy Mitch Guthrie, going from rodeo to rodeo in search of the saddle bronc championship. Mitch spent his life in rodeos while trying to convince his kid brother, Andy, it wasn't worth it. The show premiered on September 20, 1962 and ended on September 12, 1963. There were 28 episodes of the hour-long show, which ran on Thursday nights on NBC.

WIGWAM A dome-shaped lodge covered with wood and bark, used as homes by the Algonquin Indians in the northeastern United States. This term later became a generic term used by whites for Indian dwellings.

WILD BILL HICKOK See ADVENTURES OF WILD BILL HICKOK, THE.

WILD BUNCH, THE Outlaws who operated from 1896 to 1901 from Hole in the Wall, Brown's Hole and Robbers' Roost under the leadership of Butch Cassidy and his second in command, the Sundance Kid. The group was loosely organized, and approximately 100 different outlaws rode with this group at one time or another. This group was responsible for robberies at Castle Gate, Utah; Belle Fourche, South Dakota; Wilcox, Wyoming; Tipton, Wyoming; and Malta, Montana, a train robbery that was their last known job. (See also CASSIDY, BUTCH; CURRY, KID; LAY, ELZY; SUNDANCE KID, THE.)

WILD BUNCH, THE Film produced by Phil Feldman; directed by Sam Peckinpah; screenplay by Walon Green and Sam Peckinpah (from a story by Roy N. Sickner and Walon Green); music by Jerry Fielding;

The Wild Bunch   *(The Heritage Center, University of Wyoming)*

released in 1969 by Warner Brothers–Seven Arts; 134 minutes in length. Cast: William Holden, Ernest Borgnine, Robert Ryan, Edmond O'Brien, Warren Oates, Jaime Sanchez, Ben Johnson, Strother Martin, Bo Hopkins and Dub Taylor.

Like *Butch Cassidy and the Sundance Kid*, this is also a movie about the famed outlaw gang who holed up in Hole in the Wall territory. But this film, directed by Sam Peckinpah, is much more violent. Set in 1913, the Wild Bunch rides into a Texas town to rob a bank, but they are riding into an ambush; bounty hunters open fire and kill gang members and townspeople. Some of the outlaws escape, join up with another gang and head to Mexico, where they are pursued by bounty hunters. In a small village in Mexico, they rob a train and then become embroiled in the political revolution in Mexico, which leads to a gun battle in which they are killed. Told from the point of view of the outlaws, this is an important film; it showed graphically that good guys were also bad and that bad guys were also good.

WILDSIDE   TV show that starred William Smith as Brodie Hollister, J. Eddie Peck as Sutton Hollister, Howard E. Rollins, Jr. as Bannister Sparks, John DiAquinto as Varges De La Cosa, Terry Funk as Prometheus Jones, Meg Ryan as Cally Oaks, Sandy McPeak as Governor J. Wendell Summerhayes, Jon Fong as Keye Ahn, Kurt Fuller as Elliot Thogmorton, Robin Hoff as Alice Freeze, Timothy Scott as Skillet and Jason Hervey as Zeke.

Five upstanding citizens of Wildside County, California were actually a secret law enforcement group who received their orders from Governor J. Wendell Summerhayes and dispensed justice accordingly. This Disney-produced series was short lived: It premiered on March 21, 1985 and ended on April 25, 1985. The hour-long show aired on Thursday evenings on ABC.

WILD WEST C. O. W. BOYS OF MOO MESA
TV cartoon show that appeared on Saturday mornings on ABC. Created by Ryan Brown, the theme song was sung by country singer Billy Dean. The plots for this half-hour show featured mutant cows who lived in Moo Mesa, created when a comet struck and caused part of the earth to extend skyward. This was where the good guys and bad guys battled it out over the Code of the West (C. O. W.) and the good guys always won. Among the Good Guys were Marshall Moo Montana, The Dakota Dude and The Cowlorado Kid; bad guys featured Mayor

Bulloney, Sheriff Terrorbull, Boot Hill Buzzard and Saddle Sore. Other characters were saloon keeper Lily Bovine and rodeo cowgirl Cowlamity Kate. The "Code of the West" for Moo Mesa included, "Never sleep with your spurs on," "Always clean up after your horse," "Always tip your horns to a lady," "Watch your tail when crossing a field of cactus," "Eat hay only from plates," "Don't shoot 'til you see the spots of their flanks," "Never, ever, chew your cud in public" and "To err is human, to forgive bovine." The show premiered on September 12, 1992.

WILD WEST SHOW   See BUFFALO BILL'S WILD WEST SHOW

WILD, WILD WEST, THE   TV show that starred Robert Conrad as James T. West and Ross Martin as Artemus Gordon.

This show was part thrilling adventure, part pure escapism as well as a combination of the western, spy feature and action genres. James T. West worked for President Ulysses Grant as an undercover agent in the post–Civil War West. With partner Artemus Gordon he traveled on a train that had a car specially equipped with weapons and a laboratory to concoct elaborate devices to foil their adversaries. Some of the weapons and action were reminiscent of James Bond, whose exploits must have influenced the series creators. The show premiered on September 17, 1965 on CBS on

Bob Wills

"The Wild, Wild West"

Friday nights. The hour-long show was moved to Monday nights in July, 1970 and finished its run on September 7, 1970. One hundred and four episodes were shot.

WILLIAMS, BIG BOY   (b. Guinn Williams in Decatur, Texas on April 26, 1900; d. Van Nuys, California on June 6, 1962)   Williams got the name "Big Boy" (he stood over six feet and weighed over 200 pounds) from Will Rogers; he made his film debut in Rogers's film *Almost a Husband* (1919). The son of a congressman, Williams starred in his own "B" western series in 1934 and 1935 and played Tucson Smith in *Law of the 45's*, which introduced the Three Mesquiteers to moviegoers. Williams was Roy Rogers's sidekick "Teddy Bear" in *Hands across the Border* and *The Cowboy and the Senorita* and appeared as a regular in the TV series "Circus Boy."

WILLS, BOB   (b. James Robert Wills in Limestone County, Texas on March 6, 1905; d. Fort Worth, Texas on May 13, 1975)   The popularizer of western swing, a combination of big-band jazz and the Texas folk song tradition, Bob Wills brought the cowboy image to music through his cowboy dress and Texas fiddle tunes while he played big-band jazz. Wills came from rural Texas and played the fiddle at local dances; in the summer of 1929 he moved to Fort Worth and formed his first band. He formed the Light Crust Doughboys, who worked with W. Lee O'Daniel in 1930, and stayed with this group—whose nucleus included Milton Brown, another western swing pioneer—until he formed the Playboys and moved first to WACO in Waco and then to KVOO in Tulsa, where he achieved his biggest success with a big-band. His biggest hit was one he wrote, "San Antonio Rose," which his group recorded in April 1940 and then was recorded by Bing Crosby. Wills appeared in some cowboy movies and during World War II moved to California, where he played a number of large ballrooms. In 1968 he was voted into the Country Music Hall of Fame.

WILLS, CHILL   (b. Seagoville, Texas on July 18, 1903; d. Encino, California on December 16, 1978)   Wills got his nickname in one of two ways: The buggy doctor who delivered him was named Dr. Chillin, or he was born on the hottest day in his hometown. Wills began his show business career singing with his brothers in Texas and then went to vaudeville; he appeared with his group, "His Avalon Boys," in a Hopalong Cassidy film, *Bar 20 Rides Again* (1935) and then appeared with George O'Brien in six pictures in 1938 and 1939. Wills appeared in *Boom Town* with Clark Gable and Spencer Tracy, then *Rio Grande* (1950), *Giant* (1956), *The Alamo* (1960), *McLintock* (1963) and in the TV series "Frontier Circus" and "The Rounders."

WILSON, BILLY   (b. William Wilson in Trumbull County, Ohio on November 23, 1861; d. Sanderson, Texas on June 14, 1918)   Wilson joined Billy the Kid's band of fugitives after being arrested for passing counterfeit money; apparently he was paid in counterfeit money when selling a livery stable he had started in White Oaks, New Mexico. He was arrested by Pat Garrett at Stinking Springs and convicted but escaped to Santa Fe. According to legend, it was Wilson's .44 pistol, which he turned over to Garrett, that the sheriff used to kill Billy the Kid. Wilson moved to Texas and changed his name to David Anderson, but his real identity was soon discovered and he was sent back to New Mexico. Wilson returned to Texas under his real name and started a ranch in Uvalde County, married and had two children. Wilson received a presidential pardon in 1896 with the help of Pat Garrett. He became sheriff of Terrell County and had to stop drunken cowboy Ed Valentine, who was causing a disturbance at the railroad depot. When Wilson showed up, Valentine hid in the baggage shed. The sheriff demanded that Valentine give up, but the youth answered with a shot that killed Wilson. Within an hour after the incident Valentine was lynched by a mob.

WILSON, WHIP   (b. Charles Myers in Pecos, Texas on June 16, 1919; d. Hollywood, California on October 23, 1964)   Because of the success of Lash LaRue at PRC, Monogram developed Whip Wilson, who also used a bullwhip. Beginning in 1949 with *Crashing Thru,* Wilson made 22 films in the next two years. A direct

Whip Wilson

descendant of General George Armstrong Custer and a rodeo cowboy, Wilson joined the marines in World War II and received the Purple Heart; in 1952 he went back to the rodeo circuit.

WINCHESTER   Saddle gun of 1866 known as a "yellow belly" and developed from the 1860 Henry rifle. The major competition was the Spencer until Oliver Winchester bought out the company and then produced the Winchester '73, the most famous rifle of all time, which was developed by John Browning. The Winchester '73 was a .44-40 (.44 caliber with a cartridge containing 40 grains of power) and was the first center-fire repeating rifle that was succesful. It became known as "the gun that won the West" and is the most common rifle seen in cowboy movies.

WINCHESTER '73   Film produced by Aaron Rosenberg; directed by Anthony Mann; screenplay by Robert L. Richards and Borden Chase; released in 1950 by Universal-International; 92 minutes in length. Cast: James Stewart, Shelley Winters, Dan Duryea, Stephen McNally, Millard Mitchell, John McIntyre, Will Geer, Rock Hudson, Steve Brodie and Tony Curtis.

Based on a story by Stuart N. Lake, the biographer of Wyatt Earp, the film begins at a celebration in Dodge City on July 4, 1876 where a shooting contest gives the winner the prize of a Winchester '73. Two men vie for the prize; both are crack shots and both are enemies. James Stewart wants to find the man who killed his father; that man (Dan Duryea) is there competing with Stewart for the gun. Stewart wins the match and the gun, but then the rifle is stolen by Duryea, who hightails it out of town. The rifle then passes through a number of hands before a final shootout between Duryea and Stewart, which Stewart wins. This movie marked a breakthrough in star contracts; Stewart took a percentage of the box office income instead of a salary, which would set a precedent for other movie stars in the future. After this western, Jimmy Stewart would also star in *Bend of the River* (1952), *The Naked Spur* (1953), *The Far Country* (1955) and *The Man From Laramie* (1955), all directed by Mann.

WISTER, OWEN (b. Germantown, Pennsylvania on July 14, 1860; d. North Kingstown, Rhode Island on July 21, 1938)

Wister wrote *The Virginian* (1902), the first western best-seller that established the genre of western fiction in the 20th century. A privileged son, Wister graduated from Harvard University in 1882 and was intent on a musical career but was discouraged by his father. He traveled west in 1885 in an effort to improve his health and stayed at a ranch in Buffalo, Wyoming; he would spend other summers in this region in the future. Wister's first short story, "Hank's Woman," was published in 1891; a collection of stories, *Red Men and White* (1896), and two novels, *Lin McLean* (1898) and *Jimmyjohn Boss* (1900),were published before *The Virginian*. Based in part on the Powder River War in Wyoming, Wister's novel became a model for the cowboy as folk hero. Wister was a Harvard classmate of Theodore Roosevelt's, and Wister's novel and Roosevelt's presidency were major factors in the popularity of the West in general and the cowboy as a romantic hero in par-

Owen Wister *(Western Archives)*

ticular. By 1938 *The Virginian* had sold over one and a half million copies; it became a Broadway play, was made into a movie four times and then became a TV series. The phrase "When you call me that, smile!" became one of the most famous lines in western fiction. Wister never wrote another western novel after *The Virginian*, although he published a collection of short pieces, *When West Was West*, in 1928.

WOLF A rather shy animal, given to being solitary, the wolf *(Canis lupus)* can kill almost anything on four feet except a puma. The gray or timber wolf *(Canis occidentalis)* is a large wolf—about five feet in body length, three feet high and 100 pounds—which once fed on buffalo, mostly sick and weak ones on the outside of the herd. When the buffalo were eliminated, it began feeding on horses, cattle, sheep and dogs, and consequently wolves were a major threat to ranchers and settlers, who put bounties on their heads. These gray or timber wolves are nearly extinct but can still be found in some isolated regions in the Rockies, in Canada and in Alaska. Ranchers sometimes hired a wolfer, or professional hunter of wolves, to kill them, paid per animal. There are many varieties of *Canis lupus*, but "wolf" always referred to the true timber wolf, never to the little wolf, which was a coyote. (See also COYOTE.)

WOMEN IN B WESTERN MOVIES The role of women in "B" westerns was limited; in fact, only one actress, Dale Evans, emerged as a star from these movies and she has noted that even though she was the "Queen of the West," her billing was less than that of Roy, Gabby Hayes and Roy's horse, Trigger. Most women in "B" westerns were a daughter of someone who would be the target of greedy villains after she had inherited a business or ranch; she might also be a helpless schoolmarm. But many "B" westerns never even had a female lead; the Hays Office did not want sex in the movies, and the cowboy vehicles were "safe" as long as there was no romance. Actresses who appeared in "B" westerns include Rita Hayworth, Jennifer Jones, Lorraine Day, Gale Storm, Marge Champion, Ann Miller, Virginia Grey, Adele Mara, Martha Hyer, Jacqueline Wells, Louise Currie, Lois Collier and Evelyn Brent; and there were also some notable pairs, including Charles Starrett and Iris Meredith; Red Barry and Lynne Merrick; Bill Elliott and Anna Jeffreys; Monte Hale and Adrian Booth; Johnny Mack Brown and Nell O'Day; and Roy Rogers and Dale Evans. It is worth nothing that some cowboys married their leading ladies: Tex Ritter married Dorothy Fay, and Hoot Gibson married lady Sally Eilers. (See also B WESTERN MOVIES; EVANS, DALE; MOVIES.)

WOMEN IN THE WEST Popular myths and legends have tended to portray three basic roles for women in the Old West: (1) wives and mothers, who centered their lives on their homes; (2) single schoolteachers, who brought education and culture to the West but who would become wives and mothers when the right men came along; and (3) prostitutes. These views are not entirely inaccurate; carving out a new life in the West required the domestic work of women: running a household, raising children, warding off Indians, setting up schools and churches, being involved in women's clubs and in general the burden of making a wilderness a home.

The Old West was a man's world; women did not come into the West in large numbers until after the Civil War, when most of the settlement of the West occurred. There were no women in the early explorations except Sacajawea, the Indian wife of guide Toussaint Charbonneau. And there were no women with the early fur trappers except for Indian women. There were women who traveled with their families on the Oregon and California Trails in the 1840s and 1850s, and they played a key role in settling that region. But the gold rush of 1849 to California—the first example of a population explosion in the Far West—and subsequent gold and silver rushes were dominated by men. (In 1849 there were 65,000 men and 2,500 women in San Francisco.) Occasionally, a wife would come along, but the women around these early gold-digging camps were primarily prostitutes until a town was begun; then women would play the key role of bringing "civilization" to these towns, generally defined in terms of a domestic, settling influence by establishing schools, churches and homes. The women of the cattle towns were dance hall girls and prostitutes until the town became a year-round establishment; then, again, women became a settling influence.

The first women in western towns—or anywhere a group of men were gathered—were prostitutes. They were part of the saloons—generally the first place of business established in a locale—and they did a brisk, open business. The good citizens of a town never accepted prostitution; there was generally an area set aside for prostitutes away from the center of town. But as the town grew and developed, there were crusades against prostitution, and finally the prostitutes either had to leave town or learn how to conduct business in a more discreet manner.

There were several types of prostitutes, from the streetwalkers, to those who worked in rooms above the saloon, to those who worked in parlor houses in the largest cities and most wealthy towns with an exclusive, local clientele. Prostitutes were often quite young (an average age might be 19, but there were some as young as 13 or 14; rarely would a woman over 30 be a prostitute) and from very poor backgrounds. Most became prostitutes because there was simply nothing else for them to do. During the second half of the 19th century there were approximately 50,000 prostitutes in the West; they lived an extremely difficult life, and most were in debt to someone (usually a pimp or madam). Most died from violence or disease; suicide was rampant. Those who did live usually ended up in the poorhouse. If anyone did well in the prostitution business it was the madams, the most successful of whom were usually shrewd businesswomen.

Though most women in the West did not do "man's" work, vote or get involved in politics, women did play a vital role in the economic development of the West. Women of the West were milliners, shop clerks, domestic servants, teachers and nursemaids. Women could make an income by selling butter and eggs, sewing clothing, making rugs or writing. Running a household involved food processing, candle making, soap making, spinning, weaving, knitting and similar activities; in fact, in many ways a home was really a factory, and the woman was the main worker. It was a hard, demanding life; stories abound of women going crazy from frustration, loneliness and exhaustion. However, studies indicate that loneliness and frustration were prevalent when women first arrived on their homesteads, but as time passed, women learned to cope with the isolation of the plains and prairies by bonding with other women, most often through churches and religion, which provided social interaction as well as friendships, emotional support and spiritual comfort. Still, it was a hard life; women were initially afraid of Indians, although once in the West they tended to find Indians curious about the ways of whites. Of much greater concern was the weather—rain and snowstorms could devastate a home, and tornadoes could wipe out a community in moments. There was also the threat of fires, insects, rodents and reptiles. Settlers soon came to dread grasshoppers, who would eat clothing, furniture and mosquito netting, destroy woodwork and food and wipe out gardens; during the 1870s in Kansas there was a plague of grasshoppers.

Throughout the 19th century the plains and prairies were primarily a rural area, dominated by farms. Towns grew too, but for women, life in the town did not differ much from life on the farm; there were still the problems of running a home. For men, life in the rural areas was quite different from life in the cities, and they had a broader range of occupations and experiences. By 1900 about 30% of those living on the plains and prairies were in urban areas, and new inventions had come along, such as the treadle sewing machines, washing machines, clothes wringers, stoves, and flat irons with clip on handles. Few households could afford these luxuries, however, as farming equipment was considered a more essential purchase in the 19th century.

Men on the plains and prairies not only wanted wives, they needed them as co-workers and business partners on farms and ranches. It was nearly impossible to run a ranch or farm alone; help was needed, and a man and woman complemented each other. "Women's work" was essential for the survival of a family. Women who came to the plains and prairies were often unaware of how difficult it would be until they got there; homes of rough-cut logs (about 10 feet by 12 feet), a tar-paper shack or—the worst—a sod house depressed women at first. But as the homestead progressed, a better home of wood was built, and within three to five years of moving to the West, families lived in a more solidly constructed house.

The plains family was a nuclear one; during the 19th century women generally married at about 22, while men were about 26; they had a child every two or three years, and the "average" family bore 10 children, though not all survived. The average-size household on the plains was five to six people, so solitary loneliness was not generally a problem. Settlers were generally between 25 and 45 years of age, and most did not come from poor backgrounds, otherwise they could not afford the expense of getting to the plains to establish a homestead.

A little more than 10% of women on the plains never married; although marriage was generally accepted as the "ideal" way to live and it was difficult for a single woman to establish a homestead, some women elected to stay single. In many areas it was forbidden for women to own land; in other areas, it was deemed "inappropriate" for women to run a homestead. (Only about one-third of immigrants in 1880 were female.)

Women played a major role in the reform movement, begun in the 1830s and revived in the 1870s. They were particularly influential in the Temperance Movement, which began in Boston in 1826 when the American Temperance Society was formed. The Daughters of Temperance was organized in 1843, and the early wave of temperance reform peaked around 1855; it reappeared with the Prohibition Party in the 1870s. The Women's Christian Temperance Union (WCTU) formed in 1874 and was headed by Frances Willard from 1879 to 1898. It was appropriate for women to be involved in this movement because the major role for women was protecting the home and family, and alcohol was viewed as a threat to both.

The suffragist movement also involved a number of women in the 19th and early 20th century. There were two sides in this issue, and there were women in both camps. The prosuffragists society would benefit if women were active politically because they could be effective in reform and professional endeavors. Prosuffragists also believed it would be useful to the nation to have highly moral women voting on social issues. Less overt, but certainly prominent with some of the leaders of this movement, was the fact that giving women the right to vote gave them political equality to men and made them individuals in their own right.

The antisuffragists argued that women were naturally inferior and too emotional and that they simply lacked the strength to wield authority. Many—both men and women—thought women should stay in the domestic sphere; many men insisted they would reform any existing wrongs in their role as women's protectors. A much greater—though more subtle—belief was that if women were given the vote and accepted as equals, they would take jobs from men and become rivals, thus ruining the sacred institutions of marriage and family. Some believed that women would be degraded by entering polling places and that they would vote only as their husbands told them to. There was also the religious argument about the scriptural command for women to be silent; this was a strong argument for religious women, who were often heavily involved in reform movements. Finally, there was the old argument that women didn't want the vote anyway.

This movement gathered steam for 50 years before prosuffragists finally won this battle in 1920 when the 19th Amendment was passed, although Wyoming and Montana had allowed women to vote since statehood.

Although the national suffragist movement was im-portant in the history of the West, most women on the plains and prairies were involved in reforms at the local level, where they established schools, churches, libraries and other cultural institutions. Religion was usually the basis of social interaction, and women formed groups in churches for benevolent efforts. Women were also active in organizing hospital and veterans' auxiliaries, cemetery associations, sewing groups, housekeepers' societies, current-events clubs, musical groups, tourist clubs, world peace groups, physical-culture organizations and literary and study clubs. Women were active in forming chapters for Epworth Leagues, Dickens clubs, Order of the Eastern Star, Women's Relief Corps, Daughters of the American Revolution, Rebekah Lodge and Red Cross units. Since women were generally viewed as social as well as domestic housekeepers, both men and women saw involvement in these organizations as part of the role of women in society.

Although they were limited to occupations such as teacher, milliner, shop clerk and domestic servant, some women expanded these boundaries and became photographers, postmasters, nurses, writers and newspaper reporters and occasionally lawyers, dentists and professors. But women were generally admonished in speeches, sermons, newspaper articles, ladies' magazines and household guidebooks to concentrate on marriage and children, whereas men were always exhorted to dedicate their lives to "breadwinning."

Life was not all drudgery for women in the West; most found ways to live a rich and rewarding life with limited resources. They were helped by some social movements; in Oklahoma and the Dakotas it became easier for a woman to get a divorce, and by the 1860s divorce courts began to award children to the mothers instead of the fathers. Still, most women stayed married their whole life, even if the husband was unfit. Women entered into marriages after choosing a man through courtship, through arrangements by families, or as a "mail-order" bride who did not even meet her future husband until she arrived in the West.

Life was made easier at the end of the 19th century when catalogs from Sears, Roebuck and Montgomery Ward began to arrive. These catalogs allowed women who could afford them to learn about new household appliances, and they could order a wide variety of goods that were unavailable to them otherwise. Women were also kept informed and entertained through magazines such as *Harper's Bazaar*, *Godey's Lady's Book*, *Youth's Companion* and *Good Form*. The acceptability of education for women shifted in the 19th century; in 1837 the first women's college (Mount Holyoke) opened, and after the Civil War several other women's colleges (Vassar, Smith and Wellesley) opened. In 1866 the University of Kansas became the first college to admit women and men equally. Part of this was economic; there weren't enough men to fill the college. And since the role of men in the West involved manual labor, men often moved away from education while women, who were regarded as the protectors of culture and civilization, were pushed toward it.

There were, of course, some women who rejected

their traditional roles. There are examples of women dressing like men; Bill Newcomb, who fought in the Mexican War, was really Elizabeth C. Smith, and Albert Cashier, who served in the Union army, was really Jennie Hodges. Calamity Jane and Laura Bullion often dressed as men, and legendary stagecoach driver Charley Parkhurst was dead before folks knew she was really a woman. There were also some examples of real-life women outlaws: Belle Starr, Calamity Jane, Rose of Cimarron, Bronco Sue Yonker, Pike Kate and Sally Skull are some examples. But, though colorful and lively, these were the exception and not the rule for women in the West.

Women often had an important role in helping to run ranches in the West. Some women, such as Mary Ann Goodnight, were in charge of the entire ranch when their husband died. A few women went on cattle drives, primarily to help their husbands; one woman (Kate Medlin) even took her four children on a cattle drive. There was even an all-cowgirl ranch in the Texas Hill country between San Marcos and San Antonio operated by about 50 cowgirls in the mid-1880s. On ranches, as on farms on the plains and prairies, women's major role centered on the home and family, but ranches were really family-owned businesses, and each partner worked hard to make the business profitable.

From the 1870s, when popular entertainment about the West included dime novels, there were some women heroes based on real people such as Calamity Jane, as well as such fictional characters as Arietta Murdock, Rowdy Kate and Katrina Hartstein; dime novelist E. L. Wheeler was particularly adept at creating female heroines. These heroines replaced the female captive of savage Indians; these "captivity narratives" were popular and served as constant reminders that women were in a particularly dangerous and vulnerable position in the West.

The role of women changed at the end of the 19th century with the blossoming of cowboy entertainment in the form of Wild West shows and rodeos. The best example is Annie Oakley, a sharpshooter in Buffalo Bill's Wild West show and perhaps the most famous "cowgirl" in the West. Women in these shows served primarily as sharpshooters and trick riders when they had starring roles, as well as female characters in some of the dramatic reenactments. Offstage, they were usually wives of other Wild West show personnel.

The early years of rodeo are filled with examples of women who rode broncs and steers and were the trick riders and ropers. Women rode broncs at the rodeo in Cheyenne at the turn of the century—Bertha Blancett, Annie Shaffer and Prairie Rose Henderson are all examples—and female rodeo stars from the early 20th century include Lucille Mann, Florence LaDue, Alice Lee, Lottie Alridge, Babe Willets, Mabel Klein, Dot Vernon and Jane Fuller. One of the all-time great female rodeo stars was Ruth Roach, who became World's Champion All-Around Cowgirl, World's Champion Trick Rider and World's Champion Girl Bronc Rider in a career that spanned roughly 1916 to 1934. Indeed, the early years of rodeo (before 1930) are filled with women rodeo stars,

and in the 1940s, all-girl rodeos were popular for a while. But rodeos soon became dominated by men, and females were allowed only one event: barrel racing.

There are several reasons for the decline of women in rodeos. First was the male attitude that women were fragile creatures who should be protected, combined with the acute embarrassment of having to face their buddies after a female had beaten them in a roping event or bronc riding. Next was the elimination of trick riding and roping as part of rodeo; these events featured a number of females. Finally, on the practical side, there was the problem of stock contractors having to take two sets of stock to each rodeo: one for men and one for women, as the women did not ride the same broncs and steers as men. For example, since riders are judged on how well they ride as well as how hard the bronc bucks, if a female got a rather docile mount, she could lose points. Arguments would erupt that men wanted to avoid. Still, women have remained active in rodeos; the Girls' Rodeo Association was formed in 1949 in San Angelo, Texas, and the Cowgirl Hall of Fame is located in Hereford, Texas.

Clothing for women in the West underwent some major changes. First, because the long, full skirts often proved impractical on ranches, women wore split skirts so they could ride a horse like men; the sidesaddle might be appropriate for Sunday outings, but it was definitely impractical when rounding up cattle. As women became involved in Wild West shows and rodeos, they began to wear jodhpurs, high boots, fringed skirts, blouses and Stetson hats. They also added beaded belts, gloves, vests and jackets to appear more "showy." During the 1940s cowgirl clothing featured yokes in shirts and pants and fitted blouses. Women also began to wear denim jeans like men because of their comfort and practicality.

In western movies the roles of women were either limited or nonexistent; one critic notes there are three kinds of women in western movies: those who take it all off, those who keep it all on, and singing girl partners. In most western movies of the 1930s and 1940s, a woman character was usually a daughter or niece helping her father/uncle; mothers were nonexistent and presumed dead (a distinct possibility for many frontier families since so many women died in childbirth). Women were limited as a romantic interest; the cowboy was supposed to be naturally shy and scared around pretty young women, so romance was generally not revealed until the very end of a movie.

It is interesting to note the role of women in some of the most successful TV westerns. In "Gunsmoke" the only female lead is "Miss Kitty," who runs a saloon. In the Old West, she would have been a prostitute and madam, but on "Gunsmoke" her profession other than saloon keeper was not mentioned. Interestingly, in a genre that put white hats on good guys and black hats on bad guys and made blond-haired women sweet and innocent and dark-haired women dangerous and cunning, Miss Kitty had red hair. In "Bonanza" there were no women; Ben Cartwright was a single parent whose three sons came from three different mothers. Lucas

McCain in "The Rifleman" was also a single parent; in "The Big Valley" a woman ran the ranch because her husband had died. The list can go on but the point is clear; the western had a great deal of difficulty in finding a realistic role for women.

In the earliest stages, the Old West was a man's world; later it became a place for families, and here the role of women was essential. The enduring legacy of women in the West is that after men entered the West and opened it up, women made it a place worth keeping; men may have made the West a place where people could come to, but women made the West into a place where people would stay. (See also BULLION, LAURA; CALAMITY JANE; OAKLEY, ANNIE; PARKHURST, CHARLEY; STARR, BELLE; WOMEN IN B WESTERN MOVIES.)

WOUNDED KNEE MASSACRE (December 29, 1890) This tragic event, which pitted the Seventh Cavalry under Colonel James W. Forsyth against a group of about 350 Indians led by Big Foot, marked the end of the Indian Wars. The trouble was actually rooted in the ghost dance movement, begun by Wovoka, a Paiute Indian, who preached that all dead Indians would come back to life and rally together to defeat the whites. Adherents wore shirts that they believed made them invulnerable to the white man's bullets. The ghost dance movement gained steam and alarmed white settlers and the army, who feared an armed Indian uprising. A number of soldiers gathered in the South Dakota area of the Sioux reservation, and Indians, nervous about the soldiers, began leaving the reservations; they were immediately branded "hostiles" for this act. On a freezing December day after Christmas in 1890, Colonel Forsyth and his Seventh Cavalry surrounded Big Foot's group of about 350 Indians camped at Wounded Knee Creek on the Pine Ridge Reservation. Big Foot, who was sick with pneumonia, was ordered to surrender. As the soldiers began to search the Indians for concealed weapons, firing broke out and the soldiers slaughtered about 150 Indians there (including about 60 women and children—some were chased for about two miles and were slaughtered trying to escape); a total of about 300 Indians were killed before it was all over. The Seventh Cavalry had 25 dead and 39 wounded, mostly from the crossfire of their own shooting.

WRANGLER TV show that starred Jason Evers as Pitcairn, the Wrangler.

Pitcairn was a good Samaritan riding his Appaloosa horse, Sam, through various adventures in the Old West. A 1960 replacement for "The Ford Show Starring Tennessee Ernie Ford," this show premiered on August 4, 1960 and ended on September 15, 1960, on NBC on Thursday evenings. Interestingly, this half-hour series was one of the first westerns to be shot entirely on videotape.

WRANGLER The cowboy who takes care of the horses, usually a young or inexperienced hand on a trail crew. "Wrangling" is taking care of these horses, and "to wrangle" means to herd or drive them.

WRANGLERS Pants made of denim that are popular with many cowboys. The original parent firm was the Blue Bell Overall Company, started by C. C. Hudson in Greensboro, North Carolina in 1904. This company was sold in 1936 to R. W. Baker, who owned Big Ben Manufacturing and who merged these two companies to create a manufacturer of work apparel. After World War II the company hired Hollywood tailor Rodeo Ben to design jeans for cowboys; Rodeo Ben created the Wrangler jean after input from rodeo cowboys Jim Shoulders, Freckles Brown, Bill Linderman, Todd Whatley, Harry Tompkins and Gerald Roberts. The company's name officially became Wrangler in 1986 when it was acquired by the Vanity Fair Corporation; its headquarters are still in Greensboro.

WYATT, NATHANIEL ELLSWORTH See YAEGER, DICK.

WYATT EARP See LIFE AND LEGEND OF WYATT EARP, THE

XIT One of the most famous cattle brands of all time, it belonged to the largest ranch of its time. Owned by brothers John and Charles Farwell and founded by the Capitol Syndicate in the Texas panhandle, the ranch was named XIT, which stands for "Ten in Texas," because it covered all or part of 10 counties. Abe Blocker was the first to put this brand on a cow. At its peak, the XIT had three million acres in the Texas panhandle, 160,000 head of cattle, over 1,000 horses and 150 cowboys. There was also a branch ranch in Wyoming and Montana, used as grazing range where about 12,000 cattle were driven each spring so they could spend the summer getting fat on the northern grass. The XIT herd bossed by John McCanles in 1896 was supposedly the last to be driven up the Western Trail. Through the years most of the land on this ranch was sold because of rising real estate and falling cattle prices until there were only 20,000 acres left in 1950.

YAEGER, DICK (aka "Zip" and "Wild Charlie"; b. Nathaniel Ellsworth Wyatt in Indiana in 1863; d. Enid, Oklahoma on September 7, 1895)   Known as "Zip," was killed in Texas. He and two other outlaws killed E. H. Townsend, a Blaine County store owner in Todd, Oklahoma in front of his wife and children on March 29, 1894. He killed Dewey County, Oklahoma treasurer Fred Hoffman in cold blood in April 1894 and about a month later killed a telegraph operator in Whorton (Perry) Oklahoma who was typing a message for help when the outlaws held up a Santa Fe train. Zip killed Sheriff Andrew Balfour on July 4, 1894 in Pryor's Grove, Kansas. Several posses hunted Yaeger, and a large group found him asleep in a cornfield near Skeleton Creek, Oklahoma on August 3, 1895. The posse quietly got into position and then Ad Poak and Tom Smith pumped lead into him as he lay there. Taken to Enid, he died from his wounds in a few weeks.

YANCY DERRINGER   TV show that starred Jock Mahoney as Yancy Derringer, X. Brands as Pahoo-Ka-Ta-Wah, Kevin Hagen as John Colton, Julie Adams as Amanda Eaton and Frances Bergen as Madame Francine.

Yancy Derringer lived in New Orleans and carried a hidden small derringer pistol for trouble. A card shark, ladies' man and man about town, Derringer was assisted by his faithful Indian sidekick Pahoo. Ostensibly a gambler, Yancy—a former Confederate soldier—was also a special agent for the civil administrator of New Orleans, John Colton. This show ran one season, premiering on October 2, 1958 and ending September 24, 1959. The 34 half-hour episodes were shot in black and white and appeared on Thursday nights on CBS.

YELLOW ROSE, THE   TV show that starred Sam Elliott as Chance McKenzie, Cybil Shepherd as Colleen Champion, David Soul as Roy Champion, Edward Albert as Quisto Champion, Chuck Connors as Jeb Hollister, Deborah Shelton as Juliette Hollister, Susan Anspach as Grace McKenzie (1983), Noah Beery, Jr. as Luther Dillard, Ken Curtis as Hoyt Coryell, Tom Schanley as Whit Champion, Kerrie Keane as Caryn Cabrera and Will Sampson as John Stronghart.

This was a contemporary western soap opera set on a 200,000-acre west Texas ranch, The Yellow Rose. The story lines generally involved power struggles for the ranch and sexual liaisons or attractions between various members of the cast. The show premiered on October 2, 1983 on Sunday nights on NBC. It soon moved to Saturday nights, where it ran until its final telecast on May 12, 1984.

YELLOW ROSE OF TEXAS, THE   This song dates from the Texas Revolution and is supposedly about an indentured servant, Emily D. West, who served Colonel James Morgan, a plantation owner who fought for the Texas army. Also known as Emily Morgan, after her master's name, West came from New York to Texas in 1835 when Morgan tried to establish a colony of freed blacks. During the revolution, Santa Anna took control of Morgan's plantation and took custody of his servants, including the mulatto Emily. Emily was in the tent with Santa Anna on the afternoon of April 21, 1836 when Sam Houston's forces attacked the Mexican army at San Jacinto; her favors had distracted the Mexican general, who ran out into the battle in his underwear and red slippers. This lack of preparation and the ensuing chaos caused the defeat of the Mexicans. Emily's story was told to British ethnologist William Bollaert by Colonel Morgan in 1842, who conveyed the idea that the charms of the "yellow rose" were responsible for Texas independence. The song was composed soon after the Battle of San Jacinto, probably by a Tennessee volunteer. It was first published in sheet music in 1858 by Charles Brown of Jackson, Tennessee. The current melody was written by David Guion in 1930 and based on a tune he'd heard in Texas during his boyhood; this adaptation was published in 1936 in honor of the Texas Centennial. The song achieved its greatest national fame in 1955 when Mitch Miller and his group recorded it and performed it on TV and in concerts. (See also SAN JACINTO, BATTLE OF.)

YELLOW SKY   Film produced by Lamar Trotti; directed by William A. Wellman; screenplay by Lamar Trotti from a novel by W. R. Burnett; released by Twentieth Century–Fox in 1948; 98 minutes in length. Cast: Gregory Peck, Anne Baxter, Richard Widmark, Robert Arthur, John Russell, Harry Morgan, James Barton, Charles Kemperer, Jay Silverheels and Chief Yowlachie.

In 1867 some former soldiers in the Civil War hold up a bank and then are pursued into the desert by the cavalry. After wandering in the desert for days, the outlaws find a ghost town named Yellow Sky, where an old man and his granddaughter live. There is also water and a hidden treasure of gold. The gold makes everyone crazy, and the leader of the outlaws has to fight it out with his partners—and win the young lady.

YELLOWSTONE NATIONAL PARK   Yellowstone was established as a national park on March 1, 1872, the first in the national park system. Located in the northwest corner of Wyoming, with parts in Montana and Idaho, the 3,500-square-mile park contains bubbling hot springs, geysers (including Old Faithful), wild grizzly bears, buffalo, elk, moose and deep canyons. The first white person to see Yellowstone was fur trapper and mountain man John Colter in 1807–8; later Jim Bridger explored it. Both men met with disbelief when they told stories about its bubbling springs and geysers. The first published eyewitness accounts of Yellowstone were in the *Philadelphia Gazette* in 1827. The first official government expedition was led by Captain W. F. Raynold of the Corps of Topographical Engineers, who arrived in 1859. The area was a source of mystique to the Indians, who thought the hot springs and geysers contained evil spirits. White men were disbelieving of stories from those who visited there; in 1869 Montanans David Folsom, C. W. Cook and William Peterson went there to dispel rumors of its wonders; when they came back they kept silent, unwilling to "risk their reputations" by telling what they saw. In 1870 and again in 1871, official expeditions led by Henry D. Washburn and Dr. F. V. Hayden, respectively, brought back information about Yellowstone, including photographs by William Henry Jackson. The photographs, along with Hayden's 500-page report and paintings and sketches from artist Thomas Moran, convinced the Congress to establish it as the country's first national park.

YOUNG, BRIGHAM (b. Whitingham, Vermont on June 1, 1801; d. Salt Lake City, Utah on August 29, 1877) Brigham Young took over the Mormon movement in 1844 after Joseph Smith was killed in Illinois during violent anti-Mormon demonstrations. Young had converted to Mormonism in 1832, had become a missionary and was the senior member of the Quorum of Twelve Apostles in 1839, making him second in command to Smith. After Smith's death Young resolved to lead the Mormons out of non-Mormon land and establish their own colony. In the spring of 1847 he led them west until they reached the Great Salt Lake basin in Mexican Territory (now Utah), where he proclaimed the place as the Mormon colony. A horde of Mormons followed, some with push carts, as settlers laid out a city, irrigated the land and made the desert habitable. The group named its state Deseret and petitioned the Congress to become a state in 1849; Congress, fearful of the Mormons, denied their petition but established the Territory of Utah there in 1850 and named Young the governor. Later, Young was replaced as governor, a result of hostilities between the federal government and Mormons, but he remained the major power in Utah until his death. A polygamist, he had as many as 27 wives with 56 children and 17 widows at the time of his death.

YOUNG DAN'L BOONE TV show that starred Rick Moses as Daniel Boone, Devon Ericson as Rebecca Bryan, Ji-Tu Cumbuka as Hawk, John Joseph Thomas as Peter Dawes and Eloy Phil Casados as Tsiskwa.

When Fess Parker played Daniel Boone in the 1960s, the frontier hero was older—in his 40s. This program attempted to show Boone in his mid-20s and lasted only four weeks. The show premiered on September 12, 1977

on Monday nights on CBS and stayed there for three weeks. The hour-long show moved to Tuesday night for its final telecast on October 4, 1977.

YOUNGER, BOB (b. Robert Younger in Lee's Summit, Missouri on October, 1853; d. Stillwater, Minnesota on September 16, 1889) The youngest of the Younger brothers, Bob was the reason the James brothers and Youngers split after the Northfield, Minnesota robbery. Bob had been hit badly, and Jesse James insisted that Cole either abandon his brother or finish him off so they could all make their getaway. Cole refused and the gang split, with the James brothers escaping and the Youngers, who were wounded, being captured two weeks later. Bob had been hit by a rifle slug, which tore his right arm from his hand to the elbow. He was hit by Henry Wheeler, a young medical student, who was standing at a second-story window and who had just killed Clell Miller, another gang member. Bob's horse had been killed, and Cole pulled him up on his horse as he raced out of town. Bob slowed down the Youngers, and Samuel Wells and a posse tracked them to a swamp where, after a wild shootout, Wells was killed and Bob was hit in the chest. The Youngers pleaded guilty and received a life sentence. Bob studied medicine in prison but in 1889 caught tuberculosis and died. (See also JAMES, JESSE; NORTHFIELD, MINNESOTA RAID.)

YOUNGER, COLE (b. Thomas Coleman Younger in Lee's Summit, Missouri on January 15, 1844; d. Lee's Summit, Missouri on February 21, 1916) Cole Younger was the last surviving member of the outlaw Younger brothers and, in his later days, performed in a Wild West show with Frank James. Cole was the seventh child in the family of 14. He rode with Quantrill's "Bushwhackers" after his father was killed by Jayhawkers in 1862, and then joined regular Confederate troops. Cole and Myra Belle Shirley, later famous as Belle Starr, were lovers, and he fathered a daughter, Pearl, by her in Texas. Frank James, who had also ridden with Quantrill, and Cole ran into each other in Missouri after the war and held up a bank in Liberty; then he and his brothers formed a gang with Jesse and Frank James that held up a number of banks and trains in later years. After the Northfield, Minnesota raid, a posse tracked down the Younger brothers and arrested them after a shootout in which Cole received 11 wounds. He received a pardon from prison in 1903, joined Frank James for a brief venture in a Wild West show and spent his final years traveling and lecturing on the evils of crime. He died at the age of 72 in the town where he was born and grew up. (See also JAMES, FRANK; JAMES, JESSE; NORTHFIELD, MINNESOTA RAID; STARR, BELLE.)

YOUNGER, JAMES (b. Lee's Summit, Missouri on January 15, 1848; d. St. Paul, Minnesota on October 19, 1902) Like his older brother, Cole, Jim joined Quantrill's raiders during the Civil War to avenge the murder of their father. When Quantrill was killed near Smiley, Kentucky, Jim was caught and sent to the military prison in Alton, Illinois. After his release in 1865 he returned to Missouri and then joined up with Cole and

Cole Younger *(Western Archives)*

the James brothers to rob. After a series of holdups, Jim and John Younger were in Monegaw Springs, Missouri hiding at a friend's home when Pinkerton agents Louis J. Lull and John Boyle, with Deputy Sheriff Ed Daniels, came looking for them. Lull and Boyle were both killed when they encountered the Youngers on the Chalk Level Road on the afternoon of March 16, 1874; so was John Younger. Cole and Bob Younger found out about their brother's death by reading about it in a newspaper in Mississippi several weeks later and went to Arkansas, where they reunited with Jim. After the Northfield, Minnesota robbery on September 7, 1876, the James brothers went one way and the Younger brothers (Cole, Bob and Jim), along with Samuel Wells, went another to shake the posses chasing them. Two weeks later, after a gunfight in which Wells was killed, the Younger brothers surrendered to the posse. Jim was badly hurt—one of his five wounds was a bullet lodged just below his brain (the bullet had shattered his jaw). He lived in pain for three years, until he persuaded a prison hospital intern to take it out. Jim was paroled from prison in 1901 with Cole under the Deming Act, which allowed lifers out who had served a certain number of years. But he had no legal rights and had to stay in Minnesota. Jim fell in love with Alice J. Miller, a newspaper writer, but could not marry

her. In poor health, he sold insurance for a while but then learned that all the policies were no good because he was a former convict. So on October 19, 1902 he went to the Reardon Hotel in St. Paul, got a pistol and committed suicide. (See also JAMES, JESSE; NORTHFIELD, MINNESOTA RAID; YOUNGER, COLE.)

YOUNGER, JOHN (b. Lee's Summit, Missouri c. 1851; d. Monegaw Springs, Missouri on March 16, 1794)   John's father was killed by Jayhawkers, and the youth reportedly killed his first man when he was 15 after the man hit Younger with a dead fish. At 17 he was hung and beaten by a posse looking for Cole and Jim Younger. He moved to Texas with Cole and Jim but returned to Missouri after he killed a sheriff. John was with the James-Younger Gang during the train robbery at Gads Hill and hid out afterward in Monegaw Springs, Missouri with his brother Jim at a friend's home. On March 16, 1874 the brothers learned that Pinkerton detectives Louis J. Lull and John Boyle, and Deputy Sheriff Ed Daniels, were looking for them. On the Chalk Level Road, the Youngers caught up with the lawmen and disarmed them, but Lull pulled out a hidden pistol and shot John. John then killed Lull with a shotgun and Daniels with a pistol. But John had been hit badly; he fell to the ground and died.

YOUNG MAVERICK TV show that starred Charles Frank as Ben Maverick, Susan Blanchard as Nell McGarrahan and John Dehner as Marshal Edge Troy.

This show attempted to re-create the "Maverick" series but came up rather short. The show featured Ben Maverick, educated at Harvard with the Maverick penchant for gambling, humor and cowardice. Ben was the son of Beau and cousin to Bret. The show premiered on November 28, 1979 and had its last telecast on January 16, 1980. The hour-long show aired on Wednesday evenings on CBS.

YOUNG RIDERS TV show that starred Yvonne Suhor as Lou McCloud, Gregg Rainwater as Little Buck Cross, Josh Brolin as Jimmy Hickok, Ty Miller as the Kid, Stephen Baldwin as William "Billy" Cody, Travis Fine as Ike McSwain, Anthony Zerbe as Teaspoon Hunter, Melissa Leo as Emma Shannon, Brett Cullen as Marshall Sam Cain and Don Collier as Tompkins.

This was a story of young Pony Express riders and their adventures. It premiered on the ABC network on September 20, 1989 and ran until September 1, 1992. Sixty-six episodes were filmed.

YUMAN INDIANS The Yuman Indians—comprising the tribes of Yuma, Mohave, Havasupai, Maricopa, Walapai, Yavapai and Cocopah—lived in the southwestern Arizona and southeastern California area around the Gila River. These Indians farmed, hunted small game and fished. They were a primitive people; the men usually went naked, and the women wore a small barkcloth apron. They generally lived in open-sided dwellings with brush roofs. The Mohave liked tattoos, and all cremated their dead, which was very unusual for American Indians.

ZANE GREY THEATER   See DICK POWELL'S ZANE GREY THEATER.)

ZORRO   TV show that starred Guy Williams as Don Diega de la Vega (Zorro), George J. Lewis as Don Alejandro, Gene Sheldon as Bernardo, Britt Lomond as Captain Monastario, Henry Calvin as Sergeant Garcia, Jan Arvan as Nacho Torres, Eugenia Paul as Elena Torres, Vinton Hayworth as Magistrate Galindo, Jolene Brand as Anna Maria Verdugo (1958–59), Eduard Franz as Senor Gregorio Verdugo (1958–59) and Don Diamond as Captain Reyes (1958–59).

The Spanish West of California in 1820 was the setting for Zorro. Don Diego de la Vega had returned from Spain at the insistence of his father, Don Alejandro, because the area was being terrorized by a ruthless army captain. Don Diego appeared to be rather docile and effete during the day, but at night he went into a secret cave and emerged as Zorro, dressed in black with a black mask and armed with a sword with which he slashed a "Z" to let all know he had saved the day. Zorro was helped by his trusty servant Bernardo, who could not speak and most thought could not hear. Don Diego knew better, and thus he learned of fiendish plots cooked up by the inept Captain Monastario and enforced by the even more inept Sergeant Garcia from the evesdropping Bernardo. The Zorro character had appeared in several movies previously, played by actors Douglas Fairbanks and Tyrone Power. The TV Zorro rode his coal-black horse, Tornado, for three seasons, premiering on October 10, 1957 with the final telecast on September 24, 1959. This half-hour show was produced by Walt Disney and appeared on ABC on Thursday nights. There were 117 episodes filmed on the elaborately constructed lot at Disney Studios.

ZORRO AND SON   TV show that starred Henry Darrow as Don Diego de la Vega (Zorro, Sr.), Paul Regina as Don Carlos de la Vega (Zorro, Jr.), Gregory Sierra as Commandante Paco Pico, Richard Beauchamp as Sergeant Sepulveda, Bill Dana as Bernardo, Barney Martin as brothers Napa and Sonomo, John Moschitta as Corporal Cassette, Catherine Parks as Senorita Anita and Pete Leal as Peasant.

A humorous update of Zorro—actually almost a satire of the original Zorro—this show featured Don Diego de la Vega's son, Don Carlos, who came from Spain to help his father (like the original) but would rather chase

Zorro   (Guy Williams)

girls and party than administer justice. And when the young Zorro did administer justice, it was more likely to be with guns, bombs and other modern weapons instead of a sword—which drove his Dad crazy. The show was produced by Walt Disney, who produced the original, and was shot on the Disney back lot—as was the original. It premiered on April 6, 1983 on Wednesday evenings on CBS. The half-hour show ended on June 1, 1983 after just nine episodes.

ZUNI INDIANS   One of the Pueblo Indian tribes who lived in permanent adobe villages in New Mexico, the Zuni were conquered by Coronado in 1540 while the Spanish conquistador was looking for the Seven Cities of Cibola, filled with gold. In 1680 the Zuni were part of the Pueblo Revolt. The Zuni are known for their fine jewelry, with turquoise, silver and shell mosaic.

BIBLIOGRAPHY

Abbott, E. C. ("Teddy Blue"), and Helena Huntington Smith. *We Pointed Them North: Recollections of a Cowpuncher.* Norman: University of Oklahoma Press, 1966.

Adams, Alexander B. *Sitting Bull: An Epic of the Plains.* New York: Putnam, 1973.

Adams, Andy. *The Log of a Cowboy: A Narrative of the Old Trail Days.* Lincoln: University of Nebraska Press, 1964.

Adams, Les, and Buck Rainey. *Shoot-Em-Ups: The Complete Reference Guide to Westerns of the Sound Era.* Waynesville, N.C.: World of Yesterday, 1978.

Adams, Ramon F. *Burs Under the Saddle: A Second Look at Books and Histories of the West.* Norman: University of Oklahoma Press, 1989.

———. *Come and Get It: The Story of the Old Cowboy Cook.* Norman: University of Oklahoma Press, 1953.

———. *A Fitting Death for Billy the Kid.* Norman: University of Oklahoma Press, 1960.

———. *More Burs Under the Saddle: Books and Histories of the West.* Norman: University of Oklahoma Press, 1989.

———. *The Old Time Cowhand.* New York: Macmillan, 1961.

———. *Prose and Poetry of the Live Stock Industry.* New York: Antiquarian Press, Ltd. 1959.

———. *Six-Guns & Saddle Leather: A Bibliography of Books & Pamphlets on Western Outlaws and Gunmen.* Norman: University of Oklahoma Press, 1969.

———. *Western Words: A Dictionary of the Range, Cow Camp and Trail.* Norman: University of Oklahoma Press, 1968.

Alexander, Kent. *Heroes of the Wild West.* New York: Mallard Press, 1992.

Alter, J. Cecil. *Jim Bridger.* Norman: University of Oklahoma Press, 1962.

Applegate, Jesse. *A Day With the Cow Column in 1843.* Caldwell, Idaho: Caxton Club, 1934.

Arbeiter, Jean, and Linda D. Cirino. *Permanent Addresses: A Guide to the Resting Places of Famous Americans.* New York: M. Evans and Company, 1983.

Armitage, Susan, and Elizabeth Jameson, eds. *The Women's West.* Norman: University of Oklahoma Press, 1987.

Asbury, Herbert. *The Barbary Coast.* New York: Capricorn Books, 1968.

———. *Sucker's Progress.* New York: Dodd, Mead & Co., 1938.

Athearn, Robert G. *Rebel of the Rockies: A History of the Denver and Rio Grande Western Railroad.* New Haven, Conn.: Yale University Press, 1962.

———. *Union Pacific Country.* Skokie, Ill.: Rand McNally & Co., 1971.

———. *William Tecumseh Sherman and the Settlement of the West.* Norman: University of Oklahoma Press, 1956.

Atherton, Lewis. *The Cattle Kings.* Bloomington: Indiana University Press, 1961.

Autry, Gene. *Back in the Saddle Again.* Garden City, N.Y.: Doubleday, 1976.

Backes, Clarus, ed. *Growing Up Western.* New York: Alfred A. Knopf, 1990.

Baldwin, Leland D. *The Keelboat Age on Western Waters.* Pittsburgh, Pa.: University of Pittsburgh Press, 1941.

Barker, Eugene C. *The Life of Stephen F. Austin.* Austin: University of Texas Press, 1969.

Barrett, S.M., ed. *Geronimo—His Own Story.* New York: Ballantine, 1973.

Bartholomew, E. *Wild Bill Longley: A Texas Hard-Case.* Frontier Press of Texas, 1953.

———. *Wyatt Earp: The Man and the Myth.* Fort Davis, Tex.: Frontier Book Company, 1964.

———. *Wyatt Earp: The Untold Story.* Fort Davis, Tex.: Frontier Book Company, 1963.

Bartlett, Richard A. *Great Surveys of the American West.* Norman: University of Oklahoma Press, 1962.

Bayless, John. *Daniel Boone.* Harrisburg, Pa.: Stackpole Company, 1965.

Beal, Merrill D. *I Will Fight No More Forever; Chief Joseph and the Nez Perce War.* Seattle: University of Washington Press, 1963.

Bearss, Edwin C., and Arrell M. Gibson. *Fort Smith: Little Gibraltar on the Arkansas.* Norman: University of Oklahoma Press, 1969.

Beatie, Russel H. *Saddles.* Norman: University of Oklahoma Press, 1981.

Beck, W. A. *New Mexico: A History of Four Centuries.* Norman: University of Oklahoma Press, 1962.

Beck, Warren A., and Ynez D. Hasse. *Historical Atlas of the American West.* Norman: University of Oklahoma Press, 1989.

Bell, William Gardner. *Will James: The Life and Works of a Lone Cowboy.* Flagstaff, Ariz.: Northland Press, 1987.

Berry, Barbara. *Let 'Er Buck: The Rodeo.* Indianapolis: Bobbs-Merrill, 1979.

Bidwell, John. *Journey to California.* Friends of The Bancroft Library, 1964.

Billington, Ray A. *America's Frontier Heritage.* New York: Holt, Rinehart and Winston, 1966.

———. *Frederick Jackson Turner.* New York: Oxford University Press, 1973.

———. *Westward Expansion.* New York: Macmillan, 1967.

Billington, Ray A., ed. *People of the Plains and Mountains.* Westport, Conn.: Greenwood Press, 1973.

Bird, Isabella L. *A Lady's Life in the Rocky Mountains.* Norman: University of Oklahoma Press, 1960.

Blackstone, Sarah J. *Bullets, Buckskins and Business: A History of Buffalo Bill's Wild West.* Westport, Conn.: Greenwood Press, 1986.

Blevins, Winfred. *Dictionary of the American West.* New York: Facts On File, 1993.

Boessenecker, John. *Badge and Buckshot: Lawlessness in Old California.* Norman: University of Oklahoma Press, 1988.

Borthwick, J.D. *The Gold Hunters.* Highland Park, NJ: Gryphon Books, 1971.

Botkin, Benjamin A. *A Treasury of Western Folklore.* New York: Bonanza Books, 1975.

Bourke, J.G. *On the Border with Crook.* Glorieta, N.M.: Rio Grande Press, 1969.

Bowen, John (text), and Lynn Radeka (photographs). *Legendary Towns of the Old West.* New York: Mallard Books, 1990.

Bowman, John S. *The World Almanac of the American West.* New York: Pharos Book, 1986.

Brady, Cyrus T. *Indian Fights and Fighters.* Lincoln: University of Nebraska Press, 1971.

Breakenridge, William M. *Helldorado.* Glorieta, N.M.: Rio Grande Press, 1970.

Breihan, Carl W. *The Complete and Authentic Life of Jesse James.* New York: Frederick Fell, 1953, 1969.

———. *Great Gunfighters of the West.* San Antonio, Tex.: Naylor Co., 1962.

Brisbin, James S. The Beef Bonanza; or, How to Get Rich on the Plains. Norman: University of Oklahoma Press, 1959.

Brooks, Juanita. *The Mountain Meadows Massacre.* Norman: University of Oklahoma Press, 1950.

Brooks, Tim. *The Complete Directory to Prime Time TV Stars: 1946–Present.* New York: Ballantine, 1987.

Brooks, Tim, and Earle Marsh. *The Complete Directory to Prime Time Network TV Shows: 1946–Present.* New York: Ballantine, 1988.

Brown, Dee. *Bury My Heart at Wounded Knee.* New York: Holt, Rinehart and Winston, 1971.

———. *Fort Phil Kearny: An American Saga.* Lincoln: University of Nebraska Press, 1971.

———. *The Gentle Tamers: Women of the Old Wild West.* Lincoln: University of Nebraska Press, 1968.

———. *Lonesome Whistle: The Story of the First Transcontinental Railroad.* New York: Holt, Rinehart and Winston, 1980.

———. *Wondrous Times on the Frontier.* Little Rock, Ark.: August House Publishers, 1991.

Brown, Mark H. *The Flight of the Nez Perce.* New York: Putnam, 1967.

Brown, Mark, and W.R. Felton. *Before Barbed Wire.* New York: Henry Holt, 1956.

Bruce, Robert. *The Fighting Norths and Pawnee Scouts.* Lincoln: University of Nebraska Press, 1932.

Bruhl, Marshall De. *Sword of San Jacinto: A Life of Sam Houston.* New York: Random House, 1992.

Buel, James W. *The Border Bandits.* St. Louis: Historical Publishing Co., 1880.

———. *The Border Outlaws.* St. Louis: Historical Publishing Co., 1882.

Burdett, Charles. *The Life of Kit Carson.* New York: Grosset & Dunlap, 1902.

Burke, John. *Buffalo Bill, the Noblest Whiteskin.* New York: Putnam, 1973.

Burns, Walter Noble. *Tombstone: Gun-Toting, Cattle Rustling Days in Old Arizona.* New York: Grosset and Dunlap, 1929.

———. *Tombstone: An Iliad of the Southwest.* New York: Grosset and Dunlap, 1927.

Burroughs, John Rolfe. *Guardian of the Grasslands.* Bellingham, Wash.: Pioneer Printing & Stationery Co., 1971.

Burt, Nathaniel. *Jackson Hole Journal.* Norman: University of Oklahoma Press, 1984.

Burton, David H. *Theodore Roosevelt.* New York: Twayne Publishers, 1972.

Byworth, Tony. *The History of Country & Western Music.* New York: Exeter Books, 1984.

Cahill, Marie, and Lynne Piade, eds. *The History of the Union Pacific.* New York: Crescent Books, 1989.

Canfield, C.L. *Diary of a Forty-Niner.* Boston: Houghton-Mifflin, 1920.

Canfield, J.E. *The Blackfeet, Raiders on the Northwestern Plains.* Norman: University of Oklahoma Press, 1958.

Canton, Frank M. *Frontier Trails.* Norman: University of Oklahoma Press, 1966.

Capps, Benjamin (text). *The Great Chiefs,* Old West Series. Alexandra, Va.: Time-Life, 1975.

———. *The Indians,* Old West Series. Alexandra, Va.: Time-Life, 1973.

Carr, Patrick, ed. *The Illustrated History of Country Music.* New York: Dolphin, 1980.

Carrington, F.C. *My Army Life and the Fort Phil Kearny.* Philadelphia: J.B. Lippincott & Co., 1910.

Carter, Harvey Lewis. *"Dear Old Kit": The Historical Christopher Carson.* Norman: University of Oklahoma Press, 1968.

Cary, Diana. *The Hollywood Posse.* Boston: Houghton Mifflin, 1975.

Catlin, George. *North American Indians,* vols. I, II. Minneapolis: Ross & Haines, 1965.

Cawelti, John. *The Six-Gun Mystique.* Bowling Green, Ohio: Bowling Green University Popular Press, 1971.

Chafetz, H. *Play the Devil: A History of Gambling in the U.S. from 1492 to 1955.* New York: Clarkson N. Potter, 1960.

Chidsey, Donald Barr. *The War with Mexico.* New York: Crown Publishers, 1968.

Chittenden, Hiram Martin. *The American Fur Trade of the Far West,* 3 vols. F.P. Harper, 1902.

———. *The Yellowstone National Park.* Norman: University of Oklahoma Press, 1971.

Clairmonte, Glenn. *Calamity Was the Name for Jane.* Denver: Sage, 1943.

Clancy, Foghorn. *My Fifty Years in Rodeo.* San Antonio, Tex.: Naylor Co., 1952.

Clay, John. *My Life on the Range.* Norman: University of Oklahoma Press, 1962.

Cleland, Robert Glass. *The Cattle on a Thousand Hills: Southern California, 1850–1880.* San Marino, Calif.: Huntington Library, 1951.

———. *This Reckless Breed of Men, the Trappers and Fur Traders of the Southwest.* New York: Alfred A. Knopf, 1950.

Clum, John P. *It All Happened in Tombstone.* Flagstaff, Ariz.: Northland Press, 1965.

Cody, William F. *The Life of Buffalo Bill.* New York: Indian Head Books, 1991.

Collings, Ellsworth, and Alma Miller England. *The 101 Ranch.* Norman: University of Oklahoma Press, 1971.

Commager, Henry Steele, ed. in chief: *The Story of America: The Age of the West.* New York: Torstar Books, 1975.

Connor, Seymour V. *Adventure in Glory: The Saga of Texas, 1836–1849.* Austin, Tex.: Steck-Vaughn Co., 1965.

———. *Texas: A History.* New York: Thomas Y. Crowell, 1971.

Constable, George, ed. *The Gamblers,* Old West Series. Alexandria, Va.: Time-Life, 1978.

———. *The Old West,* foreword by Robert Utley. New York: Prentice Hall, 1990.

Cook, James H. *Longhorn Cowboy.* Norman: University of Oklahoma Press, 1984.

Coolidge, Dane. *California Cowboys.* Tucson: University of Arizona Press, 1985.

———. *Texas Cowboys.* Tucson: University of Arizona Press, 1981.

Cox, James. *The Cattle Industry of Texas and Adjacent Territory.* New York: Antiquarian Press, Ltd. 1959.

Crampton, Frank A. *Deep Enough: A Working Stiff in the Western Mine Camps.* Norman: University of Oklahoma Press, 1982.

Craze, Sophia. *Charles Russell.* New York: Crescent Books, 1989.

———. *Frederic Remington.* New York: Crescent Books, 1989.

Cromie, Alice. *A Tour Guide to the Old West.* Nashville: Rutledge Hill Press, 1990.

Croy, Homer. *Jesse James Was My Neighbor.* New York: Duell, Sloan and Pearce, 1949.

Culin, Stewart. *Games of the North American Indians.* New York: Dover Publications, 1975.

Cunningham, E. *Triggernometry, a Gallery of Gunfighters.* New York: Press of the Pioneers, 1934.

Curry, Larry, ed. *The American West.* New York: Viking Press, 1972.

Custer, Elizabeth B. *Boots and Saddles.* Norman: University of Oklahoma Press, 1961.

Custer, George Armstrong. *My Life on the Plains or Personal Experiences with Indians.* Norman: University of Oklahoma Press, 1962.

Dale, Edward Everett. *The Indians of the Southwest: A Century of Development Under the United States.* Norman: University of Oklahoma Press, 1949.

———. *The Range Cattle Industry: Ranching on the Great Plains from 1865 to 1925.* Norman: University of Oklahoma Press, 1969.

Dallas, Sandra. *No More Than Five in a Bed: Colorado Hotels in the Old Days.* Norman: University of Oklahoma Press, 1967.

Dalton, Emmett, and J. Jungmeyer. *When the Daltons Rode.* Garden City, N.Y.: Doubleday, Doran & Company, 1931.

Daniels, George. G., ed. *The Spanish West,* Old West Series. Alexandria, Va.: Time-Life, 1976.

Dary, David. *Cowboy Culture: A Saga of Five Centuries.* Lawrence: University Press of Kansas, 1981, 1989.

———. *Entrepreneurs of the Old West.* New York: Alfred A. Knopf, 1986.

Davis, Britton. *The Truth about Geronimo.* R.R. Donnelley & Sons, 1951.

Davis, Williams C. *The American Frontier: Pioneers, Settlers & Cowboys, 1800–1899.* New York: Smithmark, 1992.

Day, Donald. *Will Rogers: A Biography.* New York: David McKay Company, 1962.

DeArment, Robert K. *Bat Masterson: The Man and the Legend.* Norman: University of Oklahoma Press, 1979.

———. *Knights of the Green Cloth: The Saga of the Frontier Gamblers.* Norman: University of Oklahoma Press, 1982.

Debo, Angie. *Geronimo: The Man, His Time, His Place.* Norman: University of Oklahoma Press, 1976.

———. *Prairie City.* Tulsa: Council Oak Books, Ltd., 1944, 1985.

Dellar, Fred, and Roy Thompson. *The Illustrated Encyclopedia of Country Music.* New York: Harmony, 1977.

Denig, E.T. *Five Indian Tribes of the Upper Missouri.* Norman: University of Oklahoma Press, 1989.

Devol, G.H. *Forty Years a Gambler on the Mississippi.* Johnson Reprint, 1892.

Devoto, Bernard. *Across the Wide Missouri.* Boston: Houghton Mifflin, 1947.

———. *The Course of Empire.* Boston: Houghton Mifflin, 1962.

Devoto, Bernard, ed. *The Journals of Lewis and Clark.* Boston: Houghton Mifflin, 1953.

Dick, Everett N. *Conquering the Great American Desert.* Lincoln: Nebraska State Historical Society, 1975.

———. *The Lure of the Land: A Social History of the Public Lands.* Lincoln: University of Nebraska Press, 1970.

———. *The Sod House Frontier, 1854–1890.* Lincoln, Neb.: Johnsen Publishing Co., 1954.

Dimsdale, Thomas J. *The Vigilantes of Montana.* Norman: University of Oklahoma Press 1972.

Dobie, J. Frank. *The Longhorns.* Austin: University of Texas Press, 1990.

———. *The Mustangs.* Boston: Little, Brown, 1952.

———. *A Vaquero of the Brush Country.* Boston: Little, Brown, 1960.

Dodge, Richard Irving. *The Hunting Grounds of the Great West.* Chatto & Windus, 1877.

———. *The Plains of North America and Their Inhabitants.* Newark: University of Delaware Press, 1989.

Downey, Fairfax. *Indian-Fighting Army.* Ft. Collins, Colo.: Old Army Press, 1971.

Drago, Harry Sinclair. *Great American Cattle Trails.* Boston: Bramhall House, 1965.

———. *The Great Range Wars: Violence on the Grasslands.* New York: Dodd, Mead, 1970.

———. *Outlaws on Horseback.* New York: Dodd, Mead, 1964.

———. *Wild, Woolly and Wicket: The History of the Kansas Cow Towns.* New York: Clarkson N. Potter, 1960.

Dresden, Donald. *The Marquis de Mores.* Norman: University of Oklahoma Press, 1970.

Drinnon, Richard. *Facing West: The Metaphysics of Indian Hating & Empire Building.* New York: Schocken Books, 1990.

Dufour, Charles L. *The Mexican War: A Compact History, 1846–1848.* New York: Hawthorn Books, 1968.

Duke, Cordia Sloan, and Joe B. Frantz. *6,000 Miles of Fence: Life on the XIT Ranch in Texas.* Austin: University of Texas Press, 1961.

Durham, Philip, and Everett L. Jones. *The Negro Cowboys.* New York: Dodd, Mead, 1965.

Dykstra, Robert R. *The Cattle Towns.* Lincoln: University of Nebraska Press, 1968.

Eagle/Walking Turtle. *Indian America: A Traveler's Companion.* Santa Fe, N.M.: John Muir Publications, 1989.

Earp, Josephine S.M. *I Married Wyatt Earp,* ed. by Glenn G. Boyer. Tucson: University of Arizona Press, 1976.

Eastman, Mary. *Dahcotah: Life and Legends of the Sioux.* Minneapolis: Ross and Haines, Inc., 1962.

Easton, Robert. *Max Brand, The Big "Westerner."* Norman: University of Oklahoma Press, 1970.

Eckert, Edward K., and Nicholas J. Amato, eds. *Ten Years in the Saddle: The Memoir of William Woods Averell, 1851–1862.* Novato, Calif.: Presidio Press, 1978.

Edwards, Elwyn Hartley. *Encyclopedia of the Horse.* New York: Crescent Books, 1977.

Elliott, David S., and Ed Bartholomew. *The Dalton Gang and the Coffeyville Raid.* Fort Davis, Tex.: Frontier Book Co., 1968.

Emmett, Chris. *Shanghai Pierce: A Fair Likeness.* Norman: University of Oklahoma Press, 1953.

Estergreen, M. Morgan. *Kit Carson: A Portrait in Courage.* Norman: University of Oklahoma Press, 1989.

Everson, William K. *History of the Western Film.* Secaucus, N.J.: Citadel Press, 1969.

Ewers, John S. *Indian Life on the Upper Missouri.* Norman: University of Oklahoma Press, 1988.

Eyles, Allen. *The Western.* Cranbury, N.J.: A.S. Barnes, 1975.

Faragher, John M. *Daniel Boone: The Life and Legend of an American Pioneer.* New York: Henry Holt, 1993.

Faulk, Odie B. *Arizona: A Short History.* Norman: University of Oklahoma Press, 1988.

———. *Dodge City.* New York: Oxford University Press, 1977.

———. *Tombstone: Myth and Reality.* New York: Oxford University Press, 1972.

Fees, Paul, and Sarah E. Boehme. *Frontier America: Art and Treasures of the Old West from the Buffalo Bill Historical Center.* New York: Harry N. Abrams, 1988.

Fehrenbach, T.R. *Lone Star: A History of Texas and the Texans.* New York: Macmillan, 1968.

Fenin, George N., and William K. Everson. *The Western from Silents to the Seventies.* New York: Penguin Books, 1977.

Ferris, Robert G., ed. *Prospector, Cowhand, and Sodbuster.* Washington, D.C.: U.S. Department of the Interior, 1967.

Fife, Austin E. and Alta S. *Cowboy and Western Songs: A Comprehensive Anthology.* New York: Clarkson N. Potter, 1969.

Fife, Austin E. and Alta S. *Heaven on Horseback: Revivalist Songs and Verse in the Cowboy Idiom.* Logan: Utah State University Press, 1970.

Finler, Joel W. *The Hollywood Story.* New York: Crown, 1988.

Fisher, Leonard Everett. *Remington and Russell.* New York: Gallery Books, 1985.

Fisher, Ovie C., and J.C. Dykes. *King Fisher: His Life and Times.* Norman: University of Oklahoma Press, 1966.

Fisher, Vardis, and Opal Laurel Holmes. *Gold Rushes and Mining Camps of the Early American West.* Caldwell, Idaho: Caxton Printers, 1968.

Flanagan, Mike. *Out West.* New York: Harry N. Abrams, 1987.

Fletcher, Baylis John. *Up the Trail in '79.* Norman: University of Oklahoma Press, 1968.

Fletcher, Robert H. *Free Grass to Fences: The Montana Cattle Range Story.* Mattapan, Mass.: University Publishers, 1960.

Flipper, Henry Ossian. *The Colored Cadet at West Point.* New York: Homer Lee & Co., 1978.

Foner, Jack D. *Blacks and the Military in American History.* New York: Praeger, 1974.

———. *The United States Soldiers Between Two Wars: Army Life and Reforms, 1865–1989.* New York: Humanities Press, 1970.

Forbis, William H. (text). *The Cowboys,* Old West Series. Alexandria, Va.: Time-Life, 1973.

Foreman, Grant. *The Five Civilized Tribes.* Norman: University *of Oklahoma Press, 1989.*

———. *Indian Removal: The Emigration of the Five Civilized Tribes of Indians.* Norman: University of Oklahoma Press, 1989.

Forrest, Earle R. *Arizona's Dark and Bloody Ground.* Caldwell, Idaho: Caxton Printers, 1936.

Forsyth, Brevet Brigadier-General George A. *The Story of the Soldier.* D. Appleton and Company, 1900.

Fradkin, Philip L. *Sagebrush Country: Land and the American West.* New York: Alfred A. Knopf, 1989.

Frantz, J.B., and J.E. Choate. *The American Cowboy: The Myth and the Reality.* Norman: University of Oklahoma Press, 1955, 1968.

Frazer, Robert W. *Forts of the West: Military Forts and Presidios and Posts Commonly Called Forts West of the Mississippi River to 1898.* Norman: University of Oklahoma Press, 1965.

Frazier, Ian. *Great Plains.* New York: Farrar, Straus, Giroux, 1989.

Freeman, G.D. *Midnight and Noonday: Or the Incidental History of Southern Kansas and the Indian Territory, 1871–1890.* Norman: University of Oklahoma Press, 1984.

Freidel, Frank. *The Splendid Little War.* Boston: Little, Brown, 1958.

Frink, Maurice. *Cow Country Cavalcade: Eighty Years of the Wyoming Stock Growers Association.* Denver, Colo.: Old West Publishing Co., 1954.

Frink, Maurice, W. Turrentine Jackson and Agnes Wright Spring. *When Grass Was King.* Boulder: University of Colorado Press, 1956.

Frost, Lawrence. *The Custer Album: A Pictorial Biography of General George A. Custer.* Seattle, Wash.: Superior Publishing, 1964.

Fulton, Maurice G. *The Lincoln County War.* Tucson: University of Arizona Press, 1968.

Furniss, Norman F. *The Mormon Conflict.* New Haven, Conn.: Yale University Press, 1960.

Ganoe, Colonel William A. *The History of the U. S. Army.* Augusta, W.V.: Eric Lundberg, 1964.

Gard, Wayne. *The Chisholm Trail.* Norman: University of Oklahoma Press, 1969.

———. *Frontier Justice.* Norman: University of Oklahoma Press, 1949, 1968.

Garrett, Pat F. *The Authentic Life of Billy, the Kid.* Norman: University of Oklahoma Press, 1954.

Gentry, Linnell. A History and Encyclopedia of Country, Western, and Gospel Music. Nashville: Clairmont Corp, 1969.

Gilbert, Bil. *Westering Man: The Life of Joseph Walker.* Norman: University of Oklahoma Press, 1985.

Gilbert, Bil (text). *The Trailblazers,* Old West Series. Alexandria, Va.: Time-Life, 1973.

Gilfillan, Archer B. *Sheep.* Boston: Little, Brown, 1930.

Gillett, J.B. *Six Years with the Texas Rangers, 1875–1881.* Austin: University of Texas Press, 1921.

Goetzmann, William. Army Exploration in the American West, 1803–1863. New Haven, Conn.: Yale University Press, 1959.

Goldstein, Norm. *The History of Television.* New York: Portland House, 1991.

Goulart, Ron. *An Informal History of the Pulp Magazines.* New York: Ace Books, 1972.

Gragg, Rod. *The Old West Quiz & Fact Book.* New York: Harper & Row, 1986.

Graham, Colonel W.A. *The Custer Myth: A Source Book of Custeriana.* New York: Bonanza Books, 1953.

Grant, Bruce. *Concise Encyclopedia of the American Indian.* New York: Bonanza Books, 1960.

Greeley, Horace. *An Overland Journey from New York to San Francisco.* New York: Alfred A. Knopf, 1964.

Green, Donald E. *Panhandle Pioneer: Henry C. Hitch, His Ranch and His Family.* Norman: University of Oklahoma Press, 1979.

Green, Douglas B. *Country Roots: The Origins of Country Music.* New York: Hawthorne, 1976.

Green, Jonathan H. *Gambling Exposed.* Montclair, N.J.: Patterson Smith, 1973.

Gregg, Josiah. *Commerce of the Prairies.* Norman: University of Oklahoma Press, 1990.

Gregory, J., and R. Strickland. *Sam Houston and the Cherokees.* Austin: University of Texas Press, 1967.

Griffis, Ken. *Hear My Song: The Story of the Celebrated Sons of the Pioneers.* Camarillo, Calif.: Norken, 1986.

Grinnell, George B. *The Fighting Cheyennes.* Norman: University of Oklahoma Press, 1956.

———. *The Passing of the Great West: Selected Papers of George Bird Grinnell.* Norman: University of Oklahoma Press, 1985.

———. *When Buffalo Ran.* Norman: University of Oklahoma Press, 1988.

Grossman, Gary H. *Saturday Morning TV: Thirty Years of the Shows You Waited All Week to Watch.* New Rochelle, N.Y.: Arlington House, 1981.

Grover, David. *Diamondfield Jack: A Study in Frontier Justice.* Norman: University of Oklahoma Press, 1986.

Guerin, Mrs. E.J. *Mountain Charley: or the Adventures of Mrs. E.J. Guerin, who was thirteen years in male attire.* Norman: University of Oklahoma Press, 1986.

Hafen, LeRoy, ed. *The Mountain Men and the Fur Trade of the West,* 10 vols. Glendale, Calif.: Arthur H. Clark Co., 1965–1972.

Hagedorn, H. *Roosevelt, in the Badlands.* Boston: Houghton Mifflin, 1921.

Haley, J. Evetts. *Charles Goodnight: Cowman and Plainsman.* Norman: University of Oklahoma Press, 1970.

———. *The XIT Ranch of Texas and the Early Days of the Llano Estacado.* Norman: University of Oklahoma Press, 1967.

Hall, Douglas K. *Rodeo.* New York: Ballantine Books, 1976.

Hanes, Bailey C. *Bill Pickett, Bulldogger: The Biography of a Black Cowboy.* Norman: University of Oklahoma Press 1977.

Hanes, Colonel Bailey C. *Bill Doolin, Outlaw O. T.* Norman: University of Oklahoma Press, 1968.

Hanesworth, Robert D. *Daddy of 'Em All: The Story of Cheyenne Frontier Days.* Flintlock Pub. Co., 1967.

Harbaugh, William H. *The Life and Times of Theodore Roosevelt.* New York: Oxford University Press, 1975.

Hardin, John Wesley. *The Life of John Wesley Hardin as Written by Himself.* Norman: University of Oklahoma Press, 1961.

Harper's Magazine. *The West: A Collection from Harper's Magazine.* New York: Gallery Books, 1990.

Harris, Benjamin Butler. *The Gila Trail: The Texas Argonauts and the California Gold Rush.* Norman: University of Oklahoma Press, 1960.

Harris, Charles W., ed. *Six-Shooters, Songs and Sex.* Norman: University of Oklahoma Press, 1976.

Harris, Theodore, ed. *Negro Frontiersman: The Western Memoirs of Henry Ossian Flipper.* El Paso, Texas: Western College Press, 1963.

Hassrick, Peter (text). *Frederic Remington: Painting, Drawing, and Sculpture in the Amon Carter Museum and the Sid W. Richardson Foundation Collection.* New York: Harrison House, 1973.

Hassrick, P.H. *Frederic Remington: Paintings, Drawings, and Sculpture.* New York: Harrison House, 1973.

Hassrick, Peter H. *Artists of the American Frontier: The Way West.* New York: Promontory Press, 1988.

Hassrick, Royal B. *The George Catlin Book of American Indians.* New York: Promontory Press, 1977.

———. *History of Western American Art.* New York: Exeter Books, 1987.

Hassrick, Royal B.,with Dorothy Maxwell and Cile M. Bach. *The Sioux—the Life and Customs of a Warrior Society.* Norman: University of Oklahoma Press, 1989.

Haywood, C. Robert. *Cowtown Lawyers: Dodge City and Its Attorneys, 1876–1886.* Norman: University of Oklahoma Press, 1988.

———. *Trails South: The Wagon-Road Economy in the Dodge City-Panhandle Region.* Norman: University of Oklahoma Press, 1986.

Heatwole, Thelma. *Ghost Towns and Historical Haunts in Arizona.* San Marino, Calif.: Golden West, 1981.

Heitman, Francis B. *Historical Register and Dictionary of the United States Army, 1789–1903,* vol 3. Washington, D.C.: Government Printing Office, 1903.

Hendricks, Gordon. *Albert Bierstadt: Painter of the American West.* New York: Harrison House, 1988.

Henry, Stuart. *Conquering Our Great American Plains.* New York: E.P. Dutton, 1930.

Hereford, Robert A. *Old Man River.* Caldwell, Idaho: Caxton Printers, 1942.

Herr, Pamela. *Jessie Benton Fremont: A Biography.* Norman: University of Oklahoma Press, 1988.

Hieb, D.L. *Fort Laramie,* National Park Service Historical Handbook No. 20. Washington, D.C.: 1961.

Hine, Robert V. *Community on the American Frontier: Separate But Not Alone.* Norman: University of Oklahoma Press, 1980.

Hise, James Van. *Who Was That Masked Man?: The Story of the Lone Ranger.* Las Vegas: Pioneer, 1990.

Hoig, Stan. *The Sand Creek Massacre.* Norman: University of Oklahoma Press, 1961.

Hook, Jason. *American Indian Warrior Chiefs.* Firebird Books, 1989.

Hope, Holly. *Garden City: Dreams in a Kansas Town.* Norman: University of Oklahoma Press, 1988.

Hopkins, Virginia. *Pioneers of the Old West.* New York: Bonanza Books, 1988.

Horan, James D. *Desperate Men.* New York: Bonanza Books, 1969.

———. *Desperate Women.* New York: Bonanza Books, 1952.

———. *The Life and Art of Charles Schreyvogel: Painter-Historian of the Indian Fighting Army of the American West.* New York: Crown Publishers, 1969.

———. *Pictorial History of the Wild West.* New York: Crown Publishers, 1954.

Horan, J., and Howard Swiggett. *The Pinkerton Story.* New York: Putnam, 1951.

Horn, Huston (text). *The Pioneers,* Old West Series. Alexandria, Va.: Time-Life, 1974.

Horn, Tom. *Life of Tom Horn, Government Scout and Interpreter, Written by Himself, Together with His Letters and Statements by His Friends: A Vindication.* Norman: University of Oklahoma Press, 1989.

Hornung, Clarence P. *The Way It Was in the U.S.A.: The West.* New York: Smithmark, 1978.

Hough, E. *The Story of the Cowboy.* Boston: Gregg Press, 1970.

Howard, Harold P. *Sacajawea.* Norman: University of Oklahoma Press, 1971.

Howard, I.K. *Montana: High, Wide and Handsome.* New Haven, Conn.: Yale University Press, 1943.

Howes, Charles C. *This Place Called Kansas.* Norman: University of Oklahoma Press, 1952.

Hoy, Jim. *Plains Folk II: The Romance of the Landscape.* Norman: University of Oklahoma Press.

Hoy, Jim, and Tom Isern. *Plains Folk: A Commonplace of the Great Plains.* Norman: University of Oklahoma Press, 1987.

Hughes, R.B. *Pioneers Years in the Black Hills.* Glendale, Calif.: 1957.

Hughes, W.J. *Rebellious Ranger: Rip Ford and the Old Southwest.* Norman: University of Oklahoma Press, 1990.

Hunt, Frazier and Robert. *Horses and Heroes: The Story of the Horse in America for 450 Years.* New York: Charles Scribner's Sons, 1949.

———. *I Fought with Custer: The Story of Sergeant Windolph, Last Survivor of the Battle of the Little Big Horn.* New York: Charles Scribner's Sons, 1947.

Hunter, J. Marvin, ed. *The Trail Drivers of Texas,* vols I and II. New York: Argosy-Antiquarian, Ltd., 1963.

Hunter, J. Marvin and Noah H. Rose. *The Album of Gunfighters.* Hunter and Rose, 1951.

Hyams, Jay. *The Life and Times of the Western Movie.* New York: Gallery, 1983.

Hyde, Anne Farrar. *An American Vision: Far Western Landscape and National Culture, 1820–1920.* New York: New York University Press, 1990.

Hyde, George E. *Indians of the High Plains: From the Prehistoric Period to the Coming of Europeans.* Norman: University of Oklahoma Press, 1959.

———. *Red Cloud's Folk: A History of the Oglala Sioux.* Norman: University of Oklahoma Press, 1957.

Irving, Washington. *A Tour on the Prairies.* Norman: University of Oklahoma Press, 1956.

Jackson, Carlton. *Zane Grey.* New York: Twayne Publishers, 1973.

Jackson, D. *Custer's Gold: The U.S. Cavalry Expedition of 1874.* New Haven, Conn.: Yale University Press, 1966.

Jacobs, Wilbur R. *Frederick Jackson Turner's Legacy.* Lincoln: University of Nebraska Press, 1965.

Jennings, Kate F. *N.C. Wyeth.* New York: Crescent Books, 1992.

Johnannsen, Albert. *The House of Beadle and Adams and Its Dime and Nickel Novels: The Story of a Vanished Literature.* Norman: University of Oklahoma Press, 1950.

Johnson, Dorothy M. *The Bloody Bozeman: The Perilous Trail to Montana's Gold.* New York: McGraw-Hill, 1971.

Johnson, Virginia W. *The Unregimented General: A Biography of Nelson's A. Miles.* Boston: Houghton Mifflin, 1962.

Johnson, William Weber (text). *The Forty-Niners,* Old West Series. Alexandria, Va.: Time-Life, 1974.

Jones, Daryl. *The Dime Novel Western.* Bowling Green, Ohio: Bowling Green Univ. Popular Press, 1978.

Jones, Thomas R. *You Bet: How the California Pioneers Did It.* Copyright by Mrs. Lesley Mate, 1936.

Karamanski, Theodore J. *Fur Trade and Exploration: Opening the Far Northwest, 1821–1852.* Norman: University of Oklahoma Press, 1983.

Karolides, Nicholas J. *The Pioneers in the American Novel, 1900–1950.* Norman: University of Oklahoma Press, 1967.

Katz, William Loren. *The Black West.* Seattle: Open Hand Publishing, 1987.

Keleher, W.A. *Violence in Lincoln County.* Albuquerque: University of New Mexico Press, 1957.

Kennedy, Michael S. *Cowboys and Cattlemen.* New York: Hastings House, 1964.

Ketchum, Richard M. *Will Rogers: The Man and His Times.* New York: Touchstone, 1973.

Kieskalt, Charles John. *The Official John Wayne Reference Book.* Secaucus, N.J.: Citadel Press, 1989.

King, Captain Charles. *Campaigning with Crook.* Norman: University of Oklahoma, 1964.

King, Jack. *Confessions of a Poker Player.* Las Vegas, Nev.: Gambler's Book Club, 1970.

Kingsberry, Paul, ed. *Country: The Music and the Musicians.* New York: Abbeville Press, 1988.

Kirkland, K.D. *America's Premier Gunmakers.* New York: Mallard Press, 1990.

———. *America's Premier Gunmakers: Browning.* New York: Exeter Books, 1989.

Koury, Michael J. *Diaries of the Little Big Horn.* Ft. Collins, Colo.: Old Army Press, 1970.

Kupper, Winifred. *The Golden Hoof.* New York: Alfred A. Knopf, 1945.

L'Amour, Louis. *The Education of a Wandering Man.* New York: Bantam, 1989.

LaFarge, Oliver, with Arthur N. Morgan. *Santa Fe: The Autobiography of a Southwestern Town.* Norman: University of Oklahoma Press, 1959.

Lahue, Kalton C. *Winners of the West: The Sagebrush Heroes of the Silent Screen.* Cranbury, N.J.: A.S. Barnes, 1970.

Lamar, Howard, ed. *The Reader's Encyclopedia of the American West.* New York: Harper and Row, 1977.

Lane, Jack C., ed. *Chasing Geronimo: The Journal of Leonard Wood, May–September, 1886.* Albuquerque: University of New Mexico Press, 1970.

Larson, T.A. *History of Wyoming.* Norman: University of Nebraska Press, 1965.

Lavender, David. *The American Heritage History of The West.* New York: American Heritage/Bonanza Books, 1988.

———. *California.* New York: W.W. Norton & Company, 1976.

Lavine, Sigmund A. *Allan Pinkerton, America's First Private Eye.* New York: Dodd, Mead, 1963.

Lawrence, Elizabeth Atwood. *Rodeo: An Anthropologist Looks at the Wild and the Tame.* Knoxville: University of Tennessee Press, 1982.

Lawson, Don. *The United States in the Indian Wars.* New York: Abelard-Schuman, 1975.

Laycock, George. *The Mountain Men.* Danbury, Conn.: Outdoor Life Books, 1988.

Lea, R. *The King Ranch.* Boston: Little, Brown, 1957.

Leakey, John, and Nellie Snyder Yost. *The West That Was: From Texas to Montana.* Lincoln: University of Nebraska Press, 1965.

Leckie, William H. *The Buffalo Soldiers: A Narrative of the Negro Cavalry in the West.* Norman: University of Oklahoma Press, 1967.

———. *Military Conquest of the Southern Plains.* Norman: University of Oklahoma Press, 1963.

Lewis, Marvin, ed. *The Mining Frontier.* Norman: University of Oklahoma Press, 1967.

Lewis, Oscar. *Sagebrush Casinos*. Garden City, N.Y.: Doubleday, 1953.

Limerick, Patricia Nelson. *The Legacy of Conquest: The Unbroken Past of the American West*. New York: Norton, 1987.

Linderman, Frank Bird. *Recollections of Charley Russell*. Norman: University of Oklahoma Press, 1963.

Lloyd, Everett. *Law West of the Pecos*. San Antonio, Texas: Naylor Company, 1967.

Lomax, John, and Alan Lomax. *Cowboy Songs and Other Frontier Ballads*. New York: Macmillan, 1938.

Longstreet, Stephen. *Win or Lose*. Indianapolis: Bobbs-Merrill, 1977.

Love, Robertus. *The Rise and Fall of Jesse Jasmes*. New York: G.P. Putnam's Sons, 1926.

Mails, Thomas E. *The Pueblo Children of the Earth Mother*, vols. I and II. Garden City, N.Y.: Doubleday,1983.

Malone, Bill. *Country Music U.S.A.* Austin: University of Texas Press, 1968.

Malone, Bill C. *Singing Cowboys and Musical Mountaineers: Southern Culture and the Roots of Country Music*. Athens: University of Georgia Press, 1993.

Malone, Bill, and Judith McCullough, eds. *Stars of Country Music*. Urbana: University of Illinois Press, 1975.

Manchel, Frank. *Film Study: A Resource Guide*. Rutherford,N.J.: Fairleigh Dickenson University Press, 1973.

Mancini, Richard. *American Legends of the Wild West*. Philadelphia: Courage Books, 1992.

Marquis, Thomas B. *Custer on the Little Bighorn*. Endkian Publishing, 1971.

Marshall, Brigadier General S.L.A. *Crimsoned Prairie: The Indian Wars on the Great Plains*. New York: Charles Scribner's Sons, 1972.

Martin, Douglas D. *The Earps of Tombstone*. Tombstone Epitaph, 1959.

Martin, Mick, and Marsha Porter. *Video Movie Guide: 1990*. New York: Ballantine, 1989.

Maskelyne, John N. *Sharps and Flats*. Las Vegas, Nev.: Gambler's Book Club, 1971.

Mattes, Merrill J. *The Great Platte River Road*, Lincoln: Nebraska State Historical Society Publications, vol. XXV.: Nebraska State Historical Soc., 1969.

McCallum, Henry D. and Frances T. *The Wire That Fenced the West*. Norman: University of Oklahoma Press, 1965.

McClure, Arthur F., and Ken D. Jones. Heroes, Heavies and Sagebrush: A Pictorial History of the "B" Western Players. A.S. Barnes and Co., 1972.

McConnell, H.H. *Five Years a Cavalryman or, Sketches of Regular Army Life on the Texas Frontier, Twenty Odd Years Ago*. J.N. Rogers & Co. Printers, 1889.

McCoy, J.G. *Historic Sketches of the Cattle Trade of the West and Southwest*. Glendale, Calif.: Arthur H. Clark Co., 1940.

McGlashan, C.F. *History of the Donner Party*. Stanford, Calif.: Stanford University Press, 1954.

McLoughlin, Denis. *Wild and Woolly: An Encyclopedia of the Old West*. Garden City, N.Y.: Doubleday, 1975.

McNall, Scott G., and Sally Allen McNall. *Plains Families: Exploring Sociology Through Social History*. New York: St. Martin's Press, 1983.

McReynolds, Edwin C. *Oklahoma: A History of the Sooner State*. Norman: University of Oklahoma Press, 1954.

Members of the Potomoc Corral of the Westerns. *Great Western Indian Fights*. Lincoln: University of Nebraska Press, 1970.

Mercer, A.S. *The Banditti of the Plains: Or The Cattlemen's Invasion of Wyoming in 1892*. Norman: University of Oklahoma Press, 1954.

Metz, Leon C. *John Selman, Gunfighter*. Norman: University of Oklahoma Press, 1980.

———. *Pat Garrett: The Story of a Western Lawman*. Norman: University of Oklahoma Press, 1974.

Meyer, William R. *The Making of the Great Western*. New Rochelle, N.Y.: Arlington House, 1979.

Miles, Nelson A. *Personal Recollections and Observations of General Nelson A. Miles*. The Werner Co., 1896.

Miller, Don. *Hollywood Corral*. New York: Popular Library, 1976.

Miller, James Knox Polk. *The Road to Virginia City*. Norman: University of Oklahoma Press, 1960.

Miller, Nathan. *Theodore Roosevelt: A Life*. New York: Morrow, 1992.

Miller, Nyle H., and Joseph W. Snell. *Great Gunfighters of the Kansas Cowtowns, 1867–1886*. Lincoln: University of Nebraska Press, 1963.

Mintz, Lannon W. *The Trail: A Bibliography of the Travelers on the Overland Trail to California, Oregon, Salt Lake City, and Montana During the Years 1841–1864*. Albuquerque: University of New Mexico Press, 1987.

Moffat, Gwen. *The Storm Seekers: A Journey in the Footsteps of John Charles Fremont*. North Pomfret, Vt.: Secker & Warburg, 1989.

Monaco, James, and the eds. of *Baseline*. *The Encyclopedia of Film*. New York: Perigee, 1991.

Monaghan, J. *The Great Rascal: Life and Adventures of Ned Buntline*. New York: Bonanza Books, 1951.

Mooney, J. *The Ghost Dance Religion*, Bulletin 14, Bureau of American Ethnology. Washington, D.C.: Bureau of American Ethnology, 1896.

Mothershead, Harmon Ross. *The Swan Land and Cattle Company, Ltd*. Norman: University of Oklahoma Press, 1971.

Mulford, Ami F. *Fighting Indians in the 7th United States Cavalry*. Paul Lindsley Mulford, 1879.

Murray, Earl. *Ghosts of the Old West: Desert Spirits, Haunted Cabins, Lost Trails, and Other Strange Encounters*. New York: Dorset Press, 1988.

Myers, John M. *The Last Chancer: Tombstone's Early Years*. Lincoln: University of Nebraska Press, 1950.

National Geographic Society. *Wild Animals of North America*. Washington, D.C.: National Geographic Society, 1960.

National Institute of Law Enforcement and Criminal Justice. *The Development of the Law of Gambling: 1776–1976*. Washington, D.C.: U.S. Government Printing Office, November 1977.

Neihardt, John G. *Black Elk Speaks.* New York. Pocket Books, 1972.

Nevin, David (text). *The Expressmen.* Old West Series. Alexandria, Va.: Time-Life, 1974.

———. *The Mexican War,* Old West Series. Alexandria, Va.: Time-Life, 1978, 1979.

———. *The Soldiers,* Old West Series. Alexandria, Va.: Time-Life, 1974.

———. *The Texans,* Old West Series. Alexandria, Va.: Time-Life, 1975.

Newell, Gordon. *Westward to Alki.* Seattle: Superior Publishing Co., 1977.

New Hampshire Historical Society. *Abbot-Downing and the Concord Coach.* Concord: New Hampshire Historical Society, 1965.

Nichols, Alice. *Bleeding Kansas.* New York: Oxford University Press, 1954.

Nolan, William F. *Max Brand: Western Giant.* Bowling Green, Ohio: Bowling Green University Popular Press, 1985.

Nordyke, Lewis. *Great Roundup.* New York: William Morrow, 1955.

Nye, Wilbur Sturtevant. *Carbine and Lance: The Story of Old Fort Sill.* Norman: University of Oklahoma Press, 1969.

———. *Plains Indian Raiders: The Final Phases of Warfare from the Arkansas to the Red River.* Norman: University of Oklahoma Press, 1968.

O'Connor, Richard. *Sheridan the Inevitable.* Indianapolis: Bobbs-Merrill, 1953.

Ohrlin, Glenn. *The Hell-Bound Train: A Cowboy Songbook.* Urbana: University of Illinois Press, 1973.

O'Neal, Bill. *Encyclopedia of Western Gunfighters.* Norman: University of Oklahoma Press, 1979.

O'Neil, Paul (text). *The End and the Myth,* Old West Series. Alexandria, Va.: Time-Life, 1979.

———. *The Frontiersmen,* Old West Series. Alexandria, Va.: Time-Life, 1977.

———. *The Rivermen,* Old West Series. Alexandria, Va.: Time-Life, 1975.

Osgood, E.S. *The Day of the Cattleman.* Chicago: University of Chicago Press, 1929.

Ostrander, Major Alson B. *An Army Boy of the Sixties: A Story of the Plains.* World Book Co., 1924.

Parker, Watson. *Deadwood: The Golden Years.* Lincoln: University of Nebraska Press, 1981.

Parmer, Charles B. *For Gold and Glory.* Carrick and Evans, 1939.

Pearson, Edmund. *Dime Novels.* Boston: Little, Brown, 1929.

Pelzer, Louis. *The Cattleman's Frontier: A Record of the Trans-Mississippi Cattle Industry, 1850–1890.* New York: Russell and Russell, 1969.

Penrose, Dr. Charles B. *The Rustler Business.* Douglas Budget, 1959.

Phillips, Charles. *Heritage of the West.* New York: Crescent, 1992.

Pingenot, Ben E. *Siringo.* College Station, Tex.: Texas A&M Press, 1989.

Place, J.A. *The Western Films of John Ford.* Secaucus, N.J.: Citadel Press, 1973.

Pointer, Larry. *In Search of Butch Cassidy.* Norman: University of Oklahoma Press, 1977.

———. *Rodeo Champions: Eight Memorable Moments of Riding, Wrestling and Roping.* Albuquerque: University of New Mexico Press, 1985.

Poling-Kempes, Lesley. *The Harvey Girls: Women Who Opened the West.* New York: Paragon House, 1989.

Pomeroy, Earl. *In Search of the Golden West: The Tourist in Western America.* New York: Alfred A. Knopf, 1957.

Porter, Willard H. *Who's Who in Rodeo.* Oklahoma City: Powder River Book Company, no date.

Prassel, Frank Richard. *The Western Peace Officer: A Legacy of Law and Order.* Norman: University of Oklahoma Press, 1972.

Preece, Harold. *The Dalton Gang: End of an Outlaw Era.* New York: Harold Hastings House, 1963.

Pringle, Henry F. *Theodore Roosevelt, a Biography.* New York: Harcourt, Brace & World, 1956.

Prucha, Francis P. *A Guide to the Military Posts of the United States 1789–1898.* Madison: State Historical Society of Wisconsin, 1964.

Rainey, Buck. *The Shoot-Em-Ups Ride Again.* Waynesville, N.C.: World of Yesterday, 1990.

Reiter, Joan Swallow (text). *The Women,* Old West Series. Alexandria, Va.: Time-Life, 1978, 1979.

Reynolds, Lindor (text) and Lynn Radeka (photographs). *Forts & Battlefields of the Old West.* New York: Mallard Press, 1991.

Rhodes, Eugene Manlove. *The Proud Sheriff.* Norman: University of Oklahoma Press, 1968.

Rickey, Don, Jr. *Forty Miles a Day on Beans and Hay: The Enlisted Soldier Fighting the Indian Wars.* Norman: University of Oklahoma Press, 1963.

Riley, Glenda. *The Female Frontier: A Comparative View of Women on the Prairie and the Plains.* Lawrence: University Press of Kansas, 1988.

Rister, Carl C. *Border Command: General Phil Sheridan in the West.* Norman: University of Oklahoma Press, 1944.

Roach, Joyce Gibson. *The Cowgirls.* Denton: University of North Texas Press, 1977, 1990.

Robertson, M.S. *Rodeo, Standard Guide to the Cowboy Sport.* Berkeley, Calif.: Howell-North Books, 1961.

Roosevelt, Theodore. *Cowboys and Kings.* Cambridge, Mass.: Harvard University Press, 1954.

———. *Ranch Life in the Far West.* Flagstaff, Ariz.: Northland Press, 1968.

———. *Theodore Roosevelt, An Autobiography.* New York: Macmillan, 1913.

Rosa, Joseph G. *The Gunfighter: Man or Myth?* Norman: University of Oklahoma Press, 1989.

———. *They Called Him Wild Bill: The Life and Adventures of James Butler Hickok.* Norman: University of Oklahoma Press, 1987.

———. *The West of Wild Bill Hickok.* Norman: University of Oklahoma Press, 1968

Rosenberg, Bruce A. *The Code of the West.* Bloomington: Indiana University Press, 1982.

Rossi, Paul A., and David C. Hunt (text). *The Art of the Old West: From the Collection of the Gilcrease Institute.* New York: Promontory Press, 1991.

Rothel, David. *The Singing Cowboys.* Cranbury, N.J.: A.S. Barnes, 1978.

———. *Those Great Cowboy Sidekicks.* Waynesville, N.C.: WOY Publications, 1984.

Rovin, Jeff. *The Great Television Series.* Cranbury, N.J.: A.S. Barnes, 1977.

Russell, Don. *The Lives and Legends of Buffalo Bill.* Norman: University of Oklahoma Press, 1960.

———. *The Wild West: A History of the Wild West Shows.* Ft. Worth, Texas: Amon Carter Museum, 1970.

Ruxton, George Frederick. *Life in the Far West.* Norman: University of Oklahoma Press, 1951.

Salisbury, Albert and Jane. *Lewis & Clark: The Journey West.* New York: Promontory Press, 1950.

Sampson, Robert. *Yesterday's Faces: A Study of Series Characters in the Early Pulp Magazines: Vol 1: Glory Figures.* Bowling Green, Ohio: Bowling Green University Popular Press, 1983.

Samuels, Peggy and Harold. *Remington: The Complete Prints.* New York: Crown Publishers, 1990.

———. *Samuels' Encyclopedia of Artists of the American West.* Secaucus, N.J.: Castle, 1985.

Savage, William W., Jr. *The Cowboy Hero: His Image in American History and Culture.* Norman: University of Oklahoma Press, 1979.

———. *Singing Cowboys and All That Jazz: A Short History of Popular Music in Oklahoma.* Norman: University of Oklahoma Press, 1983.

Schlissel, Lillian, Byrd Gibbens, and Elizabeth Hampsten. *Far From Home: Families of the Westward Journey.* New York: Schocken Books, 1989.

Schmitt, M.F., ed. *General George Crook: His Autobiography.* Norman: University of Oklahoma Press, 1946.

Schoenberger, Dale T. *The Gunfighters.* Caldwell, Idaho: Caxton Printers, Ltd. 1971.

Settle, W.A. *Jesse James Was His Name.* Columbia: University of Missouri Press, 1966.

Shirley, Glenn. *Belle Starr and Her Times: The Literature, the Facts, and the Legends.* Norman: University of Oklahoma Press, 1982.

———. *Heck Thomas: Frontier Marshal.* Radnor, Pa.: Chilton Company, 1962.

———. *The Law West of Fort Smith.* Lincoln: University of Nebraska Press, 1968.

———. *Shotgun for Hire.* Norman: University of Oklahoma Press, 1970.

———. *Six-Gun and Silver Star.* Albuquerque: University of New Mexico Press, 1955.

———. *West of Hell's Fringe: Crime, Criminals and the Federal Peace Officer in Oklahoma Territory, 1889–1907.* Norman: University of Oklahoma Press, 1978.

Singletary, Otis A. *The Mexican War.* Chicago: The University of Chicago, 1960.

Siringo, Charles. *A Texas Cowboy or Fifteen Years on the Hurricane Deck of a Spanish Pony.* Lincoln: University of Nebraska Press, 1966.

Slatta, Richard W. *Cowboys of the Americas.* New Haven, Conn.: Yale University Press, 1990.

Slotkin, Richard. *Gunfighter Nation: The Myth of the Frontier in Twentieth-Century America.* New York: Atheneum, 1992.

Smith, Bradley. *The Horse in the West.* New York: World Publishing Co., 1969.

Smith, Duane. *Rocky Mountain Mining Camps.* Lincoln: University of Nebraska Press, 1974.

Smith, Helena Huntington. *The War on Powder River.* Lincoln: University of Nebraska Press, 1966.

Smith, Henry. *Virgin Land: The American West as Symbol and Myth.* Cambridge, Mass.: Harvard University Press, 1970.

Snell, Joseph, and Nyle H. Miller. *Why the West Was Wild.* Topeka: Kansas State Historical Society, 1963.

Sonnichsen, C.L. *Billy King's Tombstone.* Tucson: University of Arizona Press, 1972.

———. *Roy Bean: Law West of the Pecos.* New York: Macmillan, 1943.

———. *Tucson: The Life and Times of an American City.* Norman: University of Oklahoma Press, 1982.

Sprague Marshall. *A Gallery of Dudes.* Boston: Little, Brown, 1967.

Spring, Agnes Wright. *Good Little Bad Man: The Life of Colorado Charley Utter.* Boulder, Colo.: Pruett Publishing Company, 1987.

Starr, Kevin. *Americans and the California Dream.* New York: Oxford University Press, 1973.

Steckmesser, Kent Ladd. *The Western Hero in History and Legend.* Norman: University of Oklahoma Press, 1965.

Stedman, Raymond William. *The Serials: Suspense and Drama by Installment.* Norman: University of Oklahoma Press, 1977.

Steffen, Jerome O. *The American West: New Perspectives, New Dimensions.* Norman: University of Oklahoma Press, 1979.

———. *Comparative Frontiers: A Proposal for Studying the American West.* Norman: University of Oklahoma Press, 1980.

Stegner, Wallace. *Where the Bluebird Sings to the Lemonade Springs: Living and Writing in the West.* New York: Random House, 1992.

Steinberg, Cobbett. *TV Facts.* New York: Facts On File, 1980.

Steiner, Stan. *The Ranchers: A Book of Generations.* Norman: University of Oklahoma Press, 1980.

Sterling, William Warren. *Trails and Trials of a Texas Ranger.* Norman: University of Oklahoma Press, 1969.

Stewart, Edgar I. *Custer's Luck.* Norman: University of Oklahoma Press, 1971.

Stratton, Owen Tully. *Medicine Man.* Norman: University of Oklahoma Press, 1989.

Streeter, Floyd Benjamin. *Ben Thompson: Man With a Gun.* New York: Frederick Fell, 1957.

———. *Prairie Trails and Cow Towns.* Old Greenwich, Conn.: Devon Adair Co., 1963.

Stuart, Granville. *Forty Years on the Frontier.* Glendale, Calif.: A.H. Clark, 1967.

Summers, Neil. *The First Official TV Western Book.* Vienna, W.V.: Old West Shop Publishing, 1987.

———. *The Official TV Western Book,* vol 2. Vienna, W.V.: Old West Shop Publishing, 1989.

———. *The Official TV Western Book,* vol 3. Vienna, W.V.: Old West Shop Publishing, 1991.

Sunder, John E. *Bill Sublette: Mountain Man.* Norman: University of Oklahoma Press, 1959.

Sweetman, Luke D. *Backtrailing on Open Range.* Caldwell, Idaho: Caxton Printers, 1951.

Tanner, Ogden (text). *The Canadians,* Old West Series. Alexandria, Va.: Time-Life, 1977.

———. *The Ranchers,* Old West Series. Alexandria, Va.: Time-Life, 1977.

Texas State Historical Association. *History of the Cattlemen of Texas.* Austin: Texas State Historical Association, 1991.

Thorp, N. Howard "Jack." *Songs of the Cowboys.* New York: Clarkson N. Potter, 1966.

Thrapp, Dan L. *Encyclopedia of Frontier Biography.* Lincoln: University of Nebraska Press, 1988.

Tinsley, Jim Bob. *For a Cowboy Has to Sing.* Orlando: University of Central Florida Press, 1991.

———. *He Was Singin' This Song.* Orlando: University Presses of Florida, 1981.

Tobias, Michael. *Mountain People.* Norman: University of Oklahoma Press, 1986.

Tompkins, Jane. *West of Everything: The Inner Life of Westerns.* New York: Oxford University Press, 1992.

Towne, Charles Wayland and Edward Norris Wentworth. *Cattle & Men.* Norman: University of Oklahoma Press, 1955.

———. *Shepherd's Empire.* Norman: University of Oklahoma Press, 1945.

Townsend, Charles R. San Antonio Rose: The Life and Music of Bob Willis. Urbana: University of Illinois Press, 1986.

Trachtman, Paul (text). *The Gunfighters,* Old West Series. Alexandria, Va.: Time-Life, 1974.

Trafzer, Clifford Earl. *The Kit Carson Campaign: The Last Great Navajo War.* Norman: University of Oklahoma Press, 1982.

Treadwell, Edward F. *The Cattle King.* Fresno, Calif.: Valley Publishers, 1950.

Turner, Frederick Jackson. *The Frontier in American History.* New York: Henry Holt and Company, 1962.

Tuska, Jon. *The Filming of the West.* New York: Doubleday, 1976.

Tweton, D. Jerome. *The Marquis de Mores.* Fargo: North Dakota Institute for Regional Studies, 1972.

Tyson, Carol Newton. *The Red River in Southwestern History.* Norman: University of Oklahoma Press, 1981.

Utley, Robert M. *Custer Battlefield.* Washington, D.C.: National Park Service, U.S. Dept. of the Interior, 1969.

———. *Frontiersmen in Blue: The United States Army and the Indian, 1848–1865.* New York: Macmillan, 1967.

———. *The Last Days of the Sioux Nation.* New Haven, Conn.: Yale University Press, 1963.

Utley, R.M., and F.A. Ketterson. *Golden Spike,* National Park Service Historical Handbook No. 40. Washington, D.C.: National Park Service, 1969.

Van de Water, Frederick F. *The Glory Hunter: a Life of General Custer.* Indianapolis: Bobbs-Merrill, 1934.

Vestal, Stanley. *Queen of the Cowtowns: Dodge City, 1872–1886.* New York: Harper and Bros., 1952.

———. *Sitting Bull, Champion of the Sioux.* Norman: University of Oklahoma Press, 1957, 1965.

Von Richthofen, Walter Baron. *Cattle-Raising on the Plains of North America.* Norman: University of Oklahoma Press, 1969.

Wagoner, Jay J. *Arizona Territory.* Tucson: University of Arizona Press, 1970.

Walker, Henry Pickering. *The Wagonmasters: High Plains Freighting from the Earliest Days of the Santa Fe Trail to 1880.* Norman: University of Oklahoma Press, 1966.

Wallace, Ernest, and Hoebel E. Adamson. *The Comanches: Lords of the South Plains.* Norman: University of Oklahoma Press, 1952.

Wallace, Robert (text). *The Miners,* Old West Series. Alexandria, Va.: Time-Life, 1976.

Walsh, Richard J. *The Making of Buffalo Bill.* Indianapolis: Bobbs-Merrill, 1928.

Ward, Fay E. *The Cowboy at Work: All About His Job and How He Does It.* New York: Hastings House, 1958.

Waters, L. L. *Steel Rails to Santa Fe.* Lawrence, Kans.: University of Kansas Press, 1950.

Watkins, T.H. *California; An Illustrated History.* Palo Alto, Calif.: American West Pub. Co., 1973.

Watts, Peter. *A Dictionary of the Old West, 1850–1900.* New York: Alfred A. Knopf, 1977.

Wayman, Norbury L. *Life on the River.* New York: Crown Publishers, 1971.

Webb, Walter Prescott. *The Great Plains.* New York: Grosset & Dunlap, Inc., 1957.

———. *The Texas Rangers: A Century of Frontier Defense.* Austin: University of Texas Press, 1989.

Webb, Walter Prescott, and Carroll Bailey, eds. *The Handbook of Texas,* vols. I and II. Austin: Texas State Historical Association, 1952.

Weems, John Edward. *Death Song: The Last of the Indian Wars.* New York: Indian Head Books, 1976.

Wellman, Paul I. *Death on Horseback: Seventy Years of War for the American West.* Philadelphia: J.B. Lippincott Co., 1934.

———. *A Dynasty of Western Outlaws.* New York: Bonanza Books, 1960.

———. *The Trampling Herd.* New York: Cooper Square Publishers, 1974.

Westermeir, Clifford P. *Man, Beast, Dust: The Story of Rodeo.* Denver: World Press, 1947.

Weston, Jack. *The Real American Cowboy.* New York: New Amsterdam, 1985.

Wheeler, Homer. Buffalo *Days: Forty Years in the Old West: The Personal Narrative of a Cattleman, Indian Fighter and Army Officer.* Indianapolis: Bobbs-Merrill, 1925.

Wheeler, Keith (text). *The Alaskans,* Old West Series. Alexandria, Va.: Time-Life, 1977.

———. *The Chroniclers,* Old West Series. Alexandria, Va.: Time-Life, 1976.

———. *The Railroaders,* Old West Series. Alexandria, Va.: Time-Life, 1973.

———. *The Scouts,* Old West Series. Alexandria, Va.: Time-Life, 1978.

———. *The Townsmen,* Old West Series. Alexandria, Va.: Time-Life, 1975.

White, G. Edward. *The Eastern Establishment and the Western Experience.* New Haven, Conn.: Yale University Press, 1968.

White, John I. *Git Along Little Dogies: Songs and Songmakers of the American West.* Urbana: University of Illinois Press, 1975.

White, Richard. *It's Your Misfortune and None of My Own: A New History of the American West.* Norman: University of Oklahoma Press, 1991.

Williams, Richard L. (text). *The Loggers,* Old West Series. Alexandria, Va.: Time-Life, 1976.

Willis, Jack. *Roosevelt in the Rough.* Ives Washburn, 1931.

Wilson, Elinor. *Jim Beckwourth: Black Mountain Man and War Chief of the Crows.* Norman: University of Oklahoma Press, 1972.

Wilson, R.L. *Theodore Roosevelt: Outdoorsman.* New York: Winchester Press, 1971.

Winther, O.O. *Express and Stagecoach Days in California.* Stanford, Calif.: Stanford University Press, 1936.

————. *The Old Oregon Country.* Stanford, Calif.: Stanford University Press, 1950.

————. *Via Western Express and Stagecoach.* Stanford, Calif.: Stanford University Press, 1945.

Wolfenstine, Manfred R. *The Manual of Brands and Marks.* Norman: University of Oklahoma Press, 1970.

Woods, Lawrence M. *British Gentlemen in the Wild West: The Era of the Intensely English Cowboy.* London: Robson Books, 1990.

Wormser, Richard. *The Yellowlegs: The Story of the U.S. Cavalry.* Garden City, N.J.: Doubleday, 1966.

Wyman, Walker D. *Nothing But Prairie and Sky: Life on the Dakota Range in the Early Days.* Norman: University of Oklahoma Press, 1954.

————. *The Wild Horse of the West.* Lincoln: University of Nebraska Press, 1963.

Yost, Nellie Snyder. *The Call of the Range.* Denver: Sage Books, 1966.

————. *Medicine Lodge: The Story of a Kansas Frontier Town.* Chicago: Swallow Press, 1970.

Young, Frederic R. *Dodge City.* Dodge City: Boot Hill Museum, 1972.

INDEX

Boldface page numbers indicate main essays. *Italic* page numbers denote illustrations and captions.

Sullivan, C. Gardner 292
Summers, Hope 237
Summerville, Slim 304
Summit Springs, Battle of 211
sun dance 8, 183, 265, **279**
Sundance Kid, The 58, 87, **279**, 306
Sunset (Jimmy Wakely's horse) 144
Sunset Trail, The (book) 186
"Sunshine Ranch" (radio show) 268
Superstition Mountain 179
Sutter, John **279–280**
Sutter's Fort 279
Sutton, William E. **280**, 282
Sutton-Taylor Feud 129, 134, 238, **280**, 281, 282
Swackhamer, E. W. 183
Swafford, Frank 146
"Swamp Fox, The" (TV show) **280**, 300
Swan, Allan 61
Swarthout, Glenn 261
Swarthout, Miles Hood 261
Sweeney, Red 102
Sweet, A. M. 180
Swenson, Karl 174
Swerling, Jo 303
swing riders **280**
Sykes, John 11

T

Tabor, Horace A. W. 92, 164
Taeger, Ralph 140, 159
Taft, William Howard 186
tailing **280**
Tait, Arthur F. 13
Talbot, Jim **280**
"Tales of the Texas Rangers" (TV show) **281**, 283–284
"Tales of Wells Fargo" (TV show) 241, 256, **281**, 283
Taliaferro, Hal *see* Wales, Wally
Tall Bull (Cheyenne chief) 211
"Tall Man, The" (TV show) **281**
Tammen, Henry 74
Taos, New Mexico 16–17
tapaderos **281**
tarp **281**
Tarzan (Ken Maynard's horse) 144, 204
"Tate" (TV show) **281**
Taylor, Bill 238, 280, **281**, 282
Taylor, Buck 126, 243, 280, **281–282**
Taylor, Charles 178
Taylor, Cliff 163
Taylor, Doboy 134, **282**
Taylor, Dub "Cannonball" **282**, 306

Taylor, Elizabeth 116
Taylor, Jim 134, 281, **282**
Taylor, Joan 237
Taylor, Kathy 250
Taylor, Kent 250
Taylor, Robert 91
Taylor, Robert Lewis 291
Taylor, Rod 25, 217, 218
Taylor, Scrap 282
Taylor, Zachary 158, 193
Taylor-Sutton Feud *see* Sutton-Taylor Feud
team roping 243–244
Teapot Dome Scandal 111
teepee *see* tipi
Teich, Ed 223
telegraph lines *see* Pony Express
television shows **282–285**
see also specific titles (e.g., "Bonanza")
    "Acrobat Ranch," ABC 1
    "Adventures of Brisco County, Jr.," Fox 2
    "Adventures of Champion," CBS 2
    "Adventures of Jim Bowie," ABC 2–3
    "Adventures of Kit Carson," MCA 3
    "Adventures of Oky Doky," Dumont 3
    "Adventures of Rin Tin Tin," CBS 3
    "Adventures of Wild Bill Hickok," CBS/ABC 3–4
    "Alaskans," syndicated 5–6
    "Alias Smith and Jones," ABC 6
    "Americans," NBC 6
    "Annie Oakley," syndicated 7
    "Barbary Coast," ABC 23
    "Bat Masterson," NBC 24
    "Bearcats," CBS 25
    "Best of the West," ABC 27
    "Big Valley," ABC 27–28
    "Black Saddle," ABC 31
    "Bonanza," NBC 34–35
    "Boots and Saddles," NBC 37
    "Born to the Wind," NBC 37–38
    "Branded," NBC 40
    "Brave Eagle," CBS 40
    "Brave Stallion," syndicated 40
    "Bret Maverick," NBC 41
    "Broken Arrow," ABC 43
    "Bronco," ABC 43
    "Buckskin," NBC 46
    "Buffalo Bill Jr.," CBS 46
    "Cactus Jim," NBC 51
    "Cade's County," CBS 51–52
    "Californians," NBC 54

    "Call of the West," syndicated 54
    "Casey Jones," syndicated 57–58
    "Centennial," NBC 62–63
    "Cheyenne," ABC 64
    "Chisholms," CBS 66
    "Cimarron City," NBC 68
    "Cimarron Strip," CBS 68
    "Cisco Kid," syndicated 69
    "Colgate Western Theatre," syndicated 75
    "Colt .45," ABC 76
    "Concrete Cowboys," CBS 77
    "Cowboy G-Men," syndicated 80
    "Cowboy in Africa," ABC 80
    "Cowboys," ABC 83
    "Cowboys & Injuns," ABC 84
    "Cowboy Theatre," NBC 84
    "Cowtown Rodeo," ABC 84
    "Crash Corrigan's Ranch," ABC 85
    "Custer," ABC 87
    "Dakotas," ABC 89
    "Daniel Boone," NBC 90
    "Davy Crockett: King of the Wild Frontier," Disney 90
    "Death Valley Days," syndicated 91–92
    "Deputy," NBC 93
    "Destry," ABC 93
    "Dick Powell's Zane Grey Theater," CBS 94
    "Dirty Sally," CBS 94
    "Dr. Quinn, Medicine Woman," CBS 97
    "Dundee and the Culhane," CBS 99
    "Dusty's Trail," syndicated 100
    "Empire," NBC/ABC 104–105
    "Father Murphy," NBC 106
    "Frontier," NBC 112
    "Frontier Adventure," syndicated 112
    "Frontier Circus," CBS 112
    "Frontier Doctor," syndicated 112
    "Frontier Justice," syndicated 112
    "F Troop," ABC 113
    "Fury," NBC 113
    "Gabby Hayes Show," NBC 113
    "Gene Autry Show," CBS 115
    "General Electric Theatre," CBS 115
    "Gray Ghost," syndicated 120

    "Great Adventure," CBS 120
    "Guestward Ho!," ABC 123
    "Gun Shy," CBS 126
    "Gunslinger," CBS 126
    "Gunsmoke," CBS 126–128
    "Guns of Will Sonnett," ABC 128
    "Have Gun, Will Travel," CBS 132
    "Hawkeye and the Last of the Mohicans," syndicated 132
    "Hec Ramsey," NBC 133
    "High Chaparral," NBC 136–137
    "Hondo," ABC 140
    "Hopalong Cassidy," NBC 140–141
    "Hotel De Paree," CBS 144
    "Howdy Doody," NBC 145
    "How the West Was Won," ABC 145
    "Iron Horse," ABC 149
    "Jefferson Drum," NBC 152
    "Johnny Ringo," CBS 153
    "Junior Rodeo," ABC 157
    "Kentucky Jones," NBC 158
    "Klondike," NBC 159
    "Kung Fu," ABC 159–160
    "Lancer," CBS 161
    "Laramie," NBC 162
    "Laredo," NBC 163
    "Lash of the West," ABC 163
    "Lawman," ABC 164
    "Law of the Plainsman," NBC/ABC 164
    "Legend of Jesse James," ABC 165
    "Life and Legend of Wyatt Earp," ABC 168
    "Life and Times of Grizzly Adams," NBC 168
    "Life with Snarky Parker," CBS 168–169
    "Little House on the Prairie," NBC 174
    "Lone Ranger," ABC 175–177
    "Loner," CBS 175
    "Lonesome Dove," CBS 177
    "Mackenzie's Raiders," syndicated 181
    "Man Called Shenandoah," ABC 183
    "Man From Blackhawk," ABC 183
    "Man Without a Gun," syndicated 184
    "Marshal of Gunsight Pass," ABC 184–185
    "Maverick," ABC 187